AL-WĀFĪ

A THOROUGH COMMENTARY ON THE FORTY NAWĀWIYYAH

SECOND EDITION

Shaykh Muṣṭafā Dīb Al-Bughā
& Shaykh Muḥyī Ad-Dīn Dīb Mistū

Translated by
Mahdi Lock

NAWA BOOKS

We at Nawabooks would like to express our appreciation to everybody who contributed in making this book a reality. We pray that Allah ﷻ bestow His blessings upon it by guiding readers of this book closer towards Allah ﷻ and His beloved Prophet Muhammad ﷺ.

AL-WĀFĪ - *A THOROUGH COMMENTARY ON THE FORTY NAWĀWIYYAH*
Second Edition

Published by:	Nawa Books
First Edition:	December 2020
Second Edition:	March 2023
Author:	Shaykh Muṣṭafā Dīb Al-Bughā & Shaykh Muḥyī Ad-Dīn Dīb Mistū
Translated by:	Mahdi Lock

ISBN: 978-981-14-8846-7

Cover Photography: Mohammad Helal
Cover by: Muhammadan Press

CONTENTS

TRANSLATOR'S INTRODUCTION FOR THE SECOND EDITION

All praise belongs to Allah, Lord of all creation, who forgives sins and with Him alone is every success, and may His blessings and peace be upon His Final Prophet and Messenger.

We praise Allah that we have been blessed to produce a second edition of Al-Wāfī: A Thorough Commentary on the Forty Nawawiyyah.

The following changes have been made:

1. The print size and font are now much bigger, which makes it easier for the reader, or the student in class, to write notes.
2. The Qur'ānic verses are now in the Uthmānī rasm, or script.
3. Many typographical errors have been corrected.
4. The translations of certain words and expressions have been improved, and with Allah alone is every success.

If Allah so wills, this edition will bring greater benefit, and all praise belongs to Him. Only the mistakes are mine.

Mahdi Lock
18th of Rajab, 1444 (9th February, 2023)

TRANSLATOR'S INTRODUCTION & ACKNOWLEDGEMENTS FOR THE FIRST EDITION

All praise belongs to Allah, Lord of all creation, who forgives sins and with Him alone is every success. There is no power or strength except in Him. As Allah has honoured this miserable slave with the completion of such a task, all I ask is that He increase the blessings He has already bestowed upon me and to make me a better believer, cleanse my heart and grant me further strength to serve Him and the Ummah of His Beloved ﷺ.

As for the creation, I begin by thanking Ustādh Jalaluddeen of Nawa Books for arranging and running this beautiful project. He has clearly been blessed in many ways, not only by being able to study with so many high-ranking scholars in Sham, but by maintaining strong links with them. All praise be to Allah, it is through his strong relationship with Imam Muṣṭafā al-Bughā that this translation and publication was able to get off the ground and come to fruition. If Allah so wills, this work will not be the last and more books by Imam al-Bughā will be translated and published. May Allah continue to shower his blessings upon Ustādh Jalauddeen and his family in this life and the Hereafter.

Secondly, I thank Imam al-Bughā himself for answering questions that came up and for making duʿāʾ for both of us.

I must also thank two of my teachers, al-Hajj Abu Jaʿfar al-Ḥanbalī and Ustādh Hāshim Riḍā, for answering other questions that cropped up.

Lastly, but certainly not least, I thank my wife and her sister for their diligent proofreading of the entire translated text.

It is true that there are many commentaries on this collection of forty ḥadīth, about fifty in number, including by Imam an-Nawawī himself and other great luminaries such as Imam Ibn Rajab al-Ḥanbalī and Ibn Ḥajar al-Haytamī. However, what sets this commentary apart, the first English translation of which is currently in your hands,[1] is its accessibility and balanced approach. It is profound and detailed without being prolix and verbose. It is brief without leaving the reader thirsty for more.

1 There are already translations in French, Malay, and Indonesian.

This book is ideal for the one who wishes to read in isolation as well as those who would like to conducts classes. Every ḥadīth is followed by a detailed explanation of its importance, its vocabulary, and then its *fiqh* rulings along with other guidance that can be understood from it.

It is hoped that as the reader moves through the text, his understanding and appreciation of the Prophet's words ﷺ will deepen, and he will also come to see the immense wisdom in Imam an-Nawawī's choices. If Allah so wills, the reader will come out and with a much broader and more thorough understanding of Islam itself.

After covering so many aspects of theology and *fiqh*, one arrives at the last two ḥadīths, the forty-first and forty-second. The forty-first, along with the commentary, should instil the desire to obey Allah out of shame, while the forty-second, the ḥadīth that Imam an-Nawawī chose to finish with, should instil the desire to obey Allah out of love, and with Allah alone is every success.

Mahdi Lock - 1st of Rabīʿ al-Ākhar, 1442 (17th November, 2020)

دار المصـــطفى
للطباعة والنشر والتوزيع
سوريا - دمشق
هاتف 2258532 فاكس 2250982 - ص.ب : 11392
E-mail:anasbugha@hotmail.com

بســم الله الرحمـن الرحيم

إذن بالطباعة والترجمة

الحمد لله رب العالمين والصلاة والسلام على سيدنا محمد وعلى آله وصحبه إلى يوم الدين
وبعد: نحن دار المصطفى للطباعة والنشر والتوزيع ، سوريا (دمشق) أصحاب كتاب :
(الوافي في شرح الأربعين النووية) لمؤلفه الأستاذ الدكتور مصطفى ديب البغا

فقد أعطينا الإذن للأستاذ محمد جلال الدين ، مدير عام (company Nawabooks) في سنغافورة ، بترجمة وطباعة كتاب :

((الوافي في شرح الأربعين النووية)) إلى اللغة الإنكليزية

وذلك بجهود المترجم الأستاذ مهدي لوك (Mahdi Lock) وتعتبر هذه الطبعة باللغة الإنكليزية والعائدة للأستاذ محمد جلال الدين ، طبعة شرعية موافق عليها من دار المصطفى كما أننا نشكر له جهوده في نشر العلم والمعرفة .

هذا ونسال الله تعالى التوفيق

د. مصطفى البغا

دار المصطفى
المدير العام
د. أنس مصطفى البغا

PERMISSION TO PRINT AND TRANSLATE

In the Name of Allah, the All-Merciful, the Most Merciful

Praise be to Allah, Lord of all Creation, and blessings and peace be upon our master, Muḥammad, as well as his Family and his Companions, until the Day of Recompense.

To proceed:

We, Dār al-Muṣṭafā for Printing, Publishing, and Distribution, Syria (Damascus), the proprietors of the book *Al-Wāfī fī Sharḥ al-Arbaʿīn an-Nawawiyyah,* authored by Prof Dr Muṣṭafā Dīb al-Bughā

Have given permission to Ustādh Muhammad Jalaluddeen, the director of Nawa Book, Singapore, to translate and publish the book:

Al-Wāfī fī Sharḥ al-Arbaʿīn an-Nawawiyyah into the English language

This will be accomplished by the efforts of the translator, Ustādh Mahdi Lock. This English-language edition, the profits of which will be for Ustādh Muhammad Jalaluddeen, is considered a legitimate edition, authorised by Dār al-Muṣṭafā. We thank him for his efforts in spreading knowledge and learning.

We ask Allah the Exalted for success.

Dr Anas Muṣṭafā al-Bughā
General Director
Dār al-Muṣṭafā

Dr Muṣṭafā al-Bughā

AUTHORS' BIOGRAPHY

SHAYKH MUṢṬAFĀ DĪB AL-BUGHĀ

He is the beloved scholar, Prof. Dr Muṣṭafā Dīb al-Bughā al-Maydānī ad-Dimashqī ash-Shāfiʿī, born in the year 1938M/1354AH in the district of Maidan in the city of Damascus, Syria. He was sent to Maʿhad al-Tawjīh al-Islāmī at a young age of twenty-one years due to his brilliance, the very institute established by Imam Hasan H banakah al-Madanī. He graduated in 1959M. He also attained an Ijāzah in Memorisation of the Noble Qurʾān from Shaykh Khayrū Yāsīn, Damascus, 1960.

He then enrolled in Damascus University and was there for four years, graduating in 1963M with a Bachelor's degree, after which he moved onto the Azhar University in Egypt to attain his Masters and PhD, which he attained in 1974M. He specialised in Comparative Fiqh and the methods used in judging evidence according to different madhhabs.

Amongst his teachers were Imam Shaykh Ḥasan Ḥabanakah al-Maydānī and his students Khayru Yasīn al-Maydānī, Hāni al-Mubarak, Ḥusayn Khaṭṭāb, and Muḥammad Kurayyim Rājih while he was in Damascus.

Other teachers in the sciences of the Revealed Law, in both Egypt and Shām, include Mustafa as-Sibāʿī, Muḥammad al-Mubārak, Māzin al-Mubārak, Muḥammad Amin al-Maṣrī, ʿUmar al-Ḥakīm, Wahbī Sulaymān, Ghawajī al-Albānī, Muhammad ash-Shamaʿ and Muḥammad al-Muntaṣar al-Kattānī.

Shaykh Muṣṭafā al-Bughā has authored and commented upon numerous books on numerous areas in fiqh and is well-respected throughout the Muslim world for his deep knowledge and charisma in discussing intricate matters. He has taught and lectured in many different Universities throughout the world, which includes, Indonesia, Singapore, Qatar, Jordan, Malaysia, and Dagestan. To date he has published about 80 books and one encyclopaedia which includes *al-Fiqh al-Manhajī, Athar al-Adillah al-Muhktalaf Fīhā, Niẓām al-Islam, Nuzhat al-Muttaqīn Sharḥ Riyāḍ as-Ṣāliḥīn, at-Tahdhīb Fi Adillati Matan al-Ghayah wa al-Taqrīb, Uṣūl al-Fiqh: Dirāsah ʿĀmmah, al-Wāḍiḥ fī ʿUlūm al-Qurʾān*, and many more for which there is no room to mention here.

SHAYKH MUḤYĪ AD-DĪN DĪB MISTŪ

Shaykh Dr Muḥyī ad-Dīn Dīb Mistū, a professor and renowned author from Damascus Syria. He is regarded as the teacher of scholars and a respected lecturer at the Al-Fatḥ Islamic Institute, which offers undergraduate and postgraduate studies for both male and female students from all over the world.

To date, Shaykh Muḥyī ad-Dīn has either authored or co-authored eighty-two written publications of books and research papers. Most of his books are well known and used in Islamic institutions and universities throughout the world. While the majority are written in Arabic, there are some that are translated into Malay, French and Urdu.

Some of the titles that carry his name are:

- *Ḥusn al-Uswah bi-mā thabata min Allāhi wa-Rasūlihi fī al-Niswah*
- *ʿAbdullah ibn ʿUmar : as-Ṣaḥābī al-Muʾtasī bi-Rasūlillāh*
- *Kitāb ash-Shajarah an-Nabawīyyah: fī Nasab Khayr al-Barīyyah*
- *Sharḥ al-Lumaʿ*
- *Al-Āyat al-Kubrā fī Sharḥ Qiṣṣat al-Isrāʾ*
- *Manāhij at-taʾlīf fī as-Sīrah an-Nabawiyyah khilāl al-Qurūn al-Arbʿah al-Ūlā min al-Hijrah al-Nabawiyyah*
- *Al-Ḥajj wa-al-ʿUmrah: Fiqhuhu, Asrāruhu, Ḥijjat an-Nabī* ﷺ
- *Silāḥ al-Muʾmin fī ad-Duʿāʾ wa adh-Dhikr*
- *Al-Wāfī fī Sharḥ al-Arbaʿīn an-Nawawiyyah*
- *Al-ʿAqīdah al-Islāmiyyah: Arkānuhā, Ḥaqāʾiquhā, wa Mufsidātuhā*
- *Lawāmiʿ al-Anwar Sharḥ Kitāb al-Adhkār*

AUTHORS' INTRODUCTION

Praise be to Allah, the praise of those who are grateful, and blessing and peace be upon our master Muḥammad, the one sent as a mercy to all the worlds, as well as his Family, his Companions, and those who are guided by his guidance and act according to his Sunnah until the Day of Repayment.

To proceed:

It is from Allah the Exalted's favour upon us that he has granted us the success to work in compiling books of ḥadīth that are taught in Islamic schools at the preparatory and secondary levels. While commentating on 270 ḥadīths distributed over the six grades,[2] it came to our attention that the authors of the major ḥadīth works, our distinguished scholars, had referred to a number of these Prophetic ḥadīths as being **comprehensive, universal ḥadīths**, because Islam revolves around them, or half of it, or a third of it or a quarter of it. This made us devote more of our attention to certain ḥadīths to become better acquainted with their meanings, and we put more effort into commentating on them. Then an integrated curriculum started to form that comprised these comprehensive ḥadīths along with their commentary. However, the truth was spoken when someone said, 'The first has left nothing for the last.' We found that the Imam and Ḥāfiẓ[3] Abū ʿAmr ibn as-Ṣalāḥ (d.643 AH) ﷺ dictated to a gathering something called **The Comprehensive Ḥadīths**. He compiled therein these comprehensive ḥadīths, about which it had been said that Islam revolves around them or something similar, in terms of being concise and comprehensive. His gathering comprised twenty-six ḥadīths. Then Imam an-Nawawī ﷺ took these ḥadīths that Ibn as-Ṣalāḥ had dictated and added more, making them forty-two in total, and he called his book *al-Arbaʿīn*.[4] These forty became very popular and were frequently memorised. Allah brought about benefit through them because of the blessed intention of the one who compiled them, and his beautiful aspiration. Famous scholars have commentated on them and written about them, such that there are now fifty commentaries available in the Arabic language. Some of them have been published while most of them are still lost or in manuscript form.

2 (tn): i.e. six years of schools.
3 (tn): i.e. memoriser of ḥadīths.
4 (tn): i.e. *The Forty*.

We were then determined to write a commentary on *The Forty* of Imam an-Nawawī, and add the fifty-first commentary to the other commentaries on these blessed ḥadīths, not so that it would be forgotten on old library shelves and become tasty food for insects and dust. Rather, we wanted it to become, with Allah's permission, printed letters, words, and pages, so that it reaches the Muslim reader in the easiest script, the clearest method and the most beautiful garb. Our method can be summarised as follows: The first part is showing where the ḥadīth is found along with its grading, according to what the esteemed scholars of ḥadīth have said. The second part is looking into the importance of the ḥadīth so that it becomes clear why it was chosen to be in *The Forty Nawawiyyah*. Then the words and vocabulary are thoroughly explained in their linguistic sense. After that, we arrived at the most important step, which are the Legal Matters of the ḥadīth and other guidance. We have presented these under clear, numbered, marginal titles, and added the Qur'ānic verses and Prophetic ḥadīths that support the legal ruling derived from the ḥadīth, to further underscore it. We have also mentioned, as far as we have been able to, the legislative pearls of wisdom and along with the religious and worldly benefits that be realised upon adhering to and obeying the noble Prophetic ḥadīth. Likewise, in the course of doing so, we have also pointed out the Prophetic lessons and throbs of faith that constitute a healthy remedy for many of our incurable social illnesses in this age of ours.

To complete the benefit, at the end of the book we will add biographies for the narrators of the ḥadīth, so that they can be known, alongside their companionship with Allah's Messenger ﷺ and where they can be models for us in their lives. These biographies will be in alphabetical order based on the names of these narrators so that they can easily be referred to.

And by Allah, we hope that our work is useful in understanding these comprehensive ḥadīths and that they translate into conduct and action, giving and sacrifice, might and struggle.

And Allah is our goal

By The Authors

IMAM AN-NAWAWĪ'S INTRODUCTION

بِسْمِ اللهِ الرَّحْمٰنِ الرَّحِيْمِ

All praise is due to Allah, Lord of all creation, the One who sustains the heavens and the earth, the One who manages all creatures, the One who sent the Messengers to those who are legally accountable, to guide them and elucidate the laws of the Religion, with decisive evidences and clear proofs. I praise Him for all His blessings, and I ask Him for more of His favour and generosity. I bear witness that there is no god but Him, the One, the Overpowering, the Generous, the Much-Forgiving, and I bear witness that our master Muḥammad is His slave and Messenger, His beloved and His intimate friend, the best of creation, the one honoured with the Mighty Qur'ān – the ongoing miracle throughout the ages – and with the Sunnah, which illuminates for those seeking the right path. He was singled out with comprehensive speech and magnanimity of religion. May Allah's blessings and peace be upon all the Prophets and Messengers, all their families, and the rest of the righteous.

We have related from ʿAlī ibn Abī Ṭālib, ʿAbdullah ibn Masʿūd, Muʿādh ibn Jabal, Abū ad-Dardā', Ibn ʿUmar, Ibn ʿAbbās, Anas ibn Mālik, Abū Hurayrah and Abū Saʿīd al-Khudrī through many different paths with various narrations, that the Messenger of Allah ﷺ said, {Whoever preserved forty ḥadīths for my Ummah concerning the matter of their religion, Allah will resurrect him on the Day of Standing in the company of the jurists (*fuqahā'*) and scholars}.[5] In another narration: {Allah will resurrect him as a jurist and scholar}. In the narration of Abū ad-Dardā': {On the Day of Standing, I will be an intercessor and witness for him.} In the narration of Ibn Masʿūd: {It will be said to him, 'Enter from whichever door of Paradise you want.'} In the narration of Ibn ʿUmar: {He will be recorded in the company of the scholars and gathered with the martyrs.} The memorisers of ḥadīth (*ḥufāẓ*) have agreed that it is a weak ḥadīth even though it has numerous paths. The scholars have compiled innumerable books in this area, and the first person I know of to have compiled something in this area is ʿAbdullah ibn al-Mubārak, then Muḥammad ibn Aslam aṭ-Ṭūsī, the worshipful scholar, then al-Ḥasan ibn Sufyān an-Nasā'ī, Abū Bakr al-Ājurrī, Abū Bakr Muḥammad ibn

5 Collected by al-Bayhaqī from the ḥadīth of Imam Mālik and others, and he said, 'All the chains of transmission for this ḥadīth are weak. Al-Ḥāfiẓ Ibn ʿAsākir also collected it from various paths, and he said, 'This ḥadīth has been related from ʿAlī, Ibn ʿUmar, Abū Hurayrah, Abū Saʿīd and Abū Umāmah *marfūʿan* [i.e. attributed to the Messenger of Allah ﷺ] with chains of transmission that have all been commented on. There is no scope for authentification. *Al-Muʿīn ʿalā Tafahhum al-'Arbaʿīn* by Ibn Mulaqqin, 8-9 (manuscript).

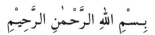

Ibrāhīm al-Aṣfahānī, ad-Dāraquṭnī, al-Ḥākim, Abū Nuʿaym, Abū ʿAbdir Raḥmān as-Sulamī, Abū Saʿīd al-Mālinī, Abū 'Uthman as-Ṣābūnī, ʿAbdullah ibn Muḥammad al-Anṣārī, Abū Bakr al-Bayhaqī, and several other people from both the early and later generations that cannot be counted.

I sought guidance from Allah the Exalted about gathering forty ḥadīths, to follows these imams, scholars, and memorisers of Islam. The scholars have unanimously agreed that it is permissible to act upon a weak ḥadīth in virtuous actions,[6] but despite that, I am not relying on this ḥadīth. Rather, I am relying on his ﷺ statement, in the authentic ḥadīths: {Let whoever of you is present convey to the absent one}[7] and his statement ﷺ: {May Allah illuminate a person who hears my words, keeps them in mind and then conveys them just as he heard them.}[8]

There are also scholars who gathered forty ḥadīths on the foundations of the Religion, some of them on the branches, some of them on *jihād*, some of them on abstinence, some of them on etiquette, some of them on public addresses, all of which are righteous intentions and may Allah be pleased with those who intended them. I saw that I should gather forty ḥadīths that are more important than all of them, and they are forty ḥadīths that comprise all of that, each one being an immense foundation of the Religion and the scholars have described it by saying that Islam revolves around it, or it is half of Islam or a third of it, and so forth.

Then I took it upon myself to ensure that these forty be authentic, and most of them are in the two *Ṣaḥīḥ* collections of al-Bukhārī and Muslim. I mention them without their chains of transmission, so their memorisation is easier and their benefit is more widespread if Allah the Exalted so wills. Then, at the end of the book, there is chapter elucidating what is hidden in their wordings.[9]

Whoever yearns for the Hereafter should know these ḥadīths, because of the important matters they comprise and because they contain that which calls attention to all acts of obedience, and this is obvious to anyone who reflects on the matter. Upon Allah is my reliance and to Him, I entrust myself, for Him is all praise and blessing, and by Him is success and protection from error.

6 (tn): i.e. not in foundational matters, such as what is lawful and unlawful.

7 Related by al-Bukhārī in the Book of Knowledge (the chapter on the Prophet's statement ﷺ: {Maybe the one conveyed to is more aware than the one who heard} as well as in the Books of Sacrifices, of the Ḥajj, Hunting, Tribulations, and other. Muslim has related it in the Book of Oaths, no.29 and 30.

8 Related by Abū Dāwūd in the Book of Knowledge (the chapter on the virtue of spreading knowledge), no.3360, at-Tirmidhī in the Book of Knowledge (the chapter on strongly encouraging the conveyance of what has been heard), and Ibn Mājah in the introduction, no.230. The text of this ḥadīth is established according to the imams.

9 This chapter is rarely found in editions of *The Forty* and its commentaries, but we will put this chapter at the end of the book, to complete the benefit, even though we have sufficiently explained and elucidated the wordings after each ḥadīth, as per our plan. However, we cannot do without the writings of our pious predecessors, because of the accuracy, trust, veracity and sincerity they contain.

THE FIRST ḤADĪTH

إِنَّمَا الْأَعْمَالُ بِالنِّيَّاتِ

عَنْ أَمِيرِ الْمُؤْمِنِينَ أَبِي حَفْصٍ عُمَرَ بْنِ الْخَطَّابِ ﵁ قَالَ: سَمِعْتُ رَسُولَ اللهِ ﷺ يَقُولُ: {إِنَّمَا الْأَعْمَالُ بِالنِّيَّاتِ وَإِنَّمَا لِكُلِّ امْرِئٍ مَا نَوَى فَمَنْ كَانَتْ هِجْرَتُهُ إِلَى اللهِ وَرَسُولِهِ فَهِجْرَتُهُ إِلَى اللهِ وَرَسُولِهِ وَمَنْ كَانَتْ هِجْرَتُهُ لِدُنْيَا يُصِيبُهَا أَوْ امْرَأَةٍ يَنْكِحُهَا فَهِجْرَتُهُ إِلَى مَا هَاجَرَ إِلَيْهِ}.

رَوَاهُ إِمَامَا الْمُحَدِّثِينَ أَبُو عَبْدِ اللهِ مُحَمَّدُ بْنُ إِسْمَاعِيلَ بْنِ إِبْرَاهِيمَ بْنِ الْمُغِيرَةِ ابْنِ بَرْدِزْبَهْ الْبُخَارِيُّ، وَأَبُو الْحُسَيْنِ مُسْلِمُ بْنُ الْحَجَّاجِ بْنِ مُسْلِمٍ الْقُشَيْرِيُّ النَّيْسَابُورِيُّ فِي صَحِيحَيْهِمَا اللَّذَيْنِ هُمَا أَصَحُّ الْكُتُبِ الْمُصَنَّفَةِ.

Actions are Only By Intentions

It is on the authority of the Commander of the Believers, Abū Ḥafs ʿUmar ibn al-Khaṭṭāb ﵁ who said, 'I heard the Messenger of Allah ﷺ, saying: {Actions are only by intentions, and for every individual is only what he intended. If someone's migration is to Allah and His Messenger, his migration is to Allah and His Messenger. If someone's migration is to acquire something worldly or to marry a woman, his migration is to what he migrated to.}'

This has been related by the two imams of the ḥadīth scholars, Abū ʿAbdillāh Muḥammad ibn Ismāʿīl ibn Ibrāhīm ibn al-Mughīrah ibn Bardizbah al-Bukhārī and Abū al-Ḥusayn Muslim ibn al-Ḥajjāj ibn Muslim al-Qushayrī al-Nīsābūrī, in their two *Ṣaḥīḥ* collections, which are the most authentic books to be compiled.

Al-Bukhārī has related it in the beginning of his *Ṣaḥīḥ* as well as in the Book of Faith (in the chapter on what has reached us regarding actions being by good intentions and every person getting what he intended) and five other places in his *Ṣaḥīḥ*. Muslim has narrated it in the Book of Rulership (in the chapter on his statement ﷺ: {Actions are only by intentions...}), no.1907. It has also been related by Abū Dāwūd in the Book of Divorce (in the chapter regarding what is meant by divorce and intention), no. 2201, at-Tirmidhī in the Book of the Virtues of Jihād (in the chapter on what has reached us regarding fighting ostentatiously and for worldly reasons), no.1646, Ibn Mājah in the Book of Abstinence (in the chapter on intentions), no. 4227, and an-Nasāʾī in the Book of Purification (in the chapter on intention *wuḍūʾ*), 1:59-60. It is also in the *Musnad* (1:25 and 43) and in the collections of ad-Dāraquṭnī, Ibn Ḥibbān and al-Bayhaqī.

Its Importance:
This is one of the more significant ḥadīths, which form the axis of Islam, as it is a foundation of the Religion and most of its rulings revolve around it. This is made clear by what the scholars have said. Abū Dāwūd said, 'This ḥadīth – actions are only by intentions – is half of Islam, because the Religion is either outward, which is action, or inward, which is intention.' Imams Aḥmad and ash-Shāfiʿī said that the ḥadīth {Actions are only by intentions...} contains a third of knowledge, because what the slave earns is by his heart, his tongue, and his limbs, and intention is in the heart, which is one of the three. This is why scholars have preferred to start their books and writings with it; al-Bukhārī places it at the beginning of his *Ṣaḥīḥ*, while an-Nawawī started three of his books with it: *Riyāḍ as-Ṣāliḥīn*, *al-Adhkār*, and *al-Arbaʿīn an-Nawawiyyah.*[10] The benefit of starting like this is to remind the student of knowledge to rectify his intention and make it sincerely for Allah the Exalted, in seeking knowledge and any other act of goodness. Part of what indicates its importance is that the Prophet ﷺ, quoted it in his *khuṭbahs*, as mentioned in al-Bukhārī's narration, and then ʿUmar did likewise. Abū ʿUbayd said, 'There is no ḥadīth that is more comprehensive, sufficient and beneficial than this ḥadīth.'

The Language of the Ḥadīth:
(حفص) *ḥafs*: a lion and Abū al-Ḥafs is an agnomen for ʿUmar ibn al-Khaṭṭāb ﷺ.

(إنما) *innama*: a tool of restriction; it affirms what follows it and negates everything else.

(النيّات) *an-niyyāt*: the plural of *niyyah*, which, linguistically, means 'intention' and in the terminology of the Revealed Law: an intention connected to an action.

(امرئ) *imriʾin*: a person, whether male or female.

10 Translator's note (tn): i.e. the Forty Ḥadīth of Imam an-Nawawī, which the book in your hands is a commentary of.

(هجرته) *hijratuhu*: linguistically, *hijrah* means to leave something, and in the Revealed Law: leaving the Abode of Disbelief (*Dār al-Kufr*) for the Abode of Islam (*Dār al-Islām*) for fear of tribulation. What is being referred to in the ḥadīth   is moving from Makkah and elsewhere to al-Madīnah before the conquest of Makkah.

(إلى الله) *ilā Allah*: to where Allah is pleased, intentionally and deliberately.

(فهجرته إلى الله ورسوله) *fa hijratuhu ilā Allahi wa Rasūlihi*: it is accepted and one is rewarded for it.

(لدنيا يصيبها) *lidunyā yaṣībuha*: for a worldly purpose that one wants to acquire.

Circumstances Surrounding the Ḥadīth:
In his *Muʿjam al-Kabīr*, with a chain of transmission whose narrators are all trustworthy, at-Ṭabarānī relates on the authority of Ibn Masʿūd ☙ that he said: 'There was a man amongst us who proposed to a woman called "Umm Qays", but she refused to marry him until he migrated, so he migrated and then married her, so we called him "the Emigrant of Umm Qays".

Saʿīd ibn Manṣūr has related in his *Sunan*, with a chain of transmission that meets the conditions of the two Sheikhs,[11] on the authority of Ibn Masʿūd, that he said, 'Whoever migrates out of desire for something, whatever he obtains from it is like the reward of the man who migrated to marry a woman called Umm Qays, and he was called "the Emigrant of Umm Qays".

Legal Matters and Other Guidance from the Ḥadīth:
1. The stipulation of intention: All scholars agree that actions performed by legally responsible[12] believers are of no consideration in the Revealed Law and do not merit any reward unless they are done with intention.

An intention in certain acts of worship, like the prayer, the Ḥajj, and fasting, is one of its pillars, and the action is not valid without it. As for that which is a means towards an act of worship, such as *wuḍūʾ* and *ghusl*, the Ḥanafīs say that they are a condition of perfection, to obtain reward. The Shāfiʿīs and others say that they, too, are a condition of validity, and thus such means are not valid without an intention.

2. The time and place of the intention: The time of the intention is at the beginning of the act of worship, such as the opening *takbīr* in the prayer and entering a state of *iḥrām* for Ḥajj. As for fasting, it suffices to have the intention in one's heart beforehand, due to the difficulty of catching the moment dawn breaks.

---

11 (tn): i.e. al-Bukhārī and Muslim.
12 Ar. *mukallaf*, i.e. sane and adolescent.

The place of one's intention is the heart; it is not stipulated that one utter it. Rather, it is recommended so that the tongue can help the heart concentrate.

It is stipulated that one specifies what is intended and distinguishes it from everything else. It does not suffice merely to intend to pray. Rather, one must specify what prayer it is, such as *Ẓuhr*, *ʿAsr*, and so forth.

3. The obligation to migrate: Migration from the lands of the disbelievers to the abodes of Islam is an obligation upon every Muslim who is not able to manifest his religion. This ruling is permanent and unrestricted. As for the report: {There is no migration after the conquest}, it means that there is no migration from Makkah after its conquest because it has become part of *Dār al-Islām*.

The word *hijrah* also applies to that which Allah has forbidden: {The emigrant[13] is the one who migrates from what Allah has forbidden.} A Muslim 'migrates' from his brother for more than three days.[14] A wife 'migrates' from her husband's bed. It could be obligatory upon a Muslim to 'migrate' from his disobedient Muslim brother, just as it would be permissible for him to 'migrate' from his recalcitrant wife to discipline her.

4. The ḥadīth informs that whoever intends a righteous action and is then prevented from doing so by an overwhelming excuse, such as an illness or death or something similar, is still rewarded. Al-Bayḍāwī said, 'Actions are not valid without an intention, because an intention without action is rewarded while an action without an intention is just dust. Intentions are connected to actions the same way spirits are connected to bodies: a body does not last without a spirit, and a spirit does not become manifest in this world unless it is attached to a body.'

5. The ḥadīth instructs us to have sincerity in our actions and our worship so that we attain reward in the Hereafter and success in this worldly life.

6. With an intention and sincerity, seeking Allah the Exalted's pleasure, every good and beneficial action becomes worship.

13 Ar. *muhājir*.

14 (tn): i.e. it is sinful for a Muslim to abandon or ignore his brother for more than three days.

THE SECOND ḤADĪTH

الإِسْلَامُ وَالإِيْمَانُ وَالإِحْسَانُ

عَنْ عُمَرَ ﷺ أَيْضًا قَالَ: {بَيْنَمَا نَحْنُ جُلُوْسٌ عِنْدَ رَسُولِ اللهِ ﷺ ذَاتَ يَوْمٍ إِذْ طَلَعَ عَلَيْنَا رَجُلٌ شَدِيْدُ بَيَاضِ الثِّيَابِ شَدِيْدُ سَوَادِ الشَّعَرِ، لَا يُرَى عَلَيْهِ أَثَرُ السَّفَرِ وَلَا يَعْرِفُهُ مِنَّا أَحَدٌ، حَتَّى جَلَسَ إِلَى النَّبِيِّ ﷺ، فَأَسْنَدَ رُكْبَتَيْهِ إِلَى رُكْبَتَيْهِ، وَوَضَعَ كَفَّيْهِ عَلَى فَخِذَيْهِ، وَقَالَ: يَا مُحَمَّدُ أَخْبِرْنِي عَنِ الإِسْلَامِ، فَقَالَ رَسُوْلُ اللهِ ﷺ: الإِسْلَامُ أَنْ تَشْهَدَ أَنْ لَا إِلَهَ إِلَّا اللهُ وَأَنَّ مُحَمَّداً رَسُوْلُ اللهِ، وَتُقِيْمَ الصَّلَاةَ، وَتُؤْتِيَ الزَّكَاةَ وَتَصُومَ رَمَضَانَ، وَتَحُجَّ الْبَيْتَ إِنِ اسْتَطَعْتَ إِلَيْهِ سَبِيْلًا. قَالَ: صَدَقْتَ. فَعَجِبْنَا لَهُ يَسْأَلُهُ وَيُصَدِّقُهُ. قَالَ: فَأَخْبِرْنِي عَنِ الْإِيْمَانِ، قَالَ: أَنْ تُؤْمِنَ بِاللهِ، وَمَلَائِكَتِهِ، وَكُتُبِهِ، وَرُسُلِهِ، وَالْيَوْمِ الْآخِرِ، وَتُؤْمِنَ بِالْقَدَرِ خَيْرِهِ وَشَرِّهِ. قَالَ صَدَقْتَ. قَالَ: فَأَخْبِرْنِي عَنِ الإِحْسَانِ، قَالَ: أَنْ تَعْبُدَ اللهَ كَأَنَّكَ تَرَاهُ فَإِنْ لَمْ تَكُنْ تَرَاهُ فَإِنَّهُ يَرَاكَ. قَالَ: فَأَخْبِرْنِي عَنِ السَّاعَةِ، قَالَ: مَا الْمَسْؤُوْلُ عَنْهَا بِأَعْلَمَ مِنَ السَّائِلِ. قَالَ: فَأَخْبِرْنِي عَنْ أَمَارَاتِهَا، قَالَ: أَنْ تَلِدَ الْأَمَةُ رَبَّتَهَا، وَأَنْ تَرَى الْحُفَاةَ الْعُرَاةَ الْعَالَةَ رِعَاءَ الشَّاءِ يَتَطَاوَلُوْنَ فِي الْبُنْيَانِ، ثُمَّ انْطَلَقَ، فَلَبِثْتُ مَلِيّاً، ثُمَّ قَالَ: يَا عُمَرُ، أَتَدْرِي مَنِ السَّائِلُ؟ قُلْتُ: اللهُ وَرَسُوْلُهُ أَعْلَمُ. قَالَ: فَإِنَّهُ جِبْرِيْلُ أَتَاكُمْ يُعَلِّمُكُمْ دِيْنَكُمْ.} رواه مسلم.

Islam, Īmān, and Iḥsān

It is on the authority of ʿUmar ؓ that he also said, 'One day, while we were sitting with the Messenger of Allah ﷺ, a man appeared before us whose clothes were extremely white and whose hair was extremely black. No traces of travel could be seen on him and none of us recognized him until he sat down close to the Prophet ﷺ, rested his knees upon his knees, placed his hands upon his thighs, and said, 'Muḥammad, tell me about Islam.' The Messenger of Allah ﷺ, said, {Islam is that you bear witness that there is no god but Allah and that Muḥammad is the Messenger of Allah, you establish the prayer, you give the zakāt, you fast Ramaḍān and you perform the Ḥajj of the House if you can make your way there.} He said, 'You have spoken the truth.' We were amazed at him asking him and then affirming that he had spoken the truth. He then said, 'Tell me about *īmān*.'[15] He replied, {That you believe in Allah, His angels, His Books, His Messengers, the Last Day, and you believe in the Decree, the good of it and the bad of it.} He said, 'You have spoken the truth.' He then said, 'Tell me about *iḥsān*.' He replied, {That you worship Allah as if you can see Him, and if you cannot see Him, He definitely sees you.} He said, 'Tell me about the Hour.' He replied, {The one who is asked about it knows no more than the one asking.} He said, 'Then tell me about its signs.' He replied, {That the female slave should give birth to her mistress, and you see poor, naked, barefoot herders of sheep and goats competing in raising tall buildings.} He then left, and I waited a while. Then he said, "Umar, do you know who the questioner was?' I replied, 'Allah and His Messenger know best.' He said {It was Jibrīl. He came to teach you your religion.} Related by Muslim.

Muslim has related it in the beginning of the Book of Faith, no. 8, as well as at-Tirmidhī in the Book of Faith, no. 2738, Abū Dāwūd in the Book of the Sunnah (the chapter on the Decree), no. 4695, and an-Nasāʾī in the Book of Faith (the chapter on the blessing of Islam), 8/97.

Its Importance:

Ibn Daqīq al-ʿĪd has said, 'This is an immense ḥadīth. It includes all the functions of both outward and inward actions. All the sciences of the Revealed Law go back to it and branch out from it, because its contents contain the sum knowledge of the Sunnah, and thus it is like the Mother of the Sunnah, just as the Fātiḥah is called the Mother of the Qurʾān because its contents contains the sum of the Qurʾān's meanings.'

---

15 (tn): i.e. faith.

It is also a mass-transmitted ḥadīth (*mutawātir*)[16] because it has been related from eight of the noble Companions: Abū Hurayrah, ʿUmar, Abū Dharr, Anas, Ibn ʿAbbās, Ibn ʿUmar, Abū ʿĀmir al-Ashʿarī, and Jarīr al-Bajalī,[17] ﷺ.

The Language of the Ḥadīth:

(بينما) *baynama*: *bayna* is an adverb of time and *ma* is additional. In one narration, the word is *baynā*.

(إذ طلع) *idh ṭalaʿa*: *idh* is a particle indicating suddenness, i.e. he appeared before us suddenly.

(ووضع كفيه على فخذيه) *wa waḍaʿa kaffayhi ʿalā fakhidayh*: i.e. on his thighs, as a well-mannered person would do. In an-Nasāʾī's narration: 'He put his hands on the Prophet's thighs ﷺ, and the first narration is more authentic and more well-known.

(أخبرني عن الإسلام) *akhbirnī ʿan al-Islām*: tell me about the reality of Islam and its legislated actions, and the same goes for (أخبرني عن الإيمان) *akhbirnī ʿan al-īmān* and (الإحسان) *iḥsān.*

(فعجبنا له يسأله ويصدقه) *fa ʿajabna lahu yasʾalahu wa yuṣaddiquhu*: i.e. we were astonished at his state, and then he asked as if he knew and was checking and verifying. Alternatively, we were astonished because his question indicated that he was ignorant about what he was asking while his affirmation indicated that he knew of it.

(أن تؤمن بالله...) *an tuʾmina billāhi*: linguistically, *īmān* is affirmation and absolute certainty in one's heart. In the Revealed Law, it is affirmation of what is mentioned in the ḥadīth.

(فأخبرني عن الساعة) *fa ʾakhbirnī an as-sāʿah*: tell me when the Day of Standing will occur.

(أماراتها) *amārātiha*: this is the plural of *amārah* (أمارة), which is sign, and what is meant by its signs is that which precedes it occurrence.

(أن تلد الأمة ربتها) *an talid al-ʾammatu rabbatahā*: i.e. her female master, and in another narration: *rabbaha,* i.e. her master. The meaning is that one of the signs of the Hour is that there will be an abundance of handmaidens whose masters will have intercourse with them, and then their children will be freemen like their fathers. A handmaiden's child by her master has the same status as her master because

16 (tn): i.e. it has been related by such a large number of people that it is rationally impossible for all of them to have conspired to lie.

17 See *al-Mutanāthir min al-Ḥadīth al-Mutawātir* by al-Kitānī, p.30.

the property of the father eventually becomes the property of the child, and this is how the child becomes her master. It has also been said that it an allusion to children not respecting their parents, such that parents come to fear their children the same way a slave fears his master. It can also be an allusion to the corruption of the age and the inversion of circumstances.

(الحفاة العراة العالة) *al-ḥufāta al-ʿurāta al-ʿālata*: *al-ḥufāt* is the plural of *ḥaf*, which refers to someone who is not wearing shoes or sandals, *al-ʿurāt* is the plural of *ʿār*, which refers to someone who is not wearing any clothes, and *al-ʿālat* is the plural of *ʿāʾil*, which is a poor person.

(رعاء الشاء) *riʿāʾa ash-shāʾi*, which is the plural of *rāʿ*, which refers to a guardian or caretaker, another plural of which is *ruʿāt*; *ash-shāʾ* is the plural of *shāt*, which is one sheep.

(يتطاولون في البنيان) *yataṭāwalūna fil-bunyān*: they build tall buildings out of vainglory and ostentation.

(فلبثت مليا) *fa labiththu maliyyan*: I waited for a long time, i.e. I was absent from the Prophet ﷺ, for three nights, as mentioned in one narration, and then I met him.

Legal Matters and Other Guidance from the Ḥadīth:

1. Beautifying one's clothes and appearance: it is advisable to wear clean clothes and to scent oneself with a pleasant fragrance before entering a masjid or attending a gathering of knowledge, and to have good manners in gatherings of knowledge and with the scholars. Jibrīl, blessings, and ﷺ came to teach people by way of his state as well as by way of his statements.

2. What is Islam? Linguistically, *islām* means submission and surrender to Allah the Exalted. In the terminology of the Revealed Law, it is based on five foundations: the testimony that there is no god but Allah and that Muḥammad is the Messenger of Allah, the establishment of the prayer on time with its conditions and pillars fulfilled, complemented by the *sunan*[18] and proper etiquette, the payment of the zakāt, fasting the month of Ramaḍān and performing the Ḥajj of the Sacred House once in one's life if one is able and can afford the travel expenses and to provide for one's family and dependents until one's return.

3. What is Īmān? Linguistically, *īmān* means affirmation. In the terminology of the Revealed Law, it means affirmation and absolute conviction that Allah the Creator exists and that He is one and has no partner.

18 (tn): which is the plural of *sunnah*, i.e. that which is recommended in the prayer.

Then there is affirmation of the existence of Allah's creation, which is the angels, and they are honoured slaves, they do not disobey Allah in respect of any order He gives them and carry out what they are ordered to do.[19] Allah created them from light. They do not eat, they are not described as male or female, they do not procreate and no one but Allah knows their number.

Then there is affirmation of the Divine Books sent down from Allah the Exalted, and that they contained Allah's legislation before people's hands corrupted them and altered them.

Then there is the affirmation of all the messengers that Allah chose to guide His creation and that the Divine Books were sent down to them, along with the conviction that the messengers are infallible humans.

Then there is the affirmation of the Last Day, in which Allah will resurrect mankind from their graves and take them to account from their actions. If they are good, they will be rewarded likewise and if they are evil, they will be rewarded likewise.

Then there is the affirmation that everything that happens in existence is according to Allah the Exalted's decree and will, in consonance with wisdom that only Allah knows.

These are the pillars of *īmān*; whoever has firm conviction in them is saved and victorious, and whoever denies them is astray and without success. Allah the Exalted has said:

﴿يَـٰٓأَيُّهَا ٱلَّذِينَ ءَامَنُوٓاْ ءَامِنُواْ بِٱللَّهِ وَرَسُولِهِۦ وَٱلْكِتَـٰبِ ٱلَّذِى نَزَّلَ عَلَىٰ رَسُولِهِۦ وَٱلْكِتَـٰبِ ٱلَّذِىٓ أَنزَلَ مِن
قَبْلُ ۚ وَمَن يَكْفُرْ بِٱللَّهِ وَمَلَـٰٓئِكَتِهِۦ وَكُتُبِهِۦ وَرُسُلِهِۦ وَٱلْيَوْمِ ٱلْـَٔاخِرِ فَقَدْ ضَلَّ ضَلَـٰلًۢا بَعِيدًا﴾

"You who believe! Believe in Allah and His Messenger and the Book He sent down to His Messenger, and the Books He sent down before. Anyone who rejects Allah, His angels, His Books, His Messengers or the Last Day has gone very far astray." [an-Nisā' 4:136]

4. Al-Islām and al-Īmān: You know from the aforementioned that *islām* and *īmān* are two distinct realities, linguistically and in the Revealed Law, and this is the default position when there are different names. However, in the Revealed Law, one term can refer to the other figuratively. No consideration is given to *īmān* without *islām* just as no consideration is given to *islām* without *īmān* because they are inseparable. There has to be faith in the heart and action in the limbs.

19 (tn): Please see Sūrat at-Taḥrīm 66:6.

5. What is Iḥsān? Iḥsān is sincerity and thoroughness, i.e. you are sincere in your worship of Allah alone with complete thoroughness as if you can see Him while you are worshipping Him, and if you cannot then remember that Allah is watching you and sees everything that you do, big or small.

6. The Hour and its Signs: Knowledge of when the Hour will occur belongs exclusively to Allah. He has not disclosed this knowledge to any of His creation, angel or messenger. This is why the Prophet ﷺ, said to Jibrīl, {The one who is asked about it knows no more than the one asking.} However, he did respond to him by informing of some of the signs that will precede its occurrence and indicate its proximity:

v. The corruption of the age and moral lassitude, such that there will be much disobedience and disrespect shown to parents by their children, and they will treat them the way a master treats his slaves.

vi. Matters will become inverted and confused, such that the lowest of people will become the kings and rulers of the Ummah and matters will fall into the hands of those who are unqualified. People will have abundant wealth and there will be lots of luxury and extravagance. People will compete in tall buildings and there will be an abundance of commodities and furnishings. Those who were once poor and wretched and used to live off the charity of other nomads and shepherds, and the like, will look down at the people and be in charge of their affairs.

7. Asking about knowledge: The Muslim only asks about that which will benefit him in this life and the Hereafter, and he does not ask about that which is of no benefit. Likewise, when someone attends a gathering of knowledge and notices that those present require a certain matter and no one has asked about it, he should ask about it even if he already knows, so that those present can benefit from the matter. It is obligatory upon whomever is asked about a matter that he does not know to say, 'I do not know', and this is evidence of his scrupulousness (*waraʿ*), his consciousness of Allah (*taqwā*) and his sound knowledge.

8. One of the methods of education is the way of question and answer. It is a very successful method, from ancient times through to today, and it was used frequently when the Messenger of Allah ﷺ, was teaching his Companions, as seen in several ḥadīths. This is because it grabs the listeners' attention and readies their ears to hear the correct answer.

THE THIRD ḤADĪTH

أَرْكَانُ الإِسْلَامِ وَدَعَائِمُهُ الْعِظَامِ

عَنْ أَبِي عَبْدِ الرَّحْمَنِ بْنِ عُمَرَ بْنِ الْخَطَّابِ ﷺ قَالَ: سَمِعْتُ رَسُولَ اللهِ ﷺ يَقُولُ: {بُنِيَ الإِسْلَامُ عَلَى خَمْسٍ: شَهَادَةِ أَنْ لَا إِلَهَ إِلَّا اللهُ وَأَنَّ مُحَمَّدًا رَسُولُ اللهِ، وَإِقَامِ الصَّلَاةِ، وَإِيْتَاءِ الزَّكَاةِ، وَحَجِّ الْبَيْتِ، وَصَوْمِ رَمَضَانَ.} رواه البُخَارِي ومُسْلِم.

The Pillars of Islam and Its Immense Supports

It is on the authority of Abū ʿAbdur Raḥmān ʿAbdullah ibn ʿUmar ibn al-Khaṭṭāb ﷺ that he said, 'I heard the Messenger of Allah ﷺ, saying: {Islam has been built from five: bearing witness that there is no god but Allah and that Muḥammad is the Messenger of Allah, establishing the prayer, paying the zakāt, making the Ḥajj of the House and fasting Ramaḍān.} Related by al-Bukhārī and Muslim.

The ḥadīth was collected by al-Bukhārī under al-Īmān (the chapter on al-Īmān and the Prophet's statement ﷺ: {Islam has been built from five}), no.8, by Muslim under al-Īmān (the chapter on explaining the pillars of Islam and its magnificent supports), no.16, at-Tirmidhī under al-Īmān (the chapter on what has reached us regarding Islam being built on five), no.2612, an-Nasāʾī under al-Īmān (the chapter on how many pillars is Islam is built upon) 8/107, and it is also in the *Musnad* of Imam Aḥmad, 2:26, 93, and 120.

Its Importance:
The ḥadīth on the 'pillars of Islam' is truly immense, as it is one of the bases of Islam and a gatherer of rulings, as it contains the knowledge of the Religion, what it relies on and all of its pillars. These pillars are specified in the Noble Qurʾān.

The Language of the Ḥadīth:
(بُنِيَ) *buniya*: this is a simple past verb in the passive voice, from *banā, yabnī, bināʾan*, i.e. it has been founded.

(على خمس) *ʿalā khams,* and in one narration *ʿala khamsah* (على خمسة), i.e. five supports or five pillars, and *ʿalā* means *min,* i.e. from.

(شهادة) *shahādah*: i.e. avowal and affirmation.

(أن لا إله إلا الله) *an lā ilāha ill Allahu*: the original phrase is *annahu la ilāha ill Allahu,* i.e. the dummy pronoun *hu* (i.e. 'it', referring to the matter at hand) has been elided.

(إقام الصلاة) *iqāmi as-ṣalāti*: i.e. to do it persistently, with all of its conditions and pillars, complemented by the *sunan* and proper etiquette.

Legal Matters and Other Guidance from the Ḥadīth:

1. The building of Islam: The Messenger of Allah ﷺ, is likening the Islam that he brought – and which takes a person out of the realm of disbelief and makes them worthy of entering Paradise and being saved from the Fire – to a solid building, standing on firmly established foundations, and he elucidates that these foundations are the following:

i. Bearing witness that there is no god but Allah and that Muḥammad is the Messenger of Allah, which means to avow Allah the Exalted's existence and oneness and to affirm the prophethood and messengership of Muḥammad ﷺ. This pillar is the foundation of all the other pillars. He ﷺ, has said, {I have been commanded to fight people until they bear witness that there is no god but Allah and that Muḥammad is the Messenger of Allah.}, as related by al-Bukhārī and Muslim. He ﷺ, has also said, {Whoever says *la ilāha ill Allah* with sincerity shall enter Paradise.} This is an authentic ḥadīth and has been collected by al-Bazzār.

ii. Establishing the prayer: i.e. maintaining the prayer and performing it in its stipulated times, fulfilling its conditions and pillars and observing its *sunan* and etiquettes, such that its benefits manifest in the Muslim's soul, and he leaves indecency and wrongdoing. The Exalted One has said:

﴿وَأَقِمِ ٱلصَّلَوٰةَ ۖ إِنَّ ٱلصَّلَوٰةَ تَنْهَىٰ عَنِ ٱلْفَحْشَآءِ وَٱلْمُنكَرِ﴾

"Establish the prayer. The prayer precludes indecency and wrongdoing." [al-ʿAnkabūt 29:45]

The prayer is the distinguishing mark of the Muslim and the sign of the believer. He ﷺ, has said, {Between a man and idolatry and disbelief is the relinquishment of the prayer.}, as collected by Muslim and others. He also said, {The prayer is the pillar of the Religion.}, which is a *ḥasan*[20] ḥadīth collected by Abū Nuʿaym.

20 (tn): i.e. the narrators in the chain of transmission are lesser in memory and precision than those in a *ṣaḥīḥ*, i.e. authentic, chain of transmission.

iii. Paying the zakāt: i.e. giving a specific portion of one's wealth – if one's wealth meets the threshold and the conditions that make it obligatory, as well as the conditions that enable it to be performed, are met – to the poor and other deserving recipients. Allah the Exalted has described the believers by saying:

﴿وَٱلَّذِينَ هُمْ لِلزَّكَوٰةِ فَـٰعِلُونَ﴾
"those who pay zakāt". [al-Mu'minūn 23:4]

He ﷻ has also said:

﴿وَٱلَّذِينَ فِىٓ أَمْوَٰلِهِمْ حَقٌّ مَّعْلُومٌ﴾
"those in whose wealth there is a known share". [al-Ma'ārij 70:24]

It is a financial form of worship and through it, societal fairness is realised. It puts an end to poverty and destitution and causes love, compassion and respect to prevail amongst Muslims.

iv. The Ḥajj: i.e. to head to the Sacred Masjid in the months of the Ḥajj, which are Shawwāl, Dhūl Qa'dah and the first ten days of Dhūl Ḥijjah, and to carry out therein the rites that the Messenger of Allah ﷺ, has elucidated. It is both a financial and physical form of worship and it brings about numerous benefits for the individual and the society at large. Furthermore, it is a large Islamic conference, an immense occasion for Muslims from every country to meet. Allah ﷻ has said:

﴿وَأَذِّن فِى ٱلنَّاسِ بِٱلْحَجِّ يَأْتُوكَ رِجَالًا وَعَلَىٰ كُلِّ ضَامِرٍ يَأْتِينَ مِن كُلِّ فَجٍّ عَمِيقٍ ﴿٢٧﴾ لِّيَشْهَدُوا۟ مَنَـٰفِعَ لَهُمْ وَيَذْكُرُوا۟ ٱسْمَ ٱللَّهِ فِىٓ أَيَّامٍ مَّعْلُومَـٰتٍ عَلَىٰ مَا رَزَقَهُم مِّنۢ بَهِيمَةِ ٱلْأَنْعَـٰمِ ۖ فَكُلُوا۟ مِنْهَا وَأَطْعِمُوا۟ ٱلْبَآئِسَ ٱلْفَقِيرَ﴾
"Announce the Ḥajj to mankind. They will come to you on foot and every sort of lean animal, coming by every distant road so that they can be present at what will profit them, and invoke Allah's name on specific days over livestock he has provided for them. Eat of them and those who are poor and in need." [al-Ḥajj 22:27-28]

This is why the reward for the Ḥajj is immense and abundant. He ﷺ, has said, {When Allah accepts a Ḥajj, there is no other reward for it apart from Paradise.} The Ḥajj was made an obligation during the sixth year of the Hijrah, when the Exalted One said:

﴿وَلِلَّهِ عَلَى ٱلنَّاسِ حِجُّ ٱلْبَيْتِ مَنِ ٱسْتَطَاعَ إِلَيْهِ سَبِيلًا﴾

"Ḥajj to the House is a duty owed to Allah by all mankind – for those who are able." [Āl ʿImrān 3:97]

v. Fasting Ramaḍān: This was made an obligation in the second year of the Hijrah, when the Exalted One said:

﴿شَهْرُ رَمَضَانَ ٱلَّذِىٓ أُنزِلَ فِيهِ ٱلْقُرْءَانُ هُدًى لِّلنَّاسِ وَبَيِّنَٰتٍ مِّنَ ٱلْهُدَىٰ وَٱلْفُرْقَانِ ۚ

فَمَن شَهِدَ مِنكُمُ ٱلشَّهْرَ فَلْيَصُمْهُ﴾

"The month of Ramaḍān is the one in which the Qur'ān was sent down as guidance for mankind, with clear signs containing guidance and discrimination. And of you who are resident for the month should fast it." [al-Baqarah 2:185]

In this worship, there is purification of one's soul, the elevation of one's spirit and health for one's body. Whoever carries it out to obey Allah's command and seek His pleasure will have his sins expiated and it will be a cause of his entering Paradise. He ﷺ, has said, {Whoever fasts Ramaḍān with firm conviction and in anticipation of Allah's reward will have all his previous sins forgiven.}

2. How the pillars are connected: Whoever carries out all of these pillars is a Muslim with complete faith, and whoever relinquishes all of them is a disbeliever. Whoever disavows one of them is not a Muslim by consensus. Whoever has firm conviction in all of them but neglects one of them – apart from the testimony of faith – out of laziness is a sinner (*fāsiq*). Whoever carries out actions and affirms them on his tongue merely out of flattery is a hypocrite (*munāfiq*).

3. The objective of worship: What is meant by worship in Islam is not its forms and shapes. Rather, what is meant is it's objective and meaning along with carrying it out. Thus, a prayer that does not preclude indecency and wrongdoing is of no benefit, and the same goes for a fast in which the fasting person does not relinquish lying and acting upon it. Likewise, any Ḥajj or zakāt that is done out of ostentation or for the sake of reputation is not accepted by Allah. This does not mean that these acts of worship should be relinquished if their benefits are not realised. Rather, one should push one's soul towards sincerity therein and to achieve what is sought.

4. The branches of faith: The matters mentioned in this ḥadīth are not everything in Islam. Rather, they are mentioned here because of their importance, and there are several matters besides them. He ﷺ, has said, {Faith has some seventy branches.}, which is an agreed-upon ḥadīth.

5. The ḥadīth shows that Islam is both creed and deed, for an action without faith is of no benefit, just as there is no faith without action.

THE FOURTH ḤADĪTH

أَطْوَارُ خَلْقِ الإِنْسَانِ وَخَاتِمَتُهُ

عَنْ أَبِي عَبْدِ الرَّحْمنِ عَبْدِ اللهِ بْنِ مَسْعُودٍ ﵁ قَالَ: حَدَّثَنَا رَسُولُ اللهِ ﷺ وَهُوَ الصَّادِقُ الْمَصْدُوقُ: {إِنَّ أَحَدَكُمْ يُجْمَعُ خَلْقُهُ فِي بَطْنِ أُمِّهِ أَرْبَعِينَ يَوْماً نُطْفَةً، ثُمَّ يَكُونُ عَلَقَةً مِثْلَ ذَلِكَ، ثُمَّ يَكُونُ مُضْغَةً مِثْلَ ذَلِكَ، ثُمَّ يُرْسَلُ إِلَيْهِ الْمَلَكُ فَيَنْفُخُ فِيهِ الرُّوحَ وَيُؤْمَرُ بِأَرْبَعِ كَلِمَاتٍ بِكَتْبِ رِزْقِهِ وَأَجَلِهِ وَعَمَلِهِ وَشَقِيٌّ أَوْ سَعِيدٌ فَوَاللهِ الَّذِي لَا إِلَهَ غَيْرُهُ إِنَّ أَحَدَكُمْ لَيَعْمَلُ بِعَمَلِ أَهْلِ الْجَنَّةِ حَتَّى مَا يَكُونُ بَيْنَهُ وَبَيْنَهَا إِلَّا ذِرَاعٌ، فَيَسْبِقُ عَلَيْهِ الْكِتَابُ فَيَعْمَلُ بِعَمَلِ أَهْلِ النَّارِ فَيَدْخُلُهَا. وَإِنَّ أَحَدَكُمْ لَيَعْمَلُ بِعَمَلِ أَهْلِ النَّارِ حَتَّى مَا يَكُونُ بَيْنَهُ وَبَيْنَهَا إِلَّا ذِرَاعٌ، فَيَسْبِقُ عَلَيْهِ الْكِتَابُ فَيَعْمَلُ بِعَمَلِ أَهْلِ الْجَنَّةِ فَيَدْخُلُهَا.} رواه البخاري ومسلم.

The Stages of Man's Creation and His End

It is on the authority of Abū ʿAbdir Raḥmān ʿAbdillāh ibn Masʿūd ﵁ that he said, 'The Messenger of Allah ﷺ, and he is the truthful one and the one who is believed, told us: {The creation of one you is gathered in the belly of his mother for forty days as a drop. Then he is likewise a clot of blood and then he is likewise a morsel of flesh. Then the angel is sent to him and breathes the spirit into him, and he is commanded with four words: with writing his provision, his life span, his deeds and whether he will be happy or wretched. By Allah, besides whom there is no other god, one of you will do the actions of the people of Paradise until there is only a cubit between him and it. Then the decree will overtake him, he will do the actions of the people of the Fire and then enter it. Likewise, one of you will do the actions of the people of the Fire until there is only a cubit between him and it. Then the decree will overtake him, he will do the actions of the people of Paradise and then enter it.} Related by al-Bukhārī and Muslim.

Al-Bukhārī has collected this ḥadīth in the Beginning of Creation (the chapter on mentioning the angels), no.3036, as well as Predestination and Prophets. Muslim has collected it in the beginning of the Book of Predestination (the chapter on how humans are created), no.2643. Abū Dāwūd has collected it in the Sunnah (the chapter on predestination), no.4708, as well as at-Tirmidhī in Predestination (the chapter on actions being according to their ends), no.2138, and Ibn Mājah in the introduction (the chapter on predestination), no.76.

Its Importance:

This ḥadīth is immense. It gathers all of man's states, from the beginning of his creation and his entrance into this worldly life through to the last of his states: eternity in the abode of bliss or the abode of wretchedness. All of it is based on what he earned and his actions in this worldly life, according to what Allah already knew of, and thus He decreed and predestined.

The Language of the Ḥadīth:

(الصادق) *as-ṣādiq*: the truthful in everything that he says; it is the veracious truth, corresponding with reality.

(المصدوق) *al-maṣdūq*: the one who is believed in what has been revealed to him, because the Angel Jibrīl came to him with the truth, and Allah ﷻ affirms him in what He has promised him.

(يجمع) *yujmaʿu*: i.e. brought together and maintained, it has also been said that he is decreed and gathered.

(خلقه) *khalquhu*: i.e. the material of his creation, which is the water that he is created from.

(في بطن أمه) *fī baṭni ummihi*: i.e. in her womb.

(نطفة) *nuṭfah*: the original meaning of which is a drop of clear water, and the meaning here is semen.

(علقة) *ʿalaqah*: a piece of blood that has not dried, and it is called *ʿalaqah*, i.e. something hangs or sticks, because it sticks to the hand that holds it.

(مضغة) *mudghah*: a piece of flesh of chewable size.

(فيسبق عليه الكتاب) *fa yasbiqu ʿalayhi al-kitāb*: i.e. that which Allah already knew, or the Preserved Tablet,[21] or that which was already in the mother's womb.

Legal Matters and Other Guidance from the Ḥadīth:

1. The embryo's phases in the womb: This ḥadīth indicates that the embryo changes over 120 days in three phases, every forty days constitutes a phase. In the first forty days, it is a drop, in the second forty days, it is a blood clot, and in the third forty days, it is a piece of flesh. Then, after 120 days, the angel breathes the spirit into it and writes these four words for it. Allah ﷻ has mentioned in His Mighty Book how the embryo changes in these phases. He ﷻ has said:

﴿يَٰٓأَيُّهَا ٱلنَّاسُ إِن كُنتُمْ فِى رَيْبٍ مِّنَ ٱلْبَعْثِ فَإِنَّا خَلَقْنَٰكُم مِّن تُرَابٍ ثُمَّ مِن نُّطْفَةٍ ثُمَّ مِنْ عَلَقَةٍ ثُمَّ مِن مُّضْغَةٍ مُّخَلَّقَةٍ﴾

"Mankind! If you are in doubt about the Resurrection, know that we created you from dust, then from a drop of sperm, then from a clot of blood, then from a lump of flesh". [al-Ḥajj 22:5]

And Allah ﷻ has said:

﴿وَلَقَدْ خَلَقْنَا ٱلْإِنسَٰنَ مِن سُلَٰلَةٍ مِّن طِينٍ ﴿١٢﴾ ثُمَّ جَعَلْنَٰهُ نُطْفَةً فِى قَرَارٍ مَّكِينٍ ﴿١٣﴾ ثُمَّ خَلَقْنَا ٱلنُّطْفَةَ عَلَقَةً فَخَلَقْنَا ٱلْعَلَقَةَ مُضْغَةً فَخَلَقْنَا ٱلْمُضْغَةَ عِظَٰمًا فَكَسَوْنَا ٱلْعِظَٰمَ لَحْمًا ثُمَّ أَنشَأْنَٰهُ خَلْقًا ءَاخَرَ ۚ فَتَبَارَكَ ٱللَّهُ أَحْسَنُ ٱلْخَٰلِقِينَ﴾

"We created man from the purest kind of clay, then made him a drop in a secure receptacle, then formed the drop into a clot and formed the clot into a lump, and formed the lump into bones and clothed the bones in flesh. Then we brought him into being as another creature. Blessed be Allah, the Best of Creators!" [al-Muʾminūn 23:12-14]

In this āyah, Allah mentions the four phases that are mentioned in the ḥadīth and adds three other phases, making them seven in total. Ibn ʿAbbās ﷺ would say, 'Allah created Adam from seven', and then he would recite this āyah.

The wisdom behind Allah the Exalted creating man in this order and according to this gradual development, from one state to another, despite His power ﷻ to bring him into existence completely in the quickest moment, is so that the creation of man is incorporated with Allah's creation of the vast universe by means, causative factors, premises and results, and this is a more profound way of demonstrating Allah's power. We can also see in this gradual process Allah the

21 Ar. *al-lawḥ al-maḥfūẓ*, please see Sūrat al-Burūj 85:22.

Exalted teaching His slaves to have deliberateness in their affairs and not to rush and be hasty. It also informs man therein that achieving his abstract perfection can only be done gradually; just as achieving his physical perfection is done gradually, as he moves from one phase of his creation to the next until he reaches physical maturity. Therefore, in his conduct, he should develop in the same way, so that he does not stumble about blindly and bumble in darkness.

2. The breathing of the spirit (*rūḥ*): the scholars agree that the spirit is breathed into the embryo 120 days after conception, which is after the completion of four months and into the fifth. This event can be witnessed and it is relied upon when there is a need for rulings, such as avowal of paternity and the obligations of expenditure. This is by relying on the movement of the foetus in the womb, and here we can see the wisdom behind a widow's waiting period (*ʿiddah*) being four months and ten days. If no signs of pregnancy have emerged after this duration of time, it can be ascertained that her womb is empty.

The spirit is that by which man lives, and it is the concern of Allah the Exalted, He has informed us in His Mighty Book:

﴿وَيَسْـَٔلُونَكَ عَنِ ٱلرُّوحِ ۖ قُلِ ٱلرُّوحُ مِنْ أَمْرِ رَبِّى وَمَآ أُوتِيتُم مِّنَ ٱلْعِلْمِ إِلَّا قَلِيلًا﴾

"They will ask you about the spirit. Say: 'The spirit is my Lord's concern. You have only been given a little knowledge'". [al-Isrāʾ 17:85]

Imam an-Nawawī says in his commentary of *Ṣaḥīḥ Muslim*, 'The spirit is a delicate mass that becomes interwoven with the body the same way water is interwoven with green stalk.' Imam al-Ghazālī says in *Iḥyāʾ ʿUlūm ad-Dīn*, 'The spirit is an abstract element that is placed in the body.'

3. Abortion has been declared unlawful: The scholars agree that abortion is unlawful after the spirit has been breathed into the embryo. They consider it a sin; it is not lawful for a Muslim to partake in it. It is a crime against a living human; their creation has been completed and they are clearly alive. Blood money (*diyah*) must be paid if the child comes out alive and then dies, and the financial penalty is less if it comes out dead.

As for abortion before the spirit has been breathed in, it is also unlawful, and this is the position of most jurists. The evidence is the authentic ḥadīths that indicate that creation starts with the drop of semen after it has settled in the womb. Muslim has related on the authority of Ḥudhayfah ibn Usayd that the Prophet ﷺ, said, {If the drop of semen has been there for forty-two night – or 'some forty nights', as in one narration – Allah sends an angel who then fashions it and creates its ears, its eyes, its skin, its flesh and its bones.}

In the book *Jāmiʿ al-ʿUlūm wa al-Ḥikam* by Imam Ibn Rajab al-Ḥanbalī, p. 42, he says, 'A group of jurists have allowed a woman to abort what is in her womb as long as the spirit has not been breathed into it, and they liken it to the withdrawal method. This is a weak position because the embryo is a child. It has coagulated and maybe even been fashioned. As for the withdrawal method, there is no child whatsoever. Rather, it is a means of preventing coagulation, and it might not prevent coagulation if Allah has willed that a child is created.'

Imam al-Ghazālī says in *Iḥyāʾ ʿUlūm ad-Dīn* (2:51), 'This – i.e. the withdrawal method – is not like abortion or burying a child alive, because they are a crime against that which exists, and existence has stages. The first state of existence is the drop of semen being placed in the womb, mixing with the woman's fluid and being prepared to receive life. To undermine that is a crime. If the drop of semen has become a blood clot, the crime is more egregious, and if the spirit has been breathed into it and it has taken shape, the crime is even more egregious. The crime is most egregious after the baby has been born.'

5. Allah the Exalted's knowledge: Allah the Exalted knows the states of creation before He creates them. There is nothing from them, be it faith and obedience or disbelief and disobedience, bliss or wretchedness, except that it is by Allah's knowledge and will, and there is an abundance of texts that mention this in the aforementioned book. In al-Bukhārī, on the authority of ʿAlī ibn Abī Ṭālib ؓ the Prophet ﷺ, said, {There is no soul that has been breathed into except that Allah has written its place in either Paradise or the Fire, whether it shall be wretched or blissful.} A man then said, 'O Messenger of Allah, do we not then rest on our book and leave off deeds?' He replied, {Do deeds, for everyone is facilitated to do what they have been created for. As for the people of bliss, they are facilitated to do the deeds of the people of bliss. As for the people of wretchedness, they are facilitated to do the deeds of the people of wretchedness.} Then he recited:

﴿فَأَمَّا مَنْ أَعْطَىٰ وَاتَّقَىٰ ۝٥ وَصَدَّقَ بِالْحُسْنَىٰ ۝٦ فَسَنُيَسِّرُهُۥ لِلْيُسْرَىٰ﴾

"As for him who gives out and is godfearing and confirms the good, We will pave his way to ease." [al-Layl 92:5-7]

Moreover, Allah's ﷻ knowledge does not lift choice and intention from the slave, because knowledge is an attribute that does not bear an effect. Allah the Exalted has commanded to have faith and to obey, and He has forbidden them from disbelief and disobedience. This is proof that the slave chooses and intends whatever he wants. Otherwise, Allah the Exalted forbidding him would be pointless, which is impossible. Allah the Exalted has said:

﴿وَنَفْسٍ وَمَا سَوَّىٰهَا ۝٧ فَأَلْهَمَهَا فُجُورَهَا وَتَقْوَىٰهَا ۝٨ قَدْ أَفْلَحَ مَن زَكَّىٰهَا ۝٩ وَقَدْ خَابَ مَن دَسَّىٰهَا﴾

"And by the soul and 'the One' who fashioned it, and inspired it with depravity or *taqwā*, successful indeed is the one who purifies it, he who corrupts it has failed." [ash-Shams 91:7-10]

5. Using predestination as an excuse: Allah the Exalted has commanded us to have faith in Him and to obey Him, and He has forbidden us from disbelieving in Him and disobeying Him. This is what He has made us legally accountable for. Whatever Allah has predestined for us or against us is unknown; we do not know of it and we are not responsible for it. Therefore, whoever is guilty of misguidance, disbelief and iniquity cannot use Allah's predestination, and what He has decreed and willed, as an excuse before doing so. Allah the Exalted has said:

﴿وَقُلِ ٱعْمَلُوا۟ فَسَيَرَى ٱللَّهُ عَمَلَكُمْ وَرَسُولُهُۥ وَٱلْمُؤْمِنُونَ﴾

"Say: 'Act, for Allah, will see your actions, and so will His Messenger and the believers.'" [at-Tawbah 9:105]

As for after one has committed what was predestined, it is allowed to use predestination as an excuse, due to the comfort that the believer finds when he submits to Allah the Exalted's decree. Allah the Exalted's decree for the believer is always good, whether it comes in the form of happiness or distress.

6. Actions are only according to their outcomes: Al-Bukhārī has related on the authority of Sahl ibn Sa'd that the Prophet ﷺ, said, {Actions are only according to their outcomes.} This means that someone who has been written to have faith and obedience at the end of their life could disbelieve in Allah and disobey Him at some point. Then Allah the Exalted grants him the success to have faith and obedience for some time towards the end of his life, and he dies on that and enters Paradise. Likewise, someone who has been written to have disbelief and iniquity at the end of their life could believe and obey at some point. Then Allah forsakes him – because of what the slave has earned, done and wanted – and thus he utters words of disbelief and does the actions of the people of the Fire. Then He dies upon that and enters the Fire.

Thus, one should not be dazzled by someone's outward state, for the lesson is in the outcomes. Likewise, one should not despair at someone's outward state, because the lesson is in the outcomes. We ask Allah the Exalted to make us firmly established upon the truth and goodness and to grant us a good end.

7. The Prophet ﷺ, would often say in his supplications, {O He who turns over the hearts, make my heart firm upon your religion.} And Muslim has related: {Indeed hearts of the children of Adam are between two of the All-Merciful's fingers ﷻ like one heart. He turns them over as He wishes.} Then he ﷺ, said, {O Allah, the One who turns over hearts, turn our hearts towards Your obedience.}

8. Imam Ibn Ḥajar al-Haytamī said, 'An evil end – and we seek refuge in Allah – is because of the slave's internal plotting. People are unaware of it. Likewise, a man can do the actions of the people of the Fire while inside of him there is a hidden trait of goodness and this trait prevails towards the end of his life, necessitating that he has a good end. It has been related that ʿAbdul ʿAzīz ibn Dāwūd said, "I was present when someone was dying and the two testimonies of faith were being dictated to him. Someone said that he did not believe in them. I then asked about him and it turned out that he had been an alcoholic." ʿAbdul ʿAzīz would say, "Be wary of sins, for that is what befell him."'[22]

9. This prophetic ḥadīth indicates the embryo's stages of growth in the womb, and the sciences of anatomy and embryology did not discover these stages until the modern age. This is a clear scientific miracle in the Noble Qurʾān and the Prophetic Sunnah.

22 *Fatḥ al-Mubīn li Sharḥ al-Arbaʿīn*, p.105.

THE FIFTH ḤADĪTH

إِبْطَالُ الْمُنْكَرَاتِ وَالْبِدَعِ

عَنْ أُمِّ الْمُؤْمِنِينَ أُمِّ عَبْدِ اللهِ عَائِشَةَ ﵂ قَالَتْ: قَالَ رَسُولُ اللهِ ﷺ: {مَنْ أَحْدَثَ فِي أَمْرِنَا هَذَا مَا لَيْسَ مِنْهُ فَهُوَ رَدٌّ}. رواه البُخَارِيُّ ومُسْلِمٌ. وفي رِوَايَةٍ لِمُسْلِمٍ {مَنْ عَمِلَ عَمَلاً لَيْسَ عَلَيْهِ أَمْرُنَا فَهُوَ رَدٌّ}.

Nullifying Reprehensible Actions and Innovations

It is on the authority of the Mother of the Believers, Umm ʿAbdillāh ʿĀʾishah ﵂ that she said, 'The Messenger of Allah ﷺ, said: {Whoever introduces something into this affair of ours that is not of it, that thing is rejected.} Related by al-Bukhārī and Muslim. In one of Muslim's narrations: {Whoever does an act that we have not commanded, that act is rejected.}

Al-Bukhārī has related it in the Book of Reconciliation (the chapter on if they agree to an unjust reconciliation, that reconciliation is rejected), no.2550 and Muslim has related it in Judgments (the chapter on negating false rulings and rejecting invented matters), no.1718. Abū Dāwūd has related it in the Sunnah (the chapter on adhering to the Sunnah), no.4606, and Ibn Mājah has done so in his introduction, no.14.

The Importance of the Ḥadīth:
This ḥadīth is one of the immense foundations of Islam. Just as the ḥadīth {Actions are only by intentions} is the standard for actions in the inward sense, and every action that is not done for Allah the Exalted is not rewarded, this ḥadīth of the Prophet ﷺ, is the standard for actions in the outward sense. Any action that does not bear Allah's command and that of His Messenger is attributed to the one who did it, and anyone who introduces something into the Religion that Allah and His Messenger have not authorised, that thing is not from the Religion whatsoever.

Imam an-Nawawī ﷺ said, 'This ḥadīth should be memorised and used to nullify reprehensible actions.'

Imam Ibn Ḥajar al-Haytamī said, 'It is one of the fundamentals of Islam and the most general of them in benefit in terms of what it articulates. This is because it is a comprehensive premise in every evidence from which a legal ruling is derived.'

The Language of the Ḥadīth:
(من أحدث) *man aḥdatha*: to originate or invent from one's ego and desires.

(في أمرنا) *fī amrina*: in our religion and our Revealed Law, which Allah is pleased with for us.

(ما ليس منه) *ma laysa minhu*: that which contradicts it and is incompatible with it, or there is no proof for it in any of its principles or general evidences.

(فهو رد) *fa huwa radd*: it is attributed to its doer[23] due to its falseness and not relied on.

Legal Matters and Other Guidance from the Ḥadīth:
1. Islam is imitation and not innovation: The Noble Messenger ﷺ, protected Islam from the excessiveness of the extremists and the distortions of liars with this ḥadīth, which is considered an example of his comprehensive speech.[24] It is derived from several āyāt in Allah's Book ﷻ which clearly stipulate that success and salvation are to be found in following the guidance of Allah's Messenger ﷺ, without adding anything or being excessive. For example, the Exalted One has said:

﴿قُلْ إِن كُنتُمْ تُحِبُّونَ ٱللَّهَ فَٱتَّبِعُونِى يُحْبِبْكُمُ ٱللَّهُ﴾

"Say: 'If you love Allah, then follow me and Allah will love you..." [Āl 'Imrān 3:31]

And He ﷻ has said:

﴿وَأَنَّ هَٰذَا صِرَٰطِى مُسْتَقِيمًا فَٱتَّبِعُوهُ ۖ وَلَا تَتَّبِعُوا۟ ٱلسُّبُلَ فَتَفَرَّقَ بِكُمْ عَن سَبِيلِهِۦ﴾

"This is My Path and it is straight, so follow it. Do not follow other ways or you will be cut off from His Way." [al-An'ām 6:153]

Muslim has related in his *Ṣaḥīḥ* that the Messenger of Allah ﷺ, would say in his khutbahs, {The best speech is the Book of Allah and the best guidance is

23 (tn): i.e. and not attributed to Islam.
24 Ar. *jawāmi' al-kalim.*

Muḥammad's guidance ﷺ. The most evil matters are newly invented ones; every newly invented matter is an innovation and every innovation is misguidance.} Al-Bayhaqī related it with the addition: {...and every misguidance is in the Fire.}

2. Rejected Actions: The ḥadīth is a clear text in rejecting every action that does not bear the Lawgiver's command, and what it clearly articulates is that actions are bound by the rulings of the Revealed Law. It is the Revealed Law that is referred to when it comes to the actions of those who are legally accountable, based on the commands and prohibitions that are found in Allah's Book or the Messenger of Allah's Sunnah ﷺ. It is absolute misguidance for such actions to go outside the scope of the Revealed Law's rulings and not be bound by them, and that such actions come to rule over the Revealed Law and not be ruled by it. At that point, it is an obligation upon every Muslim to judge such actions to be false and rejected, and they fall into two categories: pure worship (*ʿibādāt*) and transactions (*muʿāmalāt*).

A. As for ***ʿibādāt***, whatever therein that falls outside the ruling of Allah and His Messenger is rejected and attributed to its owner, and it comes under the Exalted's statement:

﴿أَمْ لَهُمْ شُرَكَٰٓؤُاْ شَرَعُواْ لَهُم مِّنَ ٱلدِّينِ مَا لَمْ يَأْذَنۢ بِهِ ٱللَّهُ﴾

"Or do they have partners who have laid down a religion for them for which Allah has not given any authority?" [ash-Shūrā 42:21]

Examples of this would include drawing nearer to Allah the Exalted by way of listening to songs, by dancing, looking at women's faces, uncovering one's head when not in *iḥrām*,[25] and similar matters that man has invented and are the product of the madness of the age. These people and others are those whom Allah the Exalted has blinded from seeing the path of truth. They are following the paths of Shayṭān while claiming that they are drawing nearer to Allah by way of the ideas and errors that they have invented. In their falsehood, they are like the Arab idolaters, who innovated acts of worship and drawing nearer to Allah for which Allah had not sent down any authority. Allah ﷻ says of them:

﴿وَمَا كَانَ صَلَاتُهُمْ عِندَ ٱلْبَيْتِ إِلَّا مُكَآءً وَتَصْدِيَةً﴾

"Their prayer at the House is nothing but whistling and clapping." [al-Anfāl 8:35]

Someone might think that whatever is a part of one act of worship can be a part of any other act of worship. An example of this would be the man in the

25 (tn): i.e. the state of ritual consecration while performing the Ḥajj or ʿUmrah.

time of the Messenger of Allah ﷺ, who vowed to stand in the sun and not sit or seek shade while fasting. The Prophet ﷺ, commanded him to sit, to seek shade and to complete his fast.

The books of *fiqh* contain detailed rulings regarding acts of worship in Islam, what parts of them are rejected and what becomes nullified upon something being added to or taken away from what ohas been established by the All-Wise Legislator.

B. As for **transactions**, such as contracts and cancellations, whatever contradicts the Revealed Law in its entirety is invalid and rejected. The evidence for this is what happened in the time of the Prophet ﷺ. A questioner came to him and wanted to change the legal punishment for fornication to paying a ransom from one's wealth and property. The Prophet ﷺ, rejected this immediately and nullified what he had brought. Al-Bukhārī and Muslim have related that a questioner came to the Messenger of Allah ﷺ, and said, 'My son has committed an act of treachery against someone and fornicated with his wife, so can I give one hundred sheep and a slave on his behalf?' The Prophet ﷺ, replied, {The one hundred sheep and the slave go back to you. Your son has to be flogged one hundred times and banished for one year.}

The same goes for any contract that the Revealed Law has forbidden, or in which the two parties have violated one of its pillars or one of its conditions, in which case it would be an invalid, rejected contract. The details of this can be found in the books of *fiqh*.

3. Accepted Actions: There are also newly invented actions and matters that do not contradict the rulings of the Revealed Law. Rather, the evidences of the Revealed Law and its principles contain that which supports them, and thus they are not rejected and attributed to their doer. Instead, they are accepted and commended. The Companions ﷺ did this often, and they would deem a matter permissible and make consensus that it had been accepted. The clearest examples of this include the gathering of the Qur'ān in one *musḥaf* in the time of Abū Bakr as-Ṣiddīq ﷺ and several copies being transcribed and sent to the major cities along with reciters in the time of 'Uthmān ibn 'Affān ﷺ. Another example would be writing down the sciences of grammar, inheritance, arithmetic, Qur'ānic exegesis, discussions about chains of transmissions and the texts of ḥadīths, as well as other theoretical sciences that serve the foundational sources of legislation. Then there the beneficial experimental sciences that serve mankind in their daily lives, and allow them to build up their strength and develop the earth, and Allah's legislation can be established and the rule is what Allah has sent down.

4. Blameworthy Innovation and Praiseworthy Innovation: After discussing accepted actions and rejected actions, we arrive at a clear and decisive conclusion. The conclusion is that some innovated actions contradict what Allah has legislated, and thus they are evil, erroneous innovations and some newly invented matters do not contradict the Revealed Law. Rather, they are consistent with it and are accepted therein. These actions are accepted and commended, and they included that which is recommended (*mandūb*) and that which is a communal obligation. It is based on this that Imam ash-Shāfiʿī said, 'Whatever is invented that contradicts the Book, the Sunnah, a consensus or a report (*athar*) is an erroneous innovation. As for a good invention that does not contradict any of the above, it is a praiseworthy innovation.'

An evil innovation could be disliked (*makrūh*) and it could be unlawful, due to its harms, its corruption and its contradiction of Islam's objectives and necessities. It could also lead a person to disbelief, deviation and misguidance, such as being a member of a group or association that denies revelation, or denies Allah's legislation, or calls for the arbitration of manmade laws and sees backwardness and weakness in having the Revealed Law arbitrate. The same goes for being a member of a group that claims *taṣawwuf* and deems it permissible to neglect what Allah has commanded. They do not stick to the boundaries of what Allah has declared lawful and unlawful, or they talk about the unity of existence (*waḥdat al-wujūd*) and divine indwelling (*al-ḥulūl*), and other states and statements that are misguidance and disbelief. One of the evil innovations found amongst the common people is the exaltation of certain things, seeking blessings from them and believing that they confer benefits, such as the exaltation of a spring, a tree or a tomb. It has been authentically narrated that the Companions, passed by a lotus tree on the way to Ḥunayn that the idolaters used to exalt and hang their weapons on. They said, 'O Messenger of Allah, give us something to hang our weapons on like they had something to hang their weapons on.' He replied, {*Allahu Akbar*, this is similar to what the people of Mūsā said, 'Let us have a god like they have a god.'} Then he said, {You are a people who do not know. You perpetrate the practices of those who went before you.}

5. The benefit of Muslim's narration: {Whoever does an act that we have not commanded, that act is rejected} is that someone who stubbornly clings to an innovation that came about before his time will argue with us by using the first narration, and say, 'I have not introduced anything into the Religion.' We then quote to him the second narration, {Whoever does an act...}, and he understands.

6. The ḥadīth clarifies that whoever innovates something in the Religion that does not agree with the Revealed Law, the sin is on him, the action is rejected and attributed to him and he deserves to be warned.

7. Something being prohibited necessitates that there is corruption therein.

8. Islam is complete and does not lack anything.

THE SIXTH ḤADĪTH

الْحَلَالُ وَالْحَرَامُ

عَنْ أَبِي عَبْدِ اللهِ النُّعْمَانِ بْنِ بَشِيرٍ رضي الله عنهما قَالَ: سَمِعْتُ رَسُولَ اللهِ ﷺ يَقُولُ: {إِنَّ الْحَلَالَ بَيِّنٌ
وَإِنَّ الْحَرَامَ بَيِّنٌ وَبَيْنَهُمَا مُشْتَبِهَاتٌ لَا يَعْلَمُهُنَّ كَثِيرٌ مِنَ النَّاسِ، فَمَنِ اتَّقَى الشُّبُهَاتِ اسْتَبْرَأَ لِدِينِهِ
وَعِرْضِهِ، وَمَنْ وَقَعَ فِي الشُّبُهَاتِ وَقَعَ فِي الْحَرَامِ، كَالرَّاعِي يَرْعَى حَوْلَ الْحِمَى يُوشِكُ أَنْ يَرْتَعَ فِيهِ، أَلَا
وَإِنَّ لِكُلِّ مَلِكٍ حِمًى أَلَا وَإِنَّ حِمَى اللهِ مَحَارِمُهُ، أَلَا وَإِنَّ فِي الْجَسَدِ مُضْغَةً إِذَا صَلَحَتْ صَلَحَ الْجَسَدُ
كُلُّهُ وَإِذَا فَسَدَتْ فَسَدَ الْجَسَدُ كُلُّهُ، أَلَا وَهِيَ الْقَلْبُ.} رَوَاهُ الْبُخَارِيُّ وَمُسْلِمٌ.

The Lawful and the Unlawful

It is on the authority of Abū ʿAbdillāh an-Nuʿmān ibn Bashīr (رضي الله عنهما) that he said, 'I heard the Messenger of Allah ﷺ, saying, {The lawful is clear and the unlawful is clear and between them are doubtful matters which many people do not know. Whoever guards himself against doubtful matters has secured his religion and his honour, and whoever falls into doubtful matters will fall into the unlawful, like the shepherd who shepherds his flock around a forbidden pasture. His flock will certainly graze in it. Indeed, every king has his forbidden pasturage and Allah's forbidden pasturage is what He has forbidden. Indeed, there is a lump of flesh in the body; if it is sound, the whole body is sound, and if it is corrupt, the whole body is corrupt. Indeed, it is the heart.}

Al-Bukhārī has related this ḥadīth in the Book of Faith (the chapter on the one who has secured his religion), no.52, as well as in the Book of Transactions. Muslim has related it in Transactions (the chapter on taking the lawful and leaving doubtful matters), no.1599, as have Abū Dāwūd (the chapter on avoiding doubtful matters), no.3329 and 3330, and at-Tirmidhī (the chapter on leaving doubtful matters), no.1205. An-Nasāʾī has related it in Sales (the chapter on avoiding doubtful matters), 7/241 and Ibn Mājah has related it in Tribulations (the chapter on stopping at doubtful matters), no.3984.

The Importance of the Ḥadīth:

No one denies the immense rank of this ḥadīth and its abundance of benefits, for it is one of the ḥadīths that Islam revolves around. A group have said that it is a third of Islam. Abū Dāwūd said that it is a quarter. If one looks closely, one will find that it comprises all of it, because it includes a clarification of the lawful, the unlawful and the doubtful, that which rectifies the heart and corrupts it, and this necessitates knowledge of the Revealed Law's rulings, its foundations and its branches. It is also a foundation for having scrupulousness (*waraʿ*), which is leaving doubtful matters.

The Language of the Ḥadīth:

(بين) *bayyin*: obvious, which means there is a clear text from Allah and His Messenger, or the Muslims have made a consensus that a specific matter is lawful or a specific matter is unlawful.

(مشتبهات) *mushtabihāt*: the plural of *mushtabih,* which is something ambiguous, because it is not clear as to whether it is lawful or unlawful.

(لا يعلمهن) *la yaʿlamuhunna*: they do not know their ruling, due to contrasting pieces of evidence; sometimes they resemble the lawful and sometimes they resemble the unlawful.

(اتقى الشبهات) *ittaqā ash-shubuhāt*: he stays away from them, and he places a barrier between himself and every doubtful or ambiguous matter.

(استبرأ لدينه وعرضه) *istabra'a li dīnihi wa ʿirḍihi*: he has sought security for his honour against defamation or he has indeed obtained it, and he has protected his religion from deficiency, and this indicates that which is connected to people and that which is connected to Allah, ﷻ.

(وقع في الشبهات) *waqaʿa fī ash-shubuhāt*: he has the audacity to engage in doubtful matters, that which appears to be lawful from one angle and unlawful from another.

(الحمى) *al-ḥimā*: a protected area, only the owner is allowed to enter. It has also been said that it is the plot of land that the Khalīfah or his representative protects so that it can be used by the beasts and animals of the *mujāhidīn,*[26] and he prevents other people from using it.

(يوشك) *yushik*: he hastens or comes close.

---

26 (tn): i.e. those engaged in martial combat.

(أَن يَرْتَع فِيه) *an yarta'a fīh*: his livestock eat from it and abide in it.

(محارمه) *maḥārimahu*: acts of disobedience that Allah the Exalted has forbidden.

(مضغة) *muḍghah*: a piece of flesh of chewable size.

Legal Matters and Other Guidance from the Ḥadīth:

1.The lawful is clear and the unlawful is clear, and between them are doubtful matters. Imam an-Nawawī ؓ said, 'The meaning is that things fall into three categories: that which is clearly lawful, its lawfulness is not hidden, such as eating bread, talking, walking and so forth; that which is clearly unlawful, such as wine, fornication and so forth. As for the doubtful matters, it means that it is not clear as to whether they are lawful or unlawful, and this is why many people do not know them. As for the scholars, they know their ruling based on a text or analogy. If something wavers between lawfulness and unlawfulness and there is no text or consensus, the *mujtahid* uses *ijtihād*[27] therein and attaches a ruling, one or the other, based on an evidence in the Revealed Law.'

It is from scrupulousness to leave doubtful matters, such as not transacting with someone whose wealth contains dubiousness, or he mixes his wealth with usury. It is also from scrupulousness not to engage a great deal in permissible matters that are better left alone.

As for that which reaches the level of demonic whisperings with regards to something being unlawful that most likely is not, this does not fall under doubtful matters that should be left alone. Examples would include avoiding marrying women from a large town for fear of one of them being a *maḥram*,[28] or not using water in an open desert for fear that it might contain filth (*najāsah*). This is not scrupulousness but rather demonic whisperings.

2. Doubtful matters have categories: Imam Ibn al-Mundhir divided them into three categories:

• Something that a person knows to be unlawful and then has doubts about it. Is it still unlawful or not? It is not permissible for him to approach it except with certainty, such as having two sheep and knowing that he slaughtered only one of them, but he does not know which one.

• The opposite is knowing that something is lawful and being uncertain as to whether it has become unlawful, such as getting married and then being uncertain as to whether one is divorced or having doubts about one's ritual purity after purifying oneself. This type of doubt is of no consequence.

---

27 (tn): i.e. the one qualified to carry out expert juridical reasoning does so.
28 (tn): i.e. a relative whom one is not permitted to marry.

• Something could be lawful or unlawful from the outset, and the best course of action is to refrain from it, such as what the Messenger of Allah 🙼, did with regards to some fallen dates. Al-Bukhārī and Muslim have related that the Messenger of Allah 🙼, said, {I returned to my family and I found some dates that had fallen on my bed. I was about to eat them and then I feared that they might be from charity (ṣadaqah), so I put them down.}

3. Statements from the First Three Generations regarding leaving doubtful matters: Abū ad-Dardā' 🙼 said, 'The perfection of *taqwā* is that the slave has *taqwā* of Allah, even down to an atom's weight. When he leaves some of what he sees as lawful, for fear that it might be unlawful, he places a barrier between himself and the unlawful.' Al-Ḥasan al-Baṣrī said, '*Taqwā* remains with the people of *taqwā* (*al-muttaqīn*) until they leave off much of the lawful for fear that it is unlawful.' Ath-Thawrī said, 'They are called the people of *taqwā* because they are wary of that which one does not need to be wary of.' It has been related from Ibn 'Umar that he said, 'I love to leave a barrier from that which is lawful between myself and the unlawful and not remove it.' Sufyān ibn 'Uyaynah said, 'A slave does not reach the reality of faith until he places between himself and the unlawful a barrier from that which is lawful, and until he leaves sin and that which resembles sin.'

It has been authentically established that Abū Bakr 🙼 ate something doubtful without knowing. When he found out, he stuck his finger in his mouth and vomited it out.

It was said to Ibrāhīm ibn Adham, 'Do you not drink the water of Zamzam?' He replied, 'If I had a bucket, I would', indicating that the bucket was from the ruler's wealth.

May Allah be pleased with the Messenger of Allah's Companions 🙼, and may Allah have mercy on those who follow them in excellence from the righteous First Three Generations, for they distanced themselves from doubtful matters and thoroughly secured their religion.

4. Every king has his forbidden pasturage, and Allah's forbidden pasturage on His earth is what He has forbidden. The purpose behind mentioning this example is to use something observable and tangible to draw attention to that which is unseen and abstract. The kings of the Arabs would protect the pasturages of their livestock and threaten anyone who came near them, and the one who feared the king's punishment would take his livestock elsewhere to graze, for fear of trespassing. As for the one who was not afraid, he would let his animals graze near these pasturages and next to them, and it would not be long before he would accidentally trespass, and thus be punished.

Allah the Glorified has his forbidden pasturage, and it is the matters He has forbidden. Whoever commits any of them deserves Allah's punishment in this life and the Hereafter, and whoever gets close to them by entering into doubtful matters will certainly fall into the unlawful.

5. The probity of the heart: The probity of the body depends on the probity of the heart, because it is the most important organ in the human body, and there is no disagreement about this from an anatomical and medical perspective. It is accepted that the heart is the source of perceptible life in man, and as long as it is healthy, pumping blood regularly to all the organs of the body, the person is fine and doing well.

The Shāfiʿīs have used this ḥadīth to support that the foundation of the intellect is in the heart, and whatever intellect is found in the head is actually from the heart, and they have also used Allah the Exalted's statement as evidence:

﴿لَهُمْ قُلُوبٌ لَّا يَفْقَهُونَ بِهَا﴾

"They have hearts they do not understand with." [al-ʾAʿrāf 7:179]

Similar to this has been related by the philosophers and scholars of *kalām*.[29]

As for the school of Imam Abū Ḥanīfah ﷺ their position is that the intellect is in the brain, similar to what has been related by physicians. They support this with the fact that when the brain is damaged, the intellect is damaged. What is apparent from modern medicine and anatomy is that the source of direct cognition is in the brain, because the senses only move based on commands from the cerebrum.

Despite that, the heart remains the source of life for all the organs, including the cerebrum. If the ḥadīth is connecting probity of the body and thinking to the heart, it is connecting them to the source. The āyah is attributing intellect to the heart because the heart is the distant source. As for the brain, it is the direct, near source of cognition.

What is meant by probity of the heart in the ḥadīth is the spiritual heart, and therefore what is meant is the probity of the soul inside of it, that which no one besides Allah knows of. It is a secret. In his book *al-Muʿīn ʿalā Tafahhum al-Arbaʿīn*, Imam Ibn al-Mulaqqin ash-Shāfiʿī says, 'The probity of the heart is in five things: reading the Qurʾān with contemplation, emptying the stomach, standing at night to pray, begging Allah before the break of dawn and keeping the company of the righteous. I added eating that which is lawful, which is the peak of the matter. How beautiful is the statement: "Food is the seed of actions. If the lawful goes in, the lawful comes out. If the unlawful goes in, the unlawful comes out. If the doubtful goes in, the doubtful comes out."'

29 (tn): i.e. scholastic theology.

A sound heart is a sign of victory with Allah ﷻ. The Exalted One has said:

﴿يَوْمَ لَا يَنفَعُ مَالٌ وَلَا بَنُونَ ۝٨٨ إِلَّا مَنْ أَتَى ٱللَّهَ بِقَلْبٍ سَلِيمٍ﴾

"the Day when neither wealth nor sons will be of any use – except to those who come to Allah with sound and flawless hearts." [ash-Shuʿarāʾ 26: 88-89]

The Prophet ﷺ, would say in his supplications, {O Allah, I ask you for a sound heart.} Imam an-Nawawī said, 'Probity of the heart is obtained by being safe from inward illnesses, such as rancour, hatred, envy, stinginess, avarice, arrogance, scorn, ostentation, reputation, deception, greed, covetousness and not being pleased with what Allah has decreed…'.

Imam Ibn Rajab said, 'A sound heart is safe from all banes and unpleasant things. It is the heart that contains nothing but the love of Allah and fear of Him, and fear of what distances one from Him'.

Al-Ḥasan al-Baṣrī once said to a man, 'Treat your heart, from what Allah needs from His slaves is the probity of their hearts'.

Probity of the hearts movements necessitates probity of the limbs' movements. When the heart is sound, it contains nothing, but Allah's will and the will of what He wants. Nothing will budge from the limbs except what Allah wants. They will hasten to where His pleasure lies and refrain from what He dislikes. This person will be wary of that which could be something He dislikes if He is not certain.[30]

6. The ḥadīth encourages doing that which is lawful, avoiding the unlawful, leaving doubtful matters, being cautious with one's religion and honour and not engaging in matters that would necessitate a bad opinion or falling into that which is prohibited.

7. Calling for one's intellectual capacity to be rectified, and the rectification of the soul inside of it, which is the rectification of the heart.

8. Blocking the means to unlawful matters and declaring unlawful that which leads to them.

30 *Jāmiʿ al-ʿUlūm wa al-Ḥikam* by Imam Ibn Rajab al-Ḥanbalī, 65-66.

THE SEVENTH ḤADĪTH

الدِّينُ النَّصِيحَةُ

عَنْ أَبِي رُقَيَّةَ تَمِيمِ بْنِ أَوْسٍ الدَّارِيِّ ﷺ: أَنَّ النَّبِيَّ ﷺ قَالَ: {الدِّينُ النَّصِيحَةُ.} قُلْنَا: لِمَنْ؟
قَالَ: {لِلَّهِ، وَلِكِتَابِهِ، وَلِرَسُولِهِ، وَلِأَئِمَّةِ الْمُسْلِمِينَ، وَعَامَّتِهِمْ.} رواه مسلم

The Religion Is Sincerity

It is on the authority of Abū Ruqayyah Tamīm ibn Aws ad-Dārī ﷺ that the Prophet ﷺ, said, {The Religion is sincerity.} We said, 'For whom?' He replied, {For Allah, His Book, His Messenger, the leaders of the Muslims and their generality.} Related by Muslim.

Muslim has related this ḥadīth in the book of Faith (the chapter clarifying that the Religion is sincerity), no.55, and it is one of the ḥadīths that only Muslim has collected. Imam an-Nawawī said, 'Tamīm ad-Dārī has nothing in *Ṣaḥīḥ al-Bukhārī* from the Prophet ﷺ, and there is nothing in *Muslim* from him apart from this ḥadīth.'

Abū Dāwūd has related it in the Book of Etiquette (the chapter on sincerity), no.4944, as well as an-Nasā'ī in the Book of Allegiance (the chapter on sincerity towards the ruler), 7/156.

The Importance of the Ḥadīth:
This ḥadīth is another example of the comprehensive speech that was exclusive to our Messenger ﷺ, which is to use concise words that comprise several meanings and significant benefits. This is so much the case that we find all the recommended acts and rulings of the Revealed Law, its foundations and its branches, falling under it, or indeed falling under one word from it, which is His Book, because Allah the Exalted's Book comprises all matters of the Religion: foundations and branches, actions and beliefs. Whoever believes in it and acts according to what it contains in the way one should, with sincerity, has gathered the entire Revealed Law.

The Exalted One has said:

﴿مَّا فَرَّطْنَا فِي ٱلْكِتَـٰبِ مِن شَيْءٍ﴾

"We have not omitted anything from the Book." [al-Anʿām 6:38]

And this is why the scholars have said that Islam revolves around this ḥadīth.

The Language of the Ḥadīth:

(الدين) *ad-dīn*: i.e. the Religion, which is the Religion of Islam, i.e. the pillar and foundation of the Religion is sincerity.

(النصيحة) *an-naṣīḥah*:[31] a word used to express that one wants good for the one being advised, and the origin of *naṣḥ* in the language is *khulūṣ*, i.e. purity and sincerity. For example, *naṣaḥtu al-ʿasl* means that I purified the honey of wax. It has also been said that it comes from a man doing *naṣḥ* of his garment, i.e. tailoring it. Thus, what the sincere advisor wants by way of giving advice is similar to someone wanting to fix a garment.

(أئمة المسلمين) *aʾimat il-muslimīn*: their rulers.

(عامتهم) *ʿāmatihim*: all other Muslims besides the rulers.

Legal Matters and other Guidance from the Ḥadīth

1. Sincerity for Allah, which is by having faith in Allah the Exalted, negating any partner for him, abandoning heresy with regards to His attributes and ascribing Him all the attributes of perfection and majesty. One must declare Him ﷻ transcendent above all deficiencies, be sincere in worshipping Him, obey Him and avoid disobeying Him, love for His sake and hate for His sake, and befriend those who obey Him and dislikes those who disobey Him. When a Muslim adheres to this in his statements and actions, the benefit comes to him in this life and the Hereafter; because He ﷻ does not need anyone's sincerity.

2. Sincerity for Allah's Book is by having faith in all of the heavenly books that have come down from Allah the Exalted, and to have faith that this Qurʾān is the seal of all of them and the witness over them. It is the inimitable speech of Allah the Exalted, preserved in hearts and written lines, and He the Glorified has guaranteed that preservation:

﴿إِنَّا نَحْنُ نَزَّلْنَا ٱلذِّكْرَ وَإِنَّا لَهُۥ لَحَـٰفِظُونَ﴾

"It is We Who have sent down the Reminder and We who will preserve it." [al-Ḥijr 15:9]

31 (tn): also translated as 'sincere advice'.

The Muslim's sincerity towards his Lord's Book ﷻ is in the following ways:

A. By reading it and memorising it, because by reading it one acquires knowledge and perspicacity, purification of the soul, clarity of conscience and an increase of *taqwā*. In reading the Qur'ān, immense rewards are written on one's scroll, and one finds intercession waiting for him on the Day of Standing. Muslim has related that the Messenger of Allah ﷺ, said, {Read the Qur'ān, for indeed it will come on the Day of Resurrection as an intercessor for its people.} As for memorising Allah the Exalted's Book in one's heart, by doing so one fills one's heart with the light of Allah's Book, and the Muslim acquires great rank and nobility and thus stands out amongst people in this world. He then ascends to a high rank in the Hereafter correspondent to how many verses and chapters He had memorised from Allah's Book. Abū Dāwūd and at-Tirmidhī have related that the Messenger of Allah ﷺ, said, {It is said to the bearer of the Qur'ān, 'Read and be elevated, and recite as you used to recite in this world, for indeed your station will be at the last verse that you recite.'}

B. Recite the Qur'ān in rhythmic tones and beautify your voice while reading it, such that reading it has an effect on the soul and it is heard in the heart. Al-Bukhārī has related that the Messenger of Allah ﷺ, said, {Whoever does not chant the Qur'ān is not one of us.}

C. Contemplating its meanings and fathoming its verses. The Exalted One has said:

﴿أَفَلَا يَتَدَبَّرُونَ ٱلْقُرْءَانَ أَمْ عَلَىٰ قُلُوبٍ أَقْفَالُهَآ﴾

"Will they not then ponder the Qur'ān or are there locks upon their hearts?" [Muḥammad 47:24]

D. Teaching it to future Muslim generations, to ensure they take up the task of preserving Allah's Book. The path to our felicity and our glory lies in learning the Qur'ān and teaching it. Al-Bukhārī has related that the Messenger of Allah ﷺ, said, {The best of you are those who learn the Qur'ān and teach it.}

E. Understanding (*tafaqquh*) and application, as there is no good in reading without understanding (*fiqh*), and no good in understanding without application. Out of all the ripe Qur'ānic fruits, we achieve the most significant after understanding and application, and it is shameful of us to know and not apply.

The Exalted One has said:

﴿يَـٰٓأَيُّهَا ٱلَّذِينَ ءَامَنُوا۟ لِمَ تَقُولُونَ مَا لَا تَفْعَلُونَ ۝٢ كَبُرَ مَقْتًا عِندَ ٱللَّهِ أَن تَقُولُوا۟ مَا لَا تَفْعَلُونَ﴾

"You who believe! Why do you say what you do not do? It is deeply abhorrent to Allah that you should say what you do not do." [as-Ṣaff 61:2-3]

3. Sincerity for Allah's Messenger is by affirming his message and having faith in everything he has brought, the Qur'ān and the Sunnah. Likewise, it is by loving him and obeying him, for in loving the Messenger of Allah ﷺ, one loves Allah the Exalted:

﴿قُلْ إِن كُنتُمْ تُحِبُّونَ ٱللَّهَ فَٱتَّبِعُونِى يُحْبِبْكُمُ ٱللَّهُ﴾

"Say, 'If you love Allah, then follow me and Allah will love you.'" [Āl ʿImrān 3:31]

And in obeying the Messenger of Allah ﷺ, one obeys Allah ﷻ:

﴿مَّن يُطِعِ ٱلرَّسُولَ فَقَدْ أَطَاعَ ٱللَّهَ﴾

"Whoever obeys the Messenger has obeyed Allah." [an-Nisāʾ 4:80]

As for sincerity for Allah's Messenger after his passing, it is required of Muslim that they read his biography in their homes, that they adopt his manners and etiquettes ﷺ, and that they adhere to his Sunnah in word and deed. They are required to extract the lessons, examples and admonitions from his life and times and to partake in spreading his Sunnah amongst mankind while refuting the accusations of biased enemies, the claims of windbags and the innovations of extremists.

4. Sincerity for the leaders of the Muslims: The leaders of the Muslims can be either the rulers and their representatives, or it can be the scholars and those who seek to rectify matters.

As for the rulers of the Muslims, they must be Muslims, such that it would be obligatory to obey them. Allah the Exalted has said,

﴿يَـٰٓأَيُّهَا ٱلَّذِينَ ءَامَنُوٓا۟ أَطِيعُوا۟ ٱللَّهَ وَأَطِيعُوا۟ ٱلرَّسُولَ وَأُو۟لِى ٱلْأَمْرِ مِنكُمْ﴾

"You who believe! Obey Allah and obey the Messenger and those in command among you." [an-Nisāʾ 4:59]

Our sincerity towards them is that we love their probity, integrity and justice, not that we love them for who they are as individuals, or because of whatever special interests of ours they can realise. We love that the Ummah comes together under the shade of their just rule, and we hate that the Ummah becomes divided, and people are lost and wasted under their tyrannical and reckless rule.

Our sincerity towards them is that we assist them in the Truth, obey them therein and remind them of it. We also remind them with gentleness, wisdom and kindness, for there is no good in an ummah that does not have sincerity towards it rulers and does not tell the oppressor that he is an oppressor. Likewise, there is no good in a ruler who disparages his people and silences those who give sincere advice and plugs his ears from hearing the truth, or indeed he hates that anyone utter it. When the Ummah becomes a herd that does not fulfil the right of sincerity towards the ruler and the ruler becomes a false god who does not accept sincerity, this means humiliation, destruction, defeat and servility. This is what can happen whenever the Ummah deviates from Islam, and its principles and ideas are distorted and perverted amongst people's statements and actions.

As for the scholars and those seeking to rectify, their responsibility in having sincerity towards Allah's Book and the Sunnah of His Messenger is great. It is required that they refute any whims and caprices that mislead using the Book and the Sunnah, and show how the Book and the Sunnah contradict all whims and caprices. Likewise, they must refute weak positions when scholars slip, and clarify what is authentic and what is weak from the ḥadīths that have been related in the *sunan*[32] books and the *musnad*[33] books. This is done by presenting them according to the rules of authentication and classification[34] and the defects that can occur in ḥadīths.

Their responsibility in sincerely advising the rulers and calling them to rule according to the Book of Allah and the Sunnah of His Messenger is greater and more immense, and Allah ﷻ will take them to account if they fall short in this responsibility, and do not strive to proclaim the truth to the rulers' faces. He ﷺ, said, {The most sublime *jihād* is a word of truth in front of a tyrannical ruler.} Allah will take them to account if they deceive the ruler by granting him respite in his oppression and transgression by way of false praise, making themselves mouthpieces and riding beasts for the rulers. There is a very big difference between them following the convoy of authorities from amongst the scholars, and becoming attendants in the convoy of the ruler's slaves.

Our sincerity towards them is that we remind them of this responsibility that is on their shoulders, and we affirm them in what they relate from ḥadīths as long as they are trustworthy. We guard our tongues against disparaging them and criticising them, for this takes away their dignity and makes them open to accusations.

5. Sincerity for the generality of the Muslims is by guiding them towards that which will benefit them in their Hereafter as well as their worldly life. Regrettably, Muslims neglect the right of sincerely advising one another, especially in matters connected to their Hereafter. Instead, they confine most of their concern to the

32 (tn): e.g. the *sunan* collections of Imams Abū Dāwūd, at-Tirmidhī, Ibn Mājah and an-Nasā'ī.

33 (tn): e.g. the *Musnad* of Imam Aḥmad ibn Ḥanbal.

34 Ar. *al-jarḥ wa at-taʿdīl.*

interests of this world and its embellishments. Sincerity must not be restricted to words. Rather, one must turn those words into action, so that sincerity is manifested in Islamic society, covering faults, plugging gaps, warding off harms, bringing about benefit, enjoining the right, forbidding the wrong, respecting the elderly, showing mercy to the young and abandoning fraud and envy, even if that harms the sincere advice-giver's wealth or worldly matters.

6. The greatest kinds of sincerity: One of the greatest kinds of sincerity between Muslims is to give sincere advice to someone who seeks guidance. The Prophet ﷺ, said, {If one of you asks his brother for advice, let him advise him.} Another great kind of sincerity is when one's brother is absent, and this is by supporting and defending him because sincerity towards someone when they are absent is evidence of the veracity of one's sincerity. He ﷺ, said, {It is a Muslim's right over another Muslim that he be sincere towards him when he is absent.}

7. Unique statements from scholars regarding sincerity: Al-Ḥasan al-Baṣrī said, 'You will not fulfil the right of your sincerity towards your brother until you urge him to what he is incapable of'. He also said, 'One of the Prophet's Companions رضي الله عنهم, said, "By the One in whose hand is my soul, if you want, I will swear to you by Allah: the most beloved of Allah's slaves to Allah are those who make Allah beloved to His slaves and make Allah's slaves beloved to Allah, and they go about the earth with sincerity"'.

8. Abū Bakr al-Muzanī said, 'Abū Bakr رضي الله عنه did not surpass Muḥammad's Companions رضي الله عنهم, by way of prayer or fasting. It was because of something in his heart'. He said, 'What was in his heart was love for Allah عز وجل and sincerity towards His creation'.

9. Al-Fuḍayl ibn ʿIyāḍ said, 'Those amongst us did not attain what they attained by way of much prayer and fasting. Rather, those amongst us attained by way of the munificence of their souls, the soundness of their hearts and being sincere towards the Ummah.'

10. The etiquette of sincere advice: Part of the etiquette of sincere advice in Islam is that the Muslim advise his Muslim brother and admonish him in private, because whoever conceals, Allah conceals him in this life and the Hereafter. One of them said, 'Whoever admonishes his brother in private has given sincere advice, and whoever admonishes him in front of people has reviled him'. Al-Fuḍayl ibn ʿIyāḍ said, 'The believer conceals and gives sincere advice. The profligate disgraces and reviles'.

11. The benefits of this ḥadīth, as stated by Ibn Baṭṭāl:

- Sincerity is the Religion of Islam, and the Religion applies to actions just as it applies to words.

- Sincerity is a communal obligation. It is sufficient if one person carries it out. Everyone else is absolved.

- Sincere advice is mandatory to the extent that one is capable if the one advising knows that his advice will be accepted, his command will be obeyed, and he feels safe that nothing untoward will happen to him. If he does fear harm for himself, he does what he can.

THE EIGHTH ḤADĪTH

حُرْمَةُ الْمُسْلِمِ

عَنْ ابْنِ عُمَرَ رضي الله عنهما أَنَّ رَسُوْلَ اللهِ ﷺ قَالَ: {أُمِرْتُ أَنْ أُقَاتِلَ النَّاسَ حَتَّى يَشْهَدُوا أَنْ لَا إِلَـهَ إِلَّا اللهُ وَأَنَّ مُحَمَّدًا رَسُوْلُ اللهِ، وَيُقِيمُوا الصَّلَاةَ، وَيُؤْتُوا الزَّكَاةَ، فَإِذَا فَعَلُوا ذَلِكَ عَصَمُوْا مِنِّي دِمَاءَهُمْ وَأَمْوَالَهُمْ إِلَّا بِحَقِّ الْإِسْلَامِ، وَحِسَابُهُم عَلَى اللهِ تَعَالَى.} رواه البخاري ومسلم.

The Muslim's Sanctity

It is on the authority of Ibn ʿUmar رضي الله عنهما that the Messenger of Allah ﷺ, said, {I have been commanded to fight people[35] until they bear witness that there is no god but Allah and that Muḥammad is the Messenger of Allah, and they establish the prayer and pay the zakāt. If they do so, they are safe from me concerning their blood and their property, except for the right of Islam, and their reckoning is with Allah the Exalted.} Related by al-Bukhārī and Muslim.

Al-Bukhārī has related this ḥadīth in the Book of Faith (the chapter on if they repent and establish the prayer), no.25, and Muslim in the Book of Faith (the chapter on the command to fight people until they say there is no god but Allah, Muḥammad is the Messenger of Allah), no.22. His statement ﷺ: {except for the right of Islam} is only found with al-Bukhārī, not Muslim.

The Importance of the Ḥadīth:
This ḥadīth is extremely immense because it comprises some of the important foundations of Islam, which are bearing witness with firm affirmation that there is no god but Allah and Muḥammad is the Messenger of Allah, establishing the prayer as it has been commanded, and paying the zakāt to those who deserve it.

The Language of the Ḥadīth:
(أمرت) *umirtu*: Allah the Exalted has commanded me

(الناس) *an-nās*: the idolaters and polytheists

35 Ar. *an-nās*.

(يقيموا الصلاة) *yuqīmū as-ṣalāta*: to perform the prayer as it has been commanded, and do so consistently and persistently.

(يؤتوا الزكاة) *yu'tū az-zakāta*: they pay it to those who deserve it.

(عصموا) *ʿasamū*: they maintain and protect, and this is the root of the expression *iʿtisamtū billāh*, i.e. by Allah's grace, I have refrained from disobeying Him.

(إلا بحق الإسلام) *illā bi ḥaqq al-Islām*: this is a disconnected exception; it means that, however, after securing their blood and their property, they must fulfil the right of Islam by carrying out their obligations and leaving prohibited matters.

(وحسابهم على الله) *wa ḥisābuhum ʿalā Allah*: the reckoning of their inward states and the veracity of their hearts is with Allah the Exalted because He the Glorified knows what they contain.

Legal Matters and Other Guidance from the Ḥadīth:

1. Narrations of the Ḥadīth: The meaning of this ḥadīth has been related from the Messenger of Allah ﷺ, from numerous paths, which clarify it and elucidate it. In the *Ṣaḥīḥ* of al-Bukhārī, on the authority of Anas ؓ, the Messenger of Allah ﷺ, said, {I have been commanded to fight people – i.e. the polytheists – until they bear witness that there is no god but Allah and that Muḥammad is His slave and messenger, and if they bear witness that there is no god but Allah and that Muḥammad is the Messenger of Allah, they pray our prayer, face our *qiblah*,[36] and eat what we have slaughtered, their blood and their property are sacred to us, except for what is a right.}

Imam Aḥmad has collected the ḥadīth of Muʿādh ibn Jabal ؓ in which the Prophet ﷺ, said, {I have been commanded to fight people until they bear witness that there is no god but Allah alone, without partner, and that Muḥammad is the Messenger of Allah, and they establish the prayer and pay the zakāt. If they do so, they are protected – or they have protected their blood and their wealth – except for what is a right, and their reckoning is with Allah ﷻ.} Ibn Mājah has collected it in an abridged form.

2. Uttering the two testimonies of faith is sufficient to protect one's self and property. It is established that the Messenger of Allah ﷺ, would accept the two testimonies of faith from whoever came to him wanting Islam, and by doing so their blood would be safe and they would be Muslim. This is supported by authentic oral ḥadīths in which establishing the prayer and paying the zakāt are not mentioned. In the collections of both al-Bukhārī and Muslim, it is on the au-

36 (tn): i.e. they pray facing the Kaʿbah in Makkah.

thority of Abū Hurayrah 🙵 that the Prophet 🙵, said, {I have been commanded to fight people until they say that there is no god but Allah. Whoever says there is no god, but Allah is safe from me concerning his property and himself, except when there is a right, and his reckoning is with Allah 🙵.} In Muslim's narration: {...until they bear witness that there is no god but Allah and believe in me and in what I have brought.}

Muslim has also related on the authority of Abū Mālik al-Ashjaʿī from his father, who said, 'I heard the Messenger of Allah 🙵, saying, {Whoever says there is no god but Allah and disbelieves in what is worshipped besides Allah, Allah has made his blood and his property sacred, and his reckoning is with Allah 🙵.}' The Prophet 🙵, rebuked Usāmah ibn Zayd for killing someone who had said there is no god but Allah, and he rebuked him sternly.

There is no contradiction between the ḥadīths. All of them are true. A person who utters the two testimonies of faith is safe and becomes a Muslim. If he establishes the prayer and pays the zakāt after his Islam, whatever is for the Muslims is for him and whatever is against them is against him. If he violates any of Islam's pillars and he is part of a group that has force, they are fought. The Exalted One has said:

﴿فَإِن تَابُواْ وَأَقَامُواْ ٱلصَّلَوٰةَ وَءَاتَوُاْ ٱلزَّكَوٰةَ فَخَلُّواْ سَبِيلَهُمْ﴾

"If they repent and establish the prayer and pay the zakāt, let them go on their way." [at-Tawbah 9:5]

He the Glorified has also said:

﴿فَإِن تَابُواْ وَأَقَامُواْ ٱلصَّلَوٰةَ وَءَاتَوُاْ ٱلزَّكَوٰةَ فَإِخْوَٰنُكُمْ فِى ٱلدِّينِ﴾

"But if they repent and establish the prayer and pay the zakāt, they are your brothers in the Religion." [at-Tawbah 9:11]

It has been established that when the Messenger of Allah 🙵, would attack a people, he would not make a move until dawn, to see if there was a call to prayer. If there was none, he would attack, even though they might have entered Islam.

3. The Difference of Opinion between Abū Bakr and ʿUmar 🙵: The difference of opinion that happened between Abū Bakr and ʿUmar 🙵 has to do with fighting those who were withholding the zakāt. It confirms what the ḥadīths have agreed upon, that the two testimonies of faith are accepted for someone to enter Islam and that a group of Muslims who refrain from establishing the prayer and paying the zakāt are fought. In the collections of al-Bukhārī and Muslim, Abū Hurayrah 🙵 said, 'When the Messenger of Allah 🙵 had passed away and Abū Bakr as-Ṣid-dīq 🙵 had been appointed his successor, and whoever disbelieved from amongst the Arabs did so, ʿUmar 🙵 said to Abū Bakr, "How can you fight people when the Messenger of Allah ﷺ has said, {I have been commanded to fight people until they say that there is no god but Allah. Whoever says there is no god but Allah is safe from me concerning his property and his person, except when there is a right, and his reckoning is with Allah ﷻ.}" Abū Bakr ؓ replied, "By Allah, I will fight anyone who differentiates between the prayer and the zakāt, for the zakāt is a monetary right. By Allah, if they withheld an *ʿiqāl*[37] from me that they used to pay to the Messenger of Allah ﷺ I would fight them for withholding it". ʿUmar said, 'By Allah, it was nothing other than that I saw Allah had open Abū Bakr's heart to fight, and I knew it was the truth"'.

Thus, Abū Bakr as-Ṣiddīq ؓ inferred fighting those who withheld the zakāt from his statement ﷺ {except for when there is a right}. ʿUmar, on the other hand, thought that merely uttering the two testimonies of faith would protect someone's blood in this life, and he inferred this from the general meaning of the first part of the ḥadīth. Then ʿUmar came to agree with Abū Bakr ؓ.

It is also affirmed that the ḥadīth of Ibn ʿUmar,[38] is a clear text regarding fighting those who withhold the zakāt, was not known to either Abū Bakr or ʿUmar. It had not reached them. Perhaps the reason is that ʿUmar did not know the difference of opinion that had happened between the two of them, due to being ill or travelling, or he forgot this ḥadīth that he had related.

This story shows that the sublimity of Abū Bakr as-Ṣiddīq's knowledge ؓ and the precision of his derivation and analogy, because it agreed with the text without him knowing the text. The story also indicates that fighting those who leave the prayer was agreed upon by the Companions. A clear text has reached us in this regard in a ḥadīth that Muslim has related from Umm Salamah, in which the Prophet ﷺ said, {Rulers will be placed over you. You will recognise some of what they do and you will disavow some of what they do. Whoever disavows is innocent, and whoever dislikes is safe. It is the one who is pleased and follows along that is guilty.} They said, 'O Messenger of Allah, should we fight them?' He replied, {No, as long as they pray.}

4. The ruling for whoever leaves all the pillars of Islam: The ruling for whoever leaves all the pillars of Islam is that if they are a group that has force, they are fought for doing so, just as those who leave the prayer and the zakāt are fought. Ibn Shihāb az-Zuhrī has related on the authority of Ḥanẓalah ibn ʿAlī ibn al-Asqaʿ that Abū Bakr as-Ṣiddīq ؓ sent Khalid ibn al-Walīd ؓ and commanded him to fight people because of five; whoever leaves one of them must be fought as if he had left all five: bearing witness that there is no god but Allah and that Muḥammad

37 (tn): i.e. a cord used for hobbling the feet of a camel.

38 (tn): i.e. the ḥadīth that Imam an-Nawawī chose as his eighth ḥadīth.

is the Messenger of Allah, establishing the prayer, paying the zakāt and fasting Ramaḍān. Saʿīd ibn Jubayr said, "Umar ibn al-Khaṭṭāb ﷺ said, "If people left the Ḥajj we would fight them just as if they had left the prayer or the zakāt"".

If a Muslim leaves one of the pillars and refrains from doing it, Imams Mālik and ash-Shāfiʿī hold that the one who refrains from prayer is executed as a legal punishment. Imams Aḥmad, Isḥāq and Ibn al-Mubārak hold that he is executed as a disbeliever. As for someone who refrains from the zakāt, from fasting or the Ḥajj, Imam ash-Shāfiʿī has said that he is not executed. Two opinions have been related from Imam Aḥmad on the matter, and the most well-known opinion from him is that one who withholds the zakāt is executed.

5. The faith that is required: The ḥadīth contains clear proof, for the verifying scholars of the First Three Generations[39] and those who have come after,[40] that the faith that is sought is a firm affirmation and firm conviction in the pillars of Islam without hesitation. As for knowing the evidences of the *kalām* scholars and using them to arrive at faith in Allah, this is not an obligation or a condition for having valid faith. The Messenger of Allah ﷺ in this ḥadīth and others, was satisfied with the affirmation of what he had brought, and did not stipulate knowledge of the evidence.

6. The meaning of his statement ﷺ {except when there is a right}: In another narration: {except for the right of Islam}, and we have seen how Abū Bakr as-Ṣiddīq ﷺ derived from this right the establishment of the prayer and the paying of the zakāt. Some scholars have derived fasting and the Ḥajj from it as well. Islam's right also includes committing that which makes a Muslim's blood permissible, if he commits something unlawful that necessitates execution. The explanation of this ḥadīth is found in what has been related by at-Ṭabarānī and Ibn Jarīr at-Ṭabarī on the authority of Anas ﷺ in which the Prophet ﷺ said, {I have been commanded to fight people until they say that there is no god but Allah. If they say so, they are safe from me concerning his property and his person, except when there is a right, and his reckoning is with Allah ﷻ.} It was said, 'What is its right?' He replied, {Fornication after getting married,[41] disbelief after faith and killing someone, and thus one is killed.} Imam Ibn Rajab said, 'Maybe the last part was said by Anas, and it has been said that the entire ḥadīth is correct. This is corroborated by what is found in the collections of al-Bukhārī and Muslim on the authority of ʿAbdullah ibn Masʿūd in which the Messenger of Allah ﷺ said, {The blood of a Muslim who

39 Ar. *as-salaf.*

40 Ar. *al-khalaf.*

41 (tn): i.e. adultery.

testifies that there is no god but Allah and that I am the Messenger of Allah does not become lawful except in three cases: the married fornicator, the murderer and the one who leaves his religion and separates from the community.}'[42]

7. The Reckoning in the Hereafter is for Allah ﷻ. He ﷻ knows all secrets and will take them to account. Whoever is a sincere believer will be entered into Paradise and whoever is a dissimulating liar, only showing his Islam, is a hypocrite and will be in the lowest level of the Fire.

As for this life, the Messenger's ﷺ mission is to remind. Allah ﷻ has said:

﴿فَذَكِّرْ إِنَّمَآ أَنتَ مُذَكِّرٌ ﴿٢١﴾ لَّسْتَ عَلَيْهِم بِمُصَيْطِرٍ ﴿٢٢﴾ إِلَّا مَن تَوَلَّىٰ وَكَفَرَ ﴿٢٣﴾

فَيُعَذِّبُهُ ٱللَّهُ ٱلْعَذَابَ ٱلْأَكْبَرَ ﴿٢٤﴾ إِنَّ إِلَيْنَآ إِيَابَهُمْ ﴿٢٥﴾ ثُمَّ إِنَّ عَلَيْنَا حِسَابَهُم﴾

"So remind them! You are only a reminder. You are not in control of them. But as for anyone who turns away and disbelieves, Allah will punish him with the Greatest Punishment. Certainly, it is to Us they will return. Then their reckoning is Our concern." [al-Ghāshiyyah 88:21-26]

Khālid ibn al-Walīd, as related by al-Bukhārī and Muslim, said, 'I have not been commanded to pierce the hearts of men, or spilt open their insides.'

8. The ḥadīth informs us of the obligation to fight idolaters that show aggression until they become Muslims.

9. The blood and property of Muslims are well-protected.

42 (tn): This is the 14th ḥadīth in Imam an-Nawawī's collection.

THE NINTH ḤADĪTH

الأَخذُ باليَسيرِ وتَرَكُ التعسير

الطَّاعَةُ وعَدَمُ التَعَنُّتِ سَبِيلُ النَّجاةِ

عَنْ أَبِي هُرَيْرَةَ عَبْدِ الرَّحْمنِ بْنِ صَخْرٍ ﷺ قَالَ: سَمِعْتُ رَسُوْلَ اللهِ ﷺ يَقُوْلُ: {مَا نَهَيْتُكُم عَنْهُ فَاجْتَنِبُوْهُ، وَمَا أَمَرْتُكُمْ بِهِ فَأْتُوْا مِنْهُ مَا اسْتَطَعْتُمْ، فَإِنَّمَا أَهْلَكَ الَّذِيْنَ مِنْ قَبْلِكُمْ كَثْرَةُ مَسَائِلِهِمْ وَاخْتِلَافُهُمْ عَلَى أَنْبِيَائِهِمْ.} رواه البخاري مسلم.

Taking the Easy Route and Avoiding Making Matters Difficult

Obedience and Lack of Obstinacy Are the Path to Success

It is on the authority of Abū Hurayrah ʿAbdir Raḥmān ibn Ṣakhr ﷺ who said, 'I heard the Messenger of Allah ﷺ saying, {Whatever I forbid you, avoid it, and whatever I command you, do as much of it as you are able. The only thing that destroyed those before you was their abundance of questions and their disagreements with their Prophets.} Related by al-Bukhārī and Muslim.

Al-Bukhārī has collected it in the Book of Adhering to the Book and the Sunnah (the chapter on following the *sunan* of the Messenger of Allah ﷺ no.6777. Muslim has collected it in the Book of Virtues (the chapter on revering him ﷺ and leaving asking him lots of questions for which there is no need), no.1337.

Its Importance:
The scholars have mentioned that this ḥadīth has profound importance and clear benefits, making it worthy of being memorised and researched:

When discussing this ḥadīth in his commentary on *Ṣaḥīḥ Muslim*, Imam an-Nawawī says, 'This is one of the important foundations of Islam, and an example of the comprehensive speech that he ﷺ was given. Countless rulings can be taken from it'.

Imam Ibn Ḥajar says in his commentary on these forty ḥadīths, 'It is a sublime ḥadīth. It contains the foundations of the Religion and the pillars of Islam. It should be memorised and paid attention to'.

Similar statements have been made by other commentators who have clarified and elucidated this ḥadīth. The importance of this ḥadīth is that it instructs us to adhere to what Allah has legislated ﷻ which is either a command or a prohibition. Then it informs us that we must stop at the bounds that Allah the Exalted's Book has clarified, and what the Sunnah of His Prophet ﷺ has outlined in detail, without excessiveness or negligence, without immoderation or slackness.

This importance will become clear in the discussion that follows, which will unveil the meaning of this ḥadīth and its objective, and elucidate the veracity and what these revered Muslim scholars have said.

Circumstances Surrounding the Ḥadīth:

The circumstances surrounding this ḥadīth and the Messenger of Allah ﷺ saying it is found in what has been related by Muslim in his *Ṣaḥīḥ*. It is on the authority of Abū Hurayrah رضي الله عنه who said, 'The Messenger of Allah ﷺ addressed us and said, {O people, Allah has made the Ḥajj an obligation upon you, so perform the Ḥajj.} A man said, 'Every year, O Messenger of Allah?' He remained quiet until the man had said it three times. Then Messenger of Allah ﷺ replied, {If I had said 'Yes', it would have been made obligatory, and you would not have been able to.} Then he said, {Leave me alone as long as I leave you alone. Those who came before you were only destroyed by their abundant questioning and their disagreeing with their Prophets. When I command you to something, do as much of it as you can. When I forbid you something, avoid it.} This is in the Book of the Ḥajj (the chapter on the Ḥajj being an obligation once in a lifetime), no.1337.

It has reached us that the questioner was al-Aqraʿ ibn Ḥābis رضي الله عنه. Ibn Mājah has related in his *Sunan* on the authority of Ibn ʿAbbās رضي الله عنهما that al-Aqraʿ ibn Ḥābis asked the Prophet ﷺ and said, 'O Messenger of Allah, is the Ḥajj every year or just once?' He replied, {Just once, and whoever is able can do so voluntarily.}[43] This is in the Ḥajj (the chapter on the obligation of the Ḥajj), no.2886.

The wording of Abū Dāwūd is: {Whoever does more than that does so voluntarily.}, no.1721. The wording in the *Mustadrak* is: {Whoever wants to can do it voluntarily}, and this is in the beginning of the Book of Rites.[44]

It has been said that this took place during the Farewell Ḥajj when the Prophet ﷺ stood before the people and was addressing them, clarifying the particularities of the Religion and teaching them the obligations of Islam.

43 (tn): i.e. one can perform the Ḥajj again if one is able, and it would not be an obligation.

44 Ar. *al-manāsik*.

The Language of the Ḥadīth:
(نهيتكم عنه) *ma nahaytukum ʿanhu*: I ask you to refrain from doing it. *Nahī* means prohibition.

(فاجتنبوه) *fajtanibūh*: put it to the side, i.e. leave it, and in another narration: *fadʿūh*, i.e. turn down.

(أمرتكم به) *amartukum bihi*: I ask you to do it.

(فأتوا) *faʾtū*: i.e. do, and in one narration the wording is *fafʿalū.*

(ما استطعتم) *ma staṭaʿtum*: what you can do and it's easy without great difficulty.

(أهلك) *ahlaka*: became the reason for their destruction, as it necessitated that they be punished in this life and the Hereafter.

(كثرة مسائلهم) *kathratu masāʾilihim*: their plethora of questions, especially regarding that which there is no need or necessity.

(اختلافهم على أنبيائهم) *ikhtilāfihim ʿalā anbiyāʾihim*: their disobedience of them, their hesitation regarding their news, and their arguing with them over the legislation they brought them.

Legal Matters and Other Guidance from the Ḥadīth:
1. Whatever I forbid you, avoid it: In Allah the Exalted's Book and in His Messenger's Sunnah ﷺ the word *nahī* has several meanings. What is intended here is one of two meanings, and they are the foundation when scholars use this word. They are unlawfulness and offensiveness.[45]

A. The prohibition of unlawfulness: There are actions that Allah ﷻ has prohibited on the tongue of His Prophet ﷺ and the evidences have established that this prohibition means unlawfulness. In other words, it is unlawful for the legally accountable person to do what has been prohibited. If he does it, he receives the resultant punishment for that action in the Revealed Law, in this life and the Hereafter.

Examples of this include the prohibition of fornication, drinking wine, consuming usury, theft, killing someone without right, revealing one's nakedness, women displaying their beauty to foreign men, lying, cheating, bribery, backbiting, slander, sowing corruption, and other matters the prohibition of which in Allah's legislation ﷻ means that they must be refrained from obligatorily and absolutely.

45 (tn): i.e. when the word is used, it either indicates that something is *ḥarām* or it is *makrūh*.

Prohibited matters like these must be avoided all at once, on the whole, and in detail. The legally accountable person is not allowed to partake in any of them, unless he is forced to by some necessity, based on the qualifications and conditions that Allah's masterful legislation has elucidated.

B. The prohibition of offensiveness: This is sometimes called *nahī at-tanzīh*[46]. The Lawgiver has prohibited certain actions but the evidences have established that this prohibition means the actions are disliked and not unlawful. In other words, it is not unlawful for the legally accountable person to partake in them, and he is not punished if he does so.

Examples of this include the prohibition of eating raw onions and garlic before attending the Friday prayer or any other congregational prayer, and the same applies to every offensive small, and other matters the prohibition of which in Allah's legislation ﷻ means that they should be refrained from but not obligatorily and absolutely.

It is permitted to partake in actions like this, in whole or in part, whether one is called to do so by necessity or not, even though it behoves the cautious Muslim to avoid them as much as possible.

2. Necessities permit forbidden matters: We know that what has been prohibited in the unlawful sense must be avoided completely, but the legally accountable person could fall into circumstances that force him to do something unlawful and compel to seek recourse in that which is prohibited, and if he refrains from doing so he will cast himself into destruction. Here we find Allah the Exalted's wise legislation granting relief to His slaves and allowing them in these situations to do that which is normally prohibited while absolving them of any blame or sin. Allah the Exalted has said:

$$﴿فَمَنِ ٱضْطُرَّ غَيْرَ بَاغٍ وَلَا عَادٍ فَلَآ إِثْمَ عَلَيْهِ إِنَّ ٱللَّهَ غَفُورٌ رَّحِيمٌ﴾$$

"But anyone who is forced to eat it – without desiring it or going to excess in it – commits no crime. Allah is Ever-Forgiving, Most Merciful." [al-Baqarah 2:173]

Acting upon this and deriving from it, the scholars have laid down this legal maxim:[47] necessities[48] permit forbidden matters.

Examples of this include the permissibility of eating carrion when one has no food and cannot find anything else, the permissibility of revealing one's nakedness in order to be treated by a physician, not amputating the hand of someone who was forced to steal by poverty and need, and so forth.

---

46 (نهي التنزيه)

47 Ar. *qāʿidah fiqhiyyah*.

48 Ar. *ad-ḍarūrāt tubīḥ al-maḥẓūrāt*.

However, something we should be aware of is what many people fall into, when they apply this maxim in the absolute sense, without defining the meaning of necessity (*ḍarūrah*), or knowing the extent to which a necessity makes something permissible. So that those who are legally accountable do not find themselves in error, the scholars of jurisprudence (*fuqahā'*) have defined the meaning of *ḍarūrah*. It is that which puts a person in danger, such that he fears for his life, or that one of his limbs will be injured or that his illness will worsen, and other matters that make it unfeasible to carry out life's interests. It could also be something that puts one in unbearable difficulty or hardship. They have also defined the extent to which a necessity makes something permissible, after which one is no longer considered to be compelled. They have laid down this maxim: the necessity is measured according to its amount. They have taken this from the Exalted One's words: **"...without desiring it or going to excess in it..."**, i.e. without intending to violate and disobey, and not transgressing the bounds of what one has been compelled to do.

Thus, someone forced to eat carrion cannot eat his fill or hoard it. Someone forced to steal to feed his dependents cannot take more than what he needs for a day and a night. Someone forced to reveal his nakedness in front of a physician cannot reveal other than the place of pain, or the place that the physician needs to examine. A woman in need of treatment cannot go to a male physician if an equally capable female physician is available.[49]

There is no compulsion whatsoever in acquiring more of this worldly life, obtaining its luxuries, having a predilection for comfort and keeping up with the rest of society in its imported customs. Someone of little capital is not forced to engage in usury to expand his trade. Someone who has an extremely small residence is not forced, likewise, such that it would be permissible for him to acquire a huge residence that is to his liking by whatever means. A woman who has a husband or guardian spending on her is not under compulsion, such that it would be permissible for her to mix with other men or be alone with them, in some job or office. Likewise, if she is forced to provide and she can work without engaging in these forbidden matters, she is not allowed to where work there is this peril.

Indeed, it is not permissible for her at all to work where she would be alone or mixing with foreign men, to ward off the causes of corruption that bring afflictions upon Allah's slaves and the lands they inhabit, acting upon the maxim: warding off the causes of corruption takes precedence over bringing about benefits. Whoever has a business is not compelled to pay bribes to make it run smoother. Whoever has relationships with people is not forced to sit with them when they are drinking wine while refraining from admonishing them. A woman

49 (tn): i.e. equally capable of providing the same treatment.

who has a lax husband is not forced to remove her decent clothes and modest outer garments, thus abandoning the legislated manners and clothes of believing women, to please and satisfy him.

3. Adhering to the command: (the categories of command and adhering to commandments)

In Allah the Exalted's Book and the Sunnah of His Prophet ﷺ the word *amr* (command) has numerous meanings. Respected scholars have agreed that the origin of *amr* is to ask (*ṭalab*), and it has two fundamental meanings: obligation and recommendation. This meaning is what is intended in his statement ﷺ: {... and whatever I command you...}, i.e. a command of obligation or a command of recommendation, which can be elucidated as follows:

A. The command of obligation: Allah the Exalted has commanded the Muslims, on the tongue of His Prophet ﷺ, to carry out certain actions, and the evidences have established that the command means obligation. In other words, the legally accountable person must carry out what this command asks. If he leaves it, he is punished, and if he does it, he is rewarded. The action that is required by way of this type of command is called *wājib* (obligatory).

Examples of this include the commands of the prayer, the zakāt, the Ḥajj and fasting, to enjoin the right and forbid the wrong, the command to fulfil contracts and carry out testimonies for those who bear them, to rule according to what Allah ﷻ has sent down, the command to establish the legal punishments, to rule with justice, to spend on one's family and children correctly and courteously, and other matters in Allah's legislation ﷻ in which the command asks the legally accountable person to do something obligatorily and absolutely.

Commandments like this must be carried out. It is not permissible to be negligent in any of them. There is no excuse for a legally accountable person to violate them, unless some of their conditions or reasons are missing, or some hindrances are preventing them from being realised, or carrying them out is mixed up with circumstances that would position the person in distress or difficulty.

B. The command of recommendation: Allah the Exalted has commanded the Muslim, on the tongue of His Prophet ﷺ to carry out several actions, and the evidences have established that this command means a recommendation. In other words, the legally accountable person is not obligated to do what the command asks of him. If he leaves it, he is not punished, and if he does it, he is rewarded. The action that is required by way of this type of command is called *mandūb* (recommended).

Examples of this include the command to pray the *sunnah rātibah* prayers along with the five daily obligatory prayers, the command to give the call to prayer, the command to increase in expenditure upon one's family and dependents, to spend in the cause of good beyond the obligatory zakāt, the command to write down debts and bear witness, and the command to eat with the right hand. These and similar matters in Allah's legislation ﷻ are commands in which the legally accountable person is requested to carry them out, but not obligatorily and absolutely. Rather, they are desirable and recommended.

It behoves the Muslim to carry out commandments like these and stick to them, even though it is permissible for him to leave them, in whole or in part, regardless of whether or not the conditions have been fulfilled and the reasons are in place, or whether or not it would put him in difficulty and hardship or ease and convenience. No sin, blame or punishment is attached to the legally accountable person who leaves any of them, even though he is blamed for leaving some of them in particular, and if he left all of them he would be blamed and censured.

4. Difficulty brings about facilitation: It is known that Allah's legislation ﷻ aims to realise absolute felicity for man, in both his worldly life and the Hereafter. Thus, He has brought facilitation for His slaves and relieved them of distress. Allah the Exalted has said:

﴿يُرِيدُ ٱللَّهُ بِكُمُ ٱلْيُسْرَ وَلَا يُرِيدُ بِكُمُ ٱلْعُسْرَ﴾

"Allah desires ease for you; He does not desire difficulty for you." [al-Baqarah 2:185]

He ﷻ has also said:

﴿مَا جَعَلَ عَلَيْكُمْ فِى ٱلدِّينِ مِنْ حَرَجٍ﴾

"He has not placed any constraint upon you in the Religion." [al-Ḥajj 22:78]

He ﷺ has said: {This religion is ease...facilitate and do not make things difficult}, as collected by al-Bukhārī.

It has been established in the Revealed Law that Allah the Exalted has allowed the ill person and the traveller to break their fast in Ramaḍān, just as the traveller is allowed to shorten and combine his prayers. Allah has allowed dry ablution (*tayammum*) for the one who has no water or would be harmed by using it. The scholars have called rulings like this *rukhaṣ* (concessions).

Based on the ease and lifting of constraint that has been established in Allah's legislation ﷻ as well as the ḥadīth of this chapter, the scholars of jurisprudence, have laid down this maxim: difficulty brings about facilitation.[50] They have deduced several branches from it in their *fiqh*, and they consider it one of the principles upon which Islamic *fiqh* is based.

50 Ar. *al-mashaqqah tajlibu at-taysīr.*

The meaning of this maxim is that when the legally accountable person finds himself in certain circumstances in which it is difficult to carry out certain obligations of the Revealed Law or carrying them out in an optimal way would put him in difficulty and hardship, that difficulty is a reason for facilitation and mitigation. Thus, it becomes easier for the obligation to be carried out, the constraint is lifted, and the legally accountable person does what he can.

Examples of the application of this maxim include certain types of filth (*najāsāt*) that are hard to avoid being excused, such as the blood of wounds and abscesses, and the mud on streets, which is rarely free of *najāsah*. Purifying oneself from these types of filth is difficult for the legally accountable person, and thus it might be hard for him to carry out many acts of worship, so he is excused out of facilitation and mitigation.

Other examples include excusing what is not known in certain contracts sometimes, such as when entering the public bathhouse. A person does not know how long he will be there and how much water he will consume. Maybe even the fee is not known in several instances. It is difficult to define these matters on the spot and clarify them in a contract every time someone enters the bathhouse, and people need it and cannot do without it. Similar to the bathhouse with regards to all of the above is hiring a barber.

Many new matters can be deduced from this maxim, such as riding on large and small means of transportation, as the foundation in the Revealed Law is that there must be a contract in which the fee is clarified as well the service, before riding.

- The limits of the hardship that necessitates facilitation: Sometimes, some legally accountable people become confused about this matter, and think that the smallest difficulty of hardship excuses them from an obligation and justifies them leaving it. Maybe many of those who are lax in the Religion use this as an excuse, and they use it a means to extricate themselves from Allah's legislation ﷻ. This is why we find that the scholars of law have elucidated the types of hardship, and laid down a general rule (*ḍābiṭ*) for the type of hardship that is taken into consideration and can be a reason for facilitation and mitigation.

- There is a type of hardship that is inseparable from the responsibilities of the Revealed Law; they are always there because they are part of the nature of a legal responsibility. Hardships like this do not affect lifting obligations or mitigating them.

Thus, one cannot break their fast in Ramaḍān because they feel extremely hungry, just as someone who can afford to perform the Ḥajj and is physically healthy cannot refrain from doing it because of the difficulty of travelling and being far from one's family and homeland. Someone cannot leave enjoining the right and forbidding the wrong because they expect some trouble or rejection, and similar matters. This is because these hardships are normal and do involve great toil or distress. The responsibilities of life are rarely free of them, and if they had an effect, there would be no legal responsibility to begin with. No Revealed Laws would have been established and the interests of Allah's slaves would be lost in both abodes.

- There is also a type of difficulty that is not from the nature of legal responsibility, and it can be separated from obligations in many cases. In fact, they are unforeseen, incidental matters, and they make legal responsibilities more difficult than they normally are. This type of difficulty has two levels:

The **first level** is when the legally accountable person expects some light hardship or constraint, such as a short journey, a slight illness or the loss of some material benefit. This type of difficulty also does not affect the incumbency of obligations. They are not taken into account or consideration. This is because the worldly and Hereafter benefits that the legally accountable person will attain by carrying out these obligations surpass the toil of these hardships, and take precedence over pushing them away.

The **second level** is extra hardship, in which the legally accountable person is threatened with danger to himself, his property or his honour. An example would be someone who can perform the Ḥajj and knows that there are brigands along the way, or he fears someone is anticipating his absence so that they can steal his property or transgress against his family, and other matters that are considered distress and constraint by people of intellect and religion. This type of difficulty is considered in the Revealed Law and it has an effect on legal responsibilities, and sometimes it necessitates the lifting of an obligation or its mitigation. This is because it is something not normally bearable and not considering it could cause those legally accountable to miss out on numerous benefits, which Allah's legislation ﷻ has come to protect.

5. That which is facilitated is not lifted because of that which has been made difficult: This is also a legal maxim that the *fuqahā'* have derived from this ḥadīth. Imam as-Suyūṭī says in *al-Ashbāh wa an-Naẓā'ir*: 'Ibn as-Subkī has said, "It is one of the most well-known maxims derived from his statement ﷺ {If I command you to something, do as much of it as you are able.}"'

It means that the legally accountable person could find himself in a situation in which it is impossible to do what is commanded in full, or it is difficult for him. However, if some of it has been facilitated and he can do it, in this situation, he is obligated to do that which has been facilitated, and the challenge or difficulty of doing some of the obligation is not a reason for the commandment to be lifted completely or there is no legal responsibility.

Examples of the application of this maxim include someone in a state of ritual impurity (*ḥadath*)[51] and he does not have enough water to lift that *ḥadath*. He is obligated to use it on some of his limbs and do *tayammum* with the rest. It is not valid for him to do *tayammum* before using the available water. Someone who finds that which can cover part of his nakedness must use it to cover as much as he can. Whoever recovers from his illness in the middle of the day is obligated to refrain from anything that would break a fast for the rest of the day, and the same applies to women whose menstruation finishes. They also must make up that fast. Whoever can give some expenditure to his poor relative must do so. Whoever can change a portion of something wrong, or to mitigate it, is obligated to do so. There are several other examples of this maxim's application.

This maxim and its application are also gathered from what has been related by al-Bukhārī on the authority of ʿImrān ibn Ḥuṣayn ﵁ who said, 'I had haemorrhoids, so I asked the Prophet ﷺ about the prayer. He said {Pray standing. If you cannot, then sitting down. If you cannot, then on your side.}'

Complete obedience and perfect imitation: Everything that Allah's legislation contains ﷻ including prohibitions of that which unlawful or disliked, commands to do what which is obligatory or recommended – as has been elucidated above, along with their exceptions, maxim and general rules – falls within the legally accountable person's capacity, because it is a legal responsibility established by the Revealed Law. Allah ﷻ does not impose on His slaves except that which they are capable of. The Exalted One has said:

﴿لَا يُكَلِّفُ ٱللَّهُ نَفْسًا إِلَّا وُسْعَهَا﴾

"Allah does not impose on any soul any more than it can bear." [al-Baqarah 2:286]

Based on this, the Muslim does not attain complete obedience except by avoiding all prohibited matters and doing everything that has been commanded, as described above. Allah the Exalted has said:

﴿وَمَآ ءَاتَىٰكُمُ ٱلرَّسُولُ فَخُذُوهُ وَمَا نَهَىٰكُمْ عَنْهُ فَٱنتَهُوا۟﴾

"Whatever the Messenger gives you, accept it, and whatever he forbids you, forgo it." [al-Ḥashr 59:7]

If someone leaves some commandments or does some prohibited actions, he has not fully obeyed what has been commanded and prohibited, and thus it is true that he is disobedient or a transgressor.

The Muslim is called to imitate Allah's Messenger ﷺ in that which has not been established to be from his unique characteristics. Allah the Exalted has said:

51 (tn): *ḥadath* is of two kinds, minor (which is lifted by *wuḍūʾ*) and a major (which is lifted by *ghusl*)..

﴿لَّقَدْ كَانَ لَكُمْ فِي رَسُولِ ٱللَّهِ أُسْوَةٌ حَسَنَةٌ لِّمَن كَانَ يَرْجُوا۟ ٱللَّهَ وَٱلْيَوْمَ ٱلْءَاخِرَ وَذَكَرَ ٱللَّهَ كَثِيرًا﴾

"You have an excellent model in the Messenger of Allah, for all who put their hope in Allah and the Last Day and remember Allah much. [al-Aḥzāb 33:21]

The Prophet ﷺ did not leave a commandment or approach something prohibited except to elucidate the legislation and clarify the type of legal responsibility.

In light of the above, one can understand his statement ﷺ: {and whatever I command you, do as much of it as you are able} and the Exalted's statement:

﴿فَٱتَّقُوا۟ ٱللَّهَ مَا ٱسْتَطَعْتُمْ وَٱسْمَعُوا۟ وَأَطِيعُوا۟﴾

"So have *taqwā* of Allah as much as you can, and listen and obey...". [at-Taghābun 64:16]

As well as other statements that convey the same meaning.

For example, he ﷺ has said, {You will not be able to and you will not do everything that I have commanded you. So do things correctly and give glad tidings.} This has been related by Aḥmad and Abū Dāwūd, and the meaning is: seek to do your actions correctly (*as-sadād* and uprightly. *As-sadād* is the intent to something justly, without immoderation or negligence.

6. Being strict in avoiding prohibited matters and uprooting corruption: Allah's legislation ﷻ constantly strives to prevent people from falling into evil, or to prevent the seeds of corruption from emerging. This is why we find the concern with prohibitions to be more emphatic, perhaps, than the concern with commandments. This does not mean negligence concerning commandments but rather strictness concerning avoiding prohibited matters in general and especially unlawful matters. This is because the Wise Lawgiver has not prohibited anything except that there is some certain corruption therein and definite harm. This is why there is no excuse for perpetrating something unlawful, unless in a situation of urgent necessity and pressing need, as you already know.

Now you can see the mistake that many Muslims fall into, especially in this age, when contradictions in people's lives are widespread. You find them keen to do acts of obedience and obligations, and maybe they are strict in adhering to what is recommended, but at the same time, you find them lax concerning prohibited matters, and maybe they yield to many unlawful matters. Thus, we find the fasting person dealing in usury, or the chaste female pilgrim adorning herself while travelling. Both of them make the excuse that they are keeping up with the times and following the crowd, thinking that this worship of theirs will save them before Allah ﷻ and be enough to enter them into the ranks of Muslims and especially the righteous on the Day everyone will be presented to the Lord of all creation. This is the opposite of what has been affirmed in Allah's wise legislation and established in the Sunnah of the Imam of the Messengers, as well as the understanding of the revered Companions, Imams and Followers, which is that the foundation of worship is to avoid what Allah ﷻ has declared unlawful.

The path to success is to strive against one's ego and one's passions and make them leave prohibited matters, and the reward for doing so surpasses much of the reward for carrying out obligations. The Messenger of Allah ﷺ said this, {Be wary of unlawful matters and you will be the most worshipful of people.}, as related by at-Tirmidhī. ʿĀ'ishah ﵂ said, 'Whoever is happy to be outstripped by someone persistent and hardworking does not need to sin.' ʿUmar ibn al-Khaṭṭāb ﵁ was asked about people who desire disobedience but do not do it. He replied, 'They are people whose hearts Allah has tested for *taqwā*. They will have forgiveness and an immense reward.'[52] ʿAbdullah ibn ʿUmar ﵄, and he is the imam of the worshippers, said, 'To refuse a sixth of a dirham from the unlawful is better than giving 100,000 for the sake of Allah.'

Al-Ḥasan al-Baṣrī ﵀, and he is the master of the Followers, said, 'Worshippers have not worshipped with anything better than leaving what Allah has prohibited'.

ʿUmar ibn ʿAbdul ʿAzīz ﵀ said, '*Taqwā* is not standing at night in prayer, fasting in the day and mixing in what is between that. Rather, *taqwā* is to carry out what Allah has obligated and to leave what Allah has declared unlawful. If this is accompanied by righteous action than that is good upon goodness'.

Thus, it has been established for us that leaving disobedience takes precedence over doing acts of obedience. This does not mean, as we have said, that the Muslim neglect his obligations, as is pleasing to some people who have diseased hearts and weak souls. These people are lax concerning Allah's legislation ﷻ and thus they do not carry out any of the obligations and they claim that they are better than those who pray and fast, on the pretext that they treat people well, and the Religion is treating one another well, and they do not commit any abomination or wrongdoing.

This position of theirs, and those before them, is a deviation from the path of guidance and a distortion of the understanding of Islam and the conduct of Muslims, as has been elucidated in what was discussed above.

7. Warding off harm takes precedence over bringing about benefit:

This is a general legal maxim. It was established by jurists based on the derivation that the Lawgiver is strict in commanding against prohibited matters. It means that if an issue comes up and the benefit and the harm are the same, such that if the benefit were observed, the harm would be realised, and if the harm were observed, the benefit would be lost, then warding off harm, by doing or refraining,

52 (tn): please see al-Ḥujurāt 49:3.

takes precedence. This is because harms spread very quickly, like fire spreading through dry wood, thus it is wise and prudent to prevent them from happening, even if doing so prevents some benefit from coming about or delays it.

Examples of this maxim being applied include refraining from selling grapes to someone you know will use them to make wine, even if he offers a higher price for them. The same applies to refraining from trading in wine and manufacturing it, even if there is material profit therein or economic benefit, and the same goes for anything unlawful in the Revealed Law. Likewise, a woman is prevented from working, even if there is some benefit in it for her, if she is going to be mixing with men or be alone with them, to avoid the harms of immorality and depravity that usually result. Indeed, men as well are prevented from such work. The applications of this maxim are many.

We can also gather this maxim and its applications from the Prophet ﷺ forbidding women from travelling alone, without her husband being with her or one of her unmarriageable male relatives. Al-Bukhārī and Muslim have related – the wording be that of the latter – on the authority of Abū Hurayrah ؓ that the Messenger of Allah ﷺ said, {It is not lawful for a woman who believes in Allah and the Last Day to travel a day's distance without being accompanied by a *maḥram*.} A *maḥram* is a man she is never permitted to marry.[53]

It is worth mentioning that considering the presence of benefit or resultant harm is based on what one thinks will most likely happen, not precise determination. That which is predominant and widespread is what is taken into account, not that which is rare. As long as an action is thought most likely to lead to harm, it is impermissible, even if we do not have any decisive proof. Likewise, if it is something that is normally expected to cause harm, it is deemed impermissible even if it were to happen several times without causing any harm.

No consideration is given to the harm that is predominated: there are actions that contain some type of harm but the realisation of clear benefit greatly surpasses the harm and predominates it. Thus, the action is permissible or even obligatory, given the predominant benefit therein. The harm is ignored because it is predominated. Examples of this include amputating an infected limb to save the life of someone legally accountable or lying to reconcile between two people quarrelling. In reality, this and similar matters go back to acting according to the lesser of two harms, to avoid the greater harm. Thus, the harm of keeping an infected limb, which could kill the legally accountable person, is a greater harm than amputating it. The harm of an ongoing quarrel between two people, which could lead to animosity and hatred taking root, and cause a great deal of tribulation, is a greater harm than a lie that is not expected to harm anyone or deprive anyone of their right.

53 (tn) e.g. her father, brother, son etc., as opposed to a brother-in-law, for example, as she is only forbidden from marrying him as long as he is married to her sister. Thus, a brother-in-law is only a temporary *maḥram* and does not carry the same ruling as a permanent *maḥram*.

8. Some reasons why nations are destroyed: The Noble Messenger ﷺ elucidated that among the reasons why nations are destroyed, why they break down and disappear, why they deserve the punishment of being uprooted – sometimes – comes down to two matters:

- Abundant questioning and unnecessary strain therein, disagreeing over matters, and not adhering to Allah's legislation ﷻ. The elucidation is as follows:

The prohibition of questioning and when it is permitted: The Messenger of Allah ﷺ forbade his Companions, in general from asking him lots of questions, for fear that it would cause them to be overburdened with legal responsibilities, and to avoid nit-picking, unnecessary strain and preoccupation with that which is of no concern. He did it to avoid questions about that which is of no benefit, even if they are not harmful, and to prevent the Muslims from going the way of those before them, in arguing and debating. Al-Bukhārī has related, as well as other, on the authority of al-Mughīrah ibn Shuʿbah ؓ: 'The Messenger of Allah ﷺ would forbid gossip, abundant questioning and wasting wealth'.

The Companions who were close to him, from the Migrants and the Helpers, understood this objective, and thus they would not ask him about something even if their souls desired to do so. This is because they were obeying his command and stopping at his prohibition. It is in their hearts that faith had become firmly established. They made their desires follow what the Messenger of Allah ﷺ was pleased with.

It also possible that they did not need to ask, as they were living with Allah's Messenger ﷺ who would immediately convey to them what had been revealed to him. The revelation of the heavens was never suspended from them. When something happened, the elucidation that they needed in their religion quickly came, without asking, so that they would not remain in any doubt:

﴿يُبَيِّنُ ٱللَّهُ لَكُمْ أَن تَضِلُّوا۟﴾

"Allah makes things clear to you so you will not go astray." [an Nisā' 4:176]

In other words, so that you do fall into error, and at that point, there is no need to ask about anything, especially before it has happened and there is no need of it. Rather, the need is to understand what has come down and to comprehend what Allah's Messenger ﷺ is informing of. Then there is the need to follow it and apply it. Ibn ʿAbbās ؓ said in his *Tafsīr* about this verse:

﴿لَا تَسْـَٔلُوا۟ عَنْ أَشْيَآءَ إِن تُبْدَ لَكُمْ تَسُؤْكُمْ﴾

"Do not ask about matters which, if they were made known to you...". [al-Mā'idah 5:101]

'The meaning is: wait. When the Qur'ān has come down, you will not ask about anything except that you will find it elucidated for you'.

As for the Bedouins and those passing through al-Madīnah, who were not able to live with the revelation like the aforementioned, Allah's Messenger ﷺ would allow them to ask. This was to show the camaraderie and make matters easy for them, and to provide them with the knowledge they needed in their religion, which they were not able to acquire any time they wanted.

Maybe this is why one of them would stay in his hometown and not migrate so that he could keep enjoying this concession because he wanted to ask about any religious matter that crossed his mind. Muslim has related on the authority of an-Nawās ibn Sam'ān ﷺ who said, 'I spent one year with the Messenger of Allah ﷺ in Madīnah. Nothing but questioning prevented me from migrating. When one of us had migrated, he did not ask the Prophet ﷺ'. In other words, he stayed in Madīnah as a visitor and did not settle there permanently, and nothing prevented him from migrating and settling other than this his love of asking, which his migration would deny him.

These visitors' questions would often coincide with the wishes of the Emigrants and Helpers, and they would rejoice at them, especially if the answer contained good news, or elucidated the path to Paradise.

Muslim has related from Anas ﷺ that he said, 'We were forbidden from asking the Messenger of Allah ﷺ about anything, and thus it pleased us when a discerning man came from the desert and asked him, and we would listen.;

Al-Bukhārī and Muslim have related from Anas ﷺ that he said, 'A man from the desert came to the Prophet ﷺ and said, "O Messenger of Allah, when will the Hour be established?" He replied, {Woe to you! What have you prepared for it?} He replied, "I have not prepared anything for it, other than that I love Allah and His Messenger." He then said, {You will be with those you love.} We then said, "And us as well?" He replied, {Yes}, and we were extremely happy that day.'

9. Questioning and Its Ruling: Questioning has types, and thus the ruling differs depending on its motive and what the possible consequences are:

A. That which is desired in the Revealed Law, and there are levels:

An **individual obligation** (*farḍ 'ayn*) upon every Muslim, meaning that it is not permissible for a Muslim to leave it and remain silent. This is a question about something he is ignorant of from the matters of the Religion and the rulings of the Revealed Law, something he is obligated to do and carry out. Examples include the rulings of purification and the prayer when one has reached maturity, the rulings of fasting when one has reached Ramaḍān and one is healthy and resident, the rulings of the zakāt and Ḥajj when one has sufficient wealth or can do so. The same applies to the rulings of buying, selling and transacting when one engages in trade, the rulings of marriage and connected matters when one wants to get married, the rulings of *jihād* when one is a soldier in the army, and so forth. The legally accountable person asks according to the situation he is in, in whatever stage of his life. Regarding this, Allah the Exalted says:

﴿فَسْـَٔلُوٓاْ أَهْلَ ٱلذِّكْرِ إِن كُنتُمْ لَا تَعْلَمُونَ﴾

"...ask the people of the Reminder if you do not know..." [an-Naḥl 16:43]

Based on this, we understand what al-Bayhaqī has related in *Shuʿab al-Īmān*[54] from his statement ﷺ {Seeking knowledge is an obligation upon every Muslim}, i.e. male and female.

Collective Obligation:
This means that it is not obligatory upon every Muslim. Rather, it suffices if some of them do it. This is asking to have more understanding (*fiqh*) of the Religion, and to know the rulings of the Revealed Law and what is connected to them, not just to apply them. This question is so there are people who preserve Allah's ﷻ religion who give *fatwā* and judge, and carry the banner of calling to Allah ﷻ. They teach other Muslims what they need to know about their religion, so they can avoid falling into error and mistake and travel the path of guidance and integrity. Regarding this, Allah the Exalted says:

﴿وَمَا كَانَ ٱلْمُؤْمِنُونَ لِيَنفِرُواْ كَآفَّةً ۚ فَلَوْلَا نَفَرَ مِن كُلِّ فِرْقَةٍ مِّنْهُمْ طَآئِفَةٌ لِّيَتَفَقَّهُواْ فِى ٱلدِّينِ وَلِيُنذِرُواْ قَوْمَهُمْ إِذَا رَجَعُوٓاْ إِلَيْهِمْ لَعَلَّهُمْ يَحْذَرُونَ﴾

"However, it is not necessary for the believers to march forth all at once. If a party from each group of them were to go out so they could increase their knowledge of the Religion, they would be able to notify their people when they returned to them, so that perhaps they would take warning!" [at-Tawbah 9:122]

In other words, the Muslims should not go out for *jihād* altogether. Rather, a group of them should stay back to seek knowledge and ask about it, and acquire *fiqh* of Allah's ﷻ religion, so that they can teach and instruct the Ummah when they come back from *jihād*.

Regarding this, he ﷺ says: {So that those present can teach those who are absent.} This ḥadīth is agreed upon.

Ibn ʿAbbās رضي الله عنهما was asked about how he obtained vast knowledge. He replied, 'I have been granted an asking tongue and an intelligent heart.'

54 (tn): i.e. The Branches of Faith.

Recommended: This means that it is recommended for the Muslim to ask about it. For example, one should ask about acts of righteousness and drawing nearer to Allah ﷻ that is beyond one's obligations, and ask questions to make sure of the validity of the obligations one has carried out, as well as about what keeps one away from forbidden matters.

B. Prohibited questioning, and it also has levels:
Unlawful: This means that the legally accountable person sins by doing so. For example:

- Asking about that which Allah the Exalted has concealed from His slaves and not granted them knowledge of, or informed us that He the Glorified has exclusive knowledge of it. Examples include asking about when the Hour will be established, about the reality and nature of the spirit (*rūḥ*), about the secret of Allah's decree and predestination, and so forth.

- Asking for the sake of jest, obstinacy and ridicule. Al-Bukhārī has related from Ibn ʿAbbās ﷺ who said, 'There were some people who would ask the Messenger of Allah ﷺ to ridicule. One man would say, "Who is my father?" A man who had lost his she-camel would say, "Where is my she-camel?" Allah ﷻ then revealed this verse:

﴿يَـٰٓأَيُّهَا ٱلَّذِينَ ءَامَنُوا۟ لَا تَسْـَٔلُوا۟ عَنْ أَشْيَآءَ إِن تُبْدَ لَكُمْ تَسُؤْكُمْ﴾

"You who believe! Do not ask about matters which, if they were made known to you, would make things difficult for you." [al-Māʾidah 5:101]

- Asking about miracles, or requesting out of stubbornness and obstinacy, or to annoy and embarrass, that the norm be suspended,[55] as the idolaters and People of the Book would do.

- Asking captious questions: Aḥmad and Abū Dāwūd have related from Muʿāwiyah ﷺ that the Prophet ﷺ forbade captious questions. He[56] said in *an-Nihāyah,* 'They are questions that seek to deceive scholars and cause them to slip, and thus stir up evil and tribulation. He forbade them because they are of no benefit in the Religion and usually they are about something that does not happen.' It has also been said that they are questions that are not needed, asking the how of this and the how of that. Asking about abstruse issues like this, which are hard to answer and only seek to aggravate, are not allowed in the Revealed Law, and they are a sign of bad manners and ill religion.

55 Ar. *khāriq al-ʿādah.*

56 (tn): i.e. Majd ad-Dīn Ibn al-Athīr in *an-Nihāyah fī Gharīb al-Ḥadīth wa al-Athar.*

Similar to asking about these kinds of issues is being preoccupied with them, researching them, relating them and presenting them to people. At-Ṭabarānī has related from Thawbān 🙵 that the Prophet 🙵 said, {There will be peoples from my Ummah whose jurists will be busy with their puzzling questions. They are the worst of my Ummah.} This is a *ṣaḥīḥ* ḥadīth according to al-Jāmiʿ aṣ-Ṣaghīr. It has been transmitted from al-Ḥasan al-Baṣrī 🙵 that he said, 'The worst of Allah's slaves are those who pursue difficult questions with which they mystify Allah's slaves.'

Disliked: i.e. the legally accountable person should leave it and he does not sin by asking it. For example:

- Asking about that which there is no need and there is no practical benefit in the answer, and maybe the answer contains something that will displease the questioner. Muslim has related from Abū Mūsā al-Ashʿarī 🙵 that he said, 'The Prophet 🙵 was being asked about things that he disliked, and when there were a lot of these questions, he became angry. He then said to the people, {Ask me about anything you want.} A man then said, "Who is my father, O Messenger of Allah?" He replied, {Your father is Ḥudhāfah.} Another person stood up and said, "Who is my father, O Messenger of Allah?" He replied, {Your father is Sālim, the client of Shaybah.} When ʿUmar saw the anger on the Messenger of Allah's face 🙵 he said, "O Messenger of Allah, we turn to Allah in repentance." Both al-Bukhārī and Muslim have something similar from Anas 🙵.

- Asking whether something is lawful or unlawful when the Revealed Law has remained silent, and it has not been made clear whether it should be required or prohibited. Questions like this can lead to legal accountability therein along with strictness, and thus the Muslims fall into constraint and hardship and the questioner is the reason why.

Muslim has related from Saʿd ibn Abī Waqāṣ 🙵 that he said, 'The Messenger of Allah 🙵 said, {The Muslims who commit the greatest offence against their fellow Muslims are those who ask about something that was not unlawful for the Muslims but then it becomes unlawful because of their questioning.}' In another narration: {...those who ask about something and examine it...}, i.e. they go to the greatest lengths in researching and investigating.

An-Nawawī 🙵 said, 'Al-Qāḍī ʿIyāḍ said, "What is meant by the offense (*jurm*) here is placing constraint upon the Muslims, not the offence or crime that is sinful and punishable." Then an-Nawawī mentions that the correct opinion is what the majority have said in commenting on this ḥadīth, which is that the meaning of offence here is sin and misdeed. Based on al-Qāḍī's position, this questioning is disliked. Based on the majority's position, it is unlawful.

An-Nawawī said, 'This prohibition is exclusive to his time ﷺ. As for after the Revealed Law had been established and was safe from being added to, the prohibition ceased because its reason had ceased.' In other words, it was no longer possible for something to be made unlawful because of questioning, because there is no revelation after Allah's Messenger ﷺ.

Al-Bukhārī and Muslim have related that a man asked Allah's Messenger ﷺ about a man who found his wife with another man and thus killed him, and this was when the verses concerning the legal punishment for fornication had come down, stipulating that it requires four witnesses. Thus, the Messenger of Allah ﷺ disliked these questions and took exception to them.

Permissible: This is what is besides the aforementioned types of questions and their rulings. In his commentary on his statement ﷺ: {The Muslims who commit the greatest offence...} An-Nawawī has transmitted from al-Khaṭṭābī ﷺ as well as others, and said, 'This ḥadīth concerns someone who asks obstinately and burdensomely about that which there is no need. As for someone who asks out of necessity, such that something has happened to him and he is asking about it, there is no sin or blame therein, because the Exalted One has said:

﴿فَسْـَٔلُوٓاْ أَهْلَ ٱلذِّكْرِ إِن كُنتُمْ لَا تَعْلَمُونَ﴾

"Ask the People of the Reminder" [al-Anbiyā' 21:7]

10. Instead of questioning, being preoccupied with understanding and obeying: What the Muslim is obligated to be interested in and concerned with is seeking that which has come from Allah the Exalted and His Messenger ﷺ. Then he must strive to understand it and know its meanings. If it has to do with knowledge, he must affirm it and have a firm conviction of it. If it is a practical matter, he must expend his effort and strive to do it as much as possible, whether it is a command to carry something out or to avoid something. Whoever does so attains felicity in this life and success in the Hereafter. Whoever contravenes this, and busies himself with his ego's whims and fancies, will fall into that which Allah's Messenger ﷺ has warned against, i.e. the condition of the People of the Book, who were destroyed by their abundant questioning and disagreeing, and lack of obedience and compliance.

This was the state of the Prophet's Companions ﷺ and those who follow them in excellence in seeking beneficial knowledge from the Book and Sunnah.

A man asked Ibn 'Umar ﷺ about touching the Stone.[57] He replied, 'I saw the Prophet ﷺ touching it and kissing it.' The man then said, 'What do you think if it

57 (tn): i.e. the Black Stone, which is in the Ka'bah.

is crowded? What if I cannot get to it?' Ibn ʿUmar ﷺ replied, 'Leave your "what if" in Yemen![58] I saw Allah's Messenger ﷺ touching it and kissing it', as has been related by al-Bukhārī and others.

What Ibn ʿUmar meant ﷺ is that there is no need to assume impossibility or difficulty in something before it has happened, for it slackens one's resolve to carry on.

11. The position of the *mujtahid* imams and jurists:

The greater part of their concern was researching the meanings of Allah's Book, and that which explains it from the authentic Sunnah, the statements of the Companions and those who follow them in excellence. As for the Sunnah of Allah's Messenger ﷺ it is knowing what is authentic and what is weak, then understanding it, comprehending it and knowing its meanings. Then comes knowing the statements of the Companions and those who follow them in excellence concerning the various sciences, such as *tafsīr*, *ḥadīth*, questions about the lawful and unlawful, the foundations of the Sunnah, abstinence and softening the hearts, and so forth. This is the way of the imams, the people of the Religion whose guidance and knowledge is agreed upon. Whoever follows other than their path is misguided and misguiding, and has taken that which is impermissible and left that which is obligatory to act upon.

12. Asking about that which has not happened:

Asking for knowledge is praiseworthy if it is for the sake of action and not with the intention of ostentation and argumentation. This is why many of the Companions and Followers disliked questions about matters that had not occurred and did not answer them.

- ʿAmr ibn Murrah said, "Umar ﷺ went out to the people and said, 'I forbid you from asking us about that which has not occurred, for it is a distraction for us'.

- It is on the authority of Ibn ʿUmar ﷺ that he said, 'Do not ask about that which has not occurred, for indeed I heard ʿUmar ﷺ cursing the one who asks about that which has not occurred'.

- When Zayd ibn Thābit ﷺ was asked about something, he would say, 'Has this happened?' If they said, 'No', he would say, 'Leave it until it does happen'.

- Masrūq said, 'I asked Ubay ibn Kaʿb ﷺ about something and he said, "Has it happened?" I said, "No". He said, "Let us be until it does happen. When we have done our *ijtihād*,[59] you will have our opinion".

58 (tn): because the man was from Yemen.

59 (tn): i.e. expert legal reasoning.

• Ash-Shaʿbī said, "ʿAmmār ⬧ was asked about an issue and he said, "Has this happened?" They replied, "No". He said, "Leave us until it does happen. Then we will exert ourselves for you"'. In other words, we will take it upon ourselves to know it and provide an answer.

Similar examples have been related from the Followers.

Regarding this, Abū Dāwūd has related in *al-Murāsīl* on the authority of Muʿādh ibn Jabal ⬧ who said, 'The Messenger of Allah ⬧ said, {Do not hasten affliction before it occurs. If you do not, there will always be someone from the Muslims who will be right and correct when he speaks. If you hasten, you will become divided, some will go here, and some will go here.}

The foundation of all of this is that one seeks Allah's countenance ⬧ and to draw near to Him by knowing what He has sent down to His Messenger, to travel his path, act accordingly and call the creation to it. Whoever does this, Allah has granted him success and guided him, inspired him and shown him the right way, and taught him what he did not know.

13. The Companions ⬧, asking for the sake of action:

The Prophet's Companions ⬧ would sometimes ask him the ruling for matters that they anticipated, that they thought were most likely to occur. These were the ones who were not always with Allah's Messenger ⬧ and thus they desired to know Allah's ⬧ ruling beforehand, so that they would know what to do when the time came. For example:

• Al-Bukhārī and Muslim have related from Rāfiʿ ibn Khadīj ⬧ who said, 'I said, "O Messenger of Allah, we might come to encounter the enemy one day and not have a knife with us. Do we slaughter with canes and reeds?" He replied {Whatever causes the blood to flow and Allah's name has been mentioned over it, eat it, but not the teeth and nails.}

• The five[60] have related from Abū Hurayrah ⬧ who said, 'A man asked the Messenger of Allah ⬧ and said, "O Messenger of Allah, we travel by sea and we only carry a little water with us. If we use it for ablution (*wuḍūʾ*), we will be thirsty. Can we do ablution with seawater?" He replied, {Its water is pure, and whatever dies therein is lawful.} In other words, any fish or the like that dies therein is lawful to eat and does not need to be slaughtered according to the Revealed Law.

14. Obedience and compliance is the path to success:

The Messenger of Allah ⬧ warned against following the path of these peoples, who hesitated and disobeyed with regards to their messengers, and thus they deserved

---

60 (tn): i.e. Imams Aḥmad, Abū Dāwūd, at-Tirmidhī, Ibn Mājah and an-Nasāʾī.

to be punished or to have their backs burdened with more legal responsibilities, and shackles. Thus, Allah the Exalted's favour towards this Ummah is immense, as he has taught them to say:

﴿سَمِعْنَا وَأَطَعْنَا غُفْرَانَكَ رَبَّنَا وَإِلَيْكَ ٱلْمَصِيرُ ۝ لَا يُكَلِّفُ ٱللَّهُ نَفْسًا إِلَّا وُسْعَهَا لَهَا مَا كَسَبَتْ وَعَلَيْهَا مَا ٱكْتَسَبَتْ رَبَّنَا لَا تُؤَاخِذْنَا إِن نَّسِينَا أَوْ أَخْطَأْنَا رَبَّنَا وَلَا تَحْمِلْ عَلَيْنَا إِصْرًا كَمَا حَمَلْتَهُ عَلَى ٱلَّذِينَ مِن قَبْلِنَا رَبَّنَا وَلَا تُحَمِّلْنَا مَا لَا طَاقَةَ لَنَا بِهِ وَٱعْفُ عَنَّا وَٱغْفِرْ لَنَا وَٱرْحَمْنَا أَنتَ مَوْلَىٰنَا فَٱنصُرْنَا عَلَى ٱلْقَوْمِ ٱلْكَٰفِرِينَ﴾

"We hear and we obey. Forgive us, our Lord! You are our journey's end... Our Lord, do not take us to task if we forget or make a mistake! Our Lord do not place on us a load like the one You placed on those before us. Our Lord do not place on us a load we have not the strength to bear! And pardon us, and forgive us, and have mercy on us. You are our Master, so help us against the people of the unbelievers." [al-Baqarah 2:285,286]

'A load like the one You placed on those before us' means legal responsibilities that are heavy and burdensome.

The truthful of this Ummah are victorious with this immense favour, as they are upon truth. Allah the Exalted has said of them:

﴿إِنَّمَا كَانَ قَوْلَ ٱلْمُؤْمِنِينَ إِذَا دُعُوٓا۟ إِلَى ٱللَّهِ وَرَسُولِهِ لِيَحْكُمَ بَيْنَهُمْ أَن يَقُولُوا۟ سَمِعْنَا وَأَطَعْنَا وَأُو۟لَٰٓئِكَ هُمُ ٱلْمُفْلِحُونَ ۝ وَمَن يُطِعِ ٱللَّهَ وَرَسُولَهُ وَيَخْشَ ٱللَّهَ وَيَتَّقْهِ فَأُو۟لَٰٓئِكَ هُمُ ٱلْفَآئِزُونَ﴾

"The reply of the believers when they are summoned to Allah and His Messenger so that he can judge between them, is to say, 'We hear and we obey'. They are the ones who are successful. All who obey Allah and His Messenger and have awe of Allah and *taqwā* of Him, they are the ones who are victorious." [an-Nūr 24:51-52]

They have not gone the way of those who said to their prophet when he commanded them to enter a land:

﴿إِنَّا لَن نَّدْخُلَهَآ أَبَدًا مَّا دَامُوا۟ فِيهَا فَٱذْهَبْ أَنتَ وَرَبُّكَ فَقَٰتِلَآ إِنَّا هَٰهُنَا قَٰعِدُونَ﴾

"We will never enter it as long as they are there. So you and your Lord go and fight. We will stay sitting here." [al-Māʾidah 5:24]

Thus, they deserved distress and destruction:

﴿فَإِنَّهَا مُحَرَّمَةٌ عَلَيْهِمْ أَرْبَعِينَ سَنَةً يَتِيهُونَ فِي ٱلْأَرْضِ﴾

"The land will be forbidden to them for forty years during which they will wander aimlessly about the earth." [al-Mā'idah 5:26]

Likewise, because of their disobedience, they deserved to be denied many delights and pleasures:

﴿فَبِظُلْمٍ مِّنَ ٱلَّذِينَ هَادُوا۟ حَرَّمْنَا عَلَيْهِمْ طَيِّبَٰتٍ أُحِلَّتْ لَهُمْ وَبِصَدِّهِمْ عَن سَبِيلِ ٱللَّهِ كَثِيرًا﴾

"Because of wrongdoing on the part of the Jews, We made unlawful for them some good things which had previously been lawful for them; and because of their obstructing many people from the Way of Allah." [an-Nisā' 4:160]

15. Warning against disagreeing and encouraging unity and agreement: Allah the Exalted has described the Muslims and the believers as one Ummah. He the Glorified has said:

﴿إِنَّ هَٰذِهِۦٓ أُمَّتُكُمْ أُمَّةً وَٰحِدَةً وَأَنَا۠ رَبُّكُمْ فَٱعْبُدُونِ﴾

"This ummah of yours in one ummah and I am your Lord, so worship Me." [al-Anbiyā' 21:92]

Thus, Muslims should strive for this unity, so that they can be a solid force against the multiple forces of evil, injustice and disbelief. Allah the Exalted and His ﷻ Chosen Messenger ﷺ have strongly warned us against disagreeing, which by its nature turns the Ummah into groups and parties, each discrediting the other, fighting the other, only concerned with itself, instead of striving against the real enemy, who is lying in wait against them. Indeed, we find the Messenger of Allah ﷺ considering it a path towards disbelief, and from the nature of the disbelievers. He ﷺ says, {Do not go back to being disbelievers after me, striking each other's necks.}[61] Likewise, the Qur'ān confirms this trait of those who disbelieve from the People of the Book:

﴿وَلَا تَكُونُوا۟ كَٱلَّذِينَ تَفَرَّقُوا۟ وَٱخْتَلَفُوا۟ مِنۢ بَعْدِ مَا جَآءَهُمُ ٱلْبَيِّنَٰتُ ۚ وَأُو۟لَٰٓئِكَ لَهُمْ عَذَابٌ عَظِيمٌ﴾

"Do not be like those who split up and differed after the Clear Signs came to them. They will have a terrible punishment." [Āl 'Imrān 3:105]

16. The consequence of those who split from the group and cause division and disagreement: Islam strongly rebukes the one who breaks from the Muslim community and causes them to disagree and become divided. The punishment of such people is to be killed in this life and burned in the Fire on the Day of Standing.

61 Al-Bukhārī and Muslim.

The Exalted One has said:

﴿وَمَن يُشَاقِقِ ٱلرَّسُولَ مِنۢ بَعۡدِ مَا تَبَيَّنَ لَهُ ٱلۡهُدَىٰ وَيَتَّبِعۡ غَيۡرَ سَبِيلِ ٱلۡمُؤۡمِنِينَ نُوَلِّهِۦ مَا تَوَلَّىٰ وَنُصۡلِهِۦ جَهَنَّمَۖ وَسَآءَتۡ مَصِيرًا﴾

"But if anyone opposes the Messenger after the guidance has become clear to him, and follows other than the path of the believers, We will hand him over to whatever he has turned to, and we will roast him in the Fire. What an evil destination!" [an-Nisā' 4:115]

And he ﷺ has said, {Whoever abandons obedience, splits from the group and then dies, dies the death of Jāhiliyyah},[62] as related by Muslim. He has also said, {If someone comes to you while you are united under one man seeking to split you up and divide your group, kill him}, which has also been related by Muslim.

17. Adhering to Allah the Exalted's law is the way to unity:

In His Book, Allah the Exalted has legislated for us the foundations of every good that humanity needs in their lives. His Chosen Messenger ﷺ has elucidated for us the most noble and encompassing of them, with what Allah ﷻ has inspired him with from the purified Sunnah. Thus, it suffices the Ummah – to achieve unity and establish solidarity and cohesion among themselves – to go back to Allah's ﷻ Book and the Sunnah of His Messenger ﷺ and by doing so they would comply with Allah's ﷻ statement:

﴿وَٱعۡتَصِمُواْ بِحَبۡلِ ٱللَّهِ جَمِيعًا وَلَا تَفَرَّقُواْ﴾

"Hold fast to the rope of Allah all together, and do not separate." [Āl 'Imrān 3:103]

They would also remember the blessing that Allah has bestowed upon them with this Islam, which by itself brought harmony between them, as well as unity, honour and rank:

﴿وَٱذۡكُرُواْ نِعۡمَتَ ٱللَّهِ عَلَيۡكُمۡ إِذۡ كُنتُمۡ أَعۡدَآءٗ فَأَلَّفَ بَيۡنَ قُلُوبِكُمۡ فَأَصۡبَحۡتُم بِنِعۡمَتِهِۦٓ إِخۡوَٰنٗا﴾

"Remember Allah's blessings to you when you were enemies and He joined your hearts together so that you became brothers by His blessing." [Āl 'Imrān 3:103]

With its guidance, they were granted success and salvation:

﴿وَكُنتُمۡ عَلَىٰ شَفَا حُفۡرَةٖ مِّنَ ٱلنَّارِ فَأَنقَذَكُم مِّنۡهَا﴾

"You were on the very brink of a pit of the Fire, and He rescued you from it." [Āl 'Imrān 3:103]

62 (tn): i.e. the pre-Islamic age of ignorance.

They looked into the matter and responded to the call of the intellect, drew conclusions from the experiences of life and then adhered and obeyed. They had the guidance that was hoped for:

﴿كَذَٰلِكَ يُبَيِّنُ ٱللَّهُ لَكُمْ ءَايَٰتِهِۦ لَعَلَّكُمْ تَهْتَدُونَ﴾

"In this way, Allah makes His signs clear to you, so that perhaps you will be guided." [Āl ʿImrān 3:103]

The Glorified's statement suffices us in this regard:

﴿وَأَنَّ هَٰذَا صِرَٰطِى مُسْتَقِيمًا فَٱتَّبِعُوهُ ۖ وَلَا تَتَّبِعُوا۟ ٱلسُّبُلَ فَتَفَرَّقَ بِكُمْ عَن سَبِيلِهِۦ ۚ ذَٰلِكُمْ وَصَّىٰكُم بِهِۦ لَعَلَّكُمْ تَتَّقُونَ﴾

"This is my path and it is straight, so follow it. Do not follow other ways or you will become cut off from His Way. This is what He instructs you to do so that perhaps, you will have *taqwā*." [al-Anʿām 6:153]

He ﷺ has said, {I have left you with two things after which you will not go astray: Allah's Book and my Sunnah}, as related by al-Ḥākim. In other words, you will not go astray after adhering to them.

18. Disagreement in the Religion:

One of the most significant causes of disunity and division in the Ummah is when the door of argumentation in knowledge and ostentation in religion is opened. They thus differ in the foundations and go their separate ways. This is why we Allah the Exalted's Book commanding us to establish Allah's legislation ﷻ this legislation that started with what was sent down to Adam عليه السلام and was perfected with what was sent down to the Seal of the Prophets and Messengers, which we adhere to and keep away from anything extraneous. We do not pay attention to any opinion or *ijtihād* that clashes with one of its texts or contradicts one of its foundations. The Exalted One has said:

﴿شَرَعَ لَكُم مِّنَ ٱلدِّينِ مَا وَصَّىٰ بِهِۦ نُوحًا وَٱلَّذِىٓ أَوْحَيْنَآ إِلَيْكَ وَمَا وَصَّيْنَا بِهِۦٓ إِبْرَٰهِيمَ وَمُوسَىٰ وَعِيسَىٰٓ ۖ أَنْ أَقِيمُوا۟ ٱلدِّينَ وَلَا تَتَفَرَّقُوا۟ فِيهِ ۚ كَبُرَ عَلَى ٱلْمُشْرِكِينَ مَا تَدْعُوهُمْ إِلَيْهِ ۚ ٱللَّهُ يَجْتَبِىٓ إِلَيْهِ مَن يَشَآءُ وَيَهْدِىٓ إِلَيْهِ مَن يُنِيبُ﴾

"He has laid down the same religion for you as He enjoined on Nūḥ: that which we have revealed to you and which we enjoined on Ibrāhīm, Mūsā and ʿĪsā: 'Establish the Religion and do not make divisions in it.'" [ash-Shūrā 42:13]

The Messenger of Allah ﷺ instructs us to study the Qurʾān, to understand its meanings and to apply what it requires. Whenever a disagreement occurs in understanding it which could lead to controversy, he commands us to stop researching until our hearts are pure and our thoughts have been enlightened. Then we go back to Allah the Exalted's Book with veracity and sincerity. Al-Bukhārī has related from Jundub ibn ʿAbdillāh al-Bajlī ؓ who said, 'Allah's Messenger ﷺ said, {Read the Qurʾān as long as your hearts are in harmony with it. If you differ, stop.} He ﷺ stopped disagreement at its root. When he was on his deathbed, he called his Companions so that he could write something down after which they would not go astray. When they differed over whether this person should write or that person should write, he tore up the document and said, {Leave me alone.} This was to repel them, restrain them and instruct them that disagreeing is the cause of loss and decline. This is why Ibn ʿAbbās ؓ would say, 'Their differing and uproar was an utter loss in what happened between the Messenger of the Allah ﷺ and writing down that document'. This was related by al-Bukhārī. He ﷺ makes it clear in the ḥadīth of this chapter: the destruction of previous nations was because they differed in their religion after contravening what their prophets had brought.

19. The danger of following one's desires:
It is an absolute calamity when disagreement in the Religion is because of interests and desires, stubbornness and greed. This is why we find Allah the Exalted's Book giving examples of people who provoked disagreement in the Religion, seeking to divide the Muslims into sects, parties and factions. We find Allah's Book taking them out of the fold of Islam and declaring His Chosen Prophet ﷺ free of them. The Exalted One has said,

﴿إِنَّ ٱلَّذِينَ فَرَّقُوا۟ دِينَهُمْ وَكَانُوا۟ شِيَعًا لَّسْتَ مِنْهُمْ فِى شَىْءٍ ۚ
إِنَّمَآ أَمْرُهُمْ إِلَى ٱللَّهِ ثُمَّ يُنَبِّئُهُم بِمَا كَانُوا۟ يَفْعَلُونَ﴾

"As for those who divide up their religion and form into sects, you have nothing whatsoever to do with them. Their case will go back to Allah and then He will inform them about what they did." [al-Anʿām 6:159]

Danger lurks in this kind of disagreement, which does seek recourse to any evidence or submit to any proof. It is this disagreement that destroys nations, and what Allah's Messenger ﷺ is referring to in his statement: {The only thing that destroyed those before you was their abundance of questions and their disagreements with their Prophets.}

This is what the Qur'ān is warning us against by saying:

﴿وَلَا تَكُونُوا۟ كَٱلَّذِينَ تَفَرَّقُوا۟ وَٱخْتَلَفُوا۟ مِنۢ بَعْدِ مَا جَآءَهُمُ ٱلْبَيِّنَـٰتُ﴾

"Do not be like those who split up and differed after the Clear Signs came to them". [Āl ʿImrān 3:105]

And emphasising it again by saying:

﴿وَمَا تَفَرَّقَ ٱلَّذِينَ أُوتُوا۟ ٱلْكِتَـٰبَ إِلَّا مِنۢ بَعْدِ مَا جَآءَتْهُمُ ٱلْبَيِّنَةُ﴾

"Those who were given the Book did not divide into sects until after the Clear Sign came to them." [al-Bayyinah 98:4]

As for disagreement that arises from evidence, and goes back to a source, this is not what is intended here, because it is disagreement in branches and not in foundations. It is disagreement that does not cause divisions and splits in the ranks of the Ummah. Rather, it is a sign of the flexibility of the legislation and freedom of opinion therein, within its basic principles and foundations. It is a sign of the uprightness of this Ummah, which do not accept to act unless they are firmly convinced that it is true and right. Perhaps the best evidence of this meaning is what al-Bukhārī has related from ʿAbdullah ibn Masʿūd ﷺ in which he heard a man reciting an āyah and it was different to what he had heard from the Prophet ﷺ. He took the man by the hand and went to the Prophet ﷺ and in one narration, 'I informed him and I saw the dislike on his face. He said {Both of you are correct. Recite and do not disagree, for those before you disagreed and were destroyed.}'

Thus, he ﷺ affirmed their different ways of reciting, because it was a disagreement based on evidence, going back to a source, which is the Qur'ān coming down in various dialects spoken by the Arabs at that time. Rather, he forbade them from disagreeing after the proof had been clarified and the evidence elucidated, which only happens because of whims and desires.

20. The ḥadīth shows that whoever is capable and can afford it is obligated to perform the Ḥajj once in a lifetime.

THE TENTH ḤADĪTH

الطَّيِّبُ الحَلالُ شَرْطُ القَبُول

عَنْ أَبِي هُرَيْرَةَ ﷺ قَالَ: قَالَ رَسُولُ اللهِ ﷺ:{إِنَّ اللهَ طَيِّبٌ لَا يَقْبَلُ إِلَّا طَيِّباً، وَإِنَّ اللهَ أَمَرَ الْمُؤْمِنِينَ بِمَا أَمَرَ بِهِ الْمُرْسَلِينَ فَقَالَ تَعَالَى: ﴿يَٰٓأَيُّهَا ٱلرُّسُلُ كُلُواْ مِنَ ٱلطَّيِّبَٰتِ وَٱعْمَلُواْ صَٰلِحًا﴾ [المؤمنون 23:51] وَقَالَ تَعَالَى ﴿يَا أَيُّهَا الَّذِينَ آمَنُوا كُلُوا مِنْ طَيِّبَاتِ مَا رَزَقْنَاكُمْ﴾ [البقرة 2:172] ثُمَّ ذَكَرَ الرَّجُلَ يُطِيلُ السَّفَرَ أَشْعَثَ أَغْبَرَ يَمُدُّ يَدَيْهِ إِلَى السَّمَاءِ يَا رَبِّ يَا رَبِّ، وَمَطْعَمُهُ حَرَامٌ، وَمَشْرَبُهُ حَرَامٌ، وَمَلْبَسُهُ حَرَامٌ، وَغُذِيَ بِالْحَرَامِ، فَأَنَّى يُسْتَجَابُ لَهُ.} رواه مسلم

The Pure and Lawful Is the Condition for Acceptance

On the authority of Abū Hurayrah ﷺ who said, 'The Messenger of Allah ﷺ said, {Allah is pure and only accepts that which is pure. Allah has commanded the believers with which He commanded the Messengers, for He the Exalted has said, **"O Messengers, eat of the good things and act rightly."** [al-Mu'minūn 23:51] and the Exalted One has said, **"You who believe! Eat of the good things We have provided for you."** [al-Baqarah 2:172]} Then he mentioned a dishevelled, dusty man lengthening his journey and stretching out his hands to the sky, 'Lord! Lord!', and his food is unlawful, his drink is unlawful and his clothing is unlawful, so how can he be answered?' Related by Muslim.

Muslim has related the ḥadīth in the Book of Zakāt (the chapter on accepting charity from pure earnings and growing it), no.1015, and at-Tirmidhī in the Book of *Tafsīr* (the chapter concerning Sūrat al-Baqarah), no.2992.

The Importance of Ḥadīth:
This is one of the ḥadīths upon which the foundations and edifices of Islam are based. It is the pillar concerning consuming the lawful and avoiding the unlawful. How wide and immense is its usefulness in creating a faithful society in which the individual loves for his brother what he loves for himself and dislikes for his

brother what he dislikes for himself. He stops at the bounds of the legislation and suffices himself with the lawful, the blessed and pure, and thus he and others live in tranquillity and prosperity.

The Language of the Ḥadīth:
(إن الله طيب) *inna Allaha ṭayyib*: i.e. pure and transcendent above any defect, and *at-Ṭayyib* is one Allah the Exalted's Beautiful Names.

(لا يقبل إلا طيبا) *la yaqbalu illa ṭayyiba*: He only accept deeds and wealth that are free from harm and corruption, or are lawful.

(أمر المؤمنين بما أمر به المرسلين) *amara al-muʾminīna bima amara bihi al-mursalīn*: He has made them equal in terms of the obligation to consume what is lawful.

(أشعث) *ashʿatha*: one's hair is frizzed because it has not been combed.

(أغبر) *aghbara*: the dust has changed the colour of his hair because he has travelled a long way for the sake of obedience, such as a Ḥajj or *jihād*.

(يمد يديه إلى السماء) *yamuddu yadayhi ilā as-samāʾi*: he raises his hands to the sky, asking Allah the Exalted and calling on Him.

(فأنى يستجاب له) *faʾanā yustajābu lahu*: how and from where can he be answered when this is his description?

Legal Matters and Other Guidance from the Ḥadīth:
1. The pure and accepted: The Prophet's statement ﷺ {Allah is pure and only accepts that which is pure} comprises deeds, wealth, statements, and doctrines:

He ﷻ does not except deeds unless they are pure and free from harm and corruption, such as ostentation and conceit.

He does not accept wealth unless it is pure and lawful. He ﷺ urged that charity be from pure, lawful earnings when he said, {...and only accepts that which is pure}, i.e. Allah does not accept charity unless it is pure and lawful.

Speech does not reach Him unless it is pure. Allah the Exalted has said,

﴿إِلَيْهِ يَصْعَدُ ٱلْكَلِمُ ٱلطَّيِّبُ وَٱلْعَمَلُ ٱلصَّـٰلِحُ يَرْفَعُهُۥ﴾
"All good words rise to Him and He elevates all virtuous deeds." [Fāṭir 35:10]

Allah the Exalted has divided speech into pure and wretched (*khabīth*). He the Glorified has said,

﴿أَلَمْ تَرَ كَيْفَ ضَرَبَ ٱللَّهُ مَثَلًا كَلِمَةً طَيِّبَةً كَشَجَرَةٍ طَيِّبَةٍ﴾

"Do you not see how Allah makes a metaphor: a good word is like a good tree..." [Ibrāhīm 14:24] and

﴿وَمَثَلُ كَلِمَةٍ خَبِيثَةٍ كَشَجَرَةٍ خَبِيثَةٍ﴾

"The metaphor of a corrupt word is that of a rotten tree." [Ibrāhīm 14:26]

No one is victorious with Him ﷻ apart from the pure believers. He the Exalted has said,

﴿ٱلَّذِينَ تَتَوَفَّىٰهُمُ ٱلْمَلَـٰٓئِكَةُ طَيِّبِينَ﴾

"those the angels take in a pure state" [an-Naḥl 16:32]

The angels greet them with peace when they enter Paradise, saying,

﴿سَلَـٰمٌ عَلَيْكُمْ طِبْتُمْ فَٱدْخُلُوهَا خَـٰلِدِينَ﴾

"Peace be upon you! You have done well so enter it timelessly, forever." [az-Zumar 39:73]

Regarding the end of this general meaning of his statement ﷺ: {...and only accepts that which is pure}, Ibn Rajab said, 'All of the believer is pure, his heart, his tongue and his body, because of the faith that abides in his heart, manifests on his tongue in remembrance and manifests in his limbs through righteous actions, which are the fruit of faith and come under its name.

2. How can deeds be accepted and pure?

One of the greatest matters that makes a believer's deeds pure and accepted is that his food is lawful. The ḥadīth bears evidence that deeds are not accepted unless one eats what is lawful, and that the unlawful corrupt actions and prevents their acceptance. This is because the Prophet ﷺ after affirming that Allah is pure and only accepts that which is pure, says, {Allah has commanded the believers with which He commanded the Messengers}, and Allah the Exalted has said, **"O Messengers, eat of the good things and act rightly."** [al-Mu'minūn 23:51] and the Exalted One has said, **"You who believe! Eat of the good things We have provided for you."** [al-Baqarah 2:172] This means that the Messengers and their ummahs are commanded to eat good pure things, which are the lawful and to act rightly, for as long as the food is lawful, the deeds are righteous. If the food is not lawful, then how can the action be accepted?'[63]

63 *Jāmiʿ al-ʿUlūm wa al-Ḥikam*, p.86, in summary.

At-Ṭabarānī has narrated from Ibn ʿAbbās 🙵 who said, 'I recited this verse in the presence of the Messenger of Allah 🙵:

﴿يَـٰٓأَيُّهَا ٱلنَّاسُ كُلُواْ مِمَّا فِى ٱلْأَرْضِ حَلَـٰلًا طَيِّبًا﴾

"Mankind! Eat what is good and lawful on the earth." [al-Baqarah 2:168]

Saʿd ibn Abī Waqqāṣ then stood up and said, "O Messenger of Allah, ask Allah to make me from those whose supplications are answered." The Prophet 🙵 replied, 'O Saʿd, purify your food and your supplications will be answered. By the One in whose hand is Muḥammad's soul, the slave will toss a morsel of the unlawful in his belly and his deeds will not be accepted for forty days. Any slave whose flesh has been nourished illegally is more deserving of the Fire.} Abū Yaḥyā al-Qattāt has related from Mujāhid, from Ibn ʿAbbās 🙵 who said, 'Allah does not accept the prayer of someone who has something unlawful in his belly'.

3. The lack of acceptance: Lack of acceptance can sometimes means, in certain ḥadīths of the Prophet 🙵 the lack of validity. For example, there is the ḥadīth: {Allah does not accept the prayers of anyone of you until you have done wuḍūʾ.} Acceptance here means one must be in a purified state before praying, and thus one has carried out one's obligation.

Lack of acceptance can also mean, as is the case in many ḥadīths, the lack of reward. For example, there is the ḥadīth: {A woman's prayer is not accepted if her husband is angry with her, nor from someone who has gone to a soothsayer, nor someone who has drunk wine, for forty days} and the ḥadīth: {...and only accepts that which is pure} and the ḥadīth: {Whoever prays in a garment whose price is ten unlawful dirhams, his prayer is not accepted.} What is meant here is the lack of completion that would necessitate reward for these actions, even though they are accepted in terms of obligations being fulfilled. Distinguishing between the two is based on external evidence.

4. How does a Muslim rid himself of the unlawful?
After being unable to discover who the owner is or to find him, a Muslim can rid himself of unlawful wealth by giving it away in charity, and the reward goes to the owner. It has been related Mālik ibn Dīnār that he said, 'I asked ʿAṭāʾ ibn Abī Rabāḥ about someone who has some unlawful wealth and he does not know who the owners are. He replied, "He should give it away in charity, and I am not saying that that suffices him"'.

The well-known position of ash-Shāfiʿī 🙵 regarding unlawful wealth is that it is put away and not given in charity until it becomes clear who deserves it.

Al-Fuḍayl ibn ʿIyāḍ held the position that someone who has unlawful wealth whose owner is not known should destroy it and toss it in the sea, not give it in charity. He said, 'One does not draw nearer to Allah except with that which is pure'. **Ibn Rajab said, 'The correct position is that it is given in charity because destroying wealth and wasting it is forbidden. Setting it aside indefinitely makes it liable to destruction and transgressors confiscating it. Rather, it should be given as charity on behalf of its owner, so that he can benefit from it in the Hereafter as he was unable to benefit from it in this life'.**

5. The reasons for supplications being answered:
A. Travelling a long distance: Traveling itself necessitates that supplications be answered, for Abū Dāwūd, Ibn Mājah and at-Tirmidhī have related from the ḥadīth of Abū Hurayrah that the Prophet ﷺ said, {Three supplications are answered and there is no doubt about them: the supplication of the oppressed, the supplication of the traveller and the supplication of the parent for his child.} If the travel is far, the supplication is closer to being answered, because it is when one expects to be broken of spirit, due to being absent from one's homeland and bearing various hardships. The brokenness of spirit is one of the greatest reasons for supplications being answered.

B. To be worn out in terms of one's clothes and appearance: He ﷺ has said in a well-known ḥadīth: {Many a dishevelled, dusty person in rags, pushed back from people's doors; if he were to call on Allah, He would answer him.} He ﷺ went out to the rain prayer in worn out clothes, humbly and submissively imploring.

C. Stretching one's hands towards the sky: It is part of the etiquette of supplication. Imam Aḥmad, Abū Dāwūd and at-Tirmidhī have related from the ḥadīth of Salmān al-Fārisī رضي الله عنه that the Prophet ﷺ said, {Allah the Exalted is alive and generous. When a man is raising his hands towards Him, He is reluctant to reject them, leaving them disappointed.} During the rain prayer, the Prophet ﷺ would raise his hands so high that the white of his armpits could be seen. On the day of Badr, when he was asking Allah for victory against the idol worshippers, he raised his hands so high that his outer garment fell from his shoulders.

D. To ask Allah ﷻ earnestly, and that is by repeatedly mentioning His Lordship ﷻ. This is one of the greatest things required for having supplications answered. Al-Bazzār has related from the ḥadīth of 'Ā'ishah رضي الله عنها from the Prophet ﷺ: {When the slave says 'O Lord!' four times, Allah says, 'I am here, My slave. Ask and you will be given.'}

6. What prevents supplications from being answered: In this ḥadīth, he ﷺ is pointing out that engaging extensively in the unlawful, be it food, drink, clothing, nourishment, prevents supplications from being answered. His statement, {...so how can he be answered?} is an expression of wonder and deeming something unlikely in the form of a question. It is not a clear text stating that such supplications cannot be answered.

7. **Supplication is the essence of worship** because the supplicating person only calls on Allah when he has lost all hope of anyone else's helping him, and that is the reality of *tawḥīd*[64] and sincerity. There is no worship above that.

8. The ḥadīth strongly encourages spending out from that which is lawful and prohibits spending out from anything else.

9. Whoever wants to supplicate must pay attention to the lawful, in what he eats and wears, so that his supplication can be accepted.

10. Allah accepts it from the believers when they spend out from that which is pure, and He causes it to grow and He blesses them therein.

64 (tn): i.e. there is no god but Allah.

THE ELEVENTH ḤADĪTH

الأَخْذُ بِاليَقِيْنِ وَالبُعْدُ عَنِ الشُّبُهَاتِ

عَنْ أَبِي مُحَمَّدٍ الحَسَنِ بْنِ عَلِيِّ بْنِ أَبِي طَالِبٍ، سِبْطِ رَسُولِ اللهِ ﷺ وَرَيْحَانَتِهِ ﷺ، قَالَ: حَفِظْتُ مِنْ رَسُوْلِ اللهِ ﷺ: {دَعْ مَا يَرِيْبُكَ إِلَى مَا لَا يَرِيْبُكَ} رواهُ التِّرْمذيُّ والنَّسَائي، وقال التِّرْمذي: حَدِيثٌ حسنٌ صحيحٌ.

Sticking To Certainty and Staying Away from Doubtful Matters

It is on the authority of Abū Muḥammad al-Ḥasan ibn ʿAlī ibn Abī Ṭālib, the grandchild of Allah's Messenger ﷺ and his offspring, that he said, 'I memorized this from Allah's Messenger ﷺ: {Leave that which gives you doubt for that which does not give you doubt.}' Related by at-Tirmidhī and an-Nasā'ī, and at-Tirmidhī said, 'It is a good, authentic[65] ḥadīth'.

At-Tirmidhī related it in the Book on Describing the Standing, the Softening of Hearts and scrupulousness (the chapter on tying your camel and relying on Allah), no.2520, and he has the additional words: {...for indeed truthfulness is tranquillity and lying is doubt.} An-Nasā'ī has related it in the Book of Drinks (the chapter on encouraging the abandonment of doubtful matters), 8/327-328. In the *Musnad* of Imam Aḥmad is it is no.1723 and Sheikh Aḥmad Shākir ﷺ says that its chain of transmission is authentic.

The Importance of the Ḥadīth:
This ḥadīth is another example of comprehensive speech, and one of the profound Prophetic wisdom. In just a few words, it has laid down an immense foundation of our Islam, which is to leave doubtful matters and stick to what is certainly lawful. This is why, at the end of his commentary on this ḥadīth, Ibn Ḥajar al-Haytamī said, 'This ḥadīth is an immense foundation of the Religion, as well as a source of scrupulousness, around which the people of *taqwā* revolve, and those who are saved from the darkness of doubts and illusions that block the light of certainty'.

65 Ar. *ḥasan ṣaḥīḥ*.

Explaining the Words of the Ḥadīth:
(دع ما يريبك) *daʿ mā yarību*k: leave dubious matters that give you doubt, and the command is one of recommendation.

(إلى ما لا يريبك) *ilā mā lā yarībuk*: for that which does not give you doubt, such as that which is clearly lawful.

Legal Matters and Other Guidance from the Ḥadīth:
1. Leaving doubtful matters: Leaving doubtful matters in worship, transactions, marriage and divorce and all other kinds of rulings, and sticking to the lawful in all matters, leads the Muslim to scrupulousness (*waraʿ*). It is also very beneficial in blocking satanic whisperings, just as it benefits the Muslim in this life and the Hereafter. It was mentioned in the sixth ḥadīth that whoever guards himself against doubtful matters has secured his religion and his honour, and that which is definitely lawful does not place any doubt or suspicion in the believer's heart. Rather, it brings tranquillity and happiness to his soul. As for doubtful matters, a person may be pleased with them outwardly, but if we were to reveal what is in his heart, we would find anxiety, unease and doubt. This psychical punishment suffices him as an abstract loss, and the greater loss and destruction is in becoming accustomed to doubtful matters and then daring to engage in the unlawful because whoever hovers around forbidden pasturage will definitely fall into it.

2. Statements from the First Three Generations regarding leaving doubt for the certainty of scrupulousness: Our righteous predecessors from the First Three Generations have clear statements and actions regarding adhering to what is purely lawful, staying away from doubtful matters and adorning oneself with scrupulousness. Here are some examples of their statements:

Abū Dharr al-Ghifārī ﷺ said, 'The perfection of *taqwā* is in leaving some of the lawful for fear that it might be unlawful'. Abū ʿAbdir Raḥmān al-ʿAmarī az-Zāhid[66] said, 'If a slave is careful, he leaves that which gives him doubt for that which does not give him doubt'. Al-Fuḍayl said, 'People claim that scrupulousness is difficult. No two matters have been presented to me except that I chose the more difficult of them. Leave what gives you doubt for what does not give you doubt'. Ḥassān ibn Abī Sinān said, 'Nothing is easier than scrupulousness. If something gives you doubt, leave it'.

As for their actions: Yazīd ibn Zariʿ turned down fifty thousand set aside as his inheritance and did not take it. His father oversaw businesses on behalf of the rulers, while Yazīd made wicker from palm leaves and lived off that until he died ﷺ.

Al-Miswar ibn Makhramah bought a huge amount of food. Then he saw some clouds in the autumn and disliked it. He said, 'Do I not see that I dislike what

66 (tn) i.e. abstinent.

benefits the Muslims?' He then swore that he would not profit from it all. Then he told 'Umar ibn al-Khaṭṭāb ؓ and 'Umar said to him, 'May Allah reward you with goodness'. It was said to Ibrāhīm ibn Adham, 'Do you not drink the water of Zamzam?' He replied, 'If I had a bucket, I would', indicating that the bucket was from the ruler's wealth and was therefore doubtful.

Someone might say, 'These statements and actions are exaggerated examples of scrupulousness'. We say that the Ummah needs a righteous model in every age, an Islamic exemplar that can be followed, whether a ruler or a scholar, so that they can stay within the bounds of the lawful and pure and do without the unlawful and filthy. If the life of this Ummah did not have the likes of these statements and actions showing such restraint concerning doubtful matters, people would plunge into the doubtful and the unlawful and indulge in it freely with astonishing insolence, because they would have lost that wise, sincerely advising guide, and they would miss that exemplar and model.

3. Doubt Contradicting Certainty: When doubt contradicts certainty, we take certainty and give it precedence and we avoid doubt. This meaning is found in the second of the legal maxims that all the rulings of the Revealed Law have determined, the text of which is: certainty is not removed by doubt. For example, someone who makes *wuḍū'* and then doubts as to whether he has nullified it is still considered to be in a state of *wuḍū'*. This goes back to what Muslim has related from the Prophet ﷺ in which he said, {If one of you felt something in his stomach and he is not sure whether he released it or not, he should not leave the masjid unless he hears a sound or notices a smell.}

4. Refraining from Doubtful Matters is for the One whose Affairs are Upright: When we call for scrutiny concerning doubtful matters and abstention from them, we are only calling on those whom all their affairs are upright, and their actions resemble one another in *taqwā* and scrupulousness. As for those who plunge into clearly unlawful matters and then want to be scrupulous about the intricate matters of that which is doubtful, this scrupulousness of theirs will be burdensome and difficult. We must reproach them for doing so and ask them to abstain from the clearly unlawful first. This is because when Ibn 'Umar ؓ was asked by the people of Iraq about the blood of a gnat, he said, 'They ask me about the blood of a gnat and they killed al-Ḥusayn, and I heard the Prophet ﷺ saying, {They are my two offspring in this life}.

A man asked Bishr ibn al-Ḥārith about a man who has a wife and his mother told him to divorce her. He replied, 'If he is dutiful to his mother in everything and nothing remains from his duty to her other than divorcing his wife, he should do so. If he is dutiful to her by divorcing his wife and then, after that, he stands up and hits his mother, he should not.

A man asked Aḥmad ibn Ḥanbal for permission to use his inkwell. He replied, 'Write. This is over-scrupulousness'. He said to someone else, 'Neither my scrupulousness nor your scrupulousness will reach this'. Imam Aḥmad said this out of modesty, for he would never write using one of his companions' inkwells. It was concerning himself that he employed this scrupulousness, and he would reproach anyone else who had not reached his level of *taqwā* and scrupulousness in all of their affairs.

5. Truthfulness is tranquillity and lying is doubt: The Prophet's statement ﷺ in at-Tirmidhī's narration: {...for indeed truthfulness is tranquillity and lying is doubt} indicates that one should seek words that are truthful and definitive. When someone needs an answer to a question or a fatwa for an issue, the sign of truthfulness is that one's heart is at ease. The sign of lying is that one has doubts, and the heart does not rest. Rather, it flees from it.

6. The ḥadīth instructs us to base our rulings and our daily affairs on certainty.

7. The lawful, the truth and veracity are tranquillity and contentment. The unlawful, the false and lying are doubt, anxiety and aversion.

THE TWELFTH ḤADĪTH

الاشْتِغَالُ بِمَا لايُفِيد

عَنْ أَبِي هُرَيْرَةَ ﷺ قَالَ: قَالَ رَسُولُ اللهِ ﷺ: ﴿مِنْ حُسْنِ إِسْلَامِ المَرْءِ تَرْكُهُ مَا لَا يَعْنِيْهِ﴾، حديثٌ حَسَنٌ رواهُ التِّرْمِذِيُّ وغَيْرُهُ هكذا.

Occupying Oneself with What Does Not Benefit

It is on the authority of Abū Hurayrah ﷺ who said, 'The Messenger of Allah ﷺ said, {From the excellence of one's Islam is leaving what does not concern one.} It is a good (*ḥasan*) ḥadīth, related by at-Tirmidhī and others as such.

At-Tirmidhī has collected this ḥadīth in the chapters of abstinence (the chapter on what has come regarding those who speak about that which does not benefit them), no.2318 and 2319. Ibn Mājah has collected it in the Book of Tribulations (the chapter on holding one's tongue in tribulation), no.3976. Mālik has related it in *al-Muwaṭṭa'* in Book of Good Manners (the chapter on what has come regarding good manners), 2/903, and az-Zarqānī says in his commentary on *al-Muwaṭṭa'*, 'Its chain of transmission is good, or indeed authentic'.

The Importance of the Ḥadīth:
Abū Hurayrah ﷺ and he is the one who kept the constant company of the Prophet ﷺ and acquired prophetic etiquette from him, is informing us of something he ﷺ said. In one brief, beneficial sentence, it elucidates that which gathers the good of this world and the bliss of the Hereafter. As the scholars have said, it is rightly an example of his comprehensive speech ﷺ matched by no one who came before him. This is because it gathers half of the Religion. After all, the Religion is doing and leaving, and it specifies leaving.

Some of them have said, 'Actually, it gathers the entire religion, because it specifies leaving and indicates doing'.

Ibn Rajab al-Ḥanbalī said, 'This ḥadīth is one of the immense foundations of etiquette'. Abū Dāwūd said, 'The foundations of the Sunnah in every discipline are four ḥadīth', and he mentioned this ḥadīth as one of them.

Please see more on the importance of this ḥadīth in the next chapter.

The Language of the Ḥadīth:
(من حسن إسلام المرء) *min ḥusni islām al-mar'i*: from the perfection and completion of his Islam, and the signs of the veracity of his faith. The meaning of 'one' is a person, male or female.

(ما لا يعنيه) *mā lā ya'nīhi*: matters of the Religion and one's worldly life that do not concern one, whether deeds or words. It is also said that it is what one cares about, i.e. one's attention to it and it is part of one's purpose and objective.

Legal Matters and Other Guidance from the Ḥadīth:
1. Establishing a distinguished society: Islam strives for the welfare of society, and that people live in harmony and unity, without there being disputes and controversies, just as it strives for the welfare of the individual, and that he live happily in this world; that he be familiar with others and they with him, that he be honoured and not harmed, and that he leaves it victorious and triumphant. The most significant cause of discord between people, corrupting society and putting people in perilous situations, is when some people meddle in other people's affairs, and especially affairs that do not concern them. Therefore, one of the signs of a Muslim's uprightness and the veracity of his faith is his not meddling in what does not concern him of other people's affairs.

2. Occupying Oneself with that which does not Concern one is a Waste and a Sign of Weak Faith: Man lives in this world and there are many people all around him, and there are all kinds of preoccupations and relations, varied and numerous. The Muslim is responsible for every action he partakes in, every moment of time he spends, every word he speaks. If a person were to occupy himself with everything around him and meddle in affairs that do not concern him, that would distract him from carrying out his obligations and fulfilling his responsibilities. He would be censured in this life and punished in the Hereafter, and that would be evidence of his weak discernment, his lack of consolidating Prophetic etiquette and that his Islam is closer to being Islam of the lips and tongue.

At-Tirmidhī has related on the authority of Anas ibn Mālik ﷺ who said, 'A man from the Companions died, so a man said, 'Rejoice at Paradise.' The Prophet ﷺ replied, {You do not know. Maybe he talked about that which did not concern him, or was stingy with that which would not diminish him.}

Ibn Ḥibbān has related in his *Ṣaḥīḥ* that he ﷺ said to Abū Dharr al-Ghifārī ﷺ: {It is sufficient evil that a person does not know about himself, and that he burden himself with what does not concern him.}

3. Turning Away from what is of no Concern is the Path of Well-being and Success: When a Muslim becomes conscious of his obligation and realises his responsibility, he becomes occupied with himself, he strives for what will benefit him in his worldly life and Hereafter. He turns away from that which is superfluous, keeps his distance from trivial matters and pays attention to that which concerns him.

If we know that the matters that concern man in this life are a few, relative to those that do not concern him, we know whoever contents himself with what concerns him will be safe from many evils and sins, and will be free to occupy himself with the interests of his Hereafter. That will be evidence of the excellence of his Islam, the firm establishment of his faith, the reality of his *taqwā*, his avoidance of his desires and whims, and his success with his Lord ﷻ.

Al-Bukhārī has related from Abū Hurayrah ؓ who said, 'The Messenger of Allah ﷺ said, ﴾When one of you has perfected his Islam, every good deed he does is written as anywhere between ten and seven hundred, while every bad deed he does is only written as one.﴿

In *al-Muwaṭṭa'*, Mālik mentions that this reached him: It was said to Luqmān, 'What made you reach what we see?' i.e. his virtue and refinement. He replied, 'Speaking the truth, fulfilling trusts, and leaving what does not concern me'.

4. The Heart that is Busy with Allah the Exalted turns away from the Affairs of the Creation that are of No Concern: The Muslim who worships Allah ﷻ as if he can see Him, and calls to mind that he is close to Allah and Allah is close to him, will not occupy himself with that which does not concern him. His not occupying himself with that which does not concern him is evidence of his truthfulness with Allah the Exalted, and his presence with Him. If someone occupies himself with that which does not concern him, that is evidence that he is not calling to mind his nearness to Allah the Exalted, that he is not being truthful with Him, that his deeds are of no avail and that he is lost.

It has been related from al-Ḥasan al-Baṣrī that he said, 'A sign that Allah has turned away from a slave is that He makes him be occupied with that which does not concern him'.

5. Matters that Concern a Person and Matters that Do Not: The matters that concern a person are that which is connected to one's livelihood, such as food, drink, clothing, shelter and so forth, and that which is connected to the success of his Hereafter. Nothing besides this concerns him.

Part of what does not concern a person are worldly objectives that are beyond one's necessities and needs, such as being extensively engaged in the world, having a variety of foods and drinks, seeking rank and positions of leadership, loving praise and commendation from people. It is a sign of a Muslim's veracity that he stay away from that, especially if there is something therein that involves compromise or flattery at the expense of his religion.

As for permissible actions, which do not benefit a person in his worldly life or Hereafter, such as playing and joking and that which violates respectability (*marūʿah*), it is better for a Muslim to leave them, because they waste his precious time in that which he was not created for, and will be taken to account for.

Excessive speech is of no concern and can lead the Muslim into unlawful speech. It is, therefore, parts of a Muslim's manners to avoid tumult and prattle and delving into every bit of gossip. At-Tirmidhī has related from Muʿādh ﷺ that he said, 'O Messenger of Allah, will we be taken to task for everything we say?' The Messenger of Allah ﷺ replied, {May your mother be bereaved of you, O Muʿādh. Are people thrown down on their nostrils in the Fire for anything other than what their tongues reaped?} He has also related that the Messenger of Allah ﷺ said, {The speech of the children of Adam is against them not for them, apart from enjoining the right, forbidding the wrong and the remembrance of Allah the Exalted.}

6. The ḥadīth instructs that it is from a Muslim's attributes to be occupied with noble matters and to be removed from trivial, petty affairs.

7. It also contains discipline and rectification for the soul from vices and shortcomings and leaving that which is of no use or benefit.

THE THIRTEENTH ḤADĪTH

أُخُوَّةُ الإِيْمَانِ وَالإِسْلام

عَنْ أَبِي حَمْزَةَ أَنَسِ بْنِ مَالِكٍ ﷺ خَادِمِ رَسُولِ اللهِ ﷺ عَنْ النَّبِيِّ ﷺ قَالَ: {لَا يُؤْمِنُ أَحَدُكُمْ حَتَّى يُحِبَّ لِأَخِيْهِ مَا يُحِبُّ لِنَفْسِه.} رَوَاهُ الْبُخَارِي ومسلم.

The Brotherhood of Īmān and Islam

It is on the authority of Abū Ḥamzah Anas ibn Mālik ﷺ the servant of the Messenger of Allah ﷺ that the Prophet ﷺ said, {None of you is a believer until he loves for his brother what he loves for himself.} Related by al-Bukhārī and Muslim.

Al-Bukhārī has collected it in Faith (the chapter on a part of faith being the loving for one's brother what one loves for oneself), no.13. Muslim has collected it in Faith (the chapter on the evidence that it is from the qualities of faith that one love the good for one's Muslim brother what one loves for oneself) no.45. An-Nasā'ī has collected it in Faith (the chapter on the sign if faith), 8/115, at-Tirmidhī has collected it in the Description of the Standing (the chapter entitled: {Rather, O Ḥanẓalah, an hour and an hour}, no.2517, and Ibn Mājah in the introduction, no.167.

Its Importance:
An-Nawawī ﷺ says in his commentary on *Ṣaḥīḥ Muslim*, 'The great Imam, Abū Muḥammad ʿAbdullah ibn Abī Zayd, the Imam of the Malikīs in the Maghreb in his time, said, "All the etiquettes of goodness branch out from four ḥadīths: the Prophet's statement ﷺ: {Whoever believes in Allah and the Last Day, let him speak well or remain silent}, his statement ﷺ: {From the excellence of one's Islam is leaving what does not concern one}, his statement ﷺ for the one whom her gave brief advice: {Do not become angry}, and his statement ﷺ: {None of you believes until he loves for his brother what he loves for himself.}"'

Perhaps this is the secret behind an-Nawawī's ﷺ choosing to include these four ḥadīths in his forty, some of which you have covered and the rest are to come, if Allah the Exalted so wills.

Al-Jurdānī says in his commentary on the Forty Nawawiyyah, 'This ḥadīth is one of the foundations of Islam'.

The Language of the Ḥadīth:

(لا يؤمن) *la yuʾminu*: belief with perfected faith.

(أحدكم) *aḥadukum*: whoever claims faith and Islam from amongst you.

(لأخيه) *li akhīhi*: male and female Muslims, and it has been said that it is one's. brother in humanity.

(ما يُحِبُّ لنفسه) *mā yuḥibbū li nafsihi*: the same goodness that he loves for himself.

Legal Matters and Other Guidance from the Ḥadīth:

1. The Muslim Community's Being Firmly Connected and Love and Amity Therein: Islam aims for all people to live in love and amity, each individual amongst them striving for the benefit of all and the felicity of the community so that justice prevails, tranquillity spreads in people's souls, and there is cooperation and solidarity between them. This cannot be realised unless every individual in the community wants for everyone else the same goodness, happiness and prosperity that he wants for himself. This is why we find him ﷺ linking it to faith and making it one of its qualities.

2. Complete Faith: The foundation of faith is realised by decisive affirmation in the heart and the heart submitting to Allah's Lordship ﷻ along with firm conviction in the remaining pillars, such as faith in the angels, the Books, the Messengers, the Last Day and the Decree and Predestination. The foundation of faith is not based on anything besides this. In this ḥadīth, the Messenger of Allah ﷺ makes it clear to us that faith does not take root in the soul, does not become consolidated in the heart and does not become perfected in the Muslim's chest unless he becomes a person of goodness, removed from selfishness and malice, hatred and envy, and thus he only loves for people what he loves for himself, such as being safe from evil and harm, enjoying a pleasant life, and being victorious with Allah the Glorified's pleasure and being close to Him ﷻ. These are some things that realise this completion in the Muslim's soul:

A. That he loves for others the good that is permissible and acts of obedience that he loves for himself, and he also despises for them the evil and disobedience that he hates from himself.

Aḥmad has collected the ḥadīth of Muʿādh ؓ in which he asked the Messenger of Allah ﷺ about the best faith: {That you love for people what you love for yourself, and you dislike for them what you dislike for yourself.}

B. That he works hard to rectify his Muslim brother if he sees his falling short in his obligations is deficient in his religion.

C. That he hastens to be just towards his Muslim brother, and to fulfil his rights, just as he would love for others to be just towards him and to fulfil his rights.

Muslim has related from ʿAbdullah ibn ʿAmr ibn al-ʿĀṣ ؓ that the Prophet ﷺ said, {Whoever would love to avoid the Fire and enter Paradise, let his wish be fulfilled as long as he believes in Allah and the Last Day, and treats people the way he would like to be treated.}

3. The Loftiness of the Muslim and his Humanity: It is a part of the Muslim's completed faith that he does not confine himself to loving good and despising evil for his fellow Muslim only. Rather, he should love that for those who are not Muslim, and especially faith. He should love for the disbeliever to become Muslim and have faith, and he should dislike and detest disbelief and iniquity for him. He ﷺ has said, {Love for people what you love yourself and you will be a Muslim}, as related by at-Tirmidhī. Therefore it is recommended to supplicate for the disbeliever's guidance.

4. Competing in Goodness is from the Perfection of Faith: It is not out of deficiency in faith or envy that the Muslim asks Allah the Exalted for virtues that other people have and make them superior to him, and to strive to reach their level. All of that is part of the perfection of faith, regarding which Allah the Exalted has said,

﴿وَفِي ذَٰلِكَ فَلْيَتَنَافَسِ ٱلْمُتَنَـٰفِسُونَ﴾

"Let the competitors compete for that." [al-Muṭaffifīn 83:26]

5. The Distinguished Community is One of the Fruits of Faith: In this ḥadīth, he ﷺ is strongly encouraging every Muslim to take it upon himself to love goodness for people, so that that can be a proof from him of the veracity of his faith and the excellence of his Islam. Furthermore, it is so that the distinguished community can be realised, because if each individual loves for everyone else the same goodness that he loves for himself, he will treat them well and protect them from harm, and then they will love him, treat him well and protect him from harm. This is how love and goodness spread amongst all people, oppression and evil are lifted and life's affairs fall into good order. This remains the case as long as each individual is aware of the interests of the group, is happy when they are happy, rejoices when they rejoice and feels pain when they feel pain, as the Chosen One ﷺ affirmed when he said, {You see the believers in their mutual love and compassion like one body. If one limb complains, the rest of the body becomes sleepless and feverish to help.} Collected by al-Bukhārī and Muslim. At that point, Allah the Exalted, grants might, nobility and supremacy to this community in this world, and an excellent reward in the Hereafter.

6. A Community Devoid of Faith is Selfish and Hateful: When faith fades from hearts and is completely extinguished, love of goodness for others also disappears, and in its place is envy and the intention to deceive. Selfishness becomes consolidated in the community and people become human wolves. Life becomes corrupt, oppression prevails, rancour and spite pervade, hatred and antipathy spread, and Allah's statement:

﴿أَمْوَاتٌ غَيْرُ أَحْيَاءٍ ۖ وَمَا يَشْعُرُونَ أَيَّانَ يُبْعَثُونَ﴾

"They are dead, not alive, and they are not aware of when they will be raised" [an-Naḥl 16:21] applies to a community like this.

7. The Ḥadīth Advises:

A. Strong encouragement of harmony between people's heart, and working to put their circumstances in good order. This is one of the most important things that Islam came for and which it strives for.

B. Making envy loathsome, because it is inconsistent with the perfection of faith. The envier hates to see anyone else doing as well as him or better, or perhaps he wishes that the person be deprived of good even if it had never reached him.

C. Faith increases and decreases. It increases with obedience and decreases with disobedience.

THE FOURTEENTH ḤADĪTH

حُرْمَةُ دَمِ الْمُسْلِمِ

عَنِ ابْنِ مَسْعُودٍ ﷺ قَالَ: قَالَ رَسُولُ اللهِ ﷺ: {لَا يَحِلُّ دَمُ امْرِئٍ مُسْلِمٍ يَشْهَدُ أَنْ لَا إِلَـهَ إِلَّا اللهُ وَأَنِّي رَسُولُ اللهِ إِلَّا بِإِحْدَى ثَلَاثٍ: الثَّيِّبُ الزَّانِي، النَّفْسُ بِالنَّفْسِ، وَالتَّارِكُ لِدِينِهِ الْمُفَارِقُ لِلْجَمَاعَةِ.} رَوَاهُ البخاري ومسلم.

The Sanctity of a Muslim's Blood

It is on the authority of Ibn Masʿūd ﷺ who said, 'The Messenger of Allah ﷺ said, {The blood of a Muslim, who bears witness that there is no god but Allah and that I am the Messenger of Allah, is not lawful except for one of three: the married fornicator, a life for a life, and someone who leaves his religion and splits from the community.} Related by al-Bukhārī and Muslim.

Al-Bukhārī has related the ḥadīth in the Book of Blood Money (the chapter on Allah the Exalted's statement: **"a life for a life"**),[67] no.6484. Muslim has related it in the Book of Oaths (the chapter on what makes a Muslim's blood permissible), no.1676, Abū Dāwūd in Legal Punishments (the chapter on the ruling regarding someone who apostates), no.4352, at-Tirmidhī in Blood Money (the chapter on what has come regarding a person's blood not being lawful except for one of three), no.1402, and an-Nasāʾī in the Unlawfulness of Blood (the chapter on what makes a Muslim's blood lawful), 7/90-91.

Its Importance:
This noble, Prophetic ḥadīth is an immense Islamic elucidation, and a masterful legislative principle in preserving a Muslim's life, as long as this Muslim is a sound human being, free of any imbalance or perturbation that would harm the safety of the society and the welfare of its individuals. As for when an individual's life becomes a danger to the life of the community, and thus he is afflicted with sickness and he deviates from normal human soundness and innate well-being, and he becomes a malignant bacterium, decimating the body of the Ummah and

67 (tn): i.e. Sūrat al-Māʾidah 5:45.

corrupting its religion, morals and dignity, causing evil and misguidance to spread therein, he no longer has the right to live. His existence is considered invalid and he must be extirpated so that the Muslim community can live in safety and prosperity.

Ibn Ḥajar al-Haytamī says regarding its importance, 'It is one the most important foundations because it is connected to the most important of things, which is blood. It elucidates what is lawful and what is unlawful, and that the basis therein is preservation. It is also rational because it is natural to love for the created human form to remain in the best shape'.[68]

Explaining the Words of the Ḥadīth:

(لا يحل دم) *la yaḥillu dam*: i.e. it is unlawful to shed it, i.e. to kill someone.

(بإحدى ثلاث) *bi iḥdā thalāth*: it is lawful to kill a Muslim because of him doing something and thus taking on of three qualities or characteristics.

(النفس بالنفس) *an-nafsu bin-nafs*: a person who kills another person deliberately without right is killed as compensation for the person killed.

(الثيب الزاني) *ath-thayyib az-zānī*: *ath-thayyib* refers to someone who is not a virgin, whether male or female, so one can say *rajul thayyib* (a non-virgin man) and *imra'ah thayyib* (a non-virgin woman). It is an active participle from the verb *thāba*, i.e. to go back, and it is used more often to refer to a woman because she returns and goes back to her family. *Az-zānī* is an active participle from the word *az-zinā*, which linguistically means fornication or debauchery. In the Revealed Law, it means a man having penetrative, frontal intercourse with a woman he is not married to.

(التارك لدينه) *at-tārik li dīnihi*: as is the wording of at-Tirmidhī; in al-Bukhārī's narration it is *al-māriq min ad-dīn*, from the word *murūq*, which means leaving. What is meant by religion is Islam. The person who has split from it or left it is an apostate.

(المفارق للجماعة) *al-mufāriq lil-jamā'ah*: the one who leaves the Muslim community by apostating.

Legal Matters and Other Guidance from the Ḥadīth:

1. The sanctity of the Muslim's blood: Whoever bears witness that there is no god but Allah and that Muḥammad is the Messenger of Allah, and thus he affirms Allah the Glorified's existence and His oneness and affirms the Prophethood of the Seal of the Messengers ﷺ and acknowledges his Messengership, has secured his blood, preserved himself and protected his life. It is not permissible or lawful for anyone to shed his blood or kill him. This protection remains inseparable from

68 (tn): i.e. this is something that be known from the Revelation as well as rationally.

the Muslim and is not stripped from him or lifted from him unless he commits one of three crimes; each one in and of itself lifts the protection from the doer and makes his blood lawful. These crimes are:

- Killing a person deliberately without the right
- Fornication after becoming married
- Apostasy

2. Stoning: The Muslims have made a consensus that the legal punishment for a married fornicator (*al-muḥṣin*) is to be stoned to death, because one has transgressed against someone else's honour and committed the abomination of fornication, after Allah ﷻ had blessed him with lawful gratification. He thus turned away from purity in favour of wretched filth and committed a crime against humanity by mixing and corrupting lineages. He also snubbed Allah's prohibition ﷻ:

﴿وَلَا تَقْرَبُوا۟ ٱلزِّنَىٰٓ ۖ إِنَّهُۥ كَانَ فَٰحِشَةً وَسَآءَ سَبِيلًا﴾

"And do not go near fornication. It is an abomination, an evil way."
[al-Isrā' 17:32]

The *muḥṣin* is the free, mature,[69] sane[70] person who had frontal intercourse within a valid marriage.

Stoning has been established from the Messenger of Allah ﷺ and he did it. The *jamāʿah*[71] have related that he stoned Māʿiz. Muslim and others have related that he ﷺ commanded that the lady from the Ghāmid tribe be stoned. There is also his statement ﷺ that the *jamāʿah* have related: {O Unays, give respite to this woman. If she confesses, stone her.} He came to her later and she confessed, so the Messenger of Allah ﷺ gave the command and she was stoned.

Stoning was in the Qur'ān and its wording was abrogated: 'If an older man and woman fornicate, stone them decidedly as an exemplary punishment from Allah, and Allah is Mighty and Wise'. Ibn 'Abbās derived stoning from the Qur'ān from the Exalted's statement:

﴿يَٰٓأَهْلَ ٱلْكِتَٰبِ قَدْ جَآءَكُمْ رَسُولُنَا يُبَيِّنُ لَكُمْ كَثِيرًا مِّمَّا كُنتُمْ تُخْفُونَ مِنَ ٱلْكِتَٰبِ وَيَعْفُوا۟ عَن كَثِيرٍ﴾

"O People of the Book, Our Messenger has come to you, making clear to you much of the Book that you have kept concealed, and passing over a lot." [al-Māʾidah 5:15]

---

69 Ar. *bāligh*.

70 Ar. *ʿāqil*.

71 (tn): i.e. Imams Aḥmad, al-Bukhārī, Muslim, Abū Dāwūd, at-Tirmidhī, Ibn Mājah and an-Nasāʾī.

He ﷺ said, 'Whoever disbelieves in stoning has disbelieved in the Qur'ān from where he does not expect'. Then he recited this āyah and said, 'Stoning was something they had concealed.' An-Nasā'ī has collected it as well as al-Ḥākim, who said, 'Its chain of transmission is authentic'.

3. Retaliation:[72] The Muslims have made a consensus that whoever kills a Muslim deliberately deserves retaliation, which is to be killed. Allah the Exalted has said,

﴿وَكَتَبْنَا عَلَيْهِمْ فِيهَآ أَنَّ ٱلنَّفْسَ بِٱلنَّفْسِ﴾

"We prescribed from them in it: a life for a life..." [al-Mā'idah 5:45]

This is so that people's lives can be safe. Allah the Exalted has also said,

﴿وَلَكُمْ فِى ٱلْقِصَاصِ حَيَوٰةٌ يَٰٓأُو۟لِى ٱلْأَلْبَٰبِ﴾

"There is life for you in retaliation, people of intelligence." [al-Baqarah 2:179]

The legally accountable person is killed if he has killed someone deliberately, regardless of whether the killer or victim is male or female. The is due to what is found in ʿAmr ibn Ḥazm's letter from the Prophet ﷺ: {A man is killed for killing a woman}, and the authentic report that he ﷺ killed a Jewish man who had killed his slave girl.}

Retaliation is dropped if the victim's guardians' pardon.

They have made consensus that retaliation is obligatory if the killer and victim are unbelievers, and they have differed if the victim is a non-combatant unbeliever, such as a *dhimmī*[73] or *musta'min*.[74] Some people – including the Ḥanafīs – hold the position that retaliation is obligatory, based on the generality of the Exalted's statement: **"a life for a life"**, and his statement ﷺ here: {a life for a life}. Others hold the position – including the Shāfiʿīs, the Ḥanbalīs and the Mālikīs, that there is no retaliation against a Muslim for killing an unbeliever. Their evidence is the statement of the Messenger of Allah ﷺ that has been related by al-Bukhārī and others: {A Muslim is not killed on account of an unbeliever.} They understand that this ḥadīth specifies the generality found in other texts regarding a life for a life.

The majority of jurists hold that a father is not killed for killing his son, and this has been authentically narrated from ʿUmar ibn al-Khaṭṭāb ﷺ.

72 Ar. *al-qiṣāṣ*.

73 (tn): i.e. an unbeliever who is a subject under Islamic governance.

74 (tn): i.e. an unbeliever who is granted temporary safety concerning his person, his wealth, his honour and his religion.

4. The Legal Punishment for Apostasy:
The Muslims have made a consensus that if a man apostates, and persists in unbelief and does not return to Islam after being asked to repent, is killed, due to what is found in the ḥadīth: {someone who leaves his religion}. There is also what al-Bukhārī and the authors of the *Sunan* works[75] have related from Ibn ʿAbbās رضي الله عنهما in which Allah's Messenger ﷺ said, {If someone changes his religion, kill him.}

They have differed over whether a woman is killed if she apostates. The majority of scholars hold that she is killed just a like a man, due to the generality of the evidences. The Ḥanafīs says that she is not killed. Instead, she is imprisoned until she becomes Muslim or dies in prison. Their evidence is what al-Bukhārī and Muslim, and others, have related regarding him ﷺ prohibiting the killing of women in war, without making a distinction between an original unbeliever and an apostate.

5. The One Who Does Not Pray: The Muslims have made a consensus that whoever leaves the prayer because he has disavowed it has committed disbelief and is considered an apostate. He receives the legal punishment for apostasy. As for someone who does not pray out of laziness while acknowledging its obligation, they have differed therein. The majority holds that he is asked to repent and if he does not repent, he is killed as a legal punishment and not because of disbelief. Imam Aḥmad and some of the Mālikīs hold that he is killed because of disbelief. The Ḥanafīs say that he is imprisoned until he prays or dies, and while in prison, he is reprimanded by being beaten, as well as other means. Allah the Exalted has said,

﴿وَأَقِيمُوا۟ ٱلصَّلَوٰةَ وَلَا تَكُونُوا۟ مِنَ ٱلْمُشْرِكِينَ﴾

"Establish the prayer. Do not be among the idolaters." [ar-Rūm 30:31]

The Glorified One has also said,

﴿فَإِن تَابُوا۟ وَأَقَامُوا۟ ٱلصَّلَوٰةَ وَءَاتَوُا۟ ٱلزَّكَوٰةَ فَإِخْوَٰنُكُمْ فِى ٱلدِّينِ﴾

"But if they repent and establish the prayer and pay the zakāt, they are your brothers in the Religion." [at-Tawbah 9:11]

The Messenger of Allah ﷺ has said, {Between a man and disbelief is leaving the prayer}, as related by Imam Aḥmad and Muslim. He ﷺ has also, said, {The covenant between us and them is the prayer. Whoever leaves it has disbelieved}, as related by Imam Aḥmad, Abū Dāwūd and at-Tirmidhī.

75 (tn): i.e. Abū Dāwūd, at-Tirmidhī, an-Nasāʾī and Ibn Mājah.

6. Who Implements Retaliation and Legal Punishments: Retaliation is implemented by the victim's guardian after the ruler has given the command. The ruler also gives the command regarding the apostate and the married fornicator, except that the ruler implements the punishment. If the guardian exacts retaliation without the ruler's permission, or someone kills the apostate or married fornicator without being commanded by the ruler, they are reprimanded for transgressing against the ruler's office. They are not killed, because the killings they did were justified.

7. The Ḥadīth Advises:

A. The Religion that is considered is what the community of Muslims are upon, and they are the vast majority of them.

B. Strong encouragement to adhere to the community of Muslims and not split from them.

C. Making these three crimes loathsome and warning against falling into them.

D. Raising a community that fears Allah the Exalted and is aware of Him in secret and in the open before implementing legal punishments.

E. Legal punishments in Islam are a deterrent. Their objective is prevention and protection.

F. According to the Ḥanafīs, retaliation is only carried out with a sword. The Shāfiʿīs say that the killer is killed in the same way he killed, and the guardian can use a sword.

THE FIFTEENTH ḤADĪTH

مِنْ خِصَالِ الإِيْمَان

الْقَوْلُ الحَسَنُ وَرِعَايَةُ حَقِّ الضَّيْفِ وَالجَّار

عَنْ أَبِي هُرَيْرَةَ ﷺ: أَنَّ رَسُولَ اللهِ ﷺ قَالَ: {مَنْ كَانَ يُؤْمِنُ بِاللهِ وَالْيَوْمِ الآخِرِ فَلْيَقُلْ خَيْراً أَوْ لِيَصْمُتْ، وَمَنْ كَانَ يُؤْمِنُ بِاللهِ وَالْيَوْمِ الآخِرِ فَلْيُكْرِمْ جَارَهُ، وَمَنْ كَانَ يُؤْمِنُ بِاللهِ وَالْيَوْمِ الآخِرِ فَلْيُكْرِمْ ضَيْفَهُ.} رواه البخاري ومسلم.

Some of the Qualities of Faith

Speaking Well and Observing the Rights of Guests and Neighbours

It is on the authority of Abū Hurayrah ﷺ that the Messenger of Allah ﷺ said, {Whoever believes in Allah and the Last Day, let him speak well or remain silent. Whoever believes in Allah and the Last Day let him honour his neighbour. Whoever believes in Allah and the Last Day let him honour his guest.} Related by al-Bukhārī and Muslim.

Al-Bukhārī has collected the ḥadīth in the Book of Etiquette (chapter: whoever believes in Allah and the Last Day, let him not harm his neighbour), no.5672. Muslim has collected it in Faith (the chapter on strongly encouraging that one honour neighbours and guests and remain silent except for speaking what is good, and all of that is from faith), no.47.

Its Importance:
Ibn Ḥajar, ﷺ, says in his commentary on the *Ṣaḥīḥ* of al-Bukhārī, 'This is an example of comprehensive speech. The ḥadīth comprises three matters that bring together good manners, both in word and deed'. One can also refer to the importance of the thirteenth ḥadīth.

The Language of the Ḥadīth:
(يؤمن) *yu'minu*: complete faith, which saves one from Allah the Exalted's punishment and leads one to His pleasure. The foundation of faith is affirmation and obedience.

(اليوم الآخر) *al-yawm al-ākhir*: the Day of Standing, which is when deeds will be rewarded and recompensed.

(يصمت) *yaṣmut*: to remain silent.

(فليكرم جاره) *falyukrim jārahu*: cause him to have goodness, and protect him from harm and evil.

(فليكرم ضيفه) *falyukrim ḍayfahu*: to give him a hospitable reception, which is to serve him a meal and the like and to treat him well.

Legal Matters and Other Guidance from the Ḥadīth:
1. Man and his relationship with the community: Man lives in this world with other people, and there are relationships and connections between him and them. He needs them and they need him. Islam strives for these relationships to be based on sound foundations and a proper way. This is realised when people honour one another, and in dealing with others, each individual adheres to the etiquette of transactions and good social relations, which includes speaking well, being a kind neighbour and showing proper hospitality. This is what the Messenger of Allah ﷺ is strongly encouraging us to do in this ḥadīth.

2. It is one of the signs of complete faith that one speaks well and remain silent concerning everything else. In this ḥadīth, the Messenger of Allah ﷺ is strongly encouraging us to have the greatest qualities of goodness and the most beneficial actions of righteousness. He is making it clear to us that it is from perfect faith and complete Islam that the Muslim speak about matters that will benefit him in his worldly life and Hereafter, and furthermore, will bring felicity and happiness to the community. While at the same time, he should remain silent concerning any matter that tends to cause harm and corruption, and thus necessitate the Lord's ﷻ anger and wrath.

Aḥmad has related in his *Musnad* on the authority of Anas ﵁ that the Prophet ﷺ said, {A slave's faith is not sound until his heart is sound, and his heart is not sound until his tongue is sound.}

At-Ṭabarānī has also collected the ḥadīth of Anas ﵁ that the Prophet ﷺ said, {A slave does not reach the reality of faith until he stores away his tongue}, i.e. he restrains it from certain speech, which is that which has no good in it.

3. Plunging into Speech is a cause of destruction, and guarding the tongue is the path to success. You have already seen his statement ﷺ: {From the excellence of one's Islam is leaving what does not concern one} and you know that speaking about that which does not concern you could be a reason for your deeds coming to nothing and you being denied Paradise. Thus, when the Muslim wants to speak he must think before he speaks. If it is clear to him that what he is talking about is, in fact, good and rewardable, he should speak. If it is clear to him that there is some harm that he is provoking or some falsehood that he is spreading, or he is not sure, he should refrain from speaking, as that is better and safer for him, because he will be reckoned for every word he utters, either rewarded or punished. Allah the Exalted has said,

﴿مَّا يَلْفِظُ مِن قَوْلٍ إِلَّا لَدَيْهِ رَقِيبٌ عَتِيدٌ﴾

"He does not utter a single word without a watcher by him pen in hand." [Qāf 50:18]

Al-Bukhārī has related from Abū Hurayrah ﵁ that the Prophet ﷺ said, {A slave will say some words that please Allah the Exalted, and he will not think much of them, but because of them Allah will raise him several ranks. Likewise, a slave will speak words that angers Allah the Exalted, and he will not think much of them, but because of them, he will descend into the Fire.} We also mention the ḥadīth of Muʿādh ﵁: {Are people thrown down on their nostrils in the Fire for anything other than what their tongues reaped?}

4. The Etiquettes of Speech: Speech in Islam has many etiquettes, such as:

A. The Muslim should be keen to speak about that which is beneficial and refrain from unlawful speech at all times. Allah the Exalted has described the believers by saying,

﴿وَٱلَّذِينَ هُمْ عَنِ ٱللَّغْوِ مُعْرِضُونَ﴾

"those who turn away from worthless talk" [al-Muʾminūn 23:3]

Worthless talk includes backbiting, slander, discrediting people's honour and so forth.

B. Not engaging in a great deal of permissible speech, because it could lead to that which is unlawful or disliked. At-Tirmidhī has related from Ibn ʿUmar ﵄ that the Prophet ﷺ said, {Do not talk a great deal without remembering Allah, for a great deal of talk without the remembrance of Allah hardens the heart, and the people most removed from Allah are the hard-hearted.} ʿUmar ﵁ said, 'Whoever talks a great deal will have many slips, and whoever has many slips will have many sins. Whoever has many sins is more deserving of the Fire'.

C. The obligation to speak when there is a need, and especially to elucidate the truth, enjoin the right and forbid the wrong, which is considered amongst the noblest qualities. Leaving it is disobedience and sin because the one who is silent about the truth is a mute demon.

5. Concern for One's Neighbour and Advising Him: It is from the perfection of one's faith and the veracity of one's Islam that one treat one's neighbour well, with righteousness, and refrain from harming him, as he ﷺ has informed. It is sufficient evidence for us that Allah the Exalted has joined between good to one's neighbour and worshipping only Him the Glorified. He has said,

﴿وَٱعْبُدُوا۟ ٱللَّهَ وَلَا تُشْرِكُوا۟ بِهِۦ شَيْـًٔا ۖ وَبِٱلْوَٰلِدَيْنِ إِحْسَٰنًا وَبِذِى ٱلْقُرْبَىٰ وَٱلْيَتَٰمَىٰ وَٱلْمَسَٰكِينِ
وَٱلْجَارِ ذِى ٱلْقُرْبَىٰ وَٱلْجَارِ ٱلْجُنُبِ وَٱلصَّاحِبِ بِٱلْجَنۢبِ وَٱبْنِ ٱلسَّبِيلِ وَمَا مَلَكَتْ أَيْمَٰنُكُمْ ۗ
إِنَّ ٱللَّهَ لَا يُحِبُّ مَن كَانَ مُخْتَالًا فَخُورًا﴾

"Worship Allah and do not associate anything with Him. Be good to your parents and relatives and to orphans and the poor, and to neighbours who are related to you and neighbours who are not related to you (*al-jār al-junub*), and to companions (*as-ṣāḥib bil-janb*)..." [an-Nisā' 4:36]

Al-jār al-junub is the neighbour who is far in terms of location or in terms of lineage, while *as-ṣāḥib bil-janb* is one's companion in travel or other circumstances.

Being good to one's neighbour and honouring him is something commanded in the Revealed Law. Indeed, concern for one's neighbour in Islam reaches a degree that is unknown in the history of social relations. Look at al-Bukhārī who has related from ʿĀ'ishah ﵂ when she said, 'The Messenger of Allah ﷺ said, {Jibrīl kept advising me regarding the neighbour until I thought that he would inherit from him.} In other words, I thought that a person would be entitled to a share of his neighbour's estate, because of how many neighbours' rights were explained to me.

6. Harming neighbours is a defect in faith and it causes destruction. Harming a neighbour is unlawful in Islam. It is an enormity; its sin is immense and its punishment from Allah ﷻ is severe. Whoever is guilty of this is prevented from reaching higher ranks of virtue and perfected faith. Al-Bukhārī and Muslim have related from Ibn Masʿūd ﵁ that the Messenger of Allah ﷺ was asked, 'What is the greatest sin?' He replied, {That you make a partner for Allah when He has created you.} It was then said, 'Then what?' He replied, {That you kill your child for fear that he will eat with you.} It was then said, 'Then what?' He replied, {That you seduce your neighbour's wife}, i.e. you seduce his wife such that she agrees to fornicate with you, and then you do so. Al-Bukhārī has related from Abū Shurayḥ رضي الله عنه that the Prophet ﷺ said, {By Allah, he does not believe. By Allah, he does not believe. By Allah, he does not believe.} It was asked, 'Who, O Messenger of Allah?' He replied, {The one whose neighbour is not safe from his calamities}, i.e. he is not safe from his evils and harms. What is meant by 'he does not believe' is not having the perfect faith that saves one from punishment with Allah ﷻ.

Aḥmad and al-Ḥākim have collected the ḥadīth of Abū Hurayrah رضي الله عنه in which he said, 'It was said to the Messenger of Allah that such-and-such woman prays at night and fasts in the day, and on her tongue is something that harms her neighbours. She is *salīṭah*. He replied, {There is no good in her. She is in the Fire.} It was then said to him that such-and-such woman prays the obligatory prayers, fasts Ramaḍān, and gives away pieces of curd for charity. She does not do anything else and she does not harm her neighbours with her tongue. He replied, {She is in Paradise.}' *Salīṭah* means that she has a vicious tongue, with which she insults others and the like.

7. The Means of Being Good to One's Neighbour: The means of showing one's neighbour righteousness are many, and they include:

A. Sharing with him when he needs it, for it is in the *Musnad* of Aḥmad, from ʿUmar رضي الله عنه: 'A believer does not satisfy himself while his neighbour is hungry.' Al-Ḥākim has related from him ﷺ {Whoever spends the night satiated while his next-door neighbour is hungry and he knows about it has not believed in me.} In the *Ṣaḥīḥ* of Muslim, it is on the authority of Abū Dharr رضي الله عنه: 'My intimate friend ﷺ advised me, {If you are cooking a broth, add more water to it. Then look to the people in your neighbour's house and give them some of it.}'

B. Helping him and procuring benefit for him, even if that would entail forgoing a right the forgoing of which would not cause harm. In the two *Ṣaḥīḥ* collections, it is on the authority of Abū Hurayrah رضي الله عنه that the Prophet ﷺ said, {Let none of you prevent his neighbour from sticking a piece of wood in his wall.}

C. Giving him gifts, and especially on special occasions. Al-Bukhārī has related on the authority of ʿĀ'ishah رضي الله عنها that the Messenger of Allah ﷺ said, {Let not a female neighbour think little of giving her female neighbour a sheep's bone with only a little meat on it.} In other words, she should give to her in any case.

8. Honouring Guests is from faith and an outward manifestation of the excellence of one's Islam. The Messenger of Allah ﷺ makes it clear in this ḥadīth that whoever hears to the laws of Islam and follows the path of the best believers, must honour any guest that comes to him, show him righteousness and be good to him. Doing so is evidence of his complete trust in Allah the Exalted and the veracity of his reliance on him. He ﷺ has said, {Whoever believes in Allah and the Last Day, let him honour his guest.}

Is hospitality a right or merely something charitable? Hospitality is part of noble manners and the etiquettes of Islam. It is from the manners of the Prophets and the righteous. Is it kindness and charity from the host, or is it a right of the guest that is obligatory upon him? The scholars have differed in this:

Aḥmad and Layth hold that it is an obligation for a day and night, due to what Ibn Mājah has related in which he ﷺ said, {The guest's night is an obligatory right upon every Muslim.} In the two *Ṣaḥīḥ* collections, it is on the authority of ʿUqbah ibn ʿĀmir ﷺ who said, 'We said, "O Messenger of Allah if you send us somewhere and we stopover at a people who do not receive us hospitably, what should we do?" The Messenger of Allah ﷺ said, {If you stopover at a people, command that you have what the guest should have and proceed. If they do not do so, take from them the guest's right that they should give.} He ﷺ also said, {let him honour his guest}, which is a command and a command indicates obligation. If hospitality is an obligation and the host withholds it, does the guest proceed to take his right or does he present his case to the ruler,[76] so that he can take his right on his behalf? Concerning this, there are two narrations from Aḥmad ﷺ.

The majority holds that hospitality is recommended and that it is part of noble manners. It is not an obligation. This is because he ﷺ said, {let him honour}, and in another narration: {let him treat him well}, neither of which indicate obligation because honouring and treating others well falls under righteousness and noble manners.

9. The Etiquette of Hospitality and Guests: It is from the etiquettes of hospitality and its generosity that one smile and show happiness to the guest, make polite conversation with him, hasten to bring him whatever food or drink one can, and feed him more than one usually feeds one's family and dependents, for a day and night. For the following two days, one feeds him as one feeds one's dependents, without inconveniencing them or harming them in any way.

Muslim has related his statement ﷺ: {Hospitality is for three days and the guest is shown preference for the first day and night. Whatever is beyond three days is a charity for him.}

As for the guest, it is from his etiquette that he not harass or annoy his host, which would include staying more than three days or staying when he can sense

76 Ar. *ḥākim*, which can also mean judge.

that the host does not have the means to accommodate him properly. Muslim has related from the ḥadīth of Abū Shurayḥ: {It is not lawful for a Muslim man to stay with his brother until he transgresses against him.} They said, 'O Messenger of Allah, how does he transgress against him?' He replied, {He stays with him and he does not have anything with which to accommodate him properly.} In this situation, he can ask him to leave, and especially after three days, because what is upon him will have expired.

10. The Importance of Applying this Ḥadīth: Applying what we know from the contents of this ḥadīth is of profound importance, because it actualises unity, brings hearts together and removes rancour and hatred. This is because everyone is someone else's neighbour, and most people are either a guest or a host. Thus, if every neighbour honoured his neighbour and every host honoured his guest, society would be sound, people's affairs would be in order and love and harmony would prevail. This would especially be the case if everyone adhered to the etiquette of the ḥadīth, and thus spoke well or remained silent.

THE SIXTEENTH ḤADĪTH

لَا تَغْضَبْ وَلَكَ الجَنَّة

عَنْ أَبِي هُرَيْرَةَ ﷺ أَنَّ رَجُلاً قَالَ لِلنَّبِيِّ ﷺ: أَوْصِنِي، قَالَ: {لَا تَغْضَبْ} فَرَدَّدَ مِرَاراً، قَالَ: {لَا تَغْضَبْ.} رواه البخاري.

Do Not Become Angry and Paradise Is Yours

It is on the authority of Abū Hurayrah ﷺ that a man said to the Prophet ﷺ 'Advise me.' He replied, {Do not become angry} and repeated it several times, saying, {Do not become angry.} Related by al-Bukhārī and Muslim.

Al-Bukhārī has related it in Etiquette (the chapter on warning against anger), no.5765.

Its Importance:
Al-Jurdānī has said that this ḥadīth is an immense ḥadīth, and it is an example of comprehensive speech because it combines the good of this life and the Hereafter.

One can also look at what is mentioned concerning the importance of the thirteenth ḥadīth.

The Language of the Ḥadīth:
(رجلا) *rajulan*: It has been said that it is Abū ad-Dardā' ﷺ as at-Ṭabarānī has narrated from him: 'I said, "O Messenger of Allah, show me an action that will enter me into Paradise." He replied, {Do not become angry and Paradise is yours.}' It has also been said that it is Jāriyah ibn Qudāmah ﷺ as Aḥmad has narrated from him that he said, 'I asked the Prophet ﷺ and said to him, "O Messenger of Allah, tell me something that is easy for me so that perhaps I will understand it." He replied, {Do not become angry.} I repeated this several times, and each time, he said, {Do not become angry.}' There is nothing preventing this event from being repeated and this question being asked by several people. (أوصني) *awṣinī*: show me an action that will benefit me.

(لا تغضب) *la taghḍab*: avoid the causes of anger and do not expose yourself to that which provokes it, or do not act upon your anger, because anger in an eruption in the soul that pushes it to desire ruthless action and revenge.

(فردد مرارا) *fa raddada mirāran*: he repeated his request for advice more than once.

Legal Matters and Other Guidance from the Ḥadīth:

1. A Muslim's Manners: A Muslim is someone who is ascribed the noblest of manners, he is adorned with forbearance and modesty, and he shows people humility and affection. At the same time, he bears the traits of masculinity, such as endurance and protecting people from harm, pardoning when he is in a position of power, patience in times of adversity, controlling his anger when someone transgresses against him or provokes him, and smiling and being cheerful in every situation. This is what the Messenger of Allah ﷺ instructed this Companion who sought his advice, asking him for something that would help him achieve his objective. The response was this concise expression, which gathers every goodness and prevents every evil: {Do not become angry.}

2. Yearning for Paradise and Seeking its Path: This advice from the Messenger of Allah ﷺ which he gave to this questioner who wanted to follow the path to Paradise. This questioner asked his teacher, his guide and the one who will lead him to the Highest Garden of Paradise (*al-Firdaws*) and Allah's ﷻ Pleasure to give him some brief advice that he could memorise, understand and comprehend its instruction. He thus answered him by granting his request and giving him what he was seeking, with this eternal advice: {Do not become angry.} In other words, have exalted manners, the manners of Prophethood, the manners of the Qur'ān, the manners of faith. If you take on these manners and they become normal for you, and they become part of your nature and character, anger will not affect you when its causes are present, and you will know the path to Allah's ﷻ pleasure and His ﷻ Paradise.

3. Forbearance and Self-Control is the Way to Victory and Pleasure: When one's human nature gets the upper hand, and human passions are stirred inside of you, if you are a Muslim seeking success, beware of giving your ego what it desires and letting anger take control of you, and thus it commands you and forbids you and you commit what Allah has forbidden. Rather, you must exert yourself to leave that which anger pushes you towards, and remember the manners of the Muslim who has *taqwā* and the believer who is pure, whom Allah the Exalted described for you when He ﷻ said,

﴿وَسَارِعُوٓاْ إِلَىٰ مَغۡفِرَةٖ مِّن رَّبِّكُمۡ وَجَنَّةٍ عَرۡضُهَا ٱلسَّمَٰوَٰتُ وَٱلۡأَرۡضُ أُعِدَّتۡ لِلۡمُتَّقِينَ ١٣٣ ٱلَّذِينَ
يُنفِقُونَ فِي ٱلسَّرَّآءِ وَٱلضَّرَّآءِ وَٱلۡكَٰظِمِينَ ٱلۡغَيۡظَ وَٱلۡعَافِينَ عَنِ ٱلنَّاسِۗ وَٱللَّهُ يُحِبُّ ٱلۡمُحۡسِنِينَ﴾

"Race each other to forgiveness from your Lord and a Garden as wide as the skies and the earth, prepared for the people who have *taqwā*: those who give in times of both ease and hardship, those who control their rage and pardon other people – Allah loves the good-doers..." [Āl 'Imrān 3:133-134]

When you protect yourself from Allah's ﷻ anger after repressing it, you will be classed amongst the people of *taqwā* and you will be from the people of Paradise, residing therein forever.

Imam Aḥmad has related from the ḥadīth of 'Abdullah ibn 'Umar ؓ that he asked the Prophet ﷺ 'What will keep me away from Allah's ﷻ anger?' He replied, {Do not become angry.}

Al-Ḥasan al-Baṣrī said, 'There are four things; whoever possesses them, Allah will protect him from Shayṭān and prevent him from entering the Fire. One should protect himself from desire, from fright, from passions and from anger'.

4. Anger is the Aggregate of Evil and Freeing Oneself from it is the Aggregate of Good: We notice in the ḥadīth that the questioning believer, when he ﷺ tells him, {Do not become angry}, understands this advice and accepts it, but he goes back and repeats his request for advice and counsel as if he is not convinced of it or thinks it is insufficient. He needs more, something that is more profound and more beneficial so that he can achieve his objective of entering Paradise. However, the Messenger of Allah ﷺ does not say anything else. Rather, he repeats what he said, twice, thrice and maybe more. Every time the man says, 'Advise me', he replies, {Do not become angry}, emphasising that it is sufficient advice and profound counsel if he understands its purport and acts accordingly.

That is when this intelligent believer becomes aware of what Allah's Messenger ﷺ is emphasising, and thus he realises the objective and knows what is intended. It has been mentioned in a narration from Imam Aḥmad that the questioner said, 'I contemplated when the Prophet ﷺ said what he said, and I realised that anger gathers all evil.' This means that if someone does not become angry, he has left all evil, and whoever leaves all evil attains every good. Thus, may the blessings and peace of Allah be upon you, O Messenger of Allah, and may Allah reward you on behalf of the Ummah with the best reward of any prophet that has been sent, for you have instructed us to have good manners and you have warned about the key to every evil.

It has been related that a man asked the Messenger of Allah ﷺ: 'What is the best action?' He replied, {Good manners, which is that you do not become angry if you are able to.}

5. Anger is Weakness and Forbearance is Strength: Being quick to anger and submitting to it is a sign of a person's weakness, even if he has strong arms and a healthy body. Al-Bukhārī and Muslim have related from Abū Hurayrah ﷺ who said, 'The Messenger of Allah ﷺ said, {A strong person is not the one who is good at wrestling. Rather, a strong person is the one who can control himself when he is angry.}

6. The Disgusting Effects of Anger: Anger is blameworthy and a bad character trait, and a lethal weapon. If a person surrenders to it, he is overcome by its evil effects, which harm the individual first and then the community.

A. As for the harms to the person, they are physical and material, moral and immaterial, as well as spiritual and religious. You can comprehend this when you picture someone in a fit of rage. His colour changes. His blood flows faster. His veins swell. His limbs tremble. His movement becomes agitated. He stutters when he talks, and his tongue unleashes obscenities. He insults and reviles. Maybe he will say something unlawful, or even something that takes him out of Islam, such as uttering blasphemy or opposing the Religion, and so forth. In addition to the aforementioned, there is the reckless behaviour this person engages in, which squanders his wealth and harms his body.

B. As for the harms to the community, it is the stirring of hatred in hearts and people bearing grudges against one another. This can lead to Muslims being harmed and forsaken, and their feeling schadenfreude when they are afflicted with some calamity. Enmity and hostility are provoked between friends, ties of kinship are cut, life is corrupted and communities collapse.

7. Repelling and Treating Anger: Anger is part of man's nature and disposition, but the Muslim who is connected to the highest *malakūt*[77] protects himself from it. He repels its evil by staying away from its causes, so that it does not emerge, and he treats it if it does emerge.

A. The causes of anger are numerous and varied, and they include: arrogance, haughtiness and pride towards people, derision and scorn towards others, abundant joking, especially when it is not true, arguing, delving into that which does

77 (tn): i.e. the unseen realm.

not concern one, and striving for extra wealth and rank. The Muslim is called to rid himself of these blameworthy traits and rise above them, and train his soul to do the opposite.

B. As for treating anger, there are many ways that Islam has shown us, which include:

• Training oneself to be adorned with noble manners, such as forbearance, patience and circumspection in matters, and carefulness in conduct and judgement. Our model for this is the Messenger of Allah ﷺ. Zayd ibn Su'nah came to him before his Islam to test him on the attributes of Prophethood, which are that his forbearance should surpass his anger, and an ignorant person's extreme ignorance should only increase him in forbearance. He thus demanded the repayment of a debt that he owed him before its repayment was actually due, showing him all kinds of rudeness and harshness. He ﷺ responded with absolute magnanimity and a wide smile. 'Umar ؓ scolded the man, so he ﷺ said, in order to teach and refine him and the man, {He and I have a greater need for other than this, O 'Umar. You should tell me to pay off the debt more efficiently and you should tell him to reclaim his debt in a better manner.} He thus commanded that the debt be paid back, and he gave him more than his right, to compensate for the fright that 'Umar ؓ had given him. This lead to him becoming Muslim ؓ and his salvation from Allah's anger and His Fire ﷻ. This has been related by Ibn Ḥibbān, al-Ḥākim and aṭ-Ṭabarānī.

• Remaining firm and controlling oneself if one is angered, and remembering the consequences of anger and the virtue of controlling one's rage and pardoning those who do wrong:

﴿وَٱلْكَـٰظِمِينَ ٱلْغَيْظَ وَٱلْعَافِينَ عَنِ ٱلنَّاسِ ۗ وَٱللَّهُ يُحِبُّ ٱلْمُحْسِنِينَ﴾

"those who control their rage and pardon other people – Allah loves the good-doers..." [Āl 'Imrān 3:134]

Aḥmad, Abū Dāwūd, at-Tirmidhī and Ibn Mājah have related that the Prophet ﷺ said, {Whoever controls his rage when he is able to act upon it, Allah will summon him on the Day of Standing at the head of all created beings, so that He can have him choose whatever maiden he wants.}

Aḥmad has also related: {There is no slave who controls himself except that his heart is filled with faith}, and according to Abū Dāwūd: {...Allah fills him with security and faith.}

- Seeking refuge in Allah from the accursed Shayṭān; Allah the Exalted has said,

﴿وَإِمَّا يَنزَغَنَّكَ مِنَ ٱلشَّيْطَـٰنِ نَزْغٌ فَٱسْتَعِذْ بِٱللَّهِ ۚ إِنَّهُۥ سَمِيعٌ عَلِيمٌ﴾

"If an evil impulse from Shayṭān provokes you, seek refuge in Allah. He is All-Hearing, All-Knowing." [al-ʾAʿrāf 7:200]

Al-Bukhārī and Muslim have related that two men were insulting each other in the Prophet's presence ﷺ and one of them was insulting his companion angrily, such that his face had turned red. The Prophet ﷺ said, '{I know some words that if he were to say them, what he finds would leave. If he were to say, 'I seek refuge in Allah from the accursed Shayṭān.'}

- Changing one's state when one is angry, for Aḥmad and Abū Dāwūd have related that the Prophet ﷺ said, {If one of you becomes angry while standing, let him sit. His anger should then leave him. If not, let him lie down.} This is because you stand when you are preparing to take revenge, which is harder to do when you are sitting or lying down.

- Not talking, because maybe you will say something that will be met with something else that makes you angrier, or you will say something that you will regret after your anger has subsided, because you never wanted to say it. Aḥmad, at-Tirmidhī and Abū Dāwūd have related: {If one of you is angry, let him remain silent.} He said it three times.

- Ablution (*wuḍūʾ*), and this is because anger stimulates heat in the body, and thus the blood flows more easily, boils, and provokes the body's vehemence. Water cools it down and returns it to its natural state. Aḥmad and at-Tirmidhī have related that he ﷺ said, {Anger is a live coal burning in the child of Adam's heart.}

This is aside from noticing that *wuḍūʾ* is a form of worship bearing the remembrance of Allah ﷻ. Shayṭān, who fans the flames of anger inside a person, withdraws when there is *dhikr*. Aḥmad and Abū Dāwūd have related, that he ﷺ said {Anger is from Shayṭān and Shayṭān was created from fire. If one of you is angry, let him perform *wuḍūʾ*.}

8. Anger for the sake of Allah the Exalted: Anger is blameworthy, and the anger that a Muslim is required to treat and stay away from its causes is that which seeks revenge for one's ego, not anger for Allah the Exalted and to give victory to His religion. As for that which is for Allah the Exalted, it is caused by a transgression against what is sacred in the Religion, such as a challenge to its theology, or an attack on its moral and manners or a disparaging of its worship. It could also be because a Muslim individual is being disparaged, or his honour or his wealth. In this case, it is a praiseworthy trait and required conduct. Allah the Exalted has said,

﴿قَـٰتِلُوهُمْ يُعَذِّبْهُمُ ٱللَّهُ بِأَيْدِيكُمْ وَيُخْزِهِمْ وَيَنصُرْكُمْ عَلَيْهِمْ وَيَشْفِ صُدُورَ قَوْمٍ مُّؤْمِنِينَ ﴿١٤﴾ وَيُذْهِبْ غَيْظَ قُلُوبِهِمْ﴾

"Fight them! Allah will punish them at your hands, and disgrace them and help you against them, and heal the hearts of those who believe. He will remove the rage from their hearts." [at-Tawbah 9:14-15]

It has been authentically reported that he ﷺ was more modest than a virgin (*al-ʿadhrāʾ*) behind her curtain, but if he saw something he disliked, we knew it from his face', as has been related by al-Bukhārī.

Al-ʿadhrāʾ means a virgin who has never been married, and a woman like this would typically have a curtain in the house that she would sit behind because she was shy to meet people.

Al-Bukhārī, Muslim and others have related that he ﷺ would not be angered by anything, but if anything Allah ﷻ, had declared inviolable was violated, nothing could stop his anger.

9. The Angry Person is Responsible for His Behaviour: If someone destroys or damages something of value while he is angry, he is responsible for it and he has to pay compensation. If he kills someone deliberately and out of hostility, he deserves retaliation (*al-qiṣāṣ*). If he utters something blasphemous, the ruling is that he has apostated from Islam until he repents. If he makes a vow, the vow stands. If he divorces his wife, the divorce is valid and in effect.

10. The ḥadīth advises that the Muslim be keen for sincere advice and be aware of the ways of goodness, and seek more beneficial knowledge and fair admonition.[78] Likewise, it advises that the Muslim speak less and work more, and follow the excellent model.[79]

---

78 (tn): Please see Sūrat an-Naḥl 16:125.

79 (tn): i.e. the Messenger of Allah ﷺ. Please see Sūrat al-Aḥzāb, 33:21.

THE SEVENTEENTH ḤADĪTH

عُمُومُ الإِحْسَانِ

عَنْ أَبِي يَعْلَى شَدَّادِ بْنِ أَوْسٍ ﷺ، عَنْ رَسُولِ اللهِ ﷺ قَالَ: {إِنَّ اللهَ كَتَبَ الْإِحْسَانَ عَلَى كُلِّ شَيْءٍ، فَإِذَا قَتَلْتُمْ فَأَحْسِنُوا الْقِتْلَةَ، وإذا ذَبَحْتُمْ فَأَحْسِنُوا الذِّبْحَةَ، وَلْيُحِدَّ أَحَدُكُمْ شَفْرَتَهُ وَلْيُرِحْ ذَبِيحَتَهُ.} رواه مسلم.

The Generality of Excellence

It is on the authority of Abū Ya'lā Shaddād ibn Aws ﷺ that the Messenger of Allah ﷺ said, {Allah has obligated excellence (*iḥsān*) in everything, so when you kill, do it with excellence. When you slaughter, do it with excellence. You should sharpen your blade and put the animal at ease.} Related by Muslim.

Muslim has related this ḥadīth in the Book of Hunting (the chapter on the command to have excellence in slaughtering and killing and to sharpen one's blade), no.1955.

The Importance of the Ḥadīth:
This ḥadīth is one of the most important foundations of the Religion, and it comprises the precision of all of Islam's teachings, because excellence in action is when it is done in accordance with the Revealed Law. Actions are connected to either a person's livelihood and how he deals with his family, his brethren and the rest of humanity, or to his Hereafter, which is his faith, which is the action of the heart, and his *islām*,[80] which is the action of the limbs. Whoever has excellence in his livelihood and his Hereafter, has acted correctly and perfectly. Such a person has achieved an immense victory and is among the joyous in both abodes, if Allah the Exalted so wills.

80 (tn): please refer to the second ḥadīth.

The Language of the Ḥadīth:
(كتب) *kataba*: required and obligated.

(الإحسان) *iḥsān*: to bring that which is excellent, which is that the Revealed Law has deemed excellent, and it is done with masterful precision.

(القتلة) *al-qitlah*: this is a type of verbal noun (*maṣdar*) that indicates how something is done.

(ليحدّ) *lyuḥidda*: to sharpen something, such as a knife.

(شفرته) *shafratahu*: the edge of the knife or whatever is used to slaughter.

Legal Matters and Other Guidance from the Ḥadīth:
1. The Obligation of Excellence: The ḥadīth stipulates the obligation of excellence, which is precision, perfection and betterment in legislated actions. Allah commanded this in His Mighty Book when He ﷻ said,

﴿إِنَّ ٱللَّهَ يَأْمُرُ بِٱلْعَدْلِ وَٱلْإِحْسَـٰنِ﴾
"Allah commands justice and excellence..." [an-Naḥl 16:90].

He the Glorified has also said,
﴿وَأَحْسِنُوٓا۟ ۛ إِنَّ ٱللَّهَ يُحِبُّ ٱلْمُحْسِنِينَ﴾
"Do excellence. Allah loves those who do excellence." [al-Baqarah 2:195]

It is required when carrying out obligations, leaving that which is unlawful and dealing with the creation. Excellence means to carry out these matters to the utmost perfection and to observe the etiquettes that rectify them and complement them. If someone does so, his deed will be accepted and his reward will be abundant.

2. Excellence in Killing: This means to improve the manner of killing by using a sharp implement and doing so swiftly, so that those whom it is permissible to kill are executed in the easiest of ways. Permissible killing is going to be in either legislated combat (*jihād*), retaliation (*qiṣāṣ*) or one of Allah the Exalted's legal punishments (*ḥadd*):

A. As for killing enemies on the battlefield for the sake of Allah, the easiest way to kill a disbeliever is to strike his neck with a sword. Allah the Exalted has said,

﴿فَإِذَا لَقِيتُمُ ٱلَّذِينَ كَفَرُوا فَضَرْبَ ٱلرِّقَابِ﴾

"Therefore when you meet those who disbelieve, strike their necks." [Muḥammad 47:4]

The Prophet ﷺ forbade *al-muthlah,* which is to cut off parts of the body,[81] regardless of whether it is before or after the person's death. It is in the *Ṣaḥīḥ* of al-Bukhārī that the Prophet ﷺ forbade *al-muthlah.* It is in the *Musnad* of Aḥmad and the *Sunan* of Abū Dāwūd, from the ḥadīth of ʿImrān ibn Ḥuṣayn and Samrah ibn Jundub, that the Prophet ﷺ would forbid *al-muthlah.* If it is permissible for Muslims to use firearms and destructive artillery weapons on the grounds of like for like.

﴿فَمَنِ ٱعْتَدَىٰ عَلَيْكُمْ فَٱعْتَدُوا عَلَيْهِ بِمِثْلِ مَا ٱعْتَدَىٰ عَلَيْكُمْ﴾

"So if anyone oversteps the limits against you, overstep against him the same as he did to you" [al-Baqarah 2:194],

It is not permissible for them, under any circumstance, to engage in combat with the objective of mutilating and maiming. Some disbelieving countries have become accustomed to asking their soldiers not to kill their enemies but to maim them instead, because the person who is maimed becomes a burden for his country. This is economic and psychological warfare, in addition to the fact that war involves shedding blood, devastation and destruction. Islam rejects such a barbaric and savage policy, and its point of departure remains excellence in everything, especially towards man.

B. As for killing out of retaliation, like for like is not permissible.[82] Rather, the person is killed with a sword. If the murderer did so deliberately by maiming the victim, Mālik, ash-Shāfiʿī and Aḥmad, according to his well-known position, hold that he is killed just as he killed. In the two *Ṣaḥīḥ* collections, it is on the authority of Anas ؓ who said, 'A slave girl who was wearing some silver jewellery went out in al-Madīnah and Jew threw stones at her. She was then brought to the Messenger of Allah ﷺ while barely alive. The Messenger of Allah ﷺ said to her, {Did so-and-so kill you?} She then raised her head. He said to her a third time, {Did so-and-so kill you?} She then lowered her head, so the Messenger of Allah ﷺ summoned him and smashed his head between two stones.

Ath-Thawrī, Abū Ḥanīfah and Aḥmad – according to another narration from him – hold that he is only killed by the sword. There is a third narration from

81 (tn): i.e. to maim.

82 (tn): i.e. the murderer is not killed in the same way that he murdered.

Aḥmad, which is that the murderer receives what he did to his victim, unless he burned him with fire or maimed him, in which case he is killed with a sword. This is because maiming and burning with fire are prohibited.

C. As for killing as a legal punishment for disbelief, most scholars hold that maiming is disliked, whether it is for original disbelief or apostasy from Islam.

3. The Prohibition of Burning with Fire: It has been established in the *Ṣaḥīḥ* of al-Bukhārī that the Messenger of Allah ﷺ initially allowed burning with fire and then he forbade it, to stress obedience and adherence therein. Al-Bukhārī has related from Ibn ʿAbbās that the Prophet ﷺ said, {Do not punish using Allah's punishment ﷻ.} This shows that the teachings of the Noble Prophet precede and predate what countries have agreed upon concerning the prohibition of incendiary bombs, even though we know that major powers do not adhere to this prohibition. It is just ink on paper!

The prohibition against burning includes animals and vermin. In the *Musnad* of Imam Aḥmad, as well as the collections of Abū Dāwūd and an-Nasāʾī, it is on the authority of Ibn Masʿūd that he said, 'We were with the Prophet ﷺ and we passed by an ant colony that had been burnt. The Prophet ﷺ became angry and said, {Humans should not punish using Allah's punishment ﷻ.}

This is why the scholars have even disliked burning vermin. Ibrāhīm an-Nakhaʿī said, 'Burning a scorpion with fire is a type of maiming'. Umm ad-Dardāʾ forbade burning fleas with fire. Aḥmad, 'A fish is not to be grilled over a fire whilst alive'. He also said, 'A locust is of less significance, because it has no blood'.

4. The prohibition against shackling[83] animals, i.e. to tie up an animal and then strike it with arrows and the like until it dies. In al-Bukhārī and Muslim, it is on the authority of Anas رضي الله عنه that the Prophet ﷺ forbade the shackling of animals. Al-Bukhārī and Muslim also related that Ibn ʿUmar رضي الله عنهما passed by some people who had erected a chicken and were shooting at it. Ibn ʿUmar said, 'Who did this? The Messenger of Allah ﷺ cursed whoever does such a thing.'

5. The prohibition against using a living thing as a target, i.e. to shoot arrows at it. In the *Musnad* of Imam Aḥmad, it is on the authority of Abū Hurayrah that the Prophet ﷺ forbade shooting at an animal and then eating it. Rather, it should be slaughtered first and then it can be used as a target.

6. Excellence in slaughtering animals: There are etiquettes in Islam that a Muslim must adhere to when slaughtering and in sum, they are a practical embodiment of excellence and gentleness. They include sharpening one's blade, so

---

83 Ar. *ṣabr.*

that the slaughter is swift and the animals dies quickly. Imam Aḥmad and Ibn Mājah have related from Ibn ʿUmar ﷺ who said, 'The Messenger of Allah ﷺ commanded that the blade be sharpened, and that it be hidden from the animal. He said, {When one of you slaughters, let him finish it off.}' They include being gentle to the animal. It should be led to the slaughter gently. In the *Sunan* of Ibn Mājah, there is the ḥadīth of Abū Saʿīd al-Khudrī in which he said, 'The Messenger of Allah ﷺ passed by a man who was dragging a sheep by its ear. The Messenger of Allah ﷺ said, {Leave its ear and take the front part of its neck.}' Imam Aḥmad said, 'It is to be led to the slaughter gently and the knife should be concealed from it. The knife should only be shown at the time of slaughter.'

Excellence in slaughtering includes cutting the jugular vein. In the *Sunan* of Abū Dāwūd, it is on the authority of Ibn ʿAbbās and Abū Hurayrah ﷺ that the Prophet ﷺ forbade the *sharīṭah* of Shayṭān, which is an animal that is slaughtered and skinned but its jugular vein has not been cut.

It is also recommended that the animal not be slaughtered in the presence of another animal, the animal should be made to face the *qiblah*, the slaughterer should say *bismillāh*[84] just before he does so, he should leave the animal until it cools down, he should have the intention of drawing nearer to Allah, and he acknowledge Allah the Exalted's favour therein, because He the Glorified has subjugated these animals for us and blessed us with them.

Excellence towards the animal includes not making it bear more than it is capable of, not mounting it while it is standing unless there is a need, and not milking it unless its child will not be harmed.

7. In addition to all of the above, this ḥadīth is one of the most important foundations of Islam, because it is a noble call from the Prophet ﷺ to have excellence in every deed.

84 (tn): i.e. in the Name of Allah.

THE EIGHTEENTH ḤADĪTH

تَقْوَى اللهِ تَعَالَى وَحُسْنُ الخُلُقِ

عَنْ أَبِي ذَرٍّ جُنْدُبِ بِنِ جُنَادَةَ، وَأَبِي عَبْدِ الرَّحْمٰنِ مُعَاذِ بْنِ جَبَلٍ ﷺ، عَنْ رَسُوْلِ اللهِ ﷺ قَالَ: {اتَّقِ اللهَ حَيْثُمَا كُنْتَ، وَأَتْبِعِ السَّيِّئَةَ الْحَسَنَةَ تَمْحُهَا، وَخَالِقِ النَّاسِ بِخُلُقٍ حَسَنٍ.} رواه الترمذي وقال: حديث حسن، وفي بعض النسخ: حسن صحيح.

Have *Taqwā* of Allah and Show People Good Manners

It is on the authority of Abū Dharr Jundub ibn Junādah and Abū ʿAbdir Raḥmān Muʿādh ibn Jabal ﷺ that the Messenger of Allah ﷺ said, {Have *taqwā* of Allah wherever you are, follow up a bad deed with a good deed that will efface it, and show people good manners.} At-Tirmidhī has related it and has said that it is a good ḥadīth, and in some copies: 'good and authentic.'

At-Tirmidhī has collected the ḥadīth in the chapters on righteousness and maintaining ties of kinship (the chapter on what has reached us regarding how to treat people), no.1988.

At-Tirmidhī grading this ḥadīth as good (*ḥasan*) is corroborated by the fact that it has numerous paths, according to Aḥmad, al-Bazzār, aṭ-Ṭabarānī, al-Ḥākim, Ibn ʿAbdul Barr and others. See *al-Futūḥāt ar-Rabbāniyyah* (7/373).

The Language of the Ḥadīth:

(اتق الله) *ittaqi llāh*: Linguistically, *taqwā* means to use a protective barrier to prevent and protect yourself from something that you fear and are wary of. *Taqwā* of Allah the Exalted means that the slave places a protective barrier between himself and what he fears, which is Allah's punishment, and thus he is protected from it. This is done by obeying His commands and avoiding what He has prohibited.

(حيثما كنت) *haythumā kunta*: i.e. whatever time and place you are in, whether you are alone or with a group, people can see you or they cannot see you.

(أتبع) *atbiʿi*: follow, do it immediately afterwards.

(السيئة) *as-sayyi'ata*: the sin that you have committed.

(تمحها) *tamḥuhā*: it removes it from the scrolls of the angelic scribes and one will not be taken to account for it.

(خالق) *khāliqi*: exert yourself and be polite and courteous with people.

(بخلق) *bikhuluq*: *khuluq* is the character and temperament that results from one's conduct, and it can be described as either good or bad.

Legal Matters and Other Guidance from the Ḥadīth:

1. Circumstances Surrounding the Ḥadīth: This advice is from the Messenger of Allah ﷺ to Abū Dharr and Muʿādh and it has been transmitted via numerous paths and on various occasions, including:

A. Ibn ʿAbdul Barr has collected in *at-Tamhīd* that Anas said, 'The Prophet ﷺ sent Muʿādh to Yemen and said, {O Muʿādh, have *taqwā* of Allah and show people good manners. If you do a bad deed, follow it up with a good deed.} He said, 'O Messenger of Allah, is *lā ilāha ill Allah*[85] a good deed?' He replied, {It is one of the greatest good deeds.}'

B. Aḥmad has collected that Abū Dharr said, 'I said, "O Messenger of Allah, teach me a deed that will bring me closer to Paradise and take me far away from the Fire." He replied, {If you do a bad deed, immediately do a good deed, for its reward is multiplied ten times.}' He said, 'I said, "O Messenger of Allah, is it a good deed to say *lā ilāha ill Allah*?" He replied, {It is the most excellent of good deeds.}'

2. Man is an Ennobled Vicegerent on Earth: Allah has created man and bestowed innumerable blessings upon him. Some people He has made messengers and sent down revelation to them from the heavens, so that they can show the rest of humanity the paths of goodness and felicity. He has commanded them to worship Him alone and not associate anything with him, to implement what He has commanded and to avoid what He has prohibited them. They must hasten to do good deeds and refrain from wrong deeds. Each individual must strive to bring about human felicity, and each must treat the other with friendship, cooperation and brotherhood. Each individual must stretch out his hand to support everyone else and show excellence, adorn himself with exalted manners, have a good soul and amicable spirit, and speak well. With all of the above, a person is victorious,

85 (tn): i.e. saying 'there is no god but Allah'.

people enjoy the good of this life and the Hereafter, and the noble vicegerency of man is realised on earth, that which distinguished Adam ﷺ from the angels that draw near:

﴿وَإِذْ قُلْنَا لِلْمَلَـٰٓئِكَةِ ٱسْجُدُوا۟ لِـَٔادَمَ فَسَجَدُوٓا۟﴾

"We said to the angels, 'Prostrate to Adam!' and they prostrated." [al-Baqarah 2:34]

This is what the Chosen Messenger ﷺ is advising us and strongly encouraging us to do in this ḥadīth.

3. Eternal Advice: How beautiful is the gift that these two revered Companions are bearing. It is a ḥadīth that both of them heard from their teacher and their beloved, Muḥammad ﷺ. Maybe in the beginning it was a gift and advice for just the two of them, and then it became guidance and instruction, and an eternal admonition for the Ummah, because of the general goodness and immense benefit that it contains. It actualises felicity in this life and gives glad tidings of the blessings of the Hereafter. It is a sublime piece of advice, gathering all of Allah the Exalted's rights and maintaining the rights of His slaves.

4. *Taqwā* is the way of salvation[86]**:** The greatest matter that the Messenger of Allah ﷺ is directing us to in this advice is *taqwā* of Allah ﷻ which brings together every goodness and protects against every evil, and because of it the believers become worthy of support and assistance from Allah the Exalted:

﴿إِنَّ ٱللَّهَ مَعَ ٱلَّذِينَ ٱتَّقَوا۟ وَّٱلَّذِينَ هُم مُّحْسِنُونَ﴾

"Allah is with those who have *taqwā* of Him and with those who do excellence." [an-Naḥl 16:128]

Because of it, Allah has promised them good provision and deliverance from adversities:

﴿وَمَن يَتَّقِ ٱللَّهَ يَجْعَل لَّهُۥ مَخْرَجًا ۝ وَيَرْزُقْهُ مِنْ حَيْثُ لَا يَحْتَسِبُ﴾

"Whoever has *taqwā* of Allah, He will give him a way out and provide for him from where he does not expect." [at-Ṭalāq 65:2-3]

Because of it, He ﷻ protects them from the scheming of their enemies:

﴿وَإِن تَصْبِرُوا۟ وَتَتَّقُوا۟ لَا يَضُرُّكُمْ كَيْدُهُمْ شَيْـًٔا﴾

86 (tn): being saved from the fire in the absolute sense.

"But if you are steadfast and have *taqwā*, their scheming will not harm you in any way." [Āl ʿImrān 3:120]

Allah has granted the people of *taqwā* a right over Himself, which is that He show them mercy:

﴿وَرَحْمَتِي وَسِعَتْ كُلَّ شَيْءٍ ۚ فَسَأَكْتُبُهَا لِلَّذِينَ يَتَّقُونَ﴾

"My mercy extends to all things, but I will prescribe it for those who have *taqwā*." [al-ʾAʿrāf 7:156]

He the Exalted has described Himself as being entitled to it and being entitled to forgive those who are characterised by it:

﴿وَمَا يَذْكُرُونَ إِلَّآ أَن يَشَآءَ ٱللَّهُ ۚ هُوَ أَهْلُ ٱلتَّقْوَىٰ وَأَهْلُ ٱلْمَغْفِرَةِ﴾

"He is entitled to be feared and entitled to forgive." [al-Mudaththir 74:56]

Finally, in the Hereafter, He ﷻ will have them reside in His ﷻ presence:

﴿إِنَّ ٱلْمُتَّقِينَ فِى جَنَّـٰتٍ وَنَهَرٍ ﴿٥٤﴾ فِى مَقْعَدِ صِدْقٍ عِندَ مَلِيكٍ مُّقْتَدِرٍۭ﴾

"The people of *taqwā* will be amid gardens and rivers, on seats of honour in the presence of an All-Powerful King." [al-Qamr 54:54-55]

There are several verses and ḥadīths about the virtue of *taqwā* and the immensity of its fruits, which is nothing strange, as *taqwā* is the way of the believers and the trait of the Prophets and Messengers:

﴿أُو۟لَـٰٓئِكَ ٱلَّذِينَ هَدَى ٱللَّهُ ۖ فَبِهُدَىٰهُمُ ٱقْتَدِهْ﴾

"They are the ones Allah has guided, so be guided by their guidance." [al-Anʿām 6:90]

It is Allah the Exalted's advice to His slaves, the first of them and the last of them, so whoever adheres to it is victorious and triumphant, and whoever turns away from it is destroyed and lost:

﴿وَلَقَدْ وَصَّيْنَا ٱلَّذِينَ أُوتُوا۟ ٱلْكِتَـٰبَ مِن قَبْلِكُمْ وَإِيَّاكُمْ أَنِ ٱتَّقُوا۟ ٱللَّهَ ۚ وَإِن تَكْفُرُوا۟ فَإِنَّ لِلَّهِ مَا فِى ٱلسَّمَـٰوَٰتِ وَمَا فِى ٱلْأَرْضِ ۚ وَكَانَ ٱللَّهُ غَنِيًّا حَمِيدًا﴾

"We have instructed those given the Book before you and you yourselves, to have *taqwā* of Allah, but if you disbelieve, what is in the heavens and in the earth belongs to Allah. Allah is Rich Beyond Need, Praiseworthy." [an-Nisāʾ 4:131]

5. The Reality of *Taqwā*: *Taqwā* is a word that includes and excludes. It comprises everything that Islam has brought: creed, worship, transactions and manners. The Exalted One has said,

﴿لَّيْسَ ٱلْبِرَّ أَن تُوَلُّوا۟ وُجُوهَكُمْ قِبَلَ ٱلْمَشْرِقِ وَٱلْمَغْرِبِ وَلَٰكِنَّ ٱلْبِرَّ مَنْ ءَامَنَ بِٱللَّهِ وَٱلْيَوْمِ
ٱلْءَاخِرِ وَٱلْمَلَٰٓئِكَةِ وَٱلْكِتَٰبِ وَٱلنَّبِيِّۦنَ وَءَاتَى ٱلْمَالَ عَلَىٰ حُبِّهِۦ ذَوِى ٱلْقُرْبَىٰ وَٱلْيَتَٰمَىٰ وَٱلْمَسَٰكِينَ
وَٱبْنَ ٱلسَّبِيلِ وَٱلسَّآئِلِينَ وَفِى ٱلرِّقَابِ وَأَقَامَ ٱلصَّلَوٰةَ وَءَاتَى ٱلزَّكَوٰةَ وَٱلْمُوفُونَ بِعَهْدِهِمْ إِذَا عَٰهَدُوا۟ ۖ
وَٱلصَّٰبِرِينَ فِى ٱلْبَأْسَآءِ وَٱلضَّرَّآءِ وَحِينَ ٱلْبَأْسِ ۗ أُو۟لَٰٓئِكَ ٱلَّذِينَ صَدَقُوا۟ ۖ
وَأُو۟لَٰٓئِكَ هُمُ ٱلْمُتَّقُونَ﴾

"Righteousness does not lie in turning your faces to the East or to the West. Rather, those with true devoutness are those who believe in Allah and the Last Day, the Angels, the Book and the Prophets, and who, despite their love for it, give away their wealth to their relatives and to orphans and the poor, and to travellers and beggars and to set slaves free, and who establish the prayer and pay the zakāt; those who honour their contracts when they make them, and are steadfast in poverty and illness and in battle. Those are the people who are true. They are the people of *taqwā*." [al-Baqarah 2:177]

Thus, according to this meaning, *taqwā* is not just a word that is uttered or a claim that is made without any evidence. Rather, it is to act assiduously in obeying Allah ﷻ while strictly avoiding disobeying Allah, Blessed and Exalted is He. The First Three Generations described *taqwā* by saying, 'It is to obey Allah and not disobey, to remember and not forget, to be grateful and not be ungrateful.' They applied this meaning and adhered to it, secretly and openly, in all circumstances and affairs, implementing Allah the Exalted's command and answering His call:

﴿يَٰٓأَيُّهَا ٱلَّذِينَ ءَامَنُوا۟ ٱتَّقُوا۟ ٱللَّهَ حَقَّ تُقَاتِهِۦ وَلَا تَمُوتُنَّ إِلَّا وَأَنتُم مُّسْلِمُونَ﴾

"You who believe! Have *taqwā* of Allah with the *taqwā* that is due to Him, and do not die except as Muslims." [Āl 'Imrān 3:102]

6. Part of the Perfection of *Taqwā* is that one steer clear of doubtful matters and whatever might be unlawful: {Whoever guards himself against doubtful matters has secured his religion and his honour}, as related by al-Bukhārī and Muslim. This meaning includes staying aloof from many permissible matters that one fears could lead to that which is unlawful. At-Tirmidhī and Ibn Mājah have related that the Prophet ﷺ said, {The slave will never be of the people of *taqwā* until he leaves that which is harmless for fear that it could be harmful.} Al-Ḥasan al-Baṣrī has said, '*Taqwā* remains with the people of *taqwā*, so much so that they leave much of the lawful for fear of the unlawful.'

7. The Condition for Realising *Taqwā*: The meanings of *taqwā* are not realised and its fruits are not borne unless the Muslim has knowledge of Allah the Exalted's religion, and thus knows how to have *taqwā* of Allah ﷻ:

﴿كَذَٰلِكَ إِنَّمَا يَخْشَى ٱللَّهَ مِنْ عِبَادِهِ ٱلْعُلَمَٰٓؤُا۟ ۗ إِنَّ ٱللَّهَ عَزِيزٌ غَفُورٌ﴾

"Only those of His slaves with knowledge have fear of Allah." [Fāṭir 35:28]

This is because the ignorant person does not know what he is obligated to do and what he is obligated to leave, and that is why knowledge is the best worship, the path that leads to Paradise and the sign that a person wants good. He ﷺ has said, {The superiority of the scholar over the ordinary worshipper is like my superiority over the least of you}, as related by at-Tirmidhī. He has also said, {Whoever travels a path seeking knowledge therein, Allah will facilitate for him the path to Paradise}, as related by Muslim. He has also said, {Whoever Allah wants good for, He gives him understanding (*fiqh*) of the Religion}, which is agreed upon.

8. Repentance from Sin and Hastening to Good Deeds is the Trait of the Believers who have *Taqwā*: A person can be overwhelmed by forgetfulness or heedlessness, his ego can tempt him or his Shayṭān can whisper to him, and thus he falls into disobedience and commits sins. It is from *taqwā* – at that point – to hasten towards repentance and to seek Allah's forgiveness ﷻ when one remembers or becomes aware. Allah has described the people of *taqwā* by saying,

﴿وَٱلَّذِينَ إِذَا فَعَلُوا۟ فَٰحِشَةً أَوْ ظَلَمُوٓا۟ أَنفُسَهُمْ ذَكَرُوا۟ ٱللَّهَ فَٱسْتَغْفَرُوا۟ لِذُنُوبِهِمْ
وَمَن يَغْفِرُ ٱلذُّنُوبَ إِلَّا ٱللَّهُ وَلَمْ يُصِرُّوا۟ عَلَىٰ مَا فَعَلُوا۟ وَهُمْ يَعْلَمُونَ﴾

"those who, when they act indecently or wrong themselves, remember Allah and ask forgiveness for their bad actions – and who can forgive bad actions except Allah? – and do not knowingly persist in what they were doing." [Āl 'Imrān 3:135]

He has also said,

﴿إِنَّ ٱلَّذِينَ ٱتَّقَوْا۟ إِذَا مَسَّهُمْ طَٰٓئِفٌ مِّنَ ٱلشَّيْطَٰنِ تَذَكَّرُوا۟ فَإِذَا هُم مُّبْصِرُونَ﴾

"As for those who have *taqwā*, when they are bothered by visitors from Shayṭān, they remember and immediately see clearly." [al-'A'rāf 7:201]

After repenting and seeking forgiveness, the Muslim who has *taqwā* hastens to do good and to increase in acts of righteousness, to expiate his sin and efface the misdeed that he committed, trusting Allah the Exalted's promise when He ﷻ said,

﴿إِنَّ ٱلْحَسَنَٰتِ يُذْهِبْنَ ٱلسَّيِّـَٔاتِ﴾

"Good actions eradicate bad actions". [Hūd 11:114]

And responding to the command of Allah's Messenger ﷺ when he said, {follow up a bad deed with a good deed that will efface it.}

9. The Light of Obedience Removes the Darkness of Disobedience: Carrying out acts of righteousness and doing so persistently, such as the prayer, fasting, the Ḥajj, the zakāt, *jihād*, the remembrance of Allah the Exalted, and other good, pious actions, efface whatever the Muslim has neglected, in terms of mistakes and sins. This has been established by several authentic ḥadīths, some of which we will mention here:

- The ḥadīth in the two *Ṣaḥīḥ* collections: {Whoever fasts Ramaḍān with faith and anticipation of reward will have his previous sins forgiven.}

- The ḥadīth in Muslim: {Shall I not show you that with which Allah effaces mistakes and raises people in rank?} They said, 'Indeed, O Messenger of Allah.' He said, {To perform *wuḍū'* properly when it is difficult (*makārih*), to take many steps to the masjid and to wait for the prayer after the prayer.} To perform *wuḍū'* properly means completely and fully. *Makārih* refers to difficult circumstances, such as extreme cold and the like.

- The ḥadīth in the two *Ṣaḥīḥ* collections: {Whoever perform the Ḥajj to this house without any obscenity or iniquity has his sins removed like the day his mother gave birth to him.}

These are in addition to the unequivocal verses in Allah's Book ﷻ concerning acts of obedience expiating bad deeds. You have seen some of them and some of them are still to come.

10. Repentance is a Condition for the Expiation of Enormities: The Muslims have made consensus that good deeds expiate minor sins. As for enormities – which refers to every sin that Allah the Exalted has threatened to punish severely, such as disobeying parents, murder, consuming usury, drinking wine and so forth – there has to be repentance. The Exalted One has said,

﴿وَإِنِّي لَغَفَّارٌ لِّمَن تَابَ وَءَامَنَ وَعَمِلَ صَٰلِحًا ثُمَّ ٱهْتَدَىٰ﴾

"But I am Ever-Forgiving to anyone who repents and believes and acts rightly, and then is guided." [Ṭaha 20:82]

This is if the sin is not connected to the right of another slave. If it is, such as in the case of theft, extortion, murder and so forth, then people's rights must be restored, or one seeks forgiveness from them and they forgive. If that is achieved, one can then hope that Allah the Exalted will accept and efface the sins, or indeed turn them into good deeds. Allah the Exalted has said,

﴿إِلَّا مَن تَابَ وَءَامَنَ وَعَمِلَ عَمَلًا صَٰلِحًا فَأُوْلَٰٓئِكَ يُبَدِّلُ ٱللَّهُ سَيِّـَٔاتِهِمْ حَسَنَٰتٍ ۗ وَكَانَ ٱللَّهُ غَفُورًا رَّحِيمًا﴾

"except for those who repent and believe and act rightly: Allah will transform the wrong actions of such people into good". [al-Furqān 25:70]

If neither redemption nor absolution is achieved, accounts will be settled on the Day of Standing.

Al-Bukhārī has related from Abū Saʿīd al-Khudrī ﷺ that the Messenger of Allah ﷺ said, {When the believers have been released from the Fire, they are detained on a bridge between Paradise and the Fire. They will settle the accounts concerning whatever wrongs they perpetrated against one another in this worldly life, until they have been purified and cleansed. Then they will be allowed to enter Paradise.} It has been said that whoever has wronged someone else, that person will get a portion of his share of Paradise.

It is from Allah's favour ﷻ that if the legally accountable person does not have any minor sins, righteous actions will have an effect on major sins. His sin will be mitigated to the extent that minor sins are expiated. If he does not have any sins, major or minor, He the Glorified will multiply his rewards.

11. Good Character is the Foundation for Establishing Human Civilization: In this advice, the Messenger of Allah ﷺ is showing that which will sort out the life of the individual and put the community in order, which is to treat people with good manners and character, to treat people the way one wants to be treated. The Muslim thus becomes amicable. He loves people and they love him. He honours them and they honour him. He treats them well and they treat him well. When every individual in a community is driven to carry out his obligations, with contentment and serenity, matters fall into order, the right values prevail and civilization is established.

Good character is valued by all nations, and it has an exalted station in Islam, which has devoted remarkable concern to it. Sufficient evidence for this is found in the plethora of verses and ḥadīth that strongly encourage noble character and elucidate the precedence of the one who adheres to it and is characterised by it.

The verses include the Exalted's statement:

﴿خُذِ ٱلْعَفْوَ وَأْمُرْ بِٱلْعُرْفِ وَأَعْرِضْ عَنِ ٱلْجَٰهِلِينَ﴾

"Make allowances for people, command what is right, and turn away from the ignorant". [al-ʾAʿrāf 7:199]

And His ﷻ statement:

﴿ٱدْفَعْ بِٱلَّتِى هِىَ أَحْسَنُ فَإِذَا ٱلَّذِى بَيْنَكَ وَبَيْنَهُۥ عَدَٰوَةٌ كَأَنَّهُۥ وَلِىٌّ حَمِيمٌ﴾

"Repel the bad with something better and, if there is enmity between you and someone else, he will be like a bosom friend." [Fuṣṣilat 41:34]

As for the ḥadīths, Ibn Ḥibbān has related his statement ﷺ in his *Ṣaḥīḥ*: {Shall I not inform you of the most beloved of you to Allah, and which of you will be sitting closest to me on the Day of Standing?} They said, 'Indeed.' He replied, {The best of you in character.} Aḥmad and Abū Dāwūd have related his statement: {The best of you are the best of you in character}, as well as his statement: {The most perfect believers in faith are the best of them in character}, and there are other verses and ḥadīth that you have seen and others that you will see while commentating on this ḥadīth, if Allah the Exalted so wills. All of the above is gathered in what al-Bukhārī has related in the Book of Etiquette, as well as al-Ḥākim and al-Bayhaqī, in which he ﷺ said, {I have only been sent to perfect noble character.}

12. Acquiring Good Character: It is possible for a person to acquire good, exalted character. It is mentioned in a narration from Muʿādh ibn Jabal رضي الله عنه related by al-Ḥākim and others with varying wordings, that he ﷺ said, {Have good character with people}, and in another wording: {Beautify your character as much as you can.} Good character can be acquired in the following ways:

- The best way is to imitate the Messenger of Allah ﷺ in good character, and Allah ﷻ commanded us to do so when He ﷻ said,

﴿لَّقَدْ كَانَ لَكُمْ فِى رَسُولِ ٱللَّهِ أُسْوَةٌ حَسَنَةٌ﴾

"You have an excellent model in the Messenger of Allah." [al-Aḥzāb 33:21]

It suffices us that his good character ﷺ was of a lofty standard, because Allah the Exalted described him in his Wise Qurʾān by saying,

﴿وَإِنَّكَ لَعَلَىٰ خُلُقٍ عَظِيمٍ﴾

"Indeed you are truly vast in character." [al-Qalam 68:4]

- Other ways of acquiring praiseworthy character include keeping the company of scholars, people of *taqwā*, and those who have virtuous character, while avoiding evil people and those that commit vile and wicked actions. Allah ﷻ said,

﴿وَٱصْبِرْ نَفْسَكَ مَعَ ٱلَّذِينَ يَدْعُونَ رَبَّهُم بِٱلْغَدَوٰةِ وَٱلْعَشِيِّ يُرِيدُونَ وَجْهَهُۥ ۖ وَلَا تَعْدُ عَيْنَاكَ عَنْهُمْ

تُرِيدُ زِينَةَ ٱلْحَيَوٰةِ ٱلدُّنْيَا ۖ وَلَا تُطِعْ مَنْ أَغْفَلْنَا قَلْبَهُۥ عَن ذِكْرِنَا وَٱتَّبَعَ هَوَىٰهُ وَكَانَ أَمْرُهُۥ فُرُطًا﴾

"Restrain yourself patiently with those who call on their Lord morning and evening, desiring His Face. Do not turn your eyes from them, desiring the attractions of this world. And do not obey someone whose heart We have made neglectful of Our remembrance and who follows his own whims and desires and whose life has transgressed all bounds." [al-Kahf 18:28]

13. Noble Character: Excellent character includes maintaining ties of kinship, pardoning and forgiving, and giving to someone who withholds from you. Al-Ḥākim and others have related from ʿUqbah ibn ʿĀmir al-Juhanī رضي الله عنه who said, 'The Messenger of Allah ﷺ said to me, {O ʿUqbah, shall I not inform you of the best character of the people of this life and the Hereafter? Maintain ties with those who cut you off, give to those who withhold from you, and forgive those who wrong you.}

In one of Aḥmad's narrations: {You pardon the one who insults you.}

Good character includes being cheerful, being forbearing and modest, showing people love and affection and not having a bad opinion of them, and protecting them from harm. He ﷺ has said, {Do not think little of any form of courtesy, even if you meet your brother with a smile on your face}, as related by Muslim. In other words, be radiant and joyful. He also said, {Let him refrain from evil, and that will be a form of charity for him}, as related by al-Bukhārī and Muslim.

14. The ḥadīth informs that good character and treating people politely and courteously are from the perfection of faith and the attributes of the people of *taqwā*. It is from the perfection of *taqwā* to dislike the people of disobedience and to refrain from socialising with them and mixing with them, if they do not take good counsel and do not refrain from that which is wrong.

THE NINETEENTH ḤADĪTH

عَوْنُ اللهِ تعالى وَحِفْظُهُ وَنَصْرُهُ وَتَأْيِيدُهُ

عَنْ أَبِي الْعَبَّاسِ عَبْدِ اللهِ بِنِ عَبَّاسٍ ﷺ قَالَ: كُنْتُ خَلْفَ النَّبِيِّ ﷺ يَوْمًا، فَقَالَ: ﴿يَا غُلَامُ،
إِنِّي أُعَلِّمُكَ كَلِمَاتٍ: احْفَظِ اللهَ يَحْفَظْكَ، احْفَظِ اللهَ تَجِدْهُ تُجَاهَكَ، إِذَا سَأَلْتَ فَاسْأَلِ اللهَ،
وَإِذَا اسْتَعَنْتَ فَاسْتَعِنْ بِاللهِ، وَاعْلَمْ أَنَّ الْأُمَّةَ لَوِ اجْتَمَعَتْ عَلَى أَنْ يَنْفَعُوكَ بِشَيْءٍ لَمْ يَنْفَعُوكَ إِلَّا
بِشَيْءٍ قَدْ كَتَبَهُ اللهُ لَكَ، وَإِنِ اجْتَمَعُوا عَلَى أَنْ يَضُرُّوكَ بِشَيْءٍ لَمْ يَضُرُّوكَ إِلَّا بِشَيْءٍ قَدْ كَتَبَهُ اللهُ
عَلَيْكَ، رُفِعَتِ الْأَقْلَامُ وَجَفَّتِ الصُّحُفُ.﴾ رواه الترمذي وقال: حديث حسن صحيح.

وفي رواية غير الترمذي: ﴿احْفَظِ اللهَ تَجِدْهُ أَمَامَكَ، تَعَرَّفْ إِلَى اللهِ فِي الرَّخَاءِ يَعْرِفْكَ فِي الشِّدَّةِ،
وَاعْلَمْ أَنَّ مَا أَخْطَأَكَ لَمْ يَكُنْ لِيُصِيبَكَ، وَمَا أَصَابَكَ لَمْ يَكُنْ لِيُخْطِئَكَ، وَاعْلَمْ أَنَّ النَّصْرَ مَعَ الصَّبْرِ،
وَأَنَّ الْفَرَجَ مَعَ الْكَرْبِ، وَأَنَّ مَعَ الْعُسْرِ يُسْرًا.﴾

Allah the Exalted's Help, Protection, Assistance and Support

It is on the authority of Abū al-ʿAbbās ʿAbdullah ibn ʿAbbās ﷺ who said, 'I was behind the Prophet ﷺ one day and he said, {Boy, I will teach you some words. Be mindful of Allah and He will be mindful of you. Be mindful of Allah and you will find Him in front of you. When you ask, ask Allah. When you seek help, seek help from Allah. If all of creation came together to benefit you with something, they would only benefit you with something that Allah had already written for you. If they came together to harm you with something, they would only harm you with something that Allah had already written against you. The pens have been lifted and the pages have dried.} At-Tirmidhī had related it and said that it is a good, authentic ḥadīth.

In a narration other than that of at-Tirmidhī: {Be mindful of Allah and you will find Him in front of you. Get to know Allah in times of ease and He will know you in times of adversity. Know that whatever misses you was never going to hit, and whatever hits you was never going to miss. Know that help is with patience, deliverance is with distress, and that with difficulty there is ease.}

At-Tirmidhī has collected this ḥadīth in the Description of the Hour, the Softening of Hearts and Carefulness from the Messenger of Allah ﷺ (in the chapter entitled: {Rather, O Ḥanẓalah, an hour and an hour}), no.2016, and Aḥmad has collected it in his *Musnad*: 1/307. The aforementioned wording has been related by ʿAbd ibn Ḥumayd in his *Musnad*, as the commentators of *The Forty* have mentioned.

The Importance of the Ḥadīth:
Ibn Rajab al-Ḥanbalī says in his book *Jāmiʿ al-ʿUlūm wa al-Ḥikam*, 'This ḥadīth comprises great advice and comprehensive principles that are some of the most important matters of the Religion, such that one of the scholars said, "I reflected on this ḥadīth and it astonished me. I was almost confused. Alas for my ignorance of this ḥadīth and my paltry understanding of its meanings"'.

The Language of the Ḥadīth:
(خلف النبي ﷺ) *khalf an-nabī*: i.e. riding behind him on a mount.

(يا غلام) *yā ghulām*: which is a boy from the time he is weaned until he is nine years of age, and he was about ten years old at that time.

(كلمات) *kalimāt*: i.e. sentences bearing advice with which Allah will benefit you.

(احفظ الله) *iḥfaẓ illāh*: know His boundaries and stay within them, adhere to the obligations He has laid down and persist in having *taqwā* of Him by doing what He has commanded and leaving what He has prohibited.

(يحفظك) *yaḥfaẓka*: He will preserve you and protect you with regards to your person and your family, your religion and your worldly life.

(تُجاهك) *tujāhak*: in front of you, i.e. you will find Him with you, protecting you and supporting you, helping you and assisting you, wherever you are.

(سألت) *sa'alta*: you want to ask for something of this world or of the Religion.

(استعنت) *istaʿanta*: you seek help on matters of this world or of the Hereafter.

(الأمة) *al-ummah*: what is meant is all other intelligent creatures.

(رفعت الأقلام) *rufiʿat al-aqlām*: they are no longer writing, what is meant is that everything has been predestined in Allah the Exalted's knowledge and it is settled.

(جفت الصحف) *jaffat as-ṣuḥuf*: what is meant by *ṣuḥuf* is what the predestinations of creatures are written on, such as the Preserved Tablet. Their dryness means that the matter is finished and settled, there will not be any change or alteration.

(الرخاء) *ar-rakhāʾ*: wealth, security, comfort, health, strength and so forth.

Legal Matters and Other Guidance from the Ḥadīth:

1. The Prophet's Endeavour ﷺ to instruct the Ummah and Raise a Model Generation of Believers: The Messenger of Allah ﷺ was keen to plant sound creed in the souls of the believers, and especially the youth amongst them, which is nothing strange. Allah the Exalted has described him by saying,

﴿لَقَدْ جَآءَكُمْ رَسُولٌ مِّنْ أَنفُسِكُمْ عَزِيزٌ عَلَيْهِ مَا عَنِتُّمْ
حَرِيصٌ عَلَيْكُم بِٱلْمُؤْمِنِينَ رَءُوفٌ رَّحِيمٌ﴾

> **"A Messenger has come to you from among yourselves. Your suffering is distressing to him; he is deeply concerned for you; he is gentle and merciful to the believers."** [at-Tawbah 9:128]

One day, he sat his cousin, ʿAbdullah ibn ʿAbbās behind him and gave him these wonderful pieces of advice, which, by their nature, make the Muslim adhere to Allah the Exalted's commands and seek help and victory from Him alone. He thus becomes brave and courageous; situations do not scare him and dangers do not frighten him. He says the truth and with Allah he does not fear the blame of those who blame, because he knows that the entire affair is in Allah's hands, the Mighty, the Wise, and that no one can harm him or benefit him except with Allah the Exalted's permission.

2. Eternal Words and a Wise Method: Ibn ʿAbbās is sharing with us this comprehensive advice that the Messenger of Allah ﷺ gave him while he was riding behind him. Due to the importance of this advice, and due to the beneficial instructions it contains that deserve a person's care and attention, he ﷺ get his attention and calls him: {Boy}, so that his mind is focused and his heart is present. He then makes him desire what he is about to say to him, and draws his attention to the preciousness of the knowledge he is giving him by saying: {I will teach you some words.} Yes, they are words, but they contain some immense principles of the Religion that refine one's thinking, sharpen one's mind, illuminate one's intellect, firmly establish one's creed and strengthen one's certainty.

3. Be Mindful of Allah and He will Be Mindful of You: Adhere to Allah the Exalted's commands, stay within His bounds, do not go near them, and beware of transgressing them. Do what Allah has obligated you and do not be negligent therein, and stay away from what He has forbidden you and place a barrier between it and you. Then, look at how Allah the Exalted preserves your religion for you and protects your creed from deviation, how He protects you from anxieties of the soul and the filth of misguidance, how He protects you from the evils of creation, from the demons amongst both humans and jinn. Look at how He repels every harm or detriment from you, you and whoever follows your path, such as your family, your dependents and your relatives. Allah the Exalted has said,

﴿لَهُۥ مُعَقِّبَـٰتٌ مِّنۢ بَيْنِ يَدَيْهِ وَمِنْ خَلْفِهِۦ يَحْفَظُونَهُۥ مِنْ أَمْرِ ٱللَّهِ﴾

"There is a succession of angels in front of him and behind him, guarding him by Allah's command." [ar-Raʿd 13:11]

The meaning is that Allah the Exalted has angels that successively come to the slave, surrounding him from every side, by the command and permission of Allah ﷻ so that they can protect him from harm. And Allah the Exalted says regarding the preservation of progeny,

﴿وَكَانَ أَبُوهُمَا صَـٰلِحًا﴾

"Their father was one of the righteous." [al-Kahf 18:82]

If you are mindful of Allah the Exalted in your worldly life, He will be mindful of you in the Hereafter, and thus protect you from the Fire and prepare for you a Garden as wide as the heavens and the earth, prepared for the people of *taqwā*:

﴿وَسَارِعُوٓا۟ إِلَىٰ مَغْفِرَةٍ مِّن رَّبِّكُمْ وَجَنَّةٍ عَرْضُهَا ٱلسَّمَـٰوَٰتُ وَٱلْأَرْضُ أُعِدَّتْ لِلْمُتَّقِينَ﴾

"Race each other to forgiveness from your Lord and a Garden as wide as the heavens and the earth, prepared for the people who are godfearing." [Āl-ʿImrān 3:133]

Angels will call on you to welcome you and honour you:

﴿هَـٰذَا مَا تُوعَدُونَ لِكُلِّ أَوَّابٍ حَفِيظٍ ﴿٣٢﴾ مَّنْ خَشِىَ ٱلرَّحْمَـٰنَ بِٱلْغَيْبِ وَجَآءَ بِقَلْبٍ مُّنِيبٍ

﴿٣٣﴾ ٱدْخُلُوهَا بِسَلَـٰمٍ ۖ ذَٰلِكَ يَوْمُ ٱلْخُلُودِ ﴿٣٤﴾ لَهُم مَّا يَشَآءُونَ فِيهَا وَلَدَيْنَا مَزِيدٌ﴾

"This is what you were promised. It is for every careful penitent: those who fear the All-Merciful in the Unseen and come with a contrite heart. Enter it in peace. This is the Day of Timeless Eternity. They will have there everything they want and with Us there is still more." [Qāf 50:32-35]

Allah the Exalted will fulfil what He ﷻ gave you the glad tidings of:

﴿وَٱلْحَـٰفِظُونَ لِحُدُودِ ٱللَّهِ ۗ وَبَشِّرِ ٱلْمُؤْمِنِينَ﴾

"...those who preserve Allah's limits: give good news to the believers." [at-Tawbah 9:112]

The Messenger of Allah ﷺ would teach his Companions to ask Allah to protect them. In the two *Ṣaḥīḥ* collections, it is mentioned that he ﷺ commanded al-Barā' ibn 'Āzib ؓ to say before sleeping, {My Lord, if You take hold my soul, have mercy on it. If You send it back, protect it with what You protect Your righteous slaves.} In the *Ṣaḥīḥ* of Ibn Ḥibbān, there is the ḥadīth of 'Umar ؓ in which the Prophet ﷺ taught him to say, {O Allah, protect me with Islam when I am standing. Protect me with Islam when I am sitting. Protect me with Islam when I am sleeping. And do not answer the supplications of my enemies or those who are envious of me.}

4. Allah the Exalted's Assistance and Support: If someone is mindful of Allah the Exalted, Allah is with him, helping him and assisting him, protecting him and supporting him, granting him success and showing him the right way, whenever he is in darkness or anguish: {Be mindful of Allah and you will find Him in front of you.} You will find Him with you, guarding and protecting, assisting and supporting:

﴿إِنَّ ٱللَّهَ مَعَ ٱلَّذِينَ ٱتَّقَوا۟ وَّٱلَّذِينَ هُم مُّحْسِنُونَ﴾

"Allah is with those who have *taqwā* of Him and with those who do excellence." [an-Naḥl 16:128]

Qatādah said, 'Whoever has *taqwā* of Allah, Allah is with him. Whoever Allah is with has a platoon with him that will never be defeated, a guard who never sleeps and a guide who never leads astray'.

However, Allah the Exalted's help and support are connected to carrying out His commands and avoiding what He has prohibited. Whoever obeys Allah the Exalted, He will assist and support him. Whoever disobeys Him, He ﷻ will forsake and humiliate him:

﴿إِن تَنصُرُوا۟ ٱللَّهَ يَنصُرْكُمْ وَيُثَبِّتْ أَقْدَامَكُمْ﴾

"if you help Allah, He will help you and make your feet firm." [Muḥammad 47:7],

﴿إِن يَنصُرْكُمُ ٱللَّهُ فَلَا غَالِبَ لَكُمْ ۖ وَإِن يَخْذُلْكُمْ فَمَن ذَا ٱلَّذِى يَنصُرُكُم مِّنۢ بَعْدِهِۦ﴾

"If Allah helps you, no one can defeat you. If He forsakes you, who can help you after that?" [Āl 'Imrān 3:160]

5. Your Youth Before Your Old Age: Whoever is mindful of Allah when He is young and strong, Allah the Exalted will be mindful of him when he is old and weak. He will grant him hearing, sight and intellect, and give him a noble station on the Day of Standing. He will shade him with the shade of His Throne when there is no shade but his shade, as is established in the two *Ṣaḥīḥ* collections: {There are seven whom Allah will shade on the Day when there is no shade but His shade: the just ruler, the youth who grows up worshipping Allah ﷻ...}. Perhaps this is the secret behind him ﷺ giving this advice to his cousin ؓ who was a young boy at the beginning of his life, so that he would take advantage of his youth and its vitality. The Messenger of Allah ﷺ spoke the truth when he said, {Take advantage of five before five: your youth before your old age...}, as related by al-Ḥākim with an authentic chain of transmission. This is especially the case when the youth are the hope of the Ummah. They are the ones who will carry the call of truth and justice, while the people of evil and falsehood strive to tempt them and entice them. They therefore desperately need more attention and instruction, so that they can be firm in the face of these devils, whether human or jinn.

6. Allah the Exalted's Grateful Slaves are the People Who Receive Help and Support from Him, Glorified is He: The believer who wins Allah the Exalted's protection, support and providence is the grateful slave, who comprehends Allah's favour ﷻ and thus knows Him as He should be known. He obeys His commands, avoids what He has prohibited, maintains His limits and observes His rights. He enjoys immense blessings while temptations surround him and passions contend with him, but he rebels against them and turns away from them. He turns to Allah ﷻ and uses these blessings to please Him, and he seeks refuge in Him to protect him from slipping. Allah inspires him to show more gratitude, so that he can continue to receive His favour, while he declares his poverty before the Rich Beyond Need, the Praiseworthy, certain that all favour is in Allah's hand, He gives it whomever He wants:

﴿وَمَا بِكُم مِّن نِّعْمَةٍ فَمِنَ ٱللَّهِ ۖ ثُمَّ إِذَا مَسَّكُمُ ٱلضُّرُّ فَإِلَيْهِ تَجْـَٔرُونَ﴾
"Any blessing you have is from Allah." [an-Naḥl 16:53]

This special knowledge of Allah is what brings the slave closer to His Lord ﷻ. Allah's love is drawn to His slave who strives for Him, He answers his supplication, He gives him what he asks for, He saves him from nuisance that disturbs his livelihood, and He protects him from anything frightful that threatens his safety: {Get to know Allah in times of ease and He will know you in times of adversity.}

At-Tirmidhī has related that the Prophet ﷺ said, {Whoever is pleased that Allah answers his supplication in times of adversity, let him make abundant supplication in times of ease.}

It is regarding the like of this slave that Allah ﷻ says in the *ḥadīth qudsī*:[87] {If he asks Me, I give him, and if he seeks refuge in Me, I grant him refuge.}[88]

7. Turning to Allah the Exalted Alone for Help and Supplication: The Messenger of Allah ﷺ is instructing his cousin – and the sincere believers who follow his path – to call on Allah ﷻ is He, the Most High, the All-Powerful, always and forever when asking for something and when seeking refuge and support. He should not ask anyone else or seek help from anyone else. Likewise, his supplication and his gratitude should only be for Him. Forgiveness should only be sought from Him and he should not bow or prostate before anyone but Him. {When you ask, ask Allah. When you seek help, seek help from Allah.} Al-Bukhārī and Muslim have related that the Prophet ﷺ said, {Allah ﷻ says, 'Is there a caller so that I can answer his call? Is there an asker so that I can give him what he is asking? Is there a seeker of forgiveness so that I can forgive him?'}

8. Supplication is for the One who is Close and Quick to Respond: Supplication is only directed towards Allah ﷻ because He alone, the Exalted, says,

﴿ٱدْعُونِىٓ أَسْتَجِبْ لَكُمْ﴾

"Call on Me and I will answer you." [Ghāfir 40:60]

He ﷻ is the One who praises His believing slaves because they supplicate to Him ﷻ and ask of Him ﷻ:

﴿إِنَّهُمْ كَانُوا۟ يُسَـٰرِعُونَ فِى ٱلْخَيْرَٰتِ وَيَدْعُونَنَا رَغَبًا وَرَهَبًا ۖ وَكَانُوا۟ لَنَا خَـٰشِعِينَ﴾

"They outdid one another in good actions, calling out to Us in yearning and in awe, and humbling themselves to Us." [al-Anbiyā' 21:90]

Because He ﷻ is Close to His slaves, He ﷻ hears their supplications and answers their requests.

﴿وَإِذَا سَأَلَكَ عِبَادِى عَنِّى فَإِنِّى قَرِيبٌ ۖ أُجِيبُ دَعْوَةَ ٱلدَّاعِ إِذَا دَعَانِ ۖ

فَلْيَسْتَجِيبُوا۟ لِى وَلْيُؤْمِنُوا۟ بِى لَعَلَّهُمْ يَرْشُدُونَ﴾

"If My slaves ask you about Me, I am near. I answer the call of the caller when he calls on Me. They should therefore respond to Me and believe in Me so that hopefully they will be rightly guided." [al-Baqarah 2:186]

---

87 (tn): i.e. a text in which the Messenger of Allah ﷺ quotes a statement from Allah and it is not from the Qur'ān. Please see the 24th ḥadīth in this book for further details.

88 (tn): this is part of Ḥadīth 38.

9. Asking The One Who Never Wearies Of Giving: It is from the perfection of *tawḥīd* to leave asking people. Instead, the Muslim asks Allah alone concerning every single one of his affairs, because He the Glorified is the One who strongly encourages His slaves to ask Him. The Exalted One has said,

﴿وَسْـَٔلُوا۟ ٱللَّهَ مِن فَضْلِهِۦٓ﴾

"but ask Allah for His bounty." [an-Nisā' 4:32]

At-Tirmidhī has related that the Prophet ﷺ said, {Ask Allah of His bounty, for indeed Allah loves to be asked.} He the Glorified never wearies of being asked and requested, because His storehouses are full and are never depleted.

﴿مَا عِندَكُمْ يَنفَدُ ۖ وَمَا عِندَ ٱللَّهِ بَاقٍ﴾

"What is with you runs out but what is with Allah goes on forever." [an-Naḥl 16:96]

Indeed, He the Glorified is angry when the slave does not ask Him. At-Tirmidhī has related that he ﷺ said, {Allah is angry with whoever does not ask him, so let each of you ask his Lord for every single one of his needs, even if the strap on his sandal is ripped.} After all the above, can someone ask and request from a human being, who wearies of giving and angers at being asked? May Allah have mercy on the one who said:

Do not ask the Children of Adam for a need
Ask the One whose doors are never hidden
Allah becomes angry if you do not ask Him
And the Children of Adam become angry when they are asked

10. Asking Other than Allah the Exalted is Humiliation and Abasement: When people are asked, either they give or they withhold. If they give, they are benevolent, and if they withhold, they show contempt and they degrade. These are all things that cut into a Muslim's soul and put hatred and distress in his heart, diminish his honour, and impinge on his dignity. Maybe this is why he ﷺ made a covenant with those who pledged allegiance to him in Islam not to ask people for anything. A group of Companions made such a pledge, including Abū Bakr as-Ṣiddīq, Abū Dharr, Thawbān and 'Awf ibn Mālik ﷺ. One of them saw his whip or halter fall from his she-camel and did not ask anyone to hand it to him. This has been related by Muslim, Abū Dāwūd and others.

11. Seeking Help from the All-Powerful, Who is Never Overcome: Help should only be sought from the All-Powerful, who is capable of helping. The slave needs help in everything, big and small, and no one besides Allah the Glorified is capable of doing so. Everyone besides Him is incapable of protecting himself from harm or bringing about benefit. Whomever Allah helps is helped and whomever He forsakes is forsaken

﴿إِن يَنصُرْكُمُ ٱللَّهُ فَلَا غَالِبَ لَكُمْ ۖ وَإِن يَخْذُلْكُمْ فَمَن ذَا ٱلَّذِى يَنصُرُكُم مِّنۢ بَعْدِهِۦ﴾

"If Allah helps you, no one can defeat you. If He forsakes you, who can help you after that?" [Āl ʿImrān 3:160]

Rather, the slaves' hearts are in Allah's hand, He does what He wants with them. He directs the slave to help someone else or to refrain from doing so. Thus, let one turn to the real mover, which is Allah the Glorified. He is the One who gives and who withholds. He bestows blessings and favours and it suffice to rely on Him:

﴿وَمَن يَتَوَكَّلْ عَلَى ٱللَّهِ فَهُوَ حَسْبُهُۥٓ﴾

"Whoever puts his trust in Allah – He will be enough for Him." [at-Ṭalāq 65:3]

So, let them turn to Him for every matter:

﴿إِيَّاكَ نَعْبُدُ وَإِيَّاكَ نَسْتَعِينُ﴾

"You alone we worship. You alone we ask for help." [al-Fātiḥah 1:5]

12. Seeking Help from Other Than Allah the Exalted is Passivity and Weakness: Seeking help necessitates that the one seeking it manifest his weakness and neediness, and this humiliation and poverty should only be for Allah alone, because it is the reality of worship. If it is for other than Allah the Exalted, it is humiliation and passivity, there is no benefit in it. Seeking help is also an acknowledgment that the one whose help is being sought has the power to help the one seeking and to fulfil his objective, or that he can bring about benefit for him or ward off harm from him. These matters are never outside what Allah ﷻ has predestined, and whoever thinks they are has failed and is lost. Whoever seeks help from a slave is seeking refuge in a support that is not strong. Allah the Exalted has said,

﴿وَإِن يَمْسَسْكَ ٱللَّهُ بِضُرٍّ فَلَا كَاشِفَ لَهُۥٓ إِلَّا هُوَ ۖ وَإِن يُرِدْكَ بِخَيْرٍ فَلَا رَآدَّ لِفَضْلِهِۦ﴾

"If Allah afflicts you with harm, no one can remove it except Him. If He desires good for you, no one can avert his favour." [Yūnus 10:107]

He has also said,

﴿مَّا يَفْتَحِ ٱللَّهُ لِلنَّاسِ مِن رَّحْمَةٍ فَلَا مُمْسِكَ لَهَا ۖ وَمَا يُمْسِكْ فَلَا مُرْسِلَ لَهُۥ مِنۢ بَعْدِهِۦ﴾

"Any mercy Allah opens up to people, no one can withhold, and any He withholds, no one can afterwards release." [Fāṭir 35:2]

13. Faith in the Decree and Predestination is Serenity and Tranquillity: After becoming confident that Allah the Exalted will protect him and support him, and that he should rely on Him alone in all affairs, the slave does not worry about what the creation contrives or what other slaves do. Rather, he knows that good and evil are predestined by Allah the Exalted, and that benefit and harm are according to His Will. The creation has no say whatsoever in the matter:

﴿قُلْ كُلٌّ مِّنْ عِندِ ٱللَّهِ﴾

"Say, 'Everything comes from Allah.'" [an-Nisā' 4:78]

The slaves are only means, so that they can obtain reward or deserve punishment: {If all of creation came together to benefit you with something, they would only benefit you with something that Allah had already written for you. If they came together to harm you with something, they would only harm you with something that Allah had already written against you.}

﴿وَإِن يَمْسَسْكَ ٱللَّهُ بِضُرٍّ فَلَا كَاشِفَ لَهُۥٓ إِلَّا هُوَ ۖ وَإِن يَمْسَسْكَ بِخَيْرٍ فَهُوَ عَلَىٰ كُلِّ شَىْءٍ قَدِيرٌ﴾

"If Allah touches you with harm, none can remove it but Him. If He touches you with good, He has power over all things." [al-An'ām 6:17]

Thus, no one can cause any harm to come to you that Allah has not predestined against you. Rather, Allah ﷻ will repel it from you. Likewise, if someone wants to benefit you, they cannot do so if Allah ﷻ has not willed it:

﴿مَآ أَصَابَ مِن مُّصِيبَةٍ فِى ٱلْأَرْضِ وَلَا فِىٓ أَنفُسِكُمْ

إِلَّا فِى كِتَٰبٍ مِّن قَبْلِ أَن نَّبْرَأَهَآ ۚ إِنَّ ذَٰلِكَ عَلَى ٱللَّهِ يَسِيرٌ﴾

"Nothing occurs, either in the earth or in yourselves, without its being in a Book before we make it happen." [al-Ḥadīd 57:22]

Aḥmad and others have related that the Prophet ﷺ said, {Everything has a reality, and a slave does not attain the reality of faith until he knows that whatever hits him was never going to miss, and what misses him was never going to hit.}

14. Faith in the Decree and Predestination is Courage and Bravery: After establishing that benefit and harm have been decisively predestined, the person only attains that which was already in Allah's knowledge ﷻ. Therefore, let the believer hasten to what Allah has commanded. Let him speak the truth, even if it is against himself, and not fear with Allah the blame of those who blame. Let him stand up courageously and bravely, without fearing death or hoping for life, declaring the veracity of his certainty in the words of Allah ﷻ that he recites:

﴿قُل لَّن يُصِيبَنَآ إِلَّا مَا كَتَبَ ٱللَّهُ لَنَا هُوَ مَوْلَىٰنَا ۚ وَعَلَى ٱللَّهِ فَلْيَتَوَكَّلِ ٱلْمُؤْمِنُونَ﴾

"Say: 'Nothing can happen to us except what Allah has ordained for us. He is Our Master. It is in Allah that the believers should put their trust.'" [at-Tawbah 9:51]

Furthermore, there is no escaping what has been decreed for one:

﴿قُل لَّوْ كُنتُمْ فِى بُيُوتِكُمْ لَبَرَزَ ٱلَّذِينَ كُتِبَ عَلَيْهِمُ ٱلْقَتْلُ إِلَىٰ مَضَاجِعِهِمْ﴾

"Say, 'Even if you had been inside your homes, those people for whom being killed was decreed would have gone out to their place of death.'" [Āl 'Imrān 3:154]

In other words, if they had not gone out to the battlefield, and stayed in their homes, whoever had been predestined to be killed would have gone out to the places that they were killed in, voluntarily, so that they could be killed there.

15. Faith, Not Surrender; Trust, Not Indifference: Faith in the decree and predestination, according to the aforementioned meaning, shows us the falsehood of the claim made by those feeble cowards, those who surrender to their passions and desires, when they try to justify their deviance and misguidance and their ongoing persistence in disobedience, they justify it by saying that Allah the Exalted predestined it against them. They say this even though Allah the Exalted, who has commanded us to believe in His decree and predestination, has also commanded us to act. The Glorified One has said,

﴿وَقُلِ ٱعْمَلُوا۟ فَسَيَرَى ٱللَّهُ عَمَلَكُمْ﴾

"Say: 'Act, for Allah will see your actions.'" [at-Tawbah 9:105]

His Messenger ﷺ who is our model in everything, has made it clear to us that the Muslim must make use of the means, by acting, striving and expending effort. Whoever leaves the means and uses predestination to justify it has disobeyed Allah the Exalted and His Messenger ﷺ and he has contravened the Revealed Law of Islam. This is because leaving the means is indifference and laziness, which Islam does not sanction. Making use of the means while relying on Allah the Exalted alone to achieve results is truth in Allah and faith. Muslim has related that the Prophet ﷺ said, {Act, for everyone is facilitated to do what they were created for.}

16. Victory is with Patience: The life of man is various battles. He is exposed therein to many enemies, of all kinds, and his victory in these battles is connected to the extent of his patience and is the consequence of it. Patience is the way to the victory that is sought. It is the effective weapon that subdues the enemy in his various forms, whether he is hidden or in the open. This is why Allah ﷻ has made it the subject of the exam for His slaves in this life, to distinguish the filthy from the pure, so that the truthful and certain is know from the doubtful hypocrite:

﴿وَلَنَبْلُوَنَّكُمْ حَتَّىٰ نَعْلَمَ الْمُجَٰهِدِينَ مِنكُمْ وَالصَّٰبِرِينَ وَنَبْلُوَاْ أَخْبَارَكُمْ﴾

"We will test you until We know the true fighters among you and those who are steadfast and test what is reported of you." [Muḥammad 47:31]

﴿لَتُبْلَوُنَّ فِي أَمْوَٰلِكُمْ وَأَنفُسِكُمْ وَلَتَسْمَعُنَّ مِنَ الَّذِينَ أُوتُواْ الْكِتَٰبَ مِن قَبْلِكُمْ وَمِنَ الَّذِينَ

أَشْرَكُوٓاْ أَذًى كَثِيرًا ۚ وَإِن تَصْبِرُواْ وَتَتَّقُواْ فَإِنَّ ذَٰلِكَ مِنْ عَزْمِ الْأُمُورِ﴾

"You will be tested in your wealth and in yourselves and you will hear many abusive words from those given the Book before you and from those who are idolaters. But if you are steadfast and have *taqwā*, that is the most resolute of matters," [Āl 'Imrān 3:186]

i.e. the matters that every sane person should be resolute in and be accustomed to, because of the perfection of virtue and honour that they contain.

Allah the Exalted has said in describing the righteous, the people of *taqwā* and the truthful,

﴿وَالصَّٰبِرِينَ فِي الْبَأْسَاءِ وَالضَّرَّاءِ وَحِينَ الْبَأْسِ ۗ أُوْلَٰٓئِكَ الَّذِينَ صَدَقُواْ ۖ وَأُوْلَٰٓئِكَ هُمُ الْمُتَّقُونَ﴾

"...and are steadfast in poverty and illness and in battle. It is they who are true in faith, and it is they who are mindful of Allah." [al-Baqarah 2:177]

Patience, as it has been defined, is to keep the ego in check, i.e. to control it, according to what is required by the intellect and the Revealed Law. Likewise, one keeps it in check and prevents it from that which the intellect and the Revealed Law prevent it from. If we were to review Allah's verses ﷻ and the ḥadīths of the Messenger of Allah ﷺ we would find that the word patience (*ṣabr*) appears in many places, and in each place it bears the abovementioned definition, aiming at one end and realising one result, which is victory and triumph. These places include:

A. Patience with doing acts of obedience and leaving disobedience: Doing what Allah the Exalted has commanded and leaving what He has prohibited is a responsibility. There is no doubt that it is a type of weight on the human soul, and therefore a person must strive to overcome his real enemy, which is embodied in the *nafs*,[89] one's passions and Shayṭān:

﴿إِنَّ ٱلنَّفْسَ لَأَمَّارَةٌۢ بِٱلسُّوٓءِ﴾

"The *nafs* commands to evil acts" [Yūsuf 12:53],

﴿وَلَا تَتَّبِعِ ٱلْهَوَىٰ فَيُضِلَّكَ عَن سَبِيلِ﴾

"...and do not follow your own passions" [Ṣād 38:26],

﴿إِنَّ ٱلشَّيْطَـٰنَ لَكُمْ عَدُوٌّ﴾

"Shayṭān is your enemy." [Fāṭir 35:6]

These hidden enemies places temptations in front of a person, and embellish for him the love of worldly appetites. They entice him to turn away from obedience and incline towards disobedience. They are tireless in what they do, never leaving him alone and never subsiding. Thus, a person must strive to subdue them, push his *nafs* to be obedient, and make his passions follow what Allah's ﷻ legislation has brought. All of this involves patience, endurance, struggle and sacrifice. Allah the Exalted has said,

﴿وَٱتَّبِعْ مَا يُوحَىٰٓ إِلَيْكَ وَٱصْبِرْ حَتَّىٰ يَحْكُمَ ٱللَّهُ ۚ وَهُوَ خَيْرُ ٱلْحَـٰكِمِينَ﴾

"Follow what has been revealed to you and be steadfast until Allah's judgment comes." [Yūnus 10:109]

He ﷻ has also said,

﴿رَّبُّ ٱلسَّمَـٰوَٰتِ وَٱلْأَرْضِ وَمَا بَيْنَهُمَا فَٱعْبُدْهُ وَٱصْطَبِرْ لِعِبَـٰدَتِهِۦ﴾

"He is Lord of the heavens and the earth and everything in between them, so worship Him and persevere in His worship." [Maryam 19:65]

He ﷺ has said, {The *mujāhid* is the one who does *jihād* against his *nafs* for the sake of Allah}, as related by at-Tirmidhī and Ibn Ḥibbān.

89 (tn): i.e. the self, or ego.

There is no doubt that whoever is able to confine his *nafs* to what pleases Allah the Exalted, and thus obey Him avoid disobeying Him, has overcome his hidden enemy and subdued his *nafs*, his Shayṭān and his passions. This is a victory that no other victory comes close to, because with it the person controls himself and becomes free from the captivity of desires, passions and the whisperings of Shayṭān. When that battle with the internal enemy has ended with him being vanquished and subdued, the truth shines forth in the believer's heart and illuminates it, and thus he follows Allah's ﷻ path:

﴿وَٱلَّذِينَ جَٰهَدُوا۟ فِينَا لَنَهْدِيَنَّهُمْ سُبُلَنَا﴾

"As for those who do *jihād* in Our Way, We will guide them to Our Paths." [al-ʿAnkabūt 29:69]

The Messenger of Allah ﷺ spoke the truth when he said, {Patience is radiant light}, as related by Muslim.[90]

B. Patience with Calamities: In this life, man is exposed to catastrophes that beset his person, his property, his family and his dependents, or his safety and serenity, and there is no doubt that this has a severe impact on a person, allowing despair to overcome him:

﴿وَإِذَا مَسَّهُ ٱلشَّرُّ كَانَ يَـُٔوسًا﴾

"When evil touches him, he despairs." [al-Isrāʾ 17:83]

Restlessness (halʿ) and anxiety (jazʿ) take over:

﴿إِنَّ ٱلْإِنسَٰنَ خُلِقَ هَلُوعًا ۝١٩ إِذَا مَسَّهُ ٱلشَّرُّ جَزُوعًا﴾

"Truly man was created restless, anxious when bad things happen." [al-Maʿārij 70:19-20]

Halʿ is more intense than jazʿ, and jazʿ is intense fear.

A person in this state is defeated. He cannot carve a path to victory in this life. This is why Allah ﷻ urges the believers to be resolute, to hold their ground in the face of these calamities, which are real, no doubt, and rise above weakness and lassitude and carve their path to victory and prosperity, arming themselves with patience, which is the foundation of exaltedness and the secret of success.

90 (tn): Please see the 23rd ḥadīth in this book.

﴿وَلَنَبْلُوَنَّكُم بِشَيْءٍ مِّنَ ٱلْخَوْفِ وَٱلْجُوعِ وَنَقْصٍ مِّنَ ٱلْأَمْوَٰلِ وَٱلْأَنفُسِ وَٱلثَّمَرَٰتِ ۗ وَبَشِّرِ ٱلصَّـٰبِرِينَ ﴿١٥٥﴾ ٱلَّذِينَ إِذَآ أَصَـٰبَتْهُم مُّصِيبَةٌ قَالُوٓا۟ إِنَّا لِلَّهِ وَإِنَّآ إِلَيْهِ رَٰجِعُونَ ﴿١٥٦﴾ أُو۟لَـٰٓئِكَ عَلَيْهِمْ صَلَوَٰتٌ مِّن رَّبِّهِمْ وَرَحْمَةٌ ۖ وَأُو۟لَـٰٓئِكَ هُمُ ٱلْمُهْتَدُونَ﴾

"We will test you with a certain amount of fear and hunger and loss of wealth and life and fruits. But give good news to the steadfast, those who, when disaster strikes them, say, 'We belong to Allah and to Him we will return.' Those are the people who will have blessings and mercy from their Lord; they are the ones who are guided." [al-Baqarah 2:155-157]

There is no doubt that these people are guided to the path of might, honour and glory, especially those who hold their ground as soon as a catastrophe strikes: {Patience is only at the first blow}, which is agreed upon. They therefore come out of it victorious, facing life with absolute courage and boldness, so that they can turn the trial that has befallen them into something good that they can benefit from, in this life and the Hereafter. Thus, their state in times of trial is no different from their state in times of ease. {How astonishing is the affair of the believer! His entire affair is good, and this is only for the believer. When something good happens to him, he is grateful, and that is good for him. When something bad happens to him, he is patient, and that is good for him.} Related by Muslim.

The Messenger of Allah ﷺ gave us the most wonderful example of this when his daughter was sent to him and she said, 'My son is approaching death, so come to us.' He sent his greeting of peace and said, {To Allah belongs what He takes and what He gives. Everything has its appointed time with him, so be patient and anticipate.} In other words, on account of her patience, she should seek reward from her Lord so that it is counted among her good deeds.

C. Patience with Harm from the Creation: A persons' life is surrounded by people with different characters and temperaments, and it is inevitable that they will perpetrate misdeeds and all kinds of harm, and if a person is unable to bear that, he fails and loses, and lives a hellish life. If he can bear with it and be patient, pardon and forgive, he will win and be victorious, and live in happiness, fulfilment and love:

﴿فَٱعْفُوا۟ وَٱصْفَحُوا۟ حَتَّىٰ يَأْتِىَ ٱللَّهُ بِأَمْرِهِۦٓ﴾

"But you should pardon and overlook until Allah gives his command." [al-Baqarah 2:109]

﴿ٱدْفَعْ بِٱلَّتِى هِىَ أَحْسَنُ فَإِذَا ٱلَّذِى بَيْنَكَ وَبَيْنَهُۥ عَدَٰوَةٌ كَأَنَّهُۥ وَلِىٌّ حَمِيمٌ﴾

"Repel the bad with something better and, if there is enmity between you and someone else, he will be like a bosom friend." [Fuṣṣilat 41:34]

There is no doubt that this is a sign of manliness.

﴿وَلَمَن صَبَرَ وَغَفَرَ إِنَّ ذَٰلِكَ لَمِنْ عَزْمِ ٱلْأُمُورِ﴾

"But if someone is steadfast and forgives, that is the most resolute course to follow." [ash-Shūrā 42:43]

No one takes this on except the one who believes in Allah ﷻ and seeks help from Him:

﴿وَجَعَلْنَا بَعْضَكُمْ لِبَعْضٍ فِتْنَةً أَتَصْبِرُونَ ۗ وَكَانَ رَبُّكَ بَصِيرًا﴾

"But We have made some of you a trial for others to see if you will be steadfast. Your Lord sees everything". [al-Furqān 25:20]

And he hopes for reward from Him:

﴿وَٱلَّذِينَ صَبَرُوا۟ ٱبْتِغَآءَ وَجْهِ﴾

"...those who are steadfast in seeking the Face of their Lord." [ar-Raʿd 13:22]

In all of this, there lies the greatest victory.

D. Patience in the Field of Calling to Allah ﷻ Enjoining the Right and Forbidding the Wrong: This is what Allah the Exalted commanded His Messengers to, and advised the wise and sincere amongst His slaves. The Exalted One has said,

﴿وَأْمُرْ أَهْلَكَ بِٱلصَّلَوٰةِ وَٱصْطَبِرْ عَلَيْهَا ۖ لَا نَسْـَٔلُكَ رِزْقًا ۖ نَّحْنُ نَرْزُقُكَ ۗ وَٱلْعَـٰقِبَةُ لِلتَّقْوَىٰ﴾

"Instruct your family to perform the prayer, and patiently persist in doing so." [Ṭaha 20:132]

He ﷻ has also said,

﴿وَأْمُرْ بِٱلْمَعْرُوفِ وَٱنْهَ عَنِ ٱلْمُنكَرِ وَٱصْبِرْ عَلَىٰ مَآ أَصَابَكَ ۖ إِنَّ ذَٰلِكَ مِنْ عَزْمِ ٱلْأُمُورِ﴾

"...and command what is right and forbid what is wrong and be steadfast in the face of all that happens to you." [Luqmān 31:17]

He ﷻ said to His Messenger ﷺ

﴿وَٱهْجُرْهُمْ هَجْرًا جَمِيلًا﴾

"...cut yourself off from them – but courteously." [al-Muzzammil 73:10]

The one who calls to Allah ﷻ has to be moulded by the trait of patience, and bear whatever comes his way on the path of calling, until decisive victory is realised for him over Allah's ﷻ enemies. The Exalted One has said,

﴿فَٱصْبِرْ إِنَّ وَعْدَ ٱللَّهِ حَقٌّ ۖ وَلَا يَسْتَخِفَّنَّكَ ٱلَّذِينَ لَا يُوقِنُونَ﴾

"So be steadfast. Allah's promise is true. Do not let those who have no certainty belittle you." [ar-Rūm 30:60]

If he hastens the result, he will fail and lose, and his striving will go to waste. Allah the Exalted said to His Chosen Messenger ﷺ

﴿فَٱصْبِرْ كَمَا صَبَرَ أُو۟لُوا۟ ٱلْعَزْمِ مِنَ ٱلرُّسُلِ وَلَا تَسْتَعْجِل لَّهُمْ﴾

"So be steadfast as the Messengers with firm resolve were also steadfast. And do not seek to hasten it for them". [al-Aḥqāf 46:35]

And He ﷻ said,

﴿فَٱصْبِرْ صَبْرًا جَمِيلًا ۝٥ إِنَّهُمْ يَرَوْنَهُۥ بَعِيدًا ۝٦ وَنَرَىٰهُ قَرِيبًا﴾

"Therefore be patient with a patience that is beautiful. They see it as something distant, but We see it as very close." [al-Maʿārij 70:5-7]

E. Patience in the Field of Battle and Fighting the Disbelievers: *Jihād* is where death and danger are expected, and souls dislike it. The Exalted One has said,

﴿كُتِبَ عَلَيْكُمُ ٱلْقِتَالُ وَهُوَ كُرْهٌ لَّكُمْ﴾

"Fighting is prescribed for you even if it is hated by you." [al-Baqarah 2:216]

Therefore, the believer who has been obligated to meet Allah's enemies ﷻ on the battlefield must arm himself, before anything else, with patience, and be more patient and forbearing than his enemy. The Exalted One has said,

﴿يَٰٓأَيُّهَا ٱلَّذِينَ ءَامَنُوا۟ ٱصْبِرُوا۟ وَصَابِرُوا۟ وَرَابِطُوا۟ وَٱتَّقُوا۟ ٱللَّهَ لَعَلَّكُمْ تُفْلِحُونَ﴾

"You who believe, be steadfast; be supreme in steadfastness; be firm on the battlefield; and have *taqwā* of Allah; so that hopefully you will be successful". [Āl ʿImrān 3:200]

Allah ﷻ joined between jihād and patience when He ﷻ said,

﴿ثُمَّ جَٰهَدُوا۟ وَصَبَرُوٓا۟﴾

"...and then did *jihād* and remained steadfast." [an-Naḥl 16:110]

He ﷻ has also made patience a condition for overcoming and subduing the enemy. He ﷻ has said,

﴿إِن يَكُن مِّنكُمْ عِشْرُونَ صَٰبِرُونَ يَغْلِبُوا۟ مِا۟ئَتَيْنِ﴾

"If there are twenty of you who are steadfast, they will overcome two hundred." [al-Anfāl 8:65]

Then He ﷻ mitigated the difference and said,

﴿فَإِن يَكُن مِّنكُم مِّائَةٌ صَابِرَةٌ يَغْلِبُواْ مِائَتَيْنِ﴾

"If there are a hundred of you who are steadfast, they will overcome two hundred." [al-Anfāl 8:66]

He ﷻ made His help and support, by way of the angels of the sky, conditional on patience when coming to blows with the enemy. The Majestic One says,

﴿بَلَىٰ إِن تَصْبِرُواْ وَتَتَّقُواْ وَيَأْتُوكُم مِّن فَوْرِهِمْ هَـٰذَا يُمْدِدْكُمْ رَبُّكُم

بِخَمْسَةِ ءَالَـٰفٍ مِّنَ ٱلْمَلَـٰئِكَةِ مُسَوِّمِينَ﴾

"Yes indeed! But if you are steadfast and have *taqwā* and they come upon you suddenly, your Lord will reinforce you with five thousand angels, clearly identified." [Āl ʿImrān 3:125]

Likewise, He the Glorified made the patience of His believing friends a condition for foiling the plots of the unbelievers, causing their plans to fail and them not being harmed by them. The Exalted One has said,

﴿وَإِن تَصْبِرُواْ وَتَتَّقُواْ لَا يَضُرُّكُمْ كَيْدُهُمْ شَيْئًا إِنَّ ٱللَّهَ بِمَا يَعْمَلُونَ مُحِيطٌ﴾

"But if you are steadfast and have *taqwā*, their scheming will not harm you in any way." [Āl ʿImrān 3:120]

This means that failure can happen to the believers and Allah the Exalted can abandon them when they do not show patience, and especially when there are other factors that necessitate it. The Exalted One has said,

﴿يَـٰٓأَيُّهَا ٱلَّذِينَ ءَامَنُوٓاْ إِذَا لَقِيتُمْ فِئَةً فَٱثْبُتُواْ وَٱذْكُرُواْ ٱللَّهَ كَثِيرًا لَّعَلَّكُمْ تُفْلِحُونَ وَأَطِيعُواْ

ٱللَّهَ وَرَسُولَهُۥ وَلَا تَنَـٰزَعُواْ فَتَفْشَلُواْ وَتَذْهَبَ رِيحُكُمْ وَٱصْبِرُوٓاْ إِنَّ ٱللَّهَ مَعَ ٱلصَّـٰبِرِينَ﴾

"You who believe! When you meet a troop, stand firm and remember Allah repeatedly so that hopefully you will be successful. Obey Allah and His Messenger and do not quarrel among yourselves lest you lose heart and your momentum disappear. And be steadfast. Allah is with the steadfast." [al-Anfāl 8:45-46]

How frequently is it that you read in the Qurʾān **"Allah loves the steadfast"** and **"Allah is with the steadfast"**. He the Glorified has made it clear that it is from the nature of those who follow the Messengers to be patient with whatever afflicts them in fields of battle, such as being killed or wounded, and not to be weak or lowly. If they do that, He the Glorified will bring them to His love and His victory. The Exalted One has said,

﴿وَكَأَيِّن مِّن نَّبِيٍّ قَـٰتَلَ مَعَهُۥ رِبِّيُّونَ كَثِيرٌ فَمَا وَهَنُواْ لِمَآ أَصَابَهُمْ فِى سَبِيلِ ٱللَّهِ
وَمَا ضَعُفُواْ وَمَا ٱسْتَكَانُواْ ۗ وَٱللَّهُ يُحِبُّ ٱلصَّـٰبِرِينَ﴾

"Many a Prophet has been killed, when there were many devout with him. They did not give up in the face of what assailed them in the Way of Allah, nor did they weaken, nor did they yield. Allah loves the steadfast." [Āl 'Imrān 3:146]

17. The Fruits of Patience:

You can deduce from the aforementioned that that the fruits of patience include: contentment, tranquillity, feeling happy, realising might, honour and goodness, and being deserving of Allah's support ﷻ as well as His victory and love. On top of all of that, there is the fruit of the Hereafter, which is embodied in that permanent blessing that they obtain in full without any reckoning:

﴿إِنَّمَا يُوَفَّى ٱلصَّـٰبِرُونَ أَجْرَهُم بِغَيْرِ حِسَابٍ﴾

"The steadfast will be paid their wages in full without any reckoning." [Az-Zumar 39:10]

They will be in a Garden as wide as the heavens and the earth, adorned with reverent angels greeting them:

﴿جَنَّـٰتُ عَدْنٍ يَدْخُلُونَهَا وَمَن صَلَحَ مِنْ ءَابَآئِهِمْ وَأَزْوَٰجِهِمْ وَذُرِّيَّـٰتِهِمْ ۖ وَٱلْمَلَـٰٓئِكَةُ يَدْخُلُونَ
عَلَيْهِم مِّن كُلِّ بَابٍ ﴿٢٣﴾ سَلَـٰمٌ عَلَيْكُم بِمَا صَبَرْتُمْ ۚ فَنِعْمَ عُقْبَى ٱلدَّارِ﴾

"Gardens of Eden which they will enter, and all of their parents, wives and children who were righteous. Angels will enter in to welcome them from every gate: 'Peace be upon you because of your steadfastness! How wonderful is the Ultimate Abode!'" [ar-Ra'd 13:23-24]

The Lord of Might turns to it with forgiveness, victory and pleasure:

﴿إِنِّى جَزَيْتُهُمُ ٱلْيَوْمَ بِمَا صَبَرُوٓاْ أَنَّهُمْ هُمُ ٱلْفَآئِزُونَ﴾

"Today I have rewarded them for being steadfast. They are the ones who are victorious." [al-Mu'minūn 23:111]

﴿وَبَشِّرِ ٱلصَّٰبِرِينَ ١٥٥ ٱلَّذِينَ إِذَآ أَصَٰبَتۡهُم مُّصِيبَةٞ قَالُوٓاْ إِنَّا لِلَّهِ وَإِنَّآ إِلَيۡهِ رَٰجِعُونَ ١٥٦ أُوْلَٰٓئِكَ عَلَيۡهِمۡ صَلَوَٰتٞ مِّن رَّبِّهِمۡ وَرَحۡمَةٞ﴾

"But give good news to the steadfast, those who, when disaster strikes them, say, 'We belong to Allah and to Him we will return.' Those are the people who will have blessings and mercy from their Lord." [al-Baqarah 2:155-157]

One should take note of the victory Allah ﷻ grants His believing slaves, the Day when neither wealth nor children will be of any benefit, except to those who come to Allah with sound hearts.[91] For everything mentioned above, patience is the best thing a person can be given. The Messenger of Allah ﷺ spoke the truth when he said, {No one has been given a greater and vaster gift than patience.} This is agreed upon.

18. Relief from Distress:

Man is constantly dealing with trials and afflictions and is exposed to various kinds of tribulation. Matters become unbearable and oppressive for him, such that he reaches a point in which grief and sorrow take over his soul, and he falls into distress. All of this is a test from Allah the Glorified, and until the believer carves his path towards Paradise with merit.

If he succeeds in the test, and is thus patient and anticipates reward in the manner that has been described, does not become exasperated or despair, realises that all of this is according to Allah the Exalted's decree and predestination and is thus content with it and his soul trusts in Him ﷻ, Allah the Exalted's solicitude seizes him, he is relieved of his grief, sorrow is removed from his soul, he is freed from every oppression and he is saved from every agony.

That is the clear victory and the immense triumph in this life and the Hereafter. This is when it becomes clear to the believing slave who has *taqwā* that light bursts forth from within darkness, that abundant rain comes from dark clouds, that the distress he was in was only for some good that was willed for him, that relief will come from within this distress, and that this was for nothing other than that the sincere slave be cut off from everything besides Allah ﷻ that he attach his heart to his Creator alone, the heart that is certain that the entire affair is in His hand. Read these meanings in Allah's words ﷻ:

﴿أَمۡ حَسِبۡتُمۡ أَن تَدۡخُلُواْ ٱلۡجَنَّةَ وَلَمَّا يَأۡتِكُم مَّثَلُ ٱلَّذِينَ خَلَوۡاْ مِن قَبۡلِكُمۖ مَّسَّتۡهُمُ ٱلۡبَأۡسَآءُ وَٱلضَّرَّآءُ وَزُلۡزِلُواْ حَتَّىٰ يَقُولَ ٱلرَّسُولُ وَٱلَّذِينَ ءَامَنُواْ مَعَهُۥ مَتَىٰ نَصۡرُ ٱللَّهِۗ أَلَآ إِنَّ نَصۡرَ ٱللَّهِ قَرِيبٞ﴾

91 (tn): this is a paraphrase of Sūrat ash-Shuʿarāʾ 26:88-89.

"Or did you suppose that you would enter Paradise without facing the same as those who came before you? Poverty and illness afflicted them and they were shaken to the point that the Messenger and those who believed with him said, 'When is Allah's help coming?' Be assured that Allah's help is very near." [al-Baqarah 2:214]

Allah the Exalted has also said,

﴿وَهُوَ ٱلَّذِى يُنَزِّلُ ٱلْغَيْثَ مِنۢ بَعْدِ مَا قَنَطُوا۟ وَيَنشُرُ رَحْمَتَهُۥ ۚ وَهُوَ ٱلْوَلِىُّ ٱلْحَمِيدُ﴾

"It is He who sends down abundant rain, after they have lost all hope, and unfolds His Mercy." [ash-Shūrā 42:28]

Maybe you can see this meaning clearly in the story of Ka'b ibn Mālik and his two companions ؓ when they stayed back from the battle of Tabūk and the Prophet ﷺ commanded people to disassociate from them. Then they were afflicted with distress that they were afflicted with, until:

﴿وَضَاقَتْ عَلَيْهِمُ ٱلْأَرْضُ بِمَا رَحُبَتْ وَضَاقَتْ عَلَيْهِمْ أَنفُسُهُمْ وَظَنُّوٓا۟ أَن لَّا مَلْجَأَ مِنَ ٱللَّهِ إِلَّآ إِلَيْهِ﴾

"the earth became narrow for them, and their own selves became constricted for them and they realised that there was no refuge from Allah except in Him". [at-Tawbah 9:118]

Then there was relief and there was mercy:

﴿ثُمَّ تَابَ عَلَيْهِمْ لِيَتُوبُوٓا۟ ۚ إِنَّ ٱللَّهَ هُوَ ٱلتَّوَّابُ ٱلرَّحِيمُ﴾

"He turned to them so that they might turn to Him. Allah is the Ever-Returning, the Most Merciful." [at-Tawbah 9:118]

You can see the same in the stories that the Qur'ān relates to us, stories of His prophets and saints being relieved of their distresses, and how Allah the Exalted honoured His prophet Muḥammad ﷺ and his Companions ؓ in these kinds of situations. This makes us trust in Allah's mercy ﷻ and desire His magnanimity, whenever calamities intensify, adversity surrounds us and distress becomes ingrained.

19. Hardship and Ease:

You will notices that the meanings of the ḥadīth are closely tied together, some of them taking from others. Hardship causes distress, and ease is one of the doors of relief. Everyone needs patience and durability, and behind that, there is triumph and victory. All of that is from Allah the Exalted's bounty and mercy towards His slaves, for He has established the norm that hardship be followed by ease or connected to it. He the Glorified says,

﴿سَيَجْعَلُ ٱللَّهُ بَعْدَ عُسْرٍ يُسْرًا﴾

"Allah will appoint after difficulty, ease". [at-Ṭalāq 65:7]

And He ﷻ has said,

﴿فَإِنَّ مَعَ ٱلْعُسْرِ يُسْرًا ۝ إِنَّ مَعَ ٱلْعُسْرِ يُسْرًا﴾

"For truly with hardship comes ease; truly with hardship comes ease". [ash-Sharḥ 94:5-6]

This is why He the Glorified has only legislated for His slaves that which contains ease:

﴿يُرِيدُ ٱللَّهُ بِكُمُ ٱلْيُسْرَ وَلَا يُرِيدُ بِكُمُ ٱلْعُسْرَ﴾

"Allah desires ease for you; He does not desire difficulty for you". [al-Baqarah 2:185]

And He ﷻ has and lifted them that which contains adversity, difficulty and hardship:

﴿وَمَا جَعَلَ عَلَيْكُمْ فِى ٱلدِّينِ مِنْ حَرَجٍ﴾

"...and He has not placed any constraint upon you in the Religion." [al-Ḥajj 22:78]

Al-Bazzār has related in his *Musnad* from the ḥadīth of Anas ؓ that the Prophet ﷺ said, {If hardship were to come and enter this hole, ease would come so that it could enter and remove it.} Allah ﷻ then revealed,

﴿فَإِنَّ مَعَ ٱلْعُسْرِ يُسْرًا ۝ إِنَّ مَعَ ٱلْعُسْرِ يُسْرًا﴾

"For truly with hardship comes ease; truly with hardship comes ease." [ash-Sharḥ 94:5-6]

His words ﷺ are emphasising that hardship and difficulty are never prolonged for a person, as long as he is content with what Allah the Glorified has predestined for him, he adheres to what Allah has commanded and forbidden, seeks refuge in Him alone and trusts Him to turn his hardship into ease:

﴿وَمَن يَتَوَكَّلْ عَلَى ٱللَّهِ فَهُوَ حَسْبُهُۥ﴾

"Whoever puts his trust in Allah – He will be enough for him." [at-Ṭalāq 65:3]

20. Legal Matters from the Ḥadīth:
If a riding animal is strong, and its rider or owner knows that it is capable of carrying more than one person, he can place one or more people behind him according to its capacity. If he knows that it is not capable, he is not permitted to do so.

Other Advice from the Ḥadīth:
1. It is advisable that the teacher catch the student's attention and mention that he wants to teach him, before starting to give him information, This will penetrate his soul, his yearning of knowledge intensifies and he accepts it wilfully.

2. Whoever is upon truth and calls to it, enjoins the right or forbids the wrong, will not be harmed by the plotting of oppressors or the trickery of Allah's enemies, who will always be thwarted.

3. A Muslim must carry out his obligations, such as doing acts of obedience and leaving that which is wrong, enjoining the right and forbidding the wrong, without listening to those who try to scare him about the consequences, those who have weak faith and certainty, because what Allah has predestined for him will inevitably hit him.

THE TWENTIETH ḤADĪTH

الحَيَاءُ مِنَ الإيْمَان

عَنْ أَبِي مَسْعُوْدٍ عُقْبَةَ بْنِ عَمْرٍو الأَنْصَارِيِّ البَدْرِيِّ ﷺ قَالَ: قَالَ رَسُوْلُ اللهِ ﷺ:

{إِنَّ مِمَّا أَدْرَكَ النَّاسُ مِنْ كَلَامِ النُّبُوَّةِ الأُوْلَى: إِذَا لَمْ تَسْتَحِي فَاصْنَعْ مَا شِئْتَ.} رواه البخاري.

Shame Is from Faith

It is on the authority of Abū Masʿūd ʿUqbah ibn ʿAmr al-Anṣārī al-Badrī ﷺ who said, 'The Messenger of Allah ﷺ said, {Part of what people understood from the prophethood of the past is: if you have no shame, do whatever you want.}' Related by al-Bukhārī.

Al-Bukhārī has related the ḥadīth towards the end of the Book of Prophets, no.3296, and in Etiquette (the chapter on if you have no shame, do whatever you want), no.5769. Abū Dāwūd has related it in Etiquette (the chapter on shame), no.3796 and Ibn Mājah has done so in Abstinence (the chapter on shame), no.4183.

The Importance of the Ḥadīth:
If the meaning of shame is to refrain from doing that which is disgraceful, to leave something or to do it for fear of the blame that will result, then calling for people to have shame and adhere to it is a call for refrain from every disobedience and evil. Moreover, shame is one of the characteristics of goodness that people strive for, and view its absence as a shortcoming and blemish. Likewise, it is from the completion and perfection of one's faith, and this is supported by what has reached us from the tongue of the Prophet ﷺ as related by al-Bukhārī and Muslim: {Shame is a branch of faith} and {Shame only brings goodness}. Indeed, in all of its rulings and teachings, Islam has only come as a call to establish goodness and truth, a sincere and fervent call to leave what is blameworthy and disgraceful. This is why Imam an-Nawawī ﷺ selected this ḥadīth for his *Forty*, and he said about it, 'Islam revolves around it', i.e. its rulings revolve around it. For example, that which is commanded is either obligatory or recommended, and thus one is ashamed to

leave it. That which is prohibited is either unlawful or disliked, and thus one is ashamed to do it. As for the permissible, the shame to do it permissible, just like the shame to leave it.

The Language of the Ḥadīth:

(إن مما أدرك الناس) *inna mimma adrak an-nās*: people (*an-nās*) can be either the subject or the object of the sentence, i.e., part of that which reached the people from what the Prophets before them said. In the ḥadīth of Ḥudhayfah ؓ according to Imam Aḥmad and al-Bazzār: {The last thing that the People of Ignorance held onto from the speech of the Prophets before them...}

(من كلام النبوة) *min kalām in-nubuwwah*: that which the Prophets have agreed on and that which they recommended and was never abrogated and mentioning prophethood informs that shame is one of the issues of prophethood that is agreed upon.
In the narration of Abū Dāwūd, Aḥmad and others: (النبوة الأولى) *in-nubuwwat il-uwlā*, i.e. the Prophets who came before our Prophet, Muḥammad ﷺ.

(إذا لم تستحي) *idhā lam tastaḥyi*: there should be one letter *yā'* at the end, the second *yā'* is elided to indicate the apocopate form (*jazm*). In one narration: (إذا لم تستح), because the verb appears in both forms: استحى (*istaḥyā*) and استحى (*istaḥā*). The first narration is more authentic and purer language. Allah the Exalted has said,

$$﴿إِنَّ ٱللَّهَ لَا يَسْتَحْىِۦٓ أَن يَضْرِبَ مَثَلًا﴾$$

"Allah is not ashamed (يستحي) to make an example..." [al-Baqarah 2:26]

(فاصنع ما شئت) *fasna' mā shi'ta*: this is in the command form, and it could either carry the meaning of a threat, i.e. if you have no shame, do what you want and you will be punished for it, or it could mean permissibility. In other words, if you want to do something and you are not ashamed to do it before Allah or people, do it. In another narration of al-Bukhārī, the wording is: (فافعل ما شئت) *faf'al mā shi'ta*

Legal Matters and Other Guidance from the Ḥadīth:

1. The Legacy of the Prophets: Shame is the foundation of noble manners, and the strongest motive for doing good and avoiding evil, and thus it is a part of the legacy of the earlier Prophets and has never been abrogated from their revealed laws. People have passed it on among themselves and inherited it successively from the Messengers, generation after generation. It became widespread and people clung to it until it reached this Muslim Ummah. If our Ummah is upon the clear legacy of all the Prophets and Messengers, as Allah the Most High, the All-Powerful, has willed, and as it is clear in the Noble Qur'ān, then it is our obligation to cling to the shame that Allah the Exalted has granted us, and to adorn ourselves with it and be characterized by it. This is so that the legacy of the Prophets remains manifest within us, and life and people prosper in goodness and truth until Allah inherits the earth and everyone on it.

2. The Meaning of the Ḥadīth: Our revered scholars have mentioned three meanings for this ḥadīth, which we shall clarify as follows:

The **first** meaning is that it is a command bearing the meaning of a threat, as if he ﷺ is saying, 'If you not have any shame, do what you want and Allah will punish you for it most severely.' This type of command is in the Noble Qur'ān when Allah addresses the disbelievers:

﴿ٱعْمَلُوا۟ مَا شِئْتُمْ﴾

"Do what you like." [Fuṣṣilat 41:40]

The **second** meaning is that it is a command bearing the meaning of informing, similar to his statement ﷺ {Let him take his seat in the Fire}, i.e. he has taken his seat. Thus, the meaning of the ḥadīth is that whoever does not have shame does whatever they want, because it is shame that prevents people from committing shameful acts. Whoever has no shame will be engrossed in every wrong and every abomination.

The **third** meaning is that it is a command bearing the meaning of permissibility, and thus the meaning is that if you are not ashamed to do something, neither before Allah nor in front of people, then do it, as it is permissible. This is because if an action is not prohibited in the Revealed Law, it is permissible.

The preferred meaning is the first. Even though Imam an-Nawawī ؒ preferred the third meaning, Abū 'Ubayd al-Qāsim ibn Salām, Ibn Qutaybah and Muḥammad ibn Naṣr al-Marwazī preferred the second meaning.

3. Shame is of Two Types:

A. The first type is natural. It is part of someone's disposition and character and not acquired, and whoever is characterised by them ascends to the noblest of manners, which Allah grants to one of His slaves and endows him with them. The one endowed with shame refrains from disobedience, shameful acts and vile character, and this is why shame is a source of good and one of the branches of faith. He ﷺ said, {Shame is a branch of faith}. The Messenger of Allah ﷺ was more modest[92] than a virgin (*al-'adhrā'*) behind her curtain. It has been related from 'Umar ؓ that he said, 'Whoever has shame, hides. Whoever hides has *taqwā*. Whoever has *taqwā* is protected.'

---

92 Ar. *ashadda hayā'an.*

B. The second type of shame is acquired. It is that which is acquired by knowing Allah, knowing His sublimity and His nearness to His slaves, His examination of them, and His knowledge, Glorified is He, of the eyes' deceit and what hearts conceal. The Muslim who strives to acquire and obtain this shame will realise within himself the highest qualities of faith and the highest ranks of excellence. This shame is brought forth by studying Allah's blessing and sensing one's own inadequacy is being grateful for them. Imam Aḥmad and at-Tirmidhī have related on the authority of Ibn Masʿūd *marfūʿan*: {Shame before Allah means that you protect your head and what it retains, your stomach and what it contains, and that you remember death and tribulation. Whoever desires the Hereafter leaves the embellishment of this world. Whoever does that has shame before Allah.} When the human soul is devoid of acquired shame the heart is devoid of natural shame, nothing remains to prevent such a person from committing despicable and disgraceful acts, and he becomes like those who have no faith, like the demons amongst men and jinn.

4. Shame that is Blameworthy: When shame restrains the soul from disgraceful acts and other shortcomings, it a praiseworthy trait for a person to have, because it completes his faith and only brings about goodness. As for when shame goes beyond its reasonable bounds and takes a person into disarray and confusion, and his soul withdraws from doing something that one should not be ashamed to do, it is a blameworthy trait. This is because it is misplaced shame, and shyness comes between a person and learning knowledge and obtaining sustenance. It has been said that a man having misplaced shame is weakness. It has been related from the *Murāsīl*[93] of al-Ḥasan al-Baṣrī that the Prophet ﷺ said, {There are two types of shame: one is from faith and the other is weakness.} Ibn Rajab al-Ḥanbalī said, 'Maybe this was said by al-Ḥasan. Likewise, Bushayr ibn Kaʿb al-ʿAdawī said to ʿImrān ibn Ḥusayn رضي الله عنه, 'We find in certain books that from it there is tranquillity and dignity and from it there is weakness.' ʿImrān then became angry and said, 'I relate to you from the Messenger of Allah ﷺ and you contradict it.' The fact of the matter, as stated by ʿImrān رضي الله عنه is that shame is praiseworthy in the Prophet's speech ﷺ and only means the trait that encourages doing good and leaving that which is disgraceful. As for weakness and incapacity, which would necessitate remissness concerning Allah's rights or those of His slaves, this is not shame but rather weakness and lassitude.

5. The Muslim Woman's Shame: The Muslim woman adorns herself with shame, and partakes with the man in developing the earth and raising generations upon the purity of a sound, female disposition. The Noble Qur'ān indicates this when Allah the Exalted talks about one of the daughters of Shuʿayb عليه السلام when she came to invite Mūsā عليه السلام,

93 (tn): i.e. the plural of *mursal.*

﴿فَجَآءَتْهُ إِحْدَىٰهُمَا تَمْشِي عَلَى ٱسْتِحْيَآءٍ قَالَتْ إِنَّ أَبِي يَدْعُوكَ لِيَجْزِيَكَ أَجْرَ مَا سَقَيْتَ لَنَا﴾

"One of them came walking shyly up to him and said, 'My father invites you so that he may pay you your wage for drawing water for us.'" [al-Qaṣaṣ 28:25]

She came with a command from her father walking like a pure, clean, chaste young woman when she meets men. There was no display of vulgar manners, no adornment of herself, no flaunting and no enticement. In addition to manifest shyness in her walk, she spoke clearly and accurately, without any stuttering or stammering. This is part of natural, sound, clean, upright shame.[94] An upright young woman is naturally shy when meeting men and talking to them, but due to her purity and uprightness, she does not become uneasy, unease that entices and arouses desire. Rather, she speaks clearly and says no more than is necessary.

As for the woman who, in the past, was described as *as-salfaʿah,*[95] constantly going in and out, in our time she is described as acting like a man, being unveiled, adorning herself, and mixing with foreign men when there is no legislated need. This does not result from the school of the Qurʾān and Islam. She has exchanged shame and obedience to Allah the Exalted for insolence, disobedience, and immorality, and she carries out what Allah enemies want for her, which is ruin and destruction in this life and the Hereafter.

6. The Fruits of Shame: The fruits of shame include virtuousness, so whoever is characterised by shame such that it governs all of his actions will be virtuous by nature, not by choice.

Its fruits also include fidelity. Al-Aḥnaf ibn Qays said, 'Two things are never combined in one person: lying and respectability'. Respectability[96] has its own fruits: truthfulness, fidelity, shame and virtuousness.

7. The Opposite of Shame: The opposite of shame is insolence, which is a blameworthy attribute, because the person who bears it will be immersed in evil and not care about any blame or censure that he receives, until he declares his wickedness openly. He ﷺ has said, {My entire Ummah is excused, apart from those who declare their wickedness openly.} When someone who has no shame before Allah or before people, there is nothing to restrain them from their ignorance apart from severe punishment and forcible seizure, as there are people who fear and have no shame, which is nothing strange, because insolence is an abandonment of one's sound, human disposition.

94 (tn): or shyness.

95 (tn): i.e. insolent and immodest.

96 Ar. *al-murūʾah.*

8. The Obligation of Parents and Educators: In a Muslim community, the obligation of parents and educators is to strive diligently towards reviving the trait of shame, and to follow tried and tested educational methods in doing so. These methods should include the supervision of the actions and behaviours of children and whatever contradicts the virtue of shame should be rectified. They should be taught how to keep righteous company and avoid bad company, and shown how to choose beneficial books and avoid corruptive films, comical plays and vulgar speech.

9. The ḥadīth informs us that shame in its entirety is good. Whoever has a lot of shame will have a lot of good, whoever has a little shame will have little good.

10. There is no shame in teaching the rulings of the Religion and no shame in seeking the truth. The Exalted One has said,

﴿وَٱللَّهُ لَا يَسْتَحْيِۦ مِنَ ٱلْحَقِّ﴾

"But Allah is not reticent with the truth." [al-Aḥzāb 33:53]

THE TWENTY-FIRST ḤADĪTH

الاسْتِقَامَةُ وَالإِيمَان

عَنْ أَبِي عَمْرٍو، وَقِيلَ أَبِي عَمْرَةَ، سُفْيَانَ بْنِ عَبْدِ اللهِ الثَّقَفِيِّ ﷺ قَالَ: قُلْتُ: يَا رَسُولَ اللهِ، قُلْ لِي فِي الإِسْلَامِ قَوْلاً، لَا أَسْأَلُ عَنْهُ أَحَداً غَيْرَكَ. قال: {قُلْ آمَنْتُ بِاللهِ ثُمَّ اسْتَقِمْ.} رواه مسلم.

Uprightness and Faith

It is on the authority of Abū ʿAmr, and it has been said 'Abū ʿAmrah', Sufyān ibn ʿAbdillāh ﷺ said, 'I said, "O Messenger of Allah, tell me something about Islam that I will not ask anyone besides you." He said, {Say, 'I believe in Allah' and then be upright.} Related by Muslim.

Muslim has related the ḥadīth in the Book of Faith (the chapter on gathering the characteristics of Islam), no.38, at-Tirmidhī in Abstinence (the chapter on what has reached us concerning guarding the tongue), no.2412, and Ibn Mājah in Tribulations (the chapter on restraining the tongue in tribulation), no.3972.

The Importance of the Ḥadīth:
This ḥadīth is an amazing example of the comprehensive speech that was unique to the Messenger of Allah ﷺ Despite its brevity, it brings together all foundations of Islam in two words: faith and uprightness. It is known that Islam is *tawḥīd* and obedience. *Tawḥīd* is the result of saying, 'I believe in Allah', and obedience is the result of uprightness, as it is compliance with everything that is commanded and avoidance of everything that is prohibited.

This includes the actions of the heart and the body, which comprise faith, excellence and Islam. The Exalted One has said,

﴿فَٱسْتَقِيمُوٓاْ إِلَيْهِ وَٱسْتَغْفِرُوهُ﴾

"Be upright with Him and ask for His forgiveness." [Fuṣṣilat 41:6]

The Language of the Ḥadīth:

(في الإسلام) *fil Islām*: i.e. in its theology and Revealed Law.

(قولا) *qawlan*: gathering the meanings of the Religion, clearly without need for explanation.

(قل آمنتُ بالله) *qul āmantu billāh*: renew your faith in Allah, remembering in your heart and mentioning on your tongue, so that you call to mind all the details of the pillars of faith.

(ثم استقم) *thumm astaqim*: i.e. be persistent and remain firm in carrying out acts of obedience and refraining from disobedience. Uprightness is not feasible when there is any sort of deviation or crookedness.

Legal Matters and Other Guidance from the Ḥadīth:

1. The meaning of uprightness: The Prophet's statement ﷺ: {Say, 'I believe in Allah' and then be upright} and his statement in another narration: {Say, 'My Lord is Allah' and then be upright} is taken from the Exalted's statement:

﴿إِنَّ ٱلَّذِينَ قَالُوا۟ رَبُّنَا ٱللَّهُ ثُمَّ ٱسْتَقَٰمُوا۟ تَتَنَزَّلُ عَلَيْهِمُ ٱلْمَلَٰئِكَةُ أَلَّا تَخَافُوا۟ وَلَا تَحْزَنُوا۟﴾

"The angels descend on those who say, 'Our Lord is Allah' and are then upright: 'Do no fear and do not grieve...'". [Fuṣṣilat 41:30]

As well the Exalted's statement:

﴿إِنَّ ٱلَّذِينَ قَالُوا۟ رَبُّنَا ٱللَّهُ ثُمَّ ٱسْتَقَٰمُوا۟ فَلَا خَوْفٌ عَلَيْهِمْ وَلَا هُمْ يَحْزَنُونَ﴾

"Those who say, 'Our Lord is Allah' and are then upright will feel no fear and know no sorrow." [al-Aḥqāf 46:13]

Abū Bakr as-Ṣiddīq ؓ commented on **"and are then upright"** by saying, 'They do not associate anything with Allah'. It has also been related that he said, 'They do not turn to a god other than Him' and that he said, 'Then they remain upright upon Allah be their Lord'. It has been related from 'Umar ibn al-Khaṭṭāb that he read this verse on the minbar, **"Those who say, 'Our Lord is Allah' and are then upright..."** and said, 'They remain upright upon His obedience and do not deviate the way a fox deviates'. What is meant by these statements is remaining upright upon complete *tawḥīd*.

Al-Qushayrī said, 'Uprightness is a rank with which matters are perfected. When it is present, goodness is obtained and put in order. Whoever is not upright in his state will see his efforts go to waste and his diligence come to nothing'. It has been said that uprightness can only be mastered by the elderly, because it means leaving that which is well known and detaching oneself from old habits, and standing before Allah the Exalted with sincerity. Al-Wāsiṭī said, 'It is the quality with which all good traits are perfected.' Ibn Rajab said, 'Uprightness is the conduct of the straight path[97] It is the correct religion, without any twisting towards the right or the left. It comprises all actions of obedience, outward and inward, and leaving everything that is prohibited. Thus, this advice gathers together every quality of goodness.'

2. Falling Short is Inevitable in Uprightness: If uprightness is the utmost degree in the perfection of realisations and states, the purity of hearts in word and deed, doctrines being free of the nonsense of innovation and misguidance, man will never achieve true uprightness. Rather, there must be some shortcoming in achieving it, and the evidence of this is Allah the Exalted's statement:

﴿فَٱسْتَقِيمُوٓا۟ إِلَيْهِ وَٱسْتَغْفِرُوهُ﴾

"Be upright with Him and ask for His forgiveness". [Fuṣṣilat 41:6]

Because the command to seek forgiveness is to compensate for what is lacking, to repent and to return to uprightness.

There is also the Prophet's statement ﷺ as related by Imam Aḥmad and Muslim: {Be upright, and you will never master it}, and his statement as related by al-Bukhārī and Muslim: {Do the right thing and come close.} Doing the right thing[98] is the core of uprightness, because it is doing what is right in every word, deed and intention, like someone who aims for a target and hits it.

3. The Uprightness of the Heart: The foundation of uprightness is the uprightness of the heart upon *tawḥīd*, as has been covered under the meaning of uprightness. When the heart is upright upon knowledge[99] of Allah and upon fear, exaltation, awe and love of Him, and it desires Him, hopes for Him and supplicates to Him, relies on Him and does not turn to anyone else, all the limbs become upright upon His obedience. This is because the heart is the king of the limbs and they are its soldiers. If the king is upright, his soldiers and subjects are upright. The Messenger of Allah ﷺ said, {Indeed, there is a lump of flesh in the body; if it is sound, the whole body is sound, and if it is corrupt, the whole body is corrupt. Indeed, it is the heart.}

4. The Uprightness of the Tongue: After the heart, the most significant limb in which uprightness must be observed is the tongue, for it is the heart's interpreter and speaks on its behalf. This is supported by what is found in at-Tirmidhī's nar-

97 Ar. *as-ṣirāṭ al-mustaqīm*.

98 Ar. *as-saddād*.

99 Ar. *maʿrifah*.

ration: 'I said, "O Messenger of Allah, what is feared the most for me?" He then grabbed his own tongue.' At-Tirmidhī then said, 'This is a good, authentic ḥadīth.' There is also what Imam Aḥmad has related in his *Musnad* on the authority of Anas ﷺ that the Prophet ﷺ said, {A slave's faith will not be upright until his heart is upright, and his heart will not be upright until his tongue is upright.} Additionally, there is what at-Tirmidhī has related on the authority of Abū Saʿīd al-Khudrī, *marfūʿan* and *mawqūfan*: {When the son of Adam wakes up, all the limbs subjugate the tongue and say, 'Have *taqwā* of Allah regarding us. We go according to you. If you are upright, we are upright. If you are crooked, we are crooked.'}

5. The Benefits of Uprightness: Uprightness is stability, triumph, vigour and victory in the battle between obedience and passions and desires. Therefore, those who are upright deserve to have angels descend upon them in this worldly life, to remove fear and grief from their lives, to give them the glad tidings of Paradise and to announce that they are at their side in this life and in the Hereafter. Allah the Exalted has said,

﴿إِنَّ ٱلَّذِينَ قَالُوا۟ رَبُّنَا ٱللَّهُ ثُمَّ ٱسْتَقَـٰمُوا۟ تَتَنَزَّلُ عَلَيْهِمُ ٱلْمَلَـٰٓئِكَةُ أَلَّا تَخَافُوا۟ وَلَا تَحْزَنُوا۟ وَأَبْشِرُوا۟
بِٱلْجَنَّةِ ٱلَّتِى كُنتُمْ تُوعَدُونَ ﴿٣٠﴾ نَحْنُ أَوْلِيَآؤُكُمْ فِى ٱلْحَيَوٰةِ ٱلدُّنْيَا وَفِى ٱلْـَٔاخِرَةِ ۖ وَلَكُمْ فِيهَا مَا
تَشْتَهِىٓ أَنفُسُكُمْ وَلَكُمْ فِيهَا مَا تَدَّعُونَ ﴿٣١﴾ نُزُلًا مِّنْ غَفُورٍ رَّحِيمٍ﴾

"The angels descend on those who say, 'Our Lord is Allah' and are then upright: 'Do no fear and do not grieve but rejoice in the Paradise you have been promised. We are your protectors in the life of this world and in the Hereafter. You will have there all that your souls could wish for. You will have there everything that you demand. Hospitality from One who is Ever-Forgiving, Most Merciful.'" [Fuṣṣilat 41:30-32]

6. The Importance of Uprightness: The importance of uprightness is evidenced by the Prophet ﷺ commanding it. Allah the Exalted has said,

﴿فَٱسْتَقِمْ كَمَآ أُمِرْتَ﴾

"Be upright as you have been commanded." [Hūd 11:112]

Ibn ʿAbbās ﷺ said, 'There was no verse that was revealed to the Messenger of Allah ﷺ in the entire Qurʾān that was harder and more difficult than this verse. When his Companions said to him, 'You have turned grey early', he replied, {Hūd and its sisters have turned me grey.} It is on the authority of al-Ḥasan that he said, 'When this verse came down, the Messenger of Allah ﷺ prepared himself and was not seen smiling.' Ibn Abī Ḥātim narrated this. Al-Qushayrī has mentioned from one of the people that he saw the Prophet ﷺ in his sleep and said to him, 'O Messenger of Allah, you said, {Hūd and its sisters have turned me grey.} What part of them made you turn grey?' He replied, 'His statement, **"Be upright as you have been commanded."**

7. The ḥadīth advises that uprightness be commanded upon *tawḥīd* and sincere worship of Allah alone.

8. The Companion's keenness to learn their religion and protect their faith.

THE TWENTY-SECOND ḤADĪTH

طَرِيْقُ الجَنَّة

عَنْ أَبِي عَبْدِ اللهِ جَابِرِ بْنِ عَبْدِ اللهِ الأَنْصَارِيِّ رضي الله عنهما أَنَّ رَجُلاً سَأَلَ رَسُولَ اللهِ ﷺ فَقَالَ: أَرَأَيْتَ إِذَا صَلَّيْتُ الصَّلَوَاتِ الْمَكْتُوْبَاتِ، وَصُمْتُ رَمَضَانَ، وَأَحْلَلْتُ الْحَلَالَ، وَحَرَّمْتُ الْحَرَامَ، وَلَمْ أَزِدْ عَلَى ذَلِكَ شَيْئاً، أَأَدْخُلُ الْجَنَّةَ؟ قَالَ {نَعَمْ.} رواه مسلم.

وَمَعْنَى حَرَّمْتُ الْحَرَامَ: اجْتَنَبْتُهُ، وَمَعْنَى أَحْلَلْتُ الْحَلَالَ: فَعَلْتُهُ مُعْتَقِداً حِلَّهُ.[100]

The Path to Paradise

It is on the authority of Jābir ibn ʿAbdillāh al-Anṣārī ﷺ that a man asked the Messenger of Allah ﷺ saying, 'What do you think? If I pray the obligatory prayers, fast Ramaḍān, consider lawful that which is lawful and consider unlawful that which is unlawful, and I do nothing more than that, will I enter Paradise?' He replied, {Yes.} Related by Muslim.

The meaning of 'consider unlawful that which is unlawful' is: 'I avoid it'. The meaning of 'I consider lawful that which is lawful' is: 'I do it believing it is lawful'.

Muslim has collected the ḥadīth in Faith (the chapter on elucidating the faith that enters one into Paradise and that whoever adheres to what he has been commanded enters Paradise), no.15.

Its Importance:
Al-Jurdānī has said in his commentary on *The Forty*, 'This ḥadīth has an immense position. Islam revolves around it because it gathers it together. This is because actions are either by the heart or by the body, and they are either authorised, which is the lawful (*ḥalāl*), or they are prohibited, which is the unlawful (*ḥarām*). If an individual considers the lawful to be lawful and the unlawful to be unlawful, he has carried out all the functions of the Religion, and he safely enters Paradise'.

---

100 (tn): This line has been included because it is from Imam an-Nawawī and part of the original text (*matn*).

The Language of the Ḥadīth:

(رجلا) *rajulan*: this is an-Nuʿmān ibn Qawqal al-Khuzāʿī – as is made clear in another narration – he was present at Badr and was martyred on the Day of Uḥud. He said on that day, 'I swear to you, O Lord of Might, the sun will not go down until I have set my lame foot in the greenery of Paradise'. After he had been martyred, the Prophet ﷺ said, {An-Nuʿmān had a good opinion of Allah ﷻ and thus he found Him to be as he thought of Him, for I have seen him treading in its greenery without any lameness or limping.}

(أرأيت) *a ra'ayta*: the letter *hamzah* (*a*) indicates a question. What is meant is 'tell me' and 'inform me'.

(المكتوبات) *al-maktūbāt*: the obligatory, which is the five daily prayers.

(رمضان) *ramaḍān*: the month of Ramaḍān.

(أحللتُ الحلال) *aḥlalt ul-ḥalāla*: I am firmly convinced that it is lawful and carry out the obligatory thereof. As for that which is not obligatory, there is no objection to not doing it. That lawful (*ḥalāl*) is that which is authorised to be done in the Revealed Law.

(حرّمتُ) *ḥarramt ul-ḥarāma*: I avoid it while being firmly convinced that it is unlawful. The unlawful (*ḥarām*) is everything that the Revealed Law has decisively prohibited.

(أدخل الجنة) *adkhul ul-jannah*: with those who went before, without any punishment preceding one's entry.

Legal Matters and Other Guidance from the Ḥadīth:

1. The Messenger of Allah ﷺ is a Mercy to all of Creation: Allah the Exalted sent His Messenger, Muḥammad ﷺ as a mercy to all of mankind, to save them from the misguidance that leads to the Fire and lead them along the path of guidance that leads to Paradise, and the path to Paradise is clear and easy. Allah the Exalted has set limits for it and obligated certain conduct therein. Whoever stays within those limits and sticks to them will reach the right destination, and whoever transgresses them and violates them will be lead into the Fire. Nevertheless, the limits that Allah the Exalted has set and what He has obligated are within man's ability and capacity, because Allah the Exalted wants ease for His slaves and does not want hardship for them. This is clearly and manifestly apparent in his guidance ﷺ as in this ḥadīth and others that bear similar meaning.

2. Yearning for Paradise and Seeking its Path: Jābir ﵁ is telling us about that believer who yearns for a Garden that is as wide as the heavens and the earth, prepared for the people of *taqwā*, so he came and asked the Messenger of Allah ﷺ about its path and what actions would enter him into its vastness. Thus, the Messenger of Allah ﷺ showed him what he wanted and his wish came true.

Questions like this and seeking guidance were repeated often by the Prophet's Companions ﷺ in different ways and on various occasions:

Al-Bukhārī and Muslim have related from Abū Ayyūb al-Anṣārī ﵁ that a man said to the Prophet ﷺ 'Tell me about a deed that will enter me into Paradise'. He replied, {That you worship Allah and not associate anything with Him, establish the prayer, pay the zakāt and maintain ties of kinship.} In Muslim's narration: 'Show me a deed I can do that will bring me closer to Paradise and take me far away from the Fire.' In both *Ṣaḥīḥ* collections, there is a similar narration from Abū Hurayrah ﵁ and it has {and fast Ramaḍān} instead of {and maintain ties of kinship}.

Aḥmad has related with his chain of transmission from Ibn al-Muntafiq ﵁ who said, 'I came to the Prophet ﷺ while he was at ʿArafāt, and I said, "I want to ask you about two things. What will save me from the Fire and what will enter me into Paradise?" He replied, {If only you had made your question brief, for you have asked about something immense, and the path to it is long. Understand the following from me. Worship Allah and do not associate anything with him. Establish the prescribed prayers. Pay the obligatory zakāt. Fast Ramaḍān. What you love people to do for you, do it for them. What you hate to be done to you, protect people from it.}

3. Adhering to Obligation and Leaving Unlawful Matters is the Foundation of Success: an-Nuʿmān ﵁ asked the Messenger of Allah ﷺ: if a person consistently performs the obligatory prayers, based on the Exalted' statement:

﴿إِنَّ ٱلصَّلَوٰةَ كَانَتْ عَلَى ٱلْمُؤْمِنِينَ كِتَـٰبًا مَّوْقُوتًا﴾

"The prayer is prescribed for the believers at specific times." [an-Nisā' 4:103]...?

And if the month of Ramaḍān comes, which is obligatory to fast, based on the Exalted's statement:

﴿شَهْرُ رَمَضَانَ ٱلَّذِىٓ أُنزِلَ فِيهِ ٱلْقُرْءَانُ هُدًى لِّلنَّاسِ

وَبَيِّنَـٰتٍ مِّنَ ٱلْهُدَىٰ وَٱلْفُرْقَانِ ۚ فَمَن شَهِدَ مِنكُمُ ٱلشَّهْرَ فَلْيَصُمْهُ﴾

"The month of Ramaḍān is the one in which the Qur'ān was sent down as guidance for mankind, with Clear Signs containing guidance and discrimination. Any of you who are resident for the month should fast it." [al-Baqarah 2:185]

And he fasts it, adhering to its etiquette and observing its sanctity…? Then, if he stays within the limits Allah ﷻ has said concerning the lawful and the unlawful, and does not consider the lawful unlawful or the unlawful lawful, but rather is firmly convinced that the lawful is what Allah has made lawful and the unlawful is what He has made unlawful, and thus he completely avoids the unlawful and carries that which obligatory from the lawful…?

The question is: if he does all of that and does not add any recommended or virtuous deeds – such as doing supererogatory acts and leaving that which is disliked,[101] and leaving certain lawful things out of carefulness sometimes – is that enough for him to be safe according to Allah the Exalted and be entered into Paradise, which is the extent of his hope and desire, along with the elite that draw near to Allah and the righteous people of before, without undergoing any punishment or castigation?

The Messenger of Allah ﷺ answers him with that which puts his soul at ease, expands his chest, brings joy to his heart and realises his desire. He says, {Yes.} In other words, the deeds that you have mentioned are sufficient for obtaining your goal of entering Paradise. How would they not? The Messenger ﷺ informs us that Allah the Exalted says, {Those who draw near to Me do not draw near with anything that matches what I have made obligatory upon them}, which is a ḥadīth qudsī related by al-Bukhārī. Indeed, for you is happiness, O believer, in Allah's ﷻ glad tidings for He ﷻ says,

﴿وَٱلْحَـٰفِظُونَ لِحُدُودِ ٱللَّهِ ۗ وَبَشِّرِ ٱلْمُؤْمِنِينَ﴾

"…those who preserve Allah's limits: give good news to the believers." [at-Tawbah 9:112]

An-Nasā'ī, Ibn Ḥibbān, and al-Ḥākim have related that the Messenger of Allah ﷺ said, {No slave prays the five prayers, fasts Ramaḍān, pays the zakāt and avoids the seven major sins except that all the doors of Paradise are opened unto him and he enters whichever one he wants.} Then he recited,

﴿إِن تَجْتَنِبُوا۟ كَبَآئِرَ مَا تُنْهَوْنَ عَنْهُ نُكَفِّرْ عَنكُمْ سَيِّـَٔاتِكُمْ وَنُدْخِلْكُم مُّدْخَلًا كَرِيمًا﴾

"If you avoid the major sins you have been forbidden, We will erase your bad actions from you and admit you by a Gate of Honour." [an-Nisā' 4:31]

The ḥadīths on this topic are many and mass-transmitted.

The seven major sins are: fornication, drinking wine, sorcery, accusing someone known to be chaste of fornication, killing someone deliberately who has not done anything wrong, dealing in usury and fleeing from the enemies of Islam on the battlefield.

101 Ar. *makrūh*, i.e. that which one is rewarded for leaving but not punished for doing.

Other major sins have been mentions in the ḥadīths, and Allah knows best.

4. This Religion is Ease: The Messenger of Allah's ﷺ position and other similar positions, show the ease of Islam, and that Allah the Exalted does not bear any of His creation with that which contains trouble and hardship. He the Glorified says,

﴿يُرِيدُ ٱللَّهُ بِكُمُ ٱلْيُسْرَ وَلَا يُرِيدُ بِكُمُ ٱلْعُسْرَ﴾

"Allah desires ease for you; He does not desire difficulty for you." [al-Baqarah 2:185]

He ﷻ also says,

﴿لَا يُكَلِّفُ ٱللَّهُ نَفْسًا إِلَّا وُسْعَهَا﴾

"Allah does not impose on any soul any more than it can bear." [al-Baqarah 2:286]

He ﷻ also says,

﴿وَمَا جَعَلَ عَلَيْكُمْ فِى ٱلدِّينِ مِنْ حَرَجٍ﴾

"...and not placed any constraint upon you in the Religion." [al-Ḥajj 22:78]

All commandments in the Islamic Revealed Law are characterised by ease, and are within the bounds of human capacity, because they are issued by the All-Wise, the All-Knowing. The intelligent person only has to hear and obey, in order to attain felicity in this life and success in the next.

5. The Muslim's Veracity and Candour: An-Nuʿmān رضي الله عنه was an example of the candid believer, in his heart and outward form. He did not want to display any *taqwā* or righteousness that was not within himself to do, or that he did not actually carry out. Rather, he was someone who wanted salvation and success, and he was prepared to adhere to whatever would lead him there. The candidness of this believer became more and more apparent when he ﷺ informed him that what he had mentioned was sufficient to attain what he wanted – as long as Allah the Exalted's pleasure is realised by way of the few easy matters He has made obligatory, and it is only a few easy matters for the believer whom Allah has made made it easy for, and hard and difficult for the one whose heart Allah has sealed.

﴿وَٱسْتَعِينُوا۟ بِٱلصَّبْرِ وَٱلصَّلَوٰةِ ۚ وَإِنَّهَا لَكَبِيرَةٌ إِلَّا عَلَى ٱلْخَـٰشِعِينَ ﴿٤٥﴾ ٱلَّذِينَ يَظُنُّونَ أَنَّهُم مُّلَـٰقُوا۟ رَبِّهِمْ وَأَنَّهُمْ إِلَيْهِ رَٰجِعُونَ﴾

"Seek help in steadfastness and prayer. But that is a very hard thing, except for the humble, those who are aware that they will meet their Lord and that they will return to Him." [al-Baqarah 2:45-46]

This candid and truthful position has been repeated by those people whose hearts faith has entered, and certainty has taken over their souls. They did not know ambiguity or hypocrisy, and they did not come anywhere near negligence or remissness concerning what Allah the Exalted had legislated. Likewise, these glad tidings were repeated by the Messenger of Allah ﷺ to them, that they would enter Paradise. In the two *Ṣaḥīḥ* collections, it is mentioned that a Bedouin came to him - Ḍammām ibn Thaʿlabah, according to Aḥmad – once and asked him about the prayers. He replied, {Five.} He said, 'Are there any other prayers I have to do?' He replied, {No. Anything else is done so voluntarily.} Then he asked him about the number of requirements and obligations, and he responded by telling him what was obligatory upon him. He then asked, 'Is there anything else I have to do?' He replied, {No. Anything else is done so voluntarily.} He said, 'By Allah, I will not do anything voluntary and I will not fall short in anything Allah the Exalted has obligated me.' He ﷺ then said, 'He has succeeded if has spoken the truth.' In another narration of Muslim: {If he sticks to what he has been commanded, he will enter Paradise.} And in another narration in the two *Ṣaḥīḥ* collections: {Whoever would be pleased to see a man from the people of Paradise, let him look at this man.}

6. The Zakāt and the Ḥajj are Two Prescribed Obligations: The zakāt is one of the pillars of Islam, it has immense rank and importance. The Exalted One has said,

﴿خُذْ مِنْ أَمْوَٰلِهِمْ صَدَقَةً تُطَهِّرُهُمْ وَتُزَكِّيهِم بِهَا﴾

"Take the zakāt from their wealth to purify and cleanse them." [at-Tawbah 9:103]

Al-Bukhārī and Muslim have related that he ﷺ said to Muʿādh when he sent him to Yemen, {Tell them that Allah has obligated the zakāt upon them. It is taken from their wealthy and given to their poor.} The Ḥajj to Allah's Sacred House is the same. Allah the Exalted has said,

﴿وَلِلَّهِ عَلَى ٱلنَّاسِ حِجُّ ٱلْبَيْتِ مَنِ ٱسْتَطَاعَ إِلَيْهِ سَبِيلًا﴾

"Ḥajj to the House is a duty owed to Allah by all mankind – those who can find a way to do it." [Āl ʿImrān 3:97]

Muslim has related that he ﷺ said, {O people, Allah has made the Ḥajj obligatory upon you, so perform the Ḥajj.}

Thus, adhering to these two pillars, which are obligatory upon him, is a fundamental condition of his salvation from the Fire and his entrance into Paradise without punishment. This has been made unequivocally clear in a narration of Aḥmad's on the authority of Ibn Muntafiq in which he asked the Prophet ﷺ

about what would enter him into Paradise. He replied, {Have *taqwā* of Allah and do not associate anything with him, establish the prayer, pay the zakāt, perform the Ḥajj to the House and fast Ramaḍān.}

An-Nuʿmān ﷺ did not mention them in particular, as he mentioned the prayer and fasting. This could be because they had not been made obligatory yet, because he was not legally accountable for them due to his poverty and lack of ability, or because they are included in the generality of his statement: '...consider lawful that which is lawful and consider unlawful that which is unlawful...', for this necessitates carrying out all obligations, because the obligatory is part of the lawful and leaving obligations is unlawful and prohibited.

7. The Importance of the Prayer and Fasting: The questioner asking this question about the obligatory prayers is clear evidence that the prayer held immense importance in the Companions' souls ﷺ and how could it not? It is the pillar of the religion and a sign that someone is Muslim; he performs it five times every day and night, maintaining its pillars and obligations, its recommended matters and etiquettes.

The Messenger of Allah ﷺ said, {The peak of this matter is Islam. Whoever becomes Muslim is safe. Its pillar is the prayer and its culmination is *jihād* for the sake of Allah}, as related by at-Ṭabarānī. He ﷺ has also said, {Whoever prays our prayer, faces our *qiblah* and eats what we have slaughtered is a Muslim who has Allah's protection and that of His Messenger}, as related by al-Bukhārī. He also said, {If you see the man who has habituated himself to the masjids, bear witness that he has faith}, as related by at-Tirmidhī and others. He also said, {There is no religion for the one who has no prayer. The prayer in relation to the religion is like the head in relation to the body}, as related by at-Ṭabarānī.

The ruling for the one who leaves the prayer: There are several ḥadīths that severely warn against leaving prayer, that it is disbelief (*kufr*) or leads to disbelief. These include what has been related by Muslim and others: {Between a man and disbelief is leaving the prayer} and what has been related by Aḥmad and the authors of the *Sunan* books: {The covenant between us and them is the prayer. Whoever leaves it has disbelieved}. Then there is what at-Tirmidhī and al-Ḥākim have related from ʿAbdullah ibn Shaqīq al-ʿUqaylī, who said, 'The Companions of Muḥammad ﷺ did'nt see leaving any deed as disbelief apart from the prayer.'

Using these texts, we can derive the ruling for the one who leaves the prayer, and it differs according to what one believes about the prayer and why it has been left:

A. If someone leaves it because they deny its obligatory nature, and reject the fact that it is one of the fundamental acts of worship in Islam, this person is a disbeliever by consensus of the Muslims and an apostate from Islam, even if he articulates the two testimonies of faith, claims to be Muslim and performs all the other deeds. He is asked to repent until he goes back on his statement and his belief. If he does not repent, he receives the legal punishment for apostasy, which is execution, and is treated like an apostate. He is not washed or prayed over, he is not buried in the graveyards of the Muslims and there is no inheritance between him and them.

B. If someone leaves it out of laziness and negligence, while affirming that it is an obligation, this person is sinful (*fāsiq*) by consensus, even though the Imams[102] have differed as to how he is treated:

Abū Ḥanīfah and his companions ﷺ say that he is to be imprisoned and reprimanded by being beaten, as well as other means, or he spends the rest of his life of his prison, so as not to be a bad example for people, or a motive for them to be negligent concerning Islam's scared rites.

The other three Imams, Mālik, ash-Shāfiʿī and Aḥmad ﷺ say that the one who leaves the prayer out of laziness is asked to repent. If he does not pray and does not repent, he is executed. However, Mālik and ash-Shāfiʿī ﷺ say that he is killed as a legal punishment. He is then washed, shrouded, prayed over and buried in the graveyards of the Muslims. As for Aḥmad ﷺ he says that the person is executed for disbelief and treated as an apostate. Aḥmad's position is also the position of several Companions, including: ʿUmar, Ibn Masʿūd and Muʿādh ﷺ and it is also the position of several Followers[103].

As for fasting, its rank is second to that of the prayer, even though it is no less of an obligation. The Ummah has made consensus that it is one of the pillars of Islam, known to be of the religion by necessity. You have already gone over several ḥadīths on this, and this is why an-Nuʿmān ﷺ mentioned it in particular after the prayer. If the prayer is repeated by a Muslim five times a day, fasting is done every year for an entire month. The Muslim undergoes therein the pain of hunger and the severity of thirst, and struggles to maintain good character traits, such as patience and strong will, freedom from the slavery of desires and the authority of the material. One experiences the feelings of poverty and indigence, and thus there is charity and support, and justice and equality are realised. This is why fasting was worthy of being mentioned in Allah's statement ﷻ: {Every deed done by the child of Adam is for him apart from fasting. It is for Me and I reward it}, which is a ḥadīth qudsī related by Muslim and others. Yes, it is protection from

102 (tn): i.e. the Imams of the Four Madhhabs.

103 (tn): The sentencing and punishment is carried out by a Qāḍī (judge).

disobedience and protection from the Fire, and a means of expiating sins and entering Paradise: {Whoever fasts Ramaḍān with faith and anticipation of reward will have his previous sins forgiven}, as related by al-Bukhārī and others. Aḥmad and others have related from Abū Umāmah 🏵 who said, 'I came to the Messenger of Allah 🏵 and I said, "Command me to a deed that will enter me into Paradise." He replied, {You must fast, for it has no equal.} Then I came to him a second time and he said, {You must fast.}'

The ruling for not fasting Ramaḍān: The Muslims have made consensus that whoever does not fast Ramaḍān because they deny its obligation is a disbeliever and apostate from Islam, and such a person is treated as an apostate. This is due to the decisive evidences that establish it being an obligation and requirement.

As for someone who does not fast out of negligence, without an acceptable excuse in the Revealed Law, this person is sinful by consensus of the Muslims, and maybe there is doubt about his Islam. It could be thought that he is hiding his disbelief and has deviated from the religion, and his negligence will lead to open disbelief.

It has been related from Ibn 'Abbās 🏵 that the Messenger of Allah 🏵 said, {The bonds of Islam and the foundations of the religion are three. The fundamentals of Islam are based on them. Whoever leaves one of them is a disbeliever and his blood is lawful: the testimony that there is no god but Allah, the obligatory prayers and fasting Ramaḍān} This has been related by Abū Yaʻlā and ad-Daylamī and adh-Dhahabī declared it authentic. Furthermore, whoever does'nt fast without a valid excuse is imprisoned and denied food and drink in the day, so he has the appearance of fasting, and this is until Ramaḍān ends.

8. The Degrees of Worship and the Believer Striving towards the Greatest Degree of Perfection: Faith is the foundation of perfection. Entering Paradise in the absolute sense depends on faith and *tawḥīd*, nothing else. Thus, whoever believes in Allah the Exalted, His Messengers, His Books, His Angels, the Last Day, the Decree and Predestination and dies without having associated anything with Allah, will absolutely enter Paradise. Leaving obligations and doing that which is unlawful prevent one from entering it along with those who are not punished. Whoever does any of that will not enter it until after accounts have been settled. In the two *Ṣaḥīḥ* collections, it is on the authority of Abū Dharr 🏵 that the Prophet 🏵 said, {There is no slave who says there is no god but Allah and then dies upon that except that he enters Paradise.} In the same collections, it is on the authority of 'Ubādah ibn aṣ-Ṣāmit 🏵 that the Prophet 🏵 said, {Whoever bears witness that there is no god but Allah alone, that Muḥammad is His Slave and Messenger, that

ʿĪsā is Allah's Slave and Messenger and His Word that He cast into Maryam and a spirit from Him,[104] that Paradise is true and that the Fire is true, Allah enters him into Paradise according to his deeds.}

Doing the Obligatory and Leaving the Unlawful is Protection from the Fire: The basis of worshipping Allah ﷻ is maintaining the obligations while leaving that which is unlawful. Whoever does so wins a great victory and achieves a huge success. Aḥmad has collected the ḥadīth of ʿAmr ibn Murrah al-Juhanī, who said, 'A man came to the Messenger of Allah ﷺ and said, "O Messenger of Allah, I have testified that there is no god but Allah and that you are the Messenger of Allah. I have prayed the five prayers, paid the zakāt from my wealth and fasted the month of Ramaḍān." The Messenger of Allah ﷺ replied, {Whoever dies upon this is with the Prophets, the truly sincere and the martyrs on the Day of Standing. This will be the case – and he put up his two fingers – as long as he does not disrespect his parents.} Disrespecting parents means one does not treat them well, as Allah ﷻ and His Messenger ﷺ have commanded.

Doing Supererogatory Deeds Takes One Closer to Allah the Exalted and Perfection: It is absolutely permissible for a Muslim to leave supererogatory and voluntary deeds, as well as to do actions that are merely allowed or disliked (*makrūh*). As long as he carries out his obligations and avoids that which is unlawful, he will not be taken to task for any of that.

This is if an individual leaves something. As for a group leaving something, such as the people of a village or a large neighbourhood in a city agreeing to completely leave a *sunnah*[105] act, the jurists[106] have mentioned that they are fought until they come back. They are taken to task for this, because it informs of their aversion to this *sunnah* and a lack of desire for it.

Likewise, an individual leaving something is not taken to task for doing so as long as his leaving it does not arise from him making light of the Sunnah or a lack of firm conviction in its superiority and legitimacy. Otherwise, it is disbelief, deviation from the religion and apostasy, for which he is asked to repent. Upon doing so, he is compelled to perform supererogatory acts. Furthermore, if someone constantly leaves them off out of laziness while being firmly convinced of their legitimacy, his respectability (*murūʾah*) is nullified and it is a type of iniquity that renders his testimony unacceptable. This is because it indicates negligence concerning the religion and its sacred rites, in addition to what the Muslim himself

104 (tn): Please see Sūrat an-Nisāʾ 4:171.

105 (tn): i.e. recommended in the Revealed Law, such that an individual is rewarded for doing it but not punished for leaving it.

106 Ar. *al-fuqahāʾ*, or legal scholars.

loses in terms of immense reward by leaving such actions, especially since these actions have been legislated to compensate for shortcomings and defects in one's obligatory deeds.

The Muslim who hopes for success and aspires to reach the highest ranks with Allah ﷻ does not leave a supererogatory act or approach anything disliked. When something is asked of him, he does not distinguish between that which is obligatory and that which is recommended, just as he does not distinguish between the disliked and the unlawful when he is asked to leave something.
This is what the Companions of the Messenger of Allah ﷺ did in general. They did not make these distinctions when they were commanded or forbidden. Rather, they adhered to Allah's statement ﷻ:

﴿وَمَآ ءَاتَىٰكُمُ ٱلرَّسُولُ فَخُذُوهُ وَمَا نَهَىٰكُمْ عَنْهُ فَٱنتَهُوا۟﴾

"Whatever the Messenger gives you, you should accept. Whatever he forbids you, you should forgo." [al-Ḥashr 59:7]

This is out of desire for reward and seeking Allah's mercy and pleasure, while shunning disobedience and prohibited matters.

The Followers, the righteous of the First Three Generations and the Imams that followed them were the same. It was the jurists who made these distinctions in their researches and elucidated the categories of legal rulings: obligatory (*wājib*), recommended (*mandūb*), permissible (*mubāḥ*, unlawful (*muḥarram*) and disliked (*makrūh*). They can use this to determine whether a legally accountable person's conduct is valid or invalid, such that it would need to be repeated or not, and other rulings.

We see the Messenger of Allah ﷺ affirming this Companion based on his statement: 'By Allah, I will not add anything to that} and did not draw his attention to the superiority of doing extra, voluntary deeds. We know that he ﷺ did this to make it easy for him, and to teach leaders and those who guide to Allah ﷻ to spread the spirit of hope amongst people and to bear the traits of magnanimity and gentleness. He also did it to affirm the facilitation and lifting of difficulty that Islam has brought. However, he ﷺ know that when this *taqwā*-bearing believer worships Allah ﷻ with what He has obligated him, and it reaches his heart, expands his chest and he feels psychical tranquillity and spiritual delight, this will push him to have a deep love of worship. He will desire to do more in order to please Allah ﷻ by supererogatory deeds and leaving that which is disliked, especially after hearing the Messenger of Allah ﷺ quoting his Lord: {My slave continues to draw nearer to me with supererogatory acts until I love him. When I love him, I am his hearing with which he hears, his sight with which he sees, his hand with which he grasps and his foot with which he walks. If he asks Me, I will definitely give him. If he seeks refuge in Me, I will definitely give him refuge. If he calls on Me, I will definitely answer him.} Related by al-Bukhārī.[107]

{I am his hearing...} means: I will help him, protect him and give him victory in all of his activities and affairs.

Thus, the believer ascends the degrees of perfection until you see him as a valiant hero in the day and a humble worshipper at night:

﴿تَتَجَافَىٰ جُنُوبُهُمْ عَنِ ٱلْمَضَاجِعِ يَدْعُونَ رَبَّهُمْ خَوْفًا وَطَمَعًا وَمِمَّا رَزَقْنَـٰهُمْ يُنفِقُونَ﴾

"Their sides eschew their beds as they call on their Lord in fear and ardent hope. And they give of what We have provided them." [as-Sajdah 32:16]

9. Declaring Matters Lawful and Unlawful is Legislation, it is Only for Allah the Exalted: You now know that the basis of faith is that the believer have firm conviction that the lawful is what Allah ﷻ has declared lawful and the unlawful is what He has declared unlawful, regardless of whether he commits the unlawful or leaves the lawful. If a person claims that he is able to declare unlawful what Allah's legislation has declared lawful ﷻ or declare lawful what has been established as unlawful, is being insolent regarding Allah's right ﷻ for He alone has the authority to legislate, to declare matters lawful and unlawful. Whoever believes that he can legislate in violation of what Allah ﷻ has legislated and what the Messenger of Allah ﷺ has elucidated, or legislates according to his whims and desires without adhering to the principles of Islamic legislation, has exited Islam. Allah the Exalted and His Messenger ﷺ are free of him. Allah the Exalted has said,

﴿يَـٰٓأَيُّهَا ٱلَّذِينَ ءَامَنُوا۟ لَا تُحَرِّمُوا۟ طَيِّبَـٰتِ مَآ أَحَلَّ ٱللَّهُ لَكُمْ وَلَا تَعْتَدُوٓا۟ ۚ إِنَّ ٱللَّهَ لَا يُحِبُّ ٱلْمُعْتَدِينَ﴾

"You who believe! Do not make unlawful the good things Allah has made lawful for you, and do not overstep the limits. Allah does not love people who overstep the limits." [al-Mā'idah 5:87]

It has been established that this verse came down concerning some Companions who wanted to deny themselves certain good things out of asceticism and abstinence, so he ﷺ said to them, {But I pray and I sleep. I fast and I do not fast. I marry women. Whoever turns away from my Sunnah is not from me.} Related by al-Bukhārī and Muslim.

10. Breaking One's Oath and Keeping It: If someone vows to do something good or that which contains obedience, it is better for him to keep his oath, i.e. do what he has vowed to do. Allah the Exalted has said,

107 (tn): Please see the 38th ḥadīth in this book.

﴿وَٱحْفَظُوٓا۟ أَيْمَـٰنَكُمْ﴾
"Keep your oaths." [al-Mā'idah 5:89]

In other words, keep them and do not break them. If someone vows to leave an obligation or commit some disobedience, he is obligated to break his oath, i.e. to violate it and not do what he has vowed to do. Abū Dāwūd and others have related that the Prophet ﷺ said, {Whoever vows to commit disobedience has no oath.}

If someone vows to leave something good that is not obligatory upon him, it is preferable for him to break it, because that is better for him. Muslim has related that he ﷺ said, {If someone makes a vow and sees something superior to it, let him do that which is superior and his vow will be expiated.}

11. The Ḥadīth Advises:

- That the Muslim ask the people of knowledge about Islam's legislations, what is obligatory upon him, what is lawful for him and what is unlawful for him if he does not know. This is so that he can be upon guidance in his daily affairs and his soul can be at ease concerning the soundness of his actions.

- That the teacher make the learner comfortable, give him good news, and treat him with ease and in a way that makes him want to learn.

THE TWENTY-THIRD ḤADĪTH

كُلُّ خَيرٍ صَدَقَة

عَنْ أَبِي مَالِكٍ الْحَارِثِ بْنِ عَاصِمٍ الأَشْعَرِي ﷺ قَالَ: قَالَ رَسُوْلُ اللهِ ﷺ: {الطُّهُوْرُ شَطْرُ الْإِيمَانِ، وَالْحَمْدُ لِلهِ تَمْلَأُ الْمِيزَانَ، وَسُبْحَانَ اللهِ وَالْحَمْدُ لِلهِ تَمْلَآنِ - أَوْ تَمْلَأُ - مَا بَيْنَ السَّمَاوَاتِ وَالْأَرْضِ، وَالصَّلَاةُ نُوْرٌ، وَالصَّدَقَةُ بُرْهَانٌ، وَالصَّبْرُ ضِيَاءٌ، وَالْقُرْآنُ حُجَّةٌ لَكَ أَوْ عَلَيْكَ، كُلُّ النَّاسِ يَغْدُو، فَبَائِعٌ نَفْسَهُ، فَمُعْتِقُهَا أَوْ مُوبِقُهَا.} رواه مسلم.

Every Good Is Charity

It is on the authority of Abū Mālik al-Ḥārith ibn ʿĀṣim al-Ashʿarī ﷺ who said, 'The Messenger of Allah ﷺ said, {Purity is half of faith, *al-ḥamdu lillāh* fills the scales, *subḥān Allah wa*[108] *al-ḥamdu lillāh* both fill – or fills – whatever is between the heavens and the earth, prayer is light, charity[109] is proof, patience is radiant light, and the Qur'ān is a proof for you or against you. Everybody goes out in the morning and sells his soul. Then he either frees it from slavery or destroys it.}' Related by Muslim.

Muslim has collected the ḥadīth at the beginning of the Book of Purification (the chapter on the superiority of *wuḍū'*), no.223.

The Language of the Ḥadīth:

(الطهور) *at-ṭuhūr*: an action that results in the lifting of *ḥadath*,[110] such as *wuḍū'* and *ghusl*,[111] or the removal of filth,[112] such as purifying ones clothes, body and place of prayer, or it can simply refer to *wuḍū'*.

(شطر) *shaṭr*: a half (*niṣf*), as mentioned in a narration belonging to Aḥmad and at-Tirmidhī: *at-ṭuhūru niṣf ul-īmān.*

108 (tn): i.e. and.
109 Ar. *ṣadaqah.*
110 (tn): i.e. ritual impurity.
111 (tn): i.e. a purificatory bath.
112 Ar. *najāsah.*

(الحمد لله) *al-ḥamdu lillāh*: a beautiful praise for Allah the Exalted for the blessings He has bestowed, and what is meant here is the reward for saying *al-ḥamdu lillāh.*

(الميزان) *al-mīzān*: the side of the scale that will have the slaves' good deeds on the Day of Standing.

(سبحان الله) *subḥān Allah*: the glorification of Allah the Exalted and declaring Him transcendent above every imperfection, and what is meant here is the reward for saying *subḥān Allah.*

(الصلاة نور) *as-ṣalātu nūr*: i.e. it guides one to doing good just as light guides one to the right path.

(برهان) *burhān*: evidence of the veracity of faith.

(الصبر) *as-ṣabr*: restraining the ego from what it desires, making it bear that which is difficult and making it firm upon the truth despite adversities.

(ضياء) *ḍiyā'*: intense light, i.e. with patience, anxieties are lifted.

(حجة) *ḥujjah*: a proof, an evidence and a guide that will defend you.

(يغدو) *yaghdu*: to go out early and strive for oneself, *al-ghadu* is to go out between the crack of dawn and sunrise.

(بائع نفسه) *bā'i'un nafasah*: to Allah by obeying Him, or to one's demon and one's passions by disobeying Allah the Exalted and angering Him.

(معتقها) *mu'tiquhā*: delivering from disgrace in this life and punishment in the Hereafter.

(موبقها) *mūbiquha*: destroying it by committing disobedience and the disgrace and punishment that result from doing so.

Legal Matters and Other Guidance from the Ḥadīth:

1. Profound Wisdom: He ﷺ was granted comprehensive speech, and how often would he advice and counsel his Companions with clear, concise words that contained every goodness and warned against every evil, without there being any complication in the wording or detriment to the meaning. The ḥadīth in front of us contains magnificent instructions, profound Prophetic wisdoms and lessons issued from the one who does not speak from whim. Rather, it is revelation that is revealed.[113] If Allah the Exalted so wills, we shall clarify these lessons in what follows.

2. Purity and its Reward:

Purification is a condition for the validity of worship, and a sign of Allah the Exalted's love. He ﷻ made it clear, putting the humble believers' hearts at ease, that what the believer does by purifying his body and his clothes, in preparation for intimate conversation with his Lord is an important and prominent sign of his faith, as it expresses his submission to His command and answering His call when He ﷻ said,

﴿يَٰٓأَيُّهَا ٱلنَّاسُ ٱعۡبُدُواْ رَبَّكُمُ ٱلَّذِي خَلَقَكُمۡ﴾

"Mankind! Worship your Lord, who created you" [al-Baqarah 2:21]

He ﷻ has also said,

﴿إِذَا قُمۡتُمۡ إِلَى ٱلصَّلَوٰةِ فَٱغۡسِلُواْ وُجُوهَكُمۡ وَأَيۡدِيَكُمۡ إِلَى ٱلۡمَرَافِقِ وَٱمۡسَحُواْ بِرُءُوسِكُمۡ

وَأَرۡجُلَكُمۡ إِلَى ٱلۡكَعۡبَيۡنِۚ وَإِن كُنتُمۡ جُنُبًا فَٱطَّهَّرُواْ﴾

"You who believe! When you get up to do the prayer, wash your faces and your hands and your arms to the elbows, and wipe over your heads, and wash your feet to the ankles. If you are in a state of major impurity, purify yourselves." [al-Mā'idah 5:6]

He ﷻ has also said,

﴿وَثِيَابَكَ فَطَهِّرۡ﴾

"Purify your clothes." [al-Mudaththir 74:4]

Thus, one will tolerate inconveniences in order to stand before Allah the Exalted in a clean and devout state, with a pleasant scent and good manners, just as Allah has made His creation beautiful. This will necessitate Allah's love for him:

﴿إِنَّ ٱللَّهَ يُحِبُّ ٱلتَّوَّٰبِينَ وَيُحِبُّ ٱلۡمُتَطَهِّرِينَ﴾

"Allah loves those who turn back from wrongdoing and He loves those who purify themselves." [al-Baqarah 2:222]

A. Half of faith: He ﷺ has made it clear that the reward for purification, whether *wuḍū'* or something else, is multiplied by Allah the Exalted until it reaches half the

113 (tn): Please see Sūrat an-Najm 53:3-4.

reward of faith. This is because faith effaces previous mistakes, major and minor, and purification – especially *wuḍū'* - effaces previous minor mistakes, so it is like half of faith.

Muslim has related from ʿUthmān ﷺ that the Prophet ﷺ said, {Whoever does *wuḍū'* and does it well, his mistakes will leave body until they leave it from under his nails.}

Furthermore, faith is a cleansing of one's inward from abstract filth, such as associating partners with Allah the Exalted, hypocrisy and so forth. Purification is a cleansing of one's outward from material filth, and thus it is a mark of the believers on the Day of Standing. He ﷺ has said, {My Ummah will be summoned on the Day of Standing and with bright faces and limbs from the effects of *wuḍū'*, so whoever is able to prolong his whiteness,[114] let him do so.}

B. Purification is Half of Prayer: Some have explained faith in the ḥadīth to mean prayer, based on the Exalted's statement:

﴿وَمَا كَانَ ٱللَّهُ لِيُضِيعَ إِيمَـٰنَكُمْ﴾

"Allah would never let your faith go to waste". [al-Baqarah 2:143]

i.e. the prayer that you prayed in Jerusalem. These people say that purification is half of faith, i.e. half of the prayer, because purification is a condition for its validity, and a condition is like a half.

C. *Wuḍū'* is the Key to Paradise: It has been mentioned in Allah the Exalted's Book that the disbelievers enter the Fire because they are not included in the ranks of the believers. Allah the Exalted has said,

﴿مَا سَلَكَكُمْ فِى سَقَرَ ۝٤٢ قَالُوا۟ لَمْ نَكُ مِنَ ٱلْمُصَلِّينَ﴾

"'What caused you to enter the melting Fire?'[115] They will say, 'We were not among those who prayed...'" [al-Mudaththir 74:42-43]

Thus, the prayer rescues one from the Fire and it is the path that leads to Paradise. Purification is the key to the prayer, and thus via the prayer it is the key to Paradise. In a narration of Muslim: {There is no Muslim who does *wuḍū'* and does it properly, then stands and does two units of prayer and devotes both his face and heart therein except that Paradise becomes necessary for him.} He has another narration: {There is not a single one of you who does *wuḍū'* and does it

114 (tn): i.e. to wash a bit more than what is obligatory while washing the face in *wuḍū'*.

115 Ar. *saqar.*

thoroughly and then says, 'I bear witness that there is no god but Allah and I bear witness that Muḥammad is His Slave and Messenger' except the eight doors of Paradise are opened unto him and he enters whichever one he wishes.

D. One of the Characteristics of Faith: *Wuḍū'* is one of the hidden characteristics of faith, which no one but the believer maintains. He ﷺ said, {No one maintains his *wuḍū'* except for a believer}, as related by Ibn Mājah and al-Ḥākim. This is because it is not obvious, in addition to the inconveniences involved, and thus the one who maintains it is closer to entering Paradise.

Ibn Khuzaymah has related in his *Ṣaḥīḥ* that the Messenger of Allah ﷺ woke up one day, called Bilāl and said, {O Bilāl, how did you get into Paradise before me? I entered Paradise yesterday and I heard your rustling in front of me.} Bilāl replied, 'O Messenger of Allah, I have never given the *adhān* without having prayed two units beforehand, and I have never entered *ḥadath* without making *wuḍū'* immediately.' He ﷺ said, {That is how.}

E. Purification is a Trust: Ibn Mājah has related from Abū Ayyūb al-Anṣārī that the Messenger of Allah ﷺ said, {The five prayers, Friday to Friday, and fulfilling trusts are an expiation for whatever is between them.} It was then said, 'What is fulfilling a trust?' He replied, {*Ghusl* when one is in a state of major ritual impurity,[116] for there is a major ritual impurity in every hair.} And there is the ḥadīth of Abū ad-Dardā' {Allah does not entrust the child of Adam with anything from the religion apart from this.} This is because it is an abstract, legal matter that exists in the body; only Allah is aware of it. No one knows about it apart from the one who has it, and it is not lifted unless the one who has it does something and does so deliberately. It is also likely that no one knows about him lifting his *janābah*, just as the intention is a hidden matter. Therefore, lifting it with purification is part of fulfilling trusts.

F. Purification of the Heart: Material purification has no value if it is not accompanied by inner purification, and thus the believer's purification of his body must be accompanied by purification of his heart, as well as a good and valid intention and upright conduct. Indeed, al-Ghazālī explained purity in this ḥadīth to mean the purification of the heart from malice, envy, hatred and other diseases of the heart, because faith is only perfect by doing so. He also explained it to be leaving disobedience and sins. The Exalted One has said on the tongue of the people of Lūṭ, when they describe Lūṭ and his family and their being removed from committing iniquity:

116 Ar. *janābah.*

﴿إِنَّهُمْ أُنَاسٌ يَتَطَهَّرُونَ﴾

"They are a people who keep themselves pure."

[al-ʾAʿrāf 7:82 and an-Naml 27:56]

3. Remembering Allah the Exalted and Being Grateful to Him: Expressing gratitude to Allah the Exalted is done by frequently remembering him, and especially with the invocations that have reached us from the Messenger of Allah ﷺ. Their reward fills the scale of righteous deeds on the Day of Standing and causes them to outnumber the evil deeds, and thus one is among the successful and those brought near to Allah the Exalted. This is especially the case if the praise of Allah is joined with declaring Him ﷻ transcendent, sanctifying Him, exalting Him, extolling His greatness,[117] glorifying Him and proclaiming His oneness.

{...*al-ḥamdu lillāh* fills the scales, *subḥān Allah wa al-ḥamdu lillāh* both fill – or fills – whatever is between the heavens and the earth...} Muslim and others have another narration: {Saying *subḥān Allah* and *Allahu akbar* fills the sky and the earth.} At-Tirmidhī has yet another narration: {There is no barrier between saying *lā ilāha ill Allah* and Allah until it reaches Him.}

The superiority of these four utterances has been mentioned in several ḥadīths. In the *Musnad* of Imam Aḥmad ﷺ it is on the authority of Abū Saʿīd and Abū Hurayrah ﷺ that the Prophet ﷺ said, {Out of all speech, Allah has chosen four utterances: *subḥān Allah, al-ḥamdu lillāh, lā ilāha ill Allah* and *Allahu akbar*. When someone says *subḥān Allah,* twenty good deeds are written for him and twenty evil deeds are effaced. It is the same when someone says *Allahu akbar,* the same when someone says *lā ilāha ill Allah* and the same when someone says *al-ḥamdu lillāh*. When someone says *al-ḥamdu lillāh Rabb il-ʿālamīn*[118] by himself, thirty good deeds are written for him and thirty evil deeds are effaced.}

Thus, whoever expresses the above with his tongue, firmly convinced of what he is uttering while it fills his heart and soul, and he reflects on their meanings in his mind, will attain an immense reward. If it were to be measured in terms of surface area and volume, it would fill whatever is between the heavens and the earth, and he would have a ladder with which to ascend the ranks of The Most High. In at-Tirmidhī's collection, there is a ḥadīth of Abū Hurayrah ﷺ in which the Prophet ﷺ said, {No slave says *lā ilāha ill Allah* sincerely except that the gates of the sky are opened unto him, until he reaches the Throne,[119] as long as he avoids major sins.} The Throne is the roof of the Highest Garden[120] in Paradise, so whoever reaches it shall dwell in the highest of abodes and attain the loftiest of ranks.

---

117 (tn): i.e. saying *Allahu akbar.*

118 (tn): i.e. all praise be to Allah, Lord of all Creation.

119 Ar. *al-ʿArsh.*

120 Ar. *al-Firdaws al-ʾAʿlā.*

Furthermore, the scholars have said that these four utterances are the 'right actions which are lasting',[121] as Allah the Exalted says,

﴿ٱلْمَالُ وَٱلْبَنُونَ زِينَةُ ٱلْحَيَوٰةِ ٱلدُّنْيَا ۖ وَٱلْبَٰقِيَٰتُ ٱلصَّٰلِحَٰتُ خَيْرٌ عِندَ رَبِّكَ ثَوَابًا وَخَيْرٌ أَمَلًا﴾

"Wealth and children are the embellishment of this worldly life. But, in your Lord's sight, right actions which are lasting bring a better reward and are a better basis for hope." [al-Kahf 18:46]

Their rewards remains with Allah ﷻ growing and becoming more magnificent, which is better than wealth, family and children.

- **The Tranquillity of the Heart:** While engaging in remembrance, the heart must be present and understand the meaning as much as possible, so that it has an effect on the Muslim's soul, brings tranquillity to his heart and his conduct becomes upright.

﴿ٱلَّذِينَ ءَامَنُوا۟ وَتَطْمَئِنُّ قُلُوبُهُم بِذِكْرِ ٱللَّهِ ۗ أَلَا بِذِكْرِ ٱللَّهِ تَطْمَئِنُّ ٱلْقُلُوبُ﴾

"...those who believe and whose hearts find peace in the remembrance of Allah. Only in the remembrance of Allah can the heart find peace." [ar-Ra'd 13:28]

- **Frequent Remembrance:** The believer is in urgent need of bringing tranquillity to his heart and stability to his soul, and thus he must engage in frequent remembrance of Allah ﷻ so that he is always connected to Him, relying on Him, seeking His support and assistance and asking for His pardon and forgiveness. It is also so that Allah ﷻ remembers him in the unseen, envelops him in His bounty and mercy and shows him the ways of guidance and truth.

﴿يَٰٓأَيُّهَا ٱلَّذِينَ ءَامَنُوا۟ ٱذْكُرُوا۟ ٱللَّهَ ذِكْرًا كَثِيرًا ۝٤١ وَسَبِّحُوهُ بُكْرَةً وَأَصِيلًا ۝٤٢ هُوَ ٱلَّذِى يُصَلِّى عَلَيْكُمْ وَمَلَٰٓئِكَتُهُۥ لِيُخْرِجَكُم مِّنَ ٱلظُّلُمَٰتِ إِلَى ٱلنُّورِ ۚ وَكَانَ بِٱلْمُؤْمِنِينَ رَحِيمًا﴾

"You who believe! Remember Allah much, and glorify Him in the morning and in the evening. It is He who calls down blessings on you, as do His angels, to bring you out of the darkness into the light. He is Most Merciful to the believers". [al-Aḥzāb 33:41-43]

'...in the morning and in the evening' means when the sun rises and when it inclines towards setting, and what is intended is all times.

121 Ar. *al-bāqiyātu s-ṣāliḥāt.*

4. The Prayer is Light: the prayer is a firm obligation and a fundamental pillar of Islam. It is – as he ﷺ has clarified – absolute light, showing the one who prays the path of goodness, protecting him from disobedience and guiding him to the way of uprightness. The Exalted One has said,

﴿إِنَّ ٱلصَّلَوٰةَ تَنْهَىٰ عَنِ ٱلْفَحْشَآءِ وَٱلْمُنكَرِ﴾

"The prayer precludes indecency and wrongdoing." [al-ʿAnkabūt 29:45]

It is thus an abstract light through which the paths of guidance and truth are illuminated, just as the straight road and the right path are illuminated by material light. It imparts awe and splendour to the Muslim in the life just as light will radiate on his face on the Day of Standing.

﴿نُورُهُمْ يَسْعَىٰ بَيْنَ أَيْدِيهِمْ وَبِأَيْمَـٰنِهِمْ﴾

"Their light will stream out ahead of them and on their right." [at-Taḥrīm 66:8]

This is because the one who is upright with Allah the Exalted and stands before him five times a day in humility and devotion will have an upright state with people and be distinguished by his manners and conduct, by his carefulness and *taqwā*, and Allah ﷻ will put light on his face just as He put light in his heart. The Exalted One has said,

﴿سِيمَاهُمْ فِى وُجُوهِهِم مِّنْ أَثَرِ ٱلسُّجُودِ﴾

"Their mark is on their faces, the traces of prostration." [al-Fatḥ 48:29]

At-Ṭabarānī has narrated from ʿUbādah ibn as-Ṣāmit ؓ *marfūʿan*: {If the slave preserves his prayer, and thus he establishes its *wuḍū'*, its bowing, its prostration and its recitation therein, the prayer will say to him, 'May Allah preserve you the way you preserved me.' Then he ascends with it into the sky and it has light, and it ends up at Allah ﷻ and intercedes for him.}

- **The Light of Congregation and the Masjid:** If the Muslim maintains the prayer in congregation then that is light upon light, and if it is in the masjid, the light is perfected and it is victory and success. He has gone ahead to Paradise with the pious and those drawn near to Him. He, peace and blessings be upon him, has said, {Whoever prays the five prayers in congregation will traverse the bridge like a flash of lightning, in the first group of forerunners,[122] and he will come on the Day of Standing like the moon when it is full}, as related by At-Ṭabarānī. He ﷺ has said, {Give glad tidings to those who walk in darkness to the masjids of perfect light on the Day of Standing}, as related by Abū Dāwūd and at-Tirmidhī.

122 Ar. *as-sābiqūn*, please see at-Tawbah 9:100.

- **The Coolness of One's Eyes and the Alleviation of Grief:** The prayer is the connection between the slave and his Lord and his intimate conversation with His creator. This is why it is the coolness of the eyes for the people of *taqwā*. They find therein comfort, serenity and security. They rush towards it whenever they feel anxious or are struck with grief, and this is nothing strange. They are merely drinking from the spring of the Master of the Messengers, who said, {The coolness of my eyes has been placed in the prayer}, as related by Aḥmad and an-Nasāʾī. 'The coolness of my eyes' means that which pleases me and which my eye enjoys. Also, if a matter befell him, he would say, {O Bilāl, establish the prayer and comfort us with it}, as related by Abū Dāwūd. A matter befalling him means a matter that caused him concern and worry.

5. Charity is Proof:

The *burhān*[123] is the rays next to the sun's face. He ﷺ has said, {When the believer's spirit leaves his body, it has a *burhān* like the sun's *burhān*.} This is why a decisive proof is called a *burhān*; it clearly shows what it is indicating.

Likewise, charity is a proof for the veracity of one's faith, and one being well-disposed towards it is a sign of the presence of faith and its taste. He ﷺ has said, {Whoever has done three things has tasted the taste of faith: the one who worships Allah alone, knows that there is no god but Allah and pays the zakāt from his wealth and his soul is well-disposed towards it, assisting him every year}, as related by Abū Dāwūd. His soul assisting him is mentioned because the ego[124] loves wealth and is stingy with it, so if it is allowing wealth to be given for the sake of Allah ﷻ this is a sign of the veracity of its faith in Allah and that it affirms His promise and His threat.

Purity and Veracity: The Muslim who has been cleansed and purified of material filth, who expresses his gratitude to Allah and carries out Allah's right over His slaves, His worship is also purified and cleansed from moral filth. The most prominent of such filth is avarice and greed, for the Muslim is always open-handed and generous, magnanimous and kind, and thus greed and faith are never gathered in the same heart. The Exalted One has said,

﴿وَمَن يُوقَ شُحَّ نَفْسِهِۦ فَأُوْلَـٰٓئِكَ هُمُ ٱلْمُفْلِحُونَ﴾

"It is the people who are safeguarded from the avarice of their own selves who are successful." [al-Ḥashr 59:9] and [at-Taghābun 64:19]

Thus, charity and spending on good causes in order to help the poor and indigent, seeking to please Allah and desiring His face, whether it is obligatory or

123 (tn): i.e. the word used for 'proof'.

124 Ar. *nafs*, which can be translated as soul or ego.

voluntary, is a decisive evidence and clear sign of the veracity of someone's faith, and that this person is among the ranks of the successful believers. The Exalted One has said,

﴿قَدْ أَفْلَحَ ٱلْمُؤْمِنُونَ ۝١ ٱلَّذِينَ هُمْ فِى صَلَاتِهِمْ خَـٰشِعُونَ ۝٢

وَٱلَّذِينَ هُمْ عَنِ ٱللَّغْوِ مُعْرِضُونَ ۝٣ وَٱلَّذِينَ هُمْ لِلزَّكَوٰةِ فَـٰعِلُونَ﴾

"It is the believers who are successful: those who are humble in their prayer; those who turn away from worthless talk; those who pay the zakāt" [al-Mu'minūn 23:1-4]

6. Patience is Radiant Light: *Ḍiyā'* is the light that bears a type of heat and burning, like the *ḍiyā'* of the sun, as opposed to the moon, which is simply light that shines without burning. Patience is radiant light because it is hard on the ego. One needs to struggle against the ego, control it and restrain it from its passions.

Patience is the Path of Victory: The Muslim remains upon that which is correct as long as he continues to be patient, because anyone living in this world is surrounded by adversities and calamities, all of which require firmness and strength. Otherwise, a person will fail and be lost. How great is the Muslim's need for patience. Obedience requires patience. Leaving disobedience requires patience. Bearing with inconveniences and adversities requires patience. Therefore, to be moulded by patience is a power like no other power, an immense light that keeps one illuminated, guided to the truth and persistent in that which is right.

The Exalted One has said in praise of Ayyūb ﷺ,

﴿إِنَّا وَجَدْنَـٰهُ صَابِرًا ۚ نِّعْمَ ٱلْعَبْدُ ۖ إِنَّهُۥٓ أَوَّابٌ﴾

"We found him steadfast. What an excellent slave!" [Ṣād 38:44]

He ﷻ has also said,

﴿وَبَشِّرِ ٱلصَّـٰبِرِينَ ۝١٥٥ ٱلَّذِينَ إِذَآ أَصَـٰبَتْهُم مُّصِيبَةٌ قَالُوٓا۟ إِنَّا لِلَّهِ وَإِنَّآ إِلَيْهِ رَٰجِعُونَ ۝١٥٦

أُو۟لَـٰٓئِكَ عَلَيْهِمْ صَلَوَٰتٌ مِّن رَّبِّهِمْ وَرَحْمَةٌ ۖ وَأُو۟لَـٰٓئِكَ هُمُ ٱلْمُهْتَدُونَ﴾

"But give good news to the steadfast, those who, when disaster strikes them, say, 'We belong to Allah and to Him we will return.' Those are the people who will have blessings and mercy from their Lord; they are the ones who are guided." [al-Baqarah 2:155-157]

Please see the detailed discussion on patience in the commentary on the nineteenth ḥadīth.

7. The Qurʾān is a Proof: The Muslim's way is the Qurʾān. His imam is Allah the Exalted's Book: he is guided by its guidance, he carries out its commands, he refrains from what it prohibits and he is moulded by its manners. Whoever does this, benefits from the Qurʾān when he recites it, and it is a guide that guides him to success in this life and a proof that will defend him on the Day of Standing.Whoever deviates from the path and from the Qurʾān's teachings will find the Qurʾān to be his adversary on the Day of Standing. The more he recites it without acting upon it, the greater his sin, because he is making himself a proof against himself, that he has deviated from the correct path:

﴿إِنَّ هَـٰذَا ٱلْقُرْءَانَ يَهْدِى لِلَّتِى هِىَ أَقْوَمُ﴾

"This Qurʾān guides to the most upright way." [al-Isrāʾ 17:9]

He ﷺ has said, {I have left with you that which if you cling to it, you will never go astray after me: the Book of Allah}, as related by Muslim. He has also said, {Read the Qurʾān, for it will come on the Day of Standing as an intercessor.}

The Cure of the Believer and the Malady of the Disbeliever and Hypocrite: In Allah the Exalted's Book, the believer finds a cure for both material and moral illnesses. Every time he reads it and contemplates it, his spirit is illuminated and his heart is expanded, and the secret of life flows through his veins. When the non-believer hears the Qurʾān, his whole body trembles with fear, his soul becomes distress and he thinks that destruction will befall him. The Exalted One has said,

﴿وَنُنَزِّلُ مِنَ ٱلْقُرْءَانِ مَا هُوَ شِفَآءٌ وَرَحْمَةٌ لِّلْمُؤْمِنِينَ ۙ وَلَا يَزِيدُ ٱلظَّـٰلِمِينَ إِلَّا خَسَارًا﴾

"We send down in the Qurʾān that which is a healing and a mercy to the believers, but it only increases the wrongdoers in loss." [al-Isrāʾ 17:82]

Someone from the First Three Generations said, 'No one sits down with the Qurʾān and stands up again and is the same. Either he profits or he loses.' Then he recited this verse.

On the Path to Paradise: He ﷺ concludes these wonderful instructions and brilliant lessons by elucidating the categories that people fall into. Every day, everyone wakes up and goes to bed, but they are in the same state. There are those who spend their night or their day in obedience to Allah ﷻ is He, and in pleasing Him. They are sincere in their dealings with Allah ﷻ and with people, and thus they have saved their souls from destruction and punishment. People like this have a free soul, a free mind and free will. They will only accept the eternal Paradise and the everlasting blessings therein. Then there are those who spend their night or their day in disobedience to Allah, violating His commands in public and in private, with Allah the Exalted and with the creation, and thus they have destroyed their souls and placed them in grave danger. They have sold their souls for a pittance: misery in this life and prison in the everlasting Fire in the end, because they are prisoners of their own desires, obeying their demons and their egos. {Everybody goes out in the morning and sells his soul. Then he either frees it from slavery or destroys it.} Every individual is striving either to destroy himself or to emancipate himself. The one who strives to obey Allah has sold his soul to Allah and liberated it from His punishment. The one who strives to disobey Allah the Exalted has sold his soul in disgrace and thrown it into sin, which necessitates Allah's anger and punishment ﷻ. The Exalted One has said,

﴿وَنَفْسٍ وَمَا سَوَّىٰهَا ۝٧ فَأَلْهَمَهَا فُجُورَهَا وَتَقْوَىٰهَا ۝٨ قَدْ أَفْلَحَ مَن زَكَّىٰهَا ۝٩ وَقَدْ خَابَ مَن دَسَّىٰهَا﴾

"and the self and what proportioned it, and inspired it with depravity or *taqwā*, he who purifies it has succeeded, he who covers it up has failed." [ash-Shams 91:7-10]

The meaning is that whoever purifies his soul by obeying Allah has succeeded, and whoever throws his soul into disobedience has failed. Obedience cleanses and purifies the soul and thus it elevates it, while disobedience corrupts the soul and represses it, and thus it sinks and becomes like something that gets buried in the soil. Allah the Exalted has said,

﴿قُلْ إِنَّ ٱلْخَـٰسِرِينَ ٱلَّذِينَ خَسِرُوٓا۟ أَنفُسَهُمْ وَأَهْلِيهِمْ يَوْمَ ٱلْقِيَـٰمَةِ ۗ أَلَا ذَٰلِكَ هُوَ ٱلْخُسْرَانُ ٱلْمُبِينُ﴾

"Say: 'The real losers are those who lose their souls and their families on the Day of Standing.' Is that not a clear loss?" [az-Zumar 39:15]

Testimony that is Accepted and Saves: In order to emancipate himself from the Fire, the believer works to polish his faith and strengthen his certainty by remembering Allah the Exalted. He ﷺ has said, {If someone says when they wake up or go to bed,

(اللهُمَّ إِنِّي أَصْبَحْتُ أُشْهِدُكَ وَأُشْهِدُ حَمَلَةَ عَرْشِكَ وَمَلائِكَتَكَ وَجَمِيعَ خَلْقِكَ أَنَّكَ أَنْتَ اللهُ

لَا إِلَهَ إِلَّا أَنْتَ وَحْدَكَ لَا شَرِيكَ لَكَ، وَأَنَّ مُحَمَّدًا عَبْدُكَ وَرَسُولُكَ.)،

'O Allah, I woke up bearing witness before You and bearing witness before those who carry Your Throne, Your angels and all of Your creation that You are Allah. There is no god but You, alone, You have no partner, and Muḥammad is Your Slave and Your Messenger', Allah emancipates a quarter of him from the Fire. If he says it twice, Allah emancipates half of him from the Fire. If he says it three times, Allah saves three quarters of him from the Fire, and if he says it four times, Allah saves him from the Fire}, as related by Abū Dāwūd. It is because this testimony puts the fear of Allah ﷻ into a person's soul, along with desire to obey him and dread of disobeying him. It will thus cause him to be far removed from the Fire and close to Allah's pleasure ﷻ. He ﷺ has also said, {Whoever says (سُبْحَانَ اللهِ وَبِحَمْدِهِ) *subḥān Allahi wa bi ḥamdihi* a thousand times when they wake up sells his soul to Allah, and at the end of his day he is emancipated from the Fire.}

There is No Sale except to Allah the Exalted: The believer is valued and noble, precious and of esteemed rank, and thus he refuses to offer his soul to other than Allah ﷻ because he will not find anyone among the creation that will give him the appropriate, proper price. How can he, when the contract between the believer and his Creator ﷻ was made in pre-eternity? The Exalted One has said,

﴿إِنَّ ٱللَّهَ ٱشْتَرَىٰ مِنَ ٱلْمُؤْمِنِينَ أَنفُسَهُمْ وَأَمْوَٰلَهُم بِأَنَّ لَهُمُ ٱلْجَنَّةَ﴾

"Allah has bought from the believers their selves and their wealth in return for Paradise." [at-Tawbah 9:111]

This is why they strive to please Allah the Exalted and avoid anything that angers him, so that they can obtain the full, available price. This world does not entice them, wealth does not deceive them, threats do not dissuade them and fear of death does not discourage them. Allah the Sublime spoke the truth when He ﷻ said,

﴿وَمِنَ ٱلنَّاسِ مَن يَشْرِى نَفْسَهُ ٱبْتِغَآءَ مَرْضَاتِ ٱللَّهِ ۗ وَٱللَّهُ رَءُوفٌۢ بِٱلْعِبَادِ﴾

"And among the people there are some who sell their souls, desiring the good pleasure of Allah. Allah is Ever-Gentle with His slaves." [al-Baqarah 2:207]

He ﷻ also said,

﴿مِّنَ ٱلْمُؤْمِنِينَ رِجَالٌ صَدَقُوا۟ مَا عَـٰهَدُوا۟ ٱللَّهَ عَلَيْهِ ۖ فَمِنْهُم مَّن قَضَىٰ نَحْبَهُۥ
وَمِنْهُم مَّن يَنتَظِرُ ۖ وَمَا بَدَّلُوا۟ تَبْدِيلًا﴾

"Among the believers there are men who have been true to the contract they made with Allah. Some of them have fulfilled their pact by death and some are still waiting to do so, not having changed in any way at all." [al-Aḥzāb 33:23]

Fulfilling their pact by death means dying as a martyr.

8. The Ḥadīth Also Advises:

A. Faith is word and deed, it increases and decreases. You increase it through righteous actions and obedience and you decrease it with disobedience and sins.

B. Deeds have weight, they can be light or heavy. This is evidenced by the texts of the Book and Sunnah and the Ummah has made consensus on it.

He ﷺ has said, {There are two words that are beloved to the All-Merciful, heavy on the scale and light on the tongue:

(سُبْحَانَ اللهِ، وَبِحَمْدِهِ سُبْحَانَ اللهِ الْعَظِيمِ),

subḥān Allahi wa bi ḥamdihi, subḥān Allah il-ʿAẓīm[125]}, related by al-Bukhārī and Muslim. He also said, {The heaviest thing that is placed on the scale is good character.}

C. Maintaining the prayers in their specified times, and performing them completely with their pillars, obligations, recommended actions and etiquettes, after fulfilling all of their conditions.

D. Frequently spending on good causes and hastening to fulfill the needs of the poor and indigent, and looking for widows, orphans, and virtuous paupers and spending on them, so that one's charity can be sincerely for the Exalted's Face.

E. Patience in the face of adversity, and especially that which the Muslim faces when enjoining the right, forbidding the wrong and calling to Allah the Exalted. The Exalted One has said,

﴿وَٱصْبِرْ عَلَىٰ مَآ أَصَابَكَ﴾

"...and be steadfast in the face of all that happens to you." [Luqmān 31:17]

He ﷻ has also said,

﴿فَٱصْبِرْ كَمَا صَبَرَ أُوْلُواْ ٱلْعَزْمِ مِنَ ٱلرُّسُلِ﴾

"So be steadfast as the Messengers with firm resolve were also steadfast." [al-Aḥqāf 46:35]

F. The Qur'ān is the Muslim's constitution. He must recite it along with understanding its meaning and acting upon it.

G. The Muslim strives to benefit from his time and his lifespan by obeying Allah ﷻ and he only busies himself with His Lord, Glorified is He and that which will benefit him in his livelihood and in his Hereafter.

125 (tn): i.e. 'Glory be to Allah the Sublime'.

THE TWENTY-FOURTH ḤADĪTH

تَحْرِيمُ الظُّلْمِ

عَنْ أَبِي ذَرٍّ الْغِفَارِيِّ ﷺ، عَنْ النَّبِيِّ ﷺ فِيمَا يَرْوِيهِ عَنْ رَبِّهِ ﷻ أَنَّهُ قَالَ: {يَا عِبَادِي إِنِّي حَرَّمْتُ الظُّلْمَ عَلَى نَفْسِي وَجَعَلْتُهُ بَيْنَكُمْ مُحَرَّماً فَلَا تَظَالَمُوا.

يَا عِبَادِي كُلُّكُمْ ضَالٌّ إِلَّا مَنْ هَدَيْتُهُ، فَاسْتَهْدُونِي أَهْدِكُمْ.

يَا عِبَادِي كُلُّكُمْ جَائِعٌ إِلَّا مَنْ أَطْعَمْتُهُ، فَاسْتَطْعِمُونِي أُطْعِمْكُمْ.

يَا عِبَادِي كُلُّكُمْ عَارٍ إِلَّا مَنْ كَسَوْتُهُ، فَاسْتَكْسُونِي أَكْسُكُمْ.

يَا عِبَادِي إِنَّكُمْ تُخْطِئُونَ بِاللَّيْلِ وَالنَّهَارِ، وَأَنَا أَغْفِرُ الذُّنُوبَ جَمِيعاً، فَاسْتَغْفِرُونِي أَغْفِرْ لَكُمْ.

يَا عِبَادِي إِنَّكُمْ لَنْ تَبْلُغُوا ضَرِّي فَتَضُرُّونِي، وَلَنْ تَبْلُغُوا نَفْعِي فَتَنْفَعُونِي.

يَا عِبَادِي لَوْ أَنَّ أَوَّلَكُمْ وَآخِرَكُمْ وَإِنْسَكُمْ وَجِنَّكُمْ كَانُوا عَلَى أَتْقَى قَلْبِ رَجُلٍ وَاحِدٍ مِنْكُمْ مَا زَادَ ذَلِكَ فِي مُلْكِي شَيْئاً.

يَا عِبَادِي لَوْ أَنَّ أَوَّلَكُمْ وَآخِرَكُمْ وَإِنْسَكُمْ وَجِنَّكُمْ كَانُوا عَلَى أَفْجَرِ قَلْبِ وَاحِدٍ مِنْكُمْ مَا نَقَصَ ذَلِكَ مِنْ مُلْكِي شَيْئاً.

يَا عِبَادِي لَوْ أَنَّ أَوَّلَكُمْ وَآخِرَكُمْ وَإِنْسَكُمْ وَجِنَّكُمْ قَامُوا فِي صَعِيدٍ وَاحِدٍ، فَسَأَلُونِي، فَأَعْطَيْتُ كُلَّ وَاحِدٍ مَسْأَلَتَهُ مَا نَقَصَ ذَلِكَ مِمَّا عِنْدِي إِلَّا كَمَا يَنْقُصُ الْمِخْيَطُ إِذَا أُدْخِلَ الْبَحْرَ.

يَا عِبَادِي إِنَّمَا هِيَ أَعْمَالُكُمْ أُحْصِيهَا لَكُمْ ثُمَّ أُوَفِّيكُمْ إِيَّاهَا، فَمَنْ وَجَدَ خَيْراً فَلْيَحْمَدِ اللَّهَ، وَمَنْ وَجَدَ غَيْرَ ذَلِكَ فَلَا يَلُومَنَّ إِلَّا نَفْسَهُ.} رواه مسلم.

Injustice Has Been Declared Unlawful

It is on the authority of Abū Dharr al-Ghifārī ﷺ that the Prophet ﷺ narrated from his Lord ﷻ that He said, {O My slaves, I have forbidden injustice for Myself and I have forbidden it between you, so do not wrong one another.

O My slaves, all of you are astray except those whom I guide, so seek guidance from Me and I will guide you.

O My slaves, all of you are hungry except those whom I feed, so ask Me for food and I will feed you.

O My slaves, all of you are naked except those whom I clothe, so ask Me for clothing and I will clothe you.

O My slaves, you make mistakes by night and by day, and I forgive all sins, so ask for My forgiveness and I will forgive you.

O My slaves, you can never reach My harm and thus harm Me, and you can never reach My benefit and thus benefit Me.

O My slaves, even if the first of you and the last of you, your human beings and your jinn, all had the heart of the most pious man among you, that would not increase My kingdom in the least.

O My slaves, even if the first of you and the last of you, your human beings and your jinn, all had the heart of the most wicked man among you, that would not decrease My kingdom in the least.

O My slaves, even if the first of you and the last of you, your human beings and your jinn, were to stand on one flat piece of land and ask Me and I gave each and every one what he asked for, that would only take away from what I have what a needle takes when it is dipped in the sea.

O My slaves, they are only your actions that I enumerate for you, and then I will reward you for them, so whoever finds good, let him praise Allah, and whoever finds other than that, let him blame no one but himself.} Related by Muslim.

Muslim has related this ḥadīth in the Book of Righteousness (the chapter on injustice being declared unlawful), no.2577.

The Importance of the Ḥadīth:
This is a *ḥadīth qudsī* that is sublime, divine and blessed. It comprises some immense principles and foundations of Islam as well as branches and etiquettes. An-Nawawī ﷺ has mentioned in his book *al-Adhkār* that Abū Idrīs al-Khawlānī – who narrated it from Abū Dharr – would fall on his knees when relating it out of exaltation and reverence for it. The men in the chain of transmission are Damascene. Aḥmad ibn Ḥanbal said, 'The people of ash-Shām[126] do not have a more distinguished ḥadīth.'

The Language of the Ḥadīth:
(حرمت الظلم) *ḥarramtu ẓ-ẓulm*: linguistically, *ẓulm* means to put something in other than its place. It is to transgress the bounds or to dispose of people's right without any right. It is impossible for Allah the Exalted. The meaning of 'I have forbidden injustice for Myself' is: 'I never do it. I am exalted and sanctified above it.'

(ضال) *ḍāl*: unaware of any Revealed Law before Messengers are sent

(إلا من هديته) *illā man hadaytuhu*: I have guided him to what the Messengers have brought and granted him success therein

(فاستهدوني) *fastahdūnī*: seek guidance from Me

(صعيد واحد) *ṣaʿīd wāḥid*: one land and one location; the origin of *ṣaʿīd* is the face of the earth. The Exalted One has said,

﴿فَتَيَمَّمُواْ صَعِيدًا طَيِّبًا﴾
"...then do tayammum with pure earth..." [an-Nisā' 4:43 and al-Mā'idah 5:6]

(المخيط) *al-mikhyaṭ*: a needle

(أحصيها لكم) *uḥṣīhā lakum*: I determine them precisely with My knowledge and My guardian angels

(أوفيكم إياها) *uwaffīkum iyyāha*: I will grant you their reward in the Hereafter

126 (tn): i.e. the Levant.

Legal Matters and Other Guidance from the Ḥadīth:

1. The Definition of Ḥadīth Qudsī: A ḥadīth qudsī is what the Messenger ﷺ narrates from his Lord ﷻ sometimes through the medium of Jibrīl ﷺ and sometimes via revelation, inspiration or in his sleep, and he is authorized to express it with whatever words he wishes. A ḥadīth qudsī only differs from a Prophetic ḥadīth in that the Messenger attributes it to his Lord, and that is why it is ascribed to Allah the Exalted in most cases. When that happens, it is an attribution of origination, because He the Glorified is the one speaking initially. It can also be ascribed to the Prophet ﷺ because he is relating from his Lord.

Part of defining a ḥadīth qudsī is to elucidate the numerous differences between it and the Noble Qur'ān:

A. The Noble Qur'ān is inimitable (*muʿjiz*) in both wording and meaning, while a ḥadīth is not inimitable.

B. It is valid to recite the Noble Qur'ān in prayer, while it is not valid to recite a ḥadīth qudsī in prayer. In fact, it would nullify the prayer.

C. The one who denies the Noble Qur'ān is a disbeliever. The one who denies a ḥadīth qudsī is sinful (*fāsiq*).

D. The Noble Qur'ān is from Allah in both wording and meaning. The wording of a ḥadīth qudsī is from the Messenger of Allah ﷺ while its meaning is revelation from Allah the Exalted.

E. It is not permissible to relate the Noble Qur'ān in meaning, while it is permissible to relate a ḥadīth qudsī in meaning.

F. No one may touch the Noble Qur'ān except the purified,[127] while purification is not a condition for touching a ḥadīth qudsī.

G. It is not permissible for someone in a state of major ritual impurity (*junub*) to recite the Qur'ān or carry it, while it is permissible for such a person to carry a ḥadīth qudsī or recite it.

H. Whoever recites one letter from Allah's Book get the rewards of ten good deeds, while there is no reward for merely reciting a ḥadīth qudsī.

127 (tn): Please see Sūrat al-Wāqiʿah 56:79.

I. It is not valid to sell the Noble Qur'ān (in one narration according to Aḥmad) or disliked to sell it (according to the Shāfiʿīs), as opposed to a ḥadīth qudsī, as it is not prohibited or disliked to sell it by consensus.

A ḥadīth qudsī can also be called *ilāhī,*[128] and there are more than one hundred of them. Some imams have compiled them, such as ʿAlī ibn Balbān in his book entitled *al-Maqāṣid as-Saniyyah fī al-Aḥādīth al-Ilāhiyyah,* in which he compiled one hundred ḥadīth.[129]

2. Injustice Being Unlawful for Allah: The wording of the ḥadīth makes it clear that Allah ﷻ has prohibited Himself from wronging His slaves: {I have forbidden injustice for Myself.} It is also clear in the Noble Qur'ān. Allah the Exalted has said,

﴿وَمَآ أَنَا۠ بِظَلَّـٰمٍ لِّلْعَبِيدِ﴾

"...and I do not wrong My slaves." [Qāf 50:29]

The Glorified One has also said,

﴿إِنَّ ٱللَّهَ لَا يَظْلِمُ ٱلنَّاسَ شَيْـًٔا﴾

"Allah does not wrong people in any way." [Yūnus 10:44] and

﴿إِنَّ ٱللَّهَ لَا يَظْلِمُ مِثْقَالَ ذَرَّةٍ﴾

"Allah does not wrong anyone by so much as the smallest speck." [an-Nisā' 4:40]

3. Injustice Being Unlawful for His Slaves: Allah ﷻ has declared injustice unlawful for His slave, and He has forbidden them from wronging one another. Thus, it is unlawful for any individual to wrong someone else, even though injustice is absolutely unlawful in and of itself. It is of two types:

The first is injustice against one's own soul, the most oppressive of which is to associate partners with Allah. The Exalted One has said,

﴿إِنَّ ٱلشِّرْكَ لَظُلْمٌ عَظِيمٌ﴾

"Associating others with Him is a terrible wrong." [Luqmān 31:13]

This is because the idolater regards a creation as having the same rank as the Creator and worships it along with Allah the Exalted, who is transcendent above having any partner.

128 (tn): i.e. divine.

129 (tn): Imam Muṣṭafā al-Bughā has done a critical edition of this book along with notes.

The injustice of associating partners with Allah is followed by disobedience and sins, minor and major, for one wrongs one's soul by making it liable to being punished and ruined in this life and the Hereafter.

The second is a person wronging someone else, and it being unlawful and warned against is repeated in the ḥadīths of the Prophet ﷺ. In the two *Ṣaḥīḥ* collections, it is on the authority of ʿAbdullah ibn ʿUmar رضي الله عنهما that the Prophet ﷺ said, {Injustice is injustices on the Day of Standing.} In the same collections, it is on the authority of Abū Mūsā al-Ashʿarī that the Prophet ﷺ said, {Allah will grant respite to the oppressor so that when He takes him, He will never let him go.} Then he recited,

﴿وَكَذَٰلِكَ أَخْذُ رَبِّكَ إِذَآ أَخَذَ ٱلْقُرَىٰ وَهِىَ ظَٰلِمَةٌ ۚ إِنَّ أَخْذَهُۥٓ أَلِيمٌ شَدِيدٌ﴾

"Such is the grip of your Lord when he seizes the cities which do wrong. His grip is painful, violent." [Hūd 11:102]

There is no doubt that establishing justice in how people deal with one another and forbidding injustice between them is one of the most important objectives and goals of Islam. This is because justice is the foundation in building the edifice of any jurisdiction or civilization. Likewise, injustice is the cause of nations declining, civilizations being destroyed and happiness being lost in this life. Likewise, it leads to Allah's wrath in the Hereafter.

4. Needing Allah: The entire creation is in need of Allah in order to bring about benefit and ward off harm in this life and the Hereafter. They are in urgent need of Allah's guidance and sustenance in this life and they need Allah's mercy and forgiveness in the Hereafter. The Muslim draws nearer to Allah ﷻ by demonstrating his need and impoverishment, and his true slavehood to Allah, Lord of all Creation, is manifested in of the three following ways:

The **first** is by asking. Allah ﷻ is He, loves it when people present their needs to Him and ask Him regarding all of their affairs, both religious and worldly, such as food, drink and clothing, and likewise when they ask him for guidance and forgiveness. In one ḥadīth: {...so let each of you ask his Lord for every single one of his needs, even the strap on his sandal if it is cut.}

The **second** is by asking for guidance.

The **third** is through complete obedience, and that is by avoiding everything that Allah the Exalted has prohibited and carrying out everything that Allah the Exalted has commanded.

THE TWENTY-FIFTH ḤADĪTH

فَضْلُ اللهِ تَعَالَى وَسِعَةُ رَحْمَتِهِ

عَنْ أَبِي ذَرٍّ ؓ: أَنَّ نَاسًا مِنْ أَصْحَابِ رَسُوْلِ اللهِ ﷺ قَالُوا لِلنَّبِيِّ ﷺ: يَا رَسُوْلَ اللهِ، ذَهَبَ أَهْلُ الدُّثُوْرِ بِالْأُجُورِ، يُصَلُّوْنَ كَمَا نُصَلِّي، وَيَصُوْمُوْنَ كَمَا نَصُوْمُ، وَيَتَصَدَّقُوْنَ بِفُضُولِ أَمْوَالِهِمْ. قَالَ: {أَوَلَيْسَ قَدْ جَعَلَ اللهُ لَكُمْ مَا تَصَدَّقُوْنَ؟ إِنَّ لَكُمْ بِكُلِّ تَسْبِيحَةٍ صَدَقَةً، وَكُلِّ تَكْبِيرَةٍ صَدَقَةً، وَكُلِّ تَحْمِيْدَةٍ صَدَقَةً، وَكُلِّ تَهْلِيْلَةٍ صَدَقَةً، وَأَمْرٍ بِالْمَعْرُوْفِ صَدَقَةً، وَنَهْيٍ عَنْ مُنْكَرٍ صَدَقَةً، وَفِي بُضْعِ أَحَدِكُمْ صَدَقَةً.} قالوا: يَا رَسُوْلَ اللهِ، أَيَأْتِي أَحَدُنَا شَهْوَتَهُ وَيَكُوْنُ لَهُ فِيهَا أَجْرٌ؟ قَالَ: {أَرَأَيْتُمْ لَوْ وَضَعَهَا فِي حَرَامٍ، أَكَانَ عَلَيْهِ وِزْرٌ؟ فَكَذَلِكَ إِذَا وَضَعَهَا فِي الْحَلَالِ كَانَ لَهُ أَجْرٌ.} رواه مسلم.

Allah the Exalted's Favour and the Vastness of His Mercy

It is on the authority of Abū Dharr ؓ that, 'Some people from the Companions of the Messenger of Allah said to the Prophet ﷺ "O Messenger of Allah, the people of great wealth have gone off with the rewards. They pray as we pray, fast as we fast and give in charity[130] with the excess of their wealth." He replied, {Has Allah not given you that which you can give in charity? Indeed, in every glorification (*tasbīḥah*) there is charity, in every magnification (*takbīrah*) there is charity, in every praise there is charity (*taḥmīdah*), in every *lā ilāha ill Allah* (*tahlīlah*) there is charity, in every command to what is right there is charity, in every forbidding of what is wrong there is charity and in the act of sexual intercourse by any one of you there is charity.} They said, "O Messenger of Allah, can one of us approach his desire and be rewarded for it?" He replied, {Do you not see that if he were to gratify himself with the unlawful, it would be a sin? Likewise, if he gratifies himself with the lawful, there is a reward.}' Related by Muslim.

Muslim has collected this ḥadīth in Zakāt (the chapter on the term *ṣadaqah* referring to every type of good), no.1006. It is agreed upon with the ḥadīth of Abū Hurayrah ؓ in other than this wording. Al-Bukhārī has collected it in the

130 Ar. *ṣadaqah.*

Description of the Prayer (the chapter on invocations after the prayer), no.807, as well as in Supplications (the chapter on supplications after the prayer), no.5970. Muslim has also collected it in Masājid and Places of Prayer (the chapter on the recommended nature of invocations after the prayer and elucidating their description), no.595.

Its Importance:
Ibn Ḥajar al-Haytamī has said in his commentary on *The Forty,* 'It is an immense ḥadīth, because it comprises some of the psychical foundations of the religion.'

The Language of the Ḥadīth:
(أن أناسا) *inna unāsan*: *unās* means the same as *nās*, and the people here are the poor amongst the Emigrants.[131]

(من أصحاب) *min aṣḥāb*: this is the plural of *ṣāḥib*, meaning *as-ṣaḥābī* (Companion), and it is everyone who met the Prophet ﷺ after his mission had been declared and before his death, and they believed in him and died upon Islam.

(الدثور) *ad-duthūr*: this is the plural of *dathr*, which is great wealth.

(فضول أموالهم) *fuḍūli amwālihim*: their wealth that is surplus to their needs.

(تصدقون) *taṣaddaqūna*: to give in charity.

(تسبيحة) *tasbīḥah*: i.e. to say *subḥān Allah.*

(تكبيرة) *takbīrah*: to say *Allahu akbar.*

(تحميدة) *taḥmīdah*: to say *al-ḥamdu lillāh*

(تهليلة) *tahlīlah*: to say *lā ilāha ill Allah.*

(صدقة) *ṣadaqah*: reward like the reward of charity.

(بضع) *buḍ'*: sexual intercourse, or the vulva itself.

(شهوته) *shahwatahu*: his pleasure and delight.

(وزر) *wizr*: sin and punishment.

131 Ar. *al-Muhājirūn.*

Legal Matters and Other Guidance from the Ḥadīth:

﴿وَفِى ذَٰلِكَ فَلْيَتَنَافَسِ ٱلْمُتَنَـٰفِسُونَ﴾
"Let those who compete, compete for that!" [al-Muṭaffifīn 83:26]

Competing in seeking more goodness and enthusiasm for righteous deeds is something that has been legislated and is desirable, and the Muslim must strive for it. Here is Abū Dharr ☙ telling us about a gathering he attended in the days of the Messenger of Allah ﷺ. He saw the posture of the Messenger of Allah ﷺ and his wise conduct therein. He also saw the mercy of Islam and the vast doors of goodness therein, through the elucidation of the one to whom the Qur'ān was sent down to make clear to mankind what had been sent down to them.[132]

This gathering was exclusively for the poor amongst the Emigrants, and maybe those like them from amongst the Helpers[133] were also present. They saw themselves as limited in terms of the good deeds and acts of charity they could do, as they did not have wealth to give in charity and could not prove the veracity of their faith and the excellence of their Islam. They had heard the Messenger of Allah ﷺ saying that charity is a proof[134] and they had recited and heard the verses of Allah the Exalted and the ḥadīths of His Messenger ﷺ that strongly encourage spending out and praise those that do, and that gardens as wide as the heavens and the earth have been prepared for them. They had seen their rich and wealthy companions and brothers rushing to give away wealth generously and munificently. One of them came with all of his wealth, another brought half, a third brought thousands and thousands, and still another placed piles in front of the Messenger of Allah ﷺ such that the Messenger of Allah ﷺ supplicated for him, was pleased with him and asked Allah the Exalted to forgive him and be pleased with him.

This is what moved the souls of these people, and their hearts aspired to have that favour, and that rank that their brother occupied. This was not out of envy for their wealth or yearning for riches. Rather, it was competition in the fields of goodness and drawing nearer to Allah the Exalted. Thus, they gathered together and came to the Messenger of Allah ﷺ and complained about their situation. They declared their destitution and their eyes welled with tears of grief because they could not find anything to give away: "O Messenger of Allah, the people of great wealth have gone off with the rewards." They people of wealth and riches have obtained every reward and claimed a monopoly at our expense, because "they pray as we pray, fast as we fast." We are equal in those matters, we have no distinction over them. However, they surpass us and have distinction over us because they

---

132 (tn): Please see Sūrat an-Naḥl 16:44.

133 Ar. *al-Anṣār*.

134 (tn): Please see the 23rd ḥadīth in this book.

"give in charity with the excess of their wealth." We do not own anything that we can give out such that we would reach their rank, and our souls desire to have their rank with Allah ﷻ, so what can we do?

2. Profound Wisdom and the Vast Doors of Goodness: The Chosen One ﷺ understood that these people longed and yearned to have a high rank with their Lord. He treated their souls with the wisdom Allah the Exalted had granted him, so he puts their minds at rest and drew their attention to the fact that the doors of goodness are vast. There are deeds whose reward is equal to that of the one who gives charity, and the one who does them has a rank close to the one who spends his wealth on others, if not a higher rank in some cases.

However, it is each according to his own.

﴿لَا يُكَلِّفُ ٱللَّهُ نَفْسًا إِلَّا وُسْعَهَا﴾

"Allah does not impose on any soul any more than it can bear." [al-Baqarah 2:286]

﴿لَا يُكَلِّفُ ٱللَّهُ نَفْسًا إِلَّا مَآ ءَاتَىٰهَا﴾

"Allah does not demand from any soul more than He has given it." [at-Ṭalāq 65:7]

{Has Allah not given you that which you can give in charity?} Indeed He has, for in your case there are several kinds of charity. Some of them are spending on people and some of them do not involve spending, but their reward is not less than spending for the sake of Allah ﷻ.

3. The Remembrance of Allah is the Greatest Charity for the Soul: If you do not have surplus wealth, glorify Allah ﷻ say *Allahu akbar,* say *al-ḥamdu lillāh* and say *lā ilāha ill Allah,* for in each of these utterances there is the reward of charity, and what a reward. And why not? We know that they are the right actions which are lasting, as Allah the Exalted has said,

﴿ٱلْمَالُ وَٱلْبَنُونَ زِينَةُ ٱلْحَيَوٰةِ ٱلدُّنْيَا ۖ وَٱلْبَٰقِيَٰتُ ٱلصَّٰلِحَٰتُ خَيْرٌ عِندَ رَبِّكَ ثَوَابًا وَخَيْرٌ أَمَلًا﴾

"But, in your Lord's sight, right actions which are lasting bring a better reward and are a better basis for hope." [al-Kahf 18:46]

The Glorified One also says,

﴿وَلَذِكْرُ ٱللَّهِ أَكْبَرُ﴾

"And remembrance of Allah is greater still". [al-'Ankabūt 29:45]

i.e. it is greater in reward.

Here is the Messenger of Allah ﷺ saying, {There is no day, no night and no hour except that Allah has some charity therein that He bestows upon whomever of His slaves that He wishes, and nothing that Allah the Exalted bestows upon His slaves is like Him inspiring him to remember Him.} This has been collected by Ibn Mājah.

Aḥmad and at-Tirmidhī have related that the Messenger of Allah ﷺ was asked, 'Who are the best slaves in the sight of Allah on the Day of Standing?' He replied, {Those who remember Allah much.}

4. Calling to Goodness is Charity for the Community: Likewise, the door of enjoining the right and forbidding the wrong is vast and open, and the reward of whoever carries out this communal obligation is not less than the one who spends in charity. Indeed, it could be several degrees greater: {Everything that is right is charity}, as related by Muslim. And how could it not be? This ummah is upon commanding the right and forbidding the wrong and it is the best ummah ever to be produced before mankind:

﴿كُنتُمْ خَيْرَ أُمَّةٍ أُخْرِجَتْ لِلنَّاسِ تَأْمُرُونَ بِٱلْمَعْرُوفِ وَتَنْهَوْنَ عَنِ ٱلْمُنكَرِ وَتُؤْمِنُونَ بِٱللَّهِ﴾

"You are the best ummah ever to be produced before mankind. You enjoin the right, forbid the wrong and believe in Allah." [Āl 'Imrān 3:110]

5. The Vastness of Allah's ﷻ Favour : Also, Allah ﷻ has laid down a reward that you can obtain every day if you have a sincere and good intention. Is it not the case that each of you spends on his family and dependents: {A man spending on his family, his wife and his dependents is charity}, as related by Muslim and others. There is also the agreed upon ḥadīth: {You do not spend anything desiring Allah the Exalted-Face except that you are rewarded for it, even the morsel of food that you put in your wife's mouth.} Indeed, is it not the case that each of you lives intimately with his wife and carries out his obligations towards her, in order to keep himself chaste and keep her away from the unlawful? Furthermore, is it not the case that he protects his own private parts, stays within Allah's limits and avoids that which is unlawful, that which if he were to commit would render him sinful and liable to be punished? Likewise, he has reward, even if he thinks that he is satisfying his desires and gratifying his passions, as long as he has a sincere intention therein and only approaches that which Allah the Exalted has made lawful for him.

6. Actions Are Only by Intentions: Part of Allah's ﷻ immense favour towards the Muslim is that through his intention a normal habit of his can become an act of worship. His acting or refraining becomes a means of him drawing nearer to His Lord ﷻ. If he consumes permissible food and drink with the intention of preserving his body and strengthening it in order to obey his Lord, it becomes an act of worship that he is rewarded for, and especially if he combines with the remembrance of Allah at the beginning of the deed and at the end. At the beginning, he invokes Allah's name[135] and at the end he praises Allah and thanks Him, as is mentioned in the Sunnah. If he has intercourse with his wife with intention of keeping both of them chaste and removed from fornication and what leads to it, or he intends to fulfil his wife's right by living with her kindly and courteously, or he intends to have a righteous child who will worship Allah the Exalted and proclaim His oneness, any one of these intentions would turn his desire into worship. It will be recorded amongst his good deeds, and especially if he is not heedless in those moments of the favour Allah the Exalted has bestowed upon him, by allowing him to have this pleasure, and he obeys the command of Allah's Messenger ﷺ and thus he remembers Allah the Exalted and supplicates to Him as he has been instructed to. He said, {When any of you approaches his wife, let him say,

(بِسْمِ اللهِ، اللهُمَّ جَنِّبْنَا الشَّيْطَانَ وَجَنِّبِ الشَّيْطَانَ مَا رَزَقْتَنَا)

'In the Name of Allah, O Allah, keep Shayṭān away from us and keep Shayṭān away from what You have provided us', and thus they will have a child and he will not harm him.} This ḥadīth is agreed upon and the meaning is that Shayṭān will not harm the child.

Likewise, the Muslim's reward with Allah ﷻ grows and increases when he refrains from what Allah the Exalted has prohibited. This is especially the case if he renews his pledge each time and calls to mind that he is refraining from disobeying Allah, Blessed and Exalted is He, and in fact obeying His command and avoiding what He has forbidden, desiring His reward and fearing His punishment, and confirming therein the description of the All-Merciful's slaves:

﴿وَٱلَّذِينَ إِذَا ذُكِّرُواْ بِـَٔايَـٰتِ رَبِّهِمْ لَمْ يَخِرُّواْ عَلَيْهَا صُمًّا وَعُمْيَانًا﴾

"...those who, when they are reminded of the signs of their Lord, do not turn their backs, deaf and blind to them." [al-Furqān 25:73]

He ﷻ has described the sincere believers by saying,

﴿إِنَّمَا ٱلْمُؤْمِنُونَ ٱلَّذِينَ إِذَا ذُكِرَ ٱللَّهُ وَجِلَتْ قُلُوبُهُمْ

وَإِذَا تُلِيَتْ عَلَيْهِمْ ءَايَـٰتُهُۥ زَادَتْهُمْ إِيمَـٰنًا وَعَلَىٰ رَبِّهِمْ يَتَوَكَّلُونَ﴾

"The believers are those whose hearts tremble when Allah is mentioned, whose faith is increased when His verses are recited to them, and who put their trust in their Lord." [al-Anfāl 8:2]

135 (tn): i.e. he says *Bismillāh* ('in the Name of Allah').

7. The Doors of Goodness are Many:

The doors of goodness and charity are not confined to what is mentioned in the ḥadīth, for there are other deeds that the Muslim can perform and anticipate the reward of charity therein. Ibn Ḥibbān has collected in his *Ṣaḥīḥ* [Places of Thirst, no.862] on the authority of Abū Dharr ﷺ that the Messenger of Allah ﷺ said, {There is no soul from the children of Adam except that it owes some charity every day that the sun rises.} It was then said, 'O Messenger of Allah, where will we get charity in order to give it out?' He replied, {The doors of goodness are many: *at-tasbīḥ, at-taḥmīd, at-takbīr, at-tahlīl,* to command right, to forbid the wrong, to remove harm from the road, to make the deaf hear, to guide the blind, to show someone the way when they ask, to strive to be there for the grieved and to strive to be there for the weak. All of this is charity from you towards you.} In the two *Ṣaḥīḥ* collections: {Keep people away from traps, for that is charity}, and according to at-Tirmidhī: {To smile at your brother is charity...to pour your bucket into your brother's bucket is charity.}[136]

8. Advice from the Ḥadīth:

A. Using wisdom to deal with situations, bringing joy to souls and putting minds to rest.

B. The virtue of the invocations that are pointed out in the ḥadīth, and that their reward is equivalent to the reward of charity for the one who does not have wealth to give out. This is especially the case after the obligatory prayers, for there is a narration in the two *Ṣaḥīḥ* collections: {Shall I not tell you about something that if you adopt it, you will catch up with those who went before you and no one after you will reach you, and you will be better than those amongst you unless they do likewise? Say *subḥān Allah, al-ḥamdu lillāh* and *Allahu akbar* thirty-three times each after every prayer.

C. It is recommended for a poor person to give in charity if it will not place constraints on himself and his dependents, just as *dhikr* is recommended for a wealthy person even if it is more than what he spends out, in order to have more goodness and reward.

D. To give in charity what one needs to spend on oneself or one's family and dependents is disliked, and it can be unlawful if it leads to one failing to spend on them what he is obligated to. He ﷺ said, {The best charity is that which is on top of wealth}, as related by al-Bukhārī and others.

136 Please see the 26th ḥadīth and its commentary. The ḥadīths on this topic are many.

E. Charity for the one who is able to and has wealth is better than *dhikr*, because the benefit of charity is more widespread and reaches others, while the benefit of *dhikr* is exclusive and confined to the one who does it. If a wealthy person combines between charity and *dhikr*, his reward with Allah ﷻ will be immense. In the narration in the two *Ṣaḥīḥ* collections, according to Muslim's wording, the poor amongst the Emigrants went back to the Messenger of Allah ﷺ and said, 'Our wealthy brethren have heard about what we are doing and they are doing likewise.' The Messenger of Allah ﷺ thus replied, {That is Allah's favour. He gives it to whomever He wishes.}

F. The superiority of the grateful wealthy person who gives charity over the patient poor person who anticipates reward.

G. The importance of enjoining the right and forbidding the wrong in a Muslim society, which is a communal obligation. If no one carries it out, everyone is in sin, and if some Muslims carry it out, the sin is lifted from everyone else. It is not specific to one group of Muslims and not another.

H. Living kindly and courteously with one's wife and fulfilling her rights, such as putting a roof over her head and food on the table. Likewise, he should be treated well, out of recognition for his kindness and gratitude for beneficence.

I. Strongly encouraging questions about that which will benefit the Muslim and raise him in degrees of perfection.

J. The one asking for a ruling can ask for the evidence if he does not know it, if he knows that the one being asked will not mind and no ill manners therein.

K. Making evidence clear for the learner, especially if it is unknown to him, so that it becomes firmly established in his heart and he has a greater incentive to obey it.

L. The legitimacy of analogy (*qiyās*) and the resultant ruling that is attached to a matter that resembles it or is equal to it.

THE TWENTY-SIXTH ḤADĪTH

الإِصْلاحُ بَيْنَ النَاسِ وَالْعَدْلُ فِيهِم

عَنْ أَبِي هُرَيْرَةَ ﷺ قَالَ: قَالَ رَسُوْلُ اللهِ ﷺ: {كُلُّ سُلَامَى مِنَ النَّاسِ عَلَيْهِ صَدَقَةٌ، كُلَّ يَوْمٍ تَطْلُعُ فِيهِ الشَّمْسُ: تَعْدِلُ بَيْنَ اثْنَيْنِ صَدَقَةٌ، وَتُعِينُ الرَّجُلَ فِي دَابَّتِهِ فَتَحْمِلُهُ عَلَيْهَا أَوْ تَرْفَعُ لَهُ مَتَاعَهُ صَدَقَةٌ، وَالْكَلِمَةُ الطَّيِّبَةُ صَدَقَةٌ، وَبِكُلِّ خَطْوَةٍ تَمْشِيهَا إِلَى الصَّلاةِ صَدَقَةٌ، وَتُمِيطُ الْأَذَى عَنِ الطَّرِيْقِ صَدَقَةٌ.} رواه البخاري ومسلم.

Conciliation between People and Establishing Justice between Them

It is on the authority of Abū Hurayrah ﷺ who said, 'The Messenger of Allah ﷺ said, {Every part (*sulāmā*) of a person's body owes charity (*ṣadaqah*) every day in which the sun rises. To establish justice between two people is charity. To help a man with his mount so that it carries him or to lift his luggage up to him when he is on it is charity. A good word is charity. Every step with which you walk to the prayer is charity, and to remove harm from the road is charity.}' Related by al-Bukhārī and Muslim.

Al-Bukhārī has related the ḥadīth in the Book of Conciliation (the chapter on the superiority of conciliation between people and establishing justice between them) and in the Book of *Jihād* (the chapter on the superiority of carrying one's luggage in travel) and (the chapter on taking passengers and the like), no.2827. Muslim has related it in the Book of Zakāt (the chapter on *ṣadaqah* referring to every goodness), no.1007 and 1009.

The Importance of the Ḥadīth:

One of the most sublime goals and objectives of Islam is to bring Muslims' hearts together in harmony, to establish the truth between them, to strengthen their might and to have them overcome Allah's enemy and their enemy. These goals and objectives cannot be realised without mutual assistance and support, and solidarity. This noble Prophetic ḥadīth is part of this because of the words and deeds it calls to, and its rulings coincide with Allah the Exalted's statement:

﴿وَتَعَاوَنُوا۟ عَلَى ٱلْبِرِّ وَٱلتَّقْوَىٰ ۖ وَلَا تَعَاوَنُوا۟ عَلَى ٱلْإِثْمِ وَٱلْعُدْوَٰنِ﴾

"Help each other in goodness and *taqwā*. Do not help each other in sin and enmity." [al-Māʾidah 5:2]

And the Prophet's statement ﷺ {In their mutual love, compassion and affection, the believers are like one body. If one limb complains, the rest of the body becomes sleepless and feverish in order to help.} Related by al-Bukhārī and Muslim.

The Language of the Ḥadīth:

(سلامى) *sulāmā*: the bones of the hand, the fingers and the feet, and what is meant here is all the parts and joints of the human body, which are three hundred and sixty in total, as Muslim has related, {Man has been created with three hundred and sixty joints. In every joint, there is charity.}

(تعدل بين اثنين) *taʿdilu bayn athnayn*: to arbitrate together with justice between two disputing parties.

(تعين الرجل في دابته) *tuʿīnu r-rajula fī dābbatihi*: the meaning of *dābbah* includes ships, cars and whatever else carries people, and it also includes carrying someone with one's hands or on one's back.

(فتحمله عليها) *fa taḥmiluhu ʿalayhā*: i.e. you put him on it, or you assist him in riding it or in fixing and maintaining his mount.

(بكل خطوة) *bi kulli khaṭwah*: a *khaṭwah* is a step while a *khuṭwah* is what is between one's feet.

(تميط الأذى) *tumīṭu l-adhā*: one can also say *tamīṭū*, because the verb can be either *māṭa* or *amāṭa*, which both mean 'to remove'. Removing harm means anything that annoys or bothers passers-by, such as rocks, thorns, or dirt.

Legal Matters and Other Guidance from the Ḥadīth:

1. The Divine Power in Creating Man's Bones and Joints: Allah has created man in the finest stature and made his bones and joints to bear the utmost uniqueness and organisation. He has asked him to look deep inside of himself and to contemplate the fineness of his senses and his bones, the cells of his flesh and the corpuscles of his blood, so that he can recognise the signs of the Unique, All-Powerful Creator. The Exalted One has said,

﴿سَنُرِيهِمْ ءَايَـٰتِنَا فِى ٱلْـَٔافَاقِ وَفِىٓ أَنفُسِهِمْ حَتَّىٰ يَتَبَيَّنَ لَهُمْ أَنَّهُ ٱلْحَقُّ﴾

"We will show them our signs on the horizon and within themselves until it is clear to them that this is the truth." [Fuṣṣilat 41:53]

The Glorified One has also said,

﴿وَفِىٓ أَنفُسِكُمْ ۚ أَفَلَا تُبْصِرُونَ﴾

"...and in yourselves as well. Do you not then see?" [adh-Dhāriyāt 51:21]

The Prophet ﷺ singled out the *sulāmā* for mention in his ḥadīth because of the organisation and beauty they contain, as well as their flexibility and symmetry. This is why Allah ﷻ has threatened every stubborn denier and disbeliever with being deprived of them by saying,

﴿بَلَىٰ قَـٰدِرِينَ عَلَىٰٓ أَن نُّسَوِّىَ بَنَانَهُۥ﴾

"On the contrary! We are able to reshape his digits." [al-Qiyāmah 75:4]

In other words, We can make his digits one thing, like the hooves of a camel or donkey, and thus he would not be able to do anything with them the way he can do things and work with separated digits that have joints.

There was that western engineer, who worked in a factory for artificial limbs, who came to realise Allah's power and returned to the fold of Islam and faith in Allah's existence after sitting one day and examining his young daughter's hand. He compared between this divine hand and what human industry has arrived at in making artificial limbs and the immense difference between the two guided him to Allah.[137]

2. Gratitude for the Soundness of One's Limbs and Organs: The soundness of a person's limbs and organs, the soundness of his senses, bones and joints, is a massive blessing that merits more gratitude to Allah the Exalted, the One who bestows blessings and favours upon His slaves. Allah the Exalted has said,

﴿يَـٰٓأَيُّهَا ٱلْإِنسَـٰنُ مَا غَرَّكَ بِرَبِّكَ ٱلْكَرِيمِ ۝٦

ٱلَّذِى خَلَقَكَ فَسَوَّىٰكَ فَعَدَلَكَ ۝٧ فِىٓ أَىِّ صُورَةٍ مَّا شَآءَ رَكَّبَكَ﴾

137 See the story in the book *al-ʿIlm yadʿū lil-Īmān* ("Science Calls to Faith").

"O man! What has deluded you concerning your Noble Lord? He who created you and formed you and proportioned you and assembled you in whatever way He willed." [al-Infiṭār 82:6-8]

The Glorified One has also said,

﴿ثُمَّ لَتُسْـَٔلُنَّ يَوْمَئِذٍ عَنِ ٱلنَّعِيمِ﴾

"Then you will be asked that Day about the pleasures (*naʿīm*) you enjoyed." [at-Takāthur 102:8]

Ibn ʿAbbās said, 'The *naʿīm* are healthy bodies and sound hearing and sight. Allah will ask the slaves, "What did you use them for?" and He knows better than they do about the matter. It is the Exalted's statement:

﴿وَلَا تَقْفُ مَا لَيْسَ لَكَ بِهِۦ عِلْمٌ ۚ إِنَّ ٱلسَّمْعَ وَٱلْبَصَرَ وَٱلْفُؤَادَ كُلُّ أُو۟لَـٰٓئِكَ كَانَ عَنْهُ مَسْـُٔولًا﴾

"Hearing, sight and hearts will all be questioned." [al-Isrāʾ 17:36]'

Ibn Masʿūd said, 'The *naʿīm* are safety and health'. At-Tirmidhī and Ibn Mājah have collected: {The first thing the slave is asked about on the Day of Standing when Allah says, 'Did We not give you a healthy body and quench your thirst with cool water?'} Abū ad-Dardāʾ said, 'Health is the growth of the body.' Wahb ibn Munabbih said, 'It is written in the wisdom of the Family of Dāwūd: "Well-being is the hidden kingdom."' In other words, it is the *naʿīm* that will be asked about on the Day of Standing.

Despite this, many people are heedless of these immense blessings and forget the soundness, health and well-being that they are in. They neglect to examine and reflect on themselves, and thus they are negligent in thanking their Creator.

3. The Types of Gratitude: Gratitude to Allah the Exalted for the blessings and He has granted increases those blessings and makes them continuous and perpetual. The Exalted One has said,

﴿وَإِذْ تَأَذَّنَ رَبُّكُمْ لَئِن شَكَرْتُمْ لَأَزِيدَنَّكُمْ﴾

"And when your Lord announced, 'If you are grateful, I will certainly give you more.'" [Ibrāhīm 14:7]

It is not sufficient for a person to be grateful on his tongue. Rather, there must be deeds alongside his words. The gratitude that is required is obligatory and recommended:

A. **Obligatory Gratitude:** This is done by carrying out all obligations and leaving everything that is unlawful, and this suffices in showing gratitude for the blessing of health, sound limbs and organs and other blessings. This is evidenced by what Abū Dāwūd has related from Abū al-Aswad ad-Dīlī, who said, 'We were with Abū Dharr and He said, "When one of you wakes up each day, each of his *sulāmā* owes charity: in every prayer there is charity for him, in a fast there is charity, in a Ḥajj there is charity, in a glorification[138] there is charity, in a magnification[139] there is charity..."' Al-Bukhārī and Muslim have related from Abū Mūsā al-Ashʿarī that the Messenger of Allah ﷺ said, {And if he cannot do so then let him refrain from evil, and that will be a form of charity for him.} This is evidence that in order to be grateful, it suffices the slave not to do anything evil, and he can only avoid evil by carrying out his obligations and avoiding the unlawful. The greatest evil is to leave obligations, and this is why one of the First Three Generations said, 'Gratitude is to leave disobedience.' One of them also said, 'Gratitude is not to use any blessing for the sake of disobedience.'

B. **Recommended Gratitude:** After fulfilling obligations and avoiding the unlawful, this is when the slave does supererogatory acts of obedience, and this is the rank of the forerunners and those who draw near to Allah in thanking the Creator ﷻ. It is what most ḥadīths that strongly encourage deeds and other types of drawing near to Allah advise, and it is the Prophet's state ﷺ for he would strive in prayer and stand until his feet became swollen and cracked. It was said to him, 'Why do you do this when Allah has forgiven for anything you could have done or could do?' He replied, {Should I not be a grateful slave?}

4. The Types of Charity that are Mentioned in the Ḥadīth and Their Ruling: It is from Allah the Exalted's additional kindness towards His slaves and His favour towards them that He has called the gratitude that is obligatory upon them and that which is recommended *ṣadaqah*. The Glorified One increased this favour by making this gratitude of theirs a *ṣadaqah* upon them as well, as if He has said, 'Make your gratitude for My blessings in your limbs and organs by using them to help My slaves, and use them to give them *ṣadaqah*.' This is while bearing in mind that *ṣadaqah* is not confined to money. These types of *ṣadaqah* include that which is transitive, such as conciliation and helping a man onto his mount, and that which is of intransitive benefit, such as walking to the prayer.

The types of charity that are mentioned in the ḥadīth are:

138 Ar. *tasbīḥ*, i.e. to say *subḥān Allah*.

139 Ar. *takbīr*, i.e. to say *Allahu akbar*.

A. Justice between two disputants or two parties who have separated: This is done through just arbitration, and by conciliating between them in a way that is permissible and does not make the lawful unlawful or the unlawful lawful.

It is one of the best ways of drawing nearer to Allah and the most complete acts of worship. Allah the Exalted has said,

﴿إِنَّمَا ٱلْمُؤْمِنُونَ إِخْوَةٌ فَأَصْلِحُوا۟ بَيْنَ أَخَوَيْكُمْ﴾

"The believers are brothers, so make peace between your brothers." [al-Ḥujurāt 49:10]

The Glorified One has also said,

﴿لَّا خَيْرَ فِى كَثِيرٍ مِّن نَّجْوَىٰهُمْ إِلَّا مَنْ أَمَرَ بِصَدَقَةٍ أَوْ مَعْرُوفٍ أَوْ إِصْلَٰحٍۭ بَيْنَ ٱلنَّاسِ﴾

"There is no good in much of their secret talk, except in the case of those who enjoin *ṣadaqah*, or what is right, or putting things right between people." [an-Nisā' 4:114]

He ﷺ said, {Shall I inform you of that which is of greater degree than the prayer, fasting and charity?} They replied, 'Yes.' He said, {Putting right that which is between you.} Putting things right between two disputants or two parties who have separated is a charity towards them, because they are being protected from the despicable actions and words that arise from disputes. This is why it is a communal obligation, andit is even permissible to lie therein by way of exaggeration in order to create harmony between Muslims.

B. Helping a man on his mount: This is by helping him regarding what he rides, and thus you help him on it, you assist him in riding or you lift his luggage up to him. This is a humane act that contains *ṣadaqah* and gratitude, because of the cooperation and chivalry therein. Al-Khaṭīb has related from Anas ؓ that the Messenger of Allah ﷺ said, {Whoever carries his brother on a sandal strap (*shisʿ*) is as if he has carried him on his mount in the path of Allah.}

A *shisʿ* is a strap that goes between two toes.

C. A good word, which includes saying 'may Allah have mercy to you'[140] to someone who sneezes, giving the greeting of peace first when meeting someone and returning it, and the right actions are lasting.[141]

﴿مَن كَانَ يُرِيدُ ٱلْعِزَّةَ فَلِلَّهِ ٱلْعِزَّةُ جَمِيعًا ۚ إِلَيْهِ يَصْعَدُ ٱلْكَلِمُ ٱلطَّيِّبُ وَٱلْعَمَلُ ٱلصَّٰلِحُ يَرْفَعُهُۥ﴾

140 Ar. *tashmīt al-ʿāṭis,* which is to say *yarḥamuk Allah.*

141 Ar. *al-bāqiyātu s-ṣāliḥāt,* please see Sūrat al-Kahf 18:46.

"All good words rise to Him and He elevates all virtuous deeds." [Fāṭir 35:10]

Good words are also in answering questions. Allah the Exalted has said,

﴿قَوْلٌ مَّعْرُوفٌ وَمَغْفِرَةٌ خَيْرٌ مِّن صَدَقَةٍ يَتْبَعُهَآ أَذًى﴾

"Correct and courteous words accompanied by forgiveness are better than ṣadaqah followed by insulting words." [al-Baqarah 2:263]

It also includes speaking well with people, because this is what brings happiness to the believer's heart and makes it rejoice, and it is one of the greatest rewards.

Then there is the word of *tawḥīd*. Allah the Exalted has said,

﴿كَلِمَةً طَيِّبَةً كَشَجَرَةٍ طَيِّبَةٍ أَصْلُهَا ثَابِتٌ وَفَرْعُهَا فِى ٱلسَّمَآءِ﴾

"...a good word is like a good tree, its roots are firm and its branches are in the sky" [Ibrāhīm 14:24]

A good word also includes remembrance and supplication, praising a Muslim deservedly, interceding on his behalf before a ruler, sincere advice, giving directions and anything else that pleases the listener and brings hearts together in harmony.

D. Walking to the prayer: This is about strongly encouraging and emphasising prayer in congregation and walking to it, so that the masjids are filled with prayers and acts of obedience, such as *al-iʿtikāf*,[142] *aṭ-ṭawāf*,[143] and attending lessons of knowledge and admonition. Al-Bukhārī and Muslim have related from Abū Hurayrah that the Prophet said, {Whoever goes to the masjid in the morning or the evening, Allah prepares hospitality[144] for him every time he goes in the morning or evening.}

Muslim and others have related from Jābir who said, 'The plots of land around the masjid were empty so the Banū Salamah wanted to move close to the masjid. This reached the Prophet so he said to them, {It has reached me that you want to move close to the masjid?} They replied, "Yes, O Messenger of Allah, we want to." He replied, {O Banū Salamah, your traces are written in your homes. Your traces are written in your homes.} They then said, "It did not please us to change."' In a narration of Muslim's that bears the same meaning, the ending contains, {...and you have a rank for every step.}

The reward also increase any time there is difficulty in walking to the masjid, especially to attend the night[145] and dawn[146] prayers in congregation. Abū Dāwūd

---

142 (tn): i.e. spiritual retreat in the masjid, especially in the last ten days of Ramaḍān.
143 (tn): i.e. in the Ḥaram in Makkah.
144 (tn): Please see Sūrat Fuṣṣilat 41:32.
145 Ar. *ʿishāʾ*.
146 Ar. *fajr*.

and at-Tirmidhī have related from Buraydah ﷺ that the Prophet ﷺ said, {Give glad tidings to those who walk in darkness to the masjids of perfect light on the Day of Standing}.

E. **Removing harm from the road:** This means to remove from the road anything that bothers the Muslims, such as rocks, thorns or filth. This *ṣadaqah* carries less reward than the charities mentioned before, due to the ḥadīth: {Faith is some seventy-seven branches, the highest of which is the testimony that there is no god but Allah and the lowest of which is removing harm from the road.} It has been said that it is recommended to say the word of *tawḥīd* when removing harm, so that one joins between the highest branch of faith and the lowest. If every Muslim adhered to this Prophetic advice, rubbish and dirt would not be thrown in other than their proper place and whatever bothers Muslims would be removed from the road, and thus Islamic countries would become the cleanest and most beautiful places on earth.

5. The Ḍuḥā Prayer Suffices in Showing Gratitude for Sound Organs and Limbs: Muslim has related from the narration of Abū al-Aswad ad-Duʾalī, from Abū Dharr, that the Prophet ﷺ said, {Every part (*sulāmā*) of your body owes charity (*ṣadaqah*) at the start of the day. Every *tasbīḥah* is charity. Every *taḥmīdah* is charity. Every *tahlīlah* is charity. Every *takbīrah* is charity. To enjoin the right is charity. To forbid the wrong is charity. Two cycles[147] of the ḍuḥā prayer suffices in that regard.}

The least ḍuḥā prayer is two cycles and the most is eight, and it is recommended to do *taslīm*[148] after every two. Its time starts when the sun is a spear's length above the horizon and ends when the sun reaches its zenith. It has been singled out for this precedence because it has not been legislated to compensate for the deficiency of something else, as opposed to all other supererogatory prayers,[149] for they compensate for the deficiencies of the obligatory prayers that precede them. Thus, they are not solely dedicated to expressing gratitude for these splendid blessings while the ḍuḥā prayer is.

If the requirement to show gratitude is repeated every day when the sun rises, the best act of worship that makes a Muslim vigilant and grateful after it has risen is the ḍuḥā prayer. However, al-Ḥāfiẓ al-ʿIrāqī holds the position that the ḍuḥā prayer has been singled out because it bear a special quality and characteristic that only Allah the Exalted knows.

147 Ar. *rakʿa.*

148 (tn): i.e. say *as-salāmu ʿālaykum* and thereby come out of the prayer.

149 Ar. *ar-rawātib*, which are the prayers done before or after the obligatory prayers.

6. Praising and Thanking Allah for His Blessings:
Abū Dāwūd and an-Nasā'ī have related that the Messenger of Allah ﷺ said, {Whoever wakes up in the morning and says,

(اللّهُمَّ ما أَصْبَحَ بِي مِنْ نِعْمَةٍ أَوْ بِأَحَدٍ مِنْ خَلْقِكَ فَمِنْكَ وَحْدَكَ لا شَرِيكَ لَكَ، فَلَكَ الْحَمْدُ وَلَكَ الشُّكْرُ)

'O Allah, whatever blessing I or anyone else from Your creation wakes up with is from You alone, You have no partner, and for You is all praise and gratitude' has fulfilled his gratitude for that day. Whoever says it in the evening has fulfilled his gratitude for that night.}

Ibn Mājah has related from the Messenger of Allah ﷺ that he said, {Allah does not bestow a blessing upon a slave and he says *al-ḥamdu lillāh* except that what he gives is better than what he takes.} Some scholars have understood from this ḥadīth that praise is better than blessings, because what is meant by blessings are those that are worldly, such as well-being and sustenance. Praise is a religious blessing. Both are blessings from Allah the Exalted, but Allah's blessing towards His slave by guiding him to thank Him by praising Him for it is better than any worldly blessings that He bestows on His slave. If these blessings are not joined with gratitude, they are a tribulation, and when Allah the Exalted grants His slave the success to have gratitude for them by praising Him and so forth, the blessing of gratitude is more complete and perfect.

7. **Sincere Intention for Allah the Exalted in all acts of Charity:** Sincere intention for Allah the Exalted alone in all the acts of righteousness and charity mentioned in this ḥadīth and others is a condition for being rewarded for them. Allah the Exalted has said,

﴿لَّا خَيْرَ فِي كَثِيرٍ مِّن نَّجْوَىٰهُمْ إِلَّا مَنْ أَمَرَ بِصَدَقَةٍ أَوْ مَعْرُوفٍ أَوْ إِصْلَـٰحٍ بَيْنَ ٱلنَّاسِ ۚ وَمَن يَفْعَلْ ذَٰلِكَ ٱبْتِغَآءَ مَرْضَاتِ ٱللَّهِ فَسَوْفَ نُؤْتِيهِ أَجْرًا عَظِيمًا﴾

"There is no good in much of their secret talk, except in the case of those who enjoin *ṣadaqah*, or what is right, or putting things right between people. If anyone does that, seeking the pleasure of Allah, We will give him an immense reward." [an-Nisā' 4:114]

Ibn Ḥibbān has related a ḥadīth in his *Ṣaḥīḥ* in which the Messenger of Allah ﷺ mentions several qualities, such as giving in charity, saying something good, assisting the weak and leaving off harm. Then he says, {By the One in whose hand is my soul, there is no one who does any of these seeking thereby what is with Allah except that I take his hand on the Day of Standing until he enters Paradise.}

It has been related from al-Ḥasan al-Baṣrī and Ibn Sirīn that doing something good is rewarded even if there is no intention. Al-Ḥasan was asked about the man who asks him for something and he despises him, but he gives it to him out of shyness. Does he get a reward? He replied, 'That is good thing to do and there is a reward for doing good things.' Ḥumayd has collected this from ibn Zanjawayh. Ibn Sirīn was asked about a man who takes part in a funeral but not because he anticipates reward. Rather, he does so because he feels shy in front of the deceased's family. Does he get a reward for that? He replied, 'One reward? He gets two rewards. One is for praying over his brother and the other is maintaining ties with the living.' This was collected by Abū Nuʿaym in *al-Ḥilyah*.[150]

8. The point of the ḥadīth is not to confine the types of *ṣadaqah* to the general meaning of what is mentioned therein. Rather, it is to draw attention to what remains of them and that *ṣadaqah* is whatever benefits oneself or others from Allah's creation. He ﷺ has said, {In every moist liver there is reward.} He has also said, {Allah has obligated excellence (*iḥsān*) in everything}. He has also said, {The creation are Allah the Exalted's dependents, and the most beloved of people to Allah the Exalted are the most compassionate of them towards His dependents.}

9. In conclusion, this ḥadīth informs us of Allah the Exalted blessing man with a healthy body and complete limbs and organs, and that he must thank Allah every day for every limb and organ. Gratitude includes doing good, spreading beneficence, helping those in need, good conduct, benefitting others and protecting them from harm and expending every good to every human being, or indeed to every creature. These are all example of transitive *ṣadaqah*.

As for intransitive *ṣadaqah*, it is the various types of *dhikr, tasbīḥ, takbīr, taḥmīd, tahlīl, istighfār,*[151] sending blessings upon the Prophet ﷺ reciting the Qur'ān, walking to the masjids and sitting therein to wait for the prayer or listen to knowledge and *dhikr*. They also include modesty in one's clothing and walking, to be dedicated to one's job, to earn the lawful and strive for it, to take oneself to account for one's previous deeds, to regret and to repent for one's previous sins, and to be saddened by them, to weep out of fear of Allah ﷻ and to contemplate the dominions of the heavens and the earth as well as the affairs of the Hereafter and what is contains, such as Paradise, the Fire, the promise and the threat.

150 *Jāmiʿ al-ʿUlūm wa al-Ḥikam*, 217-218.

151 (tn): i.e. seeking Allah's forgiveness.

THE TWENTY-SEVENTH ḤADĪTH

البِرُّ وَالإِثْمُ

عَنِ النَّوَّاسِ بِنْ سَمْعَانَ ﷺ عَنِ النَّبِيِّ ﷺ قَالَ: {البِرُّ حُسْنُ الْخُلُقِ، وَالإِثْمُ مَا حَاكَ فِيْ نَفْسِكَ وَكَرِهْتَ أَنْ يَطَّلِعَ عَلَيْهِ النَّاسُ} رواه مسلم.

وَعَنْ وَابِصَةَ بْنِ مَعْبَدٍ ﷺ قَالَ: أَتَيتُ رَسُوْلَ اللهِ ﷺ فَقَالَ: {جِئْتَ تَسْأَلُ عَنِ البِرِّ؟} قُلْتُ: نَعَمْ. فَقَالَ: {اِسْتَفْتِ قَلْبَكَ، البِرُّ مَا اطْمَأَنَّتْ إِلَيْهِ النَّفْسُ واطْمَأَنَّ إِلَيهِ الْقَلْبُ، وَالإِثْمُ مَا حَاكَ فِيْ النَّفْسِ وَتَرَدَّدَ فِيْ الصَّدْرِ وَإِنْ أَفْتَاكَ النَّاسُ وَأَفْتُوْكَ.}

حَدِيثٌ حَسَنٌ رُوِيْنَاهُ فِيْ مُسْنَدَيْ الإِمَامَيْنِ: أَحْمَدَ بْنِ حَنْبَلٍ وَالدَّارِمِيِّ، بِإِسْنَادٍ حَسَنٍ.

Righteousness and Sin

It is on the authority of an-Nawwās ibn Samʿān ﷺ that the Prophet ﷺ said, {Righteousness[152] is good character, while sin[153] is that which agitates your soul and you would not like people to know about it.} Related by Muslim.

It is on the authority of Wābiṣah ibn Maʿbad ﷺ who said, 'I came to the Messenger of Allah ﷺ and he said, {Have you come to ask about righteousness?} I replied, "Yes." He said, {Ask your heart for a judgment. Righteousness is that which the soul and heart find tranquillity, while sin is which agitates the soul and causes hesitation in the heart, even though people have repeatedly given their legal opinion [in its favour].}

This is a good (*ḥasan*) ḥadīth that we have related in the *Musnads* of the two Imams: Aḥmad ibn Ḥanbal and ad-Dārimī, with a good chain of transmission.

The ḥadīth of an-Nawwās ibn Samʿān has been related by Muslim in Righteousness and Keeping Ties (the chapter on the explanation of righteousness and sin), no.2553, while the ḥadīth of Wābiṣah ibn Maʿbad has been related by Aḥmad in the *Musnad* (4/228) and ad-Dārimī (2/246).

152 Ar. *al-birr.*
153 Ar. *al-ithm.*

The Importance of the Ḥadīth:

Ibn Ḥajar al-Haytamī said, 'This ḥadīth is an example of his comprehensive speech ﷺ. In fact, it is one of his most concise statements, as the word *birr* comprises all good actions and praiseworthy characteristics, while *ithm* comprises all evil actions and shameful deeds, whether great or small. This is why the Prophet ﷺ juxtaposed the two and made them opposites.'

The Language of the Ḥadīth:

(البر) *al-birr*: a noun that comprises goodness and every pleasing action.

(حسن الخلق) *ḥusn ul-khuluq* (or *khulq*): to be moulded by noble character, and to have the morals that Allah has legislated for His servant, by obeying His commands and avoiding what He has prohibited.

(الإثم) *al-ithm*: sin in all of its types.

(ما حاك في النفس) *ma ḥaka fin nafs*: that which causes the soul to tremble out of agitation, anxiety and aversion, and thus one's heart does not open up to it or feel tranquil regarding it.

Legal Matters and Other Guidance from the Ḥadīth:

1. The explanation of *birr*: In the ḥadīth of an-Nawwās ibn Sam'ān ﷺ the Prophet ﷺ explained it to mean good character, while in the ḥadīth of Wābiṣah, he explained it is that in which the soul and heart find tranquillity. The justification for this difference that has been related regarding the explanation of *birr* is that it means and refers to one of two specific matters:[154]

A. What is meant by *birr* is treating people well, and maybe it refers exclusively to treating parents well, and thus there is the expression *birr al-wālidayn*. It often refers to being good to the creation in general, as there is the ḥadīth of Bahz ibn Ḥakīm, from his father, from his grandfather, in which he said, 'O Messenger of Allah, who should I show righteousness (*birr*) to?' He replied, {Your mother.} He said, 'Then who?' He replied, {Your father.} He said, 'Then who?' He replied, {Then those nearest and so forth.} In the *Musnad* of Imam Aḥmad, the Messenger of Allah ﷺ was asked about the *birr* of the Ḥajj, so he said, {Give food and spread peace.}, and in another narration: {Good speech.} 'Abdullah ibn 'Umar would say, '*Birr* is a simple matter: a cheerful face and gentle words.'

154 *Jāmi' al-'Ulūm wa al-Ḥikam*, p.220-21, with slight modification.

When *birr* is connected to *taqwā*, *birr* can mean treating people well while *taqwā* refers to how you deal with the True Lord, by obeying Him and avoiding what He has declared unlawful. *Birr* can also mean carrying out obligations while *taqwā* means avoiding what has been declared unlawful. Allah the Exalted has said,

﴿وَتَعَاوَنُوا۟ عَلَى ٱلْبِرِّ وَٱلتَّقْوَىٰ﴾

"Help each other to *birr* and *taqwā*." [al-Mā'idah 5:2]

B. What is meant by *birr* is carrying out all acts of obedience, outward and inward. Allah the Exalted has said,

﴿لَّيْسَ ٱلْبِرَّ أَن تُوَلُّوا۟ وُجُوهَكُمْ قِبَلَ ٱلْمَشْرِقِ وَٱلْمَغْرِبِ وَلَـٰكِنَّ ٱلْبِرَّ مَنْ ءَامَنَ بِٱللَّهِ وَٱلْيَوْمِ
ٱلْـَٔاخِرِ وَٱلْمَلَـٰٓئِكَةِ وَٱلْكِتَـٰبِ وَٱلنَّبِيِّـۧنَ وَءَاتَى ٱلْمَالَ عَلَىٰ حُبِّهِۦ ذَوِى ٱلْقُرْبَىٰ وَٱلْيَتَـٰمَىٰ وَٱلْمَسَـٰكِينَ
وَٱبْنَ ٱلسَّبِيلِ وَٱلسَّآئِلِينَ وَفِى ٱلرِّقَابِ وَأَقَامَ ٱلصَّلَوٰةَ وَءَاتَى ٱلزَّكَوٰةَ وَٱلْمُوفُونَ بِعَهْدِهِمْ إِذَا عَـٰهَدُوا۟ ۖ
وَٱلصَّـٰبِرِينَ فِى ٱلْبَأْسَآءِ وَٱلضَّرَّآءِ وَحِينَ ٱلْبَأْسِ ۗ أُو۟لَـٰٓئِكَ ٱلَّذِينَ صَدَقُوا۟ ۖ وَأُو۟لَـٰٓئِكَ هُمُ ٱلْمُتَّقُونَ﴾

"...Rather, those with true righteousness (*birr*) are those who have faith in Allah and the Last Day, the Angels, the Book and the Prophets, and who, despite their love for it, give away their wealth to their relatives and to orphans and the very poor, and to travellers and beggars and to set slaves free, and who establish the prayer and pay the zakat; those who honour their contracts when they make them, and are steadfast in poverty and illness and in battle. Those are the people who are true. They are the people who have *taqwā*." [al-Baqarah 2:177]

According to this meaning, *birr* includes all acts of obedience, those that are inward, such as faith in Allah, His Angels, His Books, His Messengers and the Last Day, as well as those that are outward, such as spending wealth on that which Allah loves, establishing the prayer, paying the zakāt, honouring contracts and patience with what Allah has decreed, such as illness and poverty, patience with acts of obedience, such as meeting the enemy.

2. Knowing the truth is from one's natural disposition (*fiṭrah*):

The Prophet's statement ﷺ: {Righteousness is that in which the soul and the heart find tranquillity} is proof that Allah ﷻ endowed His servant with knowledge of the truth, finding tranquillity in it and accepting it. He has firmly planted love of the truth therein. He ﷺ has said, {Every child is born upon the *fiṭrah*.} Abū Hurayrah, the narrator of this ḥadīth, said, 'If you want, recite:

﴿فِطْرَتَ ٱللَّهِ ٱلَّتِى فَطَرَ ٱلنَّاسَ عَلَيْهَا﴾

"Allah's natural disposition which He has endowed man with..." [ar-Rūm 30:30]

Allah the Exalted has informed us that the believer's heart finds tranquillity and serenity in His remembrance; it expands and opens up with the light of faith. Thus, when there is ambiguity, one can turn to one's heart. If it finds tranquillity therein, it is *birr*. If not, it is *ithm*. Allah the Exalted has said,

﴿أَلَا بِذِكْرِ ٱللَّهِ تَطْمَئِنُّ ٱلْقُلُوبُ﴾

"Only in the remembrance of Allah can the hearts find peace." [ar-Ra'd 13:28]

3. The Two Signs of *Ithm*: *Ithm* has two signs, inward and outward. The inward is the unrest, anxiety, aversion and dislike that it leaves in one's soul, because it cannot find peace in it. He ﷺ said, {...*ithm* is that which agitates the soul...} It has been authentically narrated that Ibn Mas'ūd ؓ said, '*Ithm* is the ringworm of the hearts.'

The outward sign is that one would dislike for prominent people and those like them, whom one is shy in front of, to know about it, on the condition that this dislike is for a religious reason and not any normal dislike.

If both signs are present and the *ithm* is loathed by the doer as well as others if they were to know about it, this is the highest level of knowing and perceiving *ithm* when there is ambiguity.

4. Leaving the Fatwā and Adhering to It: A Muslim must leave the fatwā if it goes against what agitates his soul and causes hesitation in his heart, because the fatwā is not *taqwā* and carefulness. The *muftī* only looks at the outward, while a person knows things about his soul that the *muftī* does not know. Alternatively, it could be the case that the one who loathes the matter is someone whose heart Allah has expanded[155] and someone has given him a fatwā based merely on conjecture or an inclination towards capricious desire without any evidence in the Revealed Law.

An-Nawawī said, 'If a gift comes to you from someone whose wealth is mostly unlawful, your soul hesitates regarding its lawfulness and the *muftī* tells you it is lawful to consume it, this fatwā does not remove ambiguity. Likewise, if a woman informs a man that such-and-such woman is his milk sister and the *muftī* tells him that it is permissible for him to marry her because the minimum number has not been met,[156] such a fatwā would not remove ambiguity. Rather, one should be careful, even if been told it is permissible.'

155 (tn): Please see Sūrat al-An'ām 6:125 and Sūrat ash-Sharḥ 94:1

156 i.e. she has not been nursed the minimum number of times in order to be considered a milk sibling, which is five according to the school of Imam ash-Shāfi'ī. Please see *al-Fiqh al-Manhajī* (Damascus: Dār al-Qalam, 1433/2012), v.2, p.197.

If the fatwā is backed up by evidence in the Revealed Law, a Muslim is obligated to take it and adhere to it, even if his heart does not open up to it. Examples of this includes concessions in the Revealed Law, such as breaking one's fast when travelling or ill, or shortening one's prayer while travelling. The Prophet ﷺ would command his Companions to do things that some of their hearts were not open to, and thus they would refrain or abstain from carrying out his command. An example of this is when he commanded them to slaughter their animals and no longer proceed with their 'umrah after the treaty of al-Ḥudaybiyyah, in addition to the negotiations that took place there with the Quraysh that resulted in the Muslims heading back to Madīnah without performing the 'umrah. This was all due to their extra faith and sincerity, but what is mentioned in the text is that the believer can do nothing but obey Allah and His Messenger, as the Exalted One has said,

﴿وَمَا كَانَ لِمُؤْمِنٍ وَلَا مُؤْمِنَةٍ إِذَا قَضَى ٱللَّهُ وَرَسُولُهُۥٓ أَمْرًا أَن يَكُونَ لَهُمُ ٱلْخِيَرَةُ مِنْ أَمْرِهِمْ﴾

"When Allah and His Messenger have decided something, it is not for any man or woman of the believers to have a choice about it." [al-Aḥzāb 33:36]

One should receive this with an open heart, contentment and submission. Allah the Exalted has said,

﴿فَلَا وَرَبِّكَ لَا يُؤْمِنُونَ حَتَّىٰ يُحَكِّمُوكَ فِيمَا شَجَرَ بَيْنَهُمْ ثُمَّ لَا يَجِدُواْ فِىٓ أَنفُسِهِمْ

حَرَجًا مِّمَّا قَضَيْتَ وَيُسَلِّمُواْ تَسْلِيمًا﴾

"No, by your Lord, they are not believers until they make you their judge in the disputes that break out between them, and then find no resistance within themselves to what you decide and submit themselves completely." [an-Nisā' 4:65]

5. The Messenger's Miracle ﷺ: The Messenger of Allah ﷺ has an immense miracle in the ḥadīth of Wābiṣah, in that he informed him of what was in his soul before he spoke if it. He said to him, {Have you come to ask about righteousness?} Abū Nuʿaym has mentioned in *al-Ḥilyah* from Wābiṣah ؓ that he said, 'I came to the Messenger of Allah ﷺ and I did not want to leave anything to do with *birr* and *ithm* except that I had asked him about it, so I came to enjoy his good graces. They would say, "Wābiṣah, leave the Messenger of Allah alone" and I would reply, "Leave me to draw near to him. Out of all people, he is the one I desire most to draw near to." He then said, {Come close Wābiṣah}, and thus I came so close to him that my knees were touching his knees. He said, {Have you come to ask about *birr* and *ithm*?} I replied, 'Yes.' He then gathered his fingers and started scratching my chest, saying, {O Wābiṣah, seek a judgment from your heart. Seek a judgment from your soul. *Birr* is that in which the soul and the heart find tranquillity, while sin is that which agitates the soul and causes hesitation in the heart, even if people keep telling you that it is permissible.}'

6. Everyone Has Their Own Rank: The Prophet ﷺ told Wābiṣah to refer such matters to what his own heart understands, and he knew that he would understand that from his own soul. This is because no one grasps this unless they have a firm understanding, strong intelligence and an illuminated heart. As for the one who is coarse of character and weak in understanding, you will not get a positive response out of him to such advice, as he will not get anything out of it. Rather, what he needs are the detailed commands and prohibitions of the Revealed Law. This is from the beauty of how he ﷺ raised and nurtured his Companions. He would address them according to what their intellects could grasp, and command them according them to the fact that everybody has their own rank.

7. The Best Character: The character of the Messenger of Allah ﷺ is the best character, the noblest and the most beautiful. His character represents the character of the Revealed Law and embodies the etiquettes that Allah has refined His servant with His Mighty Book. This is why Allah praises His Noble Messenger by saying,

﴿وَإِنَّكَ لَعَلَىٰ خُلُقٍ عَظِيمٍ﴾

"Indeed you are truly vast in character." [al-Qalam 68:4]

And ʿĀʾishah ﷺ said, 'His character ﷺ was the Qurʾān.' His etiquettes were the etiquettes of the Qurʾān, and thus he carried out its commands and avoided its prohibitions. Acting according to the Qurʾān became part of his character, like an inseparable part of his nature and disposition.

8. The ḥadīth instructs us to have noble character, because beautiful character is one of the greatest qualities of *birr*.

9. The value of the heart in Islam and it being sought for judgment before action.

10. The religion is an internal inhibition and overseer, as opposed to manmade law, which is only an external inhibition.

11. The religion prevents the perpetration of *ithm*, because it makes the soul the overseer of every individual before his Lord, as opposed to manmade law, for it can only control the soul externally. It needs supervising and monitoring, which can be evaded and deceived, amongst other things.

THE TWENTY-EIGHTH ḤADĪTH

لُزومُ السُّنَّة واجْتِنابُ البِدَع

عَنْ أَبِي نَجِيحٍ العِرْباضِ بْنِ سَارِيَةَ ﷺ قَالَ: وَعَظَنَا رَسُولُ اللهِ ﷺ مَوْعِظَةً وَجِلَتْ مِنْهَا القُلُوبُ،

وَذَرَفَتْ مِنْهَا الْعُيُونُ، فَقُلْنَا: يَا رَسُولَ اللهِ، كَأَنَّهَا مَوْعِظَةُ مُوَدِّعٍ، فَأَوْصِنَا. قال: {أُوصِيكُمْ بِتَقْوَى

اللهِ عَزَّ وَجَلَّ، وَالسَّمْعِ وَالطَّاعَةِ، وَإِنْ تَأَمَّرَ عَلَيْكُمْ عَبْدٌ، فَإِنَّهُ مَنْ يَعِشْ مِنْكُمْ فَسَيَرَى اخْتِلَافاً

كَثِيراً، فَعَلَيْكُمْ بِسُنَّتِي وَسُنَّةِ الْخُلَفَاءِ الرَّاشِدِينَ الْمَهْدِيِّينَ، عَضُّوا عَلَيْهَا بِالنَّوَاجِذِ، وَإِيَّاكُمْ

وَمُحْدَثَاتِ الْأُمُورِ، فَإِنَّ كُلَّ بِدْعَةٍ ضَلَالَةٌ.} رواه أبو داود والترمذي وقال: حديث حسن صحيح.

Adhering to the Sunnah and Avoiding Innovation

It is on the authority of Abū Najīḥ al-ʿIrbāḍ ibn Sāriyah ﷺ who said, 'The Messenger of Allah ﷺ admonished us in a way that made hearts tremble with fear and eyes flow with tears, so we said, 'O Messenger of Allah, it is as if this is a farewell admonition, so advise us.' He replied, {I advise you to have *taqwā* of Allah ﷺ and to hear and obey even if a slave is given command over you. Whoever of you lives will see many disagreements, so take hold of my Sunnah and the Sunnah of the Rightly-Guided, Orthodox Khulafāʾ.[157] Bite down on it with your molar teeth. Beware of invented matters, for every invented matter is an innovation and every innovation is misguidance.}' Related by Abū Dāwūd and at-Tirmidhī, who said that it is a good, authentic ḥadīth.

Abū Dāwūd has related in the Sunnah (the chapter on adhering to the Sunnah), no.4607 and at-Tirmidhī in Knowledge (the chapter on what has reached us regarding taking hold of the Sunnah and avoiding innovation), no.2678. It is also in the *Musnad* (4/126-127) and Ibn Mājah quotes it in his introduction, no.42.

---

157 (tn): i.e. caliphs.

The Importance of the Ḥadīth:

This ḥadīth contains advice that the Messenger ﷺ gave to his Companions and to the Muslims in general. It includes advice to have *taqwā* of Allah ﷻ and to hear and obey the rulers of the Muslims, and this is how felicity is obtained in this life and the next. Likewise, he has advised the Ummah with that which will guarantee them success and guidance, which is to cling to the Sunnah and stick to the orthodox majority, while staying away from misguidance and innovations.

The Language of the Ḥadīth:

(موعظة) *mawʿiẓatan*: this comes from the word *waʿẓ*, which means to remind someone of the consequences of something. The *an* at the end indicates that it is an absolute object,[158] which is for emphasis. In other words, this was a profound admonition, and it was after the dawn prayer, as mentioned in Aḥmad's narration.

(وجلت) *wajilat*: to be afraid.

(ذرفت) *dharafat*: to flow.

(موعظة مودع) *mawʿiẓatu muwaddiʿ*: the Companions understood this from the intensity with which the Prophet ﷺ was warning them and filling them with fear, for the one bidding farewell probes and investigates like no one else.

(الراشدين) *rāshidīn*: the plural of *rāshid*, which is someone who knows the truth and follows it.

(النواجذ) *an-nawājidh*: the plural of *nājidh*, which are the last of the molar teeth and when they appear it is an indication of intellect.[159] The command to bite down on the Sunnah with one's molar teeth means it should be adhered to firmly.

(محدثات الأمور) *muḥdathāt al-umūr*: matters that are invented in the religion and have no foundation in the Revealed Law, and they are blameworthy. As for new matters that do have a foundation, they are not blameworthy.

(بدعة) *bidʿah*: linguistically, this is something that is invented without there being anything like it that preceded it. As for in the Revealed Law, it is something that is invented and goes against what the Revealed Law has commanded and its evidences.

158 Ar. *mafʿūl muṭlaq*.

159 (tn): i.e. wisdom teeth.

(ضلالة) *ḍalālah*: remoteness from the truth, because the truth is what the Revealed Law has brought, so all that does'nt go back to the truth is innovation and error

Legal Matters and Other Guidance from the Ḥadīth:

1. The Qualities of an Effective Admonition: An admonition is advice and a reminder of consequences, and for the admonition to be effective, to penetrate hearts and affect souls, the following conditions must be fulfilled:

A. Selecting the topic: One should admonish people, remind them and fill them with fear with that which will benefit them in their religious and their worldly affairs. One should not confine oneself merely to teaching them rulings and legal punishments. Rather, one chooses a topic based on wisdom and knowledge of what the people need in their daily lives. There is no doubt that when Muslims are confined to the khuṭbahs on Friday and the two ʿĪds, this has a massive effect in turning them away from the reality of their religion and removing the spirit of might and struggle[160] from their souls. This is especially the case when the khuṭbahs on Friday and the two ʿĪds are simply a job that has to be carried out and not a call that is announced and delivered properly. When they are just pages that are read from khuṭbahs that were written centuries ago, this has a part in unintentionally putting the Muslims to sleep, as well as putting up a thick barrier between the way of Islam on the one hand and the reality of life and the problems of the age on the other.

The Messenger of Allah ﷺ is an excellent model for us if we want success and prosperity. He would often admonish his Companions outside of the regular khuṭbahs, and his admonitions were effective and were an implementation of Allah the Exalted's command to him:

﴿ٱدْعُ إِلَىٰ سَبِيلِ رَبِّكَ بِٱلْحِكْمَةِ وَٱلْمَوْعِظَةِ ٱلْحَسَنَةِ﴾

"Call to the way of your Lord with wisdom and fair admonition." [an-Naḥl 16:125]

B. Eloquence in admonition: Eloquence in making people understand the meanings that are sought, making them reach the listeners' hearts by using the best words and expressions that convey the meaning; one should use the words and expressions that are the most eloquent and sweetest to the ear, which will penetrate the heart. Allah the Exalted has said,

﴿وَعِظْهُمْ وَقُل لَّهُمْ فِىٓ أَنفُسِهِمْ قَوْلًۢا بَلِيغًا﴾

"...and warn them and speak to them with words that take effect." [an-Nisāʾ 4:63]

160 Ar. *jihād*.

In the narration of Imam Aḥmad, Abū Dāwud and at-Tirmidhī, the wording is: 'The Messenger of Allah ﷺ admonished us with a profound admonition.'

C. Lack of prolixity: Lengthening an admonition causes the listeners to feel bored and annoyed, and the benefit that is sought is lost. The Prophet ﷺ would make his khuṭbahs and admonitions short and not lengthen them. Rather, he was profound and concise. In *Ṣaḥīḥ Muslim*, Jābir ibn Samurah ؓ is reported to have said, 'I prayed with the Prophet ﷺ and his prayer was thrifty and his khuṭbah was thrifty.' In the *Sunan* of Abū Dāwud: 'The Messenger of Allah would not lengthen his admonition on Friday. Rather, it was just a few words.'

D. Choosing the right opportunity and the appropriate time: This is why he ﷺ would not admonish them constantly. Rather, he would do so from time to time. Al-Bukhārī and Muslim have related from Abū Wā'il that he said, "Abdullah ibn Mas'ūd would remind us every Thursday, so a man said to him, 'O Abū 'Abdur Raḥmān, we love and desire to hear you speak, and we would like you to speak to us every day.' He replied, 'Nothing prevents me from speaking to you every day other than that I do not want to bore you. The Messenger of Allah ﷺ would only warn us from time to time because he did not want to bore us.'

2. The Qualities of a Successful Preacher: In order for the admonition to be effective, such that it wakes up heedless souls and dead consciences, it must come from a successful preacher whose personality, speech and conduct fulfill the following conditions:

A. That he believe in his own words, be affected by them and have the burning desire to make them reach his listeners' souls, and that they are thoroughly convinced of them. This is apparent in his manner of speaking and the inflections of his voice, in his state and how the contours of his face change. This is a *sunnah* of the Messenger of Allah ﷺ for his state would change when he was preaching and admonishing. Jābir ibn 'Abdillāh ؓ said, 'When the Prophet ﷺ gave a khuṭbah and mentioned the Hour, his anger would become intense, he would raise his voice and his eyes would turn red, as if he were warning an army, saying, {You could be attacked in the morning or in the evening.}

B. That he possess a heart that advices sincerely and is free of blemishes, such that his words come from a sincere heart that touches the pericardia of hearts. As for the one whose heart and soul are diseased, his words exit his mouth, go into one of the listener's ears and out the other. It is related that al-Ḥasan al-Baṣrī heard a preacher admonishing people in the Basra masjid and he was not affected by his words, so after the people had left, he said to the man, 'There must be an illness in your heart or in mine.'

C. That his words match his actions, because those who listen to his admonitions and are impressed by his eloquence will keep an eye on his deeds and actions. If his deeds match his words, they will follow him and imitate him. If they find him contradicting his own words or being negligent therein, they will make this well-known and turn away from him. It has been said, 'Whoever preaches by speaking wastes his words, and whoever preaches by doing hits the target.' It is sufficient deterrent against such misguidance that Allah the Exalted has said,

﴿يَـٰٓأَيُّهَا ٱلَّذِينَ ءَامَنُوا۟ لِمَ تَقُولُونَ مَا لَا تَفْعَلُونَ ۝ كَبُرَ مَقْتًا عِندَ ٱللَّهِ أَن تَقُولُوا۟ مَا لَا تَفْعَلُونَ﴾

"You who believe! Why do you say what you do not do? It is deeply abhorrent to Allah that you should say what you do not do." [as-Ṣaff 61:2-3]

3. The Superiority of the Companions and the Probity of Their Hearts: The fear that seized the Companions' hearts and the tears that flowed from their eyes when they heard the Prophet's admonition ﷺ is proof of precedence and probity, and ascent into the highest levels of success and ranks of faith, such that they truly became stars of guidance and integrity and became worthy of praise from their Messenger and teacher ﷺ and from their Creator ﷻ. Allah the Exalted has said,

﴿وَإِذَا سَمِعُوا۟ مَآ أُنزِلَ إِلَى ٱلرَّسُولِ تَرَىٰٓ أَعْيُنَهُمْ تَفِيضُ مِنَ ٱلدَّمْعِ مِمَّا عَرَفُوا۟ مِنَ ٱلْحَقِّ﴾

"When they listen to what has been sent down to the Messenger, you see their eyes overflowing with tears because of what they recognize of the truth." [al-Mā'idah 5:83]

The Glorified has also praised the believers in general by saying,

﴿إِنَّمَا ٱلْمُؤْمِنُونَ ٱلَّذِينَ إِذَا ذُكِرَ ٱللَّهُ وَجِلَتْ قُلُوبُهُمْ وَإِذَا تُلِيَتْ عَلَيْهِمْ ءَايَـٰتُهُۥ زَادَتْهُمْ إِيمَـٰنًا﴾

"The believers are those whose hearts tremble when Allah is mentioned, whose faith is increased when His verses are recited to them." [al-Anfāl 8:2]

4. Advising people to have *taqwā*: *Taqwā* is to obey commands and avoid prohibitions according to the obligations of the Revealed Law. Advising people to have *taqwā* was a major concern of the Prophet ﷺ because by adhering to it felicity is attained in this life and in the Hereafter. It is Allah the Exalted's advice to the first of people and the last, for Allah the Exalted has said,

﴿وَلَقَدْ وَصَّيْنَا ٱلَّذِينَ أُوتُوا۟ ٱلْكِتَـٰبَ مِن قَبْلِكُمْ وَإِيَّاكُمْ أَنِ ٱتَّقُوا۟ ٱللَّهَ﴾

"We have instructed those given the Book before you and you yourselves to have *taqwā* of Allah." [an-Nisā' 4:131]

5. Advising people to hear and obey: Hearing and obeying those in charge of the Muslims' affairs in that which is right is an obligation that Allah the Exalted has obligated in His Qur'ān:

﴿أَطِيعُوا۟ ٱللَّهَ وَأَطِيعُوا۟ ٱلرَّسُولَ وَأُو۟لِى ٱلْأَمْرِ مِنكُمْ﴾

"Obey Allah and obey the Messenger and those in command among you." [an-Nisā' 4:59]

This is why the Prophet ﷺ specifically mentioned it even though it is part of having *taqwā* of Allah ﷻ. He conjoined the specific to the general in order to emphasise it further and show how important it is. By adhering to this Prophetic advice, the Muslims attain felicity in this life, their worldly interests and livelihoods fall into place, their unity is strengthened and their worship and obedience of their Lord is manifested.

ʿAlī ibn Abī Ṭālib رضي الله عنه said, 'People will only be rectified by a righteous leader or an iniquitous one. If he is iniquitous, the believer worships his Lord therein and bears with the iniquitous leader until his appointed time. Indeed, that which weakens the Muslims and takes the wind out of their sails is when they extricate themselves from hearing and obeying their ruler, and they incline towards chaos and contravention. This, in turn, leads to tribulations and numerous disagreements and divisions, and the appearance of hypocrisy, disobedience and people chasing lowly desires.

The Prophet ﷺ said, {...even if a slave is given command over you...}. In al-Bukhārī's narration, on the authority of Anas رضي الله عنه the Prophet ﷺ said, {Hear and obey, even if an Abyssinian slave with a head like a raisin is put in charge of you.} The scholars have understood one of two matters from this:

The **first** is that he ﷺ was informing from the unseen about the circumstances of the Muslims deteriorating, and that there would be disorder in the application of the Revealed Law's rulings, such that rulership would fall into the hands of those who do not deserve it. At that point, commanding obedience is preferring the lesser of two evils, as bearing patiently with a slave's rulership, which is not permissible, is a lesser evil than the incitement of tribulation.

The **second** is that he was giving an example of something unrealistic by way of presumption and supposition. Otherwise, a slave's rulership is not valid, and it is like the ḥadīth: {Whoever builds a masjid, even if it is like a sand grouse's nest, Allah will build a house for him in Paradise.}
[A sand grouse's nest cannot be a masjid.]

6. Consistently Adhering to the Prophetic Sunnah and Sunnah of the Orthodox Khulafā': The Sunnah is the travelled path, and such adherence includes what the Prophet was upon ﷺ as well as his Orthodox Khulafā' in terms of creed, word and deed. The Prophet ﷺ linked the Sunnah of the Orthodox Khulafā' to his Sunnah because he knew that their way, which they were deriving from the Book and the Sunnah, was safe from error. The Muslims have made consensus that the term 'Rightly-Guided, Orthodox Khulafā'' refers to the four khulafā': Abū Bakr, 'Umar, 'Uthmān and 'Alī ﷺ.

There is no doubt that adhering to the Prophet's Sunnah is paramount, and the Sunnah of his four khulafā' after him is victory and success, especially when there is a great deal of disagreement and disunity.

7. Warning against Innovations: A warning like this is found in the ḥadīth that is devoted to the topic: {Whoever introduces something into this affair of ours that is not of it, that thing is rejected.} We learned from the commentary that this is an immense foundation in the religion. Anyone who introduces a matter and attributes it to the religion when it does not actually have a foundation in it, that matter is attributed to that individual instead and it is deemed blameworthy. It is erroneous innovation and the religion has nothing to do with it.

The word *bid'ah*[161] has two meanings, legal and linguistic. In the Revealed Law, it is something that is introduced that contravenes what the Lawgiver has commanded along with His general and specific evidence. This is what the Prophet is warning against in his comprehensive statement: {...every innovation is misguidance...}

As for the linguistic meaning, it is something that is invented that without there being anything like it that preceded it. It is according to this meaning that we understand certain innovations being verbally approved by a number of Companions ﷺ. An example of this is 'Umar's statement ﷺ when he had gathered the people to pray behind one imam in the masjid during the nights of Ramaḍān. He said, 'What a good innovation this is'. It has been related from Ubay ibn Ka'b that he said to him, 'This did not exist before'. 'Umar replied, 'I know, but it is good'. What he meant was that this action had been done in this way before this time, but it does have a foundation in the Revealed Law that it goes back to.

Other examples include the gathering of the *muṣḥaf* in the time of Abū Bakr, fighting those who withheld the zakāt, gathering the people upon one *muṣḥaf*, sending copies to numerous metropolises in the time of 'Uthmān, and other innovations that the Companions approved of and found foundations for in the Sunnah.

161 (tn): i.e. innovation.

It has been related from ash-Shāfiʿī that he said, '*Bidʿah* is of two types: praiseworthy and blameworthy. Whatever agrees with the Sunnah is praiseworthy, and whatever contradicts the Sunnah is blameworthy.' His proof was ʿUmar's statement ﵁: 'What a good innovation this is'.

It has also been related that he said, 'Introduced matters are of two types. There is that which contradicts something in the Book, the Sunnah, what has reached us from the Companions or a consensus, in which case it is innovation that is misguidance. An introduced matter that is good and does not contradict any of the aforementioned is not blameworthy, and there are several matters that have been introduced and the scholars have not differed as to whether they are good innovations, such that they go back to the Sunnah or not.

8. The ḥadīth is informing us of the *sunnah* of giving beneficial advice when bidding farewell, advice that leads to felicity in this life as well as the Hereafter.

9. The prohibition against introducing something into the religion that has no foundation therein.

THE TWENTY-NINTH ḤADĪTH

أَبْوابُ الخَيْرِ ومَسَالِكُ الهُدَى

عَنْ مُعَاذِ بْنِ جَبَلٍ رضي الله عنه قَالَ: قُلْتُ: يَا رَسُولَ اللهِ، أَخْبِرْنِي بِعَمَلٍ يُدْخِلُنِي الْجَنَّةَ وَيُبَاعِدُنِي عَنِ النَّارِ. قَالَ: {لَقَدْ سَأَلْتَ عَنْ عَظِيمٍ، وَإِنَّهُ لَيَسِيرٌ عَلَى مَنْ يَسَّرَهُ اللهُ تَعَالَى عَلَيْهِ: تَعْبُدُ اللهَ لَا تُشْرِكُ بِهِ شَيْئاً، وَتُقِيمُ الصَّلَاةَ، وَتُؤْتِي الزَّكَاةَ، وَتَصُومُ رَمَضَانَ، وَتَحُجُّ الْبَيْتَ}

ثُمَّ قَالَ: {أَلَا أَدُلُّكَ عَلَى أَبْوَابِ الْخَيْرِ: الصَّوْمُ جُنَّةٌ، وَالصَّدَقَةُ تُطْفِئُ الْخَطِيئَةَ كَمَا يُطْفِئُ الْمَاءُ النَّارَ، وَصَلَاةُ الرَّجُلِ فِي جَوْفِ اللَّيْلِ، ثُمَّ تَلَا: ﴿تَتَجَافَىٰ جُنُوبُهُمْ عَنِ الْمَضَاجِعِ – حَتَّى بَلَغَ – يَعْمَلُونَ﴾

ثُمَّ قَالَ: {أَلَا أُخْبِرُكَ بِرَأْسِ الْأَمْرِ وَعَمُودِهِ وَذِرْوَةِ سَنَامِهِ} قُلْتُ: بَلَى يَا رَسُولَ اللهِ. قَالَ: {رَأْسُ الْأَمْرِ الْإِسْلَامُ، وَعَمُودُهُ الصَّلَاةُ، وَذِرْوَةُ سَنَامِهِ الْجِهَادُ.}

ثُمَ قَالَ: {أَلَا أُخْبِرُكَ بِمِلَاكِ ذَلِكَ كُلِّهِ}. فَقُلْتُ: بَلَى يَا رَسُولَ اللهِ، فَأَخَذَ بِلِسَانِهِ، وَقَالَ: {كُفَّ عَلَيْكَ هَذَا} قُلْتُ: يَا نَبِيَّ اللهِ، وَإِنَّا لَمُؤَاخَذُونَ بِمَا نَتَكَلَّمُ بِهِ؟ فَقَالَ: {ثَكِلَتْكَ أُمُّكَ، وَهَلْ يَكُبُّ النَّاسَ فِي النَّارِ عَلَى وُجُوهِهِم – أَوْ قَالَ: عَلَى مَنَاخِرِهِمْ – إِلَّا حَصَائِدُ أَلْسِنَتِهِم} رَوَاهُ التِّرمذي وقال: حديث حسن صحيح.

The Doors of Goodness and the Paths of Guidance

It is on the authority of Muʿādh ibn Jabal ﷺ who said, 'I said, "O Messenger of Allah, tell me about an action that will enter me into Paradise and keep me far away from the Fire." He replied, {You have asked about something immense, and it is easy for the one whom Allah the Exalted makes it easy for: you worship Allah and do not associate anything with him, you establish the prayer, you pay the zakāt, you fast Ramaḍān and you perform the Ḥajj of the House.}

Then he said, {Shall I not show you the doors of goodness? Fasting is a shield, charity[162] extinguishes sins the way water extinguishes fire, and a man's prayer in the middle[163] of the night.} Then he recited,

﴿تَتَجَافَىٰ جُنُوبُهُمْ عَنِ ٱلْمَضَاجِعِ يَدْعُونَ رَبَّهُمْ خَوْفًا وَطَمَعًا وَمِمَّا رَزَقْنَـٰهُمْ يُنفِقُونَ ۝١٦ فَلَا تَعْلَمُ نَفْسٌ مَّآ أُخْفِىَ لَهُم مِّن قُرَّةِ أَعْيُنٍ جَزَآءًۢ بِمَا كَانُوا۟ يَعْمَلُونَ﴾

"Their sides eschew their beds as they call on their Lord in fear and ardent hope. And they give of what We have provided for them. No soul can imagine what delights are kept in store for them as a reward for what they used to do. [as-Sajdah 32:17-16]

Then he said, {Shall I not tell you about the head of the matter, its central pillar and the uppermost part of its hump?} I replied, "Yes, O Messenger of Allah." He said, {The head of the matter is Islam, its central pillar is prayer and the summit of its hump is *jihād*.}

Then he said, {Shall I not tell you what the objective is behind all of this?} I said, "Yes, O Messenger of Allah." He took hold of his tongue and said, {Restrain this.} I said, "O Prophet of Allah, will we be taken to task for what we say?" He replied, {May your mother be bereft of you! Does anything throw people into the Fire on their faces (or he said, {their nostrils}) other than the harvest of their tongues?} Related by at-Tirmidhī, who said, 'It is a good, authentic ḥadīth,'

At-Tirmidhī has related in the ḥadīth in the Doors of Faith (the chapter on what has reached us regarding the sanctity of the prayer), no.2619. There is an addition from Muʿādh ﷺ in which he said, 'I was travelling with the Prophet ﷺ. One day, I woke up and I was close to him while we were moving, so I said, 'O Messenger of Allah, tell me about an action that will enter me into Paradise...'

162 Ar. *ṣadaqah*.
163 Ar. *jawf*.

The Importance of the Ḥadīth

This ḥadīth comprises the righteous actions that will enter one into Paradise and keep one far removed from the Fire. This is an immense matter indeed, because it is for the sake of entering Paradise and salvation from the Fire that Allah sent the Messengers and revealed the Books. This is why the Prophet ﷺ said, {You have asked about something immense.} He said to a man who asked about something similar, {Your question is short in length but its subject matter is immense and vast.}

The Language of the Ḥadīth:

(الصوم جنة) *as-ṣawmu junnah*: fasting is protection from the Fire.

(الصدقة تطفئ الخطيئة) *as-ṣadaqatu tuṭfi' ul-khaṭī'atah*: i.e. charity extinguishes the effect of sin, and therefore no trace of it remains.

(جوف الليل) *jawf il-layl*: the middle of it, or during it.

(تتجافى) *tatajāfā*: to get up and move away.

(عن المضاجع) *'an il-maḍājii'*: from the bed or resting place.

(ذروة سنامه) *dhirwati sanāmih*: the *sanām* is the hump on a camel's back, the *dhirwah* is the highest part, the *dhirwatu sinām* of a matter is a metaphor for its highest part.

(ثكلتك أمك) *thakilatka ummuka*: this looks like a supplication for death, but this is not what is sought, rather it said to wake someone up from heedlessness and to express astonishment at something.

(يكب) *yakubbu*: to be thrown in the Fire.

Legal Matters and Other Guidance from the Ḥadīth:

1. Mu'ādh's Intense Concern for Righteous Deeds: Mu'ādh's question ﷺ is evidence of his intense concern for righteous deeds and to know what they are from the Messenger of Allah ﷺ. It is also evidence of his eloquence and rhetoric, for he asked a concise and profound question, and the Prophet ﷺ praised his question and marvelled at his eloquence when he said to him, {You have asked about something immense.} This is because entering Paradise and being far removed from the Fire is something immense, the cause of which is obeying every command and avoiding every prohibited matter. This is what Mu'ādh asked about ﷺ.

2. The Actions that Cause Entrance into Paradise:
This is indicated by Muʿādh's statement, 'tell me about an action that will enter me into Paradise' as well as what Allah ﷻ says in His Book:

﴿وَتِلْكَ ٱلْجَنَّةُ ٱلَّتِىٓ أُورِثْتُمُوهَا بِمَا كُنتُمْ تَعْمَلُونَ﴾

> **"This is the Paradise that you have inherited for what you did."** [az-Zukhruf 43:72]

As for the Prophet's statement ﷺ {Not a single one of you will be entered into Paradise by his deeds}, the meaning is that deeds by themselves do not make anyone deserving of Paradise. Rather, the deeds must be accepted by Allah, and this is from Allah the Exalted's mercy and grace towards His servants. Furthermore, the success to do righteous deeds in this worldly life is in Allah the Exalted's hands. If Allah facilitates guidance for someone, that person is guided and acts accordingly. If Allah does not facilitate it for someone, that person is misguided and does not do good deeds. Allah the Exalted has said,

﴿فَأَمَّا مَنْ أَعْطَىٰ وَٱتَّقَىٰ ۝٥ وَصَدَّقَ بِٱلْحُسْنَىٰ ۝٦ فَسَنُيَسِّرُهُۥ لِلْيُسْرَىٰ ۝٧

وَأَمَّا مَنۢ بَخِلَ وَٱسْتَغْنَىٰ ۝٨ وَكَذَّبَ بِٱلْحُسْنَىٰ ۝٩ فَسَنُيَسِّرُهُۥ لِلْعُسْرَىٰ﴾

> **"As for him who gives, has *taqwā* and confirms the good, We will pave his way to ease. But as for him who is stingy and self-satisfied, and denies the good, We will pave his way to difficulty."** [al-Layl 92: 5-10]

3. Carrying Out the Pillars of Islam: The Prophet ﷺ answered Muʿādh's question by mentioning Allah's Oneness ﷻ and carrying out the obligations of Islam: the prayer, the zakāt, fasting and the Ḥajj. These are the righteous deeds that will, with Allah's favour, beneficence and mercy, cause one to enter Paradise. In commenting on the third and fourth ḥadīths, we discussed how these five pillars are the supports that Islam is built upon.

4. The Doors of Goodness: In that narration of Ibn Mājah, the wording is 'doors of Paradise', and the Prophet ﷺ directed Muʿādh towards carrying out supererogatory acts after completing one's obligations. This is so that Allah's love can be manifested. The Messenger of Allah ﷺ quoted his Lord ﷻ as saying, {My slave does not draw nearer to Me with anything more beloved to Me than that which I have made obligatory upon him. My slave continues to draw nearer to Me with supererogatory acts until I love him.}[164] As for the doors of goodness and the means that leads to them, they are:

164 (tn): Please see the 38th ḥadīth in this collection.

A. Fasting is a shield: What is meant here is supererogatory fasting and not fasting Ramaḍān, because it was mentioned before. It is protection from the Fire in the Hereafter, because by fasting the Muslim refrains from his desires in obedience to Allah's command. This takes him back inside the bounds and brings him closer to *taqwā*, which is to do what Allah has commanded and leave what Allah has prohibited. Likewise, this refraining weakens the power that one's lower desires have over a person, and thus they have no control over him. By fasting, the person becomes conscious of Allah and purified and cleansed of sin.

B. Charity extinguishes sin: What is meant by charity here is other than the zakāt, because it was mentioned before. The sin that it extinguishes and the traces of which it effaces are the minor sins connected to Allah the Exalted's right, because major sins can only be effaced by repentance, while sins that are connected to another person's right can only be effaced with that person's consent. Charity is exclusively mentioned here because its benefit is transitive. At-Tirmidhī has related, as well as Ibn Ḥibbān in his *Ṣaḥīḥ*, on the authority of Anas ﷺ that the Messenger of Allah ﷺ said, {Charity extinguishes the Lord's anger and wards off an evil end.} By extinguishing sins, hope is magnified, the heart is illuminated, deeds are unpolluted, and thus charity is an immense door towards other righteous actions.

C. Prayer at night: This is voluntary prayer at night after sleeping, and the fact that 'man'[165] is mentioned in the ḥadīth is of no consequence. What is meant is whoever is legally accountable.[166] There are several verses and ḥadīths that come together to elucidate the immense virtue of praying at night. This is why the Prophet ﷺ quoted the verse: **"Their sides eschew their beds..."** [as-Sajdah 32:16] The verse mentions the virtue of praying at night as well as spending in charity, emphasising his noble words and corroborating them with the Merciful Lord's words. Allah the Exalted has said,

﴿إِنَّ ٱلْمُتَّقِينَ فِى جَنَّـٰتٍ وَعُيُونٍ ۝١٥ ءَاخِذِينَ مَآ ءَاتَىٰهُمْ رَبُّهُمْ ۚ إِنَّهُمْ كَانُوا۟ قَبْلَ ذَٰلِكَ مُحْسِنِينَ ۝١٦ كَانُوا۟ قَلِيلًا مِّنَ ٱلَّيْلِ مَا يَهْجَعُونَ ۝١٧ وَبِٱلْأَسْحَارِ هُمْ يَسْتَغْفِرُونَ﴾

"The people of *taqwā* will be among gardens and fountains, receiving what their Lord has given them. Certainly, before that they were doers of good. The part of the night they spent asleep was small and they would seek forgiveness before the dawn." [adh-Dhāriyāt 51:15-18]

Muslim has related in his *Ṣaḥīḥ* that the Messenger of Allah ﷺ said, {The best prayer after the obligatory is prayer at night.} In the *Sunan* of at-Tirmidhī, there is

165 Ar. *rajul.*

166 (tn): i.e. an adult in the Revealed Law.

the ḥadīth of Bilāl ﷺ in which the Prophet ﷺ said, {You should pray at night, for it is the habit of the righteous who went before you. Praying at night is a means of drawing nearer to Allah ﷻ. It prevents wickedness, expiates sins and wards off harm from the body.} The best time for *tahajjud* is the middle of the night, due to the Prophet's statement: {... man's prayer in the middle of the night...} The *jawf* of the night, when it is not qualified, is its middle.

5. The head of the Islamic religion, its central pillar and the uppermost part of its hump: It is as if the Messenger, the teacher ﷺ saw in the eyes of his Companion, Muʿādh, love for more Prophetic knowledge, so he increased him in clear knowledge by way of allegory and comparison. He did not share these knowledges with him until after formulating the question: {Shall I not tell you...?}, which is a successful educational method that increases the learner's attentiveness and makes him a questioner who is eager to know the answer, not just a passive recipient. These Prophetic knowledges are as follows:

A. The head of the matter is Islam. The explanation for this ḥadīth is found in Imam Aḥmad's narration, in which the Prophet ﷺ said, {The head of this matter is that you bear witness that there is no god but Allah alone, He has no partner, and that Muḥammad is His servant and Messenger.} In other words, the head of this religion is the two testimonies of faith. Whoever does not affirm them inwardly and outwardly has nothing to do with Islam. It's also been said that the head of the religion that he ﷺ was sent with is Islam with all five of its pillars.

B. Its central pillar is the prayer. In other words, the prayer is the central pillar of the religion, the support that holds it up, just as a tent is held up by its pillar. Just as a pillar raises a house and makes it ready to be used, the prayer raises the religion and makes it manifest. It makes the one who prays ready for the nobility of nearness to Allah, and the weak servant can immerse himself in his connection to his Creator, the Almighty, the Forbearing, and the Most Merciful.

C. The uppermost part of its hump is *jihād*. In other words, the highest and most elevated part of Islam is *jihād*, because through it Allah's word is exalted. Islam is manifested and it overcomes all other religions. No other act of worship bears this quality, and thus it is the highest and most elevated part from this standpoint. There are also several ḥadīths from the Messenger of Allah ﷺ that evidence that *jihād* is the best of deeds after the obligations. They include what has been related by al-Bukhārī and Muslim on the authority of Abū Dharr ﷺ: 'I said, "O Messenger of Allah, what is the best deed?" He replied, {Faith in Allah, and then *jihād* for the sake of Allah.}'

The reason why a camel was mentioned – in comparing the rank of *jihad* to the uppermost part of a camel's hump – is that it was the best of their wealth, and thus they would compare their rulers to camels.

6. The objective of the matter is guarding the tongue. The Prophet ﷺ concluded his teaching of Muʿādh, by elucidating the objectives behind these deeds and what regulates them, and makes them reach the utmost degree of perfection. It is to restrain the tongue and hold it back from evil, and we elucidated the importance of guarding the tongue and controlling it in our commentary of the ḥadīth: {Whoever believes in Allah and the Last Day, let him speak well or remain silent.}

Al-Bazzār has related in his *Musnad* on the authority of Abū Yusr 'that a man said, "O Messenger of Allah, show me an action that will enter me into Paradise." He replied, {Restrain this} and he pointed to his tongue. The man repeated the question, so he said, {May your mother be bereft of you! Does anything throw people into the Fire on their nostrils other than the harvest of their tongues?}"'

Ibn Rajab al-Ḥanbalī said, 'What is meant by the harvest of their tongues is the recompense for unlawful speech and its punishment, for through his words and his actions, man plants good deeds and bad deeds. Then, on the Day of Standing, he harvests what he planted. Whoever planted goodness by way of his words and his deeds will harvest dignity and honour, and whoever planted evil by way of his words and deeds will harvest regret tomorrow. The outward purport of Muʿādh's ḥadīth ﷺ is that the dominant factor behind people being entered into the Fire is what is uttered on their tongues, for the disobedience of utterances includes idolatry, which is the greatest sin in the sight of Allah ﷻ. It includes speaking about Allah without knowledge, which is connected to idolatry. It includes bearing false witness, which is equivalent to associating partners with Allah.[167] It includes sorcery and false accusation,[168] and other major and minor sins, such as lying, backbiting, slander...'

Imam Aḥmad and at-Tirmidhī have related on the authority of Abū Hurayrah ﷺ that the Messenger of Allah ﷺ said, {The dominant factor behind people entering the Fire are the two cavities:[169] the mouth and the private parts.} Mālik has related from Zayd ibn Aslam, who related from his father that ʿUmar entered upon Abū Bakr ﷺ and he was pulling his tongue. ʿUmar said, 'What are you doing? May Allah forgive you!' Abū Bakr replied, 'This is what causes me to fall into undesired matters.' Abū Buraydah said, 'I saw Ibn ʿAbbās ﷺ taking hold of his tongue and saying, "Woe to you! Speak good and you will benefit or say nothing evil and you will be safe. If not, know that you will have regret."' He said, 'It was said to him, "O Abū ʿAbbās, why are you saying this?" He replied, "It has reached me that the tongue – I saw him say – out of the all the parts of the body, is the part

167 (tn): i.e. it is a major sin like *shirk*.

168 Ar. *qadhf*, i.e. to accuse someone of adultery or sodomy without proof.

169 Ar. *al-ajwafān*.

that a person will be most angry at and furious with on the Day of Standing, apart from the one who made it speak good or imposed good upon it.'" Ibn Masʿūd ﷺ would swear by Allah, besides whom there is no other god, that there is nothing on earth more in need of a long prison sentence than a tongue. Al-Ḥasan al-Baṣrī said, 'The tongue is the commander of the body. If it commits a crime against the limbs in any way, they commit a crime. If it abstains, they abstain.'

7. The Best Deeds of Righteousness after the Obligations: Mālik and Abū Ḥanīfah held the position that the best deeds of righteousness after the obligations are knowledge followed by *jihād*. Ash-Shāfiʿī held the position that the best of deeds is the prayer, obligatory and supererogatory. Imam Aḥmad said it is *jihād* for the sake of Allah.

It has reached us that he ﷺ was asked which deeds are the best. One time he said it was the prayer at the beginning of its time. Another time he said it was *jihād*. Still another time he said it was showing righteousness to parents. This is understood to be according to the different circumstances of the questioners, or different times.

8. The noble ḥadīth shows the Companions seeking guidance from the Prophet ﷺ as well as his admonition. It also informs us that carrying out the five main obligations is the first thing the slave should do and is a means of entering Paradise and being far removed from the Fire.

9. The precedence of *jihād* in preserving Islam, and exalting Allah's word.

10. The significance and danger of the tongue, one will be taken to task for what it does, and it supplies the Fire through its harvests.

THE THIRTIETH ḤADĪTH

حُدُودُ اللهِ تعالى وحُرُماته

عَنْ أَبِي ثَعْلَبَةَ الخُشَنِيِّ جُرْثُومِ بْنِ نَاشِرٍ ؓ، عَنْ رَسُولِ اللهِ ﷺ قَالَ: {إِنَّ اللهَ تَعَالَى فَرَضَ فَرَائِضَ فَلَا تُضَيِّعُوْهَا، وَحَدَّ حُدُوداً فَلَا تَعْتَدُوْهَا، وَحَرَّمَ أَشْيَاءَ فَلَا تَنْتَهِكُوْهَا، وَسَكَتَ عَنْ أَشْيَاءَ - رَحْمَةً لَكُمْ غَيْرَ نِسْيَانٍ - فَلَا تَبْحَثُوْا عَنْهَا.} حديث حسن رواه الدارقطني وغيره.

Allah the Exalted's Limits and Prohibitions

On the authority of Abū Thaʿlabah al-Khushanī Jurthūm ibn Nāshir ؓ the Messenger of Allah ﷺ said, {Allah the Exalted has obligated obligations, so do not neglect them. He has defined limits, so do not transgress them. He has declared certain things unlawful, so do not approach them. He has remained silent regarding certain things, out of mercy and not forgetfulness, so do not look into them.}

This is a good ḥadīth that has been narrated by ad-Dāraquṭnī and others.

Ad-Dāraquṭnī related it on page 502. Abū Nuʿaym related it in al-Ḥilyah 9/17 on the authority of Abū ad-Dardāʾ. In ad-Dāraquṭnī's book, it is from the narration of Makḥūl on the authority of Abū Thaʿlabah al-Khushanī, and in the chain of transmission there is an interruption between Makḥūl and Abū Thaʿlabah, because Makḥūl did not hear anything directly from Abū Thaʿlabah. Ibn Muʿīn holds the position that he did hear from him. Nevertheless, the ḥadīth has other corroborations that raise it to the level of good.[170] This is why an-Nawawī ؒ in his book *al-Adhkār,* recognised that it is good, and as-Samʿānī did the same before him in his *Amālī*. Al-Ḥāfiẓ al-ʿIrāqī agreed with him in this, as did al-Ḥāfiẓ ibn Ḥajar, and Ibn as-Ṣalāḥ declared it authentic. See al-Futūḥāt ar-Rabbāniyyah,[171] 7/365.

170 Ar. *ḥasan.*

171 (tn): This is Imam Ibn ʿAllān's commentary on *al-Adhkār.*

The Importance of the Ḥadīth:
This ḥadīth is another example of the comprehensive speech that Allah the Exalted exclusively endowed our Prophet with ﷺ. It is concise and profound. Indeed, one of them said, 'There is not a single ḥadīth that is more comprehensive. It uniquely gathers the foundations of the religion and its branches.' This is because the Prophet ﷺ divided Allah's rulings into four categories: obligations, prohibitions, limits and that which nothing has been said about. Ibn as-Samʿānī said, 'Whoever acts according to it will attain reward and be safe from punishment, because he will have carried out the obligations, avoided the prohibitions, stayed within the limits and not investigated that which is not mentioned. He will have thoroughly completed the categories of virtue and fulfilled the religion's rights, because the legislations of the Revealed Law do not go outside the types mentioned in the ḥadīth.

The Language of the Ḥadīth:
(فرض فرائض) *faraḍa farāʾiḍ*: He has declared them obligatory and prescribed that they be carried out.

(فلا تضيعوها) *fala taḍayyiʿūhā*: do not leave them or neglect them until their stipulated time has elapsed. Rather, carry them out just as Allah as obligated you.

(وحد حدودا) *wa ḥadda ḥudūdan*: *ḥudūd* is the plural of *ḥadd*, which is a barrier between two things. In the Revealed Law, it is a punishment that has been decreed by the Lawgiver to restrain people from disobedience.

(فلا تعتدوها) *fala taʿtadūhā*: do not go beyond what the Revealed Law has commanded, or stay within them and do not overstep them.

(فلا تنتهكوها) *fala tantahikūhā*: do not fall into them and do not approach them.

(سكت عن أشياء) *sakat ʿan ashyāʾ*: i.e. He has not declared them obligatory or unlawful, and thus they are fundamentally permissible.

Legal Matters and Other Guidance from the Ḥadīth:
1. The Obligation to Safeguard Obligations: The obligations are that which Allah has declared obligatory for His servant and made it incumbent upon them to carry out, such as the prayer, the zakāt, fasting and the Ḥajj. The Shāfiʿīs hold the position that whatever has been obligated based on an evidence in the Revealed Law, such as from the Book, the Sunnah, Consensus or another evidence in the Revealed Law, is obligatory.[172] Thus, for them, the term *farḍ* and *wājib* are synonymous, except for in the Ḥajj. An example of a *farḍ* therein would be the

172 Ar. *farḍ*.

going-forth circumambulation.[173] If it is not performed, it cannot be compensated by a sacrifice. An example of a *wājib* would be the farewell circumambulation.[174] If not performed, it can be compensated by a sacrifice. As for the Ḥanafīs, they distinguish between the two terms. A *farḍ* is that which is established by a decisive evidence,[175] such as the prayer and the zakāt. A *wājib* is that which is established by a conjectural evidence,[176] such as something established by analogy or a singular report, such as the zakāt on ʿĪd al-Fiṭr.

Obligations fall into two categories, individual and communal. The former is that which is obligatory upon every legally accountable individual, such as the five prayer, the zakāt and fasting. As for the latter, if some Muslims carry it out, the rest are absolved of sin. If no one carries it out, they are all sinful. Examples include the funeral prayer, returning the greeting of peace, and enjoining the right and forbidding the wrong.

2. Staying Within Allah the Exalted's Limits, and they are the punishments that have been decreed to repel people from that which is unlawful, such as the *ḥadd* for fornication, the *ḥadd* for theft and the *ḥadd* for drinking wine. The Messenger of Allah ﷺ said to Usāmah ibn Zayd when he spoke to him about the Makhzūmī woman who committed theft in the year of the *Fatḥ*,[177] {Are you interceding in one of the *ḥudūd* of Allah?}, i.e. in the hand being cut off for theft. These *ḥudūd* are punishment decreed by Allah, the Creator ﷻ. They must be adhered to without any addition or subtraction. As for increasing the *ḥadd* for wine from forty lashes to eighty, this is not impermissible, even though the Messenger of Allah ﷺ and Abū Bakr confine themselves to forty, because when people started drinking more than they even had before in the time of ʿUmar ﷺ they deserved to be lashed more, as an exemplary punishment and reprimand. The increase was a juridical reasoning[178] on his part and it was valid and justified. Then ʿAlī ibn Abī Ṭālib ﷺ said, 'Both increase and its absence are *sunnah*'. This is because he ﷺ commanded that ʿUmar in particular be followed when he said, {Follow those whose come after me, Abū Bakr and ʿUmar} and in general, when he said, {take hold of my Sunnah and the Sunnah of the Rightly-Guided, Orthodox Khulafāʾ}. The Companions made consensus on this increase and their hearts became content with it when ʿAlī said to ʿUmar, 'O Commander of the Believers, whoever drinks wine has spoken irrationally, who whoever has spoken irrationally has made false accusations. The punishment for making a false accusation in Allah's Book is eighty lashes. Allah the Exalted has said,

173 Ar. *ṭawāf al-īfāḍah.*

174 Ar. *tawāf al-widāʿ.*

175 Ar. *dalīl qaṭʿī.*

176 Ar. *dalīl ẓannī,* i.e. not unequivocally proven to be *farḍ.*

177 (tn): i.e. the year Makkah was conquered.

178 Ar. *ijtihād.*

﴿وَٱلَّذِينَ يَرْمُونَ ٱلْمُحْصَنَـٰتِ ثُمَّ لَمْ يَأْتُوا۟ بِأَرْبَعَةِ شُهَدَآءَ فَٱجْلِدُوهُمْ ثَمَـٰنِينَ جَلْدَةً وَلَا تَقْبَلُوا۟ لَهُمْ شَهَـٰدَةً أَبَدًا ۚ وَأُو۟لَـٰٓئِكَ هُمُ ٱلْفَـٰسِقُونَ﴾

"But those who make accusations against chaste women and then do not produce four witnesses: flog them with eighty lashes and never again accept them as witnesses. Such people are deviators." [an-Nūr 24:4]

3. The Prohibition of Approaching Unlawful Matters and Committing Them: This means the unlawful matters that are decisively unlawful, mentioned in the Noble Qur'ān and the Prophetic Sunnah. Allah the Exalted has forbade them and prohibited approaching them, committing them and falling into them. Examples include bearing false witness, consuming an orphan's wealth and usury. Allah the Exalted has said,

﴿قُلْ إِنَّمَا حَرَّمَ رَبِّىَ ٱلْفَوَٰحِشَ مَا ظَهَرَ مِنْهَا وَمَا بَطَنَ﴾

"Say: 'My Lord has forbidden indecency, both open and hidden." [al-A'rāf 7:33]

He ﷺ said, {Every intoxicant is unlawful}, and he said, {Your blood, your property and your good reputes are unlawful for you...}[179]

If someone examines these unlawful matters closely, and looks for the rationale behind their unlawfulness with an enlightened and just intellect, will find that they are numbered and limited. All of them are evil and wicked.[180] Everything besides them remains permissible, and are of the good things. Allah the Exalted has said,

﴿يَـٰٓأَيُّهَا ٱلَّذِينَ ءَامَنُوا۟ لَا تُحَرِّمُوا۟ طَيِّبَـٰتِ مَآ أَحَلَّ ٱللَّهُ لَكُمْ﴾

"You who believe! Do not make unlawful the good things Allah has made lawful for you." [al-Mā'idah 5:87]

4. Allah's Mercy towards His Servant: The Prophet ﷺ made it clear that Allah's silence regarding the rulings for certain things, and thus He has not determined that they are obligatory or lawful or unlawful, is a mercy towards His servant and kindness. He has made them a favour. If they do them, there is no objection, and if they leave them, there is no objection. This silence from Him ﷻ is not due to a mistake or forgetfulness, may Allah be greatly exalted above that. Allah the Exalted has said,

﴿وَمَا كَانَ رَبُّكَ نَسِيًّا﴾

"Your Lord does not forget". [Maryam 19:64]

179 (tn): i.e. it is unlawful to violate someone else's blood, property or good repute.

180 Ar. *khabīth.*

And He ﷻ has said,

﴿فِي كِتَٰبٍ لَّا يَضِلُّ رَبِّي وَلَا يَنسَى﴾

"My Lord does not misplace nor does He forget." [Ṭaha 20:52]

5. Forbidding Abundant Investigating and Questioning: It is possible that the prohibition of abundant investigating and questioning mentioned in the ḥadīth is exclusive to the Prophet's time ﷺ because abundant investigating and questioning about that which had not been mentioned could have been the reason for strict revelation to come down, declaring matters obligatory or unlawful. The Exalted One has said,

﴿لَا تَسْـَٔلُوا۟ عَنْ أَشْيَآءَ إِن تُبْدَ لَكُمْ تَسُؤْكُمْ﴾

"Do not ask about matters which, if they were made known to you, would make things difficult for you." [al-Mā'idah 5:101]

It is also possible that the ḥadīth has a general application, and the prohibition therein is against penetrating deeply into the religion. He ﷺ said, {Leave me alone regarding what I have left you with. The only thing that destroyed those before you was their abundance of questions and their disagreements with their Prophets.} He ﷺ also said, {Those who delve deeply into matters[181] are destroyed.} The *mutanaṭiʿ* is the one who investigates matters that do not concern him, or the one who closely examines matters that are far-fetched. ʿAbdullah ibn Masʿūd ؓ said, 'Beware of delving deeply into matters. Beware of being too absorbed in matters. Stick to that which is ancient.' In other words, stick to what the Companions were upon ؓ.

The Companions ؓ refrained from asking him lots of questions ﷺ such that they were pleased when Bedouins would come and ask him and he would answer them, and they would listen attentively.

Investigating that which is of no concern includes investigating matters of the unseen that we have been commanded to have faith in and their how has not been made clear to us, because it could necessitate confusion and doubt and maybe even lead to denial. Ibn Isḥāq said, 'It is not permissible to ponder upon the Creator or the creation in other than that which they[182] have received on such matters.

For example, regarding the Exalted's statement,

﴿وَإِن مِّن شَىْءٍ إِلَّا يُسَبِّحُ بِحَمْدِهِۦ﴾

"There is nothing which does not glorify him with praise". [al-Isrā' 17:44]

It is not permissible to say, 'How do inanimate objects glorify with praise?'

181 Ar. *al-mutanaṭiʿūn*.

182 (tn) : i.e. the First Three Generations.

It is because the Exalted One has informed us of this, and He makes it how He wants and as He wants'.

Al-Bukhārī has related that the Messenger of Allah ﷺ said, {Shayṭān will come to one of you and say, 'Who created this? Who created this?' until he says, 'Who created your Lord?' If this happens, let one seek refuge in Allah and desist.

Muslim has collected: {People will keep asking until it is said, 'This is Allah. He created the creation, so who created Allah?' Whoever finds anything like this, let him say, 'I believe in Allah'.}

6. The ḥadīth informs us that we are commanded to carry out obligations, adhere to the limits, avoid prohibitions and not seek to get to fathom what is besides the aforementioned, out of mercy towards people.

THE THIRTY-FIRST ḤADĪTH

حَقِيقَةُ الزُّهْدِ وَثَمَراتُه

عَنْ أَبِي العَبَّاسِ سَهْلِ بْنِ سَعْدٍ السَّاعِدِيِّ ﵁ قَالَ: جَاءَ رَجُلٌ إِلَى النَّبِيِّ ﷺ فَقَالَ: يَا رَسُولَ اللهِ،

دُلَّنِي عَلَى عَمَلٍ إِذَا عَمِلْتُهُ أَحَبَّنِي اللهُ وَأَحَبَّنِي النَّاسُ. فَقَالَ: {اِزْهَدْ فِي الدُّنْيَا يُحِبَّكَ اللهُ، وَازْهَدْ فِيمَا

عِنْدَ النَّاسِ يُحِبَّكَ النَّاسُ.} حديث حسن رواه ابن ماجه وغَيْرُهُ بأسانيد حَسَنَة.

The Reality of Abstinence and its Fruits

Abū al-ʿAbbās Sahl ibn Saʿd as-Sāʿidī ﵁ said, 'A man came to the Prophet ﷺ and said, "O Messenger of Allah, show me an action which, I if do it, Allah will love me and people will love me." He replied, {Do without this worldly life and Allah will love you, and do without that which people possess and they will love you.} This is a good ḥadīth, that is related by Ibn Mājah and the others with good chains of transmission.

Ibn Mājah has related the ḥadīth in the Book of Abstinence (the chapter on abstinence in this worldly life), no.4102. As for those besides Ibn Mājah who have related it, Ibn ʿAllān has mentioned the following: at-Ṭabarānī in *al-Muʿjam al-Kabīr*, Ibn Ḥibbān in his *Rawḍat al-ʿUqalāʾ*, al-Ḥākim in the chapter on softening the hearts in *al-Mustadrak* (4/313), Abū Nuʿaym in *al-Ḥilyah* (7/136) and al-Bayhaqī in *Shuʿab al-Īmān*. Thus, the ḥadīth is good[183] with its corroborating narrations.

The Importance of the Ḥadīth:
This ḥadīth contains two sublime pieces of advice from the Prophet ﷺ:
The **first** is abstinence concerning this worldly life, and that it is a means of attaining the love that Allah the Exalted has towards His slaves.
The **second** is abstinence regarding what people have in their possession, and that it is a means of attaining people's love and appreciation.
It is emphasised in Islam that a person is not counted amongst the blissful and victorious in both abodes until after Allah's love for him has been ascertained after he has preferred the everlasting Hereafter with Allah to the fleeting life of this

---

183 Ar. *ḥasan*.

world. He also attains people's love after his soul has risen above the ephemeral things that people have in their possession. This is why Ibn Ḥajar al-Haytamī says regarding this ḥadīth, 'It is one of the four ḥadīths around which Islam revolves'.

The Language of the Ḥadīth:

(أحبني الله وأحبني الناس) *aḥabbanī Llāhu wa aḥabbanī nnāsu*: Allah will love me: through reward and beneficence. People will love me: they will naturally incline towards me because their love follows Allah's love. When Allah loves someone, He puts the love of that person into the hearts of His creation. The Exalted One has said,

﴿إِنَّ ٱلَّذِينَ ءَامَنُوا۟ وَعَمِلُوا۟ ٱلصَّـٰلِحَـٰتِ سَيَجْعَلُ لَهُمُ ٱلرَّحْمَـٰنُ وُدًّا﴾

"As for those who believe and do right actions, the All-Merciful will bestow His love on them." [Maryam 19:96]

(ازهد) *izhad*: from the word *zuhd*, which, linguistically, means to turn away from something out of disdain. It is from their[184] saying that something is *zahīd*, i.e. little. In the Revealed Law, it means to only take the necessary amount of that which is decisively lawful.

(في الدنيا) *fī d-dunyā*: to think little of it and look down on it, because Allah has debased it and degraded it and warned against being deluded by it. The Exalted One has said,

﴿فَلَا تَغُرَّنَّكُمُ ٱلْحَيَوٰةُ ٱلدُّنْيَا﴾

"So do not let the life of this world delude you." [Luqmān 31:33]

The Glorified One has also said,

﴿ٱعْلَمُوٓا۟ أَنَّمَا ٱلْحَيَوٰةُ ٱلدُّنْيَا لَعِبٌ وَلَهْوٌ وَزِينَةٌ وَتَفَاخُرٌۢ بَيْنَكُمْ وَتَكَاثُرٌ فِى ٱلْأَمْوَٰلِ وَٱلْأَوْلَـٰدِ﴾

"Know that the life of this world is merely a game and a diversion and ostentation and a cause of boasting among yourselves and trying to outdo one another in wealth and children." [al-Ḥadīd 57:20]

(يحبك الله) *yuḥibbak Allah*: the letter *bā'* is doubled and followed by a *fatḥah*, but originally it was *yuḥbibk*, which is normal for the genitive case as it is the apodosis of a command, but to avoid the coming together of two unvocalised letters and facilitate pronunciation, the *kasrah* on the *bā'* is moved back to the *ḥā'* and the second *bā'* is given a *fatḥah*. Allah's love of a slave is Him being pleased with him and kind towards Him because love is a natural inclination, which is impossible for Allah. Thus, what is meant is its end and outcome.

184 (tn): i.e. the Arabs.

Legal Matters and Other Guidance from the Ḥadīth:

1. The Meaning of Abstinence: The expressions used by the First Three Generations and the scholars that came after them have varied regarding abstinence in this worldly life, and they all go back to what Imam Aḥmad has related on the authority of Abū Idrīs al-Khawlānī ؓ in which he said, 'Abstinence in this life is not in declaring the lawful unlawful or in wasting wealth. Rather, abstinence in this life is that you have greater trust in what is with Allah than what is in your possession, and if you are afflicted with something, you have greater hope of its reward and that it will be stored for you than any desire that what you lost would have remained for you.'

This statement explains abstinence as being three matters all of which are deeds of the heart and not deeds of the limbs. This is why Abū Sulaymān ad-Dārānī would say, 'Do not testify that anyone has abstinence, for abstinence is in the heart.' These three matters are:

The **first** is that the slave has more trust in what is with Allah than what in his possession, and this comes from sound certainty, as well as trust in the provisions that Allah the Exalted has guaranteed for His slaves. Allah the Exalted has said,

﴿وَمَا مِن دَآبَّةٍ فِى ٱلْأَرْضِ إِلَّا عَلَى ٱللَّهِ رِزْقُهَا﴾

"There is no creature on the earth which is not dependent upon Allah for its provision." [Hūd 11:6]

The Glorified One has also said,

﴿وَفِى ٱلسَّمَآءِ رِزْقُكُمْ وَمَا تُوعَدُونَ﴾

"Your provision is in heaven – and what you are promised." [adh-Dhāriyāt 51:22]

The **second** is that if the slave is afflicted with an affliction in his worldly life, such as losing wealth or a child, he is more desirous of the reward for it than he is for the thing he lost to remain for him in this world. This also comes from complete certainty, and it indicates abstinence regarding this worldly life and little desire for it.

Ibn ʿUmar related from the Prophet ﷺ that he would say in his supplication,

(اللهُمَّ اقْسِمْ لَنَا مِنْ خَشْيَتِكَ مَا تَحُولُ بَيْنَنَا وَبَيْنَ مَعَاصِيكَ،

وَمِنْ طَاعَتِكَ مَا تُبَلِّغُنَا بِهِ جَنَّتَكَ، وَمِنَ الْيَقِينِ مَا تُهَوِّنُ عَلَيْنَا مَصَائِبَ الدُّنْيَا)

{O Allah, grant us the fear of You that comes between us and disobeying You, the obedience of You that causes us to reach Your Paradise and certainty that makes the hardships of this worldly life easy for us}.

This **third** is that the slave sees no difference between the one who praises him and the one who criticises him. This is one of the signs of abstinence regarding this worldly life, of looking down on it and having little desire for it. Ibn Masʿūd said, 'Certainty is that you do not please people by angering Allah'.

The expressions that explain the meaning of abstinence include the statement of al-Ḥasan al-Baṣrī: 'The abstinent person is the one who, upon seeing someone else, says, "He is better than me"'.

Wahb ibn al-Ward said, 'Abstinence in this worldly life is that you do not despair over what you have lost in it, and you do not rejoice over what comes to you from it'.

When az-Zuhrī was asked about abstinence, he said, 'The person whose patience is not overwhelmed by the unlawful and whose gratitude is not preoccupied with the lawful'.

Sufyān ibn ʿUyaynah said, 'The abstinent person is the one who is grateful when he has ease and is patient when he is being tested'.

Rabīʿah said, 'The peak of abstinence is to gather things properly and put them in their proper place'.

Sufyān ath-Thawrī said, 'Abstinence in this worldly life is to have short hope, not to eat tough food or to wear a cloak-like woollen wrap'.

Imam Aḥmad said, 'Abstinence in this worldly life is to have short hope to despair of what people possess'.

2. The Categories of Abstinence: The First Three Generations divided abstinence into three categories:

The **first** is to abstain from idolatry and from worshipping whatever is worshipped besides Allah.

The **second** is to completely abstain from the unlawful and disobedience.

The first two categories of abstinence are obligatory while the third category is not obligatory.

The **third** is to abstain from the lawful.

Ibn al-Mubārak said, 'Maʿlā ibn Abī Muṭiʿ said, 'Abstinence has three standpoints. The first is that your deeds and words are sincerely for Allah, and nothing of this worldly life is sought through them. The second is to leave what is not righteous and to act according to what is righteous. The third is to be abstinent regarding the lawful, which is voluntary, and it is the lowest type'.

Ibrāhīm ibn Adham said, 'Abstinence is of three types: obligatory abstinence, superior abstinence and safe abstinence. As for obligatory abstinence, it is to abstain from the unlawful. Superior abstinence is to be abstinent regarding the lawful. Safe abstinence is to abstain from doubtful matters'.

It has been related from Imam Aḥmad that abstinence has three standpoints. The first is to leave the unlawful, which is the abstinence of the masses. The second is to leave that which is superfluous of the lawful, which is the abstinence of the elite. The third is to leave whatever preoccupies one from Allah, which is the abstinence of those who know Him.

3. That Which Brings About Abstinence: There are several matters that bring about abstinence in someone, some of which are the following:

i. The **first** is to envision the Hereafter, and standing before the Creator on the Day of Reckoning and Reward. This will help someone overcome his demons and his passions, and turn his soul away from the delights of this worldly life and its fleeting enjoyments. The evidence for this is that when Ḥārithah ﷺ said to the Prophet ﷺ 'I woke up this morning as a true believer', he replied, {Every true believer has a reality, so what is the reality of your faith?} He replied, 'I have turned my soul away from this worldly life. Its hardships and its ease are the same to me as if I can clearly see my Lord's Throne as if I can see the people of Paradise enjoying themselves in Paradise and the people of the Fire being punished in the Fire.' He said, {O Ḥārithah. Now you know, so stick to it.}

ii. The **second** is to call to mind that the delights of this world distract one's heart from Allah the Exalted and lower one's rank with Him, necessitating that one is detained and held back for a longer period on that critical Day. One will be asked about gratitude for this life's blessings. Allah the Exalted has said,

﴿ثُمَّ لَتُسْـَٔلُنَّ يَوْمَئِذٍ عَنِ ٱلنَّعِيمِ﴾

"Then you will be asked that Day about the pleasures you enjoyed." [at-Takāthur 102:8]

iii. The **third** is to call to mind the abundance of toil and humiliation in attaining this worldly life, how often it deceives a person, how quickly it changes and comes to an end, how low people compete in seeking it and its insignificance in the sight of Allah the Exalted. He ﷺ has said, {If the life of this world were equivalent to a gnat's wing in the sight of Allah, an unbeliever would not have been given a drink of water from it.}[185]

iv. The **fourth** is to call to mind that this world is cursed. Ibn Mājah has related a good ḥadīth on the authority of Abū Hurayrah ﷺ: {This world is cursed and what it contains is cursed, apart from the remembrance of Allah and what is connected to it, or a scholar or a learner.} In another narration: {... apart from that which is done seeking Allah the Exalted's Face.}[186] In other words, this life and what it contains cause one to be remote from Allah the Exalted, apart from

---

185 Related by at-Tirmidhī and aḍ-Ḍiyā' on the authority of Sahl ibn Sa'd as-Sā'idī ﷺ and it is an authentic ḥadīth. See *al-Jāmi' as-Ṣaghīr*, 2/131.

186 (tn): this is a reference to seeing Allah in the Hereafter, please see Sūrat ar-Raḥmān 55:27.

beneficial knowledge that leads one to know Him and seeking to draw nearer to Him and the remembrance of Allah and what is connected to it that makes one draw nearer to Him, Exalted is He.

4. Scorn for this Worldly Life and Warning Against Being Deluded by it: The person who abstains from this worldly life makes himself firmer and stronger when he recites his Lord's verses ﷿ and reads the ḥadīths of His Prophet ﷺ for he finds therein scorn for this worldly life and warning against being deluded and deceived by it. Allah the Exalted has said,

﴿بَلْ تُؤْثِرُونَ ٱلْحَيَوٰةَ ٱلدُّنْيَا ﴿١٦﴾ وَٱلْءَاخِرَةُ خَيْرٌ وَأَبْقَىٰٓ﴾

"Yet still you prefer the life of this world when the Hereafter is better and longer-lasting." [al-ʿAlā 87:16-17]

The Glorified One has also said,

﴿قُلْ مَتَـٰعُ ٱلدُّنْيَا قَلِيلٌ وَٱلْءَاخِرَةُ خَيْرٌ لِّمَنِ ٱتَّقَىٰ﴾

"Say, 'The enjoyment of this world is very brief. The Hereafter is better for those who have *taqwā*.'" [an-Nisāʾ 4:77].

He ﷿ has also said,

﴿فَلَا تَغُرَّنَّكُمُ ٱلْحَيَوٰةُ ٱلدُّنْيَا وَلَا يَغُرَّنَّكُم بِٱللَّهِ ٱلْغَرُورُ﴾

"Do not let the life of this world delude you and do not let the Deluder delude you concerning Allah." [Luqmān 31:33]

He ﷿ has also said,

﴿وَفَرِحُوا۟ بِٱلْحَيَوٰةِ ٱلدُّنْيَا وَمَا ٱلْحَيَوٰةُ ٱلدُّنْيَا فِى ٱلْءَاخِرَةِ إِلَّا مَتَـٰعٌ﴾

"They rejoice in the life of this world. Yet the life of this world, compared to the Next World, is only fleeting enjoyment." [ar-Raʿd 13:26]

Muslim has related in his *Ṣaḥīḥ* on the authority of Jābir ibn ʿAbdillāh ﵁ that the Prophet ﷺ passed by the market and the people were on both sides of him. He then passed by a young goat with very short ears. He picked it up by the ear and said, {Which one of you would like this for a dirham?} They replied, 'We would not want it for anything. What would we do with it?' He said, {Would you like it for free?} They replied, 'By Allah, if it were alive, we would not want it because its ears are very short, so how could we want it when it is dead?' He said, {By Allah, this world is more insignificant in the sight of Allah than this lamb is to you.} Muslim has also related on the authority of al-Mustawrid al-Fihrī that the Prophet ﷺ said, {This world in relation to the Hereafter is like one of you dipping his finger in the open sea and seeing what he comes back with.}

5. Disparagement for this Worldly Life is not for Time or Place: This disparagement of this worldly life that is found in the Noble Qurʾān and the Prophetic Sunnah does not go back to its time, which is the night and the day succeeding each other until the Day of Standing. Allah has made both of them successors for whoever wants to remember or wants to be grateful.

Likewise, the disparagement of this world does not go back to its place, which is the earth that Allah has made a resting place and a home. It does not go back to the vegetation and trees that grow therein or the creatures that spread out across it, for all of them are part of Allah's blessings towards His slaves. There are benefits and advantages for them in these blessings, and they are evidence of Allah's power and His existence ﷻ.

Rather, the disparagement that is found goes back to people's actions that take place in this worldly life, because most of them contravene what the Messengers brought and they are harmful. Their outcome will not be beneficial. Allah the Exalted has said,

﴿ٱعْلَمُوٓا۟ أَنَّمَا ٱلْحَيَوٰةُ ٱلدُّنْيَا لَعِبٌ وَلَهْوٌ وَزِينَةٌ وَتَفَاخُرٌۢ بَيْنَكُمْ وَتَكَاثُرٌ فِى ٱلْأَمْوَٰلِ وَٱلْأَوْلَـٰدِ ۖ

كَمَثَلِ غَيْثٍ أَعْجَبَ ٱلْكُفَّارَ نَبَاتُهُۥ ثُمَّ يَهِيجُ فَتَرَىٰهُ مُصْفَرًّا﴾

"Know that the life of this world is merely a game and a diversion and ostentation and a cause of boasting among yourselves and trying to outdo one another in wealth and children: like the plant-growth after rain which delights the cultivators, but then it withers and you see it turning yellow." [al-Ḥadīd 57:20]

Ibn Rajab al-Ḥanbalī ﷺ said, 'In this life, the children of Adam are divided into two categories:

The **first** are those who deny that the slaves have an abode of reward and punishment after this life, and they are those whom Allah has described by saying,

﴿إِنَّ ٱلَّذِينَ لَا يَرْجُونَ لِقَآءَنَا وَرَضُوا۟ بِٱلْحَيَوٰةِ ٱلدُّنْيَا وَٱطْمَأَنُّوا۟ بِهَا وَٱلَّذِينَ هُمْ عَنْ ءَايَـٰتِنَا غَـٰفِلُونَ ۝٧

أُو۟لَـٰٓئِكَ مَأْوَىٰهُمُ ٱلنَّارُ بِمَا كَانُوا۟ يَكْسِبُونَ﴾

"As for those who do not expect to meet Us and are content with the life of the world and at rest in it, and those who are heedless of Our Signs, their shelter will be the Fire because of what they earned." [Yūnus 10:7-8]

The concern of these people is to enjoy themselves in this life and take advantage of its delights before they die, as the Exalted One has said,

﴿وَٱلَّذِينَ كَفَرُوا۟ يَتَمَتَّعُونَ وَيَأْكُلُونَ كَمَا تَأْكُلُ ٱلْأَنْعَـٰمُ وَٱلنَّارُ مَثْوًى لَّهُمْ﴾

"Those who disbelieve have their enjoyment, eating as cattle eat, but the Fire will be their Final residence." [Muḥammad 47:12]

Amongst these people are those who enjoin abstinence in this life because they see that increasing in it necessitates worry and anxiety. They say, "The more attached to it one becomes, to more painful it is for the soul to part from it at death", and this is the extent of their abstinence in this life.

The **second** category is those who affirm that there is an abode for reward and punishment after death, and they are affiliated with the revealed laws of the Messengers. They are broken down further into three categories: those who wrong themselves, those who are in the middle and those who outdo each other in good by Allah's permission.[187]

The **first** category is the majority. They stick to the splendour of this life by taking it with the wrong approach and using it with the wrong approach, and thus it becomes their greatest concern. These are the people of amusement, entertainment, embellishment, boasting and accumulation. None of them knows the objective behind this life, that it is merely a stopover for gathering supplies on the way to the permanent abode, even if they believe in it in general.

The **second** category takes it with the right approach but they are thoroughly engaged in its permissible matters and take delight in its permissible pleasures. Even though one is not punished for these, one's rank in the Hereafter is diminished to the extent that one engages in this worldly life. It has been authentically narrated that Ibn 'Umar ﷺ said, "No one acquires anything of this world except that it diminishes his rank in the Hereafter with Allah, even if Allah is generous towards him." At-Tirmidhī has related from Qatādah ibn an-Nu'mān that the Messenger of Allah ﷺ said, {When Allah loves a slave, He protects him from this worldly life just as one of you constantly protects an ill person he knows from water.} Al-Ḥākim related it with the following wording: {When He loves him, Allah protects His slave from this world just as you protect your ill from food and drink out of fear for them.}

Muslim has related has from 'Abdullah ibn 'Umar that the Prophet ﷺ said, {This life is the believer's prison and the unbeliever's Paradise.}

The **third** category understands what is sought from the worldly life and that Allah the Glorified has only made His slaves reside in it and shown them its pleasures and splendour to test which of them is the best in action. Someone from the First Three Generations said, 'It means who is abstinent in this life and

187 (tn): Please see Sūrat Fāṭir 35:32.

desirous of the Hereafter. The Exalted One clarified that what He had placed on the earth was an embellishment of it to test which of them is the best in action, between withdrawing from it and exhausting it, when He ﷻ said,

﴿وَإِنَّا لَجَٰعِلُونَ مَا عَلَيْهَا صَعِيدًا جُرُزًا﴾

"We will certainly make everything on it a barren wasteland." [al-Kahf 18:8]

Thus, whoever understands that this is how it will end up will be concerned with taking supplies from it for the abode of permanence. He will take what he needs from it the same way a traveller takes what he needs, just as he ﷺ says, {In this life, I am like a traveller who has taken shade under a tree. Eventually, he will get up, leave it and move on.} Then, amongst this category, there are those who have confined themselves to that which will keep them alive in this world, and this is the state of many of the abstinent.[188] Then there are those who allow themselves, sometimes, to partake in some of its permissible matters, for the soul to be strengthened and energized for action. Aḥmad and an-Nasāʾī have related that the Messenger of Allah ﷺ said, {From your world, women and scent have been made beloved to me.} Aḥmad has related that ʿĀʾishah said, 'From this world, the Messenger of Allah ﷺ loved women, scent and food. He obtained women and scent and did not obtain food.' Partaking in permissible pleasures with the intention of strengthening oneself for obedience turns those pleasures into acts of obedience, and thus they are not of this world. Al-Ḥākim has related that the Messenger of Allah ﷺ said, {How wonderful an abode this world is for the one who takes provision from it for his Hereafter to please his Lord, and how evil an abode it is when it hinders someone from their Hereafter and makes them fall short in attaining their Lord's pleasure.}

6. How do we Earn Allah the Exalted's Love? We can attain Allah the Exalted's love by being abstinent in this world, because He ﷻ loves those who obey Him. Love of Him and love of this world do not go together, as is indicated by mass-transmitted text and experience. This is why he ﷺ said, {Love of this world is the beginning of every sin.} Allah does not love sin or its people, because it is amusement and play, and Allah does not love them. It is also because the heart is an abode for the Lord, who has no partner, and thus He does not want to share His abode with love of this world or anything else. The love of this world that is prohibited is when it is preferred to fulfil desires, attain pleasure and anything else that distracts one from Allah the Exalted. As for loving it to do good deeds and draw nearer to Allah, this is praiseworthy, due to the ḥadīth, {How wonderful is righteous wealth for the righteous man who uses it to maintain ties of kinship and do what is right.} Related by Imam Aḥmad.

188 Ar. *zuhād.*

7. How do we Earn People's Love? The ḥadīth teaches us how to earn people's love, and that is by abstaining from what they possess because if we let them have what they love, they will love us. Most of their hearts are naturally inclined towards loving this world, and if someone competes with someone over something they love, they loathe and detest that person. Whoever does not oppose him he loves and deems good. Al-Ḥasan al-Baṣrī said, 'A man will remain noble to people as long as he does not covet what they possess, for, at that point, they look down on him, dislike his words and despise him'. A Bedouin said to the people of Basra, 'Who is your master?' They replied, 'Al-Ḥasan.' He said, 'How is he your master?' They replied, 'They need his knowledge and he has no need of their worldly lives'. He said, 'How excellent is this'.

The most deserving of people to earn this attribute are the rulers and the scholars. When the rulers are abstinent, the people love them and follow their way as well as their abstinence. When the scholars are abstinent, the people love them, they respect what they say and they obey them in what they admonish and instruct. Ibn Salām asked Ka'b in the presence of 'Umar رضي الله عنه 'What removes knowledge from the hearts of the scholars after they have understood and memorised it?' He replied, 'It is removed by covetousness, the ego's greed and seeking one's needs from people'. He replied, 'You have spoken the truth'.

8. The Messenger of Allah's Abstinence ﷺ and the Abstinence of his Noble Companions: If we are looking for an exemplar in the lives of the abstinent, we find it embodied in the life of the Messenger of Allah ﷺ indeed and conduct, after we have found it embodied in his statements and his advice for his Ummah. His words and deeds ﷺ which shows a preference for the Hereafter, are the fruits of divine education that Allah ﷻ raised him with. Allah the Exalted has said,

﴿وَلَا تَمُدَّنَّ عَيْنَيْكَ إِلَىٰ مَا مَتَّعْنَا بِهِۦٓ أَزْوَٰجًا مِّنْهُمْ زَهْرَةَ ٱلْحَيَوٰةِ ٱلدُّنْيَا لِنَفْتِنَهُمْ فِيهِ ۚ وَرِزْقُ رَبِّكَ خَيْرٌ وَأَبْقَىٰ﴾

"Do not direct your eyes longingly to what We have given certain of them to enjoy, the splendour of the life of this world, so that We may test them by it. Your Lord's provision is better and longer-lasting." [Ṭaha 20:131]

The Prophet ﷺ before the Migration and after it, in days of adversity and days of ease, lived a life of abstaining from the enjoyments of this world, seeking the Hereafter and being earnest in his worship. His noble Companions emulated him, and they were the masters of abstinence and exemplars for the people of abstinence. Ibn 'Umar heard a man saying, 'Where are the people of abstinence in this worldly life, those who desire the Hereafter?' He thus showed him the Prophet's grave ﷺ and that of Abū Bakr and 'Umar, and said, 'You are asking about these people.' Ibn Mas'ūd ﷺ said to his companions, 'You pray, fast and do *jihād* more than Muḥammad's Companions ﷺ and they were better than you'. They said, 'How can that be?' He replied, 'They abstained from the world more than you do and had more desire for the Hereafter than you do. The world came to them in the form of lawful wealth and they took hold of it to draw nearer to Allah the Exalted, and they spent it in the service of His religion and to make His Word uppermost'. Abū Sulaymān said, "Uthmān and 'Abdur Raḥmān ibn 'Awf ﷺ were two of Allah's treasure houses on His earth. They spent in obedience to Him and they dealt with Allah with their hearts and with their knowledge'.

9. Foreign Abstinence: The Islamic meaning of abstinence is what we have elucidated in the previous paragraphs. As for foreign abstinence, it is to completely turn away from Allah's blessings and pour scorn on them, and not let oneself enjoy any of them. Some Muslims have been influenced by this foreign understanding of abstinence, and thus we find people in the age of Abbasid weakness and afterwards wearing rags, not working or earning and living off charity while claiming to be people of abstinence.

However, the spirit of Islam rejects this lethal negativism, this fatal impotence and this humiliation and false reliance on Allah.

Muslims today are clear of this diseased mentality. They hasten towards lawful work and earnings. They compete to obtain profit and develop the earth, so much so that we have come to fear for ourselves, that we have become heedless of the Hereafter. We look for things that will calm us down and remind us of Allah the Exalted, and call us to abstain from this worldly life, and thus there would be less haste. We would not stumble and fall into Shayṭān's traps and be deluded by this world's enjoyments and its vehement passions.

THE THIRTY-SECOND ḤADĪTH

نَفْيُ الضَّرَرِ فِي الإِسْلَامِ

عَنْ أَبِي سَعِيدٍ سَعْدِ بْنِ سِنَانٍ الخُدْرِيِّ ﵁: أَنَّ رَسُولَ اللهِ ﷺ قَالَ: {لَا ضَرَرَ وَلَا ضِرَارَ.}
حَدِيثٌ حَسَنٌ، رَوَاهُ ابْنُ مَاجَهْ وَالدَّارَقُطْنِيُّ وَغَيْرُهُمَا مُسْنَداً. رواه مَالِكٌ فِي المُوَطَّأ مُرْسَلاً: عَنْ عَمْرِو بْنِ يَحْيَى، عَنْ أَبِيهِ، عَنِ النَّبِيِّ ﷺ. فَأَسْقَطَ أَبَا سَعِيدٍ. وَلَهُ طُرُقٌ يُقَوِّي بَعْضُهَا بَعْضاً.

Negating Harm in Islam

It is on the authority of Abū Saʿīd Saʿd ibn Sinān al-Khudrī ﵁ that the Messenger of Allah ﷺ said, {There is to be no harm (*ḍarar*) and no reciprocating of harm (*ḍirār*).}

It is a good ḥadīth, related by Ibn Mājah, ad-Dāraquṭnī and others with a complete chain of transmission.[189] Mālik has related in *al-Muwaṭṭāʾ mursalan*[190] on the authority of ʿAmr ibn Yaḥyā, from his father, from the Prophet ﷺ and thus Abū Saʿīd was omitted. It has other paths of transmission and they strengthen one another.

Ibn Mājah has related it in the Book of Rulings (the chapter on the one who builds within his right that which harms his neighbour), no.2340 and 2341 from the ḥadīth of ʿUbādah ibn as-Ṣāmit and Ibn ʿAbbās ﵄.

Mālik has related it in *al-Muwaṭṭāʾ* in the Book of Judgments (the chapter on judgments benefitting neighbours), no.31.

The ḥadīth of Abū Saʿīd ﵁ was collected by al-Ḥākim and al-Bayhaqī, and al-Ḥākim said, 'Its chain of transmission is authentic according to the conditions of Muslim'.

Ibn Rajab said, 'Imam Aḥmad used this ḥadīth as evidence'. He also said, 'Abū ʿAmr ibn as-Ṣalāḥ said, 'Ad-Dāraquṭnī has traced this ḥadīth from several chains, and in their totality, they strengthen the ḥadīth and make it good, and the vast

---

189 Ar. *musnadan*, which means that the chain is connected and no one has been omitted from it. Please see *al-Fatḥ al-Mubīn bi Sharḥ al-Arbaʿīn* by Imam Ibn Ḥajar al-Haytamī (Jeddah: Dār al-Minhāj, 1436/2015, p.522.)

190 (tn): According to the scholars of ḥadīth, *mursal* means that the Companion has been omitted from the chain of transmission. According to the scholars of *uṣūl al-fiqh*, it means that a narrator has been omitted, wherever in the chain that may be. (*al-Fatḥ al-Mubīn bi Sharḥ al-Arbaʿīn*, p.522.)

majority of the people of knowledge have accepted it and used it as proof'. He also said, 'Abū Dāwūd's statement, that it is one of the ḥadīths around which *fiqh* revolves, informs that it is not weak, and Allah knows best'.

The Importance of the Ḥadīth:
You have seen Abū Dāwūd's statement, that it is one of the ḥadīths around which *fiqh* revolves.

The Language of the Ḥadīth:
The scholars have differed over the meaning of *ḍarar* and *ḍirār* in the ḥadīth. Do they have the same meaning or is there a difference between them? The well-known opinion is that there is a difference, and there are opinions regarding the meaning of both. Perhaps the preferred opinion is that *ḍarar* means to harm someone who has not harmed you, while *ḍirār* means to harm someone who has harmed you in a way that is not lawful.

Both meanings are prohibited and not permissible in Allah's legislation ﷻ and you will learn the details of this in the discussion that follows.

Legal Matters and Other Guidance from the Ḥadīth:
1. What is Being Negated is Harm and not Punishment or Retaliation: What is meant by harm in the ḥadīth is that which is done without right. As for harm being done to someone who deserves it – such as someone who transgresses Allah the Exalted's bounds and is punished for his crime, or he wrongs someone and is dealt with justly and taken to task for his wrongdoing – this is not what is meant in the ḥadīth, because retaliation has been legislated by Allah ﷻ and He has placed the reality of life for people therein. The Glorified One has said,

﴿وَلَكُمْ فِي ٱلْقِصَاصِ حَيَوٰةٌ يَـٰٓأُو۟لِى ٱلْأَلْبَـٰبِ لَعَلَّكُمْ تَتَّقُونَ﴾
"There is life for you in retaliation, people of intelligence." [al-Baqarah 2:179]

And he ﷺ has said, {I have been commanded to fight people until they bear witness that there is no god but Allah and that Muḥammad is the Messenger of Allah, and they establish the prayer and pay the zakāt. If they do so, they are safe from me concerning their blood and their property, except for when there is a right, and their reckoning is with Allah the Exalted.}, which is agreed upon. In other words, if they commit a crime that makes them deserving of financial or corporal punishment, they will be taken to task for it.

Indeed, it is part of negating harm to punish criminals for their crimes and take them to task, because by doing so, significant harm is warded off from individuals and communities.

2. There is no Legal Accountability in Islam in that which Contains Harm, and no Prohibition of that which Contains Benefit: Allah the Exalted has not commanded His slaves to do something that would harm them, just as He the Glorified has not forbidden them from anything that contains benefit. This is because what He has commanded them to is the very essence of what is right and good for them in both their religious and worldly affairs, just as what He has prohibited is the very essence of what corrupts their worldly lives as well as their Hereafter. The Exalted One has said,

﴿قُلْ أَمَرَ رَبِّي بِٱلْقِسْطِ﴾

"Say: 'My Lord has commanded justice.'" [al-ʾAʿrāf 7:29]

He has also said,

﴿قُلْ إِنَّمَا حَرَّمَ رَبِّيَ ٱلْفَوَاحِشَ مَا ظَهَرَ مِنْهَا وَمَا بَطَنَ﴾

"Say: My Lord has forbidden indecency, both open and hidden." [al-ʾAʿrāf 7:33]

There is no doubt that justice contains every good and benefit, while crimes contain every act of evil and corruption.

It is clear to anyone who has an intellect and looks at Allah's legislation ﷻ that Allah the Exalted has permitted for them everything that contains wellbeing for their intellects and health for their bodies. Likewise, He has not forbidden anything for them except that it contains that which impairs their senses, capabilities and faculties, and corrupts and harms their health and their bodies. The Exalted One has said,

﴿قُلْ مَنْ حَرَّمَ زِينَةَ ٱللَّهِ ٱلَّتِيٓ أَخْرَجَ لِعِبَادِهِۦ وَٱلطَّيِّبَٰتِ مِنَ ٱلرِّزْقِ

قُلْ هِيَ لِلَّذِينَ ءَامَنُوا۟ فِى ٱلْحَيَوٰةِ ٱلدُّنْيَا خَالِصَةً يَوْمَ ٱلْقِيَٰمَةِ﴾

"Say: 'Who has forbidden the finery Allah has produced for His slaves and the good kinds of provision?' Say: 'On the Day of Standing, such things will be exclusively for those who believed during their life in this world.'" [al-ʾAʿrāf 7:32]

In other words, the finery of this world and its good things are partaken in by both believers and unbelievers, while none of the latter will share with the former in the Hereafter. The Exalted One has said,

﴿قُل لَّآ أَجِدُ فِى مَآ أُوحِىَ إِلَىَّ مُحَرَّمًا عَلَىٰ طَاعِمٍ يَطْعَمُهُۥٓ إِلَّآ أَن يَكُونَ مَيْتَةً أَوْ دَمًا مَّسْفُوحًا

أَوْ لَحْمَ خِنزِيرٍ فَإِنَّهُۥ رِجْسٌ أَوْ فِسْقًا أُهِلَّ لِغَيْرِ ٱللَّهِ بِهِۦ﴾

"Say: 'I do not find, in what has been revealed to me, any food that is unlawful to eat except for carrion, flowing blood, pork – for that is unclean – or some deviance consecrated to other than Allah.'" [al-Anʿām 6:145]

Something consecrated to other than Allah the Exalted means that a name other than Allah's is extolled when the animal is slaughtered. It is called deviance (*fisq*) because the one who does so departs from obedience to Allah ﷻ.

3. Lifting Constraint: Negating harm in Islam includes lifting constraint from those who are legally responsible and making matters easier for them when what they have been commanded to do, puts them in some abnormal hardship. This is no surprise because this religion is the religion of facilitation. Allah the Exalted has said,

﴿وَمَا جَعَلَ عَلَيْكُمْ فِي ٱلدِّينِ مِنْ حَرَجٍ﴾

"He has selected you and not placed any constraint upon you in the religion". [al-Ḥajj 22:78]

And He ﷻ has said,

﴿لَا يُكَلِّفُ ٱللَّهُ نَفْسًا إِلَّا وُسْعَهَا﴾

"Allah does not impose on any soul any more than it can bear." [al-Baqarah 2:286]

He ﷺ has said, {I have been sent with the true, magnanimous religion},[191] as related by Imam Aḥmad in his *Musnad*. It is on the authority of Ibn ʿAbbās ؓ who said, 'It was said to the Messenger of Allah ﷺ "Which religion is most beloved to Allah?"' He replied, {The true, magnanimous religion.}. This is related by Aḥmad in his *Musnad* as well as by al-Bukhārī, who commented, 'In other words, the pure religion of Allah's Oneness, in which there is no hardship and no constraint. If the commandment were to remain in its original state – regardless of situations and circumstances – a legally accountable person would be beset with profound harm.'

Examples of matters being made easier for the legally accountable when there is hardship include the following:

A. Dry ablution (*tayammum*) for the one who is ill and the one who cannot obtain water. The Exalted One has said,

﴿وَإِن كُنتُم مَّرْضَىٰٓ أَوْ عَلَىٰ سَفَرٍ أَوْ جَآءَ أَحَدٌ مِّنكُم مِّنَ ٱلْغَآئِطِ أَوْ لَٰمَسْتُمُ ٱلنِّسَآءَ فَلَمْ تَجِدُوا۟
مَآءً فَتَيَمَّمُوا۟ صَعِيدًا طَيِّبًا فَٱمْسَحُوا۟ بِوُجُوهِكُمْ وَأَيْدِيكُم مِّنْهُ ۚ مَا يُرِيدُ ٱللَّهُ لِيَجْعَلَ عَلَيْكُم
مِّنْ حَرَجٍ وَلَٰكِن يُرِيدُ لِيُطَهِّرَكُمْ وَلِيُتِمَّ نِعْمَتَهُۥ عَلَيْكُمْ لَعَلَّكُمْ تَشْكُرُونَ﴾

191 Ar. *al-ḥanīfiyyah as-samḥah.*

"But if you are ill or on a journey, or have come from the lavatory, or have touched women, and cannot find any water, do *tayammum* with pure earth, and wipe your faces and your hands. Allah does not want to make things difficult for you, but He does want to purify you and to perfect His blessing upon you so that hopefully you will be thankful." [al-Māʾidah 5:6]

B. Breaking one's fast if one is ill or travelling. The Exalted One has said,

﴿شَهْرُ رَمَضَانَ ٱلَّذِىٓ أُنزِلَ فِيهِ ٱلْقُرْءَانُ هُدًى لِّلنَّاسِ وَبَيِّنَٰتٍ مِّنَ ٱلْهُدَىٰ وَٱلْفُرْقَانِ ۚ فَمَن شَهِدَ مِنكُمُ ٱلشَّهْرَ فَلْيَصُمْهُ ۖ وَمَن كَانَ مَرِيضًا أَوْ عَلَىٰ سَفَرٍ فَعِدَّةٌ مِّنْ أَيَّامٍ أُخَرَ ۗ يُرِيدُ ٱللَّهُ بِكُمُ ٱلْيُسْرَ وَلَا يُرِيدُ بِكُمُ ٱلْعُسْرَ وَلِتُكْمِلُوا۟ ٱلْعِدَّةَ وَلِتُكَبِّرُوا۟ ٱللَّهَ عَلَىٰ مَا هَدَىٰكُمْ وَلَعَلَّكُمْ تَشْكُرُونَ﴾

"The month of Ramaḍān is the one in which the Qurʾān was sent down as guidance for mankind, with clear signs containing guidance and discrimination. Any of you who are resident for the month should fast it. But any of you who are ill or on a journey should fast a number of other days. Allah desires ease for you; He does not desire difficulty for you." [al-Baqarah 2:185]

C. No sin is incurred if one does something that is not allowed whilst in *iḥrām* because they have fallen into difficulty. The Exalted One has said,

﴿وَلَا تَحْلِقُوا۟ رُءُوسَكُمْ حَتَّىٰ يَبْلُغَ ٱلْهَدْىُ مَحِلَّهُۥ ۚ فَمَن كَانَ مِنكُم مَّرِيضًا أَوْ بِهِۦٓ أَذًى مِّن رَّأْسِهِۦ فَفِدْيَةٌ مِّن صِيَامٍ أَوْ صَدَقَةٍ أَوْ نُسُكٍ﴾

"But do not shave your heads until the sacrificial animal has reached the place of sacrifice. If any of you are ill or have a head injury, the expiation is fasting, *ṣadaqah* or a sacrifice." [al-Baqarah 2:196]

The place of sacrifice is the Sacred Precinct,[192] and it takes place on the 10th of Dhūl Ḥijjah.

D. Deferring for the debtor who is in difficulty. If someone borrows money for something permissible for a specified period and is unable to pay it back, it is obligatory upon the debtee to defer his demand for repayment until the debtor is able to. The Exalted One has said,

﴿وَإِن كَانَ ذُو عُسْرَةٍ فَنَظِرَةٌ إِلَىٰ مَيْسَرَةٍ﴾

192 Ar. *al-Ḥaram.*

"If someone is in a difficult circumstance, there should be a deferral until things are easier." [al-Baqarah 2:280]

Here, the scholars of *fiqh* affirm that is not incumbent upon him to pay off his debt by selling property the loss of which would harm him, such as his clothes, his house or his servant that he needs. The same goes for whatever he needs for trade to provide for himself and his family.

E. Not requiring that someone walk if they have vowed to perform the Ḥajj on foot. Al-Bukhārī and Muslim have related on the authority of Anas 🙵 that the Prophet 🙵 saw an old man walking between his two sons. He said, {What is this?} They replied, 'He vowed that he would walk.' He said {Allah has no need of him punishing himself like this.} Then he commanded him to ride.

It is also in the two *Ṣaḥīḥ* collections that 'Uqbah ibn 'Āmir 🙵 said, 'My sister vowed that she would walk to Allah's house, and she ordered me to ask the Prophet 🙵 on her behalf, so I did. He 🙵 said, {Let her walk or ride.}

The scholars have differed as to what is incumbent upon a person who makes such a vow:
- In one narration of Aḥmad 🙵 such a person does not have to walk and is allowed to ride, without any obligation due from him. In another narration from him, he is to fast three days and in another narration, he has to carry out the expiation for breaking an oath.[193]

- Mālik 🙵 said that it is not sufficient for him to ride. If he rides, he is obligated to make up his Ḥajj. Thus, he rides whatever he walked and he walks whatever rode, and if what he rode was more, he is obligated to make a sacrifice along with making up the Ḥajj.

- The most well-known position is that he is obligated to walk if he can. If he is not able to, he rides and there is no obligation due for him, and this is the position of Imam ash-Shāfi'ī 🙵. It has also been said that he has to carry out the expiation for breaking an oath.

4. **Manifestations of Harm:** The objective to cause harm can be manifested in two types of actions:
- Actions that a legally accountable person carries out with the sole objective of causing harm to someone else, and there is no doubt that this type is repugnant and unlawful.

---

193   Ar. *kaffārat al-yamīn*; please see *Reliance of the Traveller*, o20.0.

– Actions for which a legally accountable person has a sound, lawful objective but his objective is accompanied by or leads to someone else being harmed.

The first type of action: The Revealed Law has forbidden many actions in which the objective, in most cases, is nothing more than causing harm, such as:

i. Harmful transactions, which take on numerous forms:

The **first** is a compelled sale, which is when a person needs some commodity and cannot find the money to pay for it. He thus takes it from its seller for an exorbitantly higher price than normal, such as buying it for ten when it normally sells for five.

The prohibition of this is found in the ḥadīth of ʿAlī 🙵 as collected by Abū Dāwūd, in which he addressed the people and said, 'The time of injustice will come upon people. The wealthy person will bite down on what he has in his hands, and he has not been commanded to do so. Allah the Exalted has said,

$$﴿وَلَا تَنسَوُاْ ٱلۡفَضۡلَ بَيۡنَكُمۡ﴾$$

"Do not forget to show generosity to one another." [al-Baqarah 2:237]

People will transact under compulsion, and the Messenger of Allah 🙵 forbade compelled transactions.' Al-Ismāʿīlī added, 'The Messenger of Allah 🙵 said, {If you have some good, share it with your brother, and if not, do not add ruin to his ruin.} In other words, in this situation, it would be appropriate to give him what he needs as an act of charity, not to add to his difficulty. ʿAbdullah ibn Maʿqil said, 'A compelled sale is usury'. Ḥarb said, 'Aḥmad was asked about compelled sales and he disliked them'.

The **second** is to sell what one has purchased for a specified period for less than its monetary price. For example, a person needs some money and cannot find anyone who will lend it to him, so he buys some commodity on credit for a specified period with the intention of selling it and getting its price.

If he sells it to other than its original seller, Aḥmad has said, 'I fear that it would be a compelled sale.'

If he does sell it to its original seller, the majority has held the position that such a transaction is unlawful and invalid, and they consider it a means towards consuming usury. This is the position of Mālik, Aḥmad and Abū Ḥanīfah 🙵. They have also used as proof what has been related by ad-Dāraquṭnī, in which a woman said to ʿĀʾishah 🙵 'I sold Zayd ibn Arqam a servant for 800 dirhams on credit, as he needed its price. I then bought the servant from him before the time had elapsed for 600'. ʿĀʾishah 🙵 said, 'How evil what you have sold and purchased is. Convey to Zayd ibn Arqam that Allah the Exalted has nullified his *jihād* and his Ḥajj with the Messenger of Allah 🙵 if he does not repent'. Zayd then came to her and apologised, and she recited,

﴿فَمَن جَآءَهُۥ مَوْعِظَةٌ مِّن رَّبِّهِۦ فَٱنتَهَىٰ فَلَهُۥ مَا سَلَفَ﴾

"Whoever is given a warning by his Lord and then desists may keep what he received in the past." [al-Baqarah 2:275]

In other words, he gets the money that he spent. They said, 'This statement of hers and her reprimand is evidence that she heard this from the Prophet ﷺ.

Ash-Shāfiʿī ﵀ agreed with the three imams if the contract contains something that indicates an intention to use artful means to arrive at usury. If the contract is free of such, it is a valid sale, because it fulfils all the pillars. People are not suspected in their actions and Allah ﷻ will reckon them for their intentions.

The **third** is criminal fraud.[194] If the buyer is not good at bargaining and is willing to buy something for a highly inflated price, it is not permissible for the seller to do so. The position of Mālik and Aḥmad ﵀ is that this person has the option to nullify the sale. Al-Bukhārī, Muslim and others have related from Ibn ʿUmar ﵄ that a man who deceived people in transactions was mentioned to the Prophet ﷺ so he said, {If you transact with him, tell him, 'No deception (*khilābah*).'} The man is Ḥibbān ibn Munqidh ﵁. Aḥmad said, '*Khilābah* is deception (*khidāʿ*), which is to dupe someone in something the like of which people do not normally dupe each other. For example, someone sells something worth one dirham for five dirhams.' The Mālikīs say that if the duping reaches a third of the price, he has the option to nullify the sale.

ii. Bequests:[195] The are two scenarios in which bequests can be harmful:

The **first** is by singling out one heir to receive more than the share that Allah has allocated for him, and thus the other heirs are harmed. For this reason, the Lawgiver has prohibited this unless the other heirs give their consent. He ﷺ has said, {Allah has given everyone their right, so there is no bequest for the heir.}

The **second** is to make a bequest to someone who is not an heir to diminish that which the heirs are entitled to. For this reason, the Revealed Law has forbidden bequests to be equivalent to more than a third of one's estate, regardless of whether one intends to harm or not unless one's heirs approve. He ﷺ said, {A third, and a third is a lot.}

The Revealed Law has permitted what is within a third so that a legally accountable person can compensate for whatever good deeds he was unable to do in his lifetime and whatever aspects of spending he fell short in. This is if he does not intend to harm any of his heirs by making a bequest. If he does, his bequest is sinful in the sight of Allah ﷻ. The Exalted One has said,

194 Ar. *ghabn fāḥish.*

195 Ar. *al-waṣiyyah*, which is not the same as inheritance (*al-farāʾiḍ*). Please see *Reliance*, L1 to L3.

﴿مِنۢ بَعْدِ وَصِيَّةٍ يُوصِينَ بِهَآ أَوْ دَيْنٍ﴾

"...after any bequest you make or any debts, making sure that no one's rights are prejudiced." [an-Nisā' 4:12]

Causing harm by way of a bequest may result in one's deeds coming to nought and one's reward being nullified. It is on the authority of Abū Hurayrah that the Messenger of Allah said, {A man and a woman will act in obedience to Allah for sixty years, then death will approach them and they will cause harm by way of bequests, and thus the Fire will be necessary for them.} Then Abū Hurayrah recited, **"...after any bequest"**. This has been related by at-Tirmidhī. Ibn 'Abbās said, 'Causing harm by way of bequests is a major sin.'

Is one's bequest returned if his objective is established by way of his admission or is it carried out? The majority of scholars say that it is carried out, and it has been related from Mālik that it is returned. Ibn Rajab said, 'It is an analogy based on Aḥmad's position.'

iii. Returning to marriage: In other words, the wife is returned to the bond of marriage within the waiting period after a revocable divorce. The Exalted One has said:

﴿فَأَمْسِكُوهُنَّ بِمَعْرُوفٍ أَوْ سَرِّحُوهُنَّ بِمَعْرُوفٍ ۚ وَلَا تُمْسِكُوهُنَّ ضِرَارًا لِّتَعْتَدُوا ۚ وَمَن يَفْعَلْ ذَٰلِكَ فَقَدْ ظَلَمَ نَفْسَهُ﴾

"...then either retain them with correctness and courtesy or release them with correctness and courtesy. Do not retain them by force, those overstepping the limits. Anyone who does that has wronged himself." [al-Baqarah 2:231]

He has also said,

﴿وَبُعُولَتُهُنَّ أَحَقُّ بِرَدِّهِنَّ فِي ذَٰلِكَ إِنْ أَرَادُوٓا إِصْلَٰحًا﴾

"Their husbands have the right to take them back within that time if they desire to be reconciled." [al-Baqarah 2:228]

This shows that whoever takes his wife back intending to harm her is sinful, and the scenario is illustrated as follows: a man divorces his wife and leaves her alone until shortly before the end of her waiting period. Then he takes her back but has no desire for her. Instead, he prolongs her waiting period and prevents her from marrying anyone else until a certain time. Thus, he does not live with her the way a married couple does, and maybe he will do this repeatedly. This is why Imam Mālik took the position that if someone takes his wife back before her waiting period has elapsed and then divorces her again without having intercourse with her, and he intends to harm her by prolonging her waiting period, the waiting period is not renewed. Rather, it continues from where it left off before he took her back.

In one narration of Aḥmad: it continues from where it left off absolutely, regardless of whether or not harm was intended.

The position of the majority is that the waiting period is renewed, regardless of whether harm was intended, and the man is sinful if he intends to harm.

iv. Causing harm by way of *īlā'*, which is when a man swears not to approach his wife – i.e. not have intercourse with her – for a period of time or indefinitely. If he has intercourse with her before four months have elapsed from the time of his oath, he is considered to have taken his wife back and repented, and he is obligated to carry out the expiation for breaking an oath. If four months pass and he persists in not having intercourse with her, this is not allowed. The Exalted One has said,

﴿لِّلَّذِينَ يُؤْلُونَ مِن نِّسَآئِهِمْ تَرَبُّصُ أَرْبَعَةِ أَشْهُرٍ ۖ فَإِن فَآءُو فَإِنَّ ٱللَّهَ غَفُورٌ رَّحِيمٌ ۝٢٢٦

وَإِنْ عَزَمُوا۟ ٱلطَّلَـٰقَ فَإِنَّ ٱللَّهَ سَمِيعٌ عَلِيمٌ﴾

"Those who swear to abstain from sexual relations with their wives can wait for a period of up to four months. If they then retract their oath, Allah is Ever-Forgiving, Most Merciful. If they are determined to divorce, Allah is All-Hearing, All-Knowing." [al-Baqarah 2:226-227]

The scholars have differed as to how causing harm can be prevented. There are two positions.

The majority say that the man is brought before a judge and ordered to take back his wife or divorce her. If he refuses, the judge grants her one revocable divorce.

The Ḥanafīs say that she is divorced irrevocably once four months have elapsed from the date the oath was made.

Based on *īlā'*, the analogous conclusion is drawn for that which is similar:

- **First** of all, if a man stops having intercourse with his wife for four months with the intention of harming her but without making an oath, the outward purport of Aḥmad's statement is that his ruling is the same as someone who commits *īlā'*.

- **Secondly**, having intercourse with one's wife is obligatory – according to the Ḥanbalīs – at least once every four months. If a man abandons intercourse without an excuse and the wife demands to be separated, the separation is granted according to a group of them.[196] Is the intention to cause harm considered in such a situation or not? There is a difference of opinion.

Mālik and his companions have said that if he abandons intercourse without an excuse, the marriage is nullified, but they differ regarding how much time would have to pass before this comes into effect.

- **Thirdly**, if a man travels for a long time without an excuse, his wife requests that he return and he refuses, Mālik and Aḥmad say that the judge separates the two of them.

v. Causing harm in nursing:[197] the Exalted One has said:

﴿وَٱلْوَٰلِدَٰتُ يُرْضِعْنَ أَوْلَٰدَهُنَّ حَوْلَيْنِ كَامِلَيْنِ ۖ لِمَنْ أَرَادَ أَن يُتِمَّ ٱلرَّضَاعَةَ ۚ وَعَلَى ٱلْمَوْلُودِ لَهُۥ رِزْقُهُنَّ وَكِسْوَتُهُنَّ بِٱلْمَعْرُوفِ ۚ لَا تُكَلَّفُ نَفْسٌ إِلَّا وُسْعَهَا ۚ لَا تُضَآرَّ وَٰلِدَةٌۢ بِوَلَدِهَا وَلَا مَوْلُودٌ لَّهُۥ﴾

"Mothers should nurse their children for two full years – for those who wish to complete the full term of nursing. It is the duty of the fathers to feed and clothe them with correctness and courtesy – not a soul is charged with more than it can bear. No mother should be harmed in respect of her child nor any father in respect of his child." [al-Baqarah 2:233]

This verse comprises the prohibition against harming the mother and the prohibition against harming the father. The mother has the right to nurse her child. If she is a wife and the husband prevents her from nursing her child with the intention of making her available for his pleasure, it is permissible for him to do so. If he intends to cause her grief by doing so, it is not permissible, he is prevented from doing so and he is considered sinful. This is if he can find someone else to nurse the child. If he is unable to, because he cannot find someone else or he does find someone but the child only accepts his mother's breast, he is absolutely not allowed to prevent his wife from nursing the child, because of the harm this would cause the child.

If the mother is not a wife and is instead divorced or a widow, and she requests to nurse her child for the going rate, that is what she is entitled to. It is incumbent upon the father or his heir to accede to her request and to give the child to her. If she asks for a much larger amount than the going rate and the father or the heir find someone who will nurse the child for the going rate, it is not incumbent upon either of them to accede to her request, because she is seeking to cause harm by

---

196 (tn): i.e. Ḥanbalīs.

197 Ar. *irḍāʿ*.

asking for more. If no one else can be found to nurse the child, she is forced to nurse it for the going rate, so that no harm comes to the child or his father, by grieving over him.

The second type of actions are those in which there is a sound and legislated purpose but it is accompanied by or leads to someone else being harmed. This can be by someone using his property in a way that harms someone else, or by preventing someone else from benefitting from his property, and thus the one who is prevented is harmed.

In the first case, which is someone using their property in a way that harms someone else, there are two scenarios:

1. Someone uses their property in an abnormal or unfamiliar way, and thus it is not allowed, and someone else is harmed by their action. For example, someone lights a fire on his land on a stormy day and his neighbour's property is burnt. He is thus transgressing by doing this and he has to pay compensation.

2. Someone uses their property in a normal way, and there are issues therein in which juridical points of views differ:

The **first** issue is someone digging a well near his neighbour's well and thus causing his neighbour's well to dry up. Mālik and Aḥmad ﷺ hold that he is prohibited from doing so. If he digs it, it is filled in and obliterated, because he is harming his neighbour. Abū Dāwūd has related in *al-Murāsīl* from the ḥadīth of Abū Qilābah ﷺ who said, 'The Messenger of Allah ﷺ said: {Do not cause harm by digging. This is when a man digs next to another man to take his water.} Those besides these two have said that it is permissible.

The **second** issue is making a window or a tall building. If someone makes a window in his building and it overlooks his neighbour's property, or he builds a tall building on his land that overlooks his neighbour's property and does not grant him privacy, or it blocks out the sun and light, this is not permissible, especially if it is apparent to the judge that one intends wickedness and iniquity. Al-Kharā'iṭī has collected a ḥadīth in which he ﷺ said about the right of one's neighbour, {One must not build a tall building that blocks him from the wind unless he gives his consent.} This is the position of Aḥmad ﷺ and some of the Shāfi'īs agree with him.

The **third** issue is something happening on one's property that harms one's neighbour, such as shaking or banging and the like, or someone puts something on their property that has a disgusting odour. This is impermissible and it is the apparent position of Mālik and Aḥmad ﷺ. The Shāfi'īs says that it is impermissible if someone else's property is harmed.

The **fourth** issue is removing something that causes harm by substituting it for something if a substitute exists. This is when someone has a right in someone else's property, such as a room in a house or a shared bathhouse and the like, and when they make use of that right, someone else is harmed. He is thus forced to relinquish his right, to accept something in its place or to accept its price, so that the other person is no longer harmed.

Abū Dāwūd has narrated on the authority of Samurah ibn Jundub ﷺ that he had a short date palm within the walls of one of the men of the Helpers,[198] and the man had his family with him. Samurah would enter to get to his date palm and this would annoy the man and inconvenience him. He thus asked him to sell it, but he refused. He then asked him to exchange it for another date palm in another location, but he refused. He then went to the Prophet ﷺ and mentioned the situation to him. The Prophet ﷺ asked him to sell it, but he refused. He then asked him to exchange it for another date palm in another location, but he refused. He then said to him: {Give it to him, and you will have such-and-such}, and he mentioned things that he had a desire for, but he still refused. He then said: {You are causing harm.} The Messenger of Allah ﷺ then said to the Anṣārī man: {Go and uproot his date palm.} After this ḥadīth was mentioned to him, Aḥmad said, 'Everything that is of this nature and causes harm is not allowed. The person responsible for this should accede to the request[199] and if he does not, the ruler forces him. One is not harming one's brother therein when there's some benefit for him', i.e. something advantageous for one's brother the acquisition of it will not harm him.

Similar to this is forcing a business partner to build if he refrains from doing so and his refraining is harming his partner. Likewise, a partner can be forced to sell something that is impossible to divide, such as a shared car or a latrine, which can only be benefited from as an undivided whole, if his partner requests such.

The second type, which is preventing someone else from using their property and thus preventing them from harming others, includes the following issues:

A. A person prevents their neighbour from benefitting from and making use of their property. For example, someone has a very fragile wall. It cannot bear any more weight. He can thus prevent his neighbour from putting a piece of wood on it, even if that would not cause harm.

Ash-Shāfiʿī, Abū Ḥanīfah and Mālik ﷺ said that he can prevent him from doing anything with his property without his permission because his neighbour could do something that will cause him harm. This is due to his statement ﷺ {It is not lawful for a Muslim to take his brother's stick without his consent.} He said, {This is due to the severity with which Allah has made one Muslim's property unlawful for another Muslim.} Related by Ibn Ḥibbān.

Aḥmad ﷺ said that it is not permissible to prevent him, and there are two narrations regarding forcing him. In the two *Ṣaḥīḥ* collections, it is on the authority

198 Ar. *al-Anṣār.*

199 (tn): i.e. to sell the item, move it, or give it away, as indicated in the ḥadīth.

of Abū Hurayrah ؓ that the Prophet ﷺ said, {Let none of you prevent his neighbour from placing a piece of wood on his wall.} Abū Hurayrah ؓ said, 'Why do I see you turning away from this? By Allah, I will spread this amongst you.' 'Umar ibn al-Khaṭṭāb ؓ judged against Muḥammad ibn Maslamah that he should let his neighbour's water flow through his land. He said, 'Let it flow through, even if it goes over your stomach.'

B. Preventing water, herbage, salt and fire: Al-Bukhārī and Muslim have related on the authority of Abū Hurayrah ؓ that the Prophet ﷺ said, {Do not withhold excess water to withhold herbage.} This is because there cannot be any herbage without water passing over it, and thus withholding water can lead to withholding herbage. Abū Dāwūd has related that a man said, 'O Prophet of Allah, what is the thing that is unlawful to withhold?' He replied, {Water.} The man said, 'O Prophet of Allah, what is the thing that is unlawful to withhold?' He replied, {Salt.} The man said, 'O Messenger of Allah, what is the thing that is unlawful to withhold?' He replied, {That you do good is better for you.}

Abū Dāwūd has also related that the Prophet ﷺ said, {The Muslims are partners in three things: herbage, water and fire.}

Here is an elucidation of the ruling for these four things in light of these ḥadīths:

1. Water: Abū Ḥanīfah and ash-Shāfi'ī ؓ say that excess water that is following or gushing forth, even if it belongs to someone's land, is not withheld. Instead, it must be given freely for sowing.

   Imam Aḥmad ؓ said that is must be given freely for humans and animals to drink and irrigate crops. His speech indicates that withholding only applies when herbage is close by, such that withholding it leads to herbage being withheld.

   Imam Mālik ؓ said that it is not obligatory to give away excess water that is owned, such that its source and its stream are both owned unless it is for someone in need. It is obligatory to give away excess water that is not owned.

2. Herbage: Ash-Shāfi'ī ؓ said that the excess that one owns is withheld unless it is on uncultivated land. Abū Ḥanīfah and Aḥmad ؓ say that it is not withheld under any circumstance.

3. Salt: It is not withheld if it is in open land, i.e. not owned by anyone, and no one has been tasked with extracting it.

4. Fire: It is not permissible to prevent someone from taking some to start his own fire, just as it not permissible to prevent it from being used for light and

heat and to cook food for longer than is needed. As for items that are used to fuel the fire, if they are owned then it permissible to withhold them, even though it is more appropriate that they are not withheld.

5. A Quarter of Fiqh: As-Suyūṭī has mentioned in his book *al-Ashbāh wa an-Naẓā'ir* that the school of ash-Shāfiʿī ﵀ goes rests on four principles:

- The **first** is that **certainty is not removed by doubt**. The foundation for this is what has been related by al-Bukhārī and Muslim in which a man complained to the Prophet ﷺ that something was making him have doubts about his prayer, so he said, {One should not leave unless one hears a sound or smells an odour}. This is because one is certain that one is in a state of purification, and that certainty is not lifted by doubt as to whether one has nullified that state.

- The **second** is that **difficulty brings about facilitation**. The foundation for this is the Exalted One's statement:

  ﴿وَمَا جَعَلَ عَلَيْكُمْ فِي ٱلدِّينِ مِنْ حَرَجٍ﴾

  "He has not placed any constraint upon you in the religion". [al-Ḥajj 22:78]

  And his ﷺ statement {I have been sent with the true, magnanimous religion},[200] as related by Imam Aḥmad in his *Musnad*.

- The **third** is that **harm ceases to be**, and its foundation is his statement ﷺ {There is to be no harm and no reciprocating of harm.}

- The **fourth** is that **custom is an arbitrator**, due to his statement ﷺ {Whatever the Muslims see as good is good in the sight of Allah.}[201]

Based on the aforementioned, this ḥadīth is considered a quarter of Islamic law. The scholars of law have considered it a foundational legal principle, and they have derived numerous branches from it, such as the third principle mentioned above. Here is an elucidation of these principles along with some examples:

The foundational principle:

There is to be no harm and no reciprocating of harm.

Its branch principles include: if someone damages someone else's property, it is not permissible for his property to be damaged in turn, because that would be

200 Ar. *al-ḥanīfiyyah as-samḥah.*

201 The correct position is that this is a statement of Ibn Masʿūd ﵁ as related by Aḥmad in his *Musnad*.

an expansion of harm without any benefit. It would be reciprocating harm. Instead, the person responsible for the damaged pays for the value of what was damaged to ward off harm from the owner of that property.

The branch principles:

1) Harm is averted as much as possible.

In other words, harm must be warded off before it occurs and prevented from happening as much as possible because averting it is easier than lifting it and prevention is better than cure. Legal accountability is according to each individual's capacity.

Its juridical branches include the permissibility of imprisoning people who are known for immorality and corruption until their repentance is manifest, even if no specific judicial crime has been established on their part, to avert any harm they might cause to the society.

2) Harm ceases to be.

In other words, it is obligatory to lift harm that has taken place and to repair whatever damage has been done.

Its juridical branches include: if someone places their drainpipe over the road and it harms passersby, the drainpipe is removed and the owner compensates for any damage that was caused.

3) Harm is not removed by that which is similar to it.

In other words, it is not permissible to remove harm that has occurred by bringing about another form of harm that is similar to it or worse.

Its juridical branches include: a partner is not forced to divide shared property if it is not divisible, because dividing it would be a greater harm than that of partnership.

4) The greater harm is removed in favour of the lesser harm.

In other words, it is permissible to commit that which contains harm if by doing so a greater harm is averted.

Its juridical branches include: it is permissible for a just Muslim ruler to take money from the wealthy that exceeds the obligation of the zakāt if the proceeds of the zakāt do not meet the needs of the poor. This is because harming the wealthy by taking that from them is less than the harm that besets the poor when their needs are not met.

Two further principles bear the same meaning:

The first is: **the lesser of two evils is chosen.**

The second is: **if two causes of corruption contradict each other, the more harmful is taken into consideration.**

5) Specific harm is tolerated to avert general harm.
In other words, if a specific harm contradicts a general harm, the general harm is taken into consideration and must be averted, even if the specific harm would befall some people as a result.

Its juridical branches include: it is permissible for a just Muslim ruler to force hoarders to sell what they have hoarded at the market price, even if that would harm them because a general harm is being averted from the people.

6) Warding off the causes of corruption takes precedence over bringing about benefits.
In other words, if a cause of corruption contradicts a benefit, it is obligatory to avert the cause of corruption, even if that would lead to some benefit being lost.

Its juridical branches include: preventing the sale of narcotics, intoxicants and the like, even if there are profits and economic benefits, because of the causes of corruption they contain pertaining to morality, health and the society as a whole.

7) If preventing and necessitating contradict, preventing takes precedence.
In other words, if some matters bear warnings that it should be prevented as well as exigencies that it should be allowed and tolerated, preventing is preferred.

Its juridical branches include: preventing a partner from disposing of shared wealth in a way that would harm his partner, because it is his partners right to prevent, even though his right necessitates that his disposal is valid and permissible.

8) Harm is never old.
In other words, everything that contains harm eventually ceases to be, and there is no difference between something old and something new. The fact that it is old is not considered as long as it is fundamentally illegitimate due to the harm that it contains.

Its juridical branches include: if someone has a window in a wall that overlooks land that has not been built on and then that land is built on and that window comes to overlook women who are living in that building, the window is removed and no consideration is given to the fact that it was there first.

This principle is considered a qualification for another principle, which is:

Something old is not abandoned because it is old.

In other words, whatever is in people's possession and under their disposal, whether it be things or usufructs, remain theirs as they have always been. The fact that it has been in their possession is considered proof that it is an established right of theirs and was acquired legitimately, as long as there is no evidence to the contrary.

Its juridical branches include: if a tree stump is found belonging to a neighbour and it's bearing down on his neighbour's wall, it is not permissible for this neighbour to remove it because its oldness is evidence that it was placed rightfully and in exchange for something.

6. The ḥadīth informs us that if two men insult each other or push each other around, there is no mutual restoration of rights.[202] Rather, each of them is taken to task for his sin and the judge restores the right of each.

202 Ar. *at-taqāṣṣ*.

THE THIRTY-THIRD ḤADĪTH

أُسُسُ القَضاءِ في الإِسلام

عَنْ ابْنِ عَبَّاسٍ رضي الله عنهما: أَنَّ رَسُوْلَ اللهِ ﷺ قَالَ: {لَوْ يُعْطَى النَّاسُ بِدَعْوَاهُمْ لَادَّعَى رِجَالٌ أَمْوَالَ قَوْمٍ وَدِمَاءَهُمْ، لَكِنَّ الْبَيِّنَةَ عَلَى الْمُدَّعِي وَالْيَمِينُ عَلَى مَنْ أَنْكَرَ}

حديث حسنٌ، رَوَاهُ الْبَيْهَقِي وغَيْرُهُ هكذا، وبَعْضُهُ في الصحيحَيْنِ.

The Foundations of Judging in Islam

It is on the authority of Ibn ʿAbbās رضي الله عنهما that the Messenger of Allah ﷺ said, {If people were given according to what they claim, men would claim people's property and blood. However, clear evidence[203] is required of the claimant and an oath is required from the one who denies the claim.}

This is a good ḥadīth, related as such by al-Bayhaqī and others, and some of it is in the two *Ṣaḥīḥ* collections.

Al-Bayhaqī has related it with this wording. Al-Bukhārī has collected it in the Exegesis of Sūrat Āl ʿImrān (the chapter on the Exalted's statement: **"Those who sell Allah's contract..."**),[204] no.4219. Muslim has collected it in Judgments (the chapter on an oath being required of the defendant), no.1711, and its wording according to Muslim is: {If people were given according to what they claim, people would claim the blood of men and their property, but an oath is required of the defendant.} The wording of al-Bukhārī is: {People's blood and their wealth would go.} In a narration that they share, the Messenger of Allah ﷺ judged that an oath was required of the defendant. The authors of the *Sunan* have collected it: Abū Dāwūd (no.3619), an-Nasāʾī (8/248), at-Tirmidhī (1343) and Ibn Mājah, as well as others, with some variations in wording.

203 Ar. *al-bayyinah.*

204 (tn): Āl ʿImrān 3:77.

The Importance of the Ḥadīth:

An-Nawawī 🌸 said, 'This ḥadīth is one of the major principles that deal with rulings in the Revealed Law.' Sheikh al-Islam Ibn Daqīq al-ʿĪd said, 'This ḥadīth is one of the foundations of rulings, and the greatest reference when there are lawsuits and disputes.'

The Language of the Ḥadīth:

(يعطى الناس) *yuʿṭā n-nāsu*: given what they claim and demand is their right.

(بدعواهم) *bidaʿwāhum*: by merely saying and demanding without there being anything to corroborate their claims, and the word is derived from *duʿā*, which means to request or demand. In the terminology of legal scholars,[205] it is a statement that is accepted in the presence of a judge with which one intends to demand one's right before that of anyone else or to avert someone else from one's right.

(لادّعى رجال) *laddaʿā rijālun*: i.e. some people would regard the blood and property of others as fair game and demand it without right.

(البينة) *al-bayyinah*: which is witnesses; the word is taken from *bayyān*, which means to disclose and make manifest, or the avowal of the defendant and his affirmation of the plaintiff.

(على المدعي) *ʿalā al-muddaʿī*: the one claiming and demanding a right from another.

(اليمين) *al-yamīn*: to swear that what is being claimed against oneself is not true.

(على من أنكر) *ʿalā man ankara*: the defendant makes an oath denying the claim.

Legal Matters and Other Guidance from the Ḥadīth:

1. The Loftiness of Islamic Legislation: Islam is a complete way of life. It includes a pure theology, sincere worship, noble manners and a refined legislation, in which everyone's right is guaranteed. Every individual is protected with regards to his blood, his property and his honour. As long as the judiciary is the reference and the foundation in concluding disputes and ending lawsuits, and the decisive authority in manifesting people's right and guaranteeing them, Islam has laid down rules and principles that prevent those diseased souls from being insolent and having sway, and they protect the Ummah from nonsense and injustice. The best example of this is the ḥadīth of this chapter, which stipulates that there must be

---

205   Ar. *al-fuqahāʾ*.

evidence for the validity and veracity of the claim and it affirms what the appropriate evidence is for each of the litigants, which is what the judge will rely upon in uncovering the truth and giving a verdict accordingly.

2. *Al-Bayyinah* and Its Types: The scholars have made a consensus that what is meant by *bayyinah* is testifying, because it reveals the truth and manifests the claimant's veracity in most cases. Testifying is the means towards this revealing and manifesting because it relies on eye witnessing and being present.

Bayyinah differs, and it is testifying according to the subject matter of the claim and the effects that result from it. In Allah's legislation ﷻ there are four types of testifying that have been established:

The **first** is testifying regarding fornication. This requires four men and a woman's statement is not accepted. The Exalted One has said,

﴿وَٱلَّـٰتِي يَأْتِينَ ٱلْفَـٰحِشَةَ مِن نِّسَآئِكُمْ فَٱسْتَشْهِدُوا۟ عَلَيْهِنَّ أَرْبَعَةً مِّنكُمْ﴾

"If any of your women commit fornication, four of you must be witnesses against them." [an-Nisā' 4:15]

The Glorified One has also said,

﴿وَٱلَّذِينَ يَرْمُونَ ٱلْمُحْصَنَـٰتِ ثُمَّ لَمْ يَأْتُوا۟ بِأَرْبَعَةِ شُهَدَآءَ فَٱجْلِدُوهُمْ﴾

"But those who make accusations against chaste women and then do not produce four witnesses: flog them..." [an-Nūr 24:4]

The **second** is testifying regarding murder and crimes apart from fornication that has clearly defined punishments, such as theft, drinking wine and making a false accusation. In *fiqh*, they are called *ḥudūd* and the stipulation is two male witnesses. Again, a woman's statement is not accepted. The Exalted One has said,

﴿وَأَشْهِدُوا۟ ذَوَىْ عَدْلٍ مِّنكُمْ﴾

"Call two upright men from among yourselves as witnesses..." [at-Ṭalāq 65:2]

Some *fuqahā'*, such as the Shāfi'īs, have added testimony regarding non-financial rights to this category, such as marriage and divorce and the like, and have said that two men must testify in order for them to be established.

The **third** is testifying to establish property rights, such as buying, borrowing, renting and so forth. In these matters, testimony can be from two men or a man and two women. Allah the Exalted has said in the Verse of Debt,[206]

206 Ar. *āyat ad-dayn*.

﴿وَٱسْتَشْهِدُوا۟ شَهِيدَيْنِ مِن رِّجَالِكُمْ ۖ فَإِن لَّمْ يَكُونَا رَجُلَيْنِ

فَرَجُلٌ وَٱمْرَأَتَانِ مِمَّن تَرْضَوْنَ مِنَ ٱلشُّهَدَآءِ﴾

"Two men among you should act as witnesses. But if there are not two men, then a man and two women with whom you are satisfied as witnesses." [al-Baqarah 2:282]

Some *fuqahā'*, such as the Ḥanafīs, have considered testifying regarding all other rights, apart from the *ḥudūd* and retaliation, to be of this category, as has been discussed.

The **fourth** is testifying regarding matters pertaining to women that men are not usually privy to, such as childbirth, virginity, nursing and so forth. In these matters, women's testimony is accepted, even if there are no male witnesses whatsoever. It may even be the case that the testimony of one woman is accepted, is the position of the Ḥanafīs. Al-Bukhārī has related on the authority of 'Uqbah ibn al-Ḥārith ﷺ that he married a daughter of Abū Ihāb ibn 'Azīz. A woman then came and said, 'I nursed 'Uqbah as well as the woman he has married.' 'Uqbah replied to her, 'I didn't know that you had nursed me and you didn't tell me.' He then rode to Madīnah to ask the Messenger of Allah ﷺ and the Messenger of Allah ﷺ said, {How, when it has been said?'} 'Uqbah thus separated from her and married another woman. In other words, how can she remain with you as your wife when it has been said that she is your sister by way of nursing? No one said this apart from that woman.

Those aside from the Ḥanafīs say that there must be a plurality of women in order for their testimony to be accepted, and they understand 'Uqbah separating from his wife to be out of carefulness and to remove himself from something that could be dishonourable. They have also pointed out that the Messenger of Allah ﷺ did not explicitly command him to do so.

3. *Bayyinah* is the Plaintiff's Evidence and an Oath is the Defendant's Evidence: The Muslim judge is commanded to give his decision in favour of the person whose veracity has been established by evidence, whether it is the plaintiff or the defendant. The Wise Lawgiver has made *bayyinah* the plaintiff's evidence. If he can establish it, he deserves what he claims. Likewise, He has made an oath the defendant's evidence. If he makes an oath, he is innocent of whatever is claimed against him. The proof for this is what some narrations of the ḥadīth have clarified in which he ﷺ said, {*Bayyinah* is required of the plaintiff and an oath is required of the defendant}. Related by at-Tirmidhī. It has also been established that the Messenger of Allah ﷺ said to the plaintiff, {Your two witnesses or his oath.} Related by Muslim.

The wisdom behind this allotment is that the plaintiff is claiming something that is concealed, and thus he needs strong evidence to make it manifest. Testifying is a strong evidence because it is the statement of someone who is not an opposing party in a lawsuit, and thus it is on the side of the plaintiff. As for an oath, it is not as strong, because it is the statement of one of the two opposing parties. Furthermore, the defendant is not claiming something that is concealed. Rather, he is adhering to the original state of affairs and its continuity. Thus, it is right for him to have the weaker evidence, which is an oath, and for it to be on his side.

4. The Plaintiff's Evidence Takes Precedence Over the Defendant's: If the claim fulfils the conditions to be admissible in court, the judge listens to it. Then he asks the defendant about it, and if he avows it, the decision is given against him, because avowing is an evidence that the one avowing adheres to. If he denies it, the judge asks the plaintiff to provide witnesses to testify, and if he does, the decision is given in his favour. The judge does not take into account what the defendant says or his denial, even if he vehemently swears to be telling the truth. If the plaintiff is unable to produce witnesses, the judge asks the defendant to make an oath. If he does so, he is declared innocent and the claim is terminated.

The proof for this is what he said ﷺ to the plaintiff: {Do you have witnesses?} He replied, 'No'. He then said, {Then you have his oath.} Related by Muslim. He ﷺ asked the plaintiff about witnesses first and an oath was only required if the witnesses could not be produced. This confirms that the plaintiff's evidence takes precedence over the defendant's evidence.

5. Returning the Oath to the Plaintiff: If the defendant is demanded to give an oath but he refuses and instead requests that the judge have the plaintiff swear and then accept his claim, is his request acceded to?

Some *fuqahā'*, including the Shāfiʿīs, hold the position that his request is acceded to, because it is his right to make an oath and be cleared. If he is content with being judged against based on the opposing party's oath, he is his own judge.

Others, including the Ḥanafīs, hold that the oath is not returned to the plaintiff, because the Messenger of Allah ﷺ said to the plaintiff, {Your two witnesses or his oath. You have nothing from him but that}, as related by al-Bukhārī and Muslim, the wording is that of the latter. This is evidence that the plaintiff is not given a decision based on his oath. Also, the Messenger of Allah ﷺ allotted the evidence between the two litigants when he said, {*Bayyinah* is required of the plaintiff and an oath is required of the defendant}, as related by at-Tirmidhī. Thus, he made oaths the defendant's evidence, which proves that oaths are restricted to his side. If oaths were returned to the plaintiff then some oaths would not be on the defendant's side, and this contradicts the restrictiveness indicated by the text.

6. Judgement on Someone Refusing to Testify in Court: If the defendant is demanded to give an oath but he abstains, i.e. he refuses to swear or make an oath, he is judged against regarding the right that the plaintiff has claimed according to the Ḥanafīs and Ḥanbalīs. This is based on their details as to what can be judged as a refusal to testify is a right and what cannot be judged as such. Their evidence for this is that the Messenger of Allah ﷺ said, {an oath is required from the one who denies the claim}. This is the defendant, and the word *ʿalā*[207] indicates obligation. An intelligent and religious person would not refrain from carrying out his obligations, and therefore his refusal to testify is thus evident that he is avowing the right that is being claimed of him, or he is content with granting that right to the plaintiff. His legal responsibility is to grant his right to the other person, and thus he is judged against accordingly.

The Mālikīs and the Shāfiʿīs say that he is not judged by refusing to testify in court. Rather, the oath is returned to the plaintiff. If he makes an oath, he can take what he has claimed. If not then no. Their evidence is that the defendant is presumed innocent, and thus nothing is required of him until evidence can establish his involvement in someone else's right. Refusal to testify is not adequate evidence of this, because just as it is possible that he is wary of giving a false oath, it is also possible that he is being cautious about giving a truthful oath, and there can be no judgment when there is a possibility.

7. When Does the Defendant Make an Oath? Three of the imams, Abū Ḥanīfah, ash-Shāfiʿī and Aḥmad ﷺ say that every defendant swears an oath when he is asked to do so, and there is no difference between one defendant and another. Their evidence for this is the generality of the ḥadīths that mention making the defendant swear an oath.

Mālik ﷺ says that the defendant does not swear an oath unless some association between him and the plaintiff has been established, such as a transaction, a loan and the like, or the defendant is someone whom can conceivably be accused of what the plaintiff is claiming. His evidence in this is looking out for benefit, so that people do not use allegations as a means to harm one another and drag them into court without justification. It is also so that shameless people do not become insolent towards people of virtue and nobility, to degrade them in front of the court and make them swear oaths, or to strip them of their wealth without right.

8. What Does One Swear By? If one of the two opposing parties is asked to swear an oath, the judge makes him swear by Allah the Exalted. It is not permissible for him to swear by anything else, regardless of whether the one swearing is a Muslim

207 (tn): i.e. as in *ʿalā man ankara.*

or not. Al-Bukhārī, Muslim and others have related on the authority of Ibn ʿUmar ﷺ that the Messenger of Allah ﷺ said, '{Allah has forbidden you from swearing by your ancestors, so whoever swears, let him swear by Allah or remain silent.}

The judge can make the oath more solemn by mentioning Allah's attributes ﷻ. For example, he can say, 'Say, "By Allah, besides whom there is no other god, the Knower of the Unseen and the Visible, the All-Merciful, the Most Merciful', and other attributes that will make the oath weightier in the soul of the one swearing, or make him refrain from swearing if he knows within himself that he is lying. Another aspect of this would be to bring a *muṣḥaf* and make him swear on it if he is a Muslim, while observing the conditions for touching the Qurʾān and carrying it as well as its etiquettes. If he is a Jew, he can swear by Allah the Exalted, who sent the Torah down to Mūsā. If he is a Christian, he can swear by the One who sent down the Injīl to ʿĪsā. If he is an idolater, he can swear by Allah the Exalted, who created him and fashioned him, and so forth.

9. The Etiquettes of Swearing an Oath: When someone has been asked to swear an oath, it is recommended that the judge, and others present, admonish him before he swears, and warn him against making a false oath. They should also recite to him the verses and reports that mention the sin of doing so. Al-Bukhārī and Muslim have related that women were beading in a house or chamber. One of them then came out and the palm of her hand had been pierced with an awl, and she claimed the other woman had done it. The matter was raised before Ibn ʿAbbās ﷺ and he said, 'Remind her of Allah recite to her:

﴿إِنَّ ٱلَّذِينَ يَشۡتَرُونَ بِعَهۡدِ ٱللَّهِ﴾

"Those who sell Allah's contract..." [Āl ʿImrān 3:77].

They thus reminded her and she confessed.

If someone is asked to swear an oath and they know within themselves that it is a lie, they are obligated to admit the truth of the matter and to refrain from swearing an oath. This is because Allah the Exalted has legislated oaths in this situation so that the Muslim's right is protected against loss and destruction. It is also so that shameless people do not use allegations and claims as a means of obtaining people's wealth unlawfully, and thus make claims against them that are not true because they know that they will refrain from swearing and then the decision will be given according to what they claim.

10. Judgment Based on One Witness and an Oath: If the plaintiff cannot produce an adequate *bayyinah*, in that he produces only one witness and his claim cannot be established unless there are two, can the decision be given in his favour if he swears an oath in lieu of the other witness?

The Ḥanafīs say that no decision, in any legal case, is given based on one witness and an oath. Every claim must fulfil the conditions of *bayyinah*. If not, the defendant swears an oath while the plaintiff makes no oath whatsoever. Their proof for this is his statement ﷺ {Your two witnesses or his oath.} and the generality of his statement ﷺ {an oath is required of the defendant.}, as has already been elucidated.

The Mālikīs, Shāfiʿīs and Ḥanbalīs say that a decision can be given based on one witness and the plaintiff's oath when it comes to property rights and whatever is meant by property. Their proof for this is what Muslim has related on the authority of Ibn ʿAbbās ﵁ which is that the Messenger of Allah ﷺ gave a decision based on an oath and one witness.

11. The Plaintiff's Oath along with *Bayyinah* and The Witnesses Being Made to Swear: We know that the plaintiff's evidence is *bayyinah*. If he can produce it, the judge rules in his favour. It has been related from Imam Aḥmad ﵀ that the judge can make the plaintiff swear that his witnesses testified truthfully if he has any doubts about them. Ibn Rajab al-Ḥanbalī has mentioned in *Jāmiʿ al-ʿUlūm wa al-Ḥikam* that Imam Aḥmad ﵀ was asked about this issue, so he said, "Ali did it." The questioner then said, 'Is it right?' He said, "Ali did it." In other words, how can it not be right when ʿAli ﵁ did it? This indicates that this was his position.

Likewise, the judge in this situation can make the witnesses swear oaths, to strengthen their testimonies and dispel doubt.

12. The Judge's Decision Based on His Knowledge: If the judge has some knowledge regarding the truth of the claim that has been presented to him, it is not for him to give a verdict based on that knowledge. Rather, he gives a verdict based on the apparent evidence that is produced by the plaintiff and the defendant, even if the evidence contradicts his knowledge. The support for this is what has been related by al-Bukhārī, Muslim and others from the ḥadīth of Umm Salamah ﵂ in which the Messenger of Allah ﷺ said, {I am only a man. You bring your disputes to me and maybe some of you articulate your evidence more clearly and eloquently than others do, and thus I made a decision based on what I hear. The Messenger of Allah ﷺ is making it clear that he decides based on what he hears and not what he knows. The wisdom behind this is to block the means of oppression and corruption, so that evil judges do not get into a position of tyranny and people take hold of negative suppositions, base their claim to know the truth of the matter. Furthermore, the wisdom is that judging should be far removed from provoking suspicions and doubts when the decision does not correspond with the wishes of either of the opposing parties, and thus they accuse the judge of partiality and bias, of taking bribes, and so forth.

This is what is preferred in *fiqh*, and the schools have details that can be referred to in their proper place.

13. Judging Does Not Make the Unlawful Lawful or the Lawful Unlawful: If the judge has the means to affirm or negate the apparent evidence, such as *bayyinah* and oaths, he gives his decision accordingly, because he is commanded to follow the proofs and evidence that are apparent to him, as we know. Therefore, the recipient of a decision that is not in his favour has to implement what has been decided against him. However, this decision could contradict the truth, i.e. the fact of the matter. For example, the plaintiff could produce two false witnesses, or the defendant could swear a false oath. In this situation, the one who receives a decision in his favour cannot lawfully take what has been decided for him, when he knows within himself that it is not his right. Likewise, the one who receives a decision against him has not done anything unlawful as long as he knows that it is lawful for him and is his right.

An example would be two witnesses bearing false testimony that a woman is divorced and the husband denies that she is divorced. The judge rules that they are separated, but this does not make it lawful for her to marry another man aside from her first husband, because she is still his wife according to Allah's legislation ﷻ. Likewise, it is not unlawful for her husband to be intimate with her, because he never actually divorced her.

The foundation for this is what has reached us from the aforementioned ḥadīth of Umm Salamah ﵂ in which he ﷺ said, {Whoever is given a decision regarding his brother's right must not take it. It is only a piece of the Fire that has been cut off for him.}

He ﷺ forbade the recipient of a decision in his favour to take what he knows is not his right and informed him that it is a piece of the Fire. This indicates that the decision in his favour does not make it lawful for him, and therefore it does not make it unlawful for his opponent.

This is the position of all the respected schools.

14. The Just Judge's Reward: The judge's obligation is to expend his effort to familiarise himself with all sides of the case, and then make a decision according to what his juridical reasoning[208] leads him to believe is the truth, what he thinks is correct. This is due to his statement ﷺ – in what has been related by al-Bukhārī from the ḥadīth of Umm Salamah ﵂ – { I reckon that it is the truth and I give a decision accordingly.} If he does this, his judgement is based on justice and he

208 Ar. *ijtihād.*

is rewarded for what he has done, regardless of whether it agrees with the truth and the fact of the matter or it is mistaken. This is because he has carried out his obligation, which is to seek the truth, and he has judged according to the apparent evidence that he was commanded to judge by. Al-Bukhārī, Muslim and others have related from the ḥadīth of ʿAmr ibn al-ʿĀṣ ﷺ that he heard the Messenger of Allah ﷺ saying, {If the judge has to give a ruling and he uses juridical reasoning and is correct, he has two rewards. If he has to give a ruling, uses juridical reasoning and is then mistaken, he has one reward.}

15. A Judge in Paradise and Two Judges in the Fire: One of the conditions for being on the judiciary is that one be a scholar of the lawful and the unlawful in Allah's legislation ﷻ and that he be capable of referring to the sources of Islamic legislation and extracting rulings in the Revealed Law for cases and incidents that are presented to him. Then he is commanded – as we know – to use juridical reasoning, seek what is correct and judge according to what he thinks is the truth. If he proceeds to give a decision without deliberation and expending effort, or he is ignorant of Allah's legislation ﷻ he is sinful, even if his judgment agrees with the truth and the fact of the matter, because its agreement with the truth was not intended. Furthermore, even if he is correct one time, he will be mistaken every other time. Lastly, woe, absolute woe, be to the judge who knows the truth and judges against it in exchange for some paltry goods of this world or is motivated by personal desires, revenge and oppression.

Abū Dāwūd and others have related that the Prophet ﷺ said, {Judges are three: one is in Paradise and two are in the Fire. As for the one on Paradise, it is a man who knows the truth and judges accordingly. A man who knows the truth and judges oppressively is in the Fire, and a man who judges between people based on ignorance is in the Fire.}

THE THIRTY-FOURTH ḤADĪTH

إِزَالَةُ الْمُنْكَرِ فَرِيضَةٌ إِسْلامِيَّةٌ

عَنْ أَبِي سَعِيدٍ الخُدْرِيِّ ﵁ قَالَ: سَمِعْتُ رَسُولَ اللهِ ﷺ يَقُولُ: {مَنْ رَأَى مِنْكُمْ مُنْكَراً فَلْيُغَيِّرْهُ بِيَدِهِ، فَإِنْ لَمْ يَسْتَطِعْ فَبِلِسَانِهِ، فَإِنْ لَمْ يَسْتَطِعْ فَبِقَلْبِهِ، وَذَلِكَ أَضْعَفُ الإِيْمَانِ.}

رواه مسلم.

Removing the Reprehensible is an Islamic Obligation

It is on the authority of Abū Saʿīd al-Khudrī ﵁ who said, 'I heard the Messenger of Allah ﷺ saying, {Whoever of you sees something reprehensible, let him change it with his hand. If he is not able to then with his tongue. If he is still not able to then with his heart, and that is the weakest of faith.} Related by Muslim.

Muslim has collected the ḥadīth in Faith (the chapter elucidating that forbidding the reprehensible is part of faith, that faith increases and decreases and that commanding the good and forbidding the reprehensible are obligatory), no.49.

The Language of the Ḥadīth:

(منكم) *minkum*: i.e. legally accountable Muslims, the entire Ummah is being addressed here

(منكرا) *munkaran*: which is to leave off an obligation or commit something unlawful, even if it is small

(فليغيره) *falyughayyirhu*: let him remove it and turn it into obedience

(بيده) *biyaddihi*: if that is what changing it requires, such as breaking instruments of distractions, pouring out wine, preventing an oppressor from hitting someone, and so forth

Legal Matters and Other Guidance from the Ḥadīth:

1. The Occasion in Which Abū Saʿīd al-Khudrī Related the Ḥadīth:

Muslim has related on the authority of Ṭāriq ibn Shihāb, who said, 'The first person to start with the *khuṭbah* on ʿĪd Day was Marwān, so a man stood up and said, "The prayer is before the *khuṭbah*'. He[209] replied, 'That has been abandoned'. Abū Saʿīd said, 'As for this person, he has done what was enjoined upon him', i.e. he has carried out the obligation of rebuking a violation of the Messenger of Allah's Sunnah ﷺ. Then he said, 'I heard...' and the rest of the ḥadīth. 'That has been abandoned' means 'what you know about the prayer preceding the *khuṭbah* has been abandoned'.

According to al-Bukhārī and Muslim, Abū Saʿīd ﷺ is the one who pulled him[210] by the hand and said to him what was said, and Marwān responded as quoted above. Perhaps the man rebuked with his tongue first, and then Abū Saʿīd ﷺ tried to change the reprehensible with his hand second, and Allah the exalted knows best.

2. Fighting Against the People of Falsehood:

Truth and Falsehood have been bound together on the face of the earth since mankind came into existence, and every time the flame of faith has died down in people's souls, Allah ﷻ has sent someone to fan it and kindle it. He has prepared men who take up its cause and defend it, and thus the people of falsehood remain humbling themselves. However, when the opportunity presents itself, they spring into action to wreak havoc on the earth. At that point, the task becomes difficult for those whose hearts have merged with the joy of faith, to stand in the face of evil and strike it with word and deed, with the anger of the soul and hatred of the heart. No one acquiesces to evil tyrants, consents to their actions and submits to them except those whose hearts have seen the light of faith put out. They are pleased with disgrace for themselves in this worldly life and the humiliating punishment in the Hereafter.

Muslim has collected the ḥadīth of Ibn Masʿūd ﷺ in which the Prophet ﷺ said, {There is no prophet whom Allah has sent to a nation before me except that he had sincere followers and companions from amongst his nation. They followed his sunnah and obeyed his command. Then there were those who followed one another in evil. They said what they did not do, and they did what they did not command. Whoever fought them with his hand was a believer. Whoever fought them with his tongue was a believer, and whoever fought them with his heart was a believer. After that, there is not even a mustard seed's worth of faith.}

209 (tn): i.e. Marwān.

210 (tn): i.e. Marwān.

3. Rebuking the Reprehensible: The Ummah has made a consensus that it is obligatory to rebuke the reprehensible, and thus the Muslim is obligated to rebuke the reprehensible according to his capacity or to change it according to his ability to change it, by deed or by word, with his hand, with his tongue or with his heart:

A. Rebuking with the heart: Knowing what is right and what is reprehensible and rebuking the reprehensible in one's heart is an individual obligation that every Muslim is legally accountable for. It is not lifted from anyone under any circumstance. Whoever does not know what is right and what is reprehensible in his heart is destroyed, and if someone does not rebuke the reprehensible in his heart, that is an indication that his faith has gone. Abū Juḥayfah ﷺ has related from ʿAlī ﷺ that he said, 'The first *jihād* you employ to defeat the enemy is *jihād* with your hands, then *jihād* with your tongues and then *jihād* with your hearts. When one's heart does not know good and one's heart does not rebuke the reprehensible, matters are turned upside down. That which is above is put below.' Ibn Masʿūd ﷺ heard a man saying, 'Destroyed is the one who does not command what is good and forbid what is reprehensible.' Ibn Masʿūd then said, 'Destroyed is the man whose heart does not know what is good and what is reprehensible.'

B. The rebuke of the heart in times of incapacity: The rebuke of the heart absolves the Muslim of his responsibility when he is unable to rebuke with his hand or tongue. Ibn Masʿūd ﷺ said, 'There will soon be a time in which one of you will live and see that which is reprehensible. He will not be able to do anything other than that which Allah will know that he hates it in his heart.' Incapacity means that he fears harm will come to him, to either himself or his property, and he will not be able to bear it. If someone does not think this will most likely happen to him, the rebuke of his heart will not be enough to fulfil the obligation. Rather, he must rebuke with his hand or his tongue, according to his ability. Aḥmad and Ibn Mājah have collected the ḥadīth of Abū Saʿīd al-Khudrī ﷺ in which he said, 'I heard the Prophet ﷺ saying, {Allah will ask the slave on the Day of Standing until He says, 'What prevented you from rebuking the reprehensible when you saw it?' When Allah has dictated the slave's argument to him, he will say, 'I desired you and I separated from the people.'} In other words, I desired your pardon and forgiveness and I feared that harm would come to be from the people to either my body or my property.

C. Being content with sins and disobedience is an enormity: Whoever knows about a sin and is content with it has committed an enormity, and is guilty of one of the most disgusting unlawful actions, regardless of whether he witnessed it being done or was absent. His sin is like the sin of the one who witnessed it and did not rebuke it. Abū Dāwūd has related from al-ʿUrs ibn ʿUmayrah ﷺ that the Prophet ﷺ said, {If a sin is committed in the land, the one who witnesses it and hates it – and one time, he said, {rebukes it} – is like the one who is absent from it, and the one who is absent from it and pleased with it is like the one who witnesses it.} This is because being pleased with a sin surpasses the rebuke of the heart, which we know is an individual obligation. Abandoning an individual obligation is a major sin. His statement ﷺ {the one who witnesses it and hates it is like the one who is absent from it} means that he bears no sin, and this is if he is incapable of rebuking it with his hand or his tongue, as you know.

D. Rebuking with one's hand or tongue has two rulings:
The **first** is a communal obligation. If one sees something reprehensible or more than one Muslim knows about it, all Muslims are obligated to rebuke it and change it. If some of them do so, even if it is just one, that is sufficient and the requirement is lifted from everyone else. If no one does so, anyone who is able to without excuse and fear is sinful. The evidence that it is a communal obligation is the Exalted One's statement,

﴿وَلْتَكُن مِّنكُمْ أُمَّةٌ يَدْعُونَ إِلَى ٱلْخَيْرِ وَيَأْمُرُونَ بِٱلْمَعْرُوفِ وَيَنْهَوْنَ عَنِ ٱلْمُنكَرِ﴾

"Let there be a group[211] among you who call to the good, enjoin the right and forbid the reprehensible." [Āl 'Imrān 3:104]

The ummah is the group, which is some of the Muslims.

The **second** is an individual obligation. If one sees something reprehensible or one person knows about it, and he is able to rebuke it or change it, he is individually obligated to do so. Likewise, if a group of people see it or know about it and no one can rebuke it apart from one of them, that one person is individually obligated to do so. If he does not, he is sinful. The evidence for this is the generality of his statement ﷺ {Whoever of you sees something reprehensible...}, i.e. no one else sees it, and similar to seeing is knowing about it or being able to do something about it.

4. The Consequences for Abandoning the Removal of the Reprehensible While Being Able to do so: If forbidding the reprehensible is abandoned, the state of evil becomes worse in the land. Disobedience and iniquity become widespread. The people of corruption grow in number and they hold sway over the people of good and subdue them. These people are unable to repel them after having had power over them. Signs of virtue are blotted out and vice becomes common and prevalent. At that point, everyone deserves Allah the Exalted's anger, humiliation and revenge. Allah the Exalted has said,

211 Ar. *ummah.*

﴿لُعِنَ ٱلَّذِينَ كَفَرُوا۟ مِنۢ بَنِىٓ إِسْرَٰٓءِيلَ عَلَىٰ لِسَانِ دَاوُۥدَ وَعِيسَى ٱبْنِ مَرْيَمَ ۚ ذَٰلِكَ بِمَا عَصَوا۟ وَّكَانُوا۟ يَعْتَدُونَ ۝٧٨ كَانُوا۟ لَا يَتَنَاهَوْنَ عَن مُّنكَرٍ فَعَلُوهُ ۚ لَبِئْسَ مَا كَانُوا۟ يَفْعَلُونَ﴾

"Those among the children of Israel who disbelieved were cursed on the tongue of Dāwūd and that of ʿĪsā, son of Maryam, because they rebelled and overstepped the limits. They would not restrain one another from any of the reprehensible things that they did. How evil were the things they used to do!" [al-Māʾidah 5:78-79]

The ḥadīths on this are many, such as:

Abū Dāwūd has collected on the authority of Abū Bakr ﷺ that the Prophet ﷺ said, {There are no people among whom disobedience is committed and then they are able to change but do not change it except that Allah is about to punish all of them.} In another wording: {There are no people among whom disobedience is committed and they are greater in number than those who commit it...}.[212] He has also collected the ḥadīth of Jarīr ﷺ who heard the Prophet ﷺ saying, {There is no man who commits disobedience amongst a people and they can stop him and do not do so except that Allah afflicts them with a punishment before they die.} According to Aḥmad, the wording is: {There are no people among whom disobedience is committed and they are stronger and greater in number than those who commit it and they do not change it except that Allah punishes all of them.}

He has also collected the ḥadīth of ʿAdī ibn ʿUmayr ﷺ who said, 'I heard the Messenger of Allah ﷺ saying, {Allah does not punish the masses because of the deeds of the elite until they see the reprehensible amongst them and are able to rebuke it but do not do so. When that happens, Allah punishes the masses and the elite.} In another narration: {However, if the reprehensible is committed openly, they all deserve punishment.}

The splendid similitude that the Messenger of Allah ﷺ gave us with magnificent elucidation and comprehensive speech suffices us in this matter. He said, {The one who stays and acts within Allah's bounds is like a people who draw lots on a ship. Thus, some of them end up on top and some of them down below. When those down below want some water, they look at those above and say, 'If we made a hole in our part of the ship, we would not harm those above us.' If they let them do what they want, all of them are destroyed. If they prevent them,[213] they are saved and all of them are saved.} Related by al-Bukhārī.

The ḥadīth indicates that every reprehensible act that a person commits in his community is a dangerous breach in the well-being of that community.

212 (tn): i.e. they are greater in number and are thus able to stop a minority from committing disobedience.
213 (tn): i.e. from making a hole in the ship.

5. Correcting a Misunderstanding: Many Muslims make a mistake when they seek to justify their frustrations and shortcomings in rebuking the reprehensible by using the Exalted's statement:

﴿يَـٰٓأَيُّهَا ٱلَّذِينَ ءَامَنُوا۟ عَلَيْكُمْ أَنفُسَكُمْ ۖ لَا يَضُرُّكُم مَّن ضَلَّ إِذَا ٱهْتَدَيْتُمْ﴾

"You who believe! You are only responsible for yourselves. The misguided cannot harm you as long as you are guided." [al-Mā'idah 5:105]

However, this same verse obligates that the reprehensible be rebuked, if it is understood correctly. Abū Dāwūd and others have related from Abū Bakr ﷺ that he said, 'O people! You read this verse and you misapply it: **"You are only responsible for yourselves. The misguided cannot harm you as long as you are guided."** We heard the Prophet ﷺ saying, {When the people see an oppressor and do not prevent him, Allah is about to punish all of them.}

An-Nawawī ﷺ says in his commentary on Muslim, 'The correct position, according to the scholars who verify, is that this verse means: if you do what you have been commanded to do, you will not be harmed by the shortcomings of others, like the Exalted's statement:

﴿وَلَا تَزِرُ وَازِرَةٌ وِزْرَ أُخْرَىٰ﴾

"No bearer of burdens bears another's burden." [al-Anʿām 6:164]

If that is the case, then part of what has been commanded is to enjoin the right and forbid the reprehensible. If one does so and the one being addressed does not comply, the doer is not to be blamed at that point. He has done what he was supposed to, which is to enjoin and forbid, not accept,[214] and Allah knows best.

6. Leaving Rebuke for Fear of it Causing Corruption: If a legally accountable person is able to rebuke the reprehensible that he sees and knows but he thinks that most likely the result of his rebuke will be greater harm and evil, the obligation to rebuke is lifted in this case. This is based on the legal principle[215] that the lesser of two evils is committed to avert the greater of them.

However, one should be aware that that which lifts the obligation to rebuke is that one thinks greater harm is most likely. Merely imagining greater harm or greater harm being a mere possibility, which is the excuse that many Muslims use to justify leaving this immense obligation in Allah's legislation ﷻ is not sufficient.

---

214 (tn): i.e. he is not accountable for making people accept his commanding and forbidding.

215 Ar. *aṣl fiqhī.*

7. Commanding and Forbidding Someone Whom One Knows, or Thinks that Most Likely, Will not Accept: The scholars have held the position that it is obligatory to enjoin and forbid someone whom one knows will not accept it, so that the enjoining and forbidding Muslim will have an excuse therein. What is required of him is the rebuke, not the acceptance[216], as an-Nawawī ﷬ made clear in the statement above. This is because Allah the Exalted says,

﴿فَذَكِّرْ إِنَّمَآ أَنتَ مُذَكِّرٌ﴾

"So remind them! You are only a reminder!" [al-Ghāshiyyah 88:21]

He ﷻ also says,

﴿إِنْ عَلَيْكَ إِلَّا ٱلْبَلَـٰغُ﴾

"Your duty is only to deliver ⌜the message⌝." [ash-Shūrā 42:48]

He ﷻ also says,

﴿وَذَكِّرْ فَإِنَّ ٱلذِّكْرَىٰ تَنفَعُ ٱلْمُؤْمِنِينَ﴾

"And remind them, for truly the believers benefit from being reminded." [adh-Dhāriyāt 51:55]

This is what Abū Saʿīd meant ﷺ when he said, 'As for this person, he has done what was enjoined upon him'. Allah the Exalted has informed us of those who rebuked the transgressors on the Sabbath and they knew that there would be no benefit in admonishing them and rebuking them. The Exalted One has said,

﴿وَإِذْ قَالَتْ أُمَّةٌ مِّنْهُمْ لِمَ تَعِظُونَ قَوْمًا ۙ ٱللَّهُ مُهْلِكُهُمْ أَوْ مُعَذِّبُهُمْ عَذَابًا شَدِيدًا

قَالُوا۟ مَعْذِرَةً إِلَىٰ رَبِّكُمْ وَلَعَلَّهُمْ يَتَّقُونَ﴾

"When a group of them said, 'Why do you rebuke a people whom Allah is going to destroy or severely punish?' They said, 'So that we have an excuse to present to your Lord, and so that hopefully, they will have *taqwā*.'" [al-ʾAʿrāf 7:164]

This is an unequivocal rebuttal of those who turn away from enjoining the right and forbidding the reprehensible, and they also want to stop others from carrying out this obligation, saying, 'Don't wear yourself out. Leave the matter. There's no benefit in saying anything.' Maybe they will mistakenly use this statement of the Exalted's to buttress their argument,

﴿إِنَّكَ لَا تَهْدِى مَنْ أَحْبَبْتَ﴾

"You cannot guide those whom you would like to." [al-Qaṣaṣ 28:56]

216 (tn): i.e. the acceptance of the rebuke.

It is absent from their minds that this verse was revealed regarding Abū Ṭālib, whom the Messenger of Allah ﷺ was still calling to Islam, enjoining the right upon him and forbidding him from the reprehensible, until he breathed his last and was still upon his idolatry. The verse came down to console the Prophet ﷺ as he grieved over his uncle who had defended him and helped him, making it clear that he is not capable of putting guidance in the heart of whomever he would like to. It did not come down to forbid him from commanding and forbidding. How? Allah the Exalted says,

﴿وَإِنَّكَ لَتَهْدِى إِلَىٰ صِرَٰطٍ مُّسْتَقِيمٍ﴾

"Truly you are guiding to a straight path." [ash-Shūrā 42:52]

He ﷻ also says to him,

﴿فَٱصْدَعْ بِمَا تُؤْمَرُ﴾

"Proclaim what you have been ordered to." [al-Ḥijr 15:94]

8. Saying the Truth without Fear or Fright: The Muslim must command the right and forbid the reprehensible without looking at the state of the person he is commanding or forbidding, such as his position, rank or wealth. He must not pay attention to people's censure, nonsense and attempts to make him fail as they have failed. He must not pay attention to any material or immaterial harm that may come his way which he can handle and bear with. However, he uses wisdom therein. He addresses everyone according to what suits them. He gives every situation that which is appropriate.

At-Tirmidhī and Ibn Mājah have collected the ḥadīth of Abū Saʿīd ﵁ in which the Messenger of Allah ﷺ said in a *khuṭbah*, {Awe[217] of people should not prevent a man from saying the truth if he knows it.} Abū Saʿīd ﵁ wept and said, 'By Allah, we have seen things and we had awe.' Imam Aḥmad collected it with the additional wording: {It does not bring one's appointed time nearer or distance one from provision that the truth be said or that a powerful person be reminded.}

Aḥmad and Ibn Mājah have also collected the ḥadīth of Abū Saʿīd ﵁ in which the Prophet ﷺ said, {Let none of you degrades himself.} They said, 'O Messenger of Allah, how can one of us degrade himself?' He said, {Situations arise in which Allah has commanded him to speak but he does not say anything. Allah will thus say to him, 'What prevented you from speaking in this situation and that situation?' He will say, 'I was scared of the people'. Allah will then say, 'I had more right to be feared by you'.}

The scholars have said that these two ḥadīths are understood to refer to when it is nothing but awe that is preventing one from rebuking, not the fear that

---

217   Ar. *haybah*.

would absolve one of rebuking. In other words, and we have already mentioned this, what he fears is a greater evil or harm to himself or property that he will not be able to bear.

9. Commanding and Forbidding Rulers: Enjoining the right and forbidding the reprehensible is an obligation upon the Ummah, just as it is the Ummah's right. The Ummah is comprised of rulers and those who are ruled, and therefore, just as it is obligatory upon rulers to command and forbid their subjects, it is obligatory upon the Ummah to command and forbid their rulers, to carry out the obligation and fulfil the right. You have already seen the ḥadīth of Muslim: {Whoever fought[218] them with his hand...} Their *jihād* was to prevent them from the reprehensible things that they were doing. For example, they would pour out wine and break instruments of distraction, and not carry out whatever disobedience or oppression they commanded.

Saʿīd ibn Jubayr said, 'I said to Ibn ʿAbbās, "Do I enjoin the ruler to do what is right and forbid him from the reprehensible?" He replied, "If you fear that he will kill you then no." I then repeated the question and he gave the same response. I repeated the question again and again he gave the same response. Then he said, "If you must do so, then it is between you and him."' Ṭāwūs said, 'A man came to Ibn ʿAbbās and said, "Should I not stand up to this ruler and thus command him and forbid him?" He replied, "Do not be a tribulation for him." He said, "What if he commands me to disobey Allah?" He replied, "Is that what you mean? If that happens, be a man."'

Imam al-Ḥaramayn said, 'If the ruler of the age becomes tyrannical and his oppression is manifest, and words have not restrained him from his evil actions, it is for Those Who Loose and Bind[219] to work together towards removing him.' Imam an-Nawawī said, 'This applies if it's not feared greater harm will be caused.'

May Allah be pleased with Abū Bakr, who stood up after he had been appointed the *khalīfah* in order to lay down a sound way for the relationship between the ruler and the ruled to proceed in an upright fashion. He said, 'I have been put in charge of you and I am not the best of you. If I do well, assist me. If I do badly, correct me. Obey me as long as I obey Allah regarding you. If I disobey Him, you do not owe me any obedience.' May Allah the Exalted be pleased with ʿUmar, who distinguished between truth and falsehood,[220] for he affirmed the obligation of the ruled to give sincere advice and the obligation of the rulers to accept it. Someone said to him, 'Have *taqwā* of Allah, O ʿUmar', and he spoke to him harshly. Someone else took advantage of the situation, someone who would try to ingratiate himself with the ruler and attain his affection, said, 'Go easy on the Commander of the Believers.' ʿUmar ﷺ then said, 'There is no good in you if you do not say it – i.e. a

218 Ar. *jihād*.

219 Ar. *Ahl al-Ḥalli wa al-ʿAqd*, i.e. the highest-ranking scholars of the Ummah.

220 Ar. *fārūq*.

word of sincere advice – and there is no good in us – i.e. the rulers – if we do not accept it.' May Allah the Exalted grant success to those in charge of the Muslims' affair to follow the example of these extraordinary leaders.

10. Sincere Advice, not Tribulation: Changing the reprehensible with the sword and with weapons from which it is feared tribulations will arise and Muslims' blood will be shed is not what is sought. Rather, it is sincere advice,[221] which is the essence of the religion, as you know from the example of two Rightly-Guided Khālifahs quoted above. He ﷺ said, {The religion is sincerity.} We said, 'For whom?' He replied, {For Allah, His Book, His Messenger, the leaders of the Muslims and their generality.} Related by Muslim. Sincerity for Allah the Exalted's Book is to act in accordance with it. Sincerity for His Messenger ﷺ is to adhere to his Sunnah. Sincerity for the Muslims, the leaders and the public, is that they enjoin one another to good and forbid one another from that which is reprehensible.} The Exalted One has said,

﴿وَٱلْمُؤْمِنُونَ وَٱلْمُؤْمِنَٰتُ بَعْضُهُمْ أَوْلِيَآءُ بَعْضٍ ۚ يَأْمُرُونَ بِٱلْمَعْرُوفِ وَيَنْهَوْنَ عَنِ ٱلْمُنكَرِ وَيُقِيمُونَ

ٱلصَّلَوٰةَ وَيُؤْتُونَ ٱلزَّكَوٰةَ وَيُطِيعُونَ ٱللَّهَ وَرَسُولَهُۥٓ ۚ أُو۟لَٰٓئِكَ سَيَرْحَمُهُمُ ٱللَّهُ ۗ إِنَّ ٱللَّهَ عَزِيزٌ حَكِيمٌ﴾

"The men and women of the believers are friends of one another. They command what is right and forbid what is reprehensible. They establish the prayer and they pay the zakāt, and they obey Allah and His Messenger. They are the people on whom Allah will have mercy." [at-Tawbah 9:71]

11. Harshness and Gentleness in Commanding and Forbidding: Commanding the good and forbidding the reprehensible should be done with wisdom, as the Exalted One has said,

﴿ٱدْعُ إِلَىٰ سَبِيلِ رَبِّكَ بِٱلْحِكْمَةِ وَٱلْمَوْعِظَةِ ٱلْحَسَنَةِ﴾

"Call to the way of your Lord with wisdom and fair admonition." [an-Naḥl 16:125]

The wisdom differs according to the state of the person being commanded and forbidden, what he is being commanded to or forbidden from, and what would be the most beneficial and effective reprimand. Sometimes, one should use gentle words, courtesy and affability, and sometimes only harshness and sternness are appropriate. Addressing Mūsā and Hārūn ﷺ the Exalted One says,

﴿ٱذْهَبَآ إِلَىٰ فِرْعَوْنَ إِنَّهُۥ طَغَىٰ ﴿٤٣﴾ فَقُولَا لَهُۥ قَوْلًا لَّيِّنًا لَّعَلَّهُۥ يَتَذَكَّرُ أَوْ يَخْشَىٰ﴾

221 Ar. *munāṣaḥah.*

"Go to Fir'awn, he has overstepped the bounds. But speak to him with gentle words so that hopefully he will pay heed or show some fear." [Ṭaha 20:43-44]

The Exalted One also says,

﴿يَـٰٓأَيُّهَا ٱلنَّبِيُّ جَـٰهِدِ ٱلْكُفَّارَ وَٱلْمُنَـٰفِقِينَ وَٱغْلُظْ عَلَيْهِمْ﴾

"O Prophet, fight against the disbelievers and hypocrites and be harsh with them." [at-Tawbah 9:73]

He ﷻ also says,

﴿فَٱصْدَعْ بِمَا تُؤْمَرُ﴾

"Proclaim what you have been ordered." [al-Ḥijr 15:94]

For this reason, whoever commands and forbids must have certain qualities, the most important of them being gentleness, forbearance, justice and knowledge. Sufyān ath-Thawrī said, 'No one enjoins the right and forbids the reprehensible except someone who bears there characteristics: he is gentle in what he commands and forbids, he is just in what he commands and forbids, and he has knowledge of what he commands and forbids.' Imam Aḥmad said, 'People need affability and gentleness. The good is commanded without harshness, unless it is a man who is open about his iniquity, he is shown no deference.' Aḥmad also said, 'He commands with gentleness and humility. If they make him hear what he does not like, he does not get angry, and thus desire to give victory to his ego.' He also said, 'When Ibn Mas'ūd's companions passed by a people and saw them doing something they did not like, they would say, "Take it easy, may Allah have mercy on you. Take it easy, may Allah have mercy on you."'

12. Vying in Patience and Bearing with Suffering While Commanding and Forbidding: Ibn Shabramah said, and this is what Aḥmad stipulated, 'Commanding the good and forbidding the reprehensible is like *jihād*. One person must vie with two people in patience, and it is unlawful for him to flee from them. It is not obligatory upon him to vie in patience any more than that. If he has to bear with suffering and he can cope with it that is better. The Exalted One has said,

﴿وَأْمُرْ بِٱلْمَعْرُوفِ وَٱنْهَ عَنِ ٱلْمُنكَرِ وَٱصْبِرْ عَلَىٰ مَآ أَصَابَكَ﴾

"Command what is right, forbid what is reprehensible and be steadfast in the face of everything that happens to you." [Luqmān 31:17]

Thus, if someone fears insults or hearing unpleasant words, that does not lift his obligation to rebuke things like this.

13. Nobility, not Humiliation: Whatever suffering the Muslim may undergo while commanding or forbidding is not considered humiliation or degradation. Rather, it is honour, nobility and high standing in this life and the Hereafter, as well as a testimony for the sake of Allah ﷻ or indeed, it is the greatest testimony.

It was said to Aḥmad, 'Has it not reached us that the Messenger of Allah ﷺ said, {It is not for the believer to humiliate himself}? In other words, he should not expose himself to tribulations that he is unable to bear?' He replied, 'This is not the same as that.' In other words, someone knows that he cannot bear the suffering and be patient with it. The statement was made regarding someone who knows that he can be patient. The former rebukes with his heart and his safe, and if he rebukes with his hand that is better.

What he said is further evidence by what has been collected by Abū Dāwūd, at-Tirmidhī and Ibn Mājah, which is the ḥadīth of Abū Sa'īd ؓ in which the Messenger of Allah ﷺ said, {The best *jihād* is a word of justice in front of a tyrannical ruler.} Al-Ḥākim has collected a ḥadīth from Jābir ؓ in which the Messenger of Allah ﷺ said, {The master of the martyrs is Ḥamzah ibn 'Abdul Muṭṭalib and a man who stands in front of a tyrant and commands him and forbids him, and then the tyrant kills him.} In the *Musnad* of al-Bazzār, it is on the authority of Abū 'Ubaydah ibn al-Jarrāḥ ؓ that he said, 'I said, "O Messenger of Allah, who are the noblest martyrs in the sight of Allah?' He replied, {A man who stands in front of a tyrannical ruler, commands him to do good and forbids him from the reprehensible, and then the tyrant kills him.} Ḥamzah being the master of the martyrs means that he has the greatest reward and is nearest to Allah the Exalted.

14. Rebuking the Reprehensible that is Outward or Known, not Eavesdropping on that Which is Hidden, Suspected and Veiled:

A Muslim must rebuke the reprehensible if it is outward and he witnesses it and sees it. The evidence for this is his words ﷺ {Whoever of you sees something reprehensible} If doubt or suspicion comes to him regarding something reprehensible that is hidden and veiled from him, he does not turn his attention to it or investigate it, because that would be a type of eavesdropping that is forbidden.

Knowledge of something reprehensible takes the place of seeing it, and verifies that it is happening and where. For example, a trustworthy person could inform one of such, or there could be indications that make one think it most likely that something reprehensible is happening. In this situation, one must rebuke in a way that is appropriate and can guarantee that the reprehensible action will be put to an end, and uproot evil and corruption from communities. Can he scale walls and raid houses, and have the audacity to disclose, investigate and verify? He looks. If the reprehensible action that is being kept secret and he thinks is most likely occurring is a violation of something sacred, and the opportunity to redress it will be lost if he waits or deliberates, such as fornication or murder, he can do these things. Indeed, when it comes to matters like this, he can eavesdrop in places that are surrounded by doubts and suspicions, so that the viruses of vice do not become active in the seats of filth and sin. If the reprehensible actions are not of this nature, it is not for him to do these things. It was said to Ibn Masʿūd ﵁ 'So-and-so has wine dripping from his beard.'[222] He replied, 'Allah has forbidden us from eavesdropping.'

15. There is no Rebuking in That Which is Differed Over: The scholars have affirmed that rebuking is for doing something that the Muslims have declared unlawful by consensus, or leaving something that has been declared obligatory by consensus, such as drinking wine, dealing in usury, women revealing themselves, and so forth, or abandoning the prayer, *jihād* and other obligations.

As for that which the scholars have differed over as to whether it is unlawful or not or obligatory or no, no one is rebuked for doing them or not doing them, provided that this difference of opinion is one that the scholars recognise and is based on evidence. No consideration is given to the opinions of innovators and cults[223] that contradict the Sunnah, such as the Khawārij and the like. Likewise, no consideration is given to a divergent opinion that is weak because it has no evidence, or contradicted by the establishment of authentic evidence. Examples of this would include *nikāḥ al-mutʿah,* which is a marriage for a set period of time. It is invalid and the one who does it is rebuked. Indeed, he is considered a fornicator and is given the *ḥadd* punishment, even though some Muslim groups have affirmed it because its unlawfulness has been established by authentic, unequivocal evidence and its lawfulness has been abrogated.

16. The Generality of the Responsibility and Its Specialness: Commanding the good and forbidding the reprehensible is an obligation upon the entire Ummah. Every Muslim who knows about something reprehensible and is able to rebuke to it is obligated to do so in the way that you have learnt. There is no difference therein between the ruler and the ruled, or the scholar and the layman. The Exalted One has said,

﴿كُنتُمْ خَيْرَ أُمَّةٍ أُخْرِجَتْ لِلنَّاسِ تَأْمُرُونَ بِٱلْمَعْرُوفِ وَتَنْهَوْنَ عَنِ ٱلْمُنكَرِ﴾

"You are the best nation ever to be produced before mankind. You enjoin the right, forbid the reprehensible..." [Āl ʿImrān 3:110]

The Glorified One has also said,

﴿وَٱلْمُؤْمِنُونَ وَٱلْمُؤْمِنَـٰتُ بَعْضُهُمْ أَوْلِيَآءُ بَعْضٍ ۚ يَأْمُرُونَ بِٱلْمَعْرُوفِ وَيَنْهَوْنَ عَنِ ٱلْمُنكَرِ﴾

222 (tn): i.e. he drinks wine.
223 Ar. *firaq*.

"The men and women of the believers are friends of one another. They command what is right and forbid what is reprehensible." [at-Tawbah 9:71]

Both addresses to the nation are general, and likewise, most of the texts of the Sunnah bear a general address, for all individuals: {So that you command the good and forbid the reprehensible}, {Whoever of you sees something reprehensible, let him change it...} However, this responsibility is emphasised for two classes of people: the scholars and the rulers.

A. As for the scholars, it is because they have knowledge of Allah the Exalted's legislation that other members of the Ummah do not have. It is also because people's hearts and souls hold them in reverence and respect, which makes their commanding and forbidding more likely to be obeyed and more conducive to acceptance. It is because Allah the Exalted has granted them wisdom and fair admonition. The Exalted One has said,

﴿يَرْفَعِ ٱللَّهُ ٱلَّذِينَ ءَامَنُوا۟ مِنكُمْ وَٱلَّذِينَ أُوتُوا۟ ٱلْعِلْمَ دَرَجَـٰتٍ﴾

"Allah will raise in rank those of you who believe and those who have been given knowledge." [al-Mujādalah 58:11]

There is great danger when the scholars of the Ummah are negligent regarding this trust that Allah the Exalted has placed on their necks. Abū Dāwūd and at-Tirmidhī have related, the wording being that of the latter, on the authority of Ibn Masʿūd ﷺ who said, 'The Messenger of Allah ﷺ said, {When the Children of Israel fell into disobedience, their scholars forbade them but they did not desist. Then they started sitting with them in their gatherings, they developed relationships of mutual trust, they drank with them, and thus Allah struck their hearts against one another and cursed them on the tongues of Dāwūd and ʿĪsā the son of Maryam. That is because they overstepped the limits.}[224] The Messenger of Allah ﷺ sat down and leaned back. Then he said, {No, by the One in whose hand is my soul, until they brought them back to the truth.} In other words, they made them bear with it, they held them to it, they became attached to them and they brought them back to it.

B. As for the rulers, their responsibility is greater. The danger if they fall short in commanding and forbidding is more considerable, because the rulers have sovereign power and authority. They have the ability to implement what they command and forbid and to make people comply. No harmful consequence is to be feared from their rebuke, because the force and the weapons are in their

224 (tn): See Sūrat al-Māʾidah 5:78.

hands and people still attach importance to what the ruler commands and forbids. This is why he ﷺ said, {Those who are restrained by the ruler are more than those who are restrained by the Qur'ān.} Ibn al-Athīr has mentioned it in *an-Nihāyah*. In other words, there are people who are not affected by admonition and instruction and thus refrain from violating and instead submit to the truth, but they will be restrained and held back when the ruler shows them his stick or the lustre of his sword.

When the ruler falls short in commanding and forbidding, the people of disobedience and iniquity become covetous and spring into action to spread evil and corruption, without respecting any sanctity or revering any law. This is why one of the fundamental attributes of a ruler whom Allah supports and gives victory to, makes his kingdom firm and shows him the right way, is that he commands what is right and forbid the reprehensible. The Exalted One has said,

﴿وَلَيَنصُرَنَّ ٱللَّهُ مَن يَنصُرُهُۥٓ ۗ إِنَّ ٱللَّهَ لَقَوِىٌّ عَزِيزٌ ۝ ٱلَّذِينَ إِن مَّكَّنَّـٰهُمْ فِى ٱلْأَرْضِ أَقَامُواْ ٱلصَّلَوٰةَ وَءَاتَوُاْ ٱلزَّكَوٰةَ وَأَمَرُواْ بِٱلْمَعْرُوفِ وَنَهَوْاْ عَنِ ٱلْمُنكَرِ ۗ وَلِلَّهِ عَـٰقِبَةُ ٱلْأُمُورِ﴾

"Allah will certainly help those who help him; Allah is All-Strong, Almighty. They are those who, if We establish them firmly on the earth, will establish the prayer and pay the zakāt, and command what is right and forbid what is wrong. The end result of all affairs is with Allah." [al-Ḥajj 22:40-41]

Establishing them firmly on the earth means to makes them rulers and leaders.

Thus, when the rulers neglect this immense obligation, they betray the trust that Allah has placed on their necks, and they neglect the people that Allah the Exalted has put them in charge of.

It is an absolute calamity when the rulers themselves become immersed in reprehensible behaviour and refuse to listen to any sincere adviser or guide. Even worse is when they command the reprehensible and forbid the good, and act according to other than Allah's legislation ﷻ. Thus, it befits the rulers of the Muslims to familiarize themselves with Allah's legislation ﷻ. They should seek His protection and assistance in establishing Allah's legislation, commanding the people to good and working in spreading it, forbidding them from the reprehensible and working to uproot it from communities, and warning them against becoming those whom Allah ﷻ has described by saying,

﴿وَجَعَلْنَـٰهُمْ أَئِمَّةً يَدْعُونَ إِلَى ٱلنَّارِ ۖ وَيَوْمَ ٱلْقِيَـٰمَةِ لَا يُنصَرُونَ﴾

"We made them leaders, summoning to the Fire, and on the Day of Standing they will not be helped." [al-Qaṣaṣ 28:41]

17. Some of The Etiquettes of the One Who Commands and Forbids: Such a person should follow what he commands and avoid what he forbids, so that his commanding and forbidding has an effect on the soul of whomever he is commanding and forbidding. It is also so that his deeds will be accepted by Allah ﷻ and his conduct will not be evidence against him that will put him in the Fire on the Day of Standing. The Exalted One has said,

﴿يَـٰٓأَيُّهَا ٱلَّذِينَ ءَامَنُوا۟ لِمَ تَقُولُونَ مَا لَا تَفْعَلُونَ ۝ كَبُرَ مَقْتًا عِندَ ٱللَّهِ أَن تَقُولُوا۟ مَا لَا تَفْعَلُونَ﴾

"You who believe! Why do you say what you do not do? It is deeply abhorrent to Allah that you should say what you do not do." [as-Ṣaff 61:2-3]

Al-Bukhārī and Muslim have narrated from Usāmah ibn Zayd ﷺ who said, 'I heard the Messenger of Allah ﷺ saying, {A man will be brought on the Day of Standing and then thrown into the Fire. Then his bowels and intestines will come out, and he will go around the Fire the way a donkey goes around a quern. Then the people of the Fire will gather around him and say, 'O so-and-so? What happened to you? Did you not command the good and forbid the reprehensible?' He will reply, 'Indeed I did. I commanded the good and I did not approach it. I forbade the reprehensible and I did approach it.'}

18. Some of the Qualities of Faith: Commanding the good and forbidding the reprehensible is one of the qualities of faith. The precedence of the one who commands and forbids varies according to the degree of his commanding and forbidding. The one who changes with his hand is better than the one who changes with his tongue, and the one who changes with his tongue is better than the one who confines himself to rebuking with his heart, even if he is incapable of what is mentioned before. This is evidenced by his statement ﷺ: {... and that is the weakest of faith.} It is also evidenced by his statement ﷺ {The strong believer is better and more beloved to Allah than the weak believer, and there is good in both.}

19. The Intention and Objective Behind Commanding and Forbidding: That which motivates one to command and forbid should be the seeking of Allah the Exalted's pleasure and obeying His command, not love of fame and rank and other worldly objectives. The believer commands and forbids out of anger for the sake of Allah the Exalted when His sacred things have been violated. He does so to give sincere advice to the Muslims and to have compassion for them when he sees them do something that could expose them to Allah's wrath ﷻ and His punishment in this life and the Hereafter.

He seeks to deliver them from the evil of the woes and afflictions that occur when people immerse themselves in wrong conduct and are led by their passions and desires. Behind all of this, he seeks the reward and recompense from Allah and he protects himself from being punished in the Fire for neglecting this obligation and neglecting to command and forbid. Al-Bukhārī and Muslim have related from Jarīr ibn ʿAbdillāh al-Bajlī who said, 'I pledged allegiance to the Messenger of Allah that I would establish the prayer, pay the zakāt and give sincere advice to every Muslim.

20. True Slavehood: The believer's motive for commanding and forbidding could be his profound veneration of Allah's sublimity and his awareness that He is worthy of being obeyed and not disobeyed, of being remembered and not forgotten, of being thanked and not shown ingratitude. That kindles in his soul true love for Allah which becomes firmly established in his heart and flows throughout his spirit the way blood flows through veins.

This is why you find him preferring for the creation to be upright. He wants them to submit to the truth in every matter, and he sacrifices every precious and valuable thing he has for that cause. Indeed, he does so even if hardship and suffering come his way. He accepts that with magnanimity, and maybe he will implore Allah to forgive whoever mistreated him and to guide him to the straight path. No one reaches this rank unless he realised within his soul sincere slavehood to Allah. Look at him how his people harmed him and beat him. He started wiping the blood from his face, saying, {O Allah, forgive my people, for they do not know.} Someone from the First Three Generations said, 'I want all of the creation to obey Allah and that my flesh be cut with scissors.' ʿAbdullah ibn ʿUmar ibn ʿAbdul ʿAzīz would say to his father, 'I want me and you to be boiled in a pot for the sake of Allah the Exalted.' All of this is because of none other than the fact that their perfected faith had made them love for people what they love for themselves, as you know.

21. Summary and Instruction from a Pious Scholar:
Imam an-Nawawī – this pious scholar whose life Allah blessed and put benefit in his knowledge – says some words in his commentary on *Ṣaḥīḥ Muslim*, which are probably the choicest words on this topic as well as a comprehensive method. We wanted to present them to you here. He says, 'Know that this field, I mean the field of commanding the good and forbidding the reprehensible, has been mostly lost through the passage of time. Nothing of it remains in our times apart from a very few vestiges. It is an immense field; the foundation and basis of everything. When wretched filth[225] increases, the punishment encompasses both the righteous and the wicked. When no one takes the hand of the oppressor, Allah's punishment is about to encompass all of them:

﴿فَلْيَحْذَرِ ٱلَّذِينَ يُخَالِفُونَ عَنْ أَمْرِهِۦٓ أَن تُصِيبَهُمْ فِتْنَةٌ أَوْ يُصِيبَهُمْ عَذَابٌ أَلِيمٌ﴾

225 Ar. *khubuth.*

"Those who oppose his command should beware of a testing trial coming to them or a painful punishment striking them." [an-Nūr 24:63]

'The one who seeks the Hereafter and strives to attain Allah's pleasure ﷻ should be concerned with this field, for its benefit is immense, especially when most of it has gone, and make his intention sincere. He does not fear anyone's rebuke, because his own rank will be elevated. Allah the Exalted has said,

﴿وَلَيَنصُرَنَّ ٱللَّهُ مَن يَنصُرُهُۥٓ﴾

"Allah will certainly help those who help Him." [al-Ḥajj 22:40]

The Exalted One has also said,

﴿وَمَن يَعْتَصِم بِٱللَّهِ فَقَدْ هُدِىَ إِلَىٰ صِرَٰطٍ مُّسْتَقِيمٍ﴾

"Whoever holds fast to Allah has been guided to a straight path." [Āl 'Imrān 3:101]

The Exalted One has also said,

﴿وَٱلَّذِينَ جَٰهَدُوا۟ فِينَا لَنَهْدِيَنَّهُمْ سُبُلَنَا﴾

"As for those who struggle for Our sake, We will guide them to our paths." [al-'Ankabūt 29:69]

The Exalted One has also said,

﴿أَحَسِبَ ٱلنَّاسُ أَن يُتْرَكُوٓا۟ أَن يَقُولُوٓا۟ ءَامَنَّا وَهُمْ لَا يُفْتَنُونَ ﴿٢﴾

وَلَقَدْ فَتَنَّا ٱلَّذِينَ مِن قَبْلِهِمْ ۖ فَلَيَعْلَمَنَّ ٱللَّهُ ٱلَّذِينَ صَدَقُوا۟ وَلَيَعْلَمَنَّ ٱلْكَٰذِبِينَ﴾

"Do people imagine that they will be left to say, 'We believe', and will not be tested?' We tested those before them so that Allah would know the truthful and would know the liars." [al-'Ankabūt 29:2-3]

'Know that the reward is according to the effort one expends. One does not leave it off due to friendship, love or flattery, or to ingratiate oneself with someone and maintain one's rank with them. Friendship and love necessitate that a person has sanctity and a right, and it is their right to be given sincere advice and guided to that which will benefit them in the Hereafter and deliver them from that which will harm them therein. If someone is your friend and they love you, they strive to make your Hereafter flourish, even if that leads to some diminishment in your worldly life.

'Your enemy is the one who strives to ruin or diminish your Hereafter, even if you attain some benefit in your worldly life. Iblīs has been our enemy in this, while the Prophets ﷺ have been the believers' friends in their strive for the Hereafter and in guiding them to it. We ask Allah, the Noble, to grant us, our loved ones and all Muslims success in pleasing Him, and to gather us all under His generosity and mercy, and Allah knows best.'

He ﷺ also said, 'The one who commands the good and forbids the reprehensible should be gentle, so that he can be closer to attaining that which is sought. Imam ash-Shāfiʿī ﷺ said, "Whoever admonishes his brother privately has given him sincere advice and adorned him, and whoever admonishes him in public has dishonoured him and disgraced him." An example of people being negligent in this field is when they see someone selling defective merchandise, or something similar, and they do not rebuke him for doing so and do not inform the buyer of its defect. This is a manifest error, and the scholars have clearly stipulated that whoever knows about this is obligated to rebuke the seller and inform the buyer, and Allah knows best.

THE THIRTY-FIFTH ḤADĪTH

أُخُوَّةُ الإِسْلامِ وَحُقوقُ المُسْلِمِ

عَنْ أَبِي هُرَيْرَةَ ﷺ قَالَ: قَالَ رَسُوْلُ اللهِ ﷺ: {لَا تَحَاسَدُوْا، وَلَا تَنَاجَشُوْا، وَلَا تَبَاغَضُوْا، وَلَا تَدَابَرُوْا، وَلَا يَبِعْ بَعْضُكُمْ عَلَى بَيْعِ بَعْضٍ، وكُونُوْا عِبَادَ اللهِ إِخْوَانًا، المُسْلِمُ أَخُو المُسْلِمِ: لَا يَظْلِمُهُ وَلَا يَخْذُلُهُ وَلَا يَكْذِبُهُ، وَلَا يَحْقِرُهُ، والتَّقْوَى هٰهُنا - وَيُشِيْرُ إِلَى صَدْرِهِ ثَلَاثَ مَرَّاتٍ - بِحَسْبِ امْرِىءٍ مِنَ الشَّرِّ أَنْ يَحْقِرَ أَخَاهُ المُسْلِمَ، كُلُّ المُسْلِمِ عَلَى المُسْلِمِ حَرَامٌ: دَمُهُ وَمَالُهُ وَعِرْضُهُ.} رواه مسلم

The Brotherhood of Islam and the Muslim's Rights

It is on the authority of Abū Hurayrah ﷺ that the Messenger of Allah ﷺ said, {Do not envy one another, do not bid against one another, do not hate one another, do not turn your backs on one another and let none of you sell on top of another's sale. Be slaves of Allah, brothers. A Muslim is a brother of a Muslim. He does not wrong him, abandon him, lie to him or have contempt for him. *Taqwā* is here} and he pointed to his chest three times. {It is sufficient evil for a man that he should have contempt for his Muslim brother. Every part of the Muslim is sacred for the Muslim: his blood, his property and his honour.} Related by Muslim.

Muslim has related the ḥadīth in Book of Righteousness and Maintaining Ties of Kinship (the chapter on the unlawfulness of suspicion, spying and rivalry), no.2564.

The Importance of the Ḥadīth:
In stressing the importance of Islamic brotherhood, The Noble Messenger ﷺ does not confine himself to raising it as a slogan. Instead, he surrounds it with commands and prohibitions that makes it a tangible reality between the members of the Muslim community. This ḥadīth comprises several rulings and immense benefits connected to the attainment of this noble, Islamic objective. It also shows how it can be protected from every defect and disturbance, so that brotherhood

does not become words that people utter, or a fantasy that they dream about but never experience any trace of in their daily lives. This is what an-Nawawī, in *al-Adhkār*, said about this ḥadīth, 'How immense is its usefulness, how abundant are its benefits'.

Ibn Ḥajar al-Haytamī said, 'It is a ḥadīth that has abundant benefits. It points out the most principles and objectives. Indeed, upon reflection of its meaning and understanding its content, one can see that it comprises all the rulings of Islam, either explicitly or implicitly. It also comprises all the etiquettes, by ascertaining them or by alluding to them'.

The Language of the Ḥadīth:

(لا تحاسدوا) *la taḥāsadū*: the original verb is *la tataḥāsadū*, one of the *tā's* has been omitted for the sake of facilitation. The meaning is let none of you wishes that someone else's blessing is removed.

(لا تناجشو) *la tatanājashū*: in the language, *najsh* means deception and trickery, or rise and increase. In the Revealed Law, it means to increase the declared price of a commercial article in the market, or somewhere similar, but not out of a desire to buy it but to harm someone else.

(لا تباغضوا) *la tabāghaḍū*: do not give one another reasons to hate one another

(لا تدابرو) *la tadābarū*: Turning backs on one another (*tadābur*) means estrangement and avoidance. It comes from the word *dubr* (back), because when avoiding someone in person one turn's one back and face away from them. It is a severance of mutual relations.

(لا يخذله) *la yakhdhuluhu*: he does not fail to assist him when he is engaged in commanding the right and forbidding the wrong, or when he demands one of his rights. Rather, he helps him and assists him and protects him from harm as much as possible.

(لا يكذبه) *la yakdhibuhu*: he does not tell him something that contradicts the facts of the matter.

(لا يحقره) *la yaḥqiruhu*: he does not undervalue his significance and detract from his rank.

(بحسب امرىء من الشر) *bihasbi mrin min asharr*: it is sufficient evil for him to have contempt for his brother, i.e. this is an immense evil that is sufficient to warrant the doer's punishment for this sin.

(عرضه) *ʿirḍuhu*: *ʿirḍ* (honour) is the place of praise and blame in a person.

Legal Matters and Other Guidance from the Ḥadīth:
1. The Prohibition of Envy:
A. Definition: Envy (*ḥasad*) in the language and in the Revealed Law means to hope that the envied person's blessing is removed and given to the envier or someone else. It is a blameworthy disposition embedded firmly in human nature, because man hates to see anyone of his species surpassing him in anything good.

B. Ruling: The scholars of the Revealed Law, and others, have made a consensus that envy is unlawful and sinful, and the texts of the Revealed Law on this are many in both the Book and the Sunnah. For example, Allah the Exalted reprimands the Jews by saying:

﴿وَدَّ كَثِيرٌ مِّنْ أَهْلِ ٱلْكِتَـٰبِ لَوْ يَرُدُّونَكُم مِّنۢ بَعْدِ إِيمَـٰنِكُمْ كُفَّارًا حَسَدًا مِّنْ عِندِ أَنفُسِهِم﴾
"Many of the People of the Book would love it if they could make you revert to being unbelievers after you have become believers, showing their innate envy." [al-Baqarah 2:109]

The Exalted One has also said,

﴿أَمْ يَحْسُدُونَ ٱلنَّاسَ عَلَىٰ مَآ ءَاتَىٰهُمُ ٱللَّهُ مِن فَضْلِهِۦ﴾
"Or do they in fact envy other people for the bounty Allah has granted them?" [an-Nisāʾ 4:54]

Imam Aḥmad and at-Tirmidhī have narrated the ḥadīth of Zubayr ibn al-ʿAwām in which the Prophet ﷺ said, {The disease of the nations before you is creeping towards you: envy and hatred. Hatred is the shaver, the shaver of the religion, not the shaver of hair. By the One in whose Hand is Muḥammad's soul, you do not truly believe until you love one another. Shall I not inform you of something which, if you do it, will make you love another? Spread peace amongst yourselves.}

Imam Abū Dāwūd has narrated the ḥadīth of Abū Hurayrah in which the Prophet ﷺ said, {Beware of envy, for envy consumes good deeds the way fire consumes firewood.} Or he said, {...grass.}

Al-Ḥākim and others have narrated the ḥadīth of Abū Hurayrah in which the Prophet ﷺ said, {My Ummah will be afflicted with the disease of previous nations.} They said, 'O Prophet of Allah, what is the disease of previous nations?} He replied, {Insolence and wantonness, accumulation and competition in this worldly life, mutual hatred and envy, until there are injustice and killing.}

C. The wisdom behind its unlawfulness: It is an objection against Allah the Exalted and stubborn resistance of the fact that He has blessed someone else, along with one's attempt to nullify what The Exalted One has done and remove His bounty, Abū Ṭayyib said,

The most oppressive person on earth is the envier
Of the one who spends the night at home in His grace

Envying wearies the soul and causes it grief with no benefit and in an unlawful way. It is a vile conduct.

D. The categories of the people of envy:

i. A category who strive to remove the envied person's blessing, by being unjust towards him in word and deed. Amongst them is the person who strives to have that blessing transferred to him and amongst them is the person who strives only to have the envied person's blessing removed, without it being transferred to him, and the latter is the evilest and wretched of the two.

ii. Another category of people are those who envy someone else but do not act upon their envy. They are not unjust towards the envied person in word and deed. It has been related from al-Ḥasan al-Baṣrī that such a person is not sinful. It has been related via weak chains of transmissions *marfūʿan*.[226] There are two types:

a. One is not able to remove the envy from oneself. He is overwhelmed by it and thus he is not sinful.

b. One voluntarily provokes it within oneself, and restores it and initiates it within oneself because one finds comfort in hoping that his brother's blessing will cease to be. This is similar to someone who is resolved and determined to commit disobedience, and there is a difference of opinion amongst the scholars regarding his punishment. However, he is far from being safe from oppressing the envied person indeed, and thus being sinful, and he strives to attain similar good things, as Allah the Exalted has said,

﴿قَالَ ٱلَّذِينَ يُرِيدُونَ ٱلْحَيَوٰةَ ٱلدُّنْيَا يَـٰلَيْتَ لَنَا مِثْلَ مَآ أُوتِىَ قَـٰرُونُ﴾

"Those who desired the life of this world said, 'Oh! If only we had the same as Qārūn has been given." [al-Qaṣaṣ 28:79]

---

226 (tn): i.e. attributed to the Messenger of Allah ﷺ.

If these good things are of the religion then it is fine. The Prophet ﷺ wished for martyrdom in Allah's cause. As related by al-Bukhārī and Muslim, the Messenger of Allah ﷺ said, {There is no envy except of two: a man whom Allah has granted wealth and thus he spends night and day, and a man whom Allah has granted the Qur'ān and thus he stands with it by night and by day.} This is actually *ghibṭah*, and is only called 'envy'[227] by way of metaphor.

iii. A third category is a person who finds envy within himself and strives to remove it. He does so by acting well towards the envied person, by initiating good relations with him, supplicating for him and spreading his virtues. He strives to remove the envy that he finds within himself until he replaces it with love for the Muslim to be better than him and superior to him. This is from the highest ranks of faith. The one who bears this is a perfect believer who loves for his brother what he loves for himself.

2. The Prohibition of *Najsh*:

A. Definition: The ḥadīth includes the prohibition of *najsh*, which means to increase the declared price of a commercial article in the market, or somewhere similar, but not out of a desire to buy it but to harm someone else.

B. Ruling: It is unlawful by consensus for the one who knows about the prohibition, regardless of whether or not he has colluded with the seller, because it is fraud and deception, both of which are unlawful. It is also because it is an abandonment of the obligation to give sincere advice. The Messenger of Allah ﷺ said, {Whoever defrauds us is not from us}, and in another narration, {Whoever defrauds...}[228] Al-Bukhārī and Muslim have narrated from Ibn 'Umar that the Prophet ﷺ prohibited *najsh*. Ibn Abī Awfā said, 'The *nājish*[229] is a treacherous consumer of usury.'

Ibn 'Abdul Barr said, 'They have made a consensus that one who does it is disobeying Allah the Exalted if he knows about the prohibition.

C. The ruling for a sale that is contracted with *najsh*: The scholars have differed over this. Some have said that it is invalid, and it is a narration from Aḥmad and is the chosen position of some of his companions.

Others have said that if the *nājish* is the seller or someone who has colluded with the seller to commit *najs* then it is invalid, because the prohibition here goes back to those who contract the sale. If that is not the case, it is not invalid, because it goes back to someone who is external to the contract. Likewise, it has been related from ash-Shāfi'ī that he justified the validity of the sale on the basis that the seller is not the *nājish*, and most of the jurists have held that the sale is

227 Ar. *ḥasad*.

228 (tn): i.e. whoever defrauds anyone in the absolute sense.

229 (tn): i.e. the one who does *najsh*.

valid in the absolute sense. It is the position of Abū Ḥanīfah, Mālik, ash-Shāfiʿī and Aḥmad, in one narration from him. However, Mālik and Aḥmad have affirmed that the buyer has the option to nullify the sale if he did not know at the time and the discrepancy in price is far beyond the norm. Mālik and some of Aḥmad's companions have said that the difference should not be more than a third of the going price. If the seller wants to cancel the sale at that point, he can do so, and if he wants to hang on to his purchase, he is paid back the difference.

D. A more general explanation of *najsh*: It is valid to explain *najsh* in the Prophet's ḥadīth ﷺ in broader terms than what has been mentioned, because one of the meanings of *najsh* in the language is to stir up something through plotting, subterfuge and deception, and thus the meaning is; do not deceive one another, let none of you plot or use subterfuge against one another and do not cause harm. Allah the Exalted has said:

﴿وَلَا يَحِيقُ ٱلْمَكْرُ ٱلسَّيِّئُ إِلَّا بِأَهْلِهِۦ﴾

"But evil plotting envelops only those who do it." [Fāṭir 35:43]

There is the ḥadīth: {Plotting and deception are in the Fire}, and at-Tirmidhī has related, {Cursed is the one who harms a Muslim or plots against him}.

Thus, the prohibition of *najsh* in this ḥadīth includes all transactions that involve fraud and the like, such as hiding defects, mixing good quality items with bad quality items, and so forth. How beautiful is the statement of Abū al-ʿAtāhiyah:

There is no debt except for a debt, and the religion
Is nothing but noble manners
Plotting and deception are in the Fire
They are from the qualities of the people of hypocrisy

It is permissible to plot against someone whom it is lawful to harm, which would be someone at war with the Muslims,[230] due to his statement ﷺ {War is deception}.

3. The Prohibition of Mutual Hatred:

A. Definition: Hatred (*bughḍ*) is the aversion of something because of something repulsive that it bears, and it is a synonym of *karāhah*. The Prophet ﷺ forbade hatred between Muslim that is not for the sake of Allah but due to the passions of egos. Muslims are brothers who love one another. Allah the Exalted has said:

﴿إِنَّمَا ٱلْمُؤْمِنُونَ إِخْوَةٌ﴾

"The believers are brothers." [al-Ḥujurāt 49:10]

230 Ar. *ḥarbī*.

The Messenger of Allah ﷺ said: {By the One in whose Hand is my soul, you will not enter Paradise until you believe, and you will not believe until you love one another...}

B. Ruling: When hatred involves two people, it can be mutual or only from one side. If it is for other than Allah, it is unlawful, and it can also be obligatory or recommended. Allah the Exalted has said:

﴿يَٰٓأَيُّهَا ٱلَّذِينَ ءَامَنُواْ لَا تَتَّخِذُواْ عَدُوِّى وَعَدُوَّكُمْ أَوْلِيَآءَ﴾

"You who believe! Do not take my enemy and your enemy as friends." [al-Mumtaḥanah 60:1]

He ﷺ said: {Whoever loves for Allah, hates for Allah and gives for Allah has perfected his faith.}

What is obligatory upon the Muslim is to give sincere advice to himself, and to be wary of hatred that is based on nothing but desires or familiarity or custom. This type of hatred impairs what could be hatred for Allah's sake, and thus it should be treated as unlawful.

C. The unlawfulness of that which stirs up enmity and hatred: Allah has declared unlawful for the believers that which stirs up enmity and hatred between them. Thus, He has declared wine and gambling unlawful. The Exalted One has said:

﴿إِنَّمَا يُرِيدُ ٱلشَّيْطَٰنُ أَن يُوقِعَ بَيْنَكُمُ ٱلْعَدَٰوَةَ وَٱلْبَغْضَآءَ فِى ٱلْخَمْرِ وَٱلْمَيْسِرِ

وَيَصُدَّكُمْ عَن ذِكْرِ ٱللَّهِ وَعَنِ ٱلصَّلَوٰةِ ۖ فَهَلْ أَنتُم مُّنتَهُونَ﴾

"Shayṭān wants to stir up enmity and hatred between you by means of wine and gambling, and to debar you from remembrance of Allah and from the prayer. Will you not then give them up?" [al-Māʾidah 5:91]

Allah has also declared unlawful the spreading of slanderous rumours, because of the enmity and hatred that it stirs up, while He has granted a dispensation to lie in order to reconcile between people. There is a desire to reconcile and a renunciation of division. The Exalted One has said:

﴿لَّا خَيْرَ فِى كَثِيرٍ مِّن نَّجْوَىٰهُمْ إِلَّا مَنْ أَمَرَ بِصَدَقَةٍ أَوْ مَعْرُوفٍ أَوْ إِصْلَٰحٍۭ بَيْنَ ٱلنَّاسِ﴾

"There is no good in much of their secret talk, except in the case of those who enjoin *ṣadaqah*, or what is right, or putting things right between people." [an-Nisāʾ 4:114]

D. The rank of unity in Islam: Due to the nobility of unity and love, Allah has bestowed it upon His slaves. The Exalted One has said:

﴿وَٱذْكُرُواْ نِعْمَتَ ٱللَّهِ عَلَيْكُمْ إِذْ كُنتُمْ أَعْدَآءً فَأَلَّفَ بَيْنَ قُلُوبِكُمْ فَأَصْبَحْتُم بِنِعْمَتِهِۦٓ إِخْوَٰنًا﴾

"Remember Allah's blessing to you when you were enemies and He joined your hearts together so that you became brothers by His blessing." [Āl 'Imrān 3:103]

The Glorified One has also said:

﴿وَإِن يُرِيدُوٓاْ أَن يَخْدَعُوكَ فَإِنَّ حَسْبَكَ ٱللَّهُ ۚ هُوَ ٱلَّذِىٓ أَيَّدَكَ بِنَصْرِهِۦ وَبِٱلْمُؤْمِنِينَ ﴿٦٢﴾ وَأَلَّفَ بَيْنَ قُلُوبِهِمْ ۚ لَوْ أَنفَقْتَ مَا فِى ٱلْأَرْضِ جَمِيعًا مَّآ أَلَّفْتَ بَيْنَ قُلُوبِهِمْ وَلَٰكِنَّ ٱللَّهَ أَلَّفَ بَيْنَهُمْ ۚ إِنَّهُۥ عَزِيزٌ حَكِيمٌ﴾

"It is He who supported you with His help and with the believers, and unified their hearts. Even if you had spent everything on the earth, you could not have unified their hearts. But Allah has unified them." [al-Anfāl 8:62-63]

4. The Prohibition of Turning Backs on One Another: Turning backs on one another (*tadābur*) means estrangement and avoidance. It comes from the word *dubr* (back), because when avoiding someone in person, one turn's one back and face away from them. It is a severance of mutual relations. It is unlawful if it is for the sake of worldly matters, and is what is meant in his statement ﷺ as related by al-Bukhārī and Muslim from Abū Ayūb: {It is not lawful for the Muslim to avoid his brother for more than three days. They meet and this one turns away and this one turns away. The better of the two is the one who offers the greeting of peace.} In the *Sunan* of Abū Dāwūd, it is on the authority of Abū Kharāsh as-Sulamī that the Prophet ﷺ said: {Whoever avoids his brother for six days, it is as if he has shed his blood.}

As for avoiding for Allah, this is permissible to do for more than three days if it is for the sake of a religious matter, and this has been stipulated by Imam Aḥmad and the proof is the story of the three who stayed back from the Battle of Tabūk. The Prophet ﷺ commanded that they be avoided for fifty days, to discipline them for staying behind and out of fear that there might be hypocrisy in them. Likewise, it is permissible to avoid the people of gross innovations and those who call to desires and erroneous principles. Al-Khaṭṭābī has mentioned that it is permissible for a father to avoid his son, a husband his wife and similar relationships for the purpose of discipline, and it is permissible for it to be more than three days, because the Prophet ﷺ avoided his women for a month.

5. The Prohibition of a Sale on Top of a Sale: This prohibition has been mentioned in many ḥadīths. In al-Bukhārī and Muslim, it is on the authority of Abū Hurayrah that the Prophet ﷺ said: {The believer does not make a sale on top of his brother's sale.} This happens when a person says to someone who has just bought a commercial article and still has the option to return it,[231] 'Return it and I will sell you something better for the same price', or '...the same thing for a lower price'. The same goes for a purchase on top of a purchase, such as someone saying to the seller, 'Take it back and I will pay you more for it'. The scholars have made a consensus that a sale on top of a sale and a purchase on top of a purchase are both unlawful.

An-Nawawī said, 'This happens in buying and selling, and it is sinful and prohibited. However, if someone ventures upon it and sells or buys, the sale and the purchase stands according to the Shāfiʿīs, Abū Ḥanīfah and other jurists. It does'nt stand according to Dāwūd az-Ẓāhirī, and two narrations from Mālik.

As for offering a sale while another sale is being offered, which is when the owner of the commercial article and the one who wants it have agreed to go ahead with the sale but before they do, a third person says to the owner, 'I will pay you more for it', or he says to the one who wants it, 'I will sell you something better' or 'I will sell it to you for less', it is unlawful, just like a sale on top of a sale and a purchase on top of a purchase. This has no difference between an unbeliever and believer, as it's part of fulfilling contracts and financial obligations.

The wisdom behind this being unlawful is the damage and harm that is causes. As for an auction, which is when the article is sold to the highest bidder, this is not prohibited, because it is before any agreement or settlement. It has been established that the Messenger of Allah ﷺ was presented some commercial articles and would say: {Who will pay more?}

6. The Command to Spread Brotherhood: The Prophet ﷺ commands that brotherhood is spread amongst Muslims. He says: {Be slaves of Allah, brothers.} In other words, become brothers by leaving mutual envy, mutual *najsh*, mutual hatred and turning your backs on one another and treating one another as brothers, with love, gentleness, compassion and courteousness and working together towards good with pure hearts. Do not forget that you are Allah's slaves, and it is a distinguishing mark of slaves to obey their Master's command by being brothers and cooperating to establish His religion and manifest His sacred rites. This cannot happen without hearts being in harmony and ranks being united. The Exalted One has said: **"It is He who supported you with His help and with the believers, and unified their hearts."** [al-Anfāl 8:62-63]

231 (tn): The authors mention two terms here, *khiyār al-majlis*, which is when the two parties to the sale have not yet gone their separate ways and thus each has the right to cancel it, and *khiyār ash-sharṭ*, which is one or both parties to the sale stipulate that they have the right to cancel it within a specified time.

Brotherhood will inevitably be achieved when the Muslim gives his fellow Muslim his rights, such as greeting him with peace, saying 'May Allah have mercy on you' when he sneezes, visiting him when he is sick, accompanying his funeral procession, answering his invitation and giving him sincere advice.

Brotherhood is increased in love and affection by giving gifts and shaking hands. At-Tirmidhī has related on the authority of Abū Hurayrah that the Prophet ﷺ said: {Give gifts to one another, for gifts remove the heat in the chest}, i.e. the fraud, the hatred and the whisperings. In another narration: {Give gifts to one another and you will love one another}. In the *Musnad* of al-Bazzār: {Give gifts to one another, for gifts remove resentment and ill will.} It has been related from 'Umar ibn 'Abdul 'Azīz in a ḥadīth that is attributed to the Messenger of Allah ﷺ {Shake hands, for it removes rancour, and give gifts to one another.} Al-Ḥasan al-Baṣrī said, 'Shaking hands increases affection.'

7. The Muslim's Obligations Towards His Brother: The Muslim is commanded to treat his brothers in Islam in a way that brings hearts together. Allah the Exalted has said:

﴿إِنَّمَا ٱلْمُؤْمِنُونَ إِخْوَةٌ فَأَصْلِحُوا۟ بَيْنَ أَخَوَيْكُمْ﴾

"The believers are brothers, so make peace between your brothers." [al-Ḥujurāt 49:10]

He is forbidden from causing hearts to be disunited and in conflict, and among the most severe causes of disunion and conflict are these four matters: oppression,[232] abandonment, lying and denying, and contempt. Indeed, the Muslim does not master his Islam and perfect his faith until he loves for his brother what he loves for himself, and this includes striving to protect him from harm. After these aforementioned matters, there are no other harms that one must protect one's Muslim brother from.

Exalted character in Islam is not confined to just the Muslims. Rather, its good spreads to all of humanity. This is why these matters are unlawful, regardless of who they are done to. If an unbeliever does any of these, he does them because of his unbelief, not his personality:

i. The unlawfulness of oppressing him: No harm should come to him in terms of his body, his religion, his honour or his property without legal permission, because that is oppression and unlawful rupture of relations that contradicts the brotherhood of Islam. Oppression was discussed extensively when commenting on the ḥadīth of Abū Dharr: {O My slaves, I have forbidden injustice[233] for Myself and I have forbidden it amongst you, so do not wrong one another.}[234]

232 Ar. *ẓulm*.
233 Ar. *ẓulm*.
234 (tn): i.e. the 24th ḥadīth.

ii. The unlawfulness of abandoning him: It is emphatically unlawful for a Muslim to abandon his brother, especially if he is in need or an emergency. Allah the Exalted has said:

﴿وَإِنِ ٱسْتَنصَرُوكُمْ فِى ٱلدِّينِ فَعَلَيْكُمُ ٱلنَّصْرُ﴾

"But if they ask you for help in respect of the religion, it is your duty to help them." [al-Anfāl 8:72]

Abū Dāwūd has related: {There is no Muslim who abandons another Muslim in a situation in which his sanctity is being violated and his honour is being disparaged except that Allah abandons him in a situation in which he would like to be helped.} Imam Aḥmad has related: {If a believer is being humiliated in one's presence and one does not assist him even though one is able to, Allah will humiliate him in front of the entire creation on the Day of Standing.} Al-Bazzār has related: {Whoever assists his brother in secret and he is able to assist him, Allah will assist him in this life and the Hereafter.}

Unlawful abandonment can be worldly, such as being able to help someone who is oppressed and ward off their oppressor but not doing so, and it can be purely religious, such as being able to give someone sincere advice about his transgressions and the like and to admonish him but not doing so.

iii. The unlawfulness of lying to him or denying him: It is the Muslim's right over his fellow Muslim that he be truthful when he speaks to him, and that he believes him when he hears him speak. Islamic trust is violated when he informs him of something that contradicts actual events, or tells him something that does not correspond with the truth, especially if the one speaking bears the hallmarks of trustworthiness and credibility. In the *Musnad* of Imam Aḥmad, it is on the authority of an-Nawwās ibn Samʿān that the Prophet ﷺ said: {It is immense treachery to say something to your brother and he believes you but you are actually lying.}

Lying that is not for the purpose of bringing people together or to protect one's person or property is deceit and treachery. At-Tirmidhī has related from the Messenger of Allah ﷺ: {When the slave tells one lie, the King withdraws from him, avoiding the putrescence he has brought.}

iv. The unlawfulness of having contempt for him: It is unlawful for the Muslim to undervalue the significance of his Muslim brother and to detract from his rank, because when Allah created him, He did not show him contempt. Rather, He ennobled him, He exalted him, He addressed him and He made him legally accountable. Thus, to have contempt for him is to transgress the divine limit of pride, which is an immense sin.

This is why he ﷺ said: {It is sufficient evil for a man that he should have contempt for his Muslim brother.} Contempt stems from pride,[235] due to what Muslim has related from the Messenger of Allah ﷺ in which he said: {Pride is to disregard the truth and belittle people.} In Imam Aḥmad's narration in the *Musnad*: {Pride is to be insolent towards the truth and to have disdain for people.} In another narration: {One does not consider people and thus does not see them as anything.} This is because the proud person sees himself as perfect as everyone else as deficient, and thus he has disdain and contempt for them.

Pride is one of the most significant attributes of evil, because it takes it bearer into the Fire and far away from Paradise. In *Ṣaḥīḥ Muslim*: {Whoever has an atom's weight of arrogance in his heart will not enter Paradise.} Al-Bukhārī and Muslim have related from Ḥārithah ibn Wahb ؓ that the Prophet ﷺ said: {Shall I not tell you about the people of Paradise? They are every weak and oppressed person who, if he swears by Allah, he fulfils it. Shall I not tell you about the people of the Fire? They are every harsh, arrogant, conceited person.}

8. *Taqwā* is the Standard for Precedence and the Measure of Men:

Taqwā is to avoid Allah's punishment by doing what is commanded and leaving what is prohibited. Allah ﷻ has only ennobled man by way of his *taqwā* and the excellence of his obedience, not by way of simply who he is or his abundant wealth.

A person can be shown disdain by people because he is weak and only has a small portion of this worldly life, but he has a greater rank in the sight of Allah the Exalted than someone who is exalted by people and held in high esteem because of the counterfeit dignity he possesses, the stolen authority or the unlawful property. People differ in rank in the sight of Allah according to their deeds and to the extent of their *taqwā*, not according to their lineage and descent, not according to their appearance and colour, and not according to their wealth and property. The Exalted One has said:

﴿إِنَّ أَكْرَمَكُمْ عِندَ ٱللَّهِ أَتْقَىٰكُمْ﴾

"The noblest of you in Allah's sight is the one with the most *taqwā*." [al-Ḥujurāt 49:13]

The Messenger of Allah ﷺ was asked, 'Who is the noblest of people?' He replied: {The one who has the most *taqwā* of Allah the Exalted.}

The place of *taqwā* is the heart. The Exalted One has said,

﴿وَمَن يُعَظِّمْ شَعَٰٓئِرَ ٱللَّهِ فَإِنَّهَا مِن تَقْوَى ٱلْقُلُوبِ﴾

"As for those who honour Allah's sacred rites, that comes from the *taqwā* in their hearts." [al-Ḥajj 22:32]

235 Ar. *kibr.*

He ﷺ said: {Allah does not look at your bodies or your outward appearances. Rather, He looks at your hearts.} If *taqwā* is in the hearts then no one knows its reality apart from Allah. Likewise, one does not attain *taqwā* by performing visible deeds. Rather, it is attained by having immense fear of Allah and being consciously aware of Him. Furthermore, "Allah's look" means that He rewards and reckons according to the good and evil found in a person's heart, not their outward appearance. Thus, there can be many people who have a beautiful appearance, wealth, dignity, or leadership in this world but their hearts are devoid of *taqwā*, and someone can have none of the above but his heart is filled with *taqwā*, and thus he is the noblest in the sight of Allah. In fact, that is predominantly the case. This is why holding people in contempt is a huge crime. It violates the measure of precedence and is a clear injustice because it only considers the outward and does not consider *taqwā*, which is how men are measured.

9. The Muslim's Sanctity: The Muslim has sanctity in terms of his blood, his property and his honour. He ﷺ would mention these when addressing large gatherings. When addressing the people during his Farewell Pilgrimage, on the Day of the Sacrifice, on the Day of ʿArafah and on the second day after ʿĪd,[236] he ﷺ said: {Your blood, your wealth and your honour is sacred for you just as this day of yours is sacred in this month of yours in this land of yours...}

These are the general human rights that a safe Muslim community is built upon, in which a Muslim feels that his property is secure and thus no thief will break into it and no robber will rob it. He feels that his honour is secure, and thus no one will transgress against it. Everything is being preserved because Allah the Exalted has legislated retaliation for the loss of life and limbs. He has legislated that the thief's hand be cut off, and stoning or flogging for the fornicator.

Part of the complete preservation of the Muslim's sanctity is that his not frightened or alarmed. It is mentioned in the *Sunan* of Abū Dāwūd that one of the Companions took the rope of another and he got scared, so he ﷺ said: {It is not lawful for a Muslim to alarm another Muslim.} Aḥmad, Abū Dāwūd and at-Tirmidhī have related: {Let none of you take his brother's stick, playfully and seriously.}[237] In al-Bukhārī and Muslim: {Let no two of you have a conversation while excluding the third, for that upsets him}, and in another narration: {...that annoys the believer, and Allah hates to see the believer annoyed.}

236 Ar. *ayām at-tashrīq*.

237 This means that one takes something without intending to steal it. Rather, one wants to make the other person angry, and thus he is playing by pretending to steal and being serious by alarming him and annoying him. The wording in Abū Dāwūd and some copies of at-Tirmidhī is, {...playfully or seriously.}

10. The Ḥadīth Informs Us That:

i. Islam is not just a doctrine and worship but also manners and transactions.

ii. Blameworthy manners in the Revealed Law of Islam are an abominable crime.

iii. Intention and action are the accurate standards by which Allah measures His slaves, and He judges them accordingly.

iv. The heart is the source of one's fear of Allah.

THE THIRTY-SIXTH ḤADĪTH

جَوَامِعُ الْخَيْرِ

عَنْ أَبِيْ هُرَيْرَةَ ؓ، عَنِ النَّبِيِّ ﷺ قَالَ: ﴿مَنْ نَفَّسَ عَنْ مُؤْمِنٍ كُرْبَةً مِن كُرَبِ الدُّنْيَا نَفَّسَ اللهُ عَنْهُ كُرْبَةً مِنْ كُرَبِ يَوْمِ الْقِيَامَةِ، وَمَنْ يَسَّرَ عَلَى مُعْسِرٍ يَسَّرَ اللهُ عَلَيْهِ فِي الدُّنْيَا وَالْآخِرَةِ، وَمَنْ سَتَرَ مُسْلِماً سَتَرَهُ اللهُ فِي الدُّنْيَا وَالْآخِرَةِ، وَاللهُ فِي عَوْنِ الْعَبْدِ مَا كَانَ الْعَبْدُ فِي عَوْنِ أَخِيْهِ. وَمَنْ سَلَكَ طَرِيقاً يَلْتَمِسُ فِيْهِ عِلْماً سَهَّلَ اللهُ لَهُ بِهِ طَرِيقاً إِلَى الْجَنَّةِ. وَمَا اجْتَمَعَ قَوْمٌ فِي بَيْتٍ مِنْ بُيُوتِ اللهِ، يَتْلُوْنَ كِتَابَ اللهِ وَيَتَدَارَسُوْنَهُ بَيْنَهُمْ، إِلَّا نَزَلَتْ عَلَيْهِمُ السَّكِيْنَةُ، وَغَشِيَتْهُمُ الرَّحْمَةُ، وَحَفَّتْهُمُ الْمَلَائِكَةُ، وَذَكَرَهُمُ اللهُ فِيْمَنْ عِنْدَهُ. وَمَنْ بَطَّأَ بِهِ عَمَلُهُ لَمْ يُسْرِعْ بِهِ نَسَبُهُ.﴾ رواه بهذا اللفظ مسلم.

Comprehensive Goodness

It is on the authority of Abū Hurayrah ؓ that the Prophet ﷺ said: {Whoever removes a calamity of the world from a believer, Allah will remove a calamity of the Day of Standing from him. Whoever makes it easy for someone in difficulty, Allah will make it easy for him in this world and the Hereafter. Whoever veils a Muslim, Allah will veil him in this life and the Hereafter. Allah is in the assistance of the slave as long as the slave is in the assistance of his brother. Whoever travels a path by which to seek knowledge, Allah will pave the way to Paradise for him because of it. People do not gather in one of Allah's houses, reciting Allah's Book, studying it together and teaching it to one another except that tranquillity descends upon them, mercy covers them, the angels encircle them and Allah remembers them among those who are with Him. Whoever's deeds hold him back will not be propelled forward by his lineage.} Related by Muslim with this wording.

Muslim has collected the ḥadīth in the Book of Remembrance, Supplication, Repentance and Seeking Forgiveness (the chapter on the precedence of gathering to recite the Qur'ān and for remembrance), no.2699.

Some of its lines – from the ḥadīth of Ibn ʿUmar ؓ – have been collected by al-Bukhārī in the Book of Injustices (the chapter on the Muslim not wronging another Muslim or surrendering him to his enemy), no.2310, and in the Book of Coercion (the chapter on a man swearing to his companion that he is his brother when he fears he might be killed or the like), no.6551, as well as Muslim in the Book of Righteousness, Maintaining the Ties of Kinship and Etiquettes (the chapter on injustice being unlawful), no. 2580.

The Importance of the Ḥadīth:

An-Nawawī ﷺ said in his commentary on Muslim, 'It is an immense ḥadīth. It gathers all kinds of sciences, principles and etiquettes.' Ibn ʿAllān added, 'and virtues, benefits and rulings'.

The Language of the Ḥadīth:

(نفس) *naffasa*: in one narration in the *Ṣaḥīḥ* collection it is (فرّج) *farraja,* which means to mitigate or remove whatever is affecting someone's soul (*nafs*). The word *nafs* comes from the word *tanfīs,* which means to mitigate for someone with regards to their soul. This is from the *tanfīs* of the neck, which means to loosen it so that it can take a breath. *Farraja* is from *tafrīj,* which is more emphatic than *tanfīs* and it means to remove the effect of a calamity such that one no longer feels anxiety and distress.

(كربة) *kurbah*: immense adversity that puts a person in a state of severe distress, as if he is putting a rope around his neck and is about to cut off his air supply, and he is close to death.

(يسر على معسر) *yassara ʿalā muʿsirin*: the *muʿsir*[238] is someone who is burdened by debts and cannot pay them off. Making it easy for him would be to help him pay off those debts, either by paying the creditor directly or via someone else.

(يسر الله عليه) *yassar Allahu ʿalayhi*: Allah makes his affairs and matters easy for him.

(ستر مسلما) *satara Musliman*: if he sees him doing something shameful in the Revealed Law, he does not disclose it to other people.

(ستره الله) *satarah Ullahu*: Allah protects him from slips in this life, and if he falls short therein, Allah does not expose him in this life and does not take him to task in the Hereafter.

(عون العبد) *ʿawn il-ʿabd*: Allah assists him and guides him towards that which benefits him.

---

238 (tn): i.e. someone in difficulty.

(ما كان العبد) *ma kān al-ʿabdu*: as long as the slave is doing the following.

(عون أخيه) *ʿawni akhīh*: helping him materially and immaterially so that he can achieve his objectives and fulfil his needs.

(سلك) *salaka*: to go, or to take hold of the means.

(طريقا) *ṭarīqan*: material, such as going to gatherings of knowledge and traversing considerable distances to get to them, or immaterial, such as writing, memorizing, understanding, reading, studying and other activities that lead to the acquisition of knowledge.

(يلتمس) *yalatmisu*: to seek.

(فيه) *fīhi*: his objective and what leads to it.

(علما) *ʿilman*: beneficial.

(له) *lahu*: for the seeker of knowledge.

(به) *bihi*: because of his travelling the aforementioned path.

(طريقاً إلى الجنة) *ṭarīqan il al-jannah*: i.e. the paths of guidance are shown to him and the means of obedience are prepared for him in this life, and thus it is facilitated for him to enter Paradise in the Hereafter and he does not see the hardships that others will see on the Day of Standing, because of the reward and recompense that he deserves.

(قوم) *qawm*: three or more men, and it can refer to both men and women, as is the case here.

(بيوت الله) *buyūt illāh*: the masjids.

(يتدارسونه بينهم) *yatadārasūnahu baynahum*: each one of them reads a part of it, with contemplation and humility, trying to understand its meanings and comprehend its purposes.

(السكينة) *as-sakīnah*: what makes the heart feel at peace and the soul at ease, spreading awe and respect and provoking fear and humility.

(غشيتهم) *ghashiyathum*: covers them and encompasses them.

(الرحمة) *ar-raḥmah*: beneficence from Allah ﷻ as well as favour and pleasure.

(حفتهم) *ḥaffathum*: surrounding them from every direction.

(الملائكة) *al-malā'ikah*: those who seek out remembrance, and those who descend to earth with blessings and mercy.

(ذكرهم الله فيمن عنده) *dhakarahum ullahu fīman 'indah*: He boasts about them to the angels of the sky, praises them, accepts their deed and raises their rank.

(بطأ به عمله) *baṭṭa'a bihi 'amaluh*: his righteous deeds are deficient and few and thus fall short of the level of perfection.

(لم يسرع به نسبه) *lam yusri' bihi nasabuh*: having noble lineage will not raise his rank, and the repute of his ancestors will not make up for the elevated ranks that he fails to attain, the ranks attained by those who have perfect deeds in the sight of Allah ﷻ.

Legal Matters and Other Guidance from the Ḥadīth:

1. The Muslims are One Body: The individuals that make up the community of faith and Islam are the parts of one body. Each one of them senses what the others are feeling, and thus they share in their joys and griefs. He is happy when they have the occasion to be happy and joyous and when they enjoy familiarity, health and prosperity. He feels pain when harm comes to them, when they are afflicted with illness, and when they are struck with indigence, poverty, destitution and distress. The Messenger of Allah ﷺ said: {The believers, in their mutual love, compassion and affection, are like one body. If one part of it falls ill, the remaining parts summon one another and they experience sleeplessness and fever as a result.} One of the most important obligations that the Muslim has towards his Muslim brother is to hasten to relieve him of his calamity and to remove whatever anxiety or distress he is under.

2. The Calamities of This World are Numerous and The Ways to Relieve Them are Various: Life is filled with troubles and sorrows, and it is often the case that the Muslim is exposed to that which puts him in distress, anxiety, anguish and dire straits, which in turn necessitates that the Muslims relieve him of that. This includes:

A. Assisting him and relieving him of oppression: It is the Muslim's nature not to be a cause of oppression for his Muslim brother, but this does not suffice him in attaining Allah's pleasure ﷻ if he does not also expend effort in order to relieve him of the oppression caused by others. He ﷺ said: {The Muslim is the brother of the Muslim. He does not oppress him and he does not surrender him to his enemy}, which is agreed upon. In another narration that Muslim has: {...and he does not fail to assist him}, i.e. he does not leave him in oppression and does not leave helping him. Likewise, he ﷺ said: {Help your brother, whether he is an oppressor or ōppressed.} A man then said, 'O Messenger of Allah, I help him when he is oppressed, but if he is an oppressor, how can I help him?' He replied: {You prevent[239] him from oppressing, and that is helping him.} This is agreed upon. This is especially the case if the oppression that he has fallen into is because of his religion and him clinging to his Islam and it is being done by unbelievers or renegade sinners. The Exalted One has said:

﴿وَإِنِ ٱسۡتَنصَرُوكُمۡ فِي ٱلدِّينِ فَعَلَيۡكُمُ ٱلنَّصۡرُ﴾

"But if they ask you for help in respect of the religion, it is your duty to help them." [al-Anfāl 8:72]

It is obligatory to assist the Muslim in every situation, whether he has fallen into material or immaterial oppression, with regards to his person, his honour or his property. Imam Aḥmad has related in his *Musnad* on the authority of Sahl ibn Ḥanīf ﷺ that the Messenger of Allah ﷺ said: {If a believer is being humiliated in one's presence and one does not assist him even though one is able to, Allah will humiliate him in front of the entire creation on the Day of Standing.}

B. Rescuing him from captivity: If the Muslim is captured by the enemy, the Muslims are obligated to hasten towards rescuing him from their wicked grip, which might attempt to entice him away from his religion. It is on the authority of Abū Mūsā al-Ashʿarī ﷺ who said: {Feed the hungry, visit the sick and free the captive.} Al-Bukhārī and Abū Dāwūd have collected it.

C. Lending him money if he needs money: The Muslim can fall into financial straits and thus need expenditure to cover his basic needs such as food, drink, shelter, medical treatment and so forth. Thus, the Muslims should hasten to assist him, or at least lend him the money as a generous loan,[240] instead of using his neediness as a means of augmenting their own wealth, as is the case in societies of usury and exploitation. The Exalted One has said:

﴿وَأَقِيمُواْ ٱلصَّلَوٰةَ وَءَاتُواْ ٱلزَّكَوٰةَ وَأَقۡرِضُواْ ٱللَّهَ قَرۡضًا حَسَنٗا﴾

"And establish the prayer and pay the zakāt and lend a generous loan to Allah." [al-Muzzammil 73:20]

239 Ar. *taḥjuzuhu* or *tamnaʿuhu*.

240 Ar. *qarḍ ḥasan*.

This is how the Muslim actualises an integrated society and attains reward from Allah ﷻ. The Exalted One has said:

﴿مَّن ذَا ٱلَّذِى يُقْرِضُ ٱللَّهَ قَرْضًا حَسَنًا فَيُضَـٰعِفَهُۥ لَهُۥٓ أَضْعَافًا كَثِيرَةً﴾

"Is there anyone who will make a generous loan so that He can multiply it for him many times over?" [al-Baqarah 2:245]

He ﷺ said: {Whoever lends a Muslim a dirham twice has the same reward as someone who gives a dirham in charity once}, as related by Ibn Ḥibbān. Indeed, the reward for lending can be greater than the reward for charity, according to the state of the one receiving the loan and the one receiving the charity. Ibn Mājah has related on the authority of Anas ؓ that the Prophet ﷺ said: {On the Night Journey,[241] I saw written on the door of Paradise, 'The reward for charity is multiplied by ten and the reward for lending is multiplied by eighteen.' I said, 'O Jibrīl, how is lending better than charity.' He replied, 'Because the one who asks might do so while still possessing something, while the one seeking a loan only does so out of need.'}

3. The Calamities of the Day of Standing and Being Delivered From Them: How numerous are the calamities of the Day of Standing, how severe are their horrors, how shocking are their frights, and how great will be the Muslim's need to find some righteous deed for himself on that day, to free himself from them, give him breathing space for salvation and illuminate the path of victory in front of him, the path to Paradise. He ﷺ said: {Allah will gather the first and the last on a single plane. The caller will make them hear and sight will pierce them. The sun will come near to them and they will be so anxious and worried that they will not be able to bear it. Some people will say to one another, 'Do you not see what has reached you?' Do you see anyone who can intercede for us before your Lord?'} They have both narrated it, with the same meaning, in the two *Ṣaḥīḥ* collections on the authority of Abū Hurayrah ؓ.

It is on the authority of 'Ā'ishah ؓ who said, 'I heard the Messenger of Allah ﷺ saying: {People will be gathered on the Day of Standing barefoot, naked and uncircumcised.} I said, 'O Messenger of Allah, both men and women? Will they not look at one other?' He replied, {O 'Ā'ishah, the matter will be too severe for them to look at one another.} This is agreed upon and the wording in al-Bukhārī is: {the matter is too severe for them to be concerned about that.}

It is on the authority of Ibn 'Umar ؓ that the Prophet ﷺ said regarding the Exalted's statement:

﴿يَوْمَ يَقُومُ ٱلنَّاسُ لِرَبِّ ٱلْعَـٰلَمِينَ﴾

241 (tn): please see Sūrat al-Isrā' 17:1.

"the Day mankind will stand before the Lord of all the worlds". [al-Muṭaffifīn 83:6]

{One of them will stand with his sweat reaching the middle of his ears.} This is agreed upon.

In the vastness of these horrors, the believer will be on guard against Allah's justice ﷻ and that He recompense him for what he does in this life. If he strives to relieve the believers of their distresses and adversities, he will be relieved of distresses and adversities many times more than what he relieved them of: {Whoever removes a calamity of the world from a believer, Allah will remove a calamity of the Day of Standing from him.}

4. Making Matters Easy for the One in Difficulty: We know that the *muʿsir*[242] is someone who is burdened by debts and cannot pay them off when the time comes. The difficulty could also be because he has accumulated expenses and does not have enough to cover them. In any case, what is required of the Muslims is to make matters easy for this person in difficulty, and this can be done in one of two ways:

The **first** is that the creditor grants the debtor more time so that he can pay off his debt and get out of difficulty. This facilitation is obligatory, due to the Exalted's statemen:

﴿وَإِن كَانَ ذُو عُسْرَةٍ فَنَظِرَةٌ إِلَىٰ مَيْسَرَةٍ﴾

"If someone is in difficult circumstances, there should be a deferral until things are easier." [al-Baqarah 2:280]

The **second** is that the creditor absolve the debtor of his debt or some of it, or someone other than the creditor gives him that which will remove his difficulty. This facilitation is recommended, and it has immense virtue in the sight of Allah ﷻ. The Exalted One has said:

﴿وَإِن كَانَ ذُو عُسْرَةٍ فَنَظِرَةٌ إِلَىٰ مَيْسَرَةٍ ۚ وَأَن تَصَدَّقُوا خَيْرٌ لَّكُمْ ۖ إِن كُنتُمْ تَعْلَمُونَ﴾

"If someone is in difficult circumstances, there should be a deferral until things are easier. But making a free gift of it would be better for you if you only knew." [al-Baqarah 2:280]

He ﷺ said: {Whoever grants respite to someone in difficulty or absolves him, Allah will shade him with His shade.} He ﷺ also said: {Whoever would be pleased for Allah to save him from the calamities of the Day of Standing, let him grant respite to someone in difficulty or absolve him.} Related by Muslim. Indeed,

242 (tn): i.e. someone in difficulty.

Allah the Exalted recompenses this in this life. He ﷺ has said: {Whoever wants his supplications to be answered and to be relieved of his adversity, let him grant relief to someone in difficulty.} Related by Aḥmad.

5. Allah the Exalted is the First to Grant Facilitation: Man is undoubtedly heading towards Allah ﷻ on a Day when wealth and children will be of no benefit.

﴿ٱلْمُلْكُ يَوْمَئِذٍ ٱلْحَقُّ لِلرَّحْمَٰنِ ۚ وَكَانَ يَوْمًا عَلَى ٱلْكَٰفِرِينَ عَسِيرًا﴾

"The Kingdom that Day will belong in truth to the All-Merciful. It will be a hard day for the unbelievers." [al-Furqān 25:26]

﴿فَإِذَا نُقِرَ فِى ٱلنَّاقُورِ ۝٨ فَذَٰلِكَ يَوْمَئِذٍ يَوْمٌ عَسِيرٌ عَلَى ٱلْكَٰفِرِينَ غَيْرُ يَسِيرٍ﴾

"For when the Trumpet is blown, that Day will be a difficult day, not easy for the unbelievers." [al-Muddaththir 74:8-10]

This is when the Trumpet is blown the second time. There is no doubt that it will be a difficult day for those who were ungrateful for Allah's blessings ﷻ and thus did not worship him and did not thank him. They did not turn to Allah's creation ﷻ and assist them or treat them well. As for those who believed in Allah, worshipped Him as is His right to be worshipped, thanked Him for his blessings and favours, were generous to people and made matters easier for them because they recognised Allah the Glorified's bounty towards them, there is no doubt that Allah the Exalted will recompense them for their beneficence, pardon their evil deeds, and make that Day easy for them.

Al-Bukhārī and Muslim have related, and the wording is the latter's, on the authority of Abū Hurayrah ؓ that the Messenger of Allah ﷺ said: {There was a man who would lend to people. He would say to his slave, 'If you come to someone in difficulty, pardon him. Perhaps Allah will pardon on?' He met Allah and He pardoned him.}

In the narration of Muslim, it is on the authority of Ibn Mas'ūd ؓ who said, 'The Messenger of Allah ﷺ said: {A man from those before you was reckoned and there was nothing good that he had done apart from mixing with people. He was wealthy and he would command his servants to pardon those in difficulty.} He then said, {Allah ﷻ said, 'We have more right to that than him, so pardon him.'} 'Nothing good' means that there was nothing else that would outweigh his sins and make him worthy of directly entering Paradise.

6. In Allah's Shade ﷻ: Imam Aḥmad has related from Sahl ibn Ḥanīf ؓ who said, 'The Messenger of Allah ﷺ said: {Whoever helps someone fighting for the sake of Allah, or someone in difficulty who cannot pay off their debts, or a slave who has made an agreement with his master to buy his freedom for a certain fee, Allah will shade him on the Day when there is no shade but His shade.}'

7. Extraordinary Exemplars of Obedience and Compliance: If that was an example of those who came before us then amongst the Companions of Allah's Messenger ﷺ were extraordinary exemplars. Allah described them by saying:

﴿إِنَّمَا كَانَ قَوْلَ ٱلْمُؤْمِنِينَ إِذَا دُعُوٓاْ إِلَى ٱللَّهِ وَرَسُولِهِۦ لِيَحْكُمَ بَيْنَهُمْ أَن يَقُولُواْ سَمِعْنَا وَأَطَعْنَا﴾

"The reply of the believers when they are summoned to Allah and His Messenger so that he can judge between them is to say, 'We hear and we obey.'" [an-Nūr 24:51]

They mastered facilitation for those in difficulty. It was the fruit of taking on Prophetic character and the result of that obedience and that compliance.

A. Kaʿb ibn Mālik ﵁ demanded that Ibn Abī Ḥadrad pay back his debt to him, in the masjid. Their voices became louder until the Messenger of Allah ﷺ heard them while in his house. He lifted the curtain to his quarters and came out, saying, {O Kaʿb.} He replied, 'Here I am, O Messenger of Allah.' He said, {Bring down this debt of yours}, and he indicated to him that it should be a half. He said, 'I have done so, O Messenger of Allah.' He replied, {Stand and ask him to pay you back.}

B. ʿĀʾishah ﵂ said, 'The Messenger of Allah ﷺ heard an argument outside the door and voices being raised. One of them was asking the other to lower his debt and to help him. The other responded by saying, 'By Allah, I will not do so.' The Messenger of Allah ﷺ then came out to him and said, {Where is the one who vehemently swore by Allah that he would not do good?} He said, 'It is I, O Messenger of Allah. He can have whatever he wants.' This is agreed upon. Allah the Exalted was pleased with these people, who needed nothing more than an indication to have exemplary behaviour and upright character, to show goodness, righteousness and beneficence.

8. Veiling the Muslim: There are many texts that encourage veiling the Muslim, and warn against probing his faults, exposing them and then disgracing him in front of people. They include the ḥadīth that we are commenting on as well as the following:

Ibn Mājah has related the ḥadīth of Ibn 'Abbās ﷺ in which the Prophet ﷺ said: {Whoever veils the faults of his Muslim brother, Allah will veil his faults on the Day of Standing. Whoever reveals the faults of his Muslim brother, Allah will reveal his faults until He disgraces him with them in his own house.}

It has been related from someone of the First Three Generations that he said, 'I came across a people whose faults were not manifest. Then they mentioned the faults of others and they, in turn, mentioned their faults. I came across another people and they had faults but they refrained from the faults of others, so their faults were forgotten.'

Indeed, investigating the faults of other Muslims is one of the signs of hypocrisy. If someone's concern is to delve into people's shortcomings so that they can publicise them, this is evidence that faith has not settled in their heart. At-Tirmidhī has related from 'Abdullah ibn 'Umar ﷺ who said, 'The Messenger of Allah ascended the minbar and said and called out with a loud voice, {Those of you who have embraced Islam with their tongues while faith has not reached their hearts, do not harm the Muslims. Do not rebuke them and do not probe their faults. Whoever probes the faults of his Muslim brother, Allah will probe his faults, and when Allah probes someone's faults, He disgraces him, even if he is inside his house.}'

Abū Dāwūd and Aḥmad have related it from Abū Barzah al-Aslami ﷺ and it contains, {Do not slander the Muslims.}

9. Veiling the One who Falls into Disobedience: If the Muslim becomes aware of another's Muslims slip, does he veil it or does he publicise it? The ruling differs according to people's deeds, and people fall into two situations.

The **first** is someone whose state is veiled. In other words, he is not known amongst people to have committed any disobedience. When someone like this slip or makes a mistake, it is obligatory to veil him. It is not permissible to disclose his state or to talk about what he fell into, because that would be unlawful backbiting and spreading filth. Allah the Exalted says:

﴿إِنَّ ٱلَّذِينَ يُحِبُّونَ أَن تَشِيعَ ٱلْفَٰحِشَةُ فِى ٱلَّذِينَ ءَامَنُوا۟ لَهُمْ عَذَابٌ أَلِيمٌ فِى ٱلدُّنْيَا وَٱلْءَاخِرَةِ ۚ وَٱللَّهُ
يَعْلَمُ وَأَنتُمْ لَا تَعْلَمُونَ﴾

"People who love to see filth being spread about concerning those who believe will have a painful punishment both in this world and the Hereafter. Allah knows and you do not know." [an-Nūr 24:19]

The scholars have said that spreading filth about a believer is to mention his slips, or to accuse him of something he is innocent of. One of them said, 'Strive to veil the disobedient, for the manifestation of their disobedience is a blemish for the people of Islam. The priority is to veil blemishes.'

What is meant by the disobedient in this statement is those who are veiled and do not publicise their acts of disobedience, and the texts that encourage veiling the Muslim are understood to apply to these people.

This does not mean that one does not admonish him, does not command him to that which is right and forbid him from that which is wrong, and does not encourage him to be upright and stay away from wrong conduct. Rather, all of the above are required of him, because it is part of the Muslim's right over the Muslim.

The **second** is someone who is notorious for disobedience and declares it openly to people. Whoever is not concerned about what he commits and does not care about what is said of him is a profligate. He openly declares his iniquity, and thus there is no backbiting about him. Rather, it is recommended to expose his state to people, and maybe obligatory, so they are wary of and on guard against his evil. If his iniquity becomes unbearable, and he is not prevented by people, it is obligatory to raise the matter with the ruler, so that he can discipline him with the legal punishment that is commensurate with his iniquity, because veiling him and those like him will only make them greedy for more wrong conduct.

Thus, they wreak havoc on earth and bring widespread disaster upon the Ummah. Indeed, someone like this is sought out and followed, so that tribulation can be uprooted from the Muslim community. The evidence for this is his statement ﷺ: {O Unays, he did this with a woman. If she confesses then stone her.} This is agreed upon. This happened when two men came to him to seek a decision. The son of one of them had fornicated with the wife of the other.

10. Raising the Matter with the Ruler: When the Muslim makes a mistake, it is recommended that he veil himself and repent to his Lord ﷻ in private. Al-Bukhārī and Muslim have related, and the wording is the latter's, on the authority of ʿAbdullah ibn Masʿūd ؓ who said, 'A man came to the Prophet ﷺ and said, "O Messenger of Allah, I touched a woman on the outskirts of the city and I enjoyed myself with her but I did not have intercourse with her. Here I am. Give me whatever judgment you want." ʿUmar then said to him, "Allah veiled you. If only you had veiled yourself."' In another narration, it is mentioned that he kissed her and touched her with his hand but did not have intercourse with her.

If one raises one's matter with the ruler and thus declares his repentance without expounding the sin that he committed, it is recommended that the ruler not ask him about it. Rather, he should command him to keep it to himself and dissuade him from avowing it as much as he is able to.

Al-Bukhārī and Muslim have related from Anas Ibn Mālik ﷺ that he said, 'I was with the Messenger of Allah ﷺ and a man came and said, "O Messenger of Allah, I have done something that deserves a *ḥadd* punishment, so carry it out." He said, 'He did not ask him about it.' He said, 'I attended the prayer and he prayed with the Prophet ﷺ. When the Prophet ﷺ had finished the prayer, the man went to him and said, "O Messenger of Allah, I have done something that deserves a *ḥadd* punishment, so carry out what is in Allah's Book." He replied, {Did you not pray with us?} He said, "Yes." He then said, {Then Allah has forgiven your sin}, or he said, {your *ḥadd*}.'

Al-Bukhārī has related that Abū Hurayrah ﷺ said, 'A man came to the Messenger of Allah ﷺ while he was in the masjid and called out to him, "O Messenger of Allah, I have fornicated." The Prophet ﷺ turned away from him, so he came to the side of the Prophet's face ﷺ that he had turned away from him. When he had testified against himself four times, the Prophet ﷺ addressed him and said, {Do you have some sort of madness?} He replied, "No, O Messenger of Allah." He then said, {Are you married?} He replied, "Yes, O Messenger of Allah." He then said, {Take him and stone him.}'

It is on the authority of Ibn ʿAbbās ﷺ who said, 'When Māʿiz Ibn Mālik came to the Prophet ﷺ he said to him, {Maybe you kissed or you touched or you looked.}

This has to do with the person who commits the disobedience himself. As for others, we have learned that if his state is veiled, it is recommended to veil him and it could even be obligatory. He should not raise his matter before the ruler, and that could be disliked or unlawful. If someone is open about their disobedience, it is obligatory to raise his matter before the ruler so that appropriate punishment can be meted out, so that security is established and there is probity in societies.

11. If One Sees Someone Engaged in Disobedience: What has been mentioned above concerns someone who knows that he committed disobedience or a sin and that was the end of the matter. As for one who witnesses someone engaged in disobedience, it is not permissible to veil him or to remain silent regarding him. Rather, it is incumbent upon him to hasten to prevent him himself if he is able to. If not, he should immediately raise the matter with the ruler, acting about his statement ﷺ {Whoever of you sees something reprehensible, let him change it with his hand...} Please see the thirty-fourth ḥadīth.

12. Intercession for the One Who Has Fallen into Disobedience: When the Muslim slips and his state is veiled, and he is known amongst people to be upright and virtuous, it is recommended for people to veil him and not rebuke him for the action that was done. They should also intercede for him and act as mediators for him with regards to whomever the slip is connected to, if it is connected to anyone. He ﷺ has said, {Dismiss the slips of those who are known for righteousness.} Related by Abū Dāwūd.

As for the one who openly declares his iniquity, and is known amongst people for evil and causing harm, you know that it is disliked to veil him and it could even be unlawful. Additionally, he is not to be interceded for. Rather, he is left so that the *ḥadd* punishment can be carried out against him, so that his state can be revealed and those like him can be deterred. Mālik said, 'As for someone who is known for evil or corruption, I do not want anyone to intercede for him. He should be left so that the *ḥadd* punishment can be carried out against him.'

13. There is no Intercession in the Presence of the Ruler: What we have mentioned regarding intercession only applies to someone whose matter has not been raised before the ruler. If the matter has been raised before the ruler, intercession is unlawful, and acting as an intermediary is disobedience. Anyone who partakes in it or proceeds towards it is sinful.

Mālik said, {If someone has not been known to harm people, and a slip is made on his part, there is no harm in interceding for him as long as the ruler has not been informed.}

The basis for this is what has been related by al-Bukhārī and Muslim and the authors of the *Sunan* on the authority of 'Ā'ishah that the Quraysh were concerned with the affair of the Makhzūmī woman who had committed theft. They said, 'Who will talk to the Messenger of Allah ﷺ about her?' They then said, 'And who would be bold enough except Usāmah Ibn Zayd, who is beloved to the Messenger of Allah ﷺ?' Usāmah thus spoke to him and the Messenger of Allah ﷺ said to him, {Are you interceding regarding one of the *ḥadd* punishments?} Then he stood up to give an address and said, {Those before you were destroyed because when one of the elites amongst them committed theft, they left him alone, and when a weak person committed theft, they gave him the *ḥadd* punishment. By Allah, if Fāṭimah the daughter of Muḥammad committed theft, her hand would be chopped off.}

When the cloak of Ṣafwān ibn Ummayah was stolen, the Messenger of Allah ﷺ commanded that the thief's hand be cut off. Ṣafwān said, 'I did not want this, O Messenger of Allah. He receives charity.' The Messenger of Allah ﷺ then said, {Why did you not think of this before you brought him to me?} This has been related by an-Nasā'ī, Ibn Mājah and Mālik *mursalan*.

Mālik has related in *al-Muwaṭṭa'* that az-Zubayr ibn al-'Awwām met a man who had grabbed a thief and wanted to take him to the ruler, so az-Zubayr interceded for him. The man said, 'No, not until I have taken him to the ruler.' Az-Zubayr then said, 'Once you have reached the ruler, Allah curses the intercessor and the one who accepts the intercession.'

This is because if intercession took place in the presence of the ruler, and people could act as intermediaries before him, chaos would spread and corruption would prevail in societies. Rights would be lost and evil would worsen. The people of disobedience and iniquity would gain the upper hand and seek to curry favour with the ruler. Any reverence for him would disappear from their souls and the hopes of reformers would be dashed. The Ummah would be on the brink of collapse and destruction. This is why rulers must take this matter very seriously and follow the Messenger of Allah ﷺ by complying with the aforementioned and not contradict his guidance. Allah the Exalted says:

﴿فَلْيَحْذَرِ ٱلَّذِينَ يُخَالِفُونَ عَنْ أَمْرِهِۦٓ أَن تُصِيبَهُمْ فِتْنَةٌ أَوْ يُصِيبَهُمْ عَذَابٌ أَلِيمٌ﴾

"Those who oppose his command should beware of a testing trial coming to them or painful punishment striking them." [an-Nūr 24:63]

14. An Interesting Meaning: Ibn Ḥajar al-Haytamī has mentioned an interesting and acceptable meaning of veiling. He said, 'Or, the meaning of veiling is to veil his faults, whether tangible or immaterial, by assisting him in veiling his debt. For example, someone needs a wife and thus one helps him get married, or someone needs to earn and thus one gives him some merchandise to trade with, and so forth.'

How excellent it would be if the Muslims, especially in these days, grasped this meaning. They would deliver their society from so many calamities and avoid a great deal of evil and corruption, especially the wanton behaviour we see from young men and women because they are unable to get married, the impediments that this generation finds on the way to protecting themselves. Meanwhile, the Muslims are in tribulation and not paying attention. Imported customs and antiquated traditions hold sway over them, which have nothing to do with Islam whatsoever. Love of bragging, boasting and ostentation has taken them over, and the victim in all of this is the pure youth of this Ummah, regarding whom the Messenger of Allah ﷺ advised us. The Ummah must strive to provide its children material and spiritual habitation, so that the safety of their religion can be guaranteed as well as the security of its society, followed by salvation with their Lord ﷻ.

15. Cooperation Between Muslims and Allah ﷻ Assisting Them: The community will not be upright and straight, and it will not be strong and tenacious, unless it is based on the foundation of cooperation, solidarity and mutual responsibility between its members, and thus each individual strives to meet the needs of others, with regards to their person, their property and their dignity, until everyone feels that they are part of one body. This is what Islam calls to and what the Qur'ān commands, and what the Purified Sunnah has made a sign of the community of faith. The Exalted One has said:

﴿وَتَعَاوَنُوا۟ عَلَى ٱلْبِرِّ وَٱلتَّقْوَىٰ﴾
"Help each other to goodness and *taqwā*...". [al-Mā'idah 5:2]

And he ﷺ has said: {They believers are like one building. They strengthen one another.}

When cooperation has a great effect in the building of communities, and the life of nations and individuals is of the best deeds in the sight of Allah ﷻ and people strive for its reward the way they strive for the reward of prayer, fasting, charity and so forth, or even more so, he ﷺ has said, { To help a man with his mount so that it carries him or to lift his luggage up to him when he is on it is charity." Agreed upon.

Al-Bukhārī and Muslim have related, and the wording is the latter's, on the authority of Anas ﷺ who said, 'We were with the Messenger of Allah ﷺ on a journey.[243] Some people fasted and some people did not fast. Those who were not fasting were resolute and worked hard (in one narration: '...they shelled buildings and gave water to the riders...') while others could not work as hard because they were fasting. He said regarding this, {Those who are not fasting have taken all the reward today.}' In other words, they have obtained it, taken it as companion and run away with it. They have not left any of it for anyone else. This is hyperbole. What is meant is that their reward is like that of fasting or maybe more, because through their deeds they helped those who were fasting with their fast.

In the *Murāsīl* of Abū Dāwūd, it is on the authority of Abū Qilābah ﷺ that some people amongst the Companions of Allah's Messenger ﷺ came and said good things about a companion of theirs. They said, 'We have never seen anyone like so-and-so. He does not go anywhere except that he is reciting the Qur'ān, and we never stop somewhere except that he is in prayer.' He said, {So who takes care of his livelihood...} until he said, {...and who feeds his camel, or his mount?} They replied, 'We do.' He replied, {All of you are better than him}. In other words, each one of you has a reward similar to the reward of his recitation and prayer, or more.

At-Ṭabarānī has related on the authority of 'Umar ﷺ that the Prophet ﷺ said, {The best of deeds is to? bring happiness to the believer: clothe his nakedness, satiate his hunger or fulfil his need.}[244]

There is no doubt that that greatest fruit that the Muslim reaps from assisting his brother is that assistance and support from Allah ﷻ: {Allah is in the assistance of the slave as long as the slave is in the assistance of his brother.} How can this be otherwise, when man has no strength or power except by Allah ﷻ? It is He the Glorified who runs the entire universe. It is He who gives and withholds, whether it is sickness and health, strength and weakness, wealth and poverty. The slaves'

243 (tn): i.e. a military excursion.
244 See Ḥadīth 25 and 26 of this book.

hearts are in His hand 🕮; He turns them over as He wants. He inspires people to hasten towards assisting those who assist others, to strive to serve him, fulfil his needs and to look after his affairs. The favour is from Him and goes back to Him 🕮.

However, He has made some people serve others, and has attributed the action to them in order to reward them. This is generosity from Him:

﴿وَمَا بِكُم مِّن نِّعْمَةٍ فَمِنَ ٱللَّهِ﴾

"Any blessing you have is from Allah." [an-Naḥl 16:53]

16. The Best Exemplar and The First Three Generations: The Messenger of Allah 🕮 was the best exemplar in everything he called to. He was the best example of someone helping their companions, especially those in need.

Imam Aḥmad has related the ḥadīth of the daughter of al-Khabbāb ibn ar-Arat 🕮. She said, 'Khabbāb had gone out with a squadron, and the Prophet 🕮 had made an agreement with us that he would milk a goat into a bowl of ours, and it would be filled up until it was overflowing. When Khabbāb came and milked it, it went back to normal.

The Companions of Allah's Messenger 🕮 were outstanding students and dedicated followers. They imitated him and travelled his path, and the same goes for those who followed them in excellence, so may Allah be pleased with them and them with Him:

- Abū Bakr 🕮 would milk small cattle for his neighbours – those whose men were absent – and when he became the Caliph of the Muslims, a servant girl from amongst them said, 'Now, he does not milk them'. This reached him and he said, 'No. I do not want to change from anything that I used to do before.'

- 'Umar 🕮 would make agreements with widows and get water for them at night. Ṭalḥah ibn 'Ubaydillāh 🕮 saw him one night entering a woman's house, so Ṭalḥah entered upon her in the daytime. He saw that she was an old lady, blind and infirm, so he asked her, 'What does this man do when he is with you?' She replied, 'This man made an agreement with me from such-and-such time. He brings me what benefits me and removes harm from me.' Ṭalḥah then said, 'May your mother be bereaved of you, O Ṭalḥah! Were you probing 'Umar's faults?'

- Abū Wā'il 🕮 would visit the women of the neighbourhood as well as their elderly every day, and he would buy for them what they needed and what benefited them.

- Mujāhid said 🕮 said, 'I accompanied Ibn 'Umar 🕮 on a journey in order to serve him, and he would serve me.'

- Al-Ḥasan al-Baṣrī ﷺ sent some of his companions to take care of a man's needs, and he said to them, 'Pass by Thābit al-Bunānī and take him with you.' They came to Thābit and he said, 'I am in spiritual retreat.'[245] They thus went back to al-Ḥasan and informed him, so he said, 'Say to him, "O bleary-eyed, do you not know that you going to take care of your Muslim brother's need is better for you than one Ḥajj after another?"' They then went back to Thābit and he left his spiritual retreat and went with them.

17. Intercede and You Will Be Rewarded: Mutual assistance is not confined to that which is material, in work and the like. Rather, it includes material assistance with wealth by removing a calamity and making matters easy, as has already been discussed. It also includes immaterial assistance, such as using one's rank in the presence of the ruler or someone else to meet the needs of one's brother.

Al-Bukhārī has related from Abū Mūsā al-Ashʿārī ﷺ who said, 'Whenever a questioner came to the Messenger of Allah ﷺ or asked him for some need, he would say, {Intercede and you will be rewarded, and Allah decrees on the tongue of His Prophet ﷺ whatever He wants.} In other words, if someone presents their need to me, intercede for him with me, for if you intercede, you will attain reward, regardless of whether your intercession is accepted. Allah causes whatever He wants to flow on the tongue of his Prophet, that which will necessitate the fulfilment of someone's need or not, and that is according to Allah's decree and predestination.

Ibn Ḥajar said in *al-Fatḥ al-Bārī*, 'The ḥadīth contains the encouragement of good, by doing it and by causing it in every way. It also contains encouragement to intercede with someone powerful to remove a calamity and assist someone weak, as not everyone can gain access to the ruler and have a word with him, or explain what one wants to him so that he truly understands one's state. This is why the Messenger of Allah ﷺ would never conceal himself from people.

18. The Path to Paradise: Islam is the condition for salvation in the sight of Allah ﷻ and Islam is not established and does not exist except upon knowledge. There is no way of knowing Allah the Exalted and arriving at Him without knowledge, for it is that which indicates Allah the Glorified in the quickest way. Whoever travels its path and does not deviate from it will reach the sought objective. It is no wonder, then, that Allah's Messenger ﷺ made seeking knowledge the path to Paradise. He makes it clear that every path the Muslim takes in order to seek knowledge, by doing so he travels a path that leads him to Paradise: {Whoever travels a path by which to seek knowledge, Allah will pave the way to Paradise for him because of it.} There is nothing more indicative of what we are saying than the fact that Allah the Exalted made the opening revelation to His Messenger ﷺ a command

245 Ar. *iʿtikāf.*

to knowledge and the means of knowledge, drawing attention to the benefit of knowledge, its nobility and its importance in familiarising oneself with the sublimity of the Creator ﷻ and comprehending the secrets of the creation. The opening revelation points to established, scientific realities, for He the Glorified says:

﴿ٱقْرَأْ بِٱسْمِ رَبِّكَ ٱلَّذِى خَلَقَ ۝١ خَلَقَ ٱلْإِنسَـٰنَ مِنْ عَلَقٍ ۝٢ ٱقْرَأْ وَرَبُّكَ ٱلْأَكْرَمُ ۝٣ ٱلَّذِى عَلَّمَ بِٱلْقَلَمِ ۝٤ عَلَّمَ ٱلْإِنسَـٰنَ مَا لَمْ يَعْلَمْ﴾

"Recite in the Name of your Lord who created, created man from clots of blood. Recite, and your Lord is the Most Generous. He who taught by the pen, taught man what he did not know." [al-ʿAlaq 96:1-5]

19. The Rank of Knowledge in Islam: As long as knowledge is the path to Paradise then it has a particular rank and prestige in Islam, and the scholars have a rank with Allah ﷻ that is close to the rank of the Prophets. The Glorified One has said:

﴿يَرْفَعِ ٱللَّهُ ٱلَّذِينَ ءَامَنُوا۟ مِنكُمْ وَٱلَّذِينَ أُوتُوا۟ ٱلْعِلْمَ دَرَجَـٰتٍ﴾

"Allah will raise in rank those of you who have faith and those who have been given knowledge." [al-Mujādalah 58:11]

He ﷺ has said: {The Prophets do not leave behind any dirham or dinar as inheritance. Rather, their inheritance is knowledge, so whoever takes it has taken an abundant fortune.}

20. The Ruling of Seeking Knowledge in Islam: In Islam, seeking knowledge is an obligation, and there are two levels of obligation:

A. Individual obligation: Every Muslim is obligated to seek it, and it is that which every Muslim must know, so that his creed is sound, his worship is valid and his transactions are done properly, i.e. they are in accordance with what Allah ﷻ has legislated. This is what Allah the Exalted commanded when He ﷻ said:

﴿فَٱعْلَمْ أَنَّهُۥ لَآ إِلَـٰهَ إِلَّا ٱللَّهُ﴾

"Know that there is no god but Allah". [Muḥammad 47:19]

And it is what is meant by his statement ﷺ {Seeking knowledge is an obligation upon every Muslim.} Related by Ibn Mājah.

Every Muslim means both male and female.

B. Communal obligation: The Muslims are obligated as a group to carry it out. If one individual amongst them does it, the requirement is lifted from the rest, but if no one does it, all of them are sinful. This is to be engaged extensively in the sciences of the Revealed Law, by way of study, memorisation and research. Specialisation in each science is what the Muslim group needs, in order to preserve its essence and establish a strong, firm governance of truth and justice on earth, governance that inspires awe and is not coveted by an enemy and no renegade or profligate would dare do anything against it. This is what the Qur'ān has called us to in His statement:

﴿وَمَا كَانَ ٱلْمُؤْمِنُونَ لِيَنفِرُواْ كَآفَّةً ۚ فَلَوْلَا نَفَرَ مِن كُلِّ فِرْقَةٍ مِّنْهُمْ طَآئِفَةٌ لِّيَتَفَقَّهُواْ فِى ٱلدِّينِ
وَلِيُنذِرُواْ قَوْمَهُمْ إِذَا رَجَعُوٓاْ إِلَيْهِمْ لَعَلَّهُمْ يَحْذَرُونَ﴾

"It is not necessary for the believers to go out altogether. If a party from each group of them were to go out so they could increase their knowledge of the Religion, they would be able to notify their people when they returned to them so that hopefully they would take warning." [at-Tawbah 9:122]

Increasing knowledge of the Religion applies, via analogy, to all the sciences that the Ummah needs.

This increasing of knowledge and specialisation is recommended for every Muslim, implementing the Glorified's statement:

﴿وَقُل رَّبِّ زِدْنِى عِلْمًا﴾

"Say: 'My Lord, increase me in knowledge'". [Ṭaha 20:114]

And his statement ﷺ {Whomever Allah wants good for, He gives him an understanding of the Religion.} This is agreed upon.

21. Knowledge is Light and the Scholars are the Lighthouses of Guidance: We know that there is no path to knowing Allah the Exalted, arriving at His pleasure, and attaining nearness to Him on the Day of Standing except by knowledge. It is the light that Allah the Exalted sends His Messengers with and with which He reveals His Books. It provides guidance out of the dark layers of ignorance, and with it, one is delivered from doubts, ambiguities and delusive fantasies. The Exalted One has said:

﴿قَدْ جَآءَكُم مِّنَ ٱللَّهِ نُورٌ وَكِتَٰبٌ مُّبِينٌ ۝١٥ يَهْدِى بِهِ ٱللَّهُ مَنِ ٱتَّبَعَ رِضْوَٰنَهُۥ سُبُلَ ٱلسَّلَٰمِ
وَيُخْرِجُهُم مِّنَ ٱلظُّلُمَٰتِ إِلَى ٱلنُّورِ بِإِذْنِهِۦ وَيَهْدِيهِمْ إِلَىٰ صِرَٰطٍ مُّسْتَقِيمٍ﴾

"A Light has come to you from Allah and a Clear Book. By it, Allah guides those who follow what pleases Him to the ways of Peace. He will bring them from the darkness to the light by His permission, and guide them to a straight path." [al-Mā'idah 5:15-16]

The Glorified One has also said:

﴿فَٱلَّذِينَ ءَامَنُوا۟ بِهِۦ وَعَزَّرُوهُ وَنَصَرُوهُ وَٱتَّبَعُوا۟ ٱلنُّورَ ٱلَّذِىٓ أُنزِلَ مَعَهُۥٓ ۙ أُو۟لَٰٓئِكَ هُمُ ٱلْمُفْلِحُونَ﴾

"Those who believe in him and honour him and help him, and follow the Light that has been sent down with him, they are the ones who are successful." [al-'Aʿrāf 7:157]

Prophetic knowledge is only inherited by the scholars who implement their knowledge with sincerity: {The Prophets do not leave behind any dirham or dinar as inheritance. Rather, their inheritance is knowledge.} Related by at-Tirmidhī and others. They are the marks of truth and lighthouses of guidance by which the Ummah is guided as to how to conduct their lives, following them and being led by them in their adversities and crises, and they, in turn, show them the path to happiness and felicity and enlighten for them the meanings of might, nobility and sovereignty. He ﷺ said, {The likeness of the scholars on earth is like the stars in the sky; by them, one is guided through the layers of darkness on land and at sea. When the stars are blotted out, guides are on the verge of going astray.} Related by Aḥmad in his *Musnad*.

As long as knowledge remains in the Ummah, the people are upon guidance and goodness, civilisation and progress, uprightness and justice, and knowledge only remains as long as its bearers remain, the scholars. If the scholars go and are no longer found amongst the people, matters become disturbed and the Ummah deviates from the straight path and starts following the ways of misguidance. It sinks into the chasms of vice and corruption and throws itself into ruin and destruction. The Messenger of Allah ﷺ spoke the truth when he said, {Allah does not snatch knowledge away from the slaves. Rather, He takes it by taking back the scholars, until there is no scholar left and the people take ignoramuses as leaders. They ask them questions and they answer them without knowledge, and thus they go astray and lead others astray.} This is agreed upon.

22. "Say: 'My Lord, increase me in knowledge.'" [Ṭaha 20:114]: The Muslim does not stop at a certain point of completion. Instead, he constantly strives to ascend the ranks of superiority, and if beneficial knowledge is the sign of superiority then the Muslim is never satiated from it. How can it be otherwise when the Messenger of Allah ﷺ is his exemplar, and he is the one who responded to his Lord's ﷻ command when He said, **"Say: 'My Lord, increase me in knowledge'"**

by saying, {There is no blessing for me when the sun rises on a day in which I do not increase in knowledge that brings me closer to Allah ﷻ.} This is especially the case when the pleasure of knowledge pushes the one who has it to seek more. This is a fact that was informed of by the one whose Lord taught him and taught him excellently, refined him and refined him excellently, ﷺ when he said, {There are two covetous people who will never be satisfied: the seeker of knowledge and the seeker of the world.} Related by al-Bazzār and others. This increase in knowledge is connected to success from Allah the Exalted. When one has a sound objective and sincere intention behind seeking knowledge, and his acquisition of it is to seek Allah's pleasure ﷻ to preserve His religion and benefit His creation, Allah makes it easy for him to acquire it and prepares its means for him. When he researches one topic, the horizons of other subjects are disclosed to him, and when he pursues one science, the horizons of other sciences are opened for him. The Exalted One has said:

﴿وَلَقَدْ يَسَّرْنَا ٱلْقُرْءَانَ لِلذِّكْرِ فَهَلْ مِن مُّدَّكِرٍ﴾

"We have made the Qur'ān easy to remember. But is there anyone who remembers?" [al-Qamr 54:17]

23. If Someone Acts According to What He Knows, Allah the Exalted Bequeaths His Knowledge of What He Did Not Know: Divine providence reaches its peak and divine success reaches its objective when knowledge is joined with action and deeds are connected to words. The Exalted One has said

﴿وَٱتَّقُوا۟ ٱللَّهَ ۖ وَيُعَلِّمُكُمُ ٱللَّهُ ۗ وَٱللَّهُ بِكُلِّ شَىْءٍ عَلِيمٌ﴾

"Have *taqwā* of Allah and Allah will give you knowledge. Allah has knowledge of all things." [al-Baqarah 2:282]

Whenever the Muslim learns knowledge and implements it, he travels a path to Paradise and increases in nearness to Allah ﷻ. Increases one's nearness to Allah ﷻ increase one's success in seeking knowledge and increasing in it. Increasing in knowledge along with action increases one in guidance and *taqwā*, and so forth. The scholars who implement their knowledge never stop ascending the ranks of superiority and knowledge until they possess guidance in its complete entirety, and they achieve the rank of absolute veracity with their Powerful Owner.

﴿وَيَزِيدُ ٱللَّهُ ٱلَّذِينَ ٱهْتَدَوْا۟ هُدًى ۗ وَٱلْبَٰقِيَٰتُ ٱلصَّٰلِحَٰتُ خَيْرٌ عِندَ رَبِّكَ ثَوَابًا وَخَيْرٌ مَّرَدًّا﴾

"Allah augments those who are guided by giving them greater guidance. In your Lord's sight, right actions which are lasting are better both in reward and end result." [Maryam 19:76]

﴿وَٱلَّذِينَ ٱهْتَدَوْا۟ زَادَهُمْ هُدًى وَءَاتَىٰهُمْ تَقْوَىٰهُمْ﴾

"He increases in guidance those who are already guided and gives them their taqwā." [Muḥammad 47:17]

24. Warning against Not Acting According to Knowledge: We know that the scholars are the lighthouses of guidance in the Ummah, and if they are missing, the Ummah strays from the right path. Even worse than the absence of scholars is when these same individuals stray from the path that Allah the Exalted and His Messenger ﷺ commanded them to follow, and thus they do not act according to the knowledge they have inherited from the Prophets. Their deeds contradict their words, and they are a bad example for the Ummah, disobeying Allah ﷻ and leaving obedience to Him, doing what is wrong and leaving what is right. Allah's legislation ﷻ has warned against this path and rebuked it in the strongest terms, while elucidating its disastrous consequences for whoever follows it. Allah the Exalted has said:

﴿يَـٰٓأَيُّهَا ٱلَّذِينَ ءَامَنُوا۟ لِمَ تَقُولُونَ مَا لَا تَفْعَلُونَ ۝٢ كَبُرَ مَقْتًا عِندَ ٱللَّهِ أَن تَقُولُوا۟ مَا لَا تَفْعَلُونَ﴾

"You who believe! Why do you say what you do not do? It is deeply abhorrent to Allah that you should say what you do not do." [as-Ṣaff 61:2-3]

The Glorified One has also said:

﴿أَتَأْمُرُونَ ٱلنَّاسَ بِٱلْبِرِّ وَتَنسَوْنَ أَنفُسَكُمْ وَأَنتُمْ تَتْلُونَ ٱلْكِتَـٰبَ ۚ أَفَلَا تَعْقِلُونَ﴾

"Do you order people to devoutness and forget yourselves, when you recite the Book? Will you not use your intellect?" [al-Baqarah 2:44]

Al-Bukhārī and Muslim have related from Usāmah ibn Zayd ﵄ who said, 'I heard the Messenger of Allah ﷺ saying, {A man will be brought on the Day of Standing and then thrown into the Fire. Then his bowels and intestines will come out, and he will go around the Fire the way a donkey goes around a quern. Then the people of the Fire will gather around him and say, 'O so-and-so? What happened to you? Did you not command the good and forbid the reprehensible?' He will reply, 'Indeed I did. I commanded the good and I did not approach it. I forbade the reprehensible and I did approach it.'}

He ﷺ said: {On the Night Journey, I passed by people whose lips were being cut with scissors of fire. I said, 'Who are these people, O Jibrīl?' He replied, 'They are the preachers of your Ummah who say what they do not do.'}[246]

---

246 Al-Mundhirī has mentioned this ḥadīth in *at-Targhīb wa at-Tarhīb* after the ḥadīth that precedes it a complement for it. He said after both of them, 'Al-Bukhārī and Muslim have related it and the wording is the latter's. We have not found this addition in the two *Ṣaḥīḥ* collections, but we have found this ḥadīth in the *Musnad* of Aḥmad on the authority of Anas ﵁ with some differences in wording.'

In a narration of al-Bayhaqī: {They read Allah's Book and do not act according to it.}

He ﷺ said: {A slave's feet will not move until he is asked about his life and how he spent it, about his knowledge and how he implemented it, about his wealth and how he earned it and spent it, and about his body and how he wore it out.} Related by at-Tirmidhī, who said that it is a good, authentic ḥadīth.

25. Spreading Knowledge: Islam encourages that knowledge is to be learned and taught. The Exalted One has said:

﴿فَلَوْلَا نَفَرَ مِن كُلِّ فِرْقَةٍ مِّنْهُمْ طَآئِفَةٌ لِّيَتَفَقَّهُوا۟ فِى ٱلدِّينِ وَلِيُنذِرُوا۟ قَوْمَهُمْ إِذَا رَجَعُوٓا۟ إِلَيْهِمْ﴾

"If a party from each group of them were to go out so they could increase their knowledge of the Religion, they would be able to notify their people when they returned..." [at-Tawbah 9:122]

He ﷺ said: {Allah illuminates the person who hears something and conveys it just as he heard it, and maybe someone who conveys is more attentive than someone who hears.} Related by at-Tirmidhī and others.

The best action that a Muslim can do that will cause his reward to increase with his Lord even after his death is to teach people the knowledge that Allah the Exalted has ennobled him with and favoured him by way of its attainment. He ﷺ has said, {When a person dies, his deeds come to an end except for three: ongoing charity, knowledge that is benefitted from and a righteous child who supplicates for him.} Related by Muslim and others. He ﷺ said, {The best charity is that a Muslim learns some knowledge and then teaches it to his Muslim brother.} Related by Ibn Mājah.

26. Sincerity in Seeking Knowledge and Leaving Boastfulness and Rivalry Therein: Both the seeker of knowledge and the scholar is obligated to seek and use his knowledge sincerely for the sake of Allah the Exalted. He should only intend the preservation of His Religion, teaching it to the people and benefitting them with it. His goal behind learning knowledge and teaching it should not be to attain some position, wealth, reputation, or rank, or so that it is said that he is a scholar so that he can use his knowledge to deem himself above Allah's creation ﷻ or to debate his peers. All of this is blameworthy and will nullify one's deeds, and place one under Allah's wrath ﷻ.

Abū Dāwūd and others have related from Abū Hurayrah رضي الله عنه who said, 'The Messenger of Allah ﷺ said: {Whoever learns knowledge that is usually sought for the sake of Allah the Exalted but only learns it to attain some worldly objective will not find the scent of Paradise on the Day of Standing.}

At-Tirmidhī and others have related from Kaʿb ibn Mālik ﵁ who said, 'I heard the Messenger of Allah ﷺ saying, {Whoever seeks knowledge in order to keep pace with the scholars, argue with fools and turn people's faces towards him, Allah will put him into the Fire.}

It has reached us from the Messenger of Allah ﷺ {The first of people to be judged on the Day of Standing...a man who learned knowledge and taught it and recited the Qurʾān. He will be brought forward and shown his blessings and he will acknowledge them. He[247] will say, 'What did you do with them?' He will say, 'I learned knowledge and taught it and recited the Qurʾān for you.' He will reply, 'You have lied. You learned knowledge so that it would be said that you are a scholar. You recited the Qurʾān so that it would be said that you are a reciter, and that was said.' He will then issue a command and the man will be dragged on his face until he is thrown in the Fire.} Related by Muslim and others.

27. 'I Do Not Know' is Half of Knowledge: One of the signs of sincerity in seeking knowledge and teaching it is that the seeker of knowledge does not loathe to say, 'I do not know' regarding that which he has no knowledge of. It has often been the case that a scholar is asked about a number of issues and he answers some of them with what he knows and answers most of them with 'I do not know', such that it has been said that 'I do not know' is half of knowledge, because it is a sign that the one saying it is cautious in what he says. The Messenger of Allah – despite his exalted rank – was asked about matters and said, {The one who is asked about it knows no more than the one asking.} This is agreed upon. There is no shortcoming in this, as Allah the Exalted says:

﴿وَمَآ أُوتِيتُم مِّنَ ٱلْعِلْمِ إِلَّا قَلِيلًا﴾

"You have only been given a little knowledge." [al-Isrāʾ 17:85]

28. Some of the Etiquettes of the Seeker of Knowledge: He should strive towards the scholars and seek them out, and keep their company when they travel and when they are resident, so that he can serve them and take knowledge and manners from them.

The Exalted One has said, quoting Mūsā in his story with al-Khiḍr ﵇:

﴿فَوَجَدَا عَبْدًا مِّنْ عِبَادِنَآ ءَاتَيْنَـٰهُ رَحْمَةً مِّنْ عِندِنَا وَعَلَّمْنَـٰهُ مِن لَّدُنَّا عِلْمًا﴾

"May I follow you on condition that you teach me some of the right guidance you have been taught?" [al-Kahf 18:65]

29. Remembering Allah ﷻ: Remembering Allah ﷻ is one of the greatest acts of worship:

247 (tn): i.e. Allah.

﴿ٱتْلُ مَآ أُوحِيَ إِلَيْكَ مِنَ ٱلْكِتَٰبِ وَأَقِمِ ٱلصَّلَوٰةَ ۖ إِنَّ ٱلصَّلَوٰةَ تَنْهَىٰ عَنِ ٱلْفَحْشَآءِ وَٱلْمُنكَرِ ۗ وَلَذِكْرُ ٱللَّهِ أَكْبَرُ ۗ وَٱللَّهُ يَعْلَمُ مَا تَصْنَعُونَ﴾

"Recite what has been revealed to you of the Book and establish the prayer. The prayer precludes indecency and wrongdoing. And the remembrance of Allah is greater still. Allah knows what you do." [al-ʿAnkabūt 29:45]

This is because remembering Allah ﷻ makes a person adhere to His legislation in all of his affairs. It makes him sense Allah the Exalted is watching over him and thus watches over himself. Thus, his conduct is upright and he improves his state with Allah the Exalted and with the creation. This is why the Muslim is commanded to remember Allah ﷻ at all times and in all circumstances. The Glorified One has said:

﴿يَٰٓأَيُّهَا ٱلَّذِينَ ءَامَنُوا۟ ٱذْكُرُوا۟ ٱللَّهَ ذِكْرًا كَثِيرًا ﴿٤١﴾ وَسَبِّحُوهُ بُكْرَةً وَأَصِيلًا﴾

"You who believe! Remember Allah much, and glorify Him in the morning and evening". [al-Aḥzāb 33:41-42]

What is meant by morning and evening is all the time. The Glorified One has also said:

﴿فَإِذَا قَضَيْتُمُ ٱلصَّلَوٰةَ فَٱذْكُرُوا۟ ٱللَّهَ قِيَٰمًا وَقُعُودًا وَعَلَىٰ جُنُوبِكُمْ﴾

"When you have finished the prayer, remember Allah standing, sitting and lying on your sides." [an-Nisāʾ 4:103]

In other words, in every situation.

30. The Best Remembrance is Allah's Book: The best way that Allah ﷻ is remembered with is His Speech that He sent down to the Chosen One[248] ﷺ because it contains – in addition to remembrance – elucidation of Allah the Exalted's legislation, what the Muslim is obligated to adhere to and what he must avoid. Thus, from it, he derives the way upon which he bases his behaviour and which will lead him to victory and felicity. The Exalted One has said:

﴿وَأَنزَلْنَآ إِلَيْكَ ٱلذِّكْرَ لِتُبَيِّنَ لِلنَّاسِ مَا نُزِّلَ إِلَيْهِمْ وَلَعَلَّهُمْ يَتَفَكَّرُونَ﴾

"And We have sent down the Reminder to you so that you can make clear to mankind what has been sent down to them so that hopefully they will reflect." [an-Naḥl 16:44]

248 Ar. *al-Muṣṭafā*.

The Glorified One has also said:

﴿إِنْ هُوَ إِلَّا ذِكْرٌ وَقُرْءَانٌ مُّبِينٌ﴾

"It is simply a reminder and a clear Qur'ān." [Yā Sīn 36:69]

He has also said,

﴿هَـٰذَا ذِكْرٌ ۚ وَإِنَّ لِلْمُتَّقِينَ لَحُسْنَ مَـَٔابٍ﴾

"This is a Reminder. The godfearing will have a good Homecoming." [Ṣād 38:49]

He ﷻ has also said,

﴿وَلَقَدْ يَسَّرْنَا ٱلْقُرْءَانَ لِلذِّكْرِ فَهَلْ مِن مُّدَّكِرٍ﴾

"We have made the Qur'ān easy to remember. But is there anyone who remembers?" [al-Qamr 54:17]

31. Building Masjids: The best places for remembering Allah ﷻ reciting the Qur'ān and learning knowledge; are the masjids, the houses of Allah ﷻ. The believers build them on His earth, and building them in the true sense is that there are knowledge and remembrance alongside worship such as prayer, spiritual retreat and so forth. The Exalted One has said:

﴿فِى بُيُوتٍ أَذِنَ ٱللَّهُ أَن تُرْفَعَ وَيُذْكَرَ فِيهَا ٱسْمُهُۥ يُسَبِّحُ لَهُۥ فِيهَا بِٱلْغُدُوِّ وَٱلْـَٔاصَالِ ﴿٣٦﴾ رِجَالٌ لَّا تُلْهِيهِمْ تِجَـٰرَةٌ وَلَا بَيْعٌ عَن ذِكْرِ ٱللَّهِ وَإِقَامِ ٱلصَّلَوٰةِ وَإِيتَآءِ ٱلزَّكَوٰةِ ۙ يَخَافُونَ يَوْمًا تَتَقَلَّبُ فِيهِ ٱلْقُلُوبُ وَٱلْأَبْصَـٰرُ ﴿٣٧﴾ لِيَجْزِيَهُمُ ٱللَّهُ أَحْسَنَ مَا عَمِلُوا۟ وَيَزِيدَهُم مِّن فَضْلِهِۦ ۗ وَٱللَّهُ يَرْزُقُ مَن يَشَآءُ بِغَيْرِ حِسَابٍ﴾

"In houses which Allah has permitted to be built and in which His name is remembered, there are men who proclaim His glory morning and evening., not distracted by trade or commerce from the remembrance of Allah, the establishment of the prayer and the payment of the zakāt; fearing a day when all hearts and eyes will be in turmoil – so that Allah may reward them for the best of what they did and give them more from his unbounded favour. Allah provides for anyone He wills without reckoning". [an-Nūr 24:36-38]

32. Individual Worship, an Intercessor and Someone Accepting Intercession: Since the recitation of the Qur'ān in and of itself is a form of worship that is commanded, the Muslim is rewarded for it and it is a means of him being saved on the Day of Standing and attaining his Lord's pleasure ﷻ the Qur'ān intercedes before its Lord for the one who recites it. The Exalted One has said:

﴿وَٱتْلُ مَآ أُوحِىَ إِلَيْكَ مِن كِتَابِ رَبِّكَ﴾

"Recite what has been revealed to you of your Lord's Book". [al-Kahf 18:27]

He ﷻ has also said:

﴿ٱتْلُ مَآ أُوحِىَ إِلَيْكَ مِنَ ٱلْكِتَـٰبِ وَأَقِمِ ٱلصَّلَوٰةَ﴾

"Recite what has been revealed to you of the Book and establish the prayer". [al-ʿAnkabūt 29:45]

He ﷻ has also said on the tongue of His Prophet ﷺ:

﴿إِنَّمَآ أُمِرْتُ أَنْ أَعْبُدَ رَبَّ هَـٰذِهِ ٱلْبَلْدَةِ ٱلَّذِى حَرَّمَهَا وَلَهُۥ كُلُّ شَىْءٍ ۖ وَأُمِرْتُ أَنْ أَكُونَ مِنَ ٱلْمُسْلِمِينَ

٩١ وَأَنْ أَتْلُوَا۟ ٱلْقُرْءَانَ ۖ فَمَنِ ٱهْتَدَىٰ فَإِنَّمَا يَهْتَدِى لِنَفْسِهِۦ ۖ وَمَن ضَلَّ فَقُلْ إِنَّمَآ أَنَا۠ مِنَ ٱلْمُنذِرِينَ﴾

"I have simply been ordered to worship the Lord of this land which He has declared sacred – everything belongs to Him – and I have been ordered to be one of the Muslims and to recite the Qur'ān.' Whoever is guided is only guided to his own good; and if anyone is misguided, just say, 'I am only a warner.'" [an-Naml 27:91-92]

Al-Bukhārī and Muslim have related from ʿĀ'ishah ﵂ that the Prophet ﷺ said, {The one who reads the Qur'ān and memorises it is like one of the noble scribes.[249] The one who reads it and commits himself to it, and it is difficult for him, has two rewards.}

At-Tirmidhī has related from ʿAbdullah ibn Masʿūd ﵁ who said, 'The Messenger of Allah ﷺ said, {Whoever reads one letter from Allah's Book has the reward for one good deed, a good deed counts as ten good deeds. I do not say *alif lām mīm* is a letter. Rather, *alif* is a letter, *lām* is a letter, and *mīm* is a letter.}

Muslim has related from Abū Umāmah al-Bāhilī ﵁ who said, 'I heard the Messenger of Allah ﷺ saying, {Read the Qur'ān, for it will come on the Day of Standing as an intercessor for its people.}

The virtue of listening to the Qur'ān is not less than the virtue of reciting it. Indeed, listening silently to its recitation is a means of attaining Allah the Exalted's forgiveness and mercy. The Exalted One has said:

﴿وَإِذَا قُرِئَ ٱلْقُرْءَانُ فَٱسْتَمِعُوا۟ لَهُۥ وَأَنصِتُوا۟ لَعَلَّكُمْ تُرْحَمُونَ﴾

"When the Qur'ān is recited, listen to it and be quiet so that hopefully you will gain mercy." [al-'Aʿrāf 7:204]

249 (tn) i.e. the angels, please see Sūrat ʿAbasa 15-16.

Imam Aḥmad has related in his *Musnad* that the Messenger of Allah ﷺ said, {Whoever listens to one verse of Allah's Book has a multiplied reward written down for him, and whoever recites it has a light on the Day of Standing.}

Thus, al-Muṣṭafā ﷺ loved to listen to his Companion reciting the Qur'ān ﷺ. Al-Bukhārī and Muslim have related from ʿAbdullah ibn Masʿūd ﷺ who said, 'The Messenger of Allah said, {Recite to me.} I replied, "I recite to you and it was revealed to you?" He replied, {I long to hear it from other than myself.}' He said, 'I read an-Nisā' until I reached,

﴿فَكَيْفَ إِذَا جِئْنَا مِن كُلِّ أُمَّةٍ بِشَهِيدٍ وَجِئْنَا بِكَ عَلَىٰ هَٰٓؤُلَآءِ شَهِيدًا﴾

"How will it be when We bring a witness from every nation and bring you as a witness against them?" [an-Nisā' 4:41]

He said, {Stop.}, or {Cease.} I then saw his eyes overflowing with tears.'

33. Light Upon Light: The reward is magnified and increased and the virtue is multiplied when one's recitation and listening is combined with understanding, reflection and humility. Thus, light is gathered upon light, a noble deed is joined with a noble deed, and that is a sign of intellect and high rank in the sight of Allah ﷻ. Allah the Exalted has said:

﴿كِتَٰبٌ أَنزَلْنَٰهُ إِلَيْكَ مُبَٰرَكٌ لِّيَدَّبَّرُوٓاْ ءَايَٰتِهِۦ وَلِيَتَذَكَّرَ أُوْلُواْ ٱلْأَلْبَٰبِ﴾

"It is a Book we have sent down to you, full of blessings, so let people of intelligence ponder its signs and take heed." [Ṣād 38:29]

This is what is indicated by his statement, {People do not gather in one of Allah's houses...}, even though the virtue of remembrance and of reciting the Qur'ān mentioned in the ḥadīth is for a people who do so in any place, and especially women, for whom it is recommended to stay in their homes and not frequent places that men visit. However, remembrance in the masjids is better for men, because this is part of how they are built, as we know, and because the masjids are removed from that which distracts from Allah the Exalted's remembrance and disturbs the mind, in addition to the fact that they are protected from filth and dirt, both material and immaterial.

34. Favour From Allah the Exalted and Pleasure: Allah's favour ﷻ towards those who sit and recite His Book is immense, as He awards them four honours, each of which is evidence of their high rank and exalted standing with Him, and guarantees that they have Allah's pleasure, forgiveness and mercy ﷻ:

A. Tranquillity descends upon them: Al-Bukhārī and Muslim have related from al-Barāʾ ibn ʿĀzib رضي الله عنه who said, 'A man read al-Kahf when there was a riding beast in the house and it started bolting. He looked and there was some fog or cloud that had covered him. He mentioned this to the Prophet ﷺ and he said, {Recite O so-and-so, for indeed it is the tranquillity that descends for the Qurʾān.}

It is this tranquillity that brings peace to the heart and calmness to the soul and allows one to relax and be at ease.

The Exalted One has said:

﴿ٱلَّذِينَ ءَامَنُوا۟ وَتَطْمَئِنُّ قُلُوبُهُم بِذِكْرِ ٱللَّهِ ۗ أَلَا بِذِكْرِ ٱللَّهِ تَطْمَئِنُّ ٱلْقُلُوبُ﴾

"...those who believe and whose hearts find peace in the remembrance of Allah. Only in the remembrance of Allah can the heart find peace." [ar-Raʿd 13:28]

What an utter loss it is for those whose hearts have become empty and thus they have become heedless of Allah the Exalted and His remembrance. Thus, they live in hatred, anxiety and ruin in this world, and in the Hereafter, they will have eternal destruction in the Fire. The Exalted One has said,

﴿وَمَنْ أَعْرَضَ عَن ذِكْرِى فَإِنَّ لَهُۥ مَعِيشَةً ضَنكًا وَنَحْشُرُهُۥ يَوْمَ ٱلْقِيَـٰمَةِ أَعْمَىٰ﴾

"But if anyone turns away from My remembrance, his life will be a dark and narrow one and on the Day of Standing We will gather him blind." [Ṭaha 20:124]

The Glorified One has also said:

﴿فَوَيْلٌ لِّلْقَـٰسِيَةِ قُلُوبُهُم مِّن ذِكْرِ ٱللَّهِ ۚ أُو۟لَـٰٓئِكَ فِى ضَلَـٰلٍ مُّبِينٍ﴾

"Woe to those who hearts are hardened against the remembrance of Allah! Such people are clearly misguided." [az-Zumar 39:22]

B. Mercy covers them: Al-Ḥākim has narrated from Salmān رضي الله عنه that he was amongst a group who were remembering Allah the Exalted. The Messenger of Allah ﷺ then passed by them and said, {What were you saying? I saw mercy descend over you and I wanted to share in it with you.} This mercy is the most sublime thing that the believer enjoys and the best that the Muslim can attain as the fruit of his effort in this life. The Exalted One has said:

﴿قُلْ بِفَضْلِ ٱللَّهِ وَبِرَحْمَتِهِۦ فَبِذَٰلِكَ فَلْيَفْرَحُوا۟ هُوَ خَيْرٌ مِّمَّا يَجْمَعُونَ﴾

"Say: 'It is the favour of Allah and His mercy that should be the cause of their rejoicing. That is better than anything they accumulate.'" [Yūnus 10:58]

Thus, blessed are those to whom mercy has drawn near and therefore their recitation of Allah's Book ﷻ and studying it together and teaching it to one another is a sign that they are among the good-doers:

﴿إِنَّ رَحْمَتَ ٱللَّهِ قَرِيبٌ مِّنَ ٱلْمُحْسِنِينَ﴾
"Allah's mercy is close to the good-doers." [al-'A'rāf 7:56]

Glad tidings are for them, that they are amongst the sincere believers, those who have *taqwā* and draw near to Allah, and are saved from His punishment ﷻ. He ﷻ has said,

﴿وَٱكْتُبْ لَنَا فِى هَٰذِهِ ٱلدُّنْيَا حَسَنَةً وَفِى ٱلْءَاخِرَةِ إِنَّا هُدْنَآ إِلَيْكَ ۚ قَالَ عَذَابِىٓ أُصِيبُ بِهِۦ مَنْ أَشَآءُ ۖ
وَرَحْمَتِى وَسِعَتْ كُلَّ شَىْءٍ ۚ فَسَأَكْتُبُهَا لِلَّذِينَ يَتَّقُونَ وَيُؤْتُونَ ٱلزَّكَوٰةَ وَٱلَّذِينَ هُم بِـَٔايَٰتِنَا يُؤْمِنُونَ﴾
"He said, 'As for my punishment, I will strike with it anyone I will. My mercy extends to all things but I will prescribe it for those who have *taqwā* and pay the zakāt, and those who believe in Our signs." [al-'A'rāf 7:156]

C. The angels encircle them: Al-Bukhārī and Muslim have related from Usayd ibn Ḥuḍayr ﷺ said that while he was reciting Sūrat al-Baqarah at night and his horse was tied up nearby. The horse then suddenly moved around, and then went quiet and became still. He read again and the horse moved around again, and then it went quiet and became still again. He then read yet again and the horse moved around again, so he stopped. His son Yaḥyā was near the horse and he feared that it would step on him. After ruminating, he looked up and could no longer see the horse. When morning came, he spoke to the Prophet ﷺ and he said, {Recite, O son of Ḥuḍayr! Recite, O son of Ḥuḍayr!} He replied, 'I feared, O Messenger of Allah, that it would step on Yaḥyā, as he was close to it. I thus raised my head and went towards him. I then raised my head towards the sky and there was something resembling a lampshade containing lamps. Then it left, and I could no longer see it. He said, {Do you know what that was?} I replied, 'No'. He said, {That was angels who had come close because of your voice. If you had kept reading, morning would have come and the people would have looked at them, and they would not have disappeared from their sight.}

This is how it is. Whenever the reciters multiply, the angels multiply until they surround them from every direction.

What does the descent of these angels mean, and what is the fruit of their efforts and being surrounded? It means that these reciters, who are teaching and studying the Qur'ān together, are in security and peace. The fruit of their efforts is that they are protected from every harm, and preserved from having anything they dislike afflict them.

He ﷻ has said:

﴿لَهُۥ مُعَقِّبَٰتٞ مِّنۢ بَيۡنِ يَدَيۡهِ وَمِنۡ خَلۡفِهِۦ يَحۡفَظُونَهُۥ مِنۡ أَمۡرِ ٱللَّهِۗ﴾

"Everyone has a succession of angels in front of him and behind him, guarding him by Allah's command". [ar-Raʿd 13:11]

i.e. according to Allah's command and permission.

Perhaps the best fruit of this honour is that these angels travel between the slaves of the All-Merciful and their Creator ﷻ bringing to Him the Glorified the remembrance of Him ﷻ and the mutual study of His Book that these believers are engaged in. There is also the desire for Allah's blessings ﷻ and His pleasure that their souls are absorbed in and the dread of His wrath and fear of His punishment. This is all a cause of forgiveness, and door to victory and salvation. Al-Bukhārī and Muslim have related from Abū Hurayrah رضي الله عنه who said, 'The Messenger of Allah ﷺ said, {Allah has angels that travel about the roads seeking out the people of remembrance. When they find a people remembering Allah, they call out to one another, 'Come to your need.' They thus surround them with their wings until the lowest sky is covered.} He said, {Their Lord asks them – and He knows better than they do – 'What are My slaves saying?'} He said, {They say, 'They are saying *tasbīḥ, takbīr, taḥmīd* and proclaiming Your magnificence.'[250]}[251] He said, {He thus says, 'Have they seen me?'} He said, {They say, 'By Allah, they have not seen You.'} He said, {He thus says, 'What would they be like if they were to see me?'} He said, {They say, 'If they were to see You, they would worship You more enthusiastically, proclaim Your magnificence more enthusiastically and glorify You even more.} He said, {He says, 'What are they asking of Me?'} He said, {They say, 'They are asking You for Paradise.} He said, {He says, 'Have they seen it?} He said, {They say, 'No, by Allah, O Lord, they have not seen it.} He said, {What would they be like if they did see it?'} He said, {They say, 'If they were to see it, they would be more eager for it and they would ask for it more earnestly and with greater desire.' He said, 'What do they seek refuge from?'} He said, {They say, 'From the Fire.'} He said, {He says, "Have they seen it?} He said, {They say, 'No, by Allah, O Lord, they have not seen it.} He said, {What would they be like if they did see it?'} He said, {They say, 'If they were to see it, they would be even more eager to flee from it and more scared of it.'} He said, {He says, 'I bear witness to you that I have forgiven them.} He said, {One of the angels says, 'There is someone amongst them who is not one of them. He only came for some need.' He replies, 'They are sitting together and they are not troubled by someone sitting with them.'}

250 Ar. *at-tamjīd.*

251 All of this is attained by reciting the Qurʾān and studying it together.

D. Allah remembers them among those who are with Him: He ﷻ has said:

﴿فَاذْكُرُونِي أَذْكُرْكُمْ وَاشْكُرُوا لِي وَلَا تَكْفُرُونِ﴾

"Remember Me and I will remember you. Be grateful to Me and do not be ungrateful." [al-Baqarah 2:152]

When the believing slave remembers his Lord, by reciting His Book and listening to its verses, Allah ﷻ returns like for like and remembers him amidst His Exaltedness, and what a difference there is between the two types of remembrance! There is the high rank in Allah the Exalted remembering His slave, along with forgiveness and mercy, acceptance and pleasure.

Al-Bukhārī and Muslim have related from Abū Hurayrah ؓ who said, 'The Prophet ﷺ said, {Allah the Exalted says, 'I am as My slave thinks of Me. I am with Him when He remembers Me. If he remembers Me within Himself, I remember Him within Myself. If he remembers Me in a gathering, I remember Him in a gathering that is better than theirs. If he draws near to Me by a hand span, I draw near to him by an arm's length. If he draws near to Me by an arm's length, I draw near to him by a fathom's length. If he comes to Me walking, I come to him walking quickly.'} All of this means Allah the Exalted's acceptance and His pleasure, and that He quickly rewards the One who turns to Him ﷻ adheres to His legislation, complies with His commands, avoids His prohibitions and stay firm upon obeying Him.

In summary, the trade of these people, who have turned to Allah's Book ﷻ by reciting it, studying it, learning it, implementing it and adhering to it, is profitable. Allah the Sublime spoke the truth when He ﷻ said:

﴿إِنَّ الَّذِينَ يَتْلُونَ كِتَابَ اللَّهِ وَأَقَامُوا الصَّلَاةَ وَأَنفَقُوا مِمَّا رَزَقْنَاهُمْ سِرًّا وَعَلَانِيَةً يَرْجُونَ تِجَارَةً

لَّن تَبُورَ لِيُوَفِّيَهُمْ أُجُورَهُمْ وَيَزِيدَهُم مِّن فَضْلِهِ ۚ إِنَّهُ غَفُورٌ شَكُورٌ﴾

"Those who recite the Book of Allah and establish the prayer, and give of what We have provided them, secretly and openly, hope for a trade that will not prove profitless: that He may pay them their wages in full and give them more from His unbounded favour. He is Ever-Forgiving, Ever-Thankful." [Fāṭir 35:29-30]

It is sufficient honour for these people that their exemplar in this deed of theirs is the best of creation without exception, Muḥammad the son of ʿAbdullah ﷺ and the best angel of the heavens, Jibrīl ؑ as they would study the Qurʾān together.

Al-Bukhārī and Muslim have related from Ibn ʿAbbās ؓ who said, 'The Messenger of Allah ﷺ was the most generous of people, and he was even more generous in Ramaḍān when he met with Jibrīl. He would meet him every night in Ramaḍān and they would study the Qur'ān together. The Messenger of Allah ﷺ was more generous than the unfettered wind', i.e. the unhindered wind that is constantly blowing and spreading its benefit.

However, this profit is also attained by anyone who gathers for the remembrance of Allah the Exalted in the absolute sense. Muslim has related from Abū Hurayrah and Abū Sa'īd al-Khudrī (رضي الله عنهما) that they witnessed the Prophet ﷺ saying, {No people sit and remember Allah ﷻ except that the angels encircle them, mercy covers them, tranquillity descends upon them and Allah mentions them among those who are with Him.} It is sufficient honour for the one who remembers that Allah ﷻ mentions him in the highest gathering.

33. The Humanity and Justice of Islam (*Taqwā* and Righteous Deeds Are the Path that Leads to Allah ﷻ): Islam has affirmed the unity of humanity, and established equality between people in terms of their birth. All of them are created from one soul. There is no difference between pale and dark. There is no superiority for the Arab over the non-Arab. There is no distinction for the highborn over the commoner in terms of creation and origin:

﴿يَٰٓأَيُّهَا ٱلنَّاسُ ٱتَّقُواْ رَبَّكُمُ ٱلَّذِي خَلَقَكُم مِّن نَّفۡسٖ وَٰحِدَةٖ وَخَلَقَ مِنۡهَا زَوۡجَهَا
وَبَثَّ مِنۡهُمَا رِجَالٗا كَثِيرٗا وَنِسَآءٗ﴾

"O mankind! Have *taqwā* of your Lord, who created you from a single soul and created its mate from it, and then disseminated many men and women from the two of them." [an-Nisā' 4:1]

Divine justice in Islam is such that differentiation between people is according to righteous action and the path of drawing nearer to Allah ﷻ is to have *taqwā* of Him. One's ancestors have nothing to do with it:

﴿يَٰٓأَيُّهَا ٱلنَّاسُ إِنَّا خَلَقۡنَٰكُم مِّن ذَكَرٖ وَأُنثَىٰ وَجَعَلۡنَٰكُمۡ شُعُوبٗا وَقَبَآئِلَ لِتَعَارَفُوٓاْۚ
إِنَّ أَكۡرَمَكُمۡ عِندَ ٱللَّهِ أَتۡقَىٰكُمۡۚ إِنَّ ٱللَّهَ عَلِيمٌ خَبِيرٞ﴾

"O mankind! We created you from a male and a female, and made you into peoples and tribes so that you might come to know each other. The noblest of you in Allah's sight is the one with the most *taqwā*. Allah is All-Knowing, All-Aware." [al-Ḥujurāt 49:13]

Thus, in the sight of Allah, it does not discriminate a person to having an inferior lineage, for Allah the Exalted has made reward the consequence of righteous action, not lineage. The Glorified One has said:

﴿وَلِكُلٍّ دَرَجَٰتٌ مِّمَّا عَمِلُواْ﴾

"All have ranks according to what they did." [al-Anʿām 6:132]

Thus, the slave can only reach an elevated rank with his Lord through righteous action. Indeed, lineages come to nothing on the Day of Standing, when created beings are stood on one plane, not a single one of them looking at anyone else:

﴿فَإِذَا نُفِخَ فِى ٱلصُّورِ فَلَآ أَنسَابَ بَيْنَهُمْ يَوْمَئِذٍ وَلَا يَتَسَآءَلُونَ﴾

"Then when the Trumpet is blown, that day there will be no family ties between them, and they will not be able to question one another." [al-Mu'minūn 23:101]

This is why we find the Noble Qur'ān warning people against relying on their lineage. In conveying the call of Allah the Exalted to mankind, the Prophet ﷺ is commanded to start by warning those who are most closely related to him. Allah ﷻ says:

﴿وَأَنذِرْ عَشِيرَتَكَ ٱلْأَقْرَبِينَ﴾

"Warn your near relatives." [ash-Shuʿarā' 26:214]

We find al-Muṣṭafā ﷺ – and he is merciful and compassionate, and his tribe and his relatives are the closest of people to his mercy and compassion – we find him hastening to convey the command of his Lord. He thus climbs on top of as-Ṣafā and calls out, {O Quraysh, purchase yourselves. I will be of no benefit to you before Allah. O Children of ʿAbd Manāf, I will be of no benefit to you before Allah. O Children of ʿAbbas ibn ʿAbdul Muṭṭalib, I will be of no benefit to you before Allah. O Ṣafiyyah, the paternal aunt of Allah's Messenger, I will be of no benefit to you before Allah. O Fāṭimah, the daughter of Muḥammad – ﷺ – ask me what you want of my wealth. I will be of no benefit to you before Allah.} Agreed upon.

34. Friendship Based on Faith and Deeds, not Blood and Lineage: In the past, People would assist and befriend one another based on tribalism and blood relations. Then Islam came to cut every connection between one person and another apart from the connection of faith, and nullify all friendship except those based on the Religion and deeds, giving victory to the creed and the foundation:

﴿وَٱلْمُؤْمِنُونَ وَٱلْمُؤْمِنَٰتُ بَعْضُهُمْ أَوْلِيَآءُ بَعْضٍ يَأْمُرُونَ بِٱلْمَعْرُوفِ وَيَنْهَوْنَ عَنِ ٱلْمُنكَرِ وَيُقِيمُونَ ٱلصَّلَوٰةَ وَيُؤْتُونَ ٱلزَّكَوٰةَ وَيُطِيعُونَ ٱللَّهَ وَرَسُولَهُۥٓ أُوْلَٰٓئِكَ سَيَرْحَمُهُمُ ٱللَّهُ إِنَّ ٱللَّهَ عَزِيزٌ حَكِيمٌ﴾

"The men and women of the believers are friends of one another. They command what is right and forbid what is wrong, establish the prayer

and pay the zakāt, and obey Allah and His Messenger. They are the people on whom Allah will have mercy. Allah is Almighty, All-Wise." [at-Tawbah 9:71]

If the friendship between the believers is based on creed and religion, they have Allah's the Exalted friendship and assistance as well as the friendship and intercession of His Prophet, al-Muṣṭafā ﷺ. Whoever has the most perfect of faith will have the greatest friendship with both Allah and His Messenger, and whoever does the most deeds will be closest to Allah the Exalted and have the greatest attainment of intercession. Allah the Exalted said to His Chosen Prophet ﷺ,

﴿إِنَّ وَلِـِّۧيَ ٱللَّهُ ٱلَّذِي نَزَّلَ ٱلْكِتَـٰبَ ۖ وَهُوَ يَتَوَلَّى ٱلصَّـٰلِحِينَ﴾

"My Protector is Allah, who sent down the Book. He takes care of the righteous." [al-ʾAʿrāf 7:196]

The Glorified One has also said:

﴿وَٱللَّهُ وَلِيُّ ٱلْمُتَّقِينَ﴾

"...and Allah is the Protector of those who have *taqwā*." [al-Jāthiyyah 45:19]

He ﷻ has also said:

﴿وَٱللَّهُ وَلِيُّ ٱلْمُؤْمِنِينَ﴾

"Allah is the Protector of the Believers." [Āl ʿImrān 3:68]

The Majestic and Exalted One has also said:

﴿ذَٰلِكَ بِأَنَّ ٱللَّهَ مَوْلَى ٱلَّذِينَ ءَامَنُوا۟ وَأَنَّ ٱلْكَـٰفِرِينَ لَا مَوْلَىٰ لَهُمْ﴾

"That is because Allah is the Protector of those who believe and because those who disbelieve have no protector." [Muḥammad 47:11]

He ﷺ said, {The family of my father are not friends of mine. Rather, my friend is Allah and the righteous amongst the believers.} Agreed upon.

Regarding this meaning, one of them said,

By your life, man is nothing but his religion,
So do not leave taqwā and rely on lineage
Islam elevated Salmān the Persian
While idolatry humiliated the highborn, Abū Lahab

35. The Path to Felicity, Assistance and Salvation: If the matter is indeed as we have learned – that ranks are not attained except by way of deeds, that Allah the

Exalted's friendship and assistance are connected to *taqwā* and that the intercession of al-Muṣṭafā ﷺ and his friendship is connected to the perfection of faith – then indeed the Muslim who is distinguished by intellect and clear thinking - and he is an upright person who is balanced and positive, not a disturbed, anxious, creature – will buckle down and hasten towards good deeds, without relying on the ancestry of his parents and the nobility of his forefathers, convinced

﴿وَأَن لَّيْسَ لِلْإِنسَـٰنِ إِلَّا مَا سَعَىٰ﴾

"that man will have nothing but what he strives for". [an-Najm 53:39]

Thus, His Lord's ﷻ promise is realised for him after its condition has been fulfilled:

﴿مَنْ عَمِلَ صَـٰلِحًا مِّن ذَكَرٍ أَوْ أُنثَىٰ وَهُوَ مُؤْمِنٌ فَلَنُحْيِيَنَّهُۥ حَيَوٰةً طَيِّبَةً ۖ وَلَنَجْزِيَنَّهُمْ أَجْرَهُم بِأَحْسَنِ مَا كَانُوا۟ يَعْمَلُونَ﴾

"Anyone who acts rightly, male or female, being a believer, We will give them a good life and We will recompense them according to the best of what they did." [an-Naḥl 16:97]

Likewise, this Muslim is not pleased with any friend apart from Allah the Exalted, His Messenger ﷺ and the believers, and therefore he relinquishes any friendship that does not ascend to this level and he cuts any connection between himself and disbelief and its peoples as well as iniquity and its clique. The Exalted One has said:

﴿لَّا يَتَّخِذِ ٱلْمُؤْمِنُونَ ٱلْكَـٰفِرِينَ أَوْلِيَآءَ مِن دُونِ ٱلْمُؤْمِنِينَ﴾

"The believers should not take unbelievers as friends rather than believers". [Āl 'Imrān 3:28]

Thus, he will have triumph and victory over the forces of falsehood and tyranny on earth:

﴿إِنَّمَا وَلِيُّكُمُ ٱللَّهُ وَرَسُولُهُۥ وَٱلَّذِينَ ءَامَنُوا۟ ٱلَّذِينَ يُقِيمُونَ ٱلصَّلَوٰةَ وَيُؤْتُونَ ٱلزَّكَوٰةَ وَهُمْ رَٰكِعُونَ ﴿٥٥﴾ وَمَن يَتَوَلَّ ٱللَّهَ وَرَسُولَهُۥ وَٱلَّذِينَ ءَامَنُوا۟ فَإِنَّ حِزْبَ ٱللَّهِ هُمُ ٱلْغَـٰلِبُونَ﴾

"Your friend is only Allah and His Messenger and those who believe: those who establish the prayer and pay the zakāt, and bow. As for those who make Allah their friend, and His Messenger and those who believe: it is the party of Allah who are victorious." [al-Mā'idah 5:55-56]

﴿بَلِ ٱللَّهُ مَوْلَىٰكُمْ ۖ وَهُوَ خَيْرُ ٱلنَّـٰصِرِينَ﴾

"No, Allah is your Protector. And He is the best of helpers." [Āl ʿImrān 3:150]

36. Some of what the ḥadīth indicates:

i. Reward in the sight of Allah the Exalted is of the same type as the action that the slave puts forward, and thus the reward for removing a calamity is the removal of a calamity. The reward for removing the effect of a calamity is the removal of the effect of a calamity. Assistance is recompensed with assistance, veiling with veiling, and facilitation with facilitation. At-Tirmidhī and others have related from Abū Saʿīd al-Khudrī ؓ who said, 'The Messenger of Allah ﷺ said, {Any believer who feeds a hungry believer, Allah will feed him on the Day of Standing from the fruits of Paradise. Any believer who gives a thirsty believer something to drink, Allah will give him a drink from the Sealed Nectar[252] on the Day of Standing. Any believer who clothes a naked believer, Allah will clothe him with the greenery of Paradise.}[253] He ﷺ also said, {Allah only shows mercy to His merciful slaves.} Agreed upon.

ii. Being beneficent towards the creation is the path to Allah's love ﷻ because {the creation is Allah's dependents – i.e. He guarantees their provision and livelihood – and the most beloved of them to Him are the most beneficial of them to His dependents}, as related by at-Ṭabarānī and others. It is normal for a master and owner to love beneficence for his dependents, and what the ḥadīth mentions by way of removing calamities and so forth is beneficence towards the creation and benefit, and thus it is the path towards love.

iii. A glad tiding and promise – as informed of by the truthful one ﷺ – that whoever's disposition is to remove calamities from others, assist them and veil them will have his life sealed with goodness and he will die upon faith and Islam, because someone who is not a Muslim will not be shown mercy in the Hereafter and thus will not attain facilitation or support or the removal of a calamity.

iv. The removal of calamities and other matters that have been mentioned are general and apply to both Muslims and those who are not Muslim and have declared themselves enemies of the Muslims. Beneficence[254] towards them is sought, and maybe it extends to every creature that has a spirit. He ﷺ said, {Allah has obligated excellence (*iḥsān*) in everything.} Agreed upon.

---

252 Ar. *ar-Raḥīq al-Makhtūm*, i.e. the drink of Paradise that is sealed with musk.

253 i.e. the green clothes of Paradise.

254 Ar. *iḥsān*.

v. Warning against the penetration of ostentation when seeking knowledge, because its penetration in this is greater than its penetration in all other actions. Thus, one should correct one's intention and make it sincere so that one does not lose the reward and waste one's effort.

vi. Seeking assistance and facilitation from Allah the Exalted, because guidance is in His hand, and there is no obedience without His facilitation and kindness. Without that, knowledge is of no benefit and neither is anything else.

vii. Reciting the Qur'ān persistently and gathering to do so, and devoting oneself to understanding it, learning it and implementing, as opposed to leaving it to be recited at the beginning of gathering and special occasions, and at funeral ceremonies and over the dead.

viii. Hastening towards repentance, seeking forgiveness and righteous action. Allah the Exalted has said:

﴿وَسَارِعُوٓا۟ إِلَىٰ مَغْفِرَةٍ مِّن رَّبِّكُمْ وَجَنَّةٍ عَرْضُهَا ٱلسَّمَـٰوَٰتُ وَٱلْأَرْضُ أُعِدَّتْ لِلْمُتَّقِينَ ٱلَّذِينَ يُنفِقُونَ فِى ٱلسَّرَّآءِ وَٱلضَّرَّآءِ وَٱلْكَـٰظِمِينَ ٱلْغَيْظَ وَٱلْعَافِينَ عَنِ ٱلنَّاسِ ۗ وَٱللَّهُ يُحِبُّ ٱلْمُحْسِنِينَ﴾

"Race each other to forgiveness from your Lord and a Paradise as wide as the heavens and the earth, prepared for those who have *taqwā*, those who give in times of both ease and hardship, those who control their rage and pardon other people – Allah loves good-doers..." [Āl 'Imrān 3:133-134]

THE THIRTY-SEVENTH ḤADĪTH

عَدْلُ اللهِ تعالى وَفَضْلُهُ وَقُدْرَتُهُ

عَنِ ابْنِ عَبَّاسٍ ﵄، عَنْ رَسُولِ اللهِ ﷺ فِيمَا يَرْوِيهِ عَنْ رَبِّهِ تَبَارَكَ وَتَعَالَى قَالَ: {إِنَّ اللهَ كَتَبَ الْحَسَنَاتِ وَالسَّيِّئَاتِ ثُمَّ بَيَّنَ: فَمَنْ هَمَّ بِحَسَنَةٍ فَلَمْ يَعْمَلْهَا كَتَبَهَا اللهُ عِنْدَهُ حَسَنَةً كَامِلَةً، وَإِنْ هَمَّ بِهَا فَعَمِلَهَا كَتَبَهَا اللهُ عِنْدَهُ عَشْرَ حَسَنَاتٍ إِلَى سَبْعِمِائَةِ ضِعْفٍ إِلَى أَضْعَافٍ كَثِيرَةٍ، وَإِنْ هَمَّ بِسَيِّئَةٍ فَلَمْ يَعْمَلْهَا كَتَبَهَا اللهُ عِنْدَهُ حَسَنَةً كَامِلَةً، وَإِنْ هَمَّ بِهَا فَعَمِلَهَا كَتَبَهَا اللهُ سَيِّئَةً وَاحِدَةً.} رواه البخاري مُسْلِمٌ في صحيحيهما بهذه الحروف.

فَانْظُرْ يَا أَخِي وَفَّقَنَا اللهُ وإِيَّاكَ إِلَى عَظِيمِ لُطْفِ اللهِ تَعَالَى، وَتَأَمَّلْ هَذِهِ الْأَلْفَاظَ.

وَقَوْلُهُ: {عِنْدَهُ} إشارة إلى الاعْتِناء بها.

وقوله: {كامِلَةً} للتأكيد وشِدَّةِ الاعْتِناء بها.

وقال في السَّيِّئَةِ التي هَمَّ بها، ثُمَّ تَرَكَهَا كَتبها اللهُ عِنْدَهُ حَسَنَةً كامِلَةً، فأَكَّدها بكامِلَةٍ. وإنْ عَمِلَها كَتَبها سَيِّئَةً واحِدَةً، فأَكَّدَ تَقْليلَها بواحِدَةٍ، ولم يُؤَكِّدْها بكامِلَةٍ، فللهِ الحَمْدُ والمِنَّة، سُبْحَانَهُ لا نُحْصِي ثَنَاءً عليه، وباللهِ التوفيق.

Allah the Exalted's Justice, Bounty and Power

It is on the authority of Ibn ʿAbbās ﵄ that the Messenger of Allah ﷺ in that which he related from his Lord ﷻ said, {Allah has written the good actions and the bad actions, and then He explained that: whoever intends to do a good action but does not do it, Allah writes it down with Himself as a complete good action. If he intends to do it and does it, Allah writes it down with Himself as ten good actions, up to seven hundred multiples of it, up to many multiples of it. If he intends to do a wrong action and then does not do it, Allah writes it down with Himself as a complete good action. If he intends to do it and then does it, Allah writes it down as a single wrong action.} Al-Bukhārī and Muslim have related it in their two *Ṣaḥīḥ* collections with this wording.

Look,[255] my brother – may Allah grant both us and you success towards the sublimity of Allah the Exalted's kindness – and contemplate these words:

His statement 'with Himself' indicates his concern for it.

His statement 'complete' is for emphasis and shows His great concern for it.

He said regarding the bad action that a person intends to do and then abandons that Allah writes it with Himself as one complete good action, and he emphasised it by saying 'complete'. If he does it, it is written as a single wrong action, and he emphasised its diminution by saying 'single' and did not emphasis it by saying 'complete'. To Allah belongs all praise and benevolence. Glory be to Him, whose praise cannot be enumerated, and with Allah alone is every success.

The ḥadīth has been related by al-Bukhārī in the Book of *ar-Riqāq*[256] (the chapter on whoever intends to do a good deed or bad deed), no.6126, as well as the Book of Tawḥīd. Muslim has related it in the Book of Faith (the chapter on the slave intending a good deed and it is written for him and intending a bad deed and it is not written for him), no.131.

The Importance of the Ḥadīth:

This ḥadīth qudsī contains immense glad tidings and sublime hope for Allah's prevalent favour and overflowing mercy, which encompasses everything. It provokes radiant hope in the soul and prepares it to work and toil within Allah's surveillance and knowledge, and under His authority, hegemony, justice and kindness.

The Language of the Ḥadīth:

(كتب الحسنات والسيئات) *katab al-ḥasanāt w as-sayyi'āt*: He has commanded the guardian angels to write them both down – as they are in His knowledge – corresponding to the reality.

(هم) *hamma*: to want and intend, *hamm* is to prefer to intend to do something, and thus you have the *himmah* [ambition, resolution, determination] to do it, it is more than merely the thought of it passing through the heart.

(بحسنة) *biḥasanah*: an act of obedience that is obligatory or recommended.

(ضعف) *ḍi'fin*: like, al-Azharī said, '*Ḍi'f* in the speech of the Arabs is the similar of something, and this is the foundation. Then *ḍi'f* was used for the similar and what is added to it, and there is no limit to what is added.

(بسيئة) *bisayyi'ah*: an act of disobedience, whether small or big.

255 (tn): This part is the words of Imam an-Nawawī ﷺ.

256 (tn): i.e. that which produces mercy in the heart.

Legal Matters and Other Guidance from the Ḥadīth:
Preface:
The ḥadīth includes the writing down of good actions and bad actions and intending to do good actions and bad actions, and thus there are four categories:

1. Doing Good Actions: The believer gets ten good deeds for every good action that he does, and that is because he did not stop at mere intention and resolve. Instead, he proceeded to the field of action, and the evidence for this is the Exalted One's statement,

﴿مَن جَآءَ بِٱلْحَسَنَةِ فَلَهُۥ عَشْرُ أَمْثَالِهَا﴾

"Those who produce a good action will have ten like it." [al-Anʿām 6:160]

As for it being multiplied beyond, this is for whomever Allah wants to multiply it, and the evidence for this is Allah the Exalted's statement,

﴿مَّثَلُ ٱلَّذِينَ يُنفِقُونَ أَمْوَٰلَهُمْ فِى سَبِيلِ ٱللَّهِ كَمَثَلِ حَبَّةٍ أَنۢبَتَتْ سَبْعَ سَنَابِلَ فِى كُلِّ سُنۢبُلَةٍ مِّا۟ئَةُ حَبَّةٍ ۗ وَٱللَّهُ يُضَٰعِفُ لِمَن يَشَآءُ ۗ وَٱللَّهُ وَٰسِعٌ عَلِيمٌ﴾

"The metaphor of those who spend their wealth in the Way of Allah is that of a grain which produces seven ears; in every ear there are a hundred grains. Allah gives such multiplied increase to whomever He wills. Allah is All-Encompassing, All-Knowing." [al-Baqarah 2:261]

Muslim has related from Ibn Masʿūd that he said, 'A man came with a haltered camel and said, "O Messenger of Allah, this is for the sake of Allah." He replied, {On the Day of Standing, you will have seven hundred camels.}'

The multiplication of good deeds beyond ten is according to the perfection of one's Islam, and the completion of one's sincerity. It is also according to the superiority of the action and it being done in its proper place.

2. Doing Bad Actions: Every bad deed that the slave commits is written as one bad deed, without multiplication. The Exalted One has said,

﴿وَمَن جَآءَ بِٱلسَّيِّئَةِ فَلَا يُجْزَىٰٓ إِلَّا مِثْلَهَا وَهُمْ لَا يُظْلَمُونَ﴾

"But those who produce a bad action will only be repaid with its equivalent and they will not be wronged." [al-Anʿām 6:160]

However, a bad deed can be magnified because of the nobility of the time, the place and the person committing it.

A. A bad deed is considered increasingly unlawful in the sight of Allah if done in one of the Sacred Months, due to their nobility with Allah. He ﷻ has said:

﴿إِنَّ عِدَّةَ ٱلشُّهُورِ عِندَ ٱللَّهِ ٱثْنَا عَشَرَ شَهْرًا فِى كِتَـٰبِ ٱللَّهِ يَوْمَ خَلَقَ ٱلسَّمَـٰوَٰتِ وَٱلْأَرْضَ مِنْهَآ أَرْبَعَةٌ حُرُمٌ ۚ ذَٰلِكَ ٱلدِّينُ ٱلْقَيِّمُ ۚ فَلَا تَظْلِمُوا۟ فِيهِنَّ أَنفُسَكُمْ﴾

"There have been twelve months with Allah in the Book of Allah, from the day He first created the heavens and the earth. Four of them are sacred. That is the True Religion. So do not wrong yourselves during them." [at-Tawbah 9:36]

Al-Qatādah said regarding the exegesis of this verse, 'Know that wrongdoing in these sacred months is a greater error and sin than outside of them, even though wrongdoing is of no avail under any circumstance. However, Allah the Exalted magnifies what He wants of His affair.'

B. Sinning in the Sacred Precinct is greater due to the nobility of the place. The Exalted One has said:

﴿ٱلْحَجُّ أَشْهُرٌ مَّعْلُومَـٰتٌ ۚ فَمَن فَرَضَ فِيهِنَّ ٱلْحَجَّ فَلَا رَفَثَ وَلَا فُسُوقَ وَلَا جِدَالَ فِى ٱلْحَجِّ﴾

"The Ḥajj takes place during certain well-known months. If anyone undertakes the obligation of the Ḥajj in them, there must be no sexual intercourse, no wrongdoing, nor any quarrelling during the Ḥajj." [al-Baqarah 2:197]

Ibn 'Umar said, 'Iniquity is to commit acts of disobedience in the Sacred Precinct, and the Exalted One has said:

﴿وَمَن يُرِدْ فِيهِ بِإِلْحَادٍۭ بِظُلْمٍ نُّذِقْهُ مِنْ عَذَابٍ أَلِيمٍ﴾

"...those who desire to profane it with wrongdoing, We will let them taste a painful punishment." [al-Ḥajj 22:25]

This is why a group of the Companions and the First Three Generations were wary of living in the Sacred Precinct for fear of committing sins therein. They include Ibn 'Abbās, 'Abdullah ibn 'Amr ibn al-'Āṣ and 'Umar ibn 'Abdul 'Azīz. It has been related that 'Umar ibn al-Khaṭṭāb ؓ said, 'To commit seventy sins – meaning outside of Makkah – is more beloved to me than committing one sin inside Makkah.' It has been related from Mujāhid that he said, 'Bad deeds in Makkah are multiplied just as good deeds are multiplied.'

C. A bad deed is greater from certain slaves of Allah, due to the nobility of the one committing, the potency of their knowledge of Allah and their nearness to Him ﷻ. The Exalted One has said:

﴿يَٰنِسَآءَ ٱلنَّبِيِّ مَن يَأْتِ مِنكُنَّ بِفَٰحِشَةٍ مُّبَيِّنَةٍ يُضَٰعَفْ لَهَا ٱلْعَذَابُ ضِعْفَيْنِ ۚ وَكَانَ ذَٰلِكَ

عَلَى ٱللَّهِ يَسِيرًا ﴿٣٠﴾ وَمَن يَقْنُتْ مِنكُنَّ لِلَّهِ وَرَسُولِهِۦ وَتَعْمَلْ صَٰلِحًا نُّؤْتِهَآ أَجْرَهَا مَرَّتَيْنِ﴾

"Wives of the Prophet! If any of you commits an obvious act of indecency, she will receive double the punishment. That is an easy matter for Allah. But those of you who are obedient to Allah and His Messenger and act rightly will be given their reward twice over." [al-Aḥzāb 33:30-31]

3. Intending to Do Good Actions: The meaning of *hamm* is to want and intend, to have resolve and determination. It is not just a thought. If someone intends to do a good action, Allah writes it down with Himself as a single good action, and that is because the intention to do a good action is a cause and a beginning of doing it, and the cause of goodness is also goodness.

The explanation of *hamm* is mentioned in the ḥadīth of Abū Hurayrah as related by Muslim: {If My slaves talks about doing a good deed, I write down a good deed for him.} There is also the ḥadīth of Khuraym ibn Fātik in the *Musnad*: {If someone intends to do a good deed but does not do it, Allah knows from him that his heartfelt it and was keen to do it and He writes a good deed for him.} Abū ad-Dardā' said, {Whoever gets into bed and intends to pray at night but his eyes are too heavy until the morning, what he intended is written for him.} This has been related from him *marfūʿan*,[257] and Ibn Mājah collected it *marfūʿan*. Ad-Dāraquṭnī said, 'What has been preserved is that it is *mawqūf*.'[258] Saʿīd ibn al-Musayyib said, 'Whoever intends to pray, fast, perform a pilgrimage or partake in battle and is prevented from doing so, what he intended reaches Allah the Exalted'.

4. Intending to Do Bad Actions: If the slave intends to do a bad action and then does not do it, a complete good action is written for him. There is the ḥadīth of Abū Hurayrah as related by Muslim, {…leaving it is only for My sake}, and according to al-Bukhārī, {…if he leaves it for My sake.} This is evidence that leaving the action is qualified by it being for Allah the Exalted, and thus the one who leaves it for this reason deserves the complete good deed, because he intended righteous action, which is to please Allah the Exalted by leaving evil action. As for the person who leaves a bad action because he fears the creation or he wants to make a show before them, he does not deserve to have a good deed written for him. Rather, it

257 (tn): i.e. attributed to the Messenger of Allah ﷺ.

258 (tn): i.e. that which is attributed to a Companion and the Companion did not ascribe it to the Messenger of Allah ﷺ.

has been said that he is punished for leaving a bad deed with this intention. This is because he gave precedence to the fear of people over the fear of Allah, which is unlawful, and likewise, he intended to parade for people, which is also unlawful.

Al-Qāḍī ʿIyāḍ approved of the ḥadīth of Ibn ʿAbbās[259] being qualified by the ḥadīth of Abū Hurayrah.

Al-Ḥāfiẓ Ibn Ḥajar said, 'It is possible that one can attain a good deed simply by leaving a bad deed, without calling to mind that which qualifies it, and it would not be the same good deed mentioned in the ḥadīth. This is due to what has already been mentioned, in that leaving disobedience is to refrain from evil, and refraining from evil is good. It is also possible that one can have a good deed written for himself if he intends disobedience and then leaves it, and if he leaves it out of fear of his Lord ﷻ multiple good deeds will be written for him.

Al-Khaṭṭābī said, 'A good deed is written for leaving if the one leaving it is able to do the deed and then leaves it, because a person is not considered leaving unless he has the ability, i.e. a barrier comes between him and the deed he is keen to commit, such as a man going to fornicate with a woman and he finds the door locked and it is difficult to open it.'

5. The Sublime Bounty: Muslim's narration has this addition, {...or Allah the Exalted effaces it, and no one is destroyed before Allah the Exalted apart from someone who is destroyed.} This indicates Allah's sublime bounty, with Whom no one is destroyed apart from the one who casts himself into destruction,[260] transgresses the limits, dares to commit evil deeds and turns away from good deeds. This is why Ibn Masʿūd said, 'Woe to the one whose single deeds outnumber his tens of deeds'.

6. The Angels Being Informed of What a Person Intends: This happens to them, either by way of inspiration or the heart being disclosed to them, and it has been said that when an evil deed is intended, the angel finds a foul odour, and if it's a good deed, it finds a pleasant scent.

7. The Superiority of Fasting: Fasting is distinguished from other acts of worship because only Allah the Exalted knows the extent to which the reward is multiplied. The Messenger of Allah ﷺ said, {Every action done by the son of Adam is for him except fasting, for it is for Me and I reward it.} This is because it is the best kind of patience. Allah the Exalted has said:

﴿إِنَّمَا يُوَفَّى ٱلصَّـٰبِرُونَ أَجْرَهُم بِغَيْرِ حِسَابٍ﴾

259 (tn): i.e. the ḥadīth of this chapter.

260 (tn): Please see al-Baqarah 2:195.

"The steadfast will be paid their wages in full without any reckoning." [az-Zumar 39:10]

8. Allah's mercy towards his believing slaves is vast, His forgiveness is comprehensive and His giving is unlimited.

9. Allah the Exalted does not takes His slaves to task for what they say within themselves or if they think about disobedience unless they approve that action and implement it.

10. It is upon the Muslim to have the constant intention to do good deeds. Perhaps their reward will be written for him, and he will train himself to do good when the means have been prepared for him.

11. Sincerity in doing acts of obedience and leaving disobedience is the foundation of being rewarded as a result. The greater the sincerity, the greater the reward is multiplied and increased.

THE THIRTY-EIGHTH ḤADĪTH

وَسَائِلُ القُربِ مِنَ اللهِ تعالى ونَيْلِ مَحَبَّتِه

عَنْ أَبِي هُرَيْرَةَ ﷺ قَالَ: قَالَ رَسُوْلُ اللهِ ﷺ: {إِنَّ اللهَ تعالَى قَالَ: «مَنْ عَادَى لِي وَلِيًّا فَقَدْ آذَنْتُهُ بِالْحَرْبِ، وَمَا تَقَرَّبَ إِلَيَّ عَبْدِي بِشَيْءٍ أَحَبَّ إِلَيَّ مِمَّا افْتَرَضْتُ عَلَيْهِ، وَمَا يَزَالُ عَبْدِي يَتَقَرَّبُ إِلَيَّ بِالنَّوَافِلِ حَتَّى أُحِبَّهُ، فَإِذَا أَحْبَبْتُهُ كُنْتُ سَمْعَهُ الَّذِي يَسْمَعُ بِهِ، وَبَصَرَهُ الَّذِي يُبْصِرُ بِهِ، وَيَدَهُ الَّتِي يَبْطِشُ بِهَا، وَرِجْلَهُ الَّتِي يَمْشِي بِهَا، وَإِنْ سَأَلَنِي لَأُعْطِيَنَّهُ، وَلَئِنِ اسْتَعَاذَنِي لَأُعِيذَنَّهُ»} رَوَاهُ الْبُخَارِيُّ.

The Means of Drawing Nearer to Allah the Exalted and Attaining His Love

It is on the authority of Abū Hurayrah ﷺ who said, 'The Messenger of Allah ﷺ said, {Allah the Exalted has said, 'Whoever shows enmity to a friend of mine then I declare war on him. My slave does not draw nearer to Me with anything more beloved to Me than that which I have made obligatory upon him. My slave continues to draw nearer to Me with supererogatory acts until I love him. When I love him, I am his hearing with which he hears, his sight with which he sees, his hand with which he grasps and his foot with which he walks. If he asks Me, I will certainly give him, and if he seeks refuge in Me, I will certainly give him refuge.'} Related by al-Bukhārī.

Al-Bukhārī has related the ḥadīth in the Book of *ar-Riqāq* (the chapter on modesty), no.6137, and al-Bukhārī has the addition: {I do not hesitate in anything I do the way I hesitate regarding My believing slave. He dislikes death and I dislike it when something bad happens to him.}

The Importance of the Ḥadīth:
Allah ﷻ takes care of His friends with love and attention, and He jealously protects them from any harm coming to them. This noble ḥadīth elucidates who Allah's friends and beloveds are in the life and the Hereafter, and this is why it has been said that it is the noblest ḥadīth regarding the mention of friends.

Ash-Shawkānī said, 'The ḥadīth {Whoever transgresses against a friend of Mine...} contains numerous majestic benefits for the one who truly understands them and contemplates them as they should be contemplated.

At-Ṭukhī said, 'This ḥadīth is the foundation for one's conduct with Allah the Exalted and arriving at knowing Him and loving Him. It is the foundation of the path towards carrying obligation, both the inward, which is *īmān*, and the outward, which is *islām*, and the composite of both, which is *iḥsān*, just as the ḥadīth of Jibrīl 🙼 contains the same. *Iḥsān* contains the stations of those who travel towards Allah, such as abstinence,[261] sincerity,[262] surveillance[263] and so forth.

The Language of the Ḥadīth:

(عادى) *ʿādā*: to harm, loathe and provoke in word or deed.

(وليا) *waliyyan*: the *walī* is on the *faʿīl* pattern[264] and has the meaning of an active participle,[265] because he constantly (*walā*) worships Allah and obeys Him without the intervention of any disobedience. The meaning could also be passive,[266] because Allah the Exalted constantly maintains him and looks after him in exchange for him maintaining His limits and looking after His commands and prohibitions. It is said in the *Ṣiḥāḥ* that *walī* is the opposite of enemy, and *wilāyah*[267] is the opposite of enmity. The foundation of *wilāyah* is love and drawing near, and the foundation of enmity is hatred and remoteness. Ibn Ḥajar said in *Fatḥ al-Bārī*, 'What is meant by a *walī* of Allah is the one who knows Allah the Exalted, is devoted to obeying Him and is sincere in worshipping Him.' Allah the Exalted has said:

$$﴿أَلَا إِنَّ أَوْلِيَآءَ ٱللَّهِ لَا خَوْفٌ عَلَيْهِمْ وَلَا هُمْ يَحْزَنُونَ ۝ ٱلَّذِينَ ءَامَنُوا۟ وَكَانُوا۟ يَتَّقُونَ﴾$$

"Yes, the friends of Allah will have no fear and know no sorrow: those who have faith and *taqwā*, there is good news for them in the life of this world and in the Hereafter. There is no changing the words of Allah. That is the great victory." [Yūnus 10:62-63]

(فقد آذنته بالحرب) *faqad ādhantuhu bil-ḥarb*: *ādhantuhu* means 'I have informed him', and the meaning is that whoever harms a believer Allah informs him that He is at war with him, and when Allah the Exalted wages war against the slave, He destroys him.

---

261 Ar. *az-zuhd*.

262 Ar. *al-ikhlāṣ*.

263 Ar. *al-murāqabah*, which is knowing that Allah sees you; please refer to the ḥadīth of Jibrīl 🙼 which is the second ḥadīth in this book.

264 (tn): i.e. a pattern in Arabic that can indicate either the active or the passive.

265 Ar. *faʿil*.

266 Ar. *mafʿūl*.

267 (tn): i.e. friendship.

(النوافل) *an-nawāfil*: that which is in addition to the obligatory acts of worship; *nawāfil* is the plural of *nāfilah* and *nafl*, which means booty, gift and addition.

(استعاذني) *istaʿādhanī*: to seek refuge and protection from that which one fears.

(لأعيذنه) *laʾuʿīdhannahu*: I will protect him from that which he fears.

Legal Matters and Other Guidance from the Ḥadīth:

1. The Friends of Allah the Exalted: They are His true slaves, who obey Him with sincerity, and Allah ﷻ has described them in His Noble Book with the attributes of faith and *taqwā*. The Exalted One has said, **"Yes, the friends of Allah will have no fear and know no sorrow: those who have faith and *taqwā*."** [Yūnus 10:62-63] Thus, the first pillar of friendship is faith in Allah, and the second is *taqwā*. This makes the door wide and open for people to enter the courtyard of friendship, and shade themselves in its security and tranquillity. From there, they can ascend the ranks of obedience and sincerity until they arrive at the stratum of the pious predecessors of the Ummah of Muḥammad ﷺ which has been divided into three categories according to Allah ﷻ statement:

﴿ثُمَّ أَوْرَثْنَا ٱلْكِتَـٰبَ ٱلَّذِينَ ٱصْطَفَيْنَا مِنْ عِبَادِنَا ۖ فَمِنْهُمْ ظَالِمٌ لِّنَفْسِهِۦ وَمِنْهُم مُّقْتَصِدٌ وَمِنْهُمْ سَابِقٌۢ بِٱلْخَيْرَٰتِ بِإِذْنِ ٱللَّهِ ۚ ذَٰلِكَ هُوَ ٱلْفَضْلُ ٱلْكَبِيرُ﴾

"Then We have made our chosen slaves inherit the Book. Some of them wrong themselves, some of them are in the middle and some of them outdo each other in good by Allah's permission. That is the great favour." [Fāṭir 35:32]

Those who wrong themselves are those who have sins that they persist in. Those in the middle are those who carry out their obligations and avoid the unlawful, and these people are amongst the friends of Allah but they are in the lower stratum. Those who outdo each other in good are those who carry out their obligations as well as supererogatory acts and avoid that which is unlawful and disliked, and these are the people who ascend to the higher stratum of Allah the Exalted's friends.

The best friends of Allah the Exalted are the Prophets and Messengers, those who have been made infallible from every sin and mistake and are assisted by miracles from Allah ﷻ. The best friends after the Prophets and Messengers are the Companions of Allah's Messenger ﷺ who acted in accordance with Allah's Book and the Sunnah of His Messenger ﷺ and then those amongst the generations that followed them until today that were attributed the quality of friendship. No one can be a true friend of Allah unless faith and *taqwā* and have been realised within him, he follows the Messenger of Allah ﷺ is guided by his guidance and takes him as a model in his words and deeds.

A grave mistake that Muslims have fallen into in recent times is that they have confined friendship to just a few individuals, whom time grants them between one century and another. The great calamity[268] is that this exalted rank in Islam has come to be granted to ignorant individuals, or lying swindlers who engage in trickery and charlatanry. It is more appropriate for these people to be categorised amongst the friends of Shayṭān, and the enemies of Allah and Islam.

2. Treating Allah the Exalted's Friends as Enemies: Anyone who harms the believer who has *taqwā*, or transgresses against him regarding his property, his person or his honour, Allah the Exalted is informing him that He is at war with him, and when Allah is at war with a slave, He destroys him. He grants respite but He does not overlook. He gives wrongdoers a certain period of time and then He seizes them with the seizing of one who is Almighty, All-Powerful.[269] In some of the narrations of the ḥadīth, it is related that treating a friend as an enemy and harming him is to wage war against Allah. In the ḥadīth of ʿĀʾishah ﷺ as in the *Musnad*, the wording is, {Whoever harms a friend has regarded it as fair game to wage war against Me.} In the ḥadīth of Abū Umāmah, according to at-Ṭabarānī, the wording is, {Whoever treats a friend of Mine with contempt is openly waging war against Me.}

As for treating a friend as an enemy, as you can imagine, Ibn Ḥajar clarified this in *Fatḥ al-Bārī* when he said, 'The existence of someone treating him – i.e. the friend – as an enemy is seen as odd because enmity can only be between two parties, and it is the nature of the friend to have forbearance and to pardon people that behave foolishly towards him. I answer by saying that enmity is not confined to worldly disputes and interactions, for example. Rather, it could occur because of hatred arising from bigotry, such as the innovator having hatred towards the orthodox[270] Muslim, and thus enmity occurs between two parties. As for the side of the friend, it is for Allah the Exalted and in His cause. As for the other party, he is as described above. Likewise, the open sinner is despised by the friend, and the sinner despises him in turn because he rebukes him and constantly tries to prevent him from giving in to his evil desires. The word enmity can be used while what is meant is that only one party is actually acting it out while the other party is only responding as necessary'.

End of quote, with slight modification.

268 (tn): please see Sūrat an-Nāziʿāt 78:34.

269 (tn): please see Sūrat al-Qamar, 54:42.

270 Ar. *Sunnī*.

3. The Best Actions and the Most Beloved to Allah the Exalted are the Performance of Obligations: This benefit is explicit in Allah the Exalted's statement in this ḥadīth: {My slave does not draw nearer to Me with anything more beloved to Me than that which I have made obligatory upon him.} It has been related from 'Umar ibn al-Khaṭṭāb ؓ that he said, 'The best of actions is to carry out what Allah has made obligatory, to be wary of what Allah has made unlawful and to have a sincere intention regarding that which is with Allah the Exalted.' It is on the authority of 'Umar ibn 'Abdul 'Azīz that he said in his *khuṭbah*, 'The best acts of worship are to carry out the obligations and to avoid that which is unlawful'. This is because Allah the Exalted has only given His slaves these obligations in order to draw them nearer to Him and to make necessary for them His pleasure and His mercy. The greatest physical obligation that draws one nearer to Allah is the prayer. The Exalted One has said:

$$﴿وَٱسْجُدْ وَٱقْتَرِب﴾$$

"but prostrate and draw near." [al-'Alaq 96:19]

He ﷺ said, {The nearest moment the slave is to his Lord is when He is prostrating.}

One of the obligations that draws one nearer to Allah the Exalted is the shepherd showing justice to his flock, whether his flock is the public, like that of a ruler, or private, like the justice that individuals show towards their families and children. At-Tirmidhī has related from Abū Saʿīd al-Khudrī that the Prophet ﷺ said, {The most beloved of slaves to Allah on the Day of Standing and sitting nearest to Him is the just leader.} In *Ṣaḥīḥ Muslim*, it is on the authority of 'Abdullah ibn 'Umar that the Prophet ﷺ said, {Those who act justly in the sight of Allah are on minbars of light on the right hand of the All-Merciful, and both of His hands are right; those who showed justice in their rule, towards their families and what they were in charge of.}

4. Carrying Out Obligations Includes Leaving Acts of Disobedience, because Allah the Exalted has obligated His slaves to leave acts of disobedience. He the Glorified has informed us that whoever transgresses His bounds and disobeys him deserves painful punishment in this life and the Hereafter. Thus, from this angle, leaving disobedience comes under the general meaning of his statement: {My slave does not draw nearer to Me with anything more beloved to Me than that which I have made obligatory upon him.} Indeed, the obligations of leaving disobedience take precedence over the obligations of carrying out acts of obedience, as is evidenced by the ḥadīth of the Prophet ﷺ {When I command you to something, do as much of it as you are able to. When I forbid you from something, do not approach it.}

Ibn Rajab, in his commentary on this ḥadīth, went with the opinion that all acts of disobedience are an act of war against Allah. He quoted the statement of al-Ḥasan: 'Son of Adam, do you have the ability to wage war against Allah? Indeed, whoever disobeys Allah has waged war against him. However, whenever the sin is more shameful, the waging of war against Allah is more vehement, and this is why Allah the Exalted has described consumers of usury and highway robbers as waging war against Allah and His Messenger, due to the magnitude of their oppression of His slaves and striving to spread corruption in His lands'.

5. Drawing Nearer to Allah the Exalted Through Supererogatory Acts: This drawing nearer to Allah and endearing oneself to Him – as in the ḥadīth of Abū Umāmah – does not happen until after carrying out one's obligations, and it is by striving to carry out supererogatory acts of obedience, such as the prayer, fasting, the zakāt and Ḥajj, and to restrain oneself from intricate disliked matters out of carefulness. This makes Allah's love necessary for the slave, and whomever Allah loves, He endows him with obedience to Him and busies him with remembering Him and worshipping Him. This, in turn, necessitates that he draw nearer to Him and prosper with Him. Allah the Exalted has described His slaves who love Him and are beloved to Him by saying:

﴿مَن يَرْتَدَّ مِنكُمْ عَن دِينِهِۦ فَسَوْفَ يَأْتِى ٱللَّهُ بِقَوْمٍ يُحِبُّهُمْ وَيُحِبُّونَهُۥٓ أَذِلَّةٍ عَلَى ٱلْمُؤْمِنِينَ أَعِزَّةٍ

عَلَى ٱلْكَـٰفِرِينَ يُجَـٰهِدُونَ فِى سَبِيلِ ٱللَّهِ وَلَا يَخَافُونَ لَوْمَةَ لَآئِمٍ ۚ

ذَٰلِكَ فَضْلُ ٱللَّهِ يُؤْتِيهِ مَن يَشَآءُ ۚ وَٱللَّهُ وَٰسِعٌ عَلِيمٌ﴾

"If any of you renounce your religion, Allah will bring forward a people whom He loves and who love Him, humble to the believers, fierce to the unbelievers, who strive in the Way of Allah and do not fear the blame of any censurer. That is the unbounded favour of Allah that He gives to whomever He wills. Allah is Boundless, All-Knowing." [al-Mā'idah 5:54]

One of the greatest supererogatory acts with which the slave can draw nearer to Allah is to recite the Qur'ān often and listen to it with reflection, contemplation and understanding. At-Tirmidhī has related from Abū Umāmah *marfūʿan*, {The slave does not draw nearer to Allah like that which comes out of him}, meaning the Qur'ān. There is nothing sweeter to those who love than the speech of those they love; it is the joy of their hearts and the utmost of what they seek. Ibn Masʿūd said, 'Whoever loves the Qur'ān loves Allah and His Messenger.'

Another great supererogatory act is to remember Allah much. The Exalted One has said:

﴿فَٱذْكُرُونِىٓ أَذْكُرْكُمْ﴾

"Remember Me, I will remember you." [al-Baqarah 2:152]

Al-Bukhārī and Muslim have related that the Messenger of Allah ﷺ said, {Allah the Exalted says, 'I am as My slave thinks of Me. I am with Him when He remembers Me. If he remembers Me within himself, I remember Him within Myself. If he remembers Me in a gathering, I remember him in a gathering that is better than theirs.'}

6. The Effect of Allah's Love Towards His Friend: The effect of Allah's love towards his slave is made clear in the ḥadīth: {When I love him, I am his hearing with which he hears, his sight with which he sees, his hand with which he grasps and his foot with which he walks.} In some narrations: {...his heart with which he thinks and his tongue with which he speaks.} Ibn Rajab said, 'What is meant by these words is that whoever works hard to draw nearer to Allah by way of obligations and then supererogatory acts, He brings him nearer to him and raises him from the rank of *īmān* to the rank of *iḥsān,* and thus he comes to worship Allah with presence and surveillance, as if he is seeing Him. His heart is thus filled with knowledge of Allah along with His love and His sublimity, fear of Him and awe of Him, familiarity with Him and yearning for Him, until this knowledge that is in his heart becomes an observer of Him with the eye of insight.

When the heart is filled with Allah's sublimity, everything besides Him is eliminated from the heart. Nothing of the slave's ego or passions remains. He wants nothing except that which his Master wants from him, and at that point, the slave only articulates His remembrance, he only moves by His command. If he speaks, he speaks by Allah. If he hears, he hears by Him. If he looks, he looks by Him. If he grasps, He grasps by Him. This is what is meant by his statement, {...I am his hearing with which he hears...} Whoever indicates towards something other than this is only indicating towards heresy, such as incarnation[271] and union,[272] and Allah and His Messenger are free of this.

Ash-Shawkānī went with the opinion that what is meant is the Lord ﷻ, providing His light to those limbs, which will illuminate the paths of guidance and disperse the clouds of error. The Noble Qur'ān has articulated that Allah is the Light of the heavens and the earth, and it is has been authentically related that the Prophet ﷺ would supplicate by saying, {O Allah, put light in my heart, light in my eyes, light in my ears...}

271 Ar. *ḥulūl,* i.e. the belief that Allah is present in everything such that Allah and the thing become one.

272 Ar. *ittiḥād,* as above.

7. The Friend's Supplications Are Answered: Part of Allah's honouring of His friend is that if he asks Him, He gives to him, and if he seeks refuge in Him from something, He grants him refuge from it. If he supplicates to Him, He answers him, and thus, due to Allah's magnanimity towards him, he becomes someone whose supplications are answered. Many of the righteous of the First Three Generations were known to have their supplications answered, such as al-Barāʾ ibn Mālik, al-Barāʾ ibn ʿĀzib, Saʿd ibn Abī Waqqāṣ, and others. However, most of those whose supplications were normally answered were patient with tribulation, chose its reward, and thus did not supplicate to be relieved from it. Maybe the believer whose supplications are answered supplicates and Allah knows that what is good for him lies in something else. Thus, He does not give him what he asks and instead gives him what is good, either in this life or the Hereafter. Aḥmad, al-Bazzār and Abū Yaʿlā have collected with good chains of transmission, also al-Ḥākim, who said that its chain of transmission is authentic, the ḥadīth of Abū Saʿīd al-Khudrī where the Prophet ﷺ said: {There is no Muslim who makes a supplication that contains no sin or severing of kinship ties except that Allah gives him one of three things: either He expedites his supplication for him, He puts it aside for him in the Hereafter, or He averts similar calamity from him.}

8. What is Meant by Allah the Exalted Hesitating Regarding the Believer: The following addition is mentioned in *Ṣaḥīḥ al-Bukhārī*: {I do not hesitate in anything I do the way I hesitate regarding My believing slave. He dislikes death and I dislike it when something bad happens to him.} Ibn Ṣalāḥ said, 'It is not the literal, known hesitation that is meant here. Rather, it means that He acts towards him like someone who is reluctant and averse. In other words, due to His love for him, He dislikes something bad happening to him in the form of death, because it is the greatest of pains in this world, except for in the case of a few people, and even though it is inevitable. As has been mentioned, death has been decreed and predestined for everyone, as every soul shall taste death. This narration also informs us that He does not do this because He wants to abase him. Rather, He wants to elevate him, because it is a path that leads him to the abode of magnanimity and felicity.

9. The Legitimacy of Modesty: Al-Bukhārī used this ḥadīth as evidence for modesty, as he has mentioned it in the chapter on modesty, because drawing nearer to Allah the Exalted by way of supererogatory acts can only be with the utmost modesty. Likewise, treating the friends of Allah the Exalted as friends and not treating them as enemies can only be done with the utmost modesty and humility before Allah ﷻ. Muslim has related from the ḥadīth of ʿIyāḍ ibn Ḥammār in which the Messenger of Allah ﷺ said, {Allah the Exalted has revealed to me that you be modest such that no one vaunts himself over anyone else.}

10. The Ḥadīth Advises:

- The great rank of the friend, because he has exited from his own planning and direction and come under that of His Lord, Exalted is He. He has moved from helping himself to being helped by Allah. He does not rely on his own strength or power but instead, he sincerely relies on Allah's strength and power.

- If someone is harming a friend and then is not hastily afflicted with regards to his person, his property or his children, it should not be presumed that he is safe from Allah taking action upon him. His affliction could come in other forms, regarding something similar, such as an affliction in his religion, for example.

THE THIRTY-NINTH ḤADĪTH

رَفْعُ الحَرَجِ في الإسلام

عَن ابْنِ عَبَّاسٍ ﷺ: أَنَّ رَسُولَ اللهِ ﷺ قَالَ: {إِنَّ اللهَ تَجَاوَزَ لِي عَنْ أُمَّتِي: الخَطَأَ، وَالنِّسْيَانَ، وَمَا اسْتُكْرِهُوا عَلَيْهِ.}

حديث حسن رواه ابن ماجه والبيهقي وغيرهما.

The Lifting of Sin in Islam

It is on the authority of Ibn ʿAbbās ﷺ that the Messenger of Allah ﷺ said, {For my sake, Allah has overlooked the following from my Ummah: mistakes, forgetfulness and that which they are forced to do.}

It is a good ḥadīth that has been related by Ibn Mājah, al-Bayhaqī and others.

Ibn Mājah collected the ḥadīth in the Book of Divorce (the chapter on the divorce of someone who is forced and someone who forgets), no.2043, and his wording is, {Allah has unburdened...} Al-Bayhaqī has collected it in the Book of Faith (the chapter on comprehensive faith), 10/60.

Ibn Ḥibbān has collected it in his *Ṣaḥīḥ*, as well as al-Ḥākim and ad-Dāraquṭnī. Ibn Rajab al-Ḥanbalī said about ad-Dāraquṭnī's chain of transmission, 'Outwardly, this is an authentic chain of transmission. All of its narrators are reliable in the two *Ṣaḥīḥ* collections. (*Jāmiʿ al-ʿUlūm wa al-Ḥikam*). Ibn Ḥajar al-Haytamī said in his commentary on *The Forty*, 'It has been related *marfūʿan* from other paths, all of which indicate that it is good.

The Importance of the Ḥadīth:

An-Nawawī ﷺ said in his commentary on *The Forty*, 'This ḥadīth comprises so many important matters and benefits that if they were gathered together, they would not fit in this book'.

Ibn Ḥajar al-Haytamī said, 'Its benefit is universal, because the three matters mentioned occurs in every legal field. Its effect is sublime. It would be right to call it half of the Revealed Law, because a person's actions are comprised by his statement. Either a person acts intentionally and willingly, which is to act deliberately and consciously, or it is without intention and choice, which is due to either a mistake, forgetfulness or coercion. It is known unequivocally from this ḥadīth that actions of the latter category are pardoned, while it is understood that actions of the former category are punishable. Thus, it is half of the Revealed Law in consideration of what it articulates and it is all of the Revealed Law along with consideration of what is understood from it. In other words, if both the articulated (*manṭūq*) and the understood (*mafhūm*) are taken into consideration. The *mantūq* is that which is understood from the formulation of the wording, while the *mafhūm* is what is understood by what the text indicates.[273]

The Language of the Ḥadīth:

(تجاوز) *tajāwaza*: to pardon, from *jāza,* which means to go past something and traverse it, and here it means to lift or to leave.

(لي) *lī*: for my sake, to exalt my affair and raise my rank, and to satisfy my heart

(أمتي) *ummatī*: the Ummah who answered the call,[274] which includes everyone who has believed in him ﷺ and responded to his call.

(الخطأ) *al-khaṭa'*: the opposite of deliberateness, not the opposite of correct, such as intending to do something but one's action happens to produce other than what one intended. For example, one intends to kill an unbeliever but happens to kill a Muslim.

(النسيان) *an-nisyān*: the opposite of remembering, and the meaning here is bearing in mind, such as someone bearing something in mind and then forgetting it upon doing it.

The word can be used to mean leaving something as is, such as in the Exalted One's statement:

﴿نَسُوا۟ ٱللَّهَ فَنَسِيَهُمْ﴾

"They have forgotten Allah, so He has forgotten them". [at-Tawbah 9:67]

And the Glorified's statement:

﴿وَلَا تَنسَوُا۟ ٱلْفَضْلَ بَيْنَكُمْ﴾

"Do not forget to show generosity to one another." [al-Baqarah 2:237]

273 (tn): For example, in Allah the Exalted's statement, ﴿إِن جَآءَكُمْ فَاسِقٌۢ بِنَبَإٍ فَتَبَيَّنُوٓا۟﴾ **"If a deviator brings you a report, scrutinize it carefully..."** [al-Ḥujurāt 49:6], the *manṭūq* is that if a corrupt or untrustworthy person brings you news, you must check it. The *mafhūm* is that if a righteous or trustworthy person brings you news, you do not have to check it.

274 Ar. *ummat al-ijābah.*

(استكرهوا عليه) *ustukrihū ʿalayh*: it is said, *'akrahtuhu'*, i.e. I used compulsion to make him do something; *karh* is difficulty and *kurh* is compulsion. It has been said that *karh* is compulsion and *kurh* is difficulty and it has been said that both words convey both meanings.

Legal Matters and Other Guidance from the Ḥadīth:

1. The General Meaning of the Ḥadīth: If someone does something that Allah has forbidden or fails to fulfil something that Allah the Exalted has commanded, without intending to do or to fail to do, and the same applies to an action that is done by mistake or under compulsion, no blame is attached to that behaviour in this life and it is not punishable in the Hereafter, and this is a favour and blessing from Allah ﷻ.

2. Allah's Favour ﷻ towards this Ummah and Lifting Distress from them: This is how Allah's favour ﷻ towards this Ummah is immense, for He has mitigated legal accountability for them in matters for which other nations were punished. When the Children of Israel were commanded to do something and they forgot, or they were forbidden from something and they did it by mistake and were tempted into it, Allah the Exalted hastened punishment for them and took them to task. Meanwhile, He answers this Ummah's supplication when they supplicate with what He has inspired and instructed them with when He ﷻ said:

﴿رَبَّنَا لَا تُؤَاخِذْنَآ إِن نَّسِينَآ أَوْ أَخْطَأْنَا ۚ رَبَّنَا وَلَا تَحْمِلْ عَلَيْنَآ إِصْرًا كَمَا حَمَلْتَهُۥ عَلَى ٱلَّذِينَ مِن قَبْلِنَا ۚ رَبَّنَا وَلَا تُحَمِّلْنَا مَا لَا طَاقَةَ لَنَا بِهِۦ﴾

"Our Lord, do not take us to task if we forget or make a mistake! Our Lord, do not place on us a load like the one You placed on those before us! Our Lord, do not place on us a load we have not the strength to bear!" [al-Baqarah 2:286]

Thus, the Glorified One overlooks that which happens by mistake or out forgetfulness and does not take people to task for it. The Glorified One has said,

﴿وَلَيْسَ عَلَيْكُمْ جُنَاحٌ فِيمَآ أَخْطَأْتُم بِهِۦ وَلَـٰكِن مَّا تَعَمَّدَتْ قُلُوبُكُمْ﴾

"You are not to blame for any honest mistake you make but only for what your hearts premeditate." [al-Aḥzāb 33:5]

In other words, you will not be taken to task for what happens on your part by mistake, and the same goes for forgetfulness. However, you will be taken to task for what you intend to do. Likewise, the Glorified One has not made this Ummah legally accountable for actions that they cannot normally carry out, or burdened them with legal responsibilities that contain difficulty and distress, or adherence to them causes hardship and constraint. This is because of their compliance with Allah's ﷻ command on the tongue of His Chosen Messenger ﷺ when they said:

﴿سَمِعْنَا وَأَطَعْنَا ۖ غُفْرَانَكَ رَبَّنَا وَإِلَيْكَ ٱلْمَصِيرُ﴾

"We hear and we obey. Forgive us, our Lord! You are our journey's end." [al-Baqarah 2:285]

Muslim has related from Abū Hurayrah رضي الله عنه who said, 'When this was revealed to the Messenger of Allah ﷺ:

﴿لِّلَّهِ مَا فِى ٱلسَّمَٰوَٰتِ وَمَا فِى ٱلْأَرْضِ ۗ وَإِن تُبْدُوا۟ مَا فِىٓ أَنفُسِكُمْ أَوْ تُخْفُوهُ يُحَاسِبْكُم بِهِ ٱللَّهُ ۖ فَيَغْفِرُ لِمَن يَشَآءُ وَيُعَذِّبُ مَن يَشَآءُ ۗ وَٱللَّهُ عَلَىٰ كُلِّ شَىْءٍ قَدِيرٌ﴾

"Everything in the heavens and everything in the earth belongs to Allah. Whether you divulge what is in yourselves or keep it hidden, Allah will still call you to account for it. He forgives whomever He wills and He punishes whomever He wills. Allah has power over all things". [al-Baqarah 2:284]

It was distressing for the Companions of Allah's Messenger ﷺ.

They came to the Messenger of Allah ﷺ and made their riding mounts kneel down. They said, "O Messenger of Allah, we have been made legally accountably for actions that we are capable of: the prayer, fasting, armed combat and charity, and this āyah has been revealed to you and we are not capable of it." The Messenger of Allah ﷺ replied, {Do you want to say what the people of the two books before you said: 'We hear and we disobey?' Instead, say, 'We hear and we obey. Forgive us, our Lord! You are our journey's end.'} They said, "We hear and we obey. Forgive us, our Lord! You are our journey's end." When they had recited it and their tongues had become supple with it, Allah then revealed:

﴿ءَامَنَ ٱلرَّسُولُ بِمَآ أُنزِلَ إِلَيْهِ مِن رَّبِّهِۦ وَٱلْمُؤْمِنُونَ ۚ كُلٌّ ءَامَنَ بِٱللَّهِ وَمَلَٰٓئِكَتِهِۦ وَكُتُبِهِۦ وَرُسُلِهِۦ لَا نُفَرِّقُ بَيْنَ أَحَدٍ مِّن رُّسُلِهِۦ ۚ وَقَالُوا۟ سَمِعْنَا وَأَطَعْنَا ۖ غُفْرَانَكَ رَبَّنَا وَإِلَيْكَ ٱلْمَصِيرُ﴾

"The Messenger believes in what has been sent down to him from his Lord, as do the believers. Each one believes in Allah and His angels and His Books and His Messengers. We do not differentiate between any of His Messengers. They say, 'We hear and we obey. Forgive us, our Lord! You are our journey's end.'" [al-Baqarah 2:285]

When they had done so, Allah the Exalted abrogated it and then Allah revealed:

﴿لَا يُكَلِّفُ ٱللَّهُ نَفْسًا إِلَّا وُسْعَهَا ۚ لَهَا مَا كَسَبَتْ وَعَلَيْهَا مَا ٱكْتَسَبَتْ ۗ

رَبَّنَا لَا تُؤَاخِذْنَآ إِن نَّسِينَآ أَوْ أَخْطَأْنَا﴾

"Allah does not impose on any soul any more than it can bear. It has what it has earned and against it is what it has merited. Our Lord, do not take us to task if we forget or make a mistake." He said, {Yes.}

﴿رَبَّنَا وَلَا تَحْمِلْ عَلَيْنَآ إِصْرًا كَمَا حَمَلْتَهُۥ عَلَى ٱلَّذِينَ مِن قَبْلِنَا﴾

"Our Lord, do not place on us a load like the one You placed on those before us!" He said, {Yes.}

﴿رَبَّنَا وَلَا تُحَمِّلْنَا مَا لَا طَاقَةَ لَنَا بِهِۦ﴾

"Our Lord, do not place on us a load we have not the strength to bear!" He said, {Yes.}

﴿وَٱعْفُ عَنَّا وَٱغْفِرْ لَنَا وَٱرْحَمْنَآ ۚ أَنتَ مَوْلَىٰنَا فَٱنصُرْنَا عَلَى ٱلْقَوْمِ ٱلْكَـٰفِرِينَ﴾

"And pardon us; and forgive us; and have mercy on us. You are our Master, so help us against the unbelieving people." [al-Baqarah 2:286]

He said, {Yes.} On the authority of Ibn ʿAbbās that he said, {I have done so} instead of {Yes.}.

3. What Is Overlooked is the Sin and Not Every Consequent Ruling: If a legally accountable person does something that does not accord with the Revealed Law, there are consequent rulings, such as being taken to task and sin as well as having to compensate for something that is lost or destroyed, and so forth. The wording of the ḥadīth is general in lifting all rulings that result from such behaviour. Ibn Ḥajar al-Haytamī said, 'It is possible that the ruling is being overlooked – i.e. not the sin – or that the sin is being overlooked, or both, and this is what it looks like, as neither has preference over the other. Thus, the ḥadīth remains to be understood as is, and to understand it as only referring to the latter requires evidence.

The various evidence from the Revealed Law have established that what is meant is the lifting of the sin and being taken to task and not every consequent ruling, and the rulings are detailed. We will become familiar with them later on in the commentary on this ḥadīth. Al-Qārī said in his commentary on *The Forty*, 'It is obvious that the ruling of a mistake is more general than the sin of committing it, and the rectification that follows as a consequence.

The lifting of the sin is what is deduced from the ḥadīth, just as rectification is taken from the like of the Exalted's statement:

﴿وَمَن قَتَلَ مُؤْمِنًا خَطَـًٔا فَتَحْرِيرُ رَقَبَةٍ مُّؤْمِنَةٍ وَدِيَةٌ مُّسَلَّمَةٌ إِلَىٰٓ أَهْلِهِۦٓ﴾

"Anyone who kills a believer by mistake should free a believing slave and pay blood money to his family." [an-Nisā' 4:92]

This is what Allah's wisdom ﷻ has required: that no individual from this Ummah be taken to task unless he deliberately committed disobedience and his heart intended to violate and leave obedience, willingly and voluntarily. Ibn Ḥajar said, 'Pardoning this – i.e. the sin of what is done by mistake, out of forgetfulness or under duress – is what is required by wisdom and investigation, even though if He the Exalted were to take people to task for such actions, He would be just. This is because the benefit of legal accountability and its objective is to distinguish the obedient from the disobedient, so that those who died will die with clear proof, and those who lived would live with clear proof.[275] Both obedience and disobedience require an intention in order for reward or punishment to be attached to them and these three people have no intention. As for the first two, it is clear. As for the third, it is because the intention belongs to the one forcing and not the one being forced, as he is like an instrument. Based on this, most scholars of *uṣūl al-fiqh* have held the position that these people bear no legal accountability.

4. Examples from the Book and Sunnah: There are examples in the Book of Allah the Exalted and the Sunnah of His Messenger ﷺ in which the sin is lifted from the person who makes a mistake or forgets, while requiring that consequent rulings be carried out. For example:

A. Accidental Killing: If someone intends to shoot a game animal or an enemy and hits a Muslim or someone whose life is inviolable, no sin or crime is attached to him, but this does not exempt him from the requirements of blood money and expiation. The Exalted One has said:

﴿وَمَا كَانَ لِمُؤْمِنٍ أَن يَقْتُلَ مُؤْمِنًا إِلَّا خَطَـًٔا ۚ وَمَن قَتَلَ مُؤْمِنًا خَطَـًٔا فَتَحْرِيرُ رَقَبَةٍ مُّؤْمِنَةٍ وَدِيَةٌ مُّسَلَّمَةٌ إِلَىٰٓ أَهْلِهِۦٓ إِلَّآ أَن يَصَّدَّقُوا۟ ۚ فَإِن كَانَ مِن قَوْمٍ عَدُوٍّ لَّكُمْ وَهُوَ مُؤْمِنٌ فَتَحْرِيرُ رَقَبَةٍ مُّؤْمِنَةٍ ۖ وَإِن كَانَ مِن قَوْمٍۭ بَيْنَكُمْ وَبَيْنَهُم مِّيثَـٰقٌ فَدِيَةٌ مُّسَلَّمَةٌ إِلَىٰٓ أَهْلِهِۦ وَتَحْرِيرُ رَقَبَةٍ مُّؤْمِنَةٍ ۖ فَمَن لَّمْ يَجِدْ فَصِيَامُ شَهْرَيْنِ مُتَتَابِعَيْنِ تَوْبَةً مِّنَ ٱللَّهِ ۗ وَكَانَ ٱللَّهُ عَلِيمًا حَكِيمًا﴾

275 Please see Sūrat al-Anfāl 8:42.

"A believer should never kill another believer unless it is by mistake. Anyone who kills a believer by mistake should free a believing slave and pay blood money to his family unless they forgo it as charity. If he is from a people who are your enemies and is a believer, you should free a believing slave. Anyone who cannot find the means should fast two consecutive months. This is a concession from Allah. Allah is All-Knowing, All-Wise." [an-Nisāʾ 4:92]

B. Delaying the Prayer Beyond Its Time: If someone delays the prayer beyond its time due to an excuse, such as sleep or forgetfulness, he has not sinned, but he is required to make up the prayer as soon as he wakes up or remembers. Al-Bukhārī and Muslim and Muslim have related the ḥadīth of Anas ﷺ in which the Prophet ﷺ said, {Whoever forgets to pray let him pray when he remembers. There is no expiation due from him.

﴿وَأَقِمِ ٱلصَّلَوٰةَ لِذِكۡرِيٓ﴾

"...and establish the prayer to remember Me." [Ṭaha 20:14]}

The wording in Muslim's narration is, {Whoever forgets to pray or sleeps through it...}

C. Uttering Blasphemy: If someone is under duress to utter blasphemy, he says words that give the impression that he has uttered blasphemy, not words that unequivocally indicate it. This is unless he is under duress to unequivocal blasphemy, in which case he does so with his tongue without believing it within himself, while his heart is at peace with faith and his breast is dilated with certainty and knowledge.[276] The Exalted One has said:

﴿مَن كَفَرَ بِٱللَّهِ مِنۢ بَعۡدِ إِيمَٰنِهِۦٓ إِلَّا مَنۡ أُكۡرِهَ وَقَلۡبُهُۥ مُطۡمَئِنُّۢ بِٱلۡإِيمَٰنِ وَلَٰكِن مَّن شَرَحَ بِٱلۡكُفۡرِ صَدۡرٗا فَعَلَيۡهِمۡ غَضَبٞ مِّنَ ٱللَّهِ وَلَهُمۡ عَذَابٌ عَظِيمٞ﴾

"Those who reject Allah after having believed – except for someone forced to do it whose heart remains at rest in faith – but as for those who breasts become dilated with unbelief, anger from Allah will come down upon them. They will have a terrible punishment." [an-Naḥl 16:106]

Furthermore, if the one under duress to utter blasphemy does not do so and he bears with the harm and anticipates reward from Allah ﷻ that is better and nobler for him, even if he is killed as a result, in which case he would be a martyr. It has been related from the Messenger of Allah ﷺ that he said, {Do not

276 Ar. *ʿirfān* (or *maʿrifah*), i.e. direct knowledge of Allah, as opposed to *ʿilm*, which is learned knowledge.

associate partners with Allah, even if you are cut or burnt.} In other words, do not utter idolatry and the life if you are under compulsion to do so, even if the aforementioned is being done to you.

5. The Position on the Ruling for Mistakes and Forgetfulness in Detail: The consequences of a legally accountable person's actions, whether done by mistake or out of forgetfulness, differ depending on the deed or statement that has taken place, and it has been noticed that they fall into the following four categories:

The first is a mistake or forgetfulness occurring regarding something that has been commanded and has not been lifted. Instead, it must be rectified. An example of a mistake would be to pay one's zakāt on their wealth[277] to someone they presume to be poor but turns out to be wealthy. This does not suffice. One must pay it to the poor and has the right to reclaim it from the wealthy person.

An example of forgetfulness would be to perform dry ablution[278] and then pray while forgetting that one does indeed have water. After remembering the water, one must perform *wuḍū'* and repeat the prayer.

The second is a mistake or forgetfulness occurring regarding something that is prohibited but not connected to the damage or destruction of anything, and thus there is no consequence. An example of a mistake would be to drink alcohol while thinking that it is a non-intoxicating beverage. This person does not receive any *ḥadd* punishment or rebuke.[279] An example of forgetfulness would be for someone in *īḥrām* to scent himself or wear sewn clothes out of forgetfulness, and thus there is no consequence.

The third is a mistake or forgetfulness occurring regarding something prohibited and it is connected to the damage or destruction of something. One is not exempted from compensation. An example would be someone being served stolen food as a guest. He eats it while forgetting that it has been stolen or thinking that it was not stolen. He has to pay compensation. Another example would be killing a game animal while in a state of *iḥrām*, forgetting that one is in *iḥrām* or being ignorant of the ruling. Redemption[280] is obligatory upon such a person. Similar to this is a man telling a woman that she is divorced while thinking that she is not his wife when she is indeed his wife, in which case the divorce stands. The same ruling applies if he says, 'My wife is divorced' while forgetting that he has a wife. The divorce stands.

The fourth is a mistake or forgetfulness occurring regarding something prohibited and the actions necessitates punishment. However, the mistake or forgetfulness is an ambiguity that lifts that punishment.

---

277 Ar. *zakāt al-māl.*

278 Ar. *tayammum.*

279 Ar. *ta'zīr,* i.e. a discretionary punishment.

280 Ar. *fidyah.*

An example would be killing a Muslim in the Abode of War[281] while thinking that he is an unbeliever. There is no retaliation[282] or blood money in such a case. Likewise, if the one who mandates retaliation has pardoned the killer but the one mandated to do it carries it out due to forgetfulness, there is no further retaliation, even though blood money must be paid from his wealth.

6. That Which Does not Excuse the Forgetful Person: The aforementioned has to do with lifting punishment from someone who acts out of forgetfulness, and this person was not the cause of their forgetfulness. As for someone who is the cause, such as someone not being cautious or neglecting the means of remembering, such a person is taken to task for their behaviour, even if it happened out of forgetfulness. An example would be someone falling short in their commitment to the Qurʾān and being negligent in revising what one has memorised until one forgets. Another example would be seeing filth[283] on one's garment and (not?) taking one's time to remove it, such that one eventually forgets about it and prays in it. Such a person is regarded as negligent and is obligated to make up the prayer.

7. Legal Issues Regarding Forgetfulness:

A. Forgetting to Say *Bismillāh*[284] When Slaughtering and Hunting

Saying *bismillāh* when slaughtering is a sunnah[285] according to ash-Shāfiʿī ؒ and it is one narration from Aḥmad ؒ. Thus, if one leaves it deliberately or out of forgetfulness, the slaughtered animal is still eaten.

His evidence for this is what has been related by al-Barāʾ ؓ in which the Prophet ﷺ said, {The Muslim slaughters upon the Name of Allah, whether he says it or does not say it.} In a narration from Abū Hurayrah ؓ he ﷺ was asked about a man who slaughtered and forgot to say *bismillāh*. He said, {Allah's name is on the mouth of every Muslim.} Related by ad-Dāraquṭnī.

Abū Ḥanīfah and Mālik say, and it is the well-known position from Aḥmad ؒ that saying *bismillāh* is a condition. If one leaves it deliberately, the slaughtered animal is not eaten, due to the Exalted's statement:

﴿وَلَا تَأْكُلُوا۟ مِمَّا لَمْ يُذْكَرِ ٱسْمُ ٱللَّهِ عَلَيْهِ وَإِنَّهُۥ لَفِسْقٌ﴾

"Do not eat anything over which the name of Allah has not been mentioned. To do so is sheer deviance". [al-Anʿām 6:121]

Along with other evidence.

281 Ar. *dār al-ḥarb*, i.e. the subset of *dār al-kufr* (i.e. the abode over which unbelievers rule) in which Muslims are being persecuted or is at war with Muslims.

282 Ar. *qiṣāṣ*.

283 Ar. *najāsah*.

284 (tn): i.e. 'In the Name of Allah'.

285 (tn): i.e. recommended, one is rewarded for doing it but not punished for leaving it.

Thus, if someone leaves it out of forgetfulness, everyone agrees that the animal is eaten, due to the ḥadīth that we are discussing in this chapter.

A game animal is like a slaughtered animal, in what has been mentioned, according to Mālik, Abū Ḥanīfah and ash-Shāfiʿī ﷺ.

Aḥmad ﷺ said that if someone leaves saying *bismillāh* upon dispatching his hunting animal or shooting his weapon, out of forgetfulness or deliberately, the game animal is not eaten. This is due to his statement ﷺ {If you dispatched your dog and said the *bismillāh*, eat} and his statement, {What you hunt with your arrow and say Allah's name over, eat.} Both of these are agreed upon.

This is not necessary in the case of a slaughtered animal, because the slaughter occurs in its place, which is the neck, and this there is leniency. As for the game animal, the slaughter does not occur in its place in most cases, and thus there is no leniency. Ibn Qudāmah said, 'The difference between the game animal and the slaughtered animal is that the latter is slaughtered in its place and thus it is permissible to be lenient therein, as opposed to the game animal.

B. Accidentally Speaking in the Prayer: The position of ash-Shāfiʿī ﷺ is that the prayer is not invalidated, because the speech that invalidates the prayer is what is prohibited which does not include the speech of someone who forgets. It has been established in the two *Ṣaḥīḥ* collections that the Messenger of Allah ﷺ was praying the *ẓuhr* or *ʿasr* and he did his *taslīm*[286] after completing only two cycles, so a man called Dhūl Yadayn said to him, 'O Messenger of Allah, did you forget or was the prayer shortened?' He replied, {I did not forget and it was not shortened.} He then said to his Companions, {Is it as Dhūl Yadayn says?} They replied, 'Yes.' He thus came forward and prayed what he had left, and then prostrated twice at the end before his *taslīm*. This was related by al-Bukhārī.

The significant point in the ḥadīth is that he was speaking while believing that he was no longer in the prayer, while they were speaking thinking that the prayer had been nullified. Then, both he and they continued from where they had left off.

This is restricted to that which is commonly acknowledged[287] as a few words, because when speech is prolonged, one remembers.

This is the position that Mālik went with ﷺ

The Ḥanafīs ﷺ say that it invalidates the prayer absolutely, because speech has been forbidden due to the fact that it invalidates in and of itself, and thus there is no difference between it being deliberate or accidental. They have made an exception for accidentally eating while fasting, because there is a text that explicitly states as such. They consider the ḥadīths that prohibit speech in the prayer as abrogating those whose outward purport is that the prayer is still valid if one speaks accidentally.

286 (tn): i.e. he said *as-salām ʿalaykum*, which is the final pillar of the prayer and signifies its conclusion.

287 Ar. *ʿurf*.

There are two narrations from Aḥmad ﷺ.

C. Eating, Drinking and Having Sexual Intercourse Forgetfully While Fasting: The majority of jurists have held the position that whoever eats or drinks while forgetting that they are fasting must refrain from doing so immediately upon remembering and continue as such for the rest of the day. Their fast is not invalidated and they do not have to make it up or perform any expiation. This is due to what has been related by al-Bukhārī and Muslim, and the wording is the latter's, in which he ﷺ said, {Whoever forgets while he is fasting and thus eats or drinks let him complete his fast, for it is only that Allah fed him and gave him to drink.}

Mālik ﷺ said that he must make up the fast if it was obligatory and he does not owe any expiation, because his situation is the same as someone who forgot to pray. It is mentioned in *al-Muwaṭṭa'* that Mālik said, 'Whoever eats or drinks in Ramaḍān, absent-mindedly or forgetfully, or during any other fast that is obligatory upon him, must make up the fast for that day.'

What is apparent is that the aforementioned ḥadīth is understood to apply to voluntary fasts, for he says in *al-Muwaṭṭa'*, 'Whoever eats or drinks, absent-mindedly or forgetfully, during a voluntary fast does need to make it up. Let him complete his voluntary fast during which he ate or drank. He has not broken it.'

Similar to eating and drinking is sexual intercourse, according to Abū Ḥanīfah, ash-Shāfi'ī and Mālik ﷺ.

The well-known position from Aḥmad ﷺ is that his fast is nullified by doing so and he must make it up, and regarding him owing an expiation there are two narrations.

8. Mistakes and Forgetfulness Regarding Oaths: If someone vows to do something and then does it forgetfully or out of ignorance, i.e. he thinks that it is other than the action he swore to do, has he broken his oath or not?

Ash-Shāfi'ī ﷺ - in the more apparent of his two positions – held that he has not broken oath, even if his oath was to divorce or free a slave. However, according to the more correct position, his oath has not been dissolved, because what has taken placed is not considered to have included his oath. Otherwise, he has broken it. This is one narration from Aḥmad ﷺ.

Mālik ﷺ said that he breaks his oath regardless, because what is lifted is the sin of the mistake and forgetfulness and not the mistake and the forgetfulness themselves or their consequences.

The well-known position from Aḥmad ﷺ is that there is a difference between divorce and freeing a slave and other actions. If someone's oath concerns other than divorce and freeing a slave, his oath is not broken. If his oath does concern divorce and freeing a slave, it is broken. However, he is not sinful if he lives with his wife, as long as he does so forgetfully. When he remembers, he must separate from her immediately.

His proof for this distinction is that both divorce and freeing a slave are attached to a condition, and thus they take place when their condition is fulfilled, regardless of intention. For example, if a man says, 'You are divorced if the sun rises', she is divorced when the sun rises simply because it has risen.

9. The Consequences of a Forced Person's Action: The consequent rulings for a forced person's action differ according to the degree of compulsion and the nature of the action that one was compelled to do.

A. The compulsion could be unavoidable, meaning that the one being forced finds himself in a situation in which he has absolutely no choice regarding what he is being forced to do and he cannot refrain from it. An example would be someone who is forcibly tied up and carried and put inside a place that he swore he would never enter. By consensus, this person has committed no sin and according to the majority, his oath has not been broken.

B. The compulsion could be avoidable, meaning that the one being forced can refrain from what he is being forced to do. If a person being forced in a situation like this goes ahead with the action, there is legal accountability. An example would be someone who is beaten, or something similar, until they do something. If it is possible for him not to do it then he is choosing to do the action. However, his objective is not the action itself but to protect himself from harm. Thus, from one angle, he is making a choice and from another angle, he is not. This is why there has been a difference of opinion. Is he legally accountable or not?

10. Legal Issues Regarding Compulsion:
The first is compulsion in actions:
A. Compulsion to kill or commit fornication: Killing without right and fornication are major sins whose unlawfulness is agreed upon in every legislation that has been sent down to the Prophets and Messengers, and thus they are not permissible under any circumstance, even under duress. This means that if someone is forced to do one of them and refuses and is thus killed, he is rewarded. However, the consequences of doing either of them may differ according to the degree of compulsion, and the details are as follows:

B. Compulsion to commit fornication: In general, the scholars hold that if a woman is forced to commit fornication, she does not receive any *ḥadd* punishment. If the compulsion was unavoidable, she is not sinful, and if it was avoidable, she is sinful. Their evidence is the ḥadīth of this chapter as well as what has been related by al-Athram: 'A woman was forced in the time of the Messenger of Allah ﷺ and he did turn away from her.} Also, female slaves who had been forced upon by male slaves were brought to ʿUmar ﷺ. He thus beat the male slaves and did not beat the female slaves, because compulsion is an ambiguity and ambiguity lifts *ḥadd* punishments.

The ruling for a man is like that of a woman according to most of the people of knowledge, and it is the more correct position. Most of the Ḥanbalīs, as well as Muḥammad ibn al-Ḥasan from the Ḥanafīs, say that he is given the ḥadd punishment because intercourse can only take place if there is an erection, which contradicts compulsion. If there is an erection, compulsion is disproved, and thus there must be a *ḥadd* punishment.

Abū Ḥanīfah ﷺ said that if the compulsion is from the ruler, he does not receive a *ḥadd* punishment. If it is from someone else then he does receive a *ḥadd* punishment.

C. Compulsion to kill: Those scholars of significance are in agreement that if someone is forced to kill someone whose blood is inviolable, it is not permissible for him to kill him. If he kills him, he is sinful, because he will have killed him in order to free himself, and thus it was by choice. This goes alongside their agreement that there can be no compulsion to kill unless one is threatened with being killed or with what is feared will lead to being killed, according to conditions that have been detailed in the books of *fiqh*.

In this situation, they have differed regarding the obligation of retaliation:

- Mālik and Aḥmad – and it is the more apparent of ash-Shāfiʿīs statements – ﷺ say that retaliation is obligatory upon both of them – i.e. the one forcing and the one being forced – because they are both partaking in the killing: the one forcing is the proximate cause and the one forced is the immediate cause.

- Abū Ḥanīfah ﷺ said it is only obligatory on the one forcing, because the one being forced is like an instrument, which is one position according to the Shāfiʿīs.

- There is also a position that it is only obligatory upon the one being forced because he is the direct cause, and he is not like an instrument, because he is sinning by agreeing to it. This is the position of Zufar from amongst the Ḥanafīs and it is one position according to the Shāfiʿīs.

The second is compulsion in unlawful actions other than killing and fornication:

For example, theft, drinking wine, and so forth:

The majority of jurists have held that whoever is forced to do any of these things is allowed to do it. He must pay compensation for any property that is destroyed or damaged therein and whatever he pays in compensation is then the liability of the one who forced him, and he bears no sin and is not punished.

Some of the Mālikīs, and it is one narration from Aḥmad, have said that he is not allowed to do it. In other words, if he does anything that merits a corporal punishment, such as the *ḥadd* punishment for stealing or drinking wine, he receives that punishment. If someone else's property is damaged or destroyed therein, compensation is obligatory upon him as well as the one who forced him.

The third is compulsion to make a statement:

The majority of scholars – and they include Mālik, ash-Shāfiʿī and Aḥmad ﷺ – have held that compulsion to make any statement is supposed. Thus, whoever is put under considerable duress, without right, to make an unlawful statement, he has the right to save himself and he bears no sin. His statement is regarded as ineffectual and there are no legal consequences.

This is because Allah the Exalted has lifted the sin from the one who is forced to utter blasphemy, based on the Exalted's statement:

﴿إِلَّا مَنْ أُكْرِهَ وَقَلْبُهُۥ مُطْمَئِنٌّۢ بِٱلْإِيمَـٰنِ﴾

or someone forced to do it whose heart remains at rest in its faith..." [an-Naḥl 16:106]

Blasphemy has many rulings, the greatest of which is that it is sinful. If it is lifted, then all rulings consequent to a compelled statement are also lifted, because if the greater matter is lifted then the lesser matter is lifted with all the more reason. This is because the words of the one forced came from him while he was not content with them, and thus he is not taken to task for them in the Hereafter just as there is no legal consequence for him in this life.

There is no difference in this between one statement and another. Indeed, it applies to contracts, such as sales and marriage, just as it applies to that which cancels them, such as *khulʿ*[288] and divorce. The same also applies to vows and oaths, and the evidence is the ḥadīth of this chapter as well as what has been narrated from ʿĀ'ishah ﷺ in which the Messenger of Allah ﷺ said, {There is no divorce and no freeing of a slave when there is compulsion.}

288 (tn): i.e. a release from the marriage in exchange for a payment from the wife. For English readers, further information can be found in *Reliance of the Traveller*, section n.5, while Arabic readers can look at *al-Fiqh al-Manhājī* (Damascus, Dār al-Qalam, 1433/2012), v.2, p. 121-123.

Abū Ḥanīfah ﵀ made a distinction. There is that which can be revoked, according to him, and cancelled, such as a sale, and he said that compulsion is considered therein and thus the person forced is not obligated to do anything and there are no consequences.

And there is that which cannot be revoked and cancelled, such as marriage, divorce, vows and oaths. He said that compulsion is not considered therein and the person who makes the statement has to bear the consequences, even if he was forced.

11. The Person Forced Being Content With What He Is Being Forced To Do:
If evidence emerges that the person being forced is content with what he is being forced to do, and there is a desire on his part to do it, then the contracts and whatever else he carries out are valid. The compulsion is not taken into consideration, even if it exists, due to the validity of his intention based on the behaviour that he is exhibiting.

12. Compulsion to Carry Out A Right:
If a legally accountable person is forced to say something that is required of him, or to do something that is incumbent upon him, forcing him does not hinder the requirement of what is being forced upon him, and the consequent rulings apply. Examples include the following:

- If a *ḥarbī*[289] is forced to become Muslim and he articulates it, his Islam is valid.
- If a man vows not to approach his wife and then four months pass without him approaching her and he refuses to divorce her, the ruler forces him to divorce her and the divorce stands.
- If someone vows not to pay back a debt, the ruler forces him to pay it back, he breaks his oath and he is obligated to carry out an expiation.
- If the ruler forces someone to sell his property to pay his debts, the sale is valid.

289 (tn): i.e. an unbeliever who is at war with the Muslims.

THE FORTIETH ḤADĪTH

اغْتِنامُ الدُّنْيَا لِلْفَوزِ بِالآخِرَة

عَنْ ابْنِ عُمَرَ ﵄ قَالَ: أَخَذَ رَسُولُ اللهِ ﷺ بِمَنْكِبَيَّ فَقَالَ: {كُنْ فِي الدُّنْيَا كَأَنَّكَ غَرِيْبٌ، أَوْ عَابِرُ سَبِيْلٍ.}

كَانَ ابْنُ عُمَرَ ﵄ يَقُولُ: إِذَا أَمْسَيتَ فَلَا تَنْتَظِرِ الصَّبَاحَ، وَإِذَا أَصْبَحْتَ فَلَا تَنْتَظِرِ المَسَاءَ، وَخُذْ مِنْ صِحَّتِكَ لِمَرَضِكَ، وَمِنْ حَيَاتِكَ لِمَوْتِكَ. رَوَاهُ البُخَارِي.

Taking Advantage of This World in Order to Be Victorious in the Hereafter

Ibn ʿUmar ﵄ said, 'The Messenger of Allah ﷺ said: {Be in this world as if you are a stranger or someone traversing a path.}

Ibn ʿUmar ﵄ used to say, 'When you enter the evening, do not expect to see the morning, and when you enter the morning, do not expect to see the evening. Take from your health for your sickness, and take from your life for your death.'

Al-Bukhārī related this in the Book of *ar-Riqāq* (the chapter on the Prophet's statement ﷺ {Be in this world as if you are a stranger...}), no.6053.

The Importance of the Ḥadīth:

This is a noble ḥadīth, bearing immense rank and momentous benefits. It gathers together all kinds of goodness and admonition. It is the foundation of curtailing one's hopes in this life, for the believer should not treat this world as an abode and home and have confidence in it. Rather, he should be in it as if he is on a journey, and he is preparing his things for departure, getting ready for the Promised Day, the Day when neither wealth nor sons will be of any use – except to those who come to Allah with sound and flawless hearts.[290]

290 Please see Sūrat al-Shuʿarāʾ 26:88-89.

The Language of the Ḥadīth:
(أخذ) *akhadha*: to take hold of.

(بمنكبي) *bimankibayya*: this is the dual of *mankib*, which is where the top of the forearm meets the shoulder, and it is called as such because it rests on it.

(إذا أمسيت) *idhā amsayta*: you enter the evening, i.e. from noon until midnight.

(إذا أصبحت) *idhā aṣbaḥta*: you enter the morning, i.e. from midnight until noon.

Legal Matters and Other Guidance from the Ḥadīth:
1. The Nurturing Messenger: The Messenger of Allah ﷺ was a teacher and nurturer for his Companions, and in his teaching nurturing of them, he preceded the means and methods that the most modern scholars of pedagogy have arrived at. He would take advantage of opportunities and occasions, give them examples, and take abstract meanings and make them tangible and perceptible for them. He would admonish them and address them according to what their needs required, and in such a way that their intellects would grasp it. He would monitor their actions while approving what was correct and correcting what was mistaken, and all of this was done by being an excellent model, having patience and supreme steadfastness and watching over them.

In this ḥadīth, the Messenger of Allah ﷺ takes ʿAbdullah ibn ʿUmar by the shoulders in order to draw his attention towards the knowledge that he is about to impart to him, so that he senses its importance and his keenness to convey this knowledge to the depths of his soul and his entire alert being.

Ibn Ḥajar al-Haytamī ﷺ was aware of this noble Prophetic lesson and said, 'Therein, while teaching, the teacher or preacher touches one of the limbs of the one being taught or preached to, and it is similar to the statement of Ibn Masʿūd ﷺ: 'The Messenger of Allah ﷺ taught me the *tashahhud* by putting my hand between his hands.' The wisdom behind this is the putting at ease, awakening and reminding that it contains, since it is usually impossible to forget when someone does this. Also, in most cases, one does not do this to someone unless they incline towards them, and thus, this is evidence of his love ﷺ for Ibn ʿUmar and Ibn Masʿūd.'[291]

2. The Fleeting Nature of this World and the Everlastingness of the Hereafter: A person lives in this world for as long as Allah has willed him to live therein, and then there will inevitably be a day on which he will die:

﴿كُلُّ نَفْسٍ ذَآئِقَةُ ٱلْمَوْتِ﴾
"Every soul will taste death." [Āl ʿImrān 3:185]

291 *Fatḥ al-Mubīn li Sharḥ al-Arbaʿīn*, p.276.

﴿إِنَّكَ مَيِّتٌ وَإِنَّهُم مَّيِّتُونَ﴾
"You will die and they too will die." [az-Zumar 39:30]

A person does not know when his appointed time shall end and death will come:

﴿وَمَا تَدْرِى نَفْسٌ مَّاذَا تَكْسِبُ غَدًا ۖ وَمَا تَدْرِى نَفْسٌ بِأَىِّ أَرْضٍ تَمُوتُ﴾
"And no soul knows what it will earn tomorrow and no soul knows in what land it will die." [Luqmān 31:34]

This world is coming to an end, regardless of how long a person lives, and this is a witnessed fact. We see it every day and night. We notice it every hour and moment. Then, it is inevitable that a person will live an eternal, permanent, everlasting life, which has no end and no limit. That everlasting life is the life of the Hereafter, after Allah ﷻ has resurrected people from their graves, gathered them in order to be reckoned for their deeds and judged between them. They will either go to Paradise, which is as vast as the heavens and the earth as has been prepared for the people of *taqwā*, to abide therein forever, or to the Fire, whose fuel is men and stones and has been prepared for the unbelievers, from which they will never exit.

The intelligent believer is the one who is not deluded by this worldly life. He does not trust it or have confidence in it, or think that it is everything. Rather, he curtails his hopes therein, and he makes it a seedbed in which he plants his righteous deeds so that he can harvest their fruits in the Hereafter. He treats is as a vehicle towards salvation, over the bridge that stretches above surface of the Fire. The words of advice given by the Prophets and their followers all draw attention to this fact. Allah the Exalted says, quoting the believer from the people of Firʿawn:

﴿إِنَّمَا هَٰذِهِ ٱلْحَيَوٰةُ ٱلدُّنْيَا مَتَٰعٌ وَإِنَّ ٱلْءَاخِرَةَ هِىَ دَارُ ٱلْقَرَارِ﴾
"The life of this world is only fleeting enjoyment. It is the Hereafter that is the abode of permanence." [Ghāfir 40:39]

The Messenger of Allah ﷺ said, "How am I with this world? In this world, I am like a rider who takes shade under a tree and then he gets up and leaves it." He said, 'He sleeps in the daytime to be refreshed.'

3. This world is a bridge and path to the Hereafter: The believer therein is either a traveller or someone traversing a way. Thus, he does not rely on it, he is not distracted by it and he is not deceived by what it contains, because it is not worthy of him being attached to it and him expending his effort for its sake. It is an abode of transit and not an abode of residence.

﴿وَمَا ٱلْحَيَوٰةُ ٱلدُّنْيَآ إِلَّا مَتَـٰعُ ٱلْغُرُورِ﴾

"The life of this world is just the enjoyment of delusion." [Āl 'Imrān 3:185]

The believer is constantly and permanently aware, in his heart and in his soul, that he is living in this world like someone who is in a foreign land, far from his family and dependents. He constantly and permanently yearns for the comforts of that homeland and he longs to meet his family, his dependents, his loved ones and his close friends, regardless of how long he is in that foreign land. He does not feel at ease in it and his heart is constantly yearning to leave it. Thus, he does not erect a building therein, or look to acquire furniture or foundations. Instead, he is pleased with whatever is facilitated for him and he is able to amass and gather from this foreign land, such as gifts and presents, which he can enjoy in his homeland with his family and relatives. This is because he knows that is where he lives and permanently resides. This is how the believer abstains from this world, because it is not an abode of residence. Rather, it is fleeting moments in relation to the Hereafter.

﴿فَمَا مَتَـٰعُ ٱلْحَيَوٰةِ ٱلدُّنْيَا فِى ٱلْـَٔاخِرَةِ إِلَّا قَلِيلٌ﴾

"Yet the enjoyment of this world is very small compared to that of the Hereafter." [at-Tawbah 9:38]

﴿وَإِنَّ ٱلْـَٔاخِرَةَ هِىَ دَارُ ٱلْقَرَارِ﴾

"It is the Hereafter that is the abode of permanence." [Ghāfir 40:39]

Al-Ḥasan al-Baṣrī said, 'The believer is like a stranger. He is not worried about lowliness in this life, and he does not compete for its honours. He has his affair and the people have their affair.' Ibn Rajab said, 'When Allah created Adam ﷺ He had him and his wife live in Paradise. Then he was made to descend from it and he was promised that they would return to it along with the righteous amongst their progeny. The believer constantly yearns for his original homeland, and to love one's homeland is from faith.'

Indeed, the believer lives in this world and only settles and resides to the minimum extent that someone in a foreign land does, for it is possible for a foreigner to find a nice place to stay and to settle down with a family and dependents. This is not how the believer is in this world. Rather, he is like a traveller on a road. He passes by with dignity and his soul desires to reach his homeland and permanent abode. Whenever he gets closer, he becomes happier, and whenever he is impeding by anything, it vexes him and causes him pain. The traveller does not acquire dwellings on his journey or make friends. Rather, he suffices with the little that he has, whatever amount makes it easier for him to get closer to home and helps him reach his objective and goal. This is how the believer in this world regards dwellings and enjoyments; they assist him in realising what he seeks in the Hereafter, which is Allah's pleasure:

﴿ٱلَّذِى خَلَقَ ٱلْمَوْتَ وَٱلْحَيَوٰةَ لِيَبْلُوَكُمْ أَيُّكُمْ أَحْسَنُ عَمَلًا﴾

"He who created death and life to test which of you is best in action." [al-Mulk 67:2]

He makes close friends who show him the way, and assist him in arriving at the shore of safety.

﴿ٱلْأَخِلَّآءُ يَوْمَئِذٍۭ بَعْضُهُمْ لِبَعْضٍ عَدُوٌّ إِلَّا ٱلْمُتَّقِينَ﴾

"On that Day closest friends will be enemies to one another – except for those who have *taqwā*." [az-Zukhruf 43:67]

He is on his guard therein against thieves and highway robbers, who will take him far away from Allah ﷻ and His obedience, like a traveller in the desert:

﴿وَيَوْمَ يَعَضُّ ٱلظَّالِمُ عَلَىٰ يَدَيْهِ يَقُولُ يَٰلَيْتَنِى ٱتَّخَذْتُ مَعَ ٱلرَّسُولِ سَبِيلًا ﴿٢٧﴾ يَٰوَيْلَتَىٰ لَيْتَنِى لَمْ أَتَّخِذْ فُلَانًا خَلِيلًا ﴿٢٨﴾ لَّقَدْ أَضَلَّنِى عَنِ ٱلذِّكْرِ بَعْدَ إِذْ جَآءَنِى ۗ وَكَانَ ٱلشَّيْطَٰنُ لِلْإِنسَٰنِ خَذُولًا﴾

"the Day when a wrongdoer will bite his hands and say, 'Alas for me! If only I had gone the way of the Messenger! Alas for me! If only I had not taken so-and-so for a friend! He led me astray from the Reminder and it came to me.' Shayṭān always leaves man in the lurch." [al-Furqān 25:27-29]

The traveller gathers provisions for his journey, and the believer gathers provisions from his worldly life for his Hereafter. Allah the Exalted has said:

﴿وَتَزَوَّدُوا۟ فَإِنَّ خَيْرَ ٱلزَّادِ ٱلتَّقْوَىٰ ۚ وَٱتَّقُونِ يَٰٓأُو۟لِى ٱلْأَلْبَٰبِ﴾

"Take provision; but the best provision is taqwā of Allah. So have taqwā of Me, people of intelligence!" [al-Baqarah 2:197]

4. Ibn 'Umar's Admonition: 'Abdullah ibn 'Umar ibn al-Khaṭṭāb ﷺ receives the Messenger of Allah's admonition ﷺ with all of his limbs. He grasps it with both his heart and mind and gives it his full attention, and thus he is his teacher's, the Messenger of Allah ﷺ successful student, and he, In turn, becomes a source of light and guidance. Thus, he calls on whomever he conveys the ḥadīth of the Messenger of Allah ﷺ to have abstinence in this worldly life and thus curtail one's hopes to the utmost. If one enters the evening, one should not expect to see morning. If one enters the morning, one should not expect to see evening. Rather, one should presume that one's appointed time will come before that.

Al-Ḥākim has related a ḥadīth in his *Ṣaḥīḥ, marfūʿan,* from Ibn ʿAbbās ؓ in which the Prophet ﷺ said, {Take advantage of five before five: your youth before your old age, your health before you become ill, your wealth before your poverty, your free time before you become busy and your life before your death.}

5. The Muslim must hasten to do good deeds, and to increase in acts of obedience and righteousness, and thus one is not negligent and one does not tarry, hoping to rectify one's affairs at some point in the future, because one does not know when one's appointed time will come.

6. The Muslim must take advantage of opportunities and occasions when they present themselves to him, before they slip away.

7. The ḥadīth encourages doing without this worldly life, and turning away from its diversions. This does not mean that one should abandon working, striving and being active. Rather, what is meant is that one should not be attached to it or distracted by it from working for the Hereafter.

8. It is the Muslim's business to work hard in righteousness and to increase the ways in which he does goodness, while constantly fearing and being on guard against Allah's punishment ﷻ and thus he will increase in deeds and be more active. The business of the traveller is to expend effort in being wary and cautious, while fearing that his journey will be interrupted and that he will not arrive at his destination.

9. Being wary of evil company, those who are like highway robbers, so that they do not cause the Muslim to deviate from his intended destination and become a barrier between him and achieving his objective.

10. Worldly work is obligatory in order to restrain the ego and attain benefit, and the Muslim subjugates all of that for the sake of the Hereafter and to attain reward with Allah the Exalted.

12. A ḥadīth like this takes us back to moderation and temperance in working for this world (and the Hereafter) whenever we become more attached to the earth's soil and it causes us to be heedless of and distracted from the Hereafter.

THE FORTY-FIRST ḤADĪTH

اتِّبَاعُ شَرْعِ اللهِ تَعَالَى عِمَادُ الإِيمَان

عَنْ أَبِي مُحَمَّدٍ عَبْدِ اللهِ بْنِ عَمْرِو بْنِ الْعَاصِ ﷺ قَالَ: قَالَ رَسُولُ اللهِ ﷺ: {لَا يُؤْمِنُ أَحَدُكُمْ حَتَّى يَكُونَ هَوَاهُ تَبَعاً لِمَا جِئْتُ بِهِ.}

حديث صحيح، رُوِيْنَاهُ فِي كتاب الحُجَّة بإسنادٍ صحيح.

Following Allah the Exalted's Legislation is the Pillar of Faith

It is on the authority of Abū Muḥammad ʿAbdullah ibn ʿAmr ibn al-ʿĀṣ ﷺ who said, 'The Messenger of Allah ﷺ said, {None of you believes until his desires follow that which I have brought.} It is an authentic ḥadīth that we have related in the book *al-Ḥujjah* with an authentic chain of transmission.

The book *al-Ḥujjah* is a book on the creed of *Ahl as-Sunnah,* and it contains the foundations of the religion according to the principles of the people of ḥadīth. Its full title is *Kitāb al-Ḥujjah ʿalā Tāriki Sulūk al-Maḥjah*. Ibn Ḥajar al-Haytamī said about it, 'It is a good, beneficial book. Its author is Abū al-Fatḥ Naṣr ibn Ibrāhīm al-Maqdisī, the Shāfiʿī jurist and ascetic who lived in Damascus.' He died in 490 AH.[292]

The Language of the Ḥadīth:

(لا يؤمن) *la yu'minu*: one's faith is not perfected, or it is not valid

(هواه) *hawāhu*: what his ego loves, his heart inclines for and his nature desires

(تبعا) *tabaʿan*: he follows is such that his following of it becomes like his nature

(لما جئت به) *limā ji'tu bih*: the perfect Revealed Law that Allah the Exalted has sent me with, the commands and prohibitions therein, which have been clearly stated by the Revealed Book or instructed by the Inspired Sunnah.

292 (tn): This is information in commentaries on *The Forty,* such as those of Imams Ibn Rajab al-Ḥanbalī and Ibn Ḥajar al-Haytamī.

Legal Matters and Other Guidance from the Ḥadīth:

1. The Muslim is an Integrated Human Being: The Muslim is an integrated human being bearing the aspects of an exemplary personality, and thus there is no contradiction between his words and his deeds, between his behaviour and his thoughts. Rather, he is a person whose heart and tongue agree with the rest of his limbs and his intellect, thoughts and feelings are in harmony. His body and spirit are in equilibrium. His tongue articulates what he firmly believers and his creed is reflected by his limbs. Thus, his behaviour is upright and his conduct is upstanding. He is not taken over by desires, reprehensible innovation does not lead him into recklessness and pleasures and enjoyments do not take him down. His point of departure in all of his affairs and circumstances is Allah the Exalted's legislation, the All-Wise, that which false cannot reach from in front of it or from behind it.[293] This is what the Messenger of Allah ﷺ is affirming – and he was given comprehensive speech – when he lays down that which distinguishes the believing Muslim. He says, {None of you believes until his desires follow that which I have brought.}

2. The Reality of Desire and Its Types: The word *hawā* can be used to mean an inclination towards nothing but the truth, to love it and to be led by it. An example of this is found in the statement of ʿĀʾishah ▯ 'I only see your Lord hastening to meet your desire (*hawā*).' She said this when the Exalted One revealed His statement:

﴿تُرْجِى مَن تَشَآءُ مِنْهُنَّ وَتُـْٔوِىٓ إِلَيْكَ مَن تَشَآءُ﴾

"You may refrain from any of them you will and keep close to any of them you will." [al-Aḥzāb 33:51]

This has been collected by al-Bukhārī. There is also the statement of ʿUmar ▯ during the deliberation as to what to do with the prisoners of Badr, 'The Messenger of Allah ﷺ inclined (*yahwī*) towards what Abū Bakr had said and did not incline towards what I had said.'

It can also be used to mean inclination and love in the absolute sense, and thus it comprises inclining towards the truth and anything else. This is the meaning that is sought in the ḥadīth.

It can also be used to mean satisfying the ego's passions and realising its wishes. This is the meaning that is intended when the word *hawā* is used by itself, which is the most common use of the word. It is this meaning that the texts of the Revealed Law all censure, warn against and make loathsome. This is because in most cases it is an inclination towards other than the truth, realising base desires instead of the requirements of the Revealed Law. It thus becomes a means of misguidance and wretchedness.

293 (tn): Please see Sūrat Fuṣṣilat 41:42.

Addressing Dāwūd ﷺ Allah the Exalted says:

﴿وَلَا تَتَّبِعِ ٱلْهَوَىٰ فَيُضِلَّكَ عَن سَبِيلِ ٱللَّهِ﴾

"...and do not follow your own desires (*al-hawā*), letting them misguide you from Allah's way." [Ṣād 38:26]

3. Following Desire is the Fountainhead of Disobedience, Innovation and Avoiding the Truth: Whoever gives free rein to his passions and gives his ego what it desires will be led into disobedience and sin, and made to fall into violating Allah's legislation ﷻ. The fact of the matter is that deviators do not deviate, innovators do not innovate, and disbelievers, sinners and heretics do not turn away from the upright way and the plain truth because the truth is not clear or because they are not convinced of it – as they claim. The truth is absolutely clear while falsehood is unclear and stuttering, its only support is desires that followed. The Exalted One has said:

﴿فَإِن لَّمْ يَسْتَجِيبُوا۟ لَكَ فَٱعْلَمْ أَنَّمَا يَتَّبِعُونَ أَهْوَآءَهُمْ ۚ وَمَنْ أَضَلُّ مِمَّنِ ٱتَّبَعَ هَوَىٰهُ بِغَيْرِ هُدًى مِّنَ ٱللَّهِ﴾

"If they do not respond to you then know that they are merely following their whims and desires. And who could be further astray than someone who follows his whims and desires without any guidance from Allah?" [al-Qaṣaṣ 28:50]

4. A Followed Desire is a Deity That Is Worshipped Besides Allah ﷻ: To worship is to obey and to submit, so whoever obeys his desires and submits to his passions becomes a worshipper of them. Passions and desires do not leave a person alone until they have gained power over him and taken control of him, and thus his conduct only stems from them. He only does what they command, even if it contradicts his own thoughts and intellect and goes against his own knowledge and experience. This is how you see the slaves of desires shutting their eyes from seeing the truth and plugging their ears from hearing it, and they never know uprightness and are never guided. Ibn 'Abbās ﷺ said, 'Desire is a god that is worshipped on earth.' Then he recited

﴿أَرَءَيْتَ مَنِ ٱتَّخَذَ إِلَـٰهَهُۥ هَوَىٰهُ﴾

"Have you seen him who has taken his whims and desires to be his god?" [al-Furqān 25:43]

He ﷺ said: {Under the sky, there is no god more oppressive in the sight of Allah the Exalted than a desire that is followed.} 'More oppressive' means that it is more sinful because its evil is more extensive.

5. Following Desire is a Weakness that does not Befit an Ennobled Person: Allah ﷻ has granted man that which distinguishes him from all other creatures and made him and ennobled creation:

﴿وَلَقَدْ كَرَّمْنَا بَنِيٓ ءَادَمَ وَحَمَلْنَـٰهُمْ فِى ٱلْبَرِّ وَٱلْبَحْرِ وَرَزَقْنَـٰهُم مِّنَ ٱلطَّيِّبَـٰتِ وَفَضَّلْنَـٰهُمْ عَلَىٰ كَثِيرٍ مِّمَّنْ خَلَقْنَا تَفْضِيلًا﴾

"We have ennobled the children of Ādam and conveyed them on land and sea and provided them with good things and favoured them greatly over many we have created." [al-Isrā' 17:70]

This gift that is the sign of this ennoblement is the intellect, which makes him aware of goodness and drives him to do it and it makes him comprehend evil and become averse to approaching it. The Exalted One has said:

﴿وَنَفْسٍ وَمَا سَوَّىٰهَا ۝٧ فَأَلْهَمَهَا فُجُورَهَا وَتَقْوَىٰهَا﴾

"and the soul and what proportioned it, and inspired it with depravity or *taqwā*." [ash-Shams 91:7-8]

The human soul is disposed to both good and evil and equipped with depraved impulses as well as incentives of *taqwā*. He has been granted reason and he has been granted free will. He has the ability to go against his desires and control and restrain evil inclinations, to struggle against his ego and make it ascend the ranks of goodness and *taqwā* and thus occupy the rank that befits this ennoblement and favouring. Thus, if he does so, his conduct will be a sign of his intellect as well as of his integrated, exemplary humanity. If he allows himself to be defeated by evil inclinations, surrenders to his desires and descends the steps of vice, he diminishes his humanity and lowers his honour, and that is a sign of his foolishness and weakness. He ﷻ has said:

﴿قَدْ أَفْلَحَ مَن زَكَّىٰهَا ۝٩ وَقَدْ خَابَ مَن دَسَّىٰهَا﴾

"he who purifies it has succeeded, he who covers it up has failed." [ash-Shams 91:9-10]

He ﷺ said: {The *mujāhid* is the one who struggles against his ego. The weak person is the one who follows his ego's desires while having hopes with Allah.} He also said, {What an evil slave is the one who is led astray by his desires. What an evil slave is the one who is led by greed.}

As for struggling against the ego and rebelling against desire, it is the result of having true, direct knowledge of Allah ﷻ being aware of His sublimity and comprehending His blessings. The slave continues to struggle against his ego until he is completely stripped of slavehood to desires and it is replaced with pure slavehood to Allah ﷻ. Faith is perfected within him, certainty is firmly established and he is amongst the felicitous in both abodes. Allah the Exalted has said:

﴿وَأَمَّا مَنْ خَافَ مَقَامَ رَبِّهِۦ وَنَهَى ٱلنَّفْسَ عَنِ ٱلْهَوَىٰ ۝٤٠ فَإِنَّ ٱلْجَنَّةَ هِىَ ٱلْمَأْوَىٰ﴾

"But as for him who feared the station of his Lord and forbade the ego its desires, Paradise will be his refuge". [an-Nāziʿāt 79:40-41]

6. Following Desire is Depravity and Misguidance while Struggling against the Ego is Felicity and Salvation: Following desires, being immersed in passions and striving for delights and pleasures without caring about what is lawful and unlawful is slavehood to other than Allah ﷻ. It is oppression and tyranny, because one is allowing blessings to distract one from the Bestower of Blessings, because it contains ignorance and misguidance, and preference of the fleeting over the ever-lasting. It is a path that leads to destruction and loss, because of the arrogance and self-aggrandisement it contains, and the remoteness and subjugation that it leads to.

﴿فَأَمَّا مَن طَغَىٰ ۝٣٧ وَءَاثَرَ ٱلْحَيَوٰةَ ٱلدُّنْيَا ۝٣٨ فَإِنَّ ٱلْجَحِيمَ هِىَ ٱلْمَأْوَىٰ﴾

"As for him who overstepped the bounds and preferred the life of this world, the Blazing Fire will be his refuge". [an-Nāziʿāt 79:37-39]

7. The Ranks of Faith: When the Muslim articulates the two testimonies of faith with his tongue, in his soul he yields to Allah's legislation ﷻ and he has summoned the resolve in his heart to adhere to His commands and avoid his prohibitions, the foundation of faith has been realised within him and he has achieved the least of its ranks. He has moved from the disbelieving group to the believing group and it is expected that he will have salvation with Allah ﷻ on the Day of Standing: {Who-ever says *la ilāha ill Allah* and his heart believes in it will enter Paradise.} Related by al-Bukhārī and others.

When the Muslim adheres to Allah's way ﷻ and consolidates himself upon following it in all of his affairs, sticking to it wherever it goes, following only its commands and refraining only from its prohibitions, letting it be the arbitrator in every large and small issue, inclining towards it just as he inclines towards his lofty ambitions, making his ambitions conform to it, he thus desires that which it affirms and despises that which it negates. He declares lawful that which it declares lawful and declares unlawful that which it declares unlawful. He is wary of ambiguous matters and is careful with himself, without finding any shortcoming in his soul, or feeling and distaste or hardship. When the Muslim becomes like this, he has perfected his faith, and has reached the highest ranks of certainty, and if he is not like that then there is still some deficiency and misgiving in his faith.

As for the one who abandons Allah's legislation ﷻ out of aversion for it and desiring something else, not yielding to it the way truthful people yield, not convinced of it the way sincere people are convinced, the foundation of faith has not been established in this person, and there is no valid *islām* from him. Rather, he is amongst the ranks of the unbelievers, and on the Day of Standing he will enter the Fire forever. What an evil end.

8. Loving Allah the Exalted and His Messenger ﷺ: In order for the foundation of faith to be realised within the Muslim, and for him to travel the path that leads to its perfection, he must love what Allah the Exalted loves, love that drives him to carry out what he is obligated to and to do that which is recommended. Likewise, he must dislike that which Allah the Exalted dislikes, dislike that makes him refrain from that which is unlawful for him and that which is recommended for him to leave. This love for what Allah the Exalted loves and this dislikes for what He dislikes are never realised unless one loves Allah the Exalted and His Messenger ﷺ more than anything else, such that he would sacrifice anything for their sake and he gives them precedence over everything else. Allah the Exalted has said:

﴿قُلْ إِن كَانَ ءَابَآؤُكُمْ وَأَبْنَآؤُكُمْ وَإِخْوَٰنُكُمْ وَأَزْوَٰجُكُمْ وَعَشِيرَتُكُمْ وَأَمْوَٰلٌ ٱقْتَرَفْتُمُوهَا وَتِجَٰرَةٌ تَخْشَوْنَ كَسَادَهَا وَمَسَٰكِنُ تَرْضَوْنَهَآ أَحَبَّ إِلَيْكُم مِّنَ ٱللَّهِ وَرَسُولِهِۦ وَجِهَادٍ فِى سَبِيلِهِۦ فَتَرَبَّصُوا۟ حَتَّىٰ يَأْتِىَ ٱللَّهُ بِأَمْرِهِۦ ۗ وَٱللَّهُ لَا يَهْدِى ٱلْقَوْمَ ٱلْفَٰسِقِينَ﴾

"Say: 'If your fathers or your sons or your brothers or your wives or your tribe, or any wealth you have acquired, or any business you fear may slump, or any house which pleases you, are dearer to you than Allah and His Messenger and doing *jihād* for His sake, then wait until Allah brings about His command. Allah does not guide people who are deviators." [at-Tawbah 9:24]

Al-Bukhārī and Muslim have related from Anas ﵁ that the Messenger of Allah ﷺ said, {None of you truly believes until I am more beloved to him than himself, his children, his wife and all of mankind.} Thus, one is not a true believer until he gives precedence to love of the Messenger ﷺ over love of the entire creation, and love of the Messenger follows love of the One who sent him and necessitates it. There can be no love for him ﷺ without there being love for Allah ﷻ as is indicated by the Exalted's statement: **"...are dearer to you than Allah and His Messenger..."** [at-Tawbah 9:24]

9. The Sign of Love is Agreement and Following: True love necessitates that the lover follows the one he loves and agree with him in what he loves and dislikes, in word, deed and creed. Whoever truly loves Allah the Exalted and His Messenger ﷺ that loves bequeaths him – as we know – love of what they love and dislike of what they dislike. One of the inseparable manifestations of this is that his limbs act in accordance with this love and this dislike. Thus, he stays within the bounds of Allah's legislation ﷻ he obeys His commands and avoids His prohibitions in the most complete way, so that that can be a proof of his love and evidence of his faith. Allah ﷻ has said:

﴿قُلْ إِن كُنتُمْ تُحِبُّونَ ٱللَّهَ فَٱتَّبِعُونِى يُحْبِبْكُمُ ٱللَّهُ﴾

"Say, 'If you love Allah, then follow me and Allah will love you..." [Āl ʿImrān 3:31]

Al-Ḥasan al-Baṣrī said, 'The Prophet's Companions said, 'We deeply love our Lord', so Allah wanted to lay down a sign of His love, and thus He revealed this verse.

Whoever leaves something that Allah ﷻ and His Messenger ﷺ love and does something that they dislike while having the capacity to do what is loved and leave what is disliked, this person has a deficiency and shortcoming in his faith. He must strive to rectify it and correct it, and his love is a claim that requires clear proof.

One of them said, 'Whoever claims to love Allah the Exalted and He does not comply with His command, his claim is false. Every lover who does not fear Allah is deluded'.

Someone else said, 'Someone is not truthful if they claim to love Allah and do not stay within His bounds'.

May Allah the Exalted have mercy on the one[294] who said,

You disobey Allah and you claim to love Him,
By my life, this is an abominable deduction
If your love were truthful, you would obey Him
The lover obeys the One he loves

This is how it becomes clear to you the contradiction of those who become ecstatic when remembering Allah the Exalted or His Messenger ﷺ. Their eyes well forth with tears, their heads are lowered in humility and they make their broad claims to love Allah and His Messenger ﷺ but they are upon disobedience to Allah ﷻ such as being involved in usury, fraud and monopoly, greed and avarice, mixing with women some of whom are uncovered, and leaving the etiquettes of Allah the Exalted's masterful legislation. We ask Allah the Exalted to guide us and them to the most upright path.

294 (tn): i.e. Imam ash-Shāfiʿī, as these lines are in his *Dīwān*. Please see *at-Tafsīr al-Wasīṭ* by Imam Wahbah az-Zuḥaylī (Damascus: Dār al-Fikr, 1436/2015) v.1, p.188, as he quotes the same lines while discussing Sūrat Āl ʿImrān 3:31.

10. The Sweetness of Faith: Faith has an effect on people's souls and it is tasted in their hearts. For the believers, it is more pleasant than cold freshwater when one is thirsty and sweeter than the taste of honey after a long time of tasting bitterness. This love and that pleasantness are not felt and are not found except by the one who has perfected his faith and his love for Allah the Exalted and His Messenger ﷺ is truthful, and thus it affects his soul. He comes to love only for Allah and hate only for Allah. He does not give except for Allah and he does not withhold except for Allah.

Al-Bukhārī and Muslim have narrated from Anas ؓ that the Prophet ﷺ said, {There are three things whoever has within himself will find the sweetness of faith: that Allah and His Messenger are beloved to him than anything else, that he only love someone or not love them for the sake of Allah, and that he hate to return to disbelief – after Allah had saved him from it – just as he would hate to be thrown in the Fire.} The meaning of sweetness of faith is delight in obedience. An-Nawawī said, 'This ḥadīth is immense, and one of the foundations of Islam'.

11. Seeking Decisions from Allah's Legislation ﷻ and Being Pleased with His Ruling: One of the inseparable manifestations of faith is that the Muslim seek a decision from Allah's legislation ﷻ in his disputes and legal cases and not turn towards anything else, and he is pleased with Allah the Exalted's ruling. His ruling is established by proofs that carry weight in the Revealed Law, from the Book and Sunnah and what is derived from and branches out from both of them. He is at ease with that ruling and he submits to it, whether it is for him or against him, whether it agrees with his desires or goes against them. The Exalted One has said:

﴿وَمَا كَانَ لِمُؤْمِنٍ وَلَا مُؤْمِنَةٍ إِذَا قَضَى ٱللَّهُ وَرَسُولُهُۥٓ أَمْرًا أَن يَكُونَ لَهُمُ ٱلْخِيَرَةُ مِنْ أَمْرِهِمْ﴾

"When Allah and His Messenger have decided something, it is not for any man or woman of the believers to have a choice about it."
[al-Aḥzāb 33:36]

He ﷻ has also said:

﴿فَلَا وَرَبِّكَ لَا يُؤْمِنُونَ حَتَّىٰ يُحَكِّمُوكَ فِيمَا شَجَرَ بَيْنَهُمْ

ثُمَّ لَا يَجِدُوا۟ فِىٓ أَنفُسِهِمْ حَرَجًا مِّمَّا قَضَيْتَ وَيُسَلِّمُوا۟ تَسْلِيمًا﴾

"No, by your Lord, they are not believers until they make you their judge in the disputes that break out between them, and then find no resistance within themselves to what you decide and submit themselves completely." [an-Nisā' 4:65]

Making the Messenger of Allah ﷺ a judge after his death is done by seeking a decision from his Revealed Law and his Sunnah.

12. Loving what Allah the Exalted Dislikes and Disliking what He Loves is Disbelief and Misguidance: We know that the foundation of faith cannot be realised without the love of what Allah the Exalted loves and dislikes of what He dislikes and that the perfection of faith cannot be unless one acts accordingly. If someone does not have that love, he has lost his faith. If someone inverts the matter and thus loves what Allah the Exalted dislikes and dislikes what He loves, he has increased in disbelief and misguidance, in insolence and stubbornness. He is the greatest of losers in this life and the Hereafter. Allah the Exalted has said:

﴿وَٱلَّذِينَ كَفَرُوا۟ فَتَعْسًا لَّهُمْ وَأَضَلَّ أَعْمَـٰلَهُمْ ﴿٨﴾

ذَٰلِكَ بِأَنَّهُمْ كَرِهُوا۟ مَآ أَنزَلَ ٱللَّهُ فَأَحْبَطَ أَعْمَـٰلَهُمْ﴾

"But those who disbelieve will have utter ruin and He will make their actions go astray. This is because they hate what Allah has sent down, so He has made their actions come to nothing." [Muḥammad 47:8-9]

The Glorified One has also said:

﴿إِنَّ ٱلَّذِينَ ٱرْتَدُّوا۟ عَلَىٰٓ أَدْبَـٰرِهِم مِّنۢ بَعْدِ مَا تَبَيَّنَ لَهُمُ ٱلْهُدَى ٱلشَّيْطَـٰنُ سَوَّلَ لَهُمْ وَأَمْلَىٰ لَهُمْ ﴿٢٥﴾
ذَٰلِكَ بِأَنَّهُمْ قَالُوا۟ لِلَّذِينَ كَرِهُوا۟ مَا نَزَّلَ ٱللَّهُ سَنُطِيعُكُمْ فِى بَعْضِ ٱلْأَمْرِ ۖ وَٱللَّهُ يَعْلَمُ إِسْرَارَهُمْ
﴿٢٦﴾ فَكَيْفَ إِذَا تَوَفَّتْهُمُ ٱلْمَلَـٰٓئِكَةُ يَضْرِبُونَ وُجُوهَهُمْ وَأَدْبَـٰرَهُمْ ﴿٢٧﴾ ذَٰلِكَ بِأَنَّهُمُ ٱتَّبَعُوا۟ مَآ أَسْخَطَ
ٱللَّهَ وَكَرِهُوا۟ رِضْوَٰنَهُۥ فَأَحْبَطَ أَعْمَـٰلَهُمْ﴾

"Those who turned back in their tracks after the guidance became clear to them, it was Shayṭān who talked them into it and filled them with false hopes. This is because they said to those who hate what Allah has sent down, 'We will obey you in part of the affair.' But Allah knows their secrets. How will it be when the angels take them in death, beating their faces and their backs? That is because they followed what angers Allah and hated what is pleasing to Him. So He made their actions come to nothing." [Muḥammad 47:25-28]

13. The Model Exemplar: The Companions of Allah's Messenger ﷺ were the model exemplars in having true love for Allah the Exalted and His Messenger ﷺ and loving what pleases them and hating what angers them. They gave precedence to loving Allah and His Messenger over everything else. They made their desires conform to what the Messenger of Allah ﷺ had brought, until they expended their souls, their spirits and their wealth for its sake. They fought their fathers for it and left their wives, tribes and homelands because they knew what had the greater right and they grasped its precedence. Look at 'Umar when he said, 'You, O Messenger of Allah, are more beloved to me than everything apart from myself.' He replied, {No, by the One in whose hand is my soul, until I am more beloved to you than yourself.} He was thus quiet for a short period time, in which he realised that the Messenger of Allah's right is greater than any other right and that it has precedence over the entire creation, even the soul that one is obligated to sacrifice for his sake because he is the one who delivered it from the Fire. He then said, 'Now, by Allah, you are more beloved to me than myself.' He replied, {Now, O 'Umar.} In other words, now your faith is complete. This is why the first group of believers are worthy of the eternal praise that Allah gave them when He said,

﴿وَالسَّابِقُونَ الْأَوَّلُونَ مِنَ الْمُهَاجِرِينَ وَالْأَنصَارِ وَالَّذِينَ اتَّبَعُوهُم بِإِحْسَانٍ رَّضِيَ اللَّهُ عَنْهُمْ

وَرَضُوا عَنْهُ وَأَعَدَّ لَهُمْ جَنَّاتٍ تَجْرِي تَحْتَهَا الْأَنْهَارُ خَالِدِينَ فِيهَا أَبَدًا ۚ ذَٰلِكَ الْفَوْزُ الْعَظِيمُ﴾

"The forerunners – the first of the Emigrants and Helpers – and those who have followed them in doing good: Allah is pleased with them and they are pleased with Him. He has prepared Gardens for them with rivers flowing under them, remaining in them timelessly, forever and ever. That is the great victory." [at-Tawbah 9:100]

14. The Ḥadīth Informs:

i. That the Muslim is obligated to subject his actions to the Book and Sunnah and strive to make them in accordance with both.

ii. That whoever believes in Allah the Exalted's legislation in his heart or affirms it on his tongue and his actions go against it is a sinner, and whoever's actions agree with it and his belief and opinions go against it is a hypocrite. Furthermore, whoever conforms to whatever circumstance they are in is a renegade and heretic.

iii. One of the inseparable manifestations of faith is giving victory to the Sunnah of Allah's Messenger and defending his Revealed Law.

THE FORTY-SECOND ḤADĪTH

سَعَةُ مَغْفِرَةِ اللهِ عَزَّ وَجَل

عَنْ أَنَسٍ رضي الله عنه قَالَ: سَمِعْتُ رَسُوْلَ اللهِ ﷺ يَقُوْلُ: { قَالَ اللهُ تَعَالَى: «يَا ابْنَ آدَمَ، إِنَّكَ مَا دَعَوْتَنِي وَرَجَوْتَنِي غَفَرْتُ لَكَ عَلَى مَا كَانَ مِنْكَ وَلَا أُبَالِيْ. يَا ابْنَ آدَمَ، لَوْ بَلَغَتْ ذُنُوْبُكَ عَنَانَ السَّمَاءِ، ثُمَّ اسْتَغْفَرْتَنِي غَفَرْتُ لَكَ. إِنَّكَ لَوْ أَتَيْتَنِي بِقُرَابِ الْأَرْضِ خَطَايَا، ثُمَّ لَقِيْتَنِي لَا تُشْرِكُ بِي شَيْئًا، لَأَتَيْتُكَ بِقُرَابِهَا مَغْفِرَةً. } رواه الترمذي، وقال: حديث حسن صحيح.

The Vastness of Allah's ﷻ Forgiveness

It is on the authority of Anas رضي الله عنه who said, 'I heard the Messenger of Allah ﷺ saying, {Allah says, 'Son of Adam, as long as you call on Me and hope in Me, I will forgive whatever comes from you and I do not care. Son of Adam, even if your sins were to reach the clouds in the sky and then you were to seek My forgiveness, I would forgive you. Son of Adam, even if you were to come to Me with nearly the earth in wrong actions, and then you were to meet Me and not associate any partner with Me, I would bring you the same in forgiveness.'} Related by at-Tirmidhī, who said that it is a good, authentic ḥadīth.

At-Tirmidhī has collected it in the Book of Supplications (the chapter on sins being forgiven however great they are), no.3534, and ad-Dārimī, no.2791. As-Sakhāwī, in the derivation of *The Forty Nawawiyyah*, says, 'This ḥadīth is good'.

The Language of the Ḥadīth:

(ما دعوتني) *ma daʿawtanī*: as long as you ask Me to forgive your sins and other matters, and you worship Me through acts of obedience, supplications and so forth, for supplication is the core of worship. Furthermore, a true supplication is when the slave calls on his Lord and asks Him to help him. *Ma* is an adverb of time, i.e. as long as you are supplicating.

(رجوتني) *rajawtanī*: you fear My punishment and hope for My forgiveness, you yearn for My mercy and are afraid of My sublimity, and hope carries the meaning of fear. Hope is to hold out and expect goodness, and that it will happen soon.

(غفرت لك) *ghafartu lak*: I veil your shortcomings and efface your sins.

(على ما كان منك) *ʿalā ma kāna minka*: despite abundant sins coming from you, minor and major.

(ولا أبالي) *wa lā ubālī*: i.e. their abundance does not overwhelm Me, for indeed the slaves' crimes and the sins of stubborn people is like a tiny atom or even less next to the Lord's sublimity.

(بلغت) *balaghat*: what they reach in terms of their abundant amount or the severity of how they are committed; the intensification of what is meant is clearly illustrated here, in that the sins are so abundant that if they were tangible objects, they would fill what is between the skies and the earth.

(عنان) *ʿanān*: i.e. clouds, and it has been said that it is as far as the eye can see.

(استغفرتني) *istaghfartanī*: you sought forgiveness from Me, which is protection from the evil of sins and their veiling.

(بقراب الأرض) *bi qurāb al-ʾarḍ*: i.e. with what fills the earth or nearly fills it.

(خطايا) *khaṭāyā*: sins, major or minor.

(لقيتني) *laqaytanī*: i.e. you die and meet me on the Day of Standing.

(لا تشرك به شيئا) *la tushrik bī shayʾa*: in creed and not in deed, i.e. you believe that I have no partner in My dominion and I have neither a child nor a parent, (and do you no deed seeking other than Me)?

(مغفرة) *maghfirah*: i.e. the removal of punishment and the conveyance of reward.

Legal Matters and Other Guidance from the Ḥadīth:
This ḥadīth is the most hopeful ḥadīth in the Sunnah, because it clearly elucidates the abundance of the Exalted One's forgiveness, so that sinners do not despair of it because of their abundant sins. However, one should not be deluded by it and become engrossed in disobedience, for it may overwhelm you and become a barrier between you and Allah's forgiveness ﷻ. This is what the ḥadīth contains:

1. The Causes of Forgiveness:
There are causes and ways for a person to be forgiven for their sins, such as:
i. Supplicating while having hope that it will answered: Supplication is commanded and a response is promised. The Exalted One has said:

﴿وَقَالَ رَبُّكُمُ ٱدْعُونِىٓ أَسْتَجِبْ لَكُمْ﴾
"Your Lord says, 'Call on Me and I will answer you." [Ghāfir 40:60]

It is on the authority of Nuʿmān ibn Bashīr ؓ that the Prophet ﷺ said, {Supplication is worship.} Then he recited this verse, **"Your Lord says..."** This has been related by at-Tirmidhī and others. Allah ﷻ does not bestow bounty upon His slaves and grant them the success to call on Him and beseech Him except that He bestows upon them the bounty of acceptance and response. At-Ṭabarānī has collected a ḥadīth *marfūʿan*: {Whoever is granted supplicated is granted a response, because Allah the Exalted says, **"Call on Me and I will answer you."**} In another ḥadīth: {Allah does not? open the door of supplication for a slave and then close the door of response.}

ii. The Conditions for a Response and Its Impediments: Supplication is a means that necessitates a response when its conditions have been fulfilled and its impediments have been removed, and the response differs due to the absence of certain conditions and etiquettes or the existence of certain impediments.

a. Presence and Hope: One of the most significant conditions is the presence of the heart along with the hope of response from Allah the Exalted.

At-Tirmidhī has collected the ḥadīth of Abū Hurayrah ؓ where the Prophet ﷺ said, {Supplicate to Allah and be certain of a response, and Allah the Exalted does not accept supplication from a heart that is unmindful and inattentive.}

In the *Musnad*, it is on the authority of ʿAbdullah ibn ʿUmar ؓ that the Prophet ﷺ said, {Hearts are containers, and some of them contain more than others do. When you ask Allah ﷻ – O people – ask Him and be certain of a response, for Allah does not respond to a slave who supplicates from an unmindful heart.}

A sign of hope is proper obedience. The Exalted One has said:

﴿إِنَّ ٱلَّذِينَ ءَامَنُوا۟ وَٱلَّذِينَ هَاجَرُوا۟ وَجَٰهَدُوا۟ فِى سَبِيلِ ٱللَّهِ أُو۟لَٰٓئِكَ يَرْجُونَ رَحْمَتَ ٱللَّهِ﴾
"Those who believe and make hijrah and do *jihād* in the way of Allah can except Allah's mercy." [al-Baqarah 2:218]

b. Resolve in asking and supplicating: In other words, the slave asks with truthfulness, determination and confirmation, and does not hesitate in his heart or his words. The Messenger of Allah ﷺ forbade supplicating or seeking forgiveness by saying, 'O Allah, forgive me if You want to', 'O Allah, have mercy on me if You want to'. Rather, one should be determined in supplication, for Allah does what He wants and is not compelled to do anything.' This was related by Muslim.

It has been authentically narrated from the Prophet ﷺ who said, {When one of you supplicates, let him not say, 'O Allah, if You want to, forgive me'. Rather, let him be determined and have immense longing, for Allah the Glorified is not overwhelmed by anything that He gives.}

c. Urgency in supplication: Allah the Exalted loves for His slave to declare his slavehood to Him and his need of Him so that He answers him and complies with his request. As long as the slave has urgency in his supplication and is eager for a response without cutting his hope, he is close to a response. Whoever knocks on a door is close to having it opened for him. Allah the Exalted has said:

﴿وَٱدْعُوهُ خَوْفًا وَطَمَعًا ۚ إِنَّ رَحْمَتَ ٱللَّهِ قَرِيبٌ مِّنَ ٱلْمُحْسِنِينَ﴾

> **"Call on him fearfully and eagerly. Allah's mercy is close to those who do good."** [al-ʾAʿrāf 7:56]

In the *Mustadrak* of al-Ḥākim, it is on the authority of Anas *marfūʿan*: {Do not fail to supplicate, for no one will ever be destroyed with supplication.} He ﷺ said, {Allah is angry with whoever does not ask Him.} Related by Ibn Mājah. It has reached us from traditions[295] that when a slave supplicates to his Lord and He loves him, He says, 'O Jibrīl, do not hasten to fulfil My slave's need, for I love to hear his voice.'}

d. Hastiness and leaving supplication: The Messenger of Allah ﷺ forbade the slave from being hasty and leaving supplication due to being kept waiting for a response, and he made it one of the impediments to a response. This was so that the slave would not cut his hope for a response to a supplication, even if he has to wait a long time, for the Glorified One loves those who have urgency on their supplication. The Messenger of Allah ﷺ said, {One of you will be answered as long as he is not hasty and does not say, 'I have supplicated to my Lord and He has not answered me.'} Agreed upon.

---

295 Ar. *āthār*.

e. Lawful provision: One of the most important causes of supplications being answered is a person's provision being lawful, from legitimate sources. Likewise, one of the impediments to a response is when a person is not concerned about their provision, whether it is lawful or unlawful. It has been established that he ﷺ said, {A man will stretch his hands towards the sky, saying, 'Lord! Lord!' and his food is unlawful, his drink is unlawful and his clothing is unlawful, so how can he be answered?' Related by Muslim and others. He also said, {O Saʿd, purify your food and your supplications will be answered.} Related by at-Ṭabarānī in *as-Ṣaghīr*.

2. Asking for Forgiveness: One of the most important matters that the slave can ask his Lord is forgiveness for his sins and what would necessitate that, such as being saved from the Fire and entering Paradise. He ﷺ said, {We murmur about it.} Related by Abū Dāwūd and others, and the meaning is about asking for Paradise and being saved from the Fire. Abū Muslim al-Khawlānī said, 'No supplication came to me and I was reminded of the Fire except that I changed it to seeking refuge from the Fire.'

3. Changing the Slave's Request to that which is Good for Him: It is from Allah the Exalted's mercy towards His slave that the slave may ask Him for some worldly need and He will either answer him or give him something better. Something better could be that He will avert some harm from him, store it for him in the Hereafter or use it to forgive one of his sins. Aḥmad and at-Tirmidhī have related the ḥadīth of Jābir in which the Prophet ﷺ said, {There is no one who supplicates except that Allah gives him what he asked for or He averts harm from him that is equivalent to it, as long as he does not supplicate for something sinful or the cutting of kinship ties.} It is on the authority of Abū Saʿīd ؓ that the Prophet ﷺ said, {There is no Muslim who makes a supplication that does not contain sin or the cutting of kinship ties except that Allah gives him one of three things on account of it: either He grants him what he supplicates for, He stores it for him in the Hereafter, or He averts harm from him that is equivalent to it.} They said, 'So, we do more of it?' He replied, {Allah, do more.} In at-Ṭabarānī's narration, it is, {...or he forgives a prior sin of his.} instead of {...or He averts harm from him that is equivalent to it.}

4. Some of the Etiquettes of Supplication:
- Seeking out preferred times
- Having *wuḍūʾ* and praying beforehand
- Repentance
- Facing the *qiblah* and raising one's hands
- Starting with praise and extolment and sending prayers upon the Prophet ﷺ

- Making the sending of prayers in the middle and concluding it by saying *āmīn.*
- Not making one's supplication exclusively for oneself, but makes it general.
- Having a good opinion of Allah and hoping for a response.
- Acknowledging one's sins.
- Lowering one's voice.

5. Seeking Forgiveness However Great the Sins are: The slave's sins, however great they may be, Allah the Exalted's pardon and forgiveness is vaster and greater, and thus they are small when compared to Allah the Exalted's pardon and forgiveness. Al-Ḥākim has collected the following from Jābir ﵁: '...that a man came to the Prophet ﷺ and he was saying, 'My sins!' and he said it two or three times. The Prophet ﷺ thus said to him, {Say, 'O Allah, Your forgiveness is vaster than my sins, and Your mercy bears more hope than my deeds.'} He said it and he then said to him, {Repeat}, so he repeated it. He then said, {Repeat} again and he repeated it again. Then he said, {Stand. Allah has forgiven you.}

6. Seeking Forgiveness in the Qur'ān:

Forgiveness is mentioned often in the Qur'ān:

- Sometimes, it is commanded. The Exalted One says:

﴿وَٱسْتَغْفِرُوا۟ ٱللَّهَ ۖ إِنَّ ٱللَّهَ غَفُورٌ رَّحِيمٌۢ﴾

"And seek forgiveness from Allah, Allah is Ever-Forgiving, Most Merciful." [al-Muzzammil 73:20]

He ﷻ also says:

﴿وَأَنِ ٱسْتَغْفِرُوا۟ رَبَّكُمْ ثُمَّ تُوبُوٓا۟ إِلَيْهِ﴾

"Ask your Lord for forgiveness and then make *tawbah*[296] to him." [Hūd 11:3]

- Sometimes, its people are praised. He ﷻ says:

﴿وَٱلْمُسْتَغْفِرِينَ بِٱلْأَسْحَارِ﴾

"...and those who seek forgiveness before dawn." [Āl 'Imrān 3:17]

He also says:

﴿وَٱلَّذِينَ إِذَا فَعَلُوا۟ فَٰحِشَةً أَوْ ظَلَمُوٓا۟ أَنفُسَهُمْ ذَكَرُوا۟ ٱللَّهَ فَٱسْتَغْفَرُوا۟ لِذُنُوبِهِمْ وَمَن يَغْفِرُ ٱلذُّنُوبَ

إِلَّا ٱللَّهُ وَلَمْ يُصِرُّوا۟ عَلَىٰ مَا فَعَلُوا۟ وَهُمْ يَعْلَمُونَ﴾

296 (tn): repentance.

"those who, when they act indecently or wrong themselves, remember Allah and ask forgiveness for their bad actions – and who can forgive bad actions except Allah? – and do not knowingly persist in what they were doing." [Āl ʿImrān 3:135]

- Sometimes, forgiveness is stated to be a result of it, and Allah the Exalted mentions that He forgives those who seek His forgiveness. The Exalted One says:

﴿وَمَن يَعْمَلْ سُوٓءًا أَوْ يَظْلِمْ نَفْسَهُۥ ثُمَّ يَسْتَغْفِرِ ٱللَّهَ يَجِدِ ٱللَّهَ غَفُورًا رَّحِيمًا﴾

"Anyone who does evil or wrongs himself and then asks Allah's forgiveness will fine Allah Ever-Forgiving." [an-Nisāʾ 4:110]

This is nothing other than evidence that seeking forgiveness has an immense rank, and that it is the foundation of the slave's salvation. The slave is never separate from falling into infringements and sins, intentionally and unintentionally.

7. Repentance[297] and Seeking Forgiveness:
Seeking forgiveness is often linked to repentance:

﴿أَفَلَا يَتُوبُونَ إِلَى ٱللَّهِ وَيَسْتَغْفِرُونَهُۥ﴾

"Why do they not turn to Allah and ask for His forgiveness? Allah is Ever-Forgiving, Most Merciful". [al-Māʾidah 5:74]

﴿وَأَنِ ٱسْتَغْفِرُوا۟ رَبَّكُمْ ثُمَّ تُوبُوٓا۟ إِلَيْهِ﴾

"Ask your Lord for forgiveness and then make *tawbah* to him." [Hūd 11:3]

And there are other verses. In these situations, seeking forgiveness is an expression of one wanting to be forgiven, while repentance is an expression of one's abandonment of sins with one's heart and limbs.

Sometimes, seeking forgiveness is mentioned on its own and forgiveness is the result:

﴿قَالَ رَبِّ إِنِّى ظَلَمْتُ نَفْسِى فَٱغْفِرْ لِى فَغَفَرَ لَهُۥٓ﴾

"He said, 'My Lord, I have wronged myself. Forgive me.' So He forgave him". [al-Qaṣaṣ 28:16]

﴿وَٱسْتَغْفِرُوا۟ ٱللَّهَ ۖ إِنَّ ٱللَّهَ غَفُورٌ رَّحِيمٌۢ﴾

"And seek forgiveness from Allah. Allah is Ever-Forgiving, Most Merciful". [al-Muzzammil 73:20]

297 Ar. *at-tawbah*.

And there are other verses, and they are similar to what is mentioned in this ḥadīth and other ḥadīths.

The meaning of 'you were to seek My forgiveness' is that you make sincere repentance. This means that you regret your disobedience because it is disobedience, you refrain from it for Allah's sake, and you make the resolution not to return to it. You also make amends by making up any missed acts of obedience that you can and restoring people's rights that you transgressed against or usurped. In order to be forgiven, one must refrain from sin and rectify the situation. Allah the Exalted has said:

﴿فَمَن تَابَ مِنۢ بَعۡدِ ظُلۡمِهِۦ وَأَصۡلَحَ فَإِنَّ ٱللَّهَ يَتُوبُ عَلَيۡهِۚ إِنَّ ٱللَّهَ غَفُورٞ رَّحِيمٌ﴾

"But if anyone makes *tawbah* after his wrongdoing and puts things right, Allah will turn towards him. Allah is Ever-Forgiving, Most Merciful." [al-Mā'idah 5:39]

8. Seeking Forgiveness while Persisting in Sin:

It has been said that all the texts that mention seeking forgiveness unrestrictedly are all qualified by the lack of persistence that is mentioned in the verse in Āl 'Imrān. Allah has promised therein that He will forgive the sins of whoever seeks His forgiveness and does not persist in committing them. Abū Dāwūd and at-Tirmidhī have collected the ḥadīth of Abū Bakr ؓ in which the Prophet ﷺ said, {Whoever seeks forgiveness, even if he goes back to the sin seventy times a day, is not considered persistent therein.}

In the two *Ṣaḥīḥ* collections, it is on the authority of Abū Hurayrah ؓ that the Prophet ﷺ said, {The slave sins and says, 'My Lord, I have committed a sin, so forgive me.' Allah the Exalted says, 'My slave knows that he has a Lord who forgives sins and punishes sins. I have forgiven my slave.' Then he remains for however long Allah wants. Then he commits another sin…'} The same was then stated two more times. According to Muslim's narration, the third time, He said, 'I have forgiven My slave, so let him do what He wants.}The meaning is that as long as he is in this state, every time he commits a sin it will be forgiven. The outward purport is that seeking forgiveness is connected to a lack of persistence therein, and the complete seeking of forgiveness, which necessitates being forgiven, is that which goes hand in hand with a lack of persistence therein. Likewise, Allah the Exalted praises its people and promises to forgive them, and when He does so, He is holding out hope that there will be sincere repentance. One of the knowers of Allah said, 'If the fruit of someone's seeking of forgiveness is not the rectification of his repentance, he is lying when he seeks forgiveness.'

As for seeking forgiveness with one's tongue while one's heart persists in sin, it is nothing but a supplication. If Allah wants, He will answer it, and if He wants, He will reject it. It is hoped that it will be answered, especially if it comes from a heart that is broken because of sins, or it occurs within one of the times in which supplications are answered, such as before dawn, after the call to prayer, after the five daily prayers, and so forth. Persistence in sin can also be an impediment to being answered. In the *Musnad*, there is the ḥadīth of ʿAbdullah ibn ʿAmr *marfūʿan*: {Woe to those who knowingly persist in what they were doing.} It is on the authority of Ibn ʿAbbās ﷺ that he said, 'The one who repents from sin is like the one who has? no sin, while the one who seeks forgiveness from sin while persisting in it is like someone who mocks Allah.' This was collected by Ibn Abī ad-Dunyā. It is on the authority of Ḥudhayfah ﷺ that he said, 'It suffices as a lie to say, "I seek Allah's forgiveness" and then go back to the sin.'

9. The Liar's Repentance: Whoever says, 'I seek Allah's forgiveness and I repent to Him' while his heart persists in disobedience is lying when he says this, and he is sinning by doing so because he is not repenting. It is not permissible for him to say that he is repentant when he is not repentant. Someone like this, who says, 'O Allah, I seek your forgiveness, so turn to me' is feared for. It is feared that he will receive a severe punishment. He is like someone who hopes for a harvest but does not grow any crops, or he wants a child but never gets married.

10. Repenting and Making a Pledge: The majority of scholars hold that it is permissible for the repentant slave to say, 'I repent to Allah' and pledge to his Lord that He will not go back to disobedience. Making the firm intention to follow it through is thus immediately obligatory upon him.

11. Seeking Forgiveness Frequently: In al-Bukhārī's collection, it is on the authority of Abū Hurayrah ﷺ that the Prophet ﷺ said, {By Allah, I seek Allah's forgiveness and repent to Him more than seventy times a day.} It has reached us that Luqmān said to his son, 'My dear son, accustom your tongue to saying, "O Allah, forgive me", for indeed Allah has times in which the asker is not rejected.' Al-Ḥasan said, 'Seek forgiveness frequently; in your homes, when you sit down to eat, on your roads, in your markets, in your gatherings, and wherever else you may be, for you do not know when forgiveness will descend. In his book *ʿAml al-Yawm wa al-Laylah,*[298] an-Nasāʾī relates from Abū Hurayrah ﷺ who said, 'I have not seen anyone say, "I seek Allah's forgiveness and I repent to Him' more than the Messenger of Allah ﷺ.' In his *Sunan*, it is on the authority of Ibn ʿUmar ﷺ that he said, 'In one gathering, we would count the Messenger of Allah ﷺ saying, {My Lord, forgive me and turn to me. You are the Ever-Relenting, the Ever-Forgiving} one hundred times.

298 (tn): i.e. 'The Deeds of the Day and Night'.

12. The Master of Seeking Forgiveness:[299] When seeking forgiveness, it is recommended to say more than, (أَسْتَغْفِرُ اللهَ وَأَتُوبُ إِلَيْهِ) 'I seek Allah's forgiveness and I turn to Him.' It has been related from 'Umar ﷺ that he heard a man saying, 'I seek Allah's forgiveness and I turn to Him', so he said to him, 'Do not be silly. Say, "I turn to you as someone who cannot benefit or harm himself, cannot cause himself to live or die, or to be resurrected"'.

Al-Awzā'ī was asked about someone who seeks forgiveness by saying,

(أَسْتَغْفِرُ اللهَ العَظِيمَ الَّذِي لَا إِلَـهَ إِلَّا هُوَ الْحَيُّ الْقَيُّومُ وَأَتُوبُ إِلَيْهِ)

'I seek forgiveness from Allah the Sublime, besides Whom there is no other god, the Living, the Self-Sustaining, and I turn to him', so he said, 'This is good, but he should say, (رَبِّ اغْفِرْ لِي) "My Lord, forgive me", to complete the seeking of forgiveness'. This wording has been conveyed to us from the Messenger of Allah ﷺ by Abū Dāwūd, at-Tirmidhī, and others.

The best form of seeking forgiveness and its master, i.e. the noblest form, the one that carries the most reward and is most likely to be accepted, is for the slave to begin by praising his Lord, secondly to acknowledge his sins and finally to ask Allah for forgiveness using what has been established from the Messenger of Allah ﷺ. Al-Bukhārī has related from Shaddād ibn Aws ﷺ that the Prophet ﷺ said, {The master of seeking forgiveness is for the slave to say,

(اللهم أَنْتَ رَبِّي لَا إِلَـهَ إِلَّا أَنْتَ ، خَلَقْتَنِي وَأَنَا عَبْدُكَ ، وَأَنَا عَلَى عَهْدِكَ وَوَعْدِكَ مَا اسْتَطَعْتُ ، أَعُوذُ بِكَ مِنْ شَرِّ مَا صَنَعْتُ ، أَبُوءُ لَكَ بِنِعْمَتِكَ عَلَيَّ وَأَبُوءُ بِذَنْبِي فَاغْفِرْ لِي ، فَإِنَّهُ لَا يَغْفِرُ الذُّنُوبَ إِلَّا أَنْتَ)

'O Allah, You are my Lord, there is no god but You. You have created me and I am Your slave. I am upon Your covenant and promise to the best of my ability. I seek refuge in You from the evil that I have done. I acknowledge before You, your blessings upon me and I acknowledge my sins, so forgive me. No one forgives sins apart from You.'}

13. Seeking Forgiveness For the Sins One is Ignorant of: When someone commits many sins and evil actions and is unaware of many of them, such that they are beyond count, let him seek Allah's forgiveness ﷻ for his sins that only Allah the Exalted knows. Shaddād ibn Aws ﷺ has related from the Prophet ﷺ

(أَسْأَلُكَ مِنْ خَيْرِ مَا تَعْلَمُ وَأَعُوذُ بِكَ مِنْ شَرِّ مَا تَعْلَمُ ، وَأَسْتَغْفِرُكَ لِمَا تَعْلَمُ إِنَّكَ أَنْتَ عَلَّامُ الْغُيُوبِ)

299 Ar. *sayyid al-istighfār.*

{I ask You from the good that You know and I seek refuge in your from the evil that you know. I seek Your forgiveness for what You know, You are the Knower of the Unseen.} Allah certainly knows everything and He records it.

The Exalted One says:

﴿يَوْمَ يَبْعَثُهُمُ ٱللَّهُ جَمِيعًا فَيُنَبِّئُهُم بِمَا عَمِلُوٓاْ أَحْصَىٰهُ ٱللَّهُ وَنَسُوهُ﴾

"On the Day Allah raises up all of them together, He will inform them of what they did. Allah has recorded it while they have forgotten it." [al-Mujādalah 58:6]

14. Some of the Fruits of Seeking Forgiveness: Whoever seeks Allah the Exalted's forgiveness feels that he is seeking refuge from One who is forgiving and merciful, independent and generous, knowing and forbearing, and thus his heart is at ease and relaxed, free of anxiety and distress. He rejoices at Allah the Exalted's mercy and pleasure and his soul is optimistic; despair has no means of penetrating it. Muslim has narrated from al-Aghar al-Muzanī that the Prophet ❧ said, {It covers my heart, and I seek Allah's forgiveness one hundred times a day.} The meaning of 'covers my heart' is that I am exposed to the same preoccupations that human beings are exposed to.

In the *Sunan* of Abū Dāwūd, it is on the authority of Ibn 'Abbās ❧ that the Prophet ❧ said, {Whoever seeks Allah's forgiveness frequently, Allah grants him an opening from every anxiety, an exit from every distress and grants him provision from where he does not expect it.}

There is also the ḥadīth of Abū Dharr, *marfūʿan*: {Every malady has a remedy, and the remedy for sins is to seek forgiveness.}

Qatādah said, 'This Qur'an shows you your malady and your remedy. As for your malady, it is sins. As for your remedy, it is to seek forgiveness'.

'Ā'ishah ❧ said, 'Blessed is the one who finds much seeking of forgiveness on his page'.[300]

Abū al-Minhāl said, 'The slave in his grave has no neighbour more beloved to him than much seeking of forgiveness'.

One of them said, 'The only thing sinners can put their trust in is weeping and seeking forgiveness, so whoever is concerned about his sins let him do much seeking of forgiveness'.

Maybe one of the fruits of seeking forgiveness is that one's tongue is preoccupied from doing anything else, and thus good qualities like pardon, clemency and beautiful manners emanate from his soul. In the *Musnad* of Aḥmad, it is on the

---

300 Ar. *ṣaḥīfah*, i.e. the record of his deeds.

authority of Ḥudhayfah, who said, 'I said, "O Messenger of Allah, I have a sharp tongue and it mostly towards my family.' He replied, {Where are you in terms of seeking forgiveness? I seek Allah's forgiveness 100 times every day and night.}

Having a sharp tongue means that one does not care about what they are saying and the causticity and wicked words that are coming out of their mouth.

15. Requesting People who are Presumed to Have Few Fins to Seek Forgiveness on One's Behalf: Those who are greatly concerned about their sins, maybe they can hold on to those whose sins are few, and ask them to seek forgiveness on their behalf. 'Umar ﷺ would ask children to seek forgiveness. He would say, 'You have not committed any sins.' Abū Hurayrah ﷺ would say to young boys in the Qur'ān school, 'Say, "O Allah, forgive Abū Hurayrah"', and he would say *āmīn* after their supplication.

16. Having a Good Opinion of Allah and that He alone is Ever-Forgiving: The believing slave who seeks his Lord's forgiveness must have a good opinion of Allah ﷻ, and that He forgives His sins. It is mentioned in a *ḥadīth qudsī*: {Allah ﷻ says, 'I am as My slave thinks of Me, so let him think of Me what he wants.'} In another narration: {Do not think anything but good of Allah.} One of the greatest causes of being forgiven is that when the slave commits a sin, he does not hope for forgiveness from anyone but his Lord, and he knows that no one but Him forgives sins and takes them. Allah ﷻ describes the believers by saying:

﴿وَٱلَّذِينَ إِذَا فَعَلُوا۟ فَـٰحِشَةً أَوْ ظَلَمُوٓا۟ أَنفُسَهُمْ ذَكَرُوا۟ ٱللَّهَ فَٱسْتَغْفَرُوا۟ لِذُنُوبِهِمْ
وَمَن يَغْفِرُ ٱلذُّنُوبَ إِلَّا ٱللَّهُ﴾

"those who, when they act indecently or wrong themselves, remember Allah and ask forgiveness for their bad actions – and who can forgive bad actions except Allah?" [Āl 'Imrān 3:135]

In the two *Ṣaḥīḥ* collections, it is on the authority of 'Abdullah ibn 'Amr ﷺ that Abu Bakr ﷺ said, 'O Messenger of Allah, teach me a supplication that I can supplicate with, in my prayer.' He replied, {Say,

(اللهمَّ إِنِّي ظَلَمْتُ نَفْسِي ظُلْمًا كَثِيرًا ، وَلَا يَغْفِرُ الذُّنُوبَ إِلَّا أَنْتَ، فَاغْفِرْ لِي مَغْفِرَةً مِنْ عِنْدِكَ،
وَارْحَمْنِي، إِنَّكَ أَنْتَ الغَفُورُ الرَّحِيمُ)

O Allah, I have oppressed myself greatly, and no one forgives sins apart from You, so bestow Your forgiveness upon me and have mercy on me, you are the Ever-Forgiving, the Most Merciful.'}

The obligation to better one's opinion of Allah is emphasised when one excepts that one's time is near and that the slave is heading back to Allah ✽ so that one's hope for forgiveness is predominant. Aḥmad and at-Ṭabarānī have related from Muʿādh ibn Jabal ✽ that the Messenger of Allah ✽ said, {If you want, I will tell you the first thing that Allah says to the believers on the Day of Standing and the first thing they say to Him.} They replied, 'Yes, O Messenger of Allah.' He said, '{Allah the Exalted says to the believers, 'Did you want to meet Me?' They respond, 'Yes, our Lord.' He then says, 'Why?' They respond, 'We hoped for Your pardon and Your mercy.' He then says, 'My forgiveness has become necessary for you.'}

17. Fear and Hope: In order to realise hope, there must be fear, and thus a person must combine between the two to be safe and not confine himself to one and not the other because hope can lead to deception and fear to despair, both of which are blameworthy. There is the noble ḥadīth: {Hope and fear have sworn that if they are not combined in a person in this life, he will find the scent of the Fire, and if they are not separated in a person, he will find the scent of Paradise.}

The chosen position of the Mālikīs is that there should be more fear when one is healthy and more hope when one is ill. The preferred position of the Shāfiʿīs is that they should be equal when one is healthy, such that sometimes one looks at one's shortcomings and feels fear, and sometimes one looks at Allah's magnanimity and feels hope. As for the one who is ill, his hope should be greater than his fear, due to his statement ✽ {Let none of you die except that he has a good opinion of Allah the Exalted.}

Imam ash-Shāfiʿī ✽ said on his deathbed:

When my heart had become hard and my movement restricted
I made my hope of Your pardon a ladder
I was overwhelmed by my sins, but when I compared them
To Your pardon, my Lord, Your pardon was greater

Perhaps this is the wisdom as to why these chosen ḥadīths is concluded with this ḥadīth and takes their number to more than forty.

18. *Tawḥīd* is the Foundation of Forgiveness: *Tawḥīd* is one of the causes of forgiveness. In fact, it is the greatest cause, for whoever lacks it will never be forgiven and whoever has it has the greatest cause of forgiveness. Allah the Exalted has said:

﴿إِنَّ ٱللَّهَ لَا يَغْفِرُ أَن يُشْرَكَ بِهِۦ وَيَغْفِرُ مَا دُونَ ذَٰلِكَ لِمَن يَشَآءُ﴾

"Allah does not forgive anything being associated with Him but He forgives whomever He wills for anything other than that." [an-Nisāʾ 4:116]

Sins become small before the lights of Allah's *tawḥīd* ﷻ so whoever brings *tawḥīd* along with the earth's fill of wrong actions, Allah ﷻ meets him with the same in forgiveness. However, it depends on Allah the Exalted's will and favour. If He wants, He forgives him, and if He wants, he takes Him to task for them.

19. The Final Destination of the Bearer of *Tawḥīd* is Paradise: He will not be in the Fire forever. Instead, he will exit it and enter Paradise. He is not thrown into the Fire the way unbelievers are thrown in, nor does he remain therein as they remain therein. He ﷺ said, {Whoever says, 'There is no god but Allah'[301] and there is a wheat kernel's weight of goodness in his heart will exit the Fire.' Related by al-Bukhārī.

20. Salvation from the Fire: When the slave has perfected his *tawḥīd* and his sincerity for Allah therein, and he fulfils all the conditions, with his heart, his tongue and his limbs, or with his heart and tongue at the time of death, it necessitates that all his prior sins be forgiven and he is completely prevented from entering the Fire. He ﷺ said to Muʿādh ibn Jabal, {Do you know Allah's right over His slaves is?} He replied, 'Allah and His Messenger know best.' He said, {That they worship Him and not associate anything with Him. Do you know what their right over Him is?} He replied, 'Allah and His Messenger know best.' He said, {That He does not punish them.} Related by al-Bukhārī and others. In the *Musnad* and other collections, it is on the authority of Umm Hāni' that the Prophet ﷺ said, {*Lā ilāha ill Allah* does not leave any sin and is not preceded by any deed.}

Also in the *Musnad*, it is on the authority of Shaddād ibn Aws and ʿUbādah ibn as-Ṣāmit 'that the Prophet ﷺ said to his Companions, {Raise your hands and say *Lā ilāha ill Allah.*} So, we raised our hands for a moment. Then the Messenger of Allah ﷺ put down his hand and said, {Praise be to Allah. O Allah, You have sent me with this word and commanded me to it, and promised me Paradise based on it, and You do not break Your promise.} Then he said, {Rejoice, for Allah has forgiven you.}' This is understood in connection to what we have mentioned, i.e. it must be preceded by repentance and good action. The Exalted One has said:

﴿إِلَّا مَن تَابَ وَءَامَنَ وَعَمِلَ عَمَلًا صَٰلِحًا فَأُوْلَٰٓئِكَ يُبَدِّلُ ٱللَّهُ سَيِّـَٔاتِهِمْ حَسَنَٰتٍ ۗ

وَكَانَ ٱللَّهُ غَفُورًا رَّحِيمًا﴾

"except for those who repent and believe and act rightly: Allah will transform the wrong actions of such people into good – Allah is Ever-Forgiving, Most Merciful." [al-Furqān 25:70]

301 Ar. *lā ilāha ill Allah.*

21. Pure *Tawḥīd*: Whoever's heart is serious about the word of *tawḥīd*, everything apart from Allah the Exalted is removed from it, out of love and extolment, exaltation and awe, out of fear, hope and reliance. At that point, all sins and mistakes are burned away, even if they were like the foam on the ocean, and maybe they are turned into good deeds and the love that one has for one's Lord burns away all accidentals from one's heart. {None of you truly believes until Allah and His Messenger are more beloved to him than anything else.} Related by al-Bukhārī and others. Love of Allah's Messenger ﷺ is from the love of Allah ﷻ.

By Allah the Exalted's favour and success, the commentary on *The Forty* has been completed. May Allah's blessings be upon our master, Muḥammad, and upon his Family and Companions as well as much peace until the Day of Repayment. Praise be to Allah, Lord of all Creation.

THE CHAPTER THAT ELUCIDATES WHAT IS HIDDEN IN THE WORDINGS

Imam an-Nawawī ﵀ after mentioning they forty-second ḥadīth, said, 'This is the last of what I intended by way of expounding the ḥadīths that gather the principles of Islam, and include types of knowledge, foundations, branches and etiquettes that cannot be enumerated, and all kinds of rulings.

Here I will present a very short chapter that will elucidate what is hidden in their wordings, in order, so that no mistake is made therein and the one who is memorising them does not have to refer to any other source. Then I will proceed to explain them, if Allah the Exalted so wills, in a separate book.[302] I hope from Allah the Exalted's bounty that He will grant me the success to clarify the important subtleties and to summarise the benefits and features, the like of which a Muslim cannot do without knowing. The pure style and sublime precedence of these ḥadīths will be clear to the one who studies them, as well as the gems they comprise that I have mentioned and the important matters that I have described, and thereby one will know the wisdom as to why these forty ḥadīths were chosen, and that it is indeed a wisdom for those who look into the matter.

I have made it separate to this volume so that it will be easier to memorise on its own. Then, whoever wants to add the commentary to it can do so, and it is for Allah to graciously bestow that upon him, for he will apply himself to the precious subtleties that are derived from the speech of the one whom Allah ﷻ described by saying,

﴿وَمَا يَنطِقُ عَنِ ٱلْهَوَىٰٓ ۝٣ إِنْ هُوَ إِلَّا وَحْىٌ يُوحَىٰ﴾

"nor does he speak from whim. It is nothing but Revelation revealed." [an-Najm 53:3-4]

And for Allah is all praise, at the beginning and the end, inwardly and outwardly.

302 This book is in print.

The Chapter That Points Out Clarifications of Problematic Words

In this chapter, even though I have said 'problematic words', I will point out unequivocal words.

In the address:[303] (نَضَّرَ اللهُ امرأ) *naḍḍara Llāhū mra'an*:[304] it also been related without the *tashdīd*, i.e. *naḍara*, but with the *tashdīd* is more common, and it means to make handsome or beautiful.

The First Ḥadīth:

- (عن أمير المؤمنين عمر بن الخطاب ﷺ) 'an amīr al-mu'minīn 'Umar bin al-Khaṭṭāb raḍī Allahu 'anhu): he was the first person to be called Amīr al-Mu'minīn.
- His statement ﷺ: (إنما الأعمال بالنيات) innama l-'amālu binniyyāt means that actions in the Revealed Law are not taken into account unless there is an intention.
- His statement ﷺ: (فهجرته إلى الله ورسوله) fa hij*ratuhu ilā Llāhi wa Rasūlih* means that it is accepted.

The Second Ḥadīth:

- (لا يرى عليه أثر السفر) la yurā 'alayhi atharu as-safar: yu in yurā (as opposed to yarā) indicates the passive.
- His statement ﷺ: (تؤمن القدر خير وشره) tu'mina bil-qadari khayrihi wa sharih: i.e. you believe that Allah predestined good and evil before he created the creation, and that all beings are according to Allah the Exalted's decree and predestination and He wills them.
- His statement ﷺ: (فأخبرني عن أماراتها) fakhbirni 'an amārātiha: i.e. its signs, and amār – without the tā' marbuṭah – is also said, but the narration is amārah, i.e. with the tā' marbūṭah.
- His statement ﷺ: (تلد الأمة ربتها) talid al-ammatu rabbatahā: i.e. her female master, meaning that there will be so many slave women that a slave woman will give birth to a daughter by her master and the master's daughter will also be her master. It has also been said that so many slave women will be bought and sold that a woman will buy her mother and have her as a slave without knowing that she is her mother, and there are other positions. I have clarified this in Sharḥ Ṣaḥīḥ Muslim with its various evidence and all its paths of transmission.[305]
- His statement ﷺ: (العالة) al-'ālah: i.e. the poor, meaning the lowest of people become outwardly wealthy.

---

303 Ar. *khuṭbah*, i.e. Imam an-Nawawī's introduction to the book.

304 (tn): i.e. may Allah illuminate a person...

305 The Book of Faith, the chapter elucidation *īmān, islām* and *iḥsān*... (1/158).

- His[306] statement, 'لبثْتُ مليا' labith*tu maliyyan*: there is a *tashdīd* on the *yā*', i.e. a long time, and it was three,[307] as clarified in the narrations of Abū Dāwūd, at-Tirmidhī and others.[308]

The Fifth Ḥadīth:

- His statement ﷺ: (من أحدث في أمرنا هذا ما ليس منه فهو رد) m*an aḥdatha fī amrina mā laysa minhu fahuwa radd*: i.e. rejected, and like *khalq* (creation) bearing the meaning of *makhlūq*.

The Sixth Ḥadīth:

- His statement ﷺ: (استبرأ لدينه وعرضه) istabra'a li dīnihi wa 'irḍihi: i.e. he has protected his religion and preserved his honour from people delving into it.
- His statement ﷺ: (يوشك) yushiku: i.e. to hasten and come close.
- His statement ﷺ: (حمى الله محارمه) ḥi*mā Llāhi maḥārimuh*: i.e. that which Allah ﷻ protects and prohibits entrance are the things that He has declared unlawful.

The Seventh Ḥadīth:

- His statement: (عن أبي رقية) 'an Abī Ruqayyah, i.e. a ḍammah on the rā', a fatḥah on the qāf and a shaddah on the yā'.
- His statement: (الداري) ad-Dārī: he is attributed to an ancestor called ad-Dār, and it has been said that it is a place called *Dārīn*; it has also been said that it is *ad-Dayrī*, which is an attribution to a monastery where worship takes place. I have explained and clarified the position in the beginning of *Sharḥ Ṣaḥīḥ Muslim*.[309]

The Ninth Ḥadīth:

- His statement ﷺ: (واختلافهم) wa *khtilafuhum*: i.e. there is a *ḍammah* on the *fā'* and not *kasrah*.[310]

The Tenth Ḥadīth:

- His statement ﷺ: (غذي بالحرام) *ghudiya bil-ḥarām*: i.e. a *ḍammah* on the *ghayn* and a *kasra* on the *dhāl*.

---

306 (tn): i.e. 'Umar.

307 i.e. three days.

308 *Sunan Abī Dāwūd*: The Book of the Sunnah: the chapter on predestination (4695), at-Tirmidhī, Chapters on Faith, the chapter on what has reached us of the Prophet's ﷺ description of Jibrīl (2613), Ibn Mājah in the introduction, the chapter on faith (63), and an-Nasā'ī in the Book of Faith and Its Revealed Laws, the chapter describing Islam (8/97).

309 See the latter part of the introduction to his commentary on *Muslim* (1/142).

310 (tn): if one refers back to the ḥadīth, this distinction means that 'abundance' only applies to their questions and to their disagreements.

The Eleventh Ḥadīth:

- His statement ﷺ: (دع ما يريبك لما لا يريبك) daʿ ma yarībuk *limā lā yarībuk*: the *yā'* can be with a *fatḥah* (*ya*) or a *ḍammah* (*yu*), and the *fathah* is more eloquent and more common, and the meaning is: leave that which you have doubts about for that which you do not have doubts about.

The Twelfth Ḥadīth:

- His statement ﷺ: (يعنيه) yaʿnihi: i.e. there's a *fatḥah* on the first letter.

The Fourteenth Ḥadīth:

- His statement ﷺ: (الثيب الزاني) ath-thayyib az-zānī: i.e. the married person (muḥṣan) who commits fornication, and *al-iḥṣān* has known conditions in the books of *fiqh*.

The Fifteenth Ḥadīth:

- His statement ﷺ: (أو ليصمت) aw la*yaṣmut*: i.e. with a *ḍammah* on the *mīm*.

The Seventeenth Ḥadīth:

- (القتلة) al-qitlah and (الذبحة) adh-dhibah: both have a kasrah on the first letter.
- His statement ﷺ: (وليحد) wal *yuḥidda*: there is a *ḍammah* on the *yā'*, a *kasrah* on the *ḥā'* and a *shaddah* on the *dāl*, and the words *aḥadda*, *ḥadda* and *istiḥadda* all mean to sharpen when talking about a knife.

The Eighteenth Ḥadīth:

- His statement: (جندب) *jundub*, with a *ḍammah* on the *jīm* and a *ḍammah* or *fatḥah* on the *dāl*.

The Nineteenth Ḥadīth:

- (تجاهك) tujāhak: with a ḍammah on the tā' and a fatḥah on the hā': i.e. in front of you (amāmak), is in the other narration.
- (تعرّف إلى الله في الرخاء) *taʿarraf il Allāhī fi rrikhā'*: i.e. endear yourself to Him by adhering to His obedience and avoiding disobeying Him.

The Twentieth Ḥadīth:

- His statement ﷺ: (إذا لم تستح فاصنع ما شئت) idhā *lam tastaḥi faṣnaʿ mā shi't*: i.e. if you want to do something, if it is something that you are not ashamed to do in front of Allah and in front of people then do it. Otherwise, do not do it. This is what Islam revolves around.

The Twenty-First Ḥadīth:

- (قل آمنت بالله ثم استقم) qul āmantu billāhi thumm astaqim: be upright as you've been commanded, by obeying Allah's ﷻ commands and avoiding His prohibitions.

The Twenty-Third Ḥadīth:

- His statement ﷺ: (الطهور شطر الإيمان) at-*ṭuhūru shaṭru l-īmān*: what is meant by *ṭuhūr* is *wuḍūʾ*; it has been said that its reward is multiplied until it reaches half the reward of faith. It has also been said that faith erases[311] the sins that preceded it, just like *wuḍūʾ*, but the validity of *wuḍūʾ* is dependent on faith, and thus it becomes half. It has also been said that what is meant by faith is the prayer, and purification (*ṭuḥūr*) is a condition for its validity and thus it is like a half, and there are other opinions.
- His statement ﷺ: (الحمد لله تملأ الميزان) al-ḥamdu lillāhi tamlaʾu l-mīzān: i.e. its reward. (سبحان الله والحمد لله تملآن) subḥ*ān Allāhī wal-ḥamdū Lillāhi tamlān*: i.e. if their reward were measured in terms of tangible volume, and the reason is that they contain the declaration of Allah's ﷻ transcendence and consigning of matters to Him.
- (الصلاة نور) as-ṣalātu nūr: i.e. precludes disobedience, puts an end to indecency and guides to what is correct; it has also been that its reward is light on the Day of Standing for the person who performs it, and it has been said that it is a cause of one's heart being illuminated.
- (الصدقة برهان) as-ṣadaqatu burhān: i.e. a proof for the one who does it in carrying out the right over one's wealth, and it has been said that it is proof of the faith of the one who does it, because it is not something a hypocrite would usually do.
- (الصبر ضياء) as-ṣabru ḍiyāʾ: i.e. the patience that is loved, which is patience in obeying Allah, with the trials of calamities of this life, and refraining from disobedience. The meaning is that the person who has patience will be constantly guided towards that which is correct.
- (كل الناس يغدو فبائع نفسه) kul*lu n-nāsi yaghdu fabāʾiʿ nafsah*: the meaning is that every person strives with his soul, and thus there are those who sell it to Allah the Exalted by obeying Him and He spares them punishment, and there are those who sell it to Shayṭān and their desires by following both of them
- (فموبقها) fa muwbiquha: i.e. he destroys it, and I explained this ḥadīth in detail at the beginning of *Sharḥ Ṣaḥīḥ Muslim*,[312] so whoever wants to know more can refer to it, and with Allah is every success.

---

311 It cuts off and effaces the unbelief and disobedience that preceded it.

312 At the beginning of the Book of Purification, the chapter on the virtue of *wuḍūʾ* (3/99).

The Twenty-Fourth Ḥadīth:

- The Exalted's statement: (حرمت الظلم على نفسي): ḥaramtu z-ẓulma ʿalā nafsī: i.e. I am sanctified above that, for oppression is impossible for Allah the Exalted, because it means to transgress the bounds or dispose of someone else's property, both of which are impossible for Allah the Exalted.
- The Exalted's statement: (فلا تظالموا) *falā taẓālamū*: with a *fatḥah* on the *tā'*, i.e. do not oppress one another.
- The Exalted's statement: (إلا كما ينقص المخيط) *illā kamā yanquṣu l-mikhyaṭ*: with a *kasrah* on the *mīm*, a *sukūn* on the *khā'* and a *fatḥah* on the *yā'*, and it is a needle. The meaning is that it does not take away anything.

The Twenty-Fifth Ḥadīth:

- (الدثور) ad-duthūr: with a ḍammah on both the dhāl and thā': money, and the singular is dathr, like fals and fulūs.
- His statement ﷺ: (وفي بضع أحدكم): wa fī *buḍʿi aḥadikum*: with a *ḍammah* on the *bā'* and a *sukūn* on the *ḍad*, and it is an allusion to sexual intercourse; if one were to intend worship by it, it would be to fulfil the rights of marriage, to seek a righteous child, to keep oneself chaste and protect oneself from what is unlawful.

The Twenty-Sixth Ḥadīth:

- (السلامى) as-*sulāmā*: with a *ḍammah* on the *sīn*, no *shaddah* on the *lām* and a *fatḥah* on the *mīm*, the plural is *sulāmayāt*, with a *fatḥah* on the *mīm*, and it is the joints and organs, and there are 360 joints, as has been established in *Ṣaḥīḥ Muslim* from the Messenger of Allah ﷺ.[313]

The Twenty-Seventh Ḥadīth:

- (النوّاس) an-Nawwās: with a fatḥah on the nūn and a shaddah on the wāw, and (سمعان), which can be either samʿān or simʿān.
- His statement ﷺ: (حاك) ḥāka: i.e. one hesitates.
- (وابصة) Wābiṣah: with a kas*rah* on the *bā'*.

The Twenty-Eighth Ḥadīth:

- (العرباض) al-ʿIrbāḍ: with a kasrah on the ʿayn, (سارية) Sāriyah: with a sīn and not a shīn, and the yā' has two diacritic points under it.
- His statement ﷺ: (ذرفت) dharafat: with a fatḥah on the dhāl and rā', i.e. it flowed.
- His statement ﷺ: (بالنواجذ) bin-nawājidh: these are the canine teeth, and it is has been said that they are the molars? (البدعة) al-bidʿah: that which is done without any precedent.

313 He said, {Every person from the Children of Adam is created with 360 joints...} The Book of Zakāt, the chapter elucidating that the word *ṣadaqah* can refer to any good action, no.1009.

The Twenty-Ninth Ḥadīth:

- (ذروة السنام) dhirwati as-sinām: with kasrah or ḍammah on dhāl: i.e. its highest part.
- (ملاك الشيء) milāki sh-shay': i.e. its objective
- His statement ﷺ: (يكب) yakub*bu*: with *fatḥah* on *yā'* and a *ḍammah* on the *kāf.*

The Thirtieth Ḥadīth:

- (الخشني) al-Khushanī: with a ḍammah on the khā' and a fatḥah on the shīn followed by a nūn, attributed to Khushīnah, a well-known tribe.
- The statement: (جرثوم) Jurthūm: with a ḍammah on both the jīm and thā' and a sukūn on the rā' between them, and there is a lot of difference of opinion regarding his father's name.
- His statement ﷺ: (تنتهكوها) tantahikūhā: to violate the ḥawmah[314] means to treat it in a way that is not lawful.

The Thirty-Second Ḥadīth:

- (ولا ضرار) wa lā ḍirār: with a kasrah on the ḍād

The Thirty-Fourth Ḥadīth:

- (فإن لم يستطع فبقلبه) fa'in lam yastaṭi' fa biqalbihi: i.e. let him reject it in his heart
- (وذلك أضعف الإيمان) *wa dhālika aḍ'afu l-īmān*: i.e. the least of it in benefit

The Thirty-Fifth Ḥadīth:

- (ولا يخذله) wa lā yakhdhuluh: with a fatḥah on the yā' and a ḍammah on the dhāl
- His statement ﷺ: (بحسب امرىء من الشر) biḥas*bi mri'in min ash-sharr*: it is sufficient evil for him.

The Thirty-Eighth Ḥadīth:

- The Exalted's statement: (فقد آذنته بالحرب) faqad ādhantuhū bil-ḥarb: with an elongated hamzah: i.e. I inform him that he is at war with Me.
- The Exalted's statement: (استعاذني) ista'ādhanī: which can be with a nūn or a bā',[315] both are correct.

The Fortieth Ḥadīth:

- His statement ﷺ: (كن في الدنيا كأنك غريب أو عابر السبيل) kun fi d-d*unyā ka'annaka gharībun aw 'ābir as-sabīl*: i.e. do not rely on it and do not be concerned with it;

314 In the dictionary and elsewhere, this is the turmoil of the sea, the sand, fighting and other matters, the majority of it or the severest part of it.

315 i.e. it can be استعاذني or استعاذ بي, in *al-Fatḥ al-Bārī*, he says, 'With a *nūn* after the *dhāl* is more common'.

and do not be attached to it the same way a stranger is not attached to other than his homeland and do not be preoccupied with it the same way a stranger who wants to go home to his family is not preoccupied with it.

The Forty-Second Ḥadīth:

- His statement ﷺ: (عنان السماء) ʿanān as-samāʾ: with a fatḥāh on the ʿayn; it has been said that it is the clouds and it has been said that it is what presents itself to you from it, i.e. what appears when you raise your head
- His statement ﷺ: (بقراب الأرض) bi *qurāb al-arḍ*: with a *dāmmah* on the *qāf* or a *kasrah,* it has been related with both, but the *ḍammah* is more common; the meaning is that which almost fills it:

Section:

Know that in the ḥadīth mentioned at the beginning: {Whoever preserved forty ḥadīths for my Ummah…}, the meaning of preserve[316] is to convey them to the Muslims, even if one has not memorised them or does not know their meaning. This is the reality of its meaning, and this is how the Muslims are benefitted, not by memorising what one conveys to them, and Allah knows best what is correct.

I have finished this on the night of Thursday, the 29th of Jamād al-Uwlā of the year 668.[317]

316 Ar. *ḥafiẓa.*

317 (tn): This translation was completed on the night of Friday, the 9th of Rabīʿ al-Ākhar, 1441.

BIOGRAPHIES OF NARRATORS FROM AMONGST THE COMPANIONS ﷺ

Anas Ibn Mālik: Ḥadīth no.13 and 42
Al-Ansārī and al-Khazrajī, servant of the Messenger of Allah ﷺ. He served from the age of ten and stayed with him for ten years. The Prophet ﷺ gave him the agnomen 'Abu Ḥamzah'. His mother was Umm Sulaym. The Messenger of Allah ﷺ supplicated for him and said, {O Allah, increase his wealth and his children, grant him a long life, bless him and enter him into Paradise.} He was thus the wealthiest of people and he had some 120 children. He lived to be over 100 and died in Basra in the year 93 AH. In the books of ḥadīth, he has 2286 ḥadīths.

Tamīm Ibn Aws ad-Dārī ibn Khārijah: Ḥadīth no.7
Abu Ruqayyah, Companion, his lineage is from the clan of ad-Dār the son of Ḥāniʾ, from the tribe of Lakhm. He was a Christian and became Muslim in the year 9 AH, after which he lived in Madīnah. He moved to the Levant after the murder of ʿUthmān ibn ʿAffān and lived in Jerusalem. He often performed the night prayer.[318] He died in Palestine in the year 40 AH and he has eighteen ḥadīths in the books of ḥadīth. Abū Nuʿaym said in al-Ḥilyah, 'Tamīm ad-Dārī was the monk of the people of his age, the worshipper of the people of Palestine. He was the first to light lamps in the masjid and he was the first to narrate stories, and this was in the time of ʿUmar and with his permission.

Jābir Ibn ʿAbdillāh al-Anṣārī: Ḥadīth no.22
Al-Khazrajī, as-Sulamī, Abū ʿAbdillāh, he embraced Islam before the Hijrah and was present at al-ʿAqabah with his father, at which time he was a minor. He was a *mujāhid,* for in *Ṣaḥīḥ Muslim* it is on the authority of Jābir that he said, 'I took part in nineteen battles with the Messenger of Allah ﷺ. I did not witness Badr or Uḥud. My father prevented me. When my father had been killed, I did not stay back from any battle with the Messenger of Allah ﷺ.' He was one of those who related a lot, as he related 1540 ḥadīth. He died in Madīnah in 74 AH.

Jundub Ibn Junādah (Abū Dharr): Ḥadīth no.18, 24 and 25
The son of Sufyān the son of ʿUbayd, from the children of Ghifār, who are from Kinānah, who are in turn from Khuzaymah. He was a Companion and embraced Islam early. It has been related that he said, 'I was the fifth person to embrace

318 Ar. *tahajjud.*

Islam.' He is given as an example of truthfulness, and he was the first person that the Messenger of Allah ﷺ greeted with the greeting of Islam. He died in Rabadhah in the year 32 AH and he has 281 ḥadīths in the books of ḥadīth.

Abū Tha'labah al-Khushanī, Jurthūm Ibn Nāshir: Ḥadīth no.30
A Companion who was known by his agnomen. There has been a difference of opinion regarding his name and his father's name, some say, 'Jurthūm', some say, 'Jurthūmah, and some say 'Jurthum' or 'Jurhum'.

He was among those who pledged allegiance under the tree at al-Ḥudaybiyah. He ﷺ gave him a share of the spoils at the battle of Khaybar. The Prophet ﷺ sent him to his people from the tribe of Khushaynah and they embraced Islam. He died in the year 75 AH. He related forty ḥadīths from the Messenger of Allah ﷺ.

Al-Ḥārith Ibn 'Āṣim al-Ash'arī (Abū Mālik): Ḥadīth no.23
His lineage goes back to al-Ash'ar, a famous tribe from Yemen. He came with the Ash'arīs to the Prophet ﷺ and is considered one of the people of the Levant. He died from the plague in the time of 'Umar ibn al-Khaṭṭāb. He related twenty-seven ḥadīths from the Prophet ﷺ.

Al-Ḥasan Ibn 'Alī Ibn Abī Ṭālib: Ḥadīth no.11
Al-Hāshimī, al-Qurashī, Abū Muḥammad, the son of Fātimah az-Zahrā', born in Madīnah in the year 3 AH and raised in the Prophet's house. He was intelligent, forbearing and loved goodness. He was eloquent and one of the best regarding logical thinking and intuitive insight. The people of Iraq pledged allegiance to him to be the Caliph after his father had been martyred and the Hijaz, Yemen Iraq and Khurāsān came under his authority. After six months, he decided to spare the blood of the Muslims and thus he reconciled with Mu'āwiyah ibn Abī Sufyān ؓ and ceded the Caliphate to him with conditions. This was in the year 41 AH and thus the people called it the Year of Jamā'ah,[319] because the authority of the Muslim was united in one Caliph. Al-Ḥasan died in Madīnah in the year 50 and was buried in al-Baqī'. He related thirteen ḥadīths from his grandfather, the Messenger of Allah ﷺ.

Sa'd Ibn Mālik Ibn Sinān al-Khudrī (Abū Sa'īd): Ḥadīth no.32 and 34
His lineage goes back to Khudrat Baṭn of the Khazraj. He was not allowed to fight on the day of Uḥud because he was too young while his father died therein as a martyr. After that, he took part in twelve battles with the Messenger of Allah ﷺ.

319 (tn): i.e. the group or community.

He was one of the eminent Companions and amongst the ranks of their jurists and scholars. He died in Madīnah in the year 64 AH. There are 1170 ḥadīths related from him in the books of ḥadīth.

Sufyān Ibn ʿAbdillāh Ibn Abī Rabīʿah Ibn al-Ḥārith ath-Thaqafī: Ḥadīth no.21
A Companion from the people of aṭ-Ṭāʾif, he was governor for ʿUmar ibn al-Khaṭṭāb 🌸 over aṭ-Ṭāʾif. Muslim 🌸 has not related in his *Ṣaḥīḥ* on the authority of Sufyān ibn ʿAbdillāh from the Messenger of Allah 🌸 other than this ḥadīth, and it has been related by Imam Aḥmad, at-Tirmidhī, Ibn Mājah and an-Nasāʾī. Ibn Ḥajar said in *al-Iṣābah*, 'Sufyān embraced Islam with a delegation of Thaqīf and asked the Prophet 🌸 about a matter that he could adhere to, so he said, ﴿Say, 'My Lord is Allah' and then be upright.﴾

Sahl Ibn Saʿd as-Sāʿidī al-Anṣārī al-Khazrajī: Ḥadīth no.31
Abū al-ʿAbbās, he and both his parents are Companions; his name in *al-Jāhiliyyah* was Ḥuzn[320] so the Prophet 🌸 called him Sahl.[321] He was fifteen years old when the Prophet passed away and lived a long life, passing away in the era of al-Ḥajjāj ibn Yūsuf ath-Thaqafī in the year 88 AH, when he was over 100 years old. There are 188 ḥadīths related from him in the books of ḥadīth.

Shaddād Ibn Aws: Ḥadīth no.18
Ibn Thābit al-Khazrajī al-Anṣārī, a revered Companion and one of the rulers, ʿUmar ibn al-Khaṭṭāb made him the emir of Homs. When ʿUthmān ibn ʿAffān was killed, he isolated himself from the tribulations and devoted himself to worship. He 🌸 was eloquent, forbearing and wise. He died in Jerusalem in the year 58 AH and he has 50 ḥadīths in the books of ḥadīth.

The Mother of the Believers ʿĀʾishah the Daughter of Abū Bakr 🌸: Ḥadīth no.5
Umm ʿAbdillāh; the Messenger of Allah 🌸 gave her this name because of the son of her sister Asmāʾ, ʿAbdullah ibn az-Zubayr. The Messenger of Allah 🌸 married her in Makkah when she was six years old and consummated the marriage in Madīnah in the month of Shawwāl of the year 2 AH, after his departure from Badr. She was nine years old. When he died, she was 18 years old and she lived for another forty years. She died in the year 57 AH and Abū Hurayrah 🌸 prayed over her, and he was the emir of Madīnah under Marwan ibn al-Ḥakam. She was the most knowledgeable of women and the most proficient of them in *fiqh*. 1210 ḥadīths have been related from her.

---

320 (tn): i.e. grief, sorrow, sadness.
321 (tn): i.e. easy, facile.

ʿAbdullah Ibn ʿAbbās: Ḥadīth no.19, 33, 37 and 39
Ibn ʿAbdul Muṭṭalib al-Hāshimī, Abū al-ʿAbbās, the paternal cousin of the Messenger of Allah ﷺ. He was born in Makkah three years before the Hijrah in the gorge that the Messenger and the Muslims were blockaded in. The Prophet ﷺ supplicated for him by saying, {O Allah, give him understanding of the religion and teach him how to interpret.} ʿUmar ibn al-Khaṭṭāb ؓ would keep him close in his council and resort to his abundant knowledge and formidable intellect. He died in at-Ṭāʾif in the year 71 AH and is buried there. May Allah the Exalted have mercy on him and be pleased with him.

ʿAbdullah Ibn ʿUmar: Ḥadīth no.3, 8 and 40
He is Abū ʿAbdir Raḥmān ibn ʿUmar ibn al-Khaṭṭāb ؓ the Companion who took the Messenger of Allah ﷺ as a model.

ʿAbdullah was born after the *biʿthah*[322] and embraced Islam while still a child. He migrated with his father and mother – Zaynab bint Maẓʿūn – ؓ. He presented himself to the Prophet ﷺ on the day of Badr, when he was 13 years old, but he deemed him too young and sent him, and the same thing happened on the day of Uḥud, when he was 14. He allowed him to fight on the day of the Khandaq,[323] when he was 15, and after that, he partook in all of the Messenger of Allah's battles ﷺ.

He ؓ profited from his companionship of the Messenger of Allah ﷺ and regularly being present in Prophet's Masjid. He had vast knowledge, was one of those who memorised the Noble Qurʾān and was one of those who related many ḥadīths. 1630 ḥadīths have been related from him.

He would strictly adhere to the Sunnah, and was the most stringent of the Companions in imitating the Messenger of Allah ﷺ. The Prophet testified to his righteousness when he said, {ʿAbdullah is a righteous man.}

He died in Makkah in the year 73 AH at the age of 84, may Allah the Exalted have mercy on him.

ʿAbdullah Ibn Masʿūd: Ḥadīth no.4 and 14
ʿAbdullah ibn Masʿūd ibn Ghāfil ibn Ḥabīb al-Hudhalī, and his mother is Umm ʿAbd and also from the tribe of Hudhayl.

Ibn Masʿūd was one of the first people to embrace Islam; it has been related that he was the sixth person, and he was the first person to recite the Qurʾān aloud in Makkah. He migrated to Abyssinia and then to Madīnah. He witnessed Badr with the Messenger of Allah ﷺ as well as the *Bayʿat ar-Riḍwān*[324] and every subsequent battle, and after the Messenger of Allah ﷺ he witnessed al-Yarmūk. The Messenger of Allah loved him and honoured him, and he was the trusted

322 (tn): i.e. after the Messenger of Allah's mission ﷺ had begun.
323 (tn): i.e. the Battle of the Trench.
324 (tn): i.e. the Pledge of Satisfaction or the Pledge of the Tree, please see Sūrat al-Fatḥ 48:18.

servant of Allah's Messenger, the bearer of his secret, his attendant in everything he did. He entered upon at all times and walked with him, and carried his *siwāk*, his sandals and his washing water[325] for him.

He was one of the preeminent scholars of the Companions and one of the memorisers of the Qur'ān. The Prophet ﷺ described him by saying to him, {You are a schooled boy.} 'Umar ibn al-Khaṭṭāb looked at him one day and said, 'A vessel filled with knowledge.' 848 ḥadīths have been related from him.

After the passing of the Prophet ﷺ he was put in charge of the treasury at Kufa. Then he moved to Madīnah during the caliphate of 'Uthmān, and he died there in the year 30 AH at around sixty years of age, may Allah the Exalted have mercy on him and be pleased with him.

'Abdullah Ibn 'Amr Ibn al-'Āṣ: Ḥadīth no.41
As-Suhamī al-Qurashī, he embraced Islam before his father did, and was one of the scholars and devout worshippers of the Companion. He used to write in *al-Jāhiliyyah* and thus he sought permission from the Messenger of Allah ﷺ to write down whatever he heard from him, and he granted him that permission. He participated in wars and battles and would fight with two swords. He carried his father's banner on the day of al-Yarmūk, and witnessed Ṣiffīn with Mu'āwiyah, who put him in charge of Kufa for a short period of time. He died in the year 65 AH and he has 700 ḥadīths in the books of ḥadīth.

'Abdur Raḥmān Ibn Ṣakhr ad-Dawsī (Abū Hurayrah) Ḥadīth no.9, 10, 12, 15, 16, 26, 35, 36 and 38
The beloved Companion, he embraced Islam in the year of Khaybar and witnessed it with the Messenger of Allah ﷺ after which he was absolutely inseparable from him. He memorised the most out of all the Companions because of the blessing of Prophet's supplication ﷺ for him to be granted that, and the Prophet testified that he was eager for knowledge and ḥadīth. He died in Madīnah in the year 75 AH and he has 5374 ḥadīths in the books of ḥadīth.

Abū Najīḥ Al-'Irbāḍ Ibn Sāriyah: Ḥadīth no.28
Companion from the people of the Ṣuffah, he was one of those who wept when he wanted to partake in *jihād* and battle with the Messenger of Allah ﷺ in the Battle of Tābūk, which is also called *Ghazwat al-'Usrah,* [٣٢٦] and the Prophet ﷺ did not have sufficient equipment for them, so they left him weeping. Al-'Irbāḍ was one of the first Muslims, and we would say that he was the fourth person to embrace Islam. He settled in the Levant and lived in Homs. He died in 75 AH.

325 (tn): i.e. for *wuḍū'* and *ghusl.*

326 (tn): i.e. the battle of difficulty and distress.

'Uqbah Ibn 'Amr Al-Anṣārī: Ḥadīth no.20

He is 'Uqbah ibn 'Amr ibn Tha'labah ibn Asīrah ibn 'Aṭiyah al-Khazrajī al-Anṣārī, Abū Mas'ūd al-Badrī. He is well-known by his agnomen, even though he did not witness Badr. Rather, he resided in Badr or settled by some water in Badr and was thus attributed to it. He witnessed the second pledge of 'Aqabah, and was one of the youngest people to witness it. Then he witnessed Uḥud and the battles that followed. He resided in Kufa, and was one of the companions of 'Alī 🕮 and 'Alī left him in charge of Kufa when he went out to Ṣiffīn. There is a difference of opinion as to when he died. It has been said that he died in 41 or 42 AH, as well as 46 AH. In *al-Iṣābah*, Ibn Ḥajar prefers to say that he died after the year 40 AH, because he lived to see the emirate of al-Mughīrah ibn Shu'bah over Kufa.

'Umar Ibn Al-Khaṭṭāb: Ḥadīth no.1 and 2

He is the Commander of the Believers, 'Umar ibn al-Khaṭṭāb al-Qurashī al-'Adawī, Abū Ḥafs, the second of the Rightly-Guided Caliphs. He was an ambassador for Quraysh in *al-Jāhiliyyah* and at the beginning of the Mission, he was firmly against the Muslims. Then, he embraced Islam and his Islam was an opening for them and a relief for them from distress. 'Abdullah ibn Mas'ūd said, 'We could not pray by the Ka'bah until 'Umar had become Muslim'. His Islam was after forty men had become Muslim and eleven women, in the sixth year of the mission. He migrated openly, in front of Quraysh, and he partook in all the battles of the Messenger of Allah 🕮. He was given the pledge of allegiance as the caliph after the death of Abū Bakr as-Ṣiddīq 🕮 in the year 12 AH, based on a covenant from him.[327] He was martyred in the year 23 AH after Abū Lu'lu' al-Majūsī stabbed him in his waist while he was performing the dawn prayer. He lived for three nights after the stabbing, may Allah the Exalted have mercy on him and be pleased with him.

Mu'ādh ibn Jabal: Ḥadīth no.18 and 29

Al-Anṣārī al-Khazrajī, Abū 'Abdir Raḥmān, the foremost scholar in knowledge of the lawful and the unlawful according to the testimony of the Messenger of Allah 🕮 when he said, {The most knowledgeable of my Ummah regarding the lawful and the unlawful is Mu'ādh ibn Jabal.} He was a handsome youth, and out of all the youth of the Helpers, he was the best of them in terms of forbearance, munificence and modesty. He embraced Islam at the age of 18, and witnessed 'Aqabah, Badr and all subsequent battles. The Messenger 🕮 sent him to be in charge of Yemen. He died in the prime of his youth as a fighter in the year 18 AH from the plague of 'Amwās,[328] at the age of 34. 157 ḥadīth have been related on his authority from the Messenger of Allah 🕮.

---

327 (tn): i.e. Abū Bakr appointed to 'Umar as his successor 🕮.
328 (tn): or Emmaus.

(Abū ʿAbdillāh) An-Nuʿmān Ibn Bashīr Ibn Kaʿb al-Khazrajī al-Anṣārī: Ḥadīth no.6

He was born 14 months after the Hijrah, and was the first child born to the Helpers after the Hijrah. Both of his parents were also Companions. When the Prophet passed away he was eight years old. He lived in the Levant and Muʿāwiyah made him the emir of Homs, and Yazīd ibn Muʿāwiyah let him remain in that position. Nuʿmān ibn Bashīr was generous and endowed with deeper insight. He was killed in one of the villages of Homs because he called for ʿAbdullah ibn Zubayr to be given the pledge of allegiance, and this was in the year 56 AH. Al-Bukhārī has related six ḥadīths from him and 114 ḥadīths in total have been related from him in the books of ḥadīth.

An-Nawwās Ibn Samʿān Ibn Khālid Ibn ʿAmr Al-ʿĀmirī Al-Kilābī: Ḥadīth no.27

Companion from amongst the people of the Levant, he visited the Prophet with his father Samʿān and he supplicated for him. He lived in Madīnah with the Messenger of Allah in order to deepen his knowledge of the religion. 17 ḥadīths have been related on the authority of an-Nawwās from the Prophet.

Wābiṣah Ibn Maʿbad Ibn Mālik Ibn ʿUbayd al-Asadī: Ḥadīth no.27

A companion, he visited the Messenger of Allah in the year 9 AH and embraced Islam. He would weep a great deal and was not able to control his tears. He lived in Raqqa and died therein. Eleven ḥadīths have been related on his authority from the Messenger of Allah.

Made in the USA
Middletown, DE
21 September 2023

38995897R00256